AGING AND BEHAVIOR

Third Edition

D0945196

Jack Botwinick, Ph.D., Professor of Psychology at Washington University in St. Louis, is also Director of the Aging and Development Program of the university's Department of Psychology. Previously, he was Professor of Medical Psychology at Duke University Medical School, and Research Psychologist with the Laboratory of Psychology of the National Institute of Mental Health in Bethesda, Maryland. A past president of the Division of Adult Development and Aging of the American Psychological Association, and a past president of the Behavioral and Social Science section of the Gerontological Society of America, Professor Botwinick has served on national advisory boards and been guest lecturer at many colloquia and workshops. Among these is the prestigious "Master Lecture" series conducted by the American Psychological Association. Among the awards that he has received are the Keston Memorial Lectureship Award of the University of Southern California (1982), Kleemlier Award of the Gerontologial Society of America (1979), and the Distinguished Contribution Award of the Division of Adult Development of the American Psychological Association (1978). In addition to *Aging and Behavior*, he has published extensively in professional journals, contributed chapters to many edited volumes, and written three other books, *We Are Aging* (Springer, 1981), *Memory, Related Functions and Age* (Charles C Thomas, 1974) and *Cognitive Processes in Maturity and Old Age* (Springer, 1967).

AGING AND BEHAVIOR

A Comprehensive Integration of Research Findings

THIRD EDITION
UPDATED AND EXPANDED

Jack Botwinick

SPRINGER PUBLISHING COMPANY / NEW YORK

Copyright © 1984 by Springer Publishing Company, Inc.

Springer Publishing Company, Inc.
200 Park Avenue South
New York, New York 10003

84 85 86 87 88 / 10 9 8 7 6 5 4 3 2 1

First edition, 1973. Second edition, 1978.

Library of Congress Cataloging in Publication Data

Botwinick, Jack.
    Aging and behavior.
    Includes bibliographical references and index.
    1. Aging—Psychological aspects. 2. Aged—Psychology. I. Title. [DNLM: 1. Aging. 2.
Behavior—In old age. WT 150 B751a]
BF724.55.A35B67   1984   155.67   84-1376
ISBN 0-8261-1443-1

Printed in the United States of America

Contents

Preface to the Third Edition

The reader acquainted with previous editions of *Aging and Behavior* will find this one familiar and at the same time very different from the others. Familiarity will be found in the format, in much of the organization of materials, and in some of the material itself. Differences will be found in the extensiveness of new material in the various content areas and in the expanded scope of coverage in personality and social aging. In many ways this is a new book despite the similarity of chapter headings.

The preface of the previous, 1978 edition referred to the explosion of literature to that time. I did not then realize that the explosion was only beginning. The explosion since that time paled what had taken place before. It is mainly for this reason that more time was devoted to research and writing this revision of *Aging and Behavior* than was necessary in the original edition. If the explosion of research publication continues, it will no longer be possible to write comprehensive books on the behavioral aspects of aging and still keep them to manageable size. Future books will have to be limited to specialty areas, as, for example, information processing and memory in relation to age.

The literature explosion posed a problem in writing this present edition. Some of the new information supplanted the old but much of it simply added to it. How was all this new and old information to be integrated without making for a volume twice this size? This was the challenge in the present revision. A decision was made to introduce new important areas of research, maintain as much of the old areas as possible, but be more selective in covering related literature than in past editions when more comprehensive coverage was the goal. The reader will note that despite this, many, many research studies and references are noted.

When *Aging and Behavior* first appeared in 1973, it was one of only a few books on the topic. Now there are many, so many in fact that a year or two ago a reviewer of another book commented that there are now more books on aging available than one can read or even cares to read. Why, then, a new revision of *Aging and Behavior?* This book has served a need that remains and grows, but the 1978 edition was fast becoming out of date. The field is now full-blown with a lot of student interest. There are undergraduate and graduate courses on aging in many colleges and universities and there are many university programs and centers of aging. *Aging and Behavior* can continue its role as a major university text on aging.

In revising this book, Mrs. Wanda Meek must be singled out for special gratitude. Her labors in typing and retyping and typing again the main manuscript pages, her editorial assistance, her checking of references, all this and more were continuous, uncomplaining, and thoroughly reliable. I thank you, Wanda Meek. My wife, Joan, receives my gratitude in a different way. Once again, in writing I was often unavailable when needed. She was also uncomplaining and she was patient, making the process easier for me. I thank Joan, too.

1
Who Are the Aged?

THE PERSON

Who are the aged? The aged are not easy to categorize because they are so varied. They are so varied, in fact, that for years it had commonly been held that there are greater differences among old people than among young people, and we know how varied the young are. A recent study put doubt into this commonly held idea (Bornstein & Smircina, 1982), but no one doubts that no two old people are alike, just as no two young people are. We can expect large individual differences among the elderly. First, we start with the large individual differences among the young. Then, as people grow old, some functions decline, some remain essentially the same, and, up to a point at least, some improve. Thus, the range of function varies from poor to very good and this range is very large among the elderly.

This large variation among older adults makes generalizations about them difficult. The situation is not unlike that of the actuarial tables of life insurance companies where the companies bet on people and events and almost always win. We like to think that as individuals we can outlive the life expectancies of the actuarial tables and that we can outperform the expected averages. It would not be very smart, however, to arrange our lives betting heavily that we will win by outliving and outperforming the averages.

Is age 55 old? Is 75? Neugarten (1975) suggested that older adults are best thought of in terms of two groupings: one group is the young-old, ranging in age from 55 to 75, and the other group is the old-old, comprising people over 75. These two groups are very different—the young-old are healthier than the old-old, their abilities are greater, and the ratio of men to women in this younger group is larger. Why only two groupings? We can think of the young-old (55–64), middle-old (65–74), and the old-old (75 and over). Perhaps in the over-75 category it would be well to make another distinction: the old-old (75–84) are different from the very old (85 and over group). Each of these groups is different. The more numerous and differentiated the groupings, the more we can learn about aging and the individual.

Why, then, think about aging and not just the individual? First, older adults do have a lot in common even with their great individual differences. Second, we can best understand the aging individual with knowledge of how he or she compares to those younger, to age peers, and to those older. It is for this reason that group trends, from early life to old age, are important to study.

This book is about the psychology of aging—the behavioral changes. These are seen as consequences both of changes going on in the body and of pressures people experience in their circumstances in the social world. When we see the older person who has responded well to these internal and social stimulations, we might think to ourselves, "There *with* the grace of God go I."

WHEN DOES AGING BEGIN?

There are different answers to the question, When does aging begin? No single answer is adequate for all purposes. Some scientists maintain that aging starts at birth and is continuous, with no specific age or period marking off the onset of senescence. Others believe that aging begins with sexual maturity. No one, it seems, is satisfied with calendar age as part of the definition of aging or old age.

Still, in a very real sense, we all think in terms of calendar time and, by necessity, legal systems are based on such thought. For example, without intent, perhaps, lawmakers have effectively defined old age for us and in most instances it is 65 and over. This is changing now. This quasi-legal definition, 65, goes back at least to the time of Chancellor Bismarck of Germany when in 1883 he initiated a program of social security for people aged 65 and over. The United States followed a similar practice when in 1935 social security benefits became available with mandatory retirement at age 65 in most occupations. Age 65, therefore, became an important marker in life. What was law became social fact; old age started at 65. Attitudes and expectations were formed on the basis of age 65, and it is not unreasonable to believe that many people became old at this age because they and the world around them accepted this *de facto* definition.

Recent social security laws have been changed so that in the future, eligibility for full social security benefits will not begin until age 67. Furthermore, not long ago United States law was changed so that mandatory age retirement was extended to age 70 (for all but a relatively few people in special occupations and for those self-employed). It is probable that in the near future, mandatory retirement based on any age will be outlawed; many states already have such statutes. Given this, and the fact that people are living longer and are in better physical condition than years ago, what will be future attitudes and expectations of aging? What will be old age at that time?

Retirement age in the future will be more variable. Some will retire later than age 70, some much earlier. There are predictions that in two or so decades, retirement at age 55 will be common (Neugarten, 1975). Even now, Butler (1980, p. 7), discussing "current definitions of aging," points out that age 60 defines old age in terms of eligibility for a federal nutrition program but 62 for a housing program and 65 for Medicare.

In brief, no single year defines old age. It is a matter of convenience and custom.

WHAT IS AGING?

Models

In a general way, everyone knows what aging is, yet when it comes to describing and understanding it, no one definition seems very adequate. The reason for this is that there is more than one kind of aging. Havighurst (1957) was concerned with social competence and concluded that this does not decline with age. Shock (1972) was concerned with biological organ systems, which clearly decline with age. Likewise, many behavioral functions and abilities decline with age, but there is no one-to-one correspondence between these and biological aging. Thus, *sociological models* of aging, *biological*, and *behavioral models* of aging are more or less independent, each describing or encompassing just a part of the total.

Physicians are trained to think in terms of disease processes. Since the frequency of diseases increases with age, it is not surprising that many physicians seem to suggest that if diseases of the heart were completely understood, if cancer and cerebrovascular diseases were understood, much of aging would be understood. Just as *biostatistical models* define aging in terms of the probability of survival, and sociologists define aging in terms of social factors, physicians tend to see aging as accumulating disease processes. Theirs is a *medical model* of aging.

The shortcoming of the medical model is that it cannot account for the old man who is without apparent disease. There are such people: one study reported on them (Birren, Butler, Greenhouse, Sokoloff, & Yarrow, 1963). The men who were examined in this study were old by years, by appearance, by behavioral and other test functioning, but there were no apparent disease processes. The medical model of aging would be inadequate in dealing with these men.

The fact is, even if cures for the major killers were found, aging would go on. If the major cardiovascular and renal diseases were eliminated, there would be a gain in life expectancy of about 11 to 12 years. If cancer was eliminated, life expectancy would increase less—only about 2 years. (See Siegel, 1980, Table IV-11, p. 306). There is much more to aging than the associated disease processes.

Theories

Through the years scientists have tried to understand aging by formulating theories. Most of these are not theories in the formal sense; in fact, many are hardly more than untestable ideas. Many psychological theories take the form of developmental stages. Sociological theories often take the form of social constraints and expectations that dictate what older people should do and very often, therefore, what they actually do. Some of the psychological and sociological theories are presented in Chapter 9.

Biological Theories. Another set of theories are biological. These theories have in common the idea that cells or organs of the body function less well with advancing age. They function less well because of (1) genetic factors, (2) breakdown with use, or (3) assaults from the environment. Gene theories are discussed in Chapter 3. Here, it is simply indicated that gene theories have it that cells or organ systems and, thus, the whole person are genetically programmed to function optimally for only a limited time.

There are several breakdown theories and one of them is hardly more than the idea that in the course of living there is *wear and tear* of cells and organs. Another breakdown theory is that over time, a binding or *cross-linking* of cell molecules takes place and this makes for imperfect cell functioning. Another is that in the course of years of continuous function, there is an accumulation of harmful chemical by-products that have deleterious effects. This theory has the colorful name of *clinker* theory.

More vague are environmental insult theories. It is thought that decline with age is due to damage to cells and membranes resulting from accidental events in both the external and internal environment. The longer one lives, the greater the opportunity for accidental damage. If the insult is a random event, prediction is hardly possible, except in the grossest actuarial sense. (For more detail of biological theories of aging, see Rockstein & Sussman, 1979, pp. 37–43; or Shock, 1977, pp. 103–115).

The Autoimmune Theory. There is one biological theory that seems particularly promising and growing in importance because it lends itself to research. It is the *autoimmune* theory; some investigators tie this theory to genetic theories. When bacteria or viruses invade the body, or when there is a transplant of tissue or organ from someone else, a biochemical system is called into play to defend against these foreign substances. Even harmful substances produced by the self are attacked in this way. This is an adaptive process where immunity is built up by antibodies protecting against such harmful external and internal invasions.

Normally, the antibodies attack only these harmful substances but do not attack substances of the self that are beneficial or not harmful. It is believed that in the course of aging, this system falters in two ways: one, the antibodies fail to recognize a foreign body as foreign, that is, not part of the self; or, the antibodies fail to recognize harmful substances produced by the self. The person is thus left unprotected. For this reason, it is believed, diseases such as cancer and arthritis are more prevalent in old age. Two, the immune system falters in that tissues and organs of the self that are not harmful are mistakenly recognized as foreign, invading substances. Self parts are thus attacked. It is possible that the deterioration of the circulatory and other systems results from this faulty autoimmune process.

Parts of this theory have support in the laboratory (Weksler, 1981), holding promise that if the immune system can be brought under control, diseases of old age will diminish, conceivably even be eradicated. This is a hope, a dream. For the present, it must be said that despite all our models and all our theories, we really do not know very much about why people and animals age or why major organ systems decline. Perhaps it is this mystery that makes the study of aging so interesting for many scientists.

LIFE EXPECTANCY

Life Span versus Life Expectancy

There are more old people living today than ever before. This fact would not surprise many people. It is less well known, however, that although more people are living longer than ever before, our maximum *life span*, as determined by our genes, has hardly increased since biblical times, and probably not over the last 100,000 years (e.g., Hayflick, 1978). This may sound paradoxical, but the fact is that over the centuries, more and more people have lived closer to the length of life that their genes have programmed. In other words, *life expectancy* has gotten closer to the maximum life span, considered by some to be between 95 and 110 years.

Biomedical progress has drastically reduced infant and child death and also has led to greater control of acute diseases of young adulthood and middle age. These advances, plus improved knowledge of what is good for us and what is not, have permitted life expectancies to approach the maximum life span. Thus, life expectancy has increased but life span has not, or has increased very, very little.

The increase in life expectancy has been considerable. For example,

Hayflick (1978) pointed out that 2,000 years ago in Rome, the average length of life was about 22 years; in the late 1600s, it was about 33 years. As late as 1900 in the United States, it was only about 50 years; in 1946 it was 66 years. Today, a person's life expectancy is in the mid-70s. If this trend of increasing life expectancy continues, a strange phenomenon that some scientists are predicting may occur: nearly everyone will reach the age of the maximum life span of about 95 to 110 years. This is called the "rectangular survival curve"—everyone reaches approximately the same age and then everyone dies at approximately this age. Some scientists believe that death will result from a faulty biochemical process involving protein metabolism.

Life Expectancy is a Function of Age

People who are 45 years old have already lived almost as long as the average person born in 1900 could have expected to live. In the United States, men aged 45 have an average life expectancy of an additional 27 years, that is, age 72. For women the life expectancy is nearly 5 years longer. At age 65, life expectancy for men is about 79 and for women, 83 years. (Data are from United States Bureau of the Census, 1972, 1973; Siegel, 1980, p. 302). It is seen, therefore, that a person's life expectancy depends on the age of the person.

Figure 1.1 shows that the older a person is, the longer the life is expected to be. Thus, the figure shows that at age 85, the expected life duration is 90.3. At age 70, expectation is that life will continue to age 82. Another way of saying this is that at age 85, another 5.3 years are expected. At age 70, another 12 years are expected.

Special Concerns

Demographic Patterns. Life expectancy is not a static statistic; it changes. From 1955 to 1965, there was little change in life expectancy at age 65. But since 1968, mortality rates of older people have begun to fall, that is, older adults were living longer (Siegel, 1980, pp. 299–300).* Will this continue into the future?

Yes it will. There will be more and more old people and this will change the face of our society. The age-group 65 and over is expected to approximately double in the next 40 years; there is an expected increase from 23 million in 1976, to 32 million in the year 2000, to 45 million in 2020. Very important, all age segments of the elderly population are expected to grow rapidly, but the growth of "the extreme aged" will be especially large.

*All demographic data in this chapter are from Siegel (1980), except as indicated.

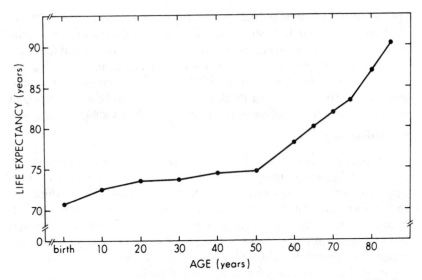

FIGURE 1.1: Life expectancy as a function of age in the United States, 1969–1971. (Data from Table 3.4 of Rockstein & Sussman, 1979, p. 26.)

Increases in the number of older adults is not only a U.S. phenomenon, it is worldwide. A United Nations periodical (1971) reported that the world's people over age 65 then numbered about 200 million. Of special note, there were 24 million more people over 65 in 1971 than there were just five years prior to that time. Most of the increase, as might be expected, was due to medical advances that took place in the "developed countries." A United Nations report 10 years later reported population patterns in terms of age over 60, rather than 65 as in the earlier report. In 1980, there were about 200 million people over age 60 in the "developing world" alone. The number is expected to reach 350 million by the year 2000.

Social Factors. Not only will the number of older people increase, their proportion in the population is expected to rise. The proportion is dependent not only on the number of old people in the population but also on birthrates, both past and future. There is an interesting history of shifts in the age structure that points to important social concerns.

Several indices have been developed to determine the ratio of "producers" to "dependents." These are called *"dependency ratios"* or "dependency indices." One such ratio is of the number of persons aged 65 and over ("dependents") to the number of persons of usual working age, 18 to 64 ("producers"). This ratio has more than doubled between 1920 and 1960 and is expected to rise slowly in the next several decades. It is expected to hit a high peak in the year 2020 because of the large number of births during the "baby boom" (1950–1960) and the small number of births during the "baby bust"

(1970–1980). During year 2020, the baby boom cohort will be 60 to 70 and the baby bust cohort 40 to 50. During this year, and the years following, the smaller number of "baby bust people" will need to support and aid the larger number of "baby boom people" by way of taxes and other means. Such population shifts must be planned for or else there can be much social discomfort and unrest. Are we planning for this? If not, there can be a polarization of age-groups as there are of racial groups and possibly sex groups.

Sex Differences

It was indicated earlier that the life expectancy of women is greater than men. They live longer than men and thus constitute a larger segment of the older population. This trend appears to be increasing. The "natural life span" of women relative to men may be longer than commonly recognized. Figure 1.2 shows that, although among those under 25 years men outnumber women slightly, the reverse is true after this age and the trend becomes progressive. Figure 1.2 also shows that in the very oldest age-group, there are more than two women for each man still alive.

The ratio of women to men has been increasing through the years. Figure 1.3 shows that from 1950 to 1976, there was a dramatic increase in the ratio of older women to older men. From 1980 to 2020, however, projected figures reflect only slight increases to come.

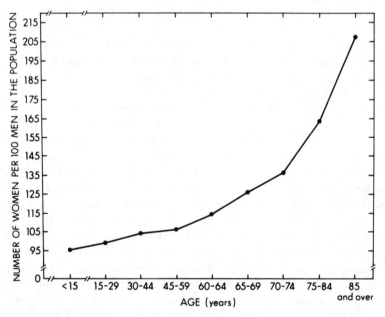

FIGURE 1.2: The number of American women relative to men in 1976 as a function of age. (Data computed from Table IV-5 of Siegel, 1980, p. 297).

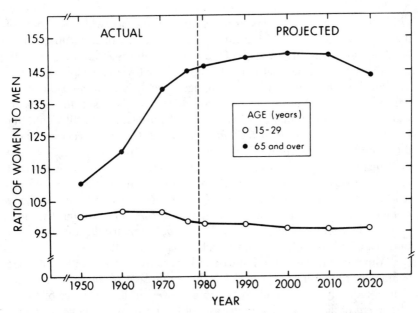

FIGURE 1.3: The number of American women relative to men during different time periods. (Data computed from Table IV-5 of Siegel, 1980, p. 297.)

Women are thus more often widowed than are men. Most old men are married; most old women are not. Why do women outlive men? Some believe the reasons are in the genes but others think it is lifestyle or environment. This will be discussed in Chapter 3.

Race Differences

Whites live longer than nonwhites, but this difference in longevity has been greatly reduced in recent years. The reduction has been due to improvements in black mortality, suggesting that medical and nutritional factors have improved over the years. Still, whites live about five years longer.

The more favorable life expectancy of whites is mainly below age 65. Above this age, there is little race difference in life expectancy and it has been small for decades. In fact, at age 75 to 79, deaths of nonwhites have occurred at later ages than they have for whites. Siegel (1980, p. 304) does not believe that this is an artifact, due only to statistics.

HEALTH

Illnesses that start with relative suddenness and often have a peak period of discomfort, but are of short duration, are called *acute diseases*. These decrease with age. On the other hand, *chronic diseases*, those that come on gradually and persist for years, if not a lifetime, increase with age. Some of the chronic diseases, such as arthritis, are painful and often incapacitating, but they do not result in death. Other chronic diseases, however, do kill.

The same diseases that kill old people also kill young people, but their incidence or prevalence increases with age. The diseases of old age that are the major causes of death are, first, the diseases of the heart, then cancer, and next, cerebrovascular problems, mainly stroke (see National Center for Health Statistics, *Health in the Later Years of Life*, 1971). Together these three conditions account for 70 percent of the deaths of people aged 45 and over; heart diseases alone account for over 50 percent. Among those dying of diseases of the heart, approximately five times as many men over 65 are represented as those between 45 and 64 years; more than 10 times as many women over 65 are represented as those younger. A more startling statistic is provided by Atchley (1980, p. 38): "At age 75, the probability of death from cardiovascular disease is 150 times higher than at age 35."

Although the pattern of increase of heart disease from youth to old age is dramatic, the percentage of death due to diseases of the heart does not change radically from age 65 to age 85 and over. In the age range 65 to 74, 41 percent of deaths are due to diseases of the heart. In the range 75 to 84, 44 percent are due to heart, and in those 85 and over, 48 percent. (See Table 3.1 in Chapter 3.)

There are other disease killers of old age such as cancers and strokes. The old require extensive medical attention. At present, those over 65 have medical expenditures three-and-a-half times those of people under 65. Much of this expenditure comes about at the very time when income is limited. Governmental programs provide help but need is still great. Whereas 10 or 11 percent of the population is over 65, as much as 52 percent of the amount paid for health care by these programs is spent on older people. Can social machinery and funds be developed to keep up with the increasing proportions of older people that are expected?

INCOME

It is difficult to generalize about the aged. Some are poor, some are rich, and some are in between. Among the poor, jobs are needed; they are hard to get. Older workers find it hard to get jobs once they have become unemployed. In 1900 almost two-thirds of older men were still in the work force; now it is only slightly more than one-quarter. Women show a different pattern. Of those over 65, the proportion of those working rose from about 8 percent in 1900 to about 10 percent in 1970.

Many Older People are Poor

Above and below the Poverty Line. It is strange that something as basic and seemingly simple as income analysis could give rise to almost opposite viewpoints. Until recently, there was one viewpoint only and it was that a high percentage of the old are poor. For example, in 1975, half of the families with heads of household 65 or over earned little more than half what younger families earned. Half the older families earned about $8,000 per year or less whereas the median income of younger families was approximately $15,000. There were nearly seven million older people who either lived alone or lived with nonrelatives. Half of these had incomes less than $2,000 per year. These data may best be understood against an "official poverty level threshold." In 1975, this poverty level for a couple was $3,232 and for an individual $2,572. Clearly, a summary statement of all this is that many of the old are poor (Brotman, 1977).

Relative Improvement. Hurd and Shoven (1982) presented another viewpoint. The incomes of the elderly, as a group, have kept pace with the cost of living, unlike other groups. The inflation of the 1970s and early 1980s has reduced the buying power of many people but this has not been so for many of the elderly. The reason for this is that most of the assets of older people are in housing, Social Security, Medicare, and Medicaid. These assets, particularly those of the government programs, have been "inflation protected." That is, the amount of money provided by the government has been tied to the cost of living. This protected older people to the point where their real incomes (buying power) were stable, while at the same time the real incomes of younger people were going down. In a *relative* sense, therefore, "the income per household of the elderly has increased more rapidly than the rest of the population. . . ." (Hurd & Shoven, 1982, see their abstract). Moreover, they pointed out, even though the total income of elderly households is much smaller than the incomes of non-elderly households (it was only 58 percent of the non-elderly's income in 1978), their household sizes are smaller. Looking at it this way, "The elderly have higher per capita income than non-elderly. . . ." (p. 7).

Thus, with the combination of keeping pace with inflation and having smaller households, many of the elderly have moved from a dismal state of poverty to being relatively comfortable. This relative income picture, however, may be misleading. It is true, the incomes of the elderly have improved, but as Hurd and Shoven indicated, 14 percent of the elderly families had incomes below the poverty level in 1978; as many as 27 percent of the elderly living alone were below the poverty level. The lot of many older people has improved, but the actual number of dollars coming into the homes of many older people remains small. Hurd and Shoven agree that many older adults are poor, but their emphasis on relative gain against inflation makes for this conclusion: "The wealthy are most vulnerable to inflation" (see their abstract). It is so—the wealthy have lost more of their buying power than did the poor, but they remain affluent and can buy many things. The poorest of the elderly have benefited the most from the government "inflation-protected" benefits, but they remain poor.

Complaining about Income. An interesting fact was disclosed in a 1981 Louis Harris poll (as told in a news service report in the *St. Louis Post-Dispatch*, November 19, 1981, p. 15A). The poll disclosed that old and young viewed financial and other affairs differently. Of the 3,400 people who were polled, 68 percent of those under 65 said that a lack of money was a very serious problem for most older people. In contrast, only 17 percent of those over 65 found money a personal problem. (In similar fashion, other concerns were seen differently between the age-groups—loneliness, crime, medical care, and transportation problems. The younger adults saw these as more dire problems for the aged than the aged saw these as problems for themselves.)

Harris, the author of the study, said "the elderly are perceived as being in much more desperate shape than they actually are." This conlcusion may be correct. It may not. It is known that elderly respondents tend not to complain and not to voice problems even when their conditions of life are such as to make younger adults express discomforts (e.g., Carp & Carp, 1981a, b).

Many Older People Are Wealthy

Poverty and relative improvement are not the whole story. In 1981, the Andrus Gerontology Center in Los Angeles put together a "fact sheet" listing the assets of people aged 55 and over (Unlisted Author, 1981). People of this age had 30 percent of the total U.S. personal income, they had nearly 80 percent of savings and loan money, and they made 25 percent of the total U.S. consumer expenditures. People of this age, therefore, constituted a powerful constituency and an important target for business marketing. It is to be noted that these data are of people aged 55 and over; a major share of this wealth and consumption rests with the age-group 55 and 64 years.

WHERE OLD PEOPLE LIVE

Statistics regarding where old people live sometimes seem to give contradictory information, but that is only because one set of statistics focuses on the *proportion of older people* in an area and another set focuses on the *number of older people* in an area. The largest proportion of older people in an area is found in rural-nonfarm communities populated by 1,000–2,500 people. This is mainly because of out-migration of young people to larger places. In terms of proportions, the Midwestern farm belt states are leaders (Iowa, Kansas, Missouri, Nebraska, and South Dakota). Florida is also a leader but, unlike the other states, this is probably due to the in-migration of older adults.

In terms of the number of older people, geographic patterns of older adults are similar to those of younger ones. Older people live mostly in the larger states, with New York, California, and Pennsylvania the leaders. One-quarter of all older Americans live in these three states (see U.S. Census Report, 1973). In 1970, 34 percent of people over 65 lived in the central cities and 27 percent in rural areas.

Most older people live in a family setting, usually in their own households. It may be hard to believe, but it has been reported that 70 percent of persons over 65 live in homes they own (Carp, 1976, p. 251). This is not to say that most older people live in fine houses in affluent neighborhoods. Just the opposite—many live in deteriorating houses in deteriorating neighborhoods.

There is a continuing and growing trend for older people to live away from their children. Of every 100 older people, 28 live alone or with nonrelatives. It comes as a surprise to many that only four percent of old people live in institutions. Although this is so, it is also true that the percentage of old people who will have to be institutionalized eventually is much greater. Kastenbaum and Candy (1973) found that 4 percent of those aged 65 and older were in institutions (mostly nursing homes), but among those aged 85 and above, 17 percent were institutionalized. The percentage of adults who are institutionalized increases with age past 65.

Overall, then, although most young people live in the suburbs, most old people live in the central city in their own homes. As indicated, however, an appreciable percentage live outside of metropolitan areas altogether.

SUMMARY

It is well to begin the study of aging with the recognition that the aged are not homogeneous. There are large individual differences and it is difficult, therefore, to generalize about them. Actually, the aged constitute several subgroups of ages. We might classify the aged as young-old (55–64), middle-old (66–74), old-old (75–84), and very old (85 and over). Each of these subgroups is different from the others in terms of health, ability, and the ratio of surviving women to men. They are different in other ways, too. Although this age classification is no less arbitrary than any other one, it does point out that there is much, varied life after the onset of senescence.

In the end, the individual is a person who is also a member of many groups and subgroups.

This classification suggests that old age starts at 55. Actually, for most legal purposes, at least, old age might be thought to start sometime during one's 60s. It is during this age that, historically, people planned retirement from work and looked forward to financial benefits from government and private pension plans. Recent legislation in the United States moved the age of mandatory retirement to 70, and it is expected that mandatory retirement based on any age will soon be illegal. When this happens, old age might be seen differently. Old age is continuous with young age. There really is no specific age or period to mark the start of aging or old age.

Scientists develop models and theories so that they can better understand what aging is. It seems that, at best, aging can be understood only in parts. For example, there is aging of the social self, the psychological self, the biological self. These models of aging are not correlated. Social competence is retained in late life, although biological integrity is not. People develop chronic illness as they get old, but we cannot understand aging by the study of disease. Not everyone develops chronic ailments, but everyone living long enough becomes old. Even if all the killing diseases were cured, people would still get old.

Biological theories of aging are of three types. One type, breakdown theory, hardly seems useful, simply indicating that tissue and organ systems break down in the course of living. It is thought that in the course of continuous functioning, an accumulation of harmful chemical by-products brings on deleterious aging effects, or that damage to cells and membranes occurs by random, unpredictable attacks by events in both the external and internal environments. The second type of biological theory relates the breakdown to genetic control. It is believed by some that cells or organ systems and, thus, the whole person are genetically programmed to function optimally for only a limited time before breakdown occurs. The third type of biological theory seems most useful because it can be put to test by laboratory studies. It is believed that with age there is a breakdown of the autoimmune system, giving rise to a wide variety of diseases.

People today are living longer than ever before; life expectancies have risen dramatically over the centuries and even over the last decades. Medical advances underlie most of this increase in life expectancy. Despite this increase, however, the maximum life span of people over the centuries has not increased very much, if at all. In other words, medical advances have permitted us to come closer to living the length of life that seems possible. Today, life expectancy at birth is in the 70s; the maximum life span may be between 95 and 110 years. If this is so, we have far to go to improve life expectancy.

We have even farther to go to improve the expected quality of life. As life expectancy has increased, as life expectancy of the future increases, the number of older people increases. Not only this, but the proportion of older people in the population increases, depending on birthrates and other factors. Old people require more medical attention than younger people, they tend not to be in the labor force in large percentages, and they tend to play roles of "dependents" not "producers." The ratio of dependents to producers has doubled between 1920 and 1960 and is increasing almost continuously. Such population shifts must be planned for or else there can be much social and fiscal chaos.

It was said that the aged require more medical care than the young. Much of the care relates to diseases of the heart. About five times as many men over 65 die from heart problems as men aged 45 to 64. Cancer is also a killer, as are other chronic diseases.

To date, these diseases have attacked men more than women and this, in part, is the reason there are so many more women alive than older men. Men outnumber women slightly among those under 25, but at very old age, there are more than two women for every man. From age 25 on, the percentage of women in the population increases.

Whites live longer than nonwhites, but this pattern is diminishing with the more favorable social and medical conditions of nonwhites. Income is a problem for many of the aged, both nonwhite and white. For example, heads of household age 65 and over tend to have about half the income of younger families; however, their families are smaller. Many of the old are poor but, as indicated, individual differences are large, and many elderly are wealthy. Since so much of the assets of older people are inflation-protected—assets such as the government benefit programs of Social Security, Medicare, and Medicaid—the elderly have not been ravaged as much as younger people by the inflationary 1970s.

Most older people live in a family setting, usually in their own households. The households are usually in the city, rather than the suburbs, but an appreciable percentage of older people live outside of metropolitan areas altogether.

REFERENCES

Atchley, R. C. *The social forces in later life.* Belmont, Calif.: Wadsworth, 1980.

Birren, J. E., Butler, R. N., Greenhouse, S. W., Sokoloff, L., & Yarrow, M. *Human aging.* Washington, D.C.: Public Health Service Publication No. 986, 1963.

Bornstein, R., & Smircina, M. T. The status of empirical support for the hypothesis of increased variability in aging populations. *The Gerontologist,* 1982, *22,* 258–260.

Brotman, H. B. Income and poverty in the older population in 1975. *The Gerontologist,* 1977, *17,* 23–26.

Butler, R. N. Introduction. In S. G. Haynes & M. Feinleib (Eds.), *Epidemiology of aging.*

Washington, D.C.: U.S. Govt. Printing Office (NIH Publication No. 80–969), 1980, pp. 1–4.

Carp, F. M. Housing and living arrangements of older people. In R. H. Binstock & E. Shanas (Eds.), *Handbook of aging and social sciences*. New York: Van Nostrand Reinhold, 1976, pp. 244–271.

Carp, F. M., & Carp, A. It may not be the answer, it may be the question. *Research in Aging*, 1981, 3, 85–100. (a)

Carp, F. M., & Carp, A. Age, deprivation and personal competence. *Research in Aging*, 1981, 3, 279–298. (b)

Havighurst, R. J. *The sociological meaning of aging*. Address given at the General Session of the International Congress in Merano, Italy, July 15, 1957.

Hayflick, L. *The biology of aging*. Master lecture of the series on the Psychology of Aging, 86th Annual Convention of the American Psychological Association, 1978.

Hurd, M. D., & Shoven, J. B. *The economic status of the elderly* (Working Paper Series No. 914). Cambridge, Mass.: National Bureau of Economic Research, 1982.

Kastenbaum, R. J., & Candy, S. E. The 4% fallacy: a methodological and empirical critique of extended care facility population statistics. *International Journal of Aging*, 1973, 4, 15–21.

National Center for Health Statistics (USPHS). *Health in the later years of life*. Stock No. 1722-0178, October 1971.

Neugarten, B. L. The future and the young-old. *The Gerontologist*, 1975, 15 (No. 1, Part 2), 4–9.

Rockstein, M., & Sussman, M. *Biology of aging*. Belmont, Calif.: Wadsworth, 1979.

Shock, N. W. Energy metabolism, caloric intake and physical activity of the aging. In L. A. Carlson (Ed.), *Nutrition in old age* (X Symposium of the Swedish Nutrition Foundation). Uppsala, Sweden: Almqvist and Wiksell, 1972, pp. 12–23.

Shock, N. W. Biological theories of aging. In J. E. Birren & K. W. Schaie (Eds.), *Handbook of the psychology of aging*. New York: Van Nostrand Reinhold, 1977, pp. 103–115.

Siegel, J. S. Recent and prospective demographic trends for the elderly population and some implications for health care. In S. G. Haynes & M. Feinleib (Eds.), *Epidemiology of aging*. Washington, D.C.: U.S. Govt. Printing Office (NIH Publication No. 80–969), 1980, pp. 289–315.

United Nations General Assembly. *Question of the elderly and the aged*. A/8364, August 31, 1971.

United Nations Secretariat's *Bulletin on Aging*, Vol. VI, No. 1, 1981.

United States Bureau of the Census. *Current population reports. Illustrative population projection for the United States: The demographic effects of alternative paths to zero growth*. Series P-25, No. 476, April 1972.

United States Bureau of the Census. *Census of the population: Characteristics of the population*. Part 1, Section 1, 1973.

Unlisted Author. *A profile of maturing America*. Los Angeles: Ethel Percy Andrus Gerontology Center, Fall, 1981.

Weksler, M. E. The senescence of the immune system. *Hospital Practice*, 1981, 16, 53–64.

2
Person-Perception: Stereotyping the Elderly

BELIEFS AND ATTITUDES

Many studies carried out in different ways over the years indicate that beliefs about the elderly and attitudes toward them are generally negative. Beliefs and attitudes are not identical. Beliefs may be correct, such as old people are slow, or they may be wrong, such as old people cannot learn. Attitudes, on the other hand, are likes and dislikes, often based on these beliefs. A dislike based on false belief is wrong. Atchley (1980, pp. 253–260) made this distinction between beliefs and attitudes, but the literature tends to fuzz it. It is well to keep this distinction in mind, however, because regardless of the correctness of the beliefs, attitudes are simply emotional postures, phasing to bias and prejudice.

Even when beliefs regarding the elderly are true, they are often viewed as being more universal than they actually are. Chapter 1 emphasized individual differences and the importance of not making the mistake that the elderly constitute a homogeneous population. True or otherwise, beliefs can stigmatize large numbers of people—they "provide justification for those who would discriminate against older persons" (Atchley, 1980, p. 254).

Stereotypes

Stereotypes are combinations of beliefs, but this word is often used to suggest attitudes. Quadagno (1980, p. 123) indicated that it "is difficult to pinpoint the source of these stereotypes" of the elderly. She indicated that much of the research is based on surveys and questionnaires, and it is their formats that make people appear prejudiced rather than what they really believe. Most of these surveys and questionnaires provide negative statements about the elderly, and respondents are asked to agree or disagree with them. This does not provide opportunity to express positive statements. As will be seen,

17

this applies more to the earlier studies than the more recent ones, but it applies to some of the more recent ones too. Brubaker and Powers (1976) believe that people carry both positive and negative stereotypes of the elderly.

Not everyone agrees that it is the questionnaires that make people appear prejudiced. Quadagno also pointed out that people such as Butler (1969) believe that "these stereotypes have deeper roots." Butler believes the stereotypes reflect a distaste for growing old; they reflect a fear of becoming powerless or useless.

The Old Perform Well

The concept "stereotype," as indicated, suggests that the opinions and beliefs are not necessarily founded in fact. Hess (1974, p. 127) emphasized this by listing some facts that are not compatible with the stereotypes. She surveyed the literature and concluded that, overall, old people in the labor force perform as well as younger people. They are "as likely as not" to give help to adult children. Many old people are heads of households. They are responsible citizens, having higher voting rates than younger people. Old people have positive self-evaluations across a variety of traits, even though old people share many of the stereotypes of the young.

The world all around, however, helps perpetuate these negative opinions. Francher (1980, p. 134) analyzed 100 television commercials and concluded that "the young complex serves to disenfranchise the aged." Francher believes that the kind of message seen in these commercials may produce "anxiety [and induce] symptoms of senility." Whether this is so, it is clear that there are many messages, explicit and implicit, that say young is good, old is not.

EARLY STUDIES

The early studies were of surveys and questionaaires in which a series of statements were endorsed, either by a simple yes or no, or by indicating extent of endorsement (do not agree, agree, agree very much, etc.). These questionnaire studies have a long history now, going back at least to 1953 with a study of Tuckman and Lorge. Only a few of these studies will be discussed, and these in only little detail. The more recent studies are more sophisticated and greater reliance can be placed on them. These will be described in more detail. Each of these studies is listed in Table 2.1 (see pp. 26–27) with notes to help follow the very many details.

Questionnaire and Survey Studies

In the main, the early questionnaire studies were very clear not only in maintaining that negative stereotypes were held toward the elderly but that the elderly themselves harbored such stereotypes. For example, Axelrod and Eisdorfer (1961) reported that beliefs about people became more negative with each decade from 35 to 75 years. Tuckman and Lorge (1954) also showed that older adults held negative opinions. It should not be very surprising that some old people harbor negative stereotypes. After all, they were young once, and this is a legacy of their youth. Among the most recent of this type of study was a major survey by the National Council on the Aging conducted by the pollster Louis Harris (1975). "The results of 4,250 interviews make abundantly clear that adult Americans harbor many misconceptions about what old age is really like" (Aiken, 1982, p. 168). Most Americans seem to have an exaggerated picture of what is negative in later life.

These many questionnaire and survey studies notwithstanding, not all investigators concluded that negative stereotypes characterized most people. For example, Kogan (1961) concluded otherwise. He developed a questionnaire that had a set of 17 items in two forms regarding old people. One form expressed negative sentiments and the other form expressed positive ones. These items were interspersed among other items to disguise this opposite character of the questionnaire items. The disguise items were selected from personality and other types of tests.

Kogan gave this questionnaire to college students who, unlike those in other studies, tended to have a more favorable than unfavorable attitude toward old people. Those students who showed unfavorable attitudes also showed them toward ethnic minorities and a variety of disabled groups. The "more nurturant students" were more positively disposed toward the elderly.

Sentence Completion Tasks

Less quantitative than questionnaire studies, but richer in expression, was a series of sentence completion studies to assess attitudes toward the elderly. First, Golde and Kogan (1959) developed an "instrument" where items were, again, presented in two ways: one, where the items were stated in terms of "most old people . . ."; and two, where they were stated in terms of "most people. . . ." The hypothesis under test was that "attitudes toward old people are qualitatively different from those concerning the broader class of 'people in general" (p. 355). Again, the "instrument" was given to college students.

The hypothesis was confirmed but not "always in the direction unfavorable to old people" (Golde & Kogan, 1959, p. 359). Some items did reflect negative feelings, however, as for example, not wishing to become interpersonally involved with old people. Also, these young respondents believed that happiness and pleasures lie in the past for old adults, not the future.

This sentence completion test was then given to adults ranging in age from 49 to 92 (Kogan & Shelton, 1962a). Their response reflected a fear of loneliness, isolation, and dependence. They resented rejection, condescension, and references to age. These older adults seemed to dislike "anything suggestive of special treatment because of age" (p. 14). The need for companionship was seen as particularly important. They saw the lives of old people in more negative terms than the lives of people in general, lacking stimulation and happiness.

Following this study, adults aged 50 to 92 were compared to undergraduate students in their responses to the sentence completion task (Kogan & Shelton, 1962b). The differences between the age-groups were apparent in several items. The older responder was again resentful or fearful of being set apart, or thought of as different. The young, particularly women, saw the old as unattractive physically; the older group saw this less so. Paradoxically, perhaps, certainly in conflict with stereotypes, the young indicated an "interest in family" whereas the older people indicated an interest in "companionship and love." Kogan and Shelton (1962b, p. 104) suggested that this finding is "highly supportive of . . . views regarding a disengagement process in aging. . . ." (Disengagement will be discussed in great detail in Chapter 5.)

DENYING OLD AGE

Taken as a whole, these questionnaire and sentence completion studies showed that although not all attitudes and beliefs about the elderly are negative, and certainly not all people harbor negative attitudes, there is sufficient evidence that the aged are targets for negative opinion. Life can hardly be pleasant in such circumstances. Denial of old age might be one way out; it seems that people do not want to be old.

Few See Themselves as Old

"There is substantial literature showing that older persons often deny their own aging; that they tend to tenaciously cling to conceptions of themselves as 'middle-aged' or even 'young' . . . despite . . . the onset of old age. . . ." So wrote Bultena and Powers (1978, p. 748) in providing a half dozen literature references going back to 1968 and continuing almost to the date of their longitudinal study as documentation of this contention. There were earlier studies that also showed denial of aging. For example, Wallach and Kogan (1961) found evidence that people aged 54 to 92 years, with an average of 71, were more likely to see themselves as "not elderly" than "elderly." In similar fashion, Streib (1965) analyzed survey data of persons over 60 and found that the majority of people considered themselves "middle-aged"; it was only among those over 65 that there was any noticeable tendency to identify themselves as "old" or "elderly." The cutoff age was somewhere between 67 and 70 years. It is now a well-documented finding—many old people do not see themselves as old; at least they say they do not.

In the longitudinal study by Bultena and Powers (1978) the same question was asked of older people in 1960 and again in 1970. The question was, "Which of the following statements best describes the way you think of yourself: an old man, an elderly man, or a middle-aged man?" (The word *woman* was used in place of *man* when questioning female respondents.)

There were 611 respondents questioned in 1960 with 235 of them again questioned in 1970. All were 70 years or older in 1970, with 30 percent being 80 or older. One-third of these people thought of themselves as "middle-aged." One-quarter did think of themselves as "old" while 38 percent identified themselves as "elderly." This was in distinction to the identification 10 years previously, in 1960, when 70 percent identified themselves as "middle-aged." At that time the respondents were over 60. Only 6 percent identified themselves as "old" and 19 percent as "elderly."

Bultena and Powers recognized that "elderly" has been seen as interchangeable with "old," or as a euphemism for it, but they provided these categories "in the possibility that an elderly status might be viewed as less stigmatizing than being old" (p. 750). Still, it may be surprising that only 25 percent of the sample aged 70 and over identified themselves as old. Further, the denial of old age was not confined to only those aged 70, but also to those over 80. Of those over 85 years, only 48 percent identified themselves as old, the rest as "middle-aged" or "elderly."

Feeling Age

Some people feel old and some do not, and this feeling is only partly related to one's actual age. By and large, it seems, people of lower socioeconomic status (SES) see old age beginning at about 60, and higher SES people see it starting 10 years later (Neugarten & Peterson, 1957). This difference is probably due to the markers people use in feeling old. Poor health, loss of independence, and other such factors hit low SES people earlier and harder, and these make a person feel old.

Linn and Hunter (1979) categorized people aged 65 and older according to whether they felt younger than their age, or as old or older than their actual age. Those who felt younger than their age had more internal locus of control. (They tended to see life events as depending on their own efforts and abilities rather than on chance or fate.) The younger-feeling group was more satisfied with life and had better self-esteem, which related to minimum disability and impairment. Those who felt younger had higher intelligence, but this was more a matter of SES than of an intrinsic tie between intelligence and how old a person feels.

Thus, in sum, those feeling younger were more satisfied, had higher self-esteem, and felt in control. They were brighter. Surprisingly, perhaps, Linn and Hunter reported that those who felt younger than their age seemed no less anxious or depressed, and had no fewer physical complaints.

IDENTIFYING THE OLDER PERSON

The old person is easily told apart from the young person, but how easily differentiated are people in more similar age categories? Are opinions of people and preferences for them based on how old they appear and little else? At least some studies show that this is so.

Age Categories and Preferences

Kogan (1979) had photographs of men and women of wide age range and asked people to estimate the ages of the persons photographed. They were also asked to categorize persons in the photographs as either young, middle-aged, or elderly.

Kogan found that the older the estimating group, the older was the average assigned age. Men in the photographs were assigned older ages than women. Interestingly, the older the estimating group, the "greater the boundary permeability." That is, older people differentiated age categories less clearly than younger ones. For the older estimators, young, middle-aged, and elderly were less distinguishable. Although men in the photographs were assigned older ages than women, paradoxically, the older age categories were assigned to the women. Thus, women were perceived to age more quickly than men.

Kogan also asked his estimators to select three men and three women in the photographs whom they liked most. Men selected photos of people of median age 40; women selected people of median age 45. This difference resulted from the fact that the women preferred men and women in the photographs of similar age. Men, however, preferred women in the photograph some eight years younger than the men.

Stereotyping from Voice Alone

Just as Kogan wanted to see whether ages could be identified from photographs, Ryan and Capadano (1978) wanted to see whether ages could be identified from voice recordings. Tapes were made of very brief readings by men and women ranging in age from 12 to 71. These tapes were then played for young university students, who estimated the ages of the speakers. The correspondence between estimated age and actual age was excellent, especially from adolescence to about age 45. The older speakers, aged 60 to 71 years, tended to be perceived as younger, in the mid-50s.

Ryan and Capadano then carried out a procedure common to several studies described in the next section. They had their age-estimators rate each speaker (from the tape alone) on the basis of six adjectives describing personality characteristics. Each of the six was presented as a continuum from one extreme to the other—thus six "bipolar adjectives." The personality trait continua were: Weak—Strong, Outgoing—Reserved, Active—Passive, With-it—Out-of-it, Insecure—Self-assured, and Inflexible—Flexible. Each of these adjectives was rated on a seven-point scale such that a rating of "4" would be an in-between rating, while a rating of "1" would be extremely "Weak," for example, and a rating of "7" would be extremely "Strong."

It was found that older female speakers were rated as more reserved, passive, out-of-it, and inflexible than younger speakers. Older male speakers came out better; they were perceived only as more inflexible than younger speakers. Here it is seen that preconceived ideas, that is, stereotypes about the elderly, were present in the face of no information about them other than their voice and speech.

AGE IS NOT THE ONLY TARGET OF ATTRIBUTION

Age and Sex

Studies such as that by Ryan and Capadano utilizing bipolar adjectives to describe personality traits have become popular, possibly because these adjective ratings can be analyzed to develop independent domains of personality. For example, O'Connell and Rotter (1979) presented to undergraduate college students 32 bipolar items clustered into three factors, that is, the items represented three main traits of personality. The traits were effectiveness, independence, and personal acceptance.

The undergraduates rated the 32 bipolar items with regard to an average 25-year-old, an average 50-year-old, and an average 75-year-old. Half the ratings were based on men and half on women. It is to be noted that in this study, as well as all the others, the ratings of the "average person" or "people in general" indicate stereotypes of different age-groups since no particular person is singled out.

Effectiveness "was seen as decreasing sharply and linearly with age." Independence was seen as maintained from age 25 to 50 but as diminishing afterwards. The "25-year-old was judged to be more personally acceptable . . . than the 75-year-old (O'Connell & Rotter, 1979, p. 223).

Men were judged more effective and more independent than women as both 25- and 50-year-olds, but not as 75-year-olds. Thus, as Ryan and Capadano found, women were judged more harshly than men. Men tended to judge men more positively than they judged women. Women, on the other hand, judged the sexes similarly. This is compatible with Kogan's (1979) data of age preferences where women were more even-handed in regard to the sexes than men. Although men were seen as more effective and independent, they were also seen lower in personal acceptability at each of the three ages.

Age and Occupation

Bassili and Reil (1981) had young (16–49) and older (65–90) people rate 61 bipolar adjective scales. Theirs was a complex study in that the ratings were not only of age categories (35 or 70) and the two sexes, but of occupation (engineer or bus driver) and ethnic group (Canadian Indian or white Canadian). The target or stimulus person that was judged involved some combination of two of these four attributes: for example, one judgment was of a 70-year-old Canadian Indian; another was a 35-year-old man, or a 70-year-old former engineer. (The older target person's occupation was presented in terms of "former" while the younger person was presented as "still on the job.")

There was similarity in the ratings of old and young respondents. Their stereotyped views of the older target person were more homogeneous than those of the younger target person. This suggests that "observers stereotype young mature adults in terms of a variety of features; however, they stereotype old people mainly in terms of their age" (Bassili & Reil, 1981, p. 682). Among the traits characterizing the 70-year-old target person were: traditional, conservative, and present-oriented. Bassili and Reil concluded that these stereotypes overrode the stereotypes of sex, occupation, and ethnicity. The one exception was perception of the 70-year-old former engineer by the young raters. The 70-year-old former engineer was seen as scientific, industrious, and efficient.

If Bassili and Reil (1981) were more impressed with age as a stimulus for trait attribution than occupation, this was not true for Kogan and Shelton (1960) in a study carried out some 20 years earlier. Undergraduate college students were presented with short sketches or stories in which either a 33-year-old person or a 75-year-old retired person was depicted. The person was either a steelworker, assistant manager of a factory, or a university professor. The undergraduates categorized the central character in the sketches in terms of 45 traits, some of which were from popular attitude questionnaires in use at that time.

It was found that "occupation is a more critical determinant than age of the impression formed of a person" (Kogan & Shelton, 1960, pp. 206, 209). In fact, only a small number of traits were applied differently to young and old sketch characters, possibly because "age effects have no opportunities to manifest themselves" in the face of the overriding impact of occupational status. Since the first two traits in the list reflected an age effect, and few of the others did, Kogan and Shelton (1960, p. 209) concluded that, "One might infer that Ss [the respondents] had age in mind when they started to fill out the trait list, but forgot about it as the task proceeded."

A second part of the study involved sketches where age and occupation were not in as much competition, and here age stereotypes were found. The "older stimulus . . . is more likely to be considered 'absent minded,' 'conservative,' 'sad,' 'sluggish' . . ." but, interestingly, also "wise" (p. 211). Thus, Table 2.1 indicates both the presence and absence of stereotypes. Kogan and Shelton's study suggests that age-stereotypes will be seen when overriding opportunities for other stereotyping are not present.

PERSON-PERCEPTION: MORE REALISTIC EVALUATIONS

Up to now, each of the studies was based on either ratings of traits in terms of "more likely," "less likely," or some similar continuum, or ratings of traits was on the continuum of bipolar adjectives. Although the more recent of these studies are improvements over the early questionnaire studies, they remain artificial, yielding little more than a list of traits with limited meanings.

A new series of studies has been initiated that is more meaningful and realistic in what the judges are asked to rate. These studies in attribution are a long way from the simple questionnaire studies in that several important

TABLE 2.1
Investigations Reviewed in this Chapter, in Order of Their Presentation in Text

Investigators	Type of Study	Who Tested	Age-Stereotype?	Other Characteristics
Axelrod & Eisdorfer (1961)	Questionnaire	Young	Yes	—
Tuckman & Lorge (1954)	Questionnaire	Young and old	Yes	—
Harris (1975)	Survey	Young and old	Yes	—
Kogan (1961)	Questionnaire	Young	No	—
Golde & Kogan (1959)	Sentence completion	Young	Yes, but[*]	—
Kogan & Shelton (1962a)	Sentence completion	Old	Yes	—
Kogan & Shelton (1962b)	Sentence completion	Young and old	Yes	—
Bultena & Powers (1978)	Questionnaire	Old	—	Denied age
Wallach & Kogan (1961)	Questionnaire	Old	—	Denied age
Streib (1965)	Questionnaire	Old	—	Denied age
Neugarten & Peterson (1957)	Interview	Middle-age	—	SES—age identification
Linn & Hunter (1979)	Questionnaire & tests	Old	—	Age identification
Kogan (1979)	Rate photographs	Young and old	—	Age identification and preferences

Investigators	Type of Study	Who Tested	Age-Stereotype?	Other Characteristics
Ryan & Capadano (1978)	Rate voice recordings	Young	Yes	Age–sex differences
O'Connell & Rotter (1979)	Rate bipolar adjectives	Young	Yes	Age–sex differences
Bassili & Reil (1981)	Rate bipolar adjectives	Young and old	yes	Age more than occupation
Kogan & Shelton (1960)	Rate sketch	Young	Yes and no*	Occupation more than age
Connor et al. (1978)	Rate sketch	Young	No, but*	—
Locke-Connor & Walsh (1980)	Rate sketch	Young and old	No, but*	Subtle age differences
Weinberger & Millham (1975)	Questionnaire & rate sketch	Young	Yes and no*	No age–sex interaction Age–sex interaction
Reno (1979)	Estimate probability	Young	No, but*	None
Banziger & Drevenstedt (1982)	Rate sketch	Young	Yes	Subtle stereotype
Walsh & Connor (1979)	Rate sketch	Young	No, but*	Young women and old men stereotyped
Drevenstedt (1981)	Rate sketch	Young	No	No age–sex interaction
Crockett et al. (1979)	Evaluate sketch	Young	Yes, but*	—

*See text.

variables are varied simultaneously. Many of these studies are very complex. Although studies carried out in the 1950s or early 1960s, with exceptions, showed negative age stereotypes, these more recent, 1980s studies tend not to show them or, when they do, to show more subtle stereotyping. Have values and beliefs changed during a generation such that there is better acceptance of the aging and the aged? Are the different methods of investigation the reason for the differences in findings? It may be the latter because one of these complex studies included an attitude questionnaire that showed negative stereotypes although the main body of the study actually showed more positive attitudes toward the old than the young.

The general formats or experimental designs of these newer attribution studies have in common the following: Transcripts are presented to raters under the guise that they are true recordings of real interviews or real biographies of people. Sometimes a photograph of the person is presented with the transcripts.

The principal character in the transcript is depicted as either young or old. Often, both the young and the old character are portrayed as male for some raters and female for others. Thus, there is a young man and a young woman, and an older man and an older woman, most usually in an identical situation, differing only with regard to their ages and sexes. Often there is another simultaneous variation or two. For example, in job interview situations described next, the rater was told either that the applicant was hired or that the applicant was not hired. Or the applicant was portrayed as more able or less able.

The raters themselves are often both young and old, male and female. In such studies, rater ages and sexes are examined in interaction with the ages and sexes of the principal characters. These interactions will not be highlighted here, although some will be indicated.

Generalized Old People versus a Particular Person

Two studies were based on hypothetical job interviews. In the first study, a fictional transcript of the interview was distributed to college students to evaluate the applicant (Connor, Walsh, Litzelman, & Alvarez, 1978). The "applicant," a Mrs. Virginia Johnson, was either 24 or 63. Half the students were given a transcript for a position as a switchboard operator, the other half were given transcripts for a teacher's aid. One-third were told that the applicant had been hired, one-third were told that she was not hired, and one-third were told that the outcome was unknown.

Traits and the Person. Judgments were made regarding the applicant's ability in the interview, her motivation and her potential value as an employee (ability to handle job, background experience, ability to get along with co-workers). Judges also indicated how likely they would be to hire the applicant.

"Overall, there were no differences in the assessment of old and young job applicants" (Connor et al., 1978, p. 251). Those applicants who had been identified as "not hired" were rated less favorably than the others regardless of age. Connor et al. pointed out that these results are different from current employment practices that make it less likely for older adults to be hired than younger ones. The reason for this, they indicated, is that although, "The participants in our study did not react to age of the stimulus person, *per se* . . . they did react to . . . a situation, rejection for a job. . . ." Lack of money, or poor health, or physical unattractiveness may lead to negative evaluations for jobs and these characteristics may be true of more old people than young. They suggested that it is these characteristics, not age *per se*, that are the target of negative stereotypes, and by implication, related to hiring practices.

Although it is true that a distinction can be made between age *per se* and traits common to more of the old than young, negative stereotypes of the old remain. If there is negative response to people with these traits, and there are more such elderly than young people, there is age bias.

Competence and the Old Person. The second study of simulated job interviews focused on the competence of the applicant and, once again, on the success of obtaining the job (Locke-Connor & Walsh, 1980). Competence was varied by having two different transcripts, one reflecting competence and the other not. Each concerned a 25- or a 65-year-old man or woman applying for a job as a travel agent. The raters themselves were of two age-groups: a college student group and a group aged 25 to 64 of average age 38.

The findings of this study were similar to those of the previous one. Age of applicant was not an important factor in the evaluations, although the older applicant was seen as less active. This was equally true in the ratings of the younger and older responders. Despite the fact that age was not seen to affect competence evaluations, older age and other demographic factors were given as the reasons for the poor quality of the applicant who was not hired. When a younger applicant was not hired, lack of effort or ability was given as the reason. Thus, older age was seen as a basis for not getting the job, not younger age. Sex of applicant was not a factor in the evaluation, at least not in relation to age.

Contributions to Society. In the first job interview study, Connor et al. gave their raters an attitude scale and found that the responses to this questionnaire of "people in general" were not correlated with the evaluations of the individual person. This was also found by Weinberger and Millham (1975). They gave an attitude scale to undergraduates who rated a "representative 25-year-old" and a "representative 70-year-old" and found more negative attitudes toward the older person. At the same time, they presented brief biographical sketches, and here the reverse was found: the 70-year-old was more favorably judged than the 25-year-old.

One finding militated against the blanket conclusion that the particular aged person is not singled out for negative stereotype, only "people in general" are. The 70-year-old woman was seen as contributing less to society than the younger woman. The older and younger men, however, were seen as contributing equally. Thus, unlike the Locke-Connor and Walsh study, an age–sex interaction was observed. Once again, women were viewed in harsher terms than men; in this case, however, it was limited to older women.

Ability versus Effort. A somewhat different type of study was carried out by Reno (1979) where, again, an age bias was not found, except, perhaps, in a subtle way. College students estimated the probability (on a scale from 1 to 10) that a 25-year-old man or a 63-year-old man would succeed in college. They also estimated his grade-point average (1 to 4) and the causes for success or failure.

The estimations were no different regarding the 25-year-old than the 70-year-old, but the failure on the part of the older person was attributed to lack of ability and difficulty of the work. On the other hand, failure on the part of the younger person was attributed to the lack of effort. This suggests some subtle bias—it is as if the young could if they would; the success of the old is hampered by ability and difficulty of the work. It may be noted that although lack of ability was the reason given for the failure of the old in this study, it was the reason given for the failure of the young in the study by Locke-Connor and Walsh (1980). That study suggested that age and other demographic characteristics were the reasons for failure.

Age and Failure. Banziger and Drevenstedt (1982) presented under-graduate women with a situation involving an academic course in nutrition. The transcript variations included age (30 or 70 years), performance history of the person (succes or failure), and outcome of the course work (success or failure). It told that the course in nutrition would enable "Mrs. Smith" to plan better meals. In a second study, a sketch about retaking a driver's license test was presented both to college students and adults aged 55 to 82. In addition, the raters were told about "performance levels of others" and the outcome of the driver's test. Each student rated the situation on the basis of whether the outcome was due to effort, ability, age, luck, or task difficulty.

In the driver's test situation, old age was seen as the basis of failure in the case of the older person, and young age was seen as the basis of success in the case of the younger person. It was as if the old were expected to fail and the young to succeed. In the academic situation, the older person's failure was seen as due to inability. The investigators saw aspects of these results as inconsistent with those of Reno (1979), who examined estimations of likely success in college. The findings of both studies are similar, however, in the sense that both pointed to failure of the elderly as due to poor ability—but not for the young.

Ambiguous Situation?   Under the heading, "Contributions to Society," it was seen that Locke-Connor and Walsh (1980) did not find age-sex combinations of principal characters important in the evaluations, but Weinberger and Millham (1975) did. They found attributions such that old women contributed less to society than young women, whereas old and younger men contributed similarly. Walsh and Connor (1979) also reported significant age–sex interactions. They gave college students an essay to evaluate. The essay described a work of art and was either well-written or poorly written. Information regarding the author of the essay was given in brief biographical sketches. The author was either a man or woman, aged either 25 or 64. The evaluations were of how knowledgeable the author seemed to be about art, how likely the respondent would be to ask for advice, how well the author expressed ideas, and how likely they would be to publish the article.

Young women and old men "may be targets of subtle prejudice," the investigators wrote (Walsh & Connor, 1979, p. 561): their essays were devalued. Essays by the young man and old woman were seen to be of better quality. Locke-Connor and Walsh (1980) referred to this interaction between age and sex, and to the fact that their study did not show such an interaction. They suggested that ambiguous situations more often bring out stereotypic responses, and they believe that Walsh and Connor's situation was more ambiguous than theirs.

Role Appropriateness.   Following the procedure of Walsh and Connor, Drevenstedt (1981) presented a "newspaper article" on gardening as well as accompanying biographical sketches. She did not find that old and young principal characters were responded to differently; neither did she find a significant interaction between age and sex of the character. Drevenstedt attributed this to the perceived appropriateness of the role played by the women in the article.

Drevenstedt presented college undergraduates with a manuscript in which the principal character was either 25 or 64 years and the manuscript was either well-written or poorly written. The principal character was either a man or a woman, as were the judges. The judges rated the quality of the article on gardening and also rated the expertise of the "author." Drevenstedt believed that when "the field of endeavor (such as writing gardening articles) was compatible with age and sex stereotypes," age–sex bias would not be seen (p. 454). Drevenstedt referred to studies on sex bias showing that it occurs mainly, or only, when the sex role is seen as relatively inappropriate to the particular field of endeavor. The implication is that age bias would be seen mainly when the role is "age-inappropriate."

Favoring the Aged

The last study in this section follows a similar format in that a hypothetical 36-year-old is compared to a hypothetical 76-year-old (Crockett, Press, & Osterkamp, 1979). Each is a widow who "talked" about her life in an interview that was "recorded" and typed in manuscript.

This study was different from the others in that the interviews were in two pages of dialogue (not brief paragraphs) and men and women university students wrote their impressions of the women, as well as filled out rating scales. The impressions were based on instructions "to describe everything they 'know, think and feel' about her." Each impression protocol was "content analyzed for the number of statements in which specific reference was made to age" (Crockett et al., 1979, p. 370).

The ratings of the 76-year-old woman were more favorable than of the 36-year-old, "even when her behavior corresponded to negative stereotypes of older persons" (p. 368). Crockett et al. (1979, p. 373) concluded from the protocols that "when a person is mentally alert, is actively involved in social affairs, or does and says things that are of interest to a younger person, the older person will be perceived as deviating from the norm of that age and will be evaluated more positively than would a younger person who showed the same level of activity."

In a way, this conclusion is compatible with that of Connor et al. (1978), who, it will be recalled, made a distinction betwen aging *per se* and negative traits. Crockett et al. suggested that if the elderly are interesting to the young (are like the young?), then they are positively regarded, even more so than the young are. What if the elderly are not interesting to the young? Are they then stereotyped negatively?

Conclusion

Eight person-perception studies were described, each complex and similar to the others, yet different in detail and focus. Collectively, they tell an interesting story, even if not each and every study points in exactly the same direction.

First, most of the studies did not show negative evaluations of the old. In fact, two studies showed evaluations more favorable to the old. Taken at this level, it would seem that while the old questionnaire studies reflected age stereotypes, these more sophisticated studies on attribution did not. This is compatible with the idea that people may be biased toward age-groups in general, but not necessarily toward a particular individual. It is also compatible with what was suggested at the very beginning of this chapter, *viz.*, questionnaires themselves make people appear negative in attitude since negative statements are presented and some kind of endorsement response is required (disagree, agree, agree very much, etc.). This idea was supported further in one study where a questionnaire was given along with the attribution questions. The questionnaire responses showed negative stereotypes of the old and the attribution evaluations showed favorable response.

Left at this level, mistaken impressions may be maintained. Although little blatant or apparent age bias tends to be seen in these studies, subtle ones are apparent. In one study, when the old failed, failure was attributed to inability; when the young failed, failure was attributed to a lack of effort. In another study, when failure of the young was seen due to lack of ability, failure of the old was seen as due to age. In another study, age was the reason for the failure of the old, while at the same time age was seen as the reason for the success of the young.

Even more subtle, and even harder to combat, is a type of bias that is not based on "age *per se*" but on traits more common to the old than to the young, or bias based not on age but on characteristics not of interest to a younger person. This type of bias suggests that an old person will be responded to positively if that person has traits more common to the young than the old, or if the young find the old person interesting. The latter may simply mean that if the old person is more like a young person the old person will be viewed more positively.

Some of these studies showed an age–sex interaction; some did not. The data were mixed. In one study, the older women were seen in a more negative light than the younger women, with men of the two age-groups seen similarly. In another study, young women and old men were seen as targets of prejudice. It was claimed that if the role was ambiguously described, it was more likely to elicit a sex bias, perhaps along with an age bias. This idea is compatible with the greater bias seen with "old people in general" versus the "particular older person." It was also claimed that if the role was seen as "appropriate" to the age and sex group, little or no bias would be seen. Otherwise, bias would be apparent.

PAST, PRESENT, AND FUTURE

It was seen that studies carried out in 1950s and the early 1960s reflected generally negative opinions held by both young and old regarding the elderly. One study showed that the negative stereotypes increased toward those in each decade from 35 to 75. More current, more sophisticated studies reflected less negatively held beliefs, but those that were held were more subtle. Thus there is much work to do in education, work to demonstrate the unfairness and tragedy of bias. Negative attitudes can only make a person feel negative about him- or herself just because of being old or becoming old. Much of the life span can be painful, even ruined, simply by negative stereotype.

Old age is not synonymous with bad life. Borges and Dutton (1976) asked people in an extended age range to rate their own lives in terms of a continuum ranging from "very good" to "very bad." They also asked young people to rate their lives as foreseen or projected in the future. The older respondents rated their lives as better than the younger respondents did when they projected themselves into the future as older people. In other words, the young saw old age in more negative terms than did the old.

Older people are in better physical shape now than ever before. People have longer life expectancies. What had been considered old decades ago is not considered old today. Very many people at age 60 are vibrant, and many at 70 can look forward to exciting things. In 1980 a man was elected to the presidency of the United States at age 70. People at 80 are old, but even at this age there are wide individual differences.

Much can be pleasant in life at age 80 and older, but not if the world around the elderly thinks negatively and harbors negative stereotypes of them. This is not to say that older adults should deny their ages or failing abilities or fool themselves regarding difficulties. It is to say, however, that acceptance of these realities with positive outlook of what can be done and what is enjoyable to do will make the end years better years. The old are not to be thought of as "they." The old are but people with strengths and with weaknesses, just like anyone else.

SUMMARY

Beliefs about old people are different from attitudes toward them, although the research literature does not often make this distinction. It is important to make the distinction nevertheless because one should not bear on the other in any major way. If a person believes that old people are unattractive, for example, this is no reason to have a negative attitude toward them. Negative attitudes are dislikes just one step away from bias and prejudice.

The early studies on beliefs and attitudes were based mainly on questionnaires and surveys. Most of these showed that young people were generally negative about the elderly. Some studies showed that older people held similar negative beliefs and attitudes. After all, they had been young once, and then grew into old age only to keep their same ideas.

Not every questionnaire study showed negative attitudes, although most did. Some showed attitudes more favorable toward old people than unfavorable. It has been suggested by some investigators that it is the way questions are asked in these studies that brings out negative responses—that questionnaires do not reflect the positive attitudes that are present. Not everyone endorses this position, however. Some maintain that negative attitudes are real, reflecting a distaste for growing old. Possibly because of this, old people often deny their ages. In one study, for example, the majority of people age 60 and over saw themselves as middle-aged. In another study, even among those over 85, half identified themselves as middle-aged or elderly, rather than old.

Some of the questionnaires and surveys showed that young people tended to see the lives of older people in less desirable terms than the older people themselves saw it. This could mean that the young do not know much about the old. It could also mean, as was suggested in the previous chapter, that the old do not complain very much, at least not about circumstances that would bring complaint from younger adults.

Old people are readily told apart from young people on the basis of physical appearance, but age categories close together are not easily told apart, especially among old people themselves. One study showed that elderly people do not seem to be as preferred as the middle-aged. This study also showed that the preferred age of women is younger than the preferred age of men. Older women seem to be seen in more negative terms relative to younger women than are older men relative to younger ones.

Age and sex are not the only factors in evaluation. Occupational categories are also important, so important, in fact, that one study saw them as overriding age. That is, the impact of occupational status on attitudes was so great in this study that age considerations became minor. Another study reported otherwise, however—the age impact was greater than occupation.

A new type of study has developed that is superior to the questionnaire studies. In these new studies, typewritten manuscripts are presented under the guise that they are true transcriptions of interviews or are true biographical accounts. In these transcriptions, the principal character is sometimes a man, sometimes a woman; sometimes the character is young, sometimes old. The transcription may be of a job interview or an article written by the principal character, or something similar. Most often, there are simultaneous experimental variations—for instance, the written quality of the transcript or the degree of success of the character.

Unlike the earlier studies, these tend to show that evaluations of the elderly are not negative. It has been suggested that the earlier studies recorded attitudes of "old people in general," whereas the more recent ones recorded attitudes of a specific person in a specific context. The former may show negative stereotypes, the latter usually do not.

The latter studies based on specific persons, however, sometimes show subtle bias. For example, in one study, when the old failed, it was attributed to inability; when the young failed it was attributed to lack of effort. In another study, old age was seen as the basis of failure while at the same time, young age was seen as the basis of success. It was also concluded that it is not age *per se* that elicits negative attitude, but traits more common to the old than to the young. This hardly constitutes acceptance of the old.

It is more difficult to combat subtle bias than the more blatant bias seen in questionnaire studies. Older people do very well in a wide variety of areas: they perform well in the labor force, they often help adult children, they are responsible citizens. Old people are in better shape now than ever before. There is now a long old age to be enjoyed. The old are people with strengths and weaknesses, just like you and me.

REFERENCES

Aiken, L. R. *Later life.* New York: Holt, Rinehart and Winston, 1982.

Atchley, R. C. *The social forces in later life.* Belmont, Calif.: Wadsworth, 1980.

Axelrod, S. & Eisdorfer, C. Attitudes toward old people: an empirical analysis of the stimulus-group validity of the Trackman-Lorge questionnaire. *Journal of Gerontology*, 1961, 16, 75–80.

Banziger, G., & Drevenstedt, J. Achievement attributions by young and old judges as a function of perceived age of stimulus person. *Journal of Gerontology*, 1982, 37, 468–474.

Bassili, J. N., & Reil, J. E. On the dominance of the old-age stereotype. *Journal of Gerontology*, 1981, 36, 682–688.

Borges, M. A., & Dutton, L. J. Attitudes toward aging. *The Gerontologist*, 1976, 16, 220–224.

Brubaker, T., & Powers, E. The stereotype of "old": a review and an alternative approach. *Journal of Gerontology*, 1976, 31, 441–447.

Bultena, G. L., & Powers, E. A. Denial of aging: age identification and reference group orientations. *Journal of Gerontology*, 1978, 33, 748–754.

Butler, R. Ageism—another form of bigotry. *The Gerontologist*, 1969, 9, 243–246.

Connor, C. L., Walsh, P., Litzelman, D. K., & Alvarez, M. G. Evaluation of job applicants: The effects of age versus success. *Journal of Gerontology*, 1978, 33, 246–252.

Crockett, W. H., Press, A. N., & Osterkamp, M. The effect of deviations from stereotyped expectations upon attitudes toward older persons. *Journal of Gerontology*, 1979, 34, 368–374.

Drevenstedt, J. Age bias in the evaluation of achievement: What determines? *Journal of Gerontology*, 1981, 36, 453–454.

Francher, J. S. "It's the Pepsi generation": accelerated aging and the television commercial. In J. S. Quadagno (Ed.), *Aging, the individual and society.* New York: St. Martin's Press, 1980, pp. 134–143.

Golde, P., & Kogan, N. A sentence completion procedure for assessing attitudes toward old people. *Journal of Gerontology*, 1959, *14*, 355–363.

Harris, L., & Associates. *The myth and reality of aging in America*. Washington, D.C.: National Council on Aging, 1975.

Hess, B. B. Stereotypes of the aged. *Journal of Communication*, 1974, *24*, 76–85.

Kogan, N. A study of age categorization. *Journal of Gerontology*, 1979, *34*, 358–367.

Kogan, N. Attitudes toward old people: the development of a scale and an examination of correlates. *Journal of Abnormal and Social Psychology*, 1961, *62*, 44–54.

Kogan, N., & Shelton, F. C. Differential cue value of age and occupation in impression formation. *Psychological Reports*, 1960, *7*, 203–216.

Kogan, N., & Shelton, F. C. Images of "old people" and "people in general" in an older sample. *Journal of Genetic Psychology*, 1962, *100*, 3–21. (a)

Kogan, N., & Shelton, F. C. Beliefs about "old people": a comparative study of older and younger samples. *Journal of Genetic Psychology*, 1962, *100*, 93–111. (b)

Linn, M. W., & Hunter, K. Perception of age in the elderly. *Journal of Gerontology*, 1979, *34*, 46–52.

Locke-Connor, C., & Walsh, P. Attitudes toward the older job applicant: just as competent but more likely to fail. *Journal of Gerontology*, 1980, *35*, 920–927.

Neugarten, B. L., & Peterson, W. A. A study of the American age-grade system. *Proceedings of the Fourth Congress of the International Association of Gerontology*, 1957, *3*, 497–502.

O'Connell, A. N., & Rotter, N. G. The influence of stimulus age and sex on person perception. *Journal of Gerontology*, 1979, *34*, 220–228.

Quadagno, J. S. *Aging, the individual and society*. New York: St. Martin's Press, 1980.

Reno, R. Attribution for success and failure as a function of perceived age. *Journal of Gerontology*, 1979, *34*, 709–715.

Ryan, E. B., & Capadano, H. L. Age perceptions and evaluative reactions toward adult speakers. *Journal of Gerontology*, 1978, *33*, 98–102.

Streib, G. F. Are the aged a minority group? In A. W. Gouldner & S. M. Miller (Eds.), *Applied sociology*. New York: Free Press of Glencoe, 1965, pp. 311–328.

Tuckman, J., & Lorge, I. Attitudes toward old people. *Journal of Social Psychology*, 1953, *37*, 249–260.

Tuckman, J., & Lorge, I. Old people's appraisal of adjustment over the life-span. *Journal of Personality*, 1954, *22*, 417–422.

Wallach, M. A., & Kogan, N. Aspects of judgment and decision making: Interrelationships and changes with age. *Behavioral Sciences*, 1961, *6*, 23–36.

Walsh, R. P., & Connor, C. L. Old men and young women: how objectively are their skills assessed? *Journal of Gerontology*, 1979, *34*, 561–568.

Weinberger, L. E., & Millham, J. A multi-dimensional, multiple method analysis of attitudes toward the elderly. *Journal of Gerontology*, 1975, *30*, 343–348.

3
Biological Factors in Longevity and Survival

Biologists and other investigators have sought to discover why some people live long and some die early in life. Although most of the important answers—and perhaps most of the important questions—are not known, a body of information is developing that permits some control over our own longevities.

This chapter deals mainly with biological factors of longevity and survival and the next chapter deals mainly with psychological and social factors. All these factors are related so that distinctions among them are at least partly arbitrary. Even those factors that at first may appear to be purely biological are influenced by environmental, social, and personal events.

GENETIC CONTROL

Chapter 1 included a very brief review of biological theories of aging. The autoimmune theory was discussed in more detail than the others since it seems an especially promising theory. The basic idea is that with aging, a point is reached where foreign, invading substances are not always recognized as foreign, and tissues and organs of the body are not always recognized as the self. Thus there is an attack on the self and a failure to ward off harmful effects from invaders.

It is believed by some that such a breakdown with age results in the increase of chronic diseases that can lead to death. Why the breakdown? One answer, an obvious one, although not necessarily correct, is that, from the moment of birth, there is a genetic program for such breakdown. All genetic theories have this character: some genetic defects are seen soon after birth, cerebral palsy, for example; others are not developed until late in life, such as immunological breakdown. It should be very clear, however, that as adequate as genetic theory may be, whether it relates to immunological breakdown or to other mechanisms, no evidence has yet been found for genes that control delayed programming (breakdown starting late in life).

Evolutionary Considerations

If there are such things as genes responsible for breakdown and the time of breakdown and, thus, for the length of life, they may be expected to play a role in an evolutionary sense, even if a limited one. Fries and Crapo (1981, pp. 37–40) briefly summarized some of the ideas regarding evolution and aging, indicating that a basic tenet of evolutionary theory is that the fittest reproduce and the others do not, or do not as readily. This protects the species because, in time, it is made up of the fittest. After the reproductive period, however, the parents' state of fitness does not contribute to the fitness of the offspring. The job has already been accomplished, so to speak—the genes have already been passed on. Thus after the reproductive years, after the 20s or 30s, there is no evolutionary, biological advantage to long-life genes.

The credence of genetic theory does not rest on evolutionary theory, but traditionally the two are linked. What are some of the indirect evolutionary advantages to genes of long life? There are speculations: as Fries and Crapo indicated, one advantage may be that children living with long-lived parents are more likely to be protected until their 20s or 30s, when they reproduce. Psychological development in humans progresses beyond the age of reproduction—perhaps there is a selective advantage for the offspring to have long-lived parents. There is another possible advantage. It is beneficial to have a reserve of whatever is required for survival. The beneficial reserve for living to the age of reproduction may keep people from breaking down after this period to survive well into old age.

Aging genes or otherwise, long life is limited to system breakdowns, such as the immune system. The foregoing suggests that the breakdowns are under genetic control. It may be the other way around, however. It may be that the breakdown limits the genetic potential.

Cellular Aging: Time Clocks

Is there evidence of genetic control of longevity on the level of a single cell? There seems to be. Certain kinds of animal cells have what might be thought of as built-in "time clocks." These clocks function as if they count off the amount of life already lived and program the time still left. Hayflick (1974) summarized some details of this discovery in a nontechnical address, speculating on how much of our future lives relate to such cell groups.

Hayflick started with the simple goal of developing human cell cultures free from disease. He chose to do this with embryonic tissue because such tissue is most likely to be free of disease. "The major surprise . . . was the finding that the normal cell populations grew and divided perfectly for many months, then slowed down, stopped dividing, and ultimately died" (Hayflick, 1974, pp. 37–38). He focused on some strains of human fibroblasts derived from embryos (cells giving rise to connective tissue—a tissue that deteriorates with age). Hayflick noted that the fibroblasts undergo 50 population doublings and then die. Strains derived from young adults rather than embryos, however, undergo only about 30 population doublings before dying. Furthermore, strains from old adults undergo even fewer doublings, about 20. This finite lifetime of cultured normal cells may well be "a manifestation of biological aging at the cellular level. . . . Cultured normal cells are mortal just as are the animals from which they are taken" (pp. 38–39).

There seems to be some biochemical mechanism—some clock—within the cells that counts the doublings and allows only so many more. Hayflick speculated that functional losses occur in cells prior to the loss of their capacity to double and that these functional losses produce age changes.

Longevity of Different Species

The different lengths of life of various animal groups provide strong evidence in support of the concept of a genetic basis of longevity. In a review entitled *General Biology of Senescence*, two tables were presented listing the length of life of various animals (Lansing, 1959, pp. 121–122). Normal life for man was estimated as 70 to 80 years, with a possible potential for living 110 years. The chimpanzee tends to live 15 to 20 years, although it may have a life potential greater than 30 years. The range of the different life spans of mammals is very great: the rat lives about two to three years; it is possible that the fin whale lives several hundred years. These great specie differences are consistent over the generations. What other than genes can account for this? The fact that long- and short-lived animals can be developed through genetic inbreeding in the laboratory leaves little room for doubt regarding genetic control of life span (Rockstein & Sussman, 1979, p. 30).

A distinction was made in the first chapter between life span and life expectancy. Although man's genetic destiny may not include life beyond the age of 110, from his limited time perspective there is much life between the ages of 70 to 80, when he now dies, and 110, that may be achievable.* Belief in genetic control is not synonymous with personal destiny. As will be seen, we can shorten our lives by poor habits and we can maximize life duration by good ones.

*Life spans much longer than 110 years were reported among two different groups of people living in relatively primitive and isolated surroundings: one group was in the Ecuadorian valley of Vilcabamba and the other in Abkhazia of the Georgian Soviet Socialist Republic (e.g., Leaf, 1973). Hayflick (1974, p. 43) contended, "In none of these reports is adequate scientific proof given to substantiate the claims for longevity that are made." Fries and Crapo (1981, pp. 12–

Long-lived Parents Make for Long-lived Offspring

Biologists like to say, "If you want to live long, choose long-lived parents." There is some scientific evidence for the contention that there is a relationship between parental longevity and that of the offspring, but the evidence is sparse. One major study to which reference is often made was first reported in 1918 by Alexander Graham Bell and then published more widely in 1922 by Pearl. The longevities of 4,000 descendants of one family were examined in relation to age of parents at death. Figure 3.1 is based upon these observations and suggests some correlation between age at death of parents and age at death of offspring.

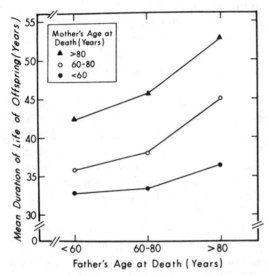

FIGURE 3.1: Longevity of offspring as a function of the longevity of mother and father. (From Table 16 of Pearl, 1922.)

These early data seem to constitute much of the basis for a belief in genetic determination of the human life span, but there are other studies as well. Rockstein (1958) reported that Beeton and Pearson (1899) examined data of 1,000 fathers and their sons, and 2,000 pairs of brothers. Very small correlations were seen between father–son longevities, and somewhat larger ones for brother–brother longevities. A more recent study involved the records of American and Canadian life insurance companies. Higher death

13) reviewed studies investigating over 600 people over 100 years of age. The oldest confirmed age was 114, thus, ". . . it can be rather confidently stated that there are no" people over age 120 in the Western developed countries.

rates of the policy holders were seen when their parents died before ages 50 and 60 than when they died later in life (Dublin, Lotka, & Spiegelman, 1949).

Perhaps more impressive was the study by Jalavisto (1951), who examined the longevities of nearly 13,000 Finnish and Swedish couples. These data, as discussed by Kallmann and Jarvik (1959), also indicated a positive relationship between the longevities of parent and offspring. The maternal influences were greater than the paternal ones, and the life spans of daughters had a greater relationship to parental life spans than those of sons. Kallman and Jarvik were able to confirm the parent–offspring longevity relationship but not the findings regarding the greater maternal influence or the greater influence on the daughter. Paradoxically, Palmore (1982, pp. 515–516) found support, although weak support, for just the opposite conclusion. "Mother's age at death was not a significant predictor [of offspring longevity] but father's age of death was [for men]. . . ." Neither "father's nor mother's longevity significantly predicted longevity among women."

Palmore emphasized that even the father–son longevity relationship was not strong. Actually, none of the studies produced correlations that are very high. Even had they been, however, it still would have been a mistake to automatically attribute the relationship between parental and offspring longevities to genetic factors alone. Data such as seen in Figure 3.1 could result from a variety of factors. Long-lived parents may be healthier, wealthier, and wiser than short-lived parents in ways unrelated to a longevity gene pool but related to longevity, nevertheless. It is reasonable to expect that favorable cultural and intellectual factors alone could lengthen the life span of both parent and child. Rockstein (1958) recognized this but maintained a respect for the genetic hypothesis on the basis of parent–offspring longevity correlations seen in the data on lower animal forms, especially those often used in laboratory experiments.

Study of Twins

The genetic hypothesis in human studies receives great support in the examination of longevities of twin pairs. The relevant data were summarized by Kallmann and Jarvik (1959), most of them being their own. Beginning in 1945, more than 2,500 twin cases were identified, and records were kept of those living to age 60 and over. Genetic control of longevity was inferred from the fact that the life spans of twins born of one egg were more similar than those born of two eggs. Identical twins died on an average of about four years apart, and fraternal twins died on an average of about five-and-a-half years apart. It was also found, however, that as late old age was approached, the similarity in life spans of the one-egg twins decreased, and the similarity of two-egg twins increased. This latter trend was attributed, at least in part, to artifacts of the experimental problem. For example, if one of the dizygotic twin pair dies at age 97, the other cannot die very many years after this. Nevertheless, even at the ages over 80, "intrapair differences in life span were still less for MZ [one-egg twins] than for DZ [two-egg] partners . . ." (Bank & Jarvik, 1978,p. 305).

The evidence, overall, does seem to support the contention that "If you want to live long, choose long-lived parents." But, again, it is obvious that within the broad limits that may be established by the germ plasm, there are many years that are vital or not, depending upon other biological factors, and certainly upon environmental and psychological factors.

Women Live Longer Than Men

The fact that the female outlives the male was made clear in Chapter 1 with Figure 1.2. Is the basis for this in the genes? Is it due to social or cultural factors? It seems that the answer to both these questions is yes.

Rockstein (1958) evolved a table on the basis of a detailed literature search showing the the female outlives the male in a wide variety of animal groups—for example, rats, black widow spiders, mealworms, fruitflies, the common housefly, and other species. He pointed out that, with human beings, the female is not only the longer-lived but, with only a few exceptions, whatever the specific disease causing death, the female fares better at every adult age level. Such evidence is compatible with a genetic explanation of the longer life of women, but there is another type of evidence arguing otherwise.

Environmental arguments point to lifestyles as the basis of the age difference in longevity—for example, the pressure men experience in the competitive, assertive world of work and career. This argument may apply to the oldest of age-groups; it is not as compatible with the youngest of age-groups since young women have joined the work force in large numbers. Further, the environmental argument does not receive support by the data of Figure 1.3. It is seen in this figure that from 1950 to 1976, the pattern has been for increasing sex differences in longevity. It was during this time that women came a long way from the care of home to the world of work in joining the labor force. Data from the Soviet Union also argue against environmental explanations. In the USSR, more than in the United States, occupational roles of the two sexes are equal, yet Siegel (1980, pp. 301–302) pointed out that women outlive men by about 10 years in the USSR.

A more vital argument in support of the environmental or lifestyle position was seen in a conclusion by Retherford (as referred to by Siegel, 1980, p. 301). Two-thirds of the difference in longevity between the sexes "in most of the century was due to smoking." The sex difference in mortality is due mainly to coronary heart disease that, as will be seen later, is related to smoking. There are other killer diseases that are also more prevalent among men than women. Lung cancers are more frequent among men, as are emphysema and cirrhosis of the liver (Waldron, 1980, p. 163). More cigarette smoking among men accounts for much of the emphysema and lung cancer, and more alcohol drinking accounts for the cirrhosis.

These data argue for environmental factors as contributors to the sex difference in longevity. They certainly suggest the notion that whatever the genetic basis, it is not the whole basis. Cross-cultural data also support this contention. The sex mortality ratio varies widely, "from 0.9 in Honduras . . . to 2.1 in Canada and the United States among American countries . . . and from 1.3 in Greece . . . to 2.1 in France . . . among the European countries" (p. 165). It seems that sex differences in length of life "are smaller in predominantly rural, agricultural countries" (p. 171).

MAINTAINING HEALTH

Killer Diseases

The prevalence of chronic disease increases with age, and these diseases are the main cause of death in later years. It may be seen in Table 3.1 that in 1976 diseases of the heart and blood vessels alone accounted for well over 40 percent of deaths among the over-65-year-olds. It is unclear whether, when a fatal disease occurs, it "hits" in a random fashion or whether with age there is a change in the "genetic program" that makes the "hit" more likely. It is known that in mice, at least, different genetic strains are differentially susceptible to disease processes that shorten the life span (e.g., Curtis, 1966, p. 95). In man, susceptibility to diabetes is inheritable, and this too is a killer in old age (see Table 3.1). Curtis is unequivocal in his opinion about disease in later adulthood: ". . . mutations occur which predispose an individual to the development of a particular disease" (Curtis, 1966, p. 12). The particular disease often relates to a breakdown of a particular organ system, for example, the cardiovascular system.

TABLE 3.1
Percent Death Rates for Leading Causes of Death for Ages 65 and Over During 1976*

Cause of Death by Rank	65 Years and Over	65 to 74 Years	75 to 84 Years	85 Years and Over
	All Causes: Deaths per 100,000 Population			
	5,428.9	3,127.6	7,331.6	15,486.9
	Percent Death Rate			
Diseases of the heart	44[†]	41	44	48
Malignant neoplasms	18	25	17	09
Cerebrovascular diseases	13	09	14	17
Influenza and pneumonia	04	02	04	06
Arteriosclerosis	02	01	02	05
Diabetes mellitus	02	02	02	01
Accidents	02	02	02	02

*Calculated from Table IV-10 of Siegel (1980, p. 305).
[†]To determine the number of deaths per 100,000 population from percentages, multiply the respective percentages by the number of deaths for all causes. For example, .44 (5,428.9) equals the number of deaths per 100,000 of all those 65 years and over due to diseases of the heart.

The Major Organ Systems

The long list of how organ systems of the body lose efficiency and deteriorate with age can be discouraging, even depressing, unless two important related concepts are kept in mind—the concepts of *plasticity* and *lifestyle*. Plasticity means that defects can be helped, at least to some degree, and lifestyle bears on health habits that minimize decline and maximize efficiency. Plasticity and lifestyle are related factors that can bring life expectancy closer to life span.

Rockstein and Sussman (1979), among others, described in fine detail the major organ systems of the body and how they change with age. They discussed the cardiovascular system, the nervous system, the respiratory system, the gastrointestinal system, the urinary system, the endocrine system, the reproductive system, and skin, bones, and muscle. Each of these show negative age changes, some of which are important to life, some not. Here, only the first two systems will be discussed, not in any great detail, but sufficient to indicate what happens to these systems with age, and how plasticity and lifestyle come into play.

The Cardiovascular System. Blood vessels narrow with age (atherosclerosis) and they harden (arteriosclerosis), making for a loss of elasticity.

This keeps an adequate blood supply from reaching all the tissues and organs of the body. Adequate blood supply brings nutrients and oxygen to the tissues and, at the same time, removes waste products.

When there is blood vessel constriction, blood pressure is elevated; if the blood pressure is high enough, the blood vessels can burst. The heart itself loses efficiency. There is a diminished capability of the heart to compensate to stress. Except in broad statistical terms, however, deterioration of cardiovascular function with age is not preordained (Fries & Crapo, 1981, p. 91). The rate of organ deterioration can be slowed, the onset of infirmity can be pushed off, and satisfactory function can be extended. In other words, the organ system is plastic. Lifestyles can affect the plasticity in both directions—hastening infirmity and death, or delaying it. Drug use and, as already indicated, cigarettes, hasten deterioration of cardiovascular and other processes. Good dietary and exercise habits can retard deterioration processes. Since 1970, public awareness of these habits has had the effect of a steady decline of cardiovascular disease. (These health habits will be described in greater detail later.)

Nervous System. This major organ system—the brain, spinal cord, and mass of neural connections—is the central coordinating system of the body. It innervates other organ systems and maintains contact with the external world and internal environment. It evaluates information and processes it; it is the system of all mental life. The nervous system is made up of billions of nerve cells (neurons). These are connected by nerve fibers that conduct nerve impulses away from the cell (axons) and also conduct impulses toward the cell (dendrites).

Cells of the brain decrease in number as people age. The loss starts very early in life, at about age 20. Since neurons do not regenerate, the cell loss is permanent. In the cerebral cortex, the decrease is about 45 percent by the ninth decade (Brody & Vijayashanker, 1977, pp. 244–245). There is also cell loss in the cerebellar cortex and other brain areas (Bondareff, 1981 p. 143). The human brain has so many cells, however, that not all of them are needed for optimal functioning; there seems to be a reserve. It is believed that the gradual cell loss with age is no special problem, not at least until some threshold level is reached. Beyond this level, problems in cognition might be expected, although it has never been demonstrated that cell loss is the basis of any cognitive problem. Thus, the impact of neuron loss, if any, has yet to be determined.

There is also a decrease with age in the number of dendrites and number of synapses (points where impulses pass from one neuron to another). This may be the result of the loss of neurons, but it is not certain that this is so (see Bondareff, 1981, pp. 140–147). Again, the functional importance of these changes is uncertain. There are other brain changes as well. The white matter of the brain becomes more cream-colored because of yellowish "aging pigments" (called lipofuscin or lipochrome). The presence of "aging pigment" is seen early in life so that by age 32, as many as 84 percent of the cells contain the pigment. Even more than cell loss, "aging pigment" is of questionable functional significance (see Rockstein & Sussman, 1979, pp. 57–58).

Thus, there are losses in the number of brain cells, synapses, and dendrites with age. There is also the accumulation of "aging pigments" that changes the arrangements of components within some neurons. These changes make for what Bondareff (pp. 146–148) called "changes in the organization of the brain." He suggested that reorganization, or redistribution of brain components, might make for an adaptive process to compensate for what otherwise would result in functional loss. He suggests that in this way there is a plasticity in the nervous system to prolong function.

These are normal or expected changes with age. There are also abnormal or pathological nervous system changes, which are discussed in Chapter 8.

Health Habits

There are both avoidable and unavoidable stressors in life that affect the functioning of the major organ systems that, in turn, make for disability, disease, and even death. Even some of the unavoidable ones can be controlled, however, even if to a limited extent. For example, high levels of radiation make for degenerative diseases as well as for defects at birth. Some radiation exposure can be minimized. Fries and Crapo (1981, p. 88) emphasize that such threats to health and life can sometimes be controlled by group efforts. They point to asbestos and other chemical pollutants as life-endangering. Other threats may come from the consumption of saccharin and some food dyes. These may be dangerous, although all the data are not yet in. One problem with controlling such environmental pollutants and toxins is that it is costly. The trade-off between dollars and community health is a community decision.

Other environmental insults are under direct personal control. It is these that are a matter of one's lifestyle affecting major organ systems and disease processes.

Alcohol. Drugs and alcohol affect nervous system and cardiovascular functioning. Taken to excess, these chemical agents make for permanent damage. Damage to the nervous system affects all other systems. Moderate alcohol consumption may actually be healthful—say, two ounces per day. Not all persons, however, can limit themselves to moderate drinking and there is the danger of excess consumption. Heavy drinking can cause hemorrhages of the stomach; it could shorten life duration (Fries & Crapo,

1981, p. 87). It can make for a reduction in brain cells, an enlargement of the ventricles of the brain, and a loss of cognitive ability (Brewer & Perrett, 1971; Cala, Jones, Mastaglia, & Wiley, 1978).

Cigarette Smoking. Much has already been said here about the negative effects of smoking. Just about everyone now knows that cigarette smoking can be damaging to health, but how damaging is only now being disclosed.

Early in 1982, the Surgeon General of the U.S. Public Health Service, C. Everett Koop, issued a report that leaves little doubt about smoking. He reported that death due to cancer is twice as likely among men who smoke than men who do not. Deaths due to heart, lung, and respiratory diseases, among others, are also attributed to smoking. Pipes, cigars, snuff, and chewing tobacco can also cause cancer. Even nonsmokers exposed to smoke-filled rooms are in danger. Smoking during pregnancy is dangerous because it can result in premature births, miscarriages, and birth defects.

This Surgeon General's report is not different from the many that preceded it, unless, perhaps, that it focused on the many varieties of cancer that are smoking-related. Formerly, the problem was pretty much limited to men; now it includes women. Despite the projection of the ratio of women to men in Figure 1.3, it is possible that death due to smoking among women of the future will be so great as to diminish the sex differences in mortality rates.

If there is any single health fact that may be pleasing to smokers, it is that stopping smoking helps even if damage is already done. Kannell and Gordon (1980, pp. 65–66) reported that, "there is a halving of the risk [of cardiovascular disease] in those who give up smoking. . . ." This, however, does not apply to people aged over 65. After this age, cigarette smoking does not seem to play a role—there "is no discernible benefit" in stopping. This lack of benefit after 65 applies to cardiovascular disease; there does not appear to be evidence that it applies to cancers and lung diseases.

Very recent studies have shown that most cigarette smokers have high levels of carbon monoxide in the blood. These high levels are potentially dangerous, increasing the chance of complications from heart disease. Even when there is no history of heart ailments, there may be subclinical vascular disease that can be aggravated by carbon monoxide.

Knowledge of the detrimental effects of smoking is not new. Twenty years prior to the 1982 Surgeon General's report it was declared, "There is no longer any doubt that cigarette smokers have a higher death rate than nonsmokers. New biological studies help to explain how tobacco smoke damages the lungs, heart and other body tissues" (Hammond, 1962). Figure 3.2 shows the percent of people in the United States during the one year between 1964 and 1965 who developed chronic health problems in relation

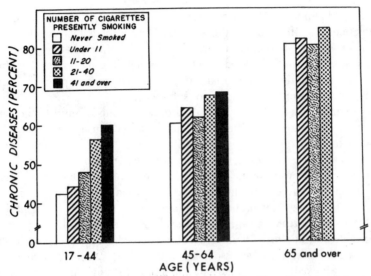

FIGURE 3.2: Percent of people with one or more chronic health problems in relation to the quantity of cigarettes smoked. Smoking has a greater effect on the health of young adults than on older people. (Data from Table 3, USPHS Report, 1967.)

to smoking. This figure shows that smoking and chronic health conditions go hand in hand, at least among the young. The more cigarettes smoked, the greater the frequency of chronic disease.

There is the interesting idea that genetic factors may predispose some people both to smoking and to the related illnesses; genes, not smoking, are the "cause" of the illnesses. As reviewed by Seltzer (1967), twin studies have shown that identical twin pairs are much more alike in their smoking habits than fraternal twin pairs. Diseases such as lung cancer have been found more in some families than in others irrespective of smoking habits. Some investigators maintain that, even if there is not a genetic basis for both smoking and cancer, the genetic predisposition to cancer is exacerbated by smoking. This contention received support in an editorial written years ago ("Counterblast to Tobacco," *The Lancet*, Jan. 9, 1971, pp. 69–70).

> The epidemiological and chronical evidence of reduced risk of lung cancer and chronic bronchitis after stopping smoking is especially important insofar as it counters both the genetic theory of causation of lung cancer and the argument that there is no point stopping after essential damage has been done.

Diet. Gross obesity in adulthood is one road to heart attacks. Gross obesity makes the heart work harder and stresses the blood vessels. On the other hand, there is the suggestion that too little weight also reduces longevity (e.g., Palmore, 1980, p. 57). Related to obesity are fatty deposits, called cholesterol, in the walls of the arteries. Certain foods increase the cholesterol deposits and so their intake should be minimized—eggs, red meat, creams, butter, and processed cheeses. Although it is not certain that cholesterol causes arteriosclerosis, many physicians advise their patients, particularly men, to avoid eating much of such foods.

Actually, there are two types of cholesterol, one harmful to the cardiovascular system and the other not. There is a low-density lipoprotein (LDL) that is harmful, and a high-density liproprotein (HDL) that may even be beneficial to the cardiovascular system. Recent reports, however, indicate that too high consumption rates of either type of cholesterol may increase the likelihood of certain cancers. The idea, then, is to decrease LDL consumption and be careful about too much HDL. Examples of harmful cholesterol were already given; examples of HDL cholesterol are margarine, vegetable oils, and fish—the polyunsaturated foods. Vegetables and fruits are the safest foods, being unassociated with either cancer or cardiovascular disease. Smoked, pickled, and salt-cured foods, on the other hand, may be related to high cancer rates.*

Cholesterol is one type of fat. Another type is triglycerides. Along with LDL, triglycerides are to be consumed in moderation. This is done by minimizing the intake of sugars, carbohydrates, and alcohol. If people reduce their consumption of eggs, meat, sugar, carbohydrates, and alcohol without reducing the overall quantity of food consumed, it is likely that they will reduce their weight. It is not a general dietary restriction that is the probable element in longevity, but the type of nutriments restricted.

As with the reduction of cigarette smoking, Kannell and Gordon (1980, p. 65) indicated that LDL reduction is important mainly during the younger years. "The impact of serum cholesterol . . . definitely diminishes with advancing age."

Exercise and Activity. Three factors keep recurring as important to health and long life. Proper food and no cigarette smoking are two of these; the third is exercise and activity. Palmore (1971) attempted to determine from the data of a longitudinal study which of these three practices was most associated with longevity. He concluded that activity might be. It is difficult to determine just how important exercise is in contrast to the other factors. For example, as Palmore (1980, p. 58) pointed out, people who are grossly overweight tend to be sedentary. Both obesity and sedentary existence are negative factors in long life. Is it the lack of activity or is it the obesity that contributes more in this negative way? Similarly, people who are less

---

*Information regarding the association between foods and cancers, and the recommended safe foods, is from *Time* magazine, June 28, 1982, p. 77.

healthy tend to be less active—is it this, or is it that sedentary existence makes for poor health?

These important questions bear only indirectly to the practical matter that activity and exercise go hand in hand with good health and life prolongation. This is seen in several studies, as for example, one by Bartko, Patterson, and Butler (1971, p. 135). They reported the results of an 11-year follow-up of a multidisciplinary study that was different from most others in that, at the start, the elderly men studied were in extraordinarily good health. Very many measurements were made, but two of them "correctly classified about 80 percent of both survivors and nonsurvivors." One of these was activity. The activity was assessed on the basis of a five-point scale ranging from carrying out a few routine chores to involvement in many activities of a structured, planned, and self-initiated type. Here again, however, good health may have led to the activity rather than have resulted from it. Another study was designed to understand more fully the problems of coronary heart disease. The role of activity was again very clear: ". . . sedentary males were more susceptible to lethal episodes of coronary heart disease . . . than were physically active males. . . ." (Kannell, 1971, p. 62).

The studies on exercise and health in relation to longevity have not concentrated on the obvious distinction between the more vigorous activities such as walking and bicycling and the less vigorous ones such as gardening or even reading. Obviously, walking does more for the cardiovascular system than does reading. Palmore's study (1982, p. 514) is an exception but even here, too little distinction was made between vigorous and less vigorous activity. In his study, "physical mobility" and longevity were related among women but not among men. Among men, less vigorous activity and longevity were related.

Under normal conditions, some reduction in activity with age might be expected, although perhaps not as great a reduction as some people might think. Lawton (1983) reviewed the literature and found that cross-sectional studies show much decline in activity with age but longitudinal studies do not. It is mainly vigorous activity that drops out with age, not other kinds. In fact, Lawton's review of longitudinal studies shows increases with age in reading, watching TV, and gardening. Future studies would do well to examine the relation between health status and longevity regarding different types of exercise and activity.

SUMMARY

Biologists and other investigators have contributed an interesting and important body of information bearing on problems of longevity and survival. It is well known that genes underlie the fact that some people live long and some do not. Genes even play a role on the level of individual cells. Some cells have built-in "biological clocks" that set the limits of their longevity. Perhaps the most impressive evidence for genetic control of longevity is the extreme diversity in the lengths of lives of various animals. For example, the rat lives about two to three years and the fin whale may live several hundred years. Breeding experiments in laboratories are additional evidence of genetic control of longevity. There are also data suggesting that long-lived parents tend to sire long-lived offspring. Additionally, identical twins live to about the same age, more so at least than do fraternal twins.

Women outlive men, and there is evidence that at least part of the reason for this is also genetic. For example, the female outlives the male in animal groups such as rats, spiders, flies, and others. On the other hand, there is evidence that part of the sex difference in longevity relates to environmental factors. Lifestyles of men and women have been different, certainly in terms of their smoking and drinking habits. These make for differential longevities. The major basis of the longer life of women is their greater resistance to coronary heart disease. Smoking is known to increase the incidence of this problem. It also increases the incidence of many different types of cancer. Men drink more alcohol than women and, in excess, this too can kill.

Just as smoking and drinking maximize the likelihood of chronic disease, good dietary habits minimize the likelihood. Cardiovascular disease is more likely with excessive consumption of one kind of cholesterol (LDL) and good health is more likely with moderate consumption of another kind (HDL). Excessive consumption, however, of either type of cholesterol may lead to cancers. Examples of LDL foods are fatty red meat, eggs, and butter. Examples of HDL food are vegetable oils, fish, and margarine. Fruits and vegetables are the safest foods.

In addition to LDL cholesterol, excessive triglyceride consumption should be avoided—food such as sugars, carbohydrates, and alcohol. One will not get fat with eating large quantities of HDL and low triglyceride foods. Grossly obese people are more prone to heart attacks than thinner people, although too little weight also reduces life expectancy. Obesity and sedentary existence go hand in hand. Sedentary existence is clearly related to cardiovascular problems and thus longevity. The three health habits that contribute to longer life are proper diet, exercise, and no cigarette smoking.

Chronic disease results from the breakdown of or damage to major organ systems. Two systems were discussed: the cardiovascular and the nervous systems. In the course of aging, blood vessels narrow and harden, making for a loss of elasticity. This can keep an adequate blood supply from reaching all the tissues and organs of the body. Adequate blood supply brings nutrients and oxygen to the tissues and, at the same time, removes waste products.

When there is blood vessel constriction, blood pressure is elevated; if the blood pressure is high enough the blood vessels can burst. The heart itself loses efficiency. With age, there is a diminished capability of the heart to compensate to stress. Public awareness of good health habits, however, has had the effect of a steady decline of cardiovascular disease.

The nervous system, which includes the brain, spinal cord, and mass of neural connections, is the central coordinating system of the body. It innervates all other organ systems. Cells of the brain decrease in number as people age, with the decrease starting at about age 20. Since neurons do not regenerate, the cell loss is permanent. The human brain has so many cells, however, that not all of them are needed for optimal functioning. It is believed that the gradual loss with age is no special problem, not at least until some threshold level is reached. Beyond this level, problems in cognition might be expected, although it has never been demonstrated that cell loss is the basis of any cognitive problem. Thus, the impact of neuron loss, if any, has yet to be determined.

There is also a decrease with age in the number of dendrites and number of synapses. There is also an accumulation of "aging pigments" that changes the arrangements of components within some neurons. Again, these age changes are of questionable meaning in terms of function. In fact, it has been suggested that these age changes, in making for an overall change in the organization of the brain, might have adaptive value. The reorganization might compensate for what otherwise would result in functional loss. In this way there is a plasticity in the nervous system to prolong function.

REFERENCES

Bank, L., & Jarvik, L. F. A longitudinal study of aging human twins. In E. L. Schneider (Ed.), *The genetics of aging.* New York: Plenum Press, 1978, pp. 303–333.

Bartko, J. J., Patterson, R. D., & Butler, R. N. Biomedical and behavioral predictors of survival among normal aged men: a multivariate analysis. In E. Palmore & F. C. Jeffers (Eds.), *Prediction of life span.* Lexington, Mass.: D. C. Heath, 1971, pp. 123–137.

Beeton, M., & Pearson, K. Data for the problem of evolution in man. II. A first study of the inheritance of longevity and the selective death rate of man. *Proceedings Royal Society,* 1899, LXV, 290–305.

Bell, A. G. The duration of life and conditions associated with longevity, a study of the Hyde genealogy. Washington, privately printed, 1918.

Bondareff, W. The neurobiological basis of age-related changes in neuronal connectivity. In J. L. McGaugh & S. B. Kiesler (Eds.), *Aging: biology and behavior.* New York: Academic Press, 1981, pp. 141–157.

Brewer, C., & Perrett, L. Brain damage due to alcohol consumption: an air-encephalographic, psychometric and electroencephalographic study. *British Journal of Addictions,* 1971, 66, 170–182.

Brody, H., & Vijayashanker, N. Anatomical changes in the nervous system. In C. E. Finch &

L. Hayflick (Eds.), *Handbook of the biology of aging.* New York: Van Nostrand Reinhold, 1977, pp. 241–261.

Cala, L. A., Jones, B., Mastaglia, F. L., & Wiley, B. Brain atrophy and intellectual impairment in heavy drinkers—a clinical, psychometric and computerized tomography study. *Australian and New Zealand Journal of Medicine,* 1978, *8,* 147–153.

Curtis, H. J. *Biological mechanisms of aging.* Springfield, Ill.: Charles C Thomas, 1966.

Dublin, L. I., Lotka, A. J., & Spiegelman, M. *Length of life.* New York: Ronald Press, 1949.

Fries, J. F., & Crapo, L. M. *Vitality and aging.* San Francisco: W. H. Freeman, 1981.

Hammond, E. C. The effects of smoking. *Scientific American,* 1962, *207,* 39–51.

Hayflick, L. The strategy of senescence. *Journal of Gerontology,* 1974, *14,* 37–45.

Jalavisto, E. Inheritance of longevity according to Finnish and Swedish genealogies. *Annals Medicinae Internae Fenniae,* 1951, *40,* 263–274.

Kallmann, F. J., & Jarvik, L. F. Individual differences in constitution and genetic background. In J. E. Birren (Ed.), *Handbook of aging and the individual: Psychological and biological aspects.* Chicago: University of Chicago Press, 1959, pp. 216–263.

Kannell, W. B. Habits and heart disease mortality. In E. Palmore & F. C. Jeffers (Eds.), *Prediction of life span.* Lexington, Mass.: D. C. Heath, 1971, pp. 61–69.

Kannell, W. B., & Gordon, T. Cardiovascular risk factors in the aged: The Framingham study. In S. G. Haynes & M. Feinleib (Eds.), *Epidemiology of aging.* Washington, D.C.: U.S. Govt. Printing Office (NIH Publication No. 80-969), 1980, pp. 65–89.

Lansing, A. I. General biology of senescence. In J. E. Birren (Ed.), *Handbook of aging and the individual: Psychological and biological aspects.* Chicago: University of Chicago Press, 1959, pp. 119–135.

Lawton, M. P. Activities and leisure. In C. Eisdorfer (Ed.), *Annual review of gerontology and geriatrics* (Vol. 4). New York: Springer Publishing Co., 1983.

Leaf, A. Every day is a gift when you are over 100. *National Geographic,* 1973, *143,* 93–119.

Palmore, E. Health practices, illness and longevity. In E. Palmore & F. C. Jeffers (Eds.), *Prediction of life span.* Lexington, Mass.: D. C. Heath, 1971, pp. 71–77.

Palmore, E. Predictors of longevity. In S. G. Haynes & M. Feinleib (Eds.), *Epidemiology of aging.* Washington, D.C.: U.S. Govt. Printing Office (NIH Publication No. 80-969), 1980, pp. 57–64.

Palmore, E. Predictors of longevity difference: a 25-year follow up. *The Gerontologist,* 1982, *22,* 513–518.

Pearl, R. *The biology of death.* Philadelphia: Lippincott, 1922.

Rockstein, M. Heredity and longevity in the animal kingdom. *Journal of Gerontology,* 1958, Supplement No. 2, *13,* 7–12.

Rockstein, M., & Sussman, M. *Biology of aging.* Belmont, Calif.: Wadsworth, 1979.

Seltzer, C. C. Constitution and heredity in relation to tobacco smoking. *Annals of the New York Academy of Sciences,* 1967, *142,* 322–330.

Siegel, J. S. Recent and prospective demographic trends for the elderly population and some implications for health care. In S. G. Haynes & M. Feinleib (Eds.), *Epidemiology of aging.* Washington, D.C.: U.S. Govt. Printing Office (NIH Publication No. 80-969), 1980, pp. 289–315.

Surgeon General's Report, *The health consequences of smoking.* U.S. Dept. of Health and Human Services (PHS). Washington, D.C.: U.S. Govt. Printing Office, 1982.

United States Public Health Service. *Cigarette smoking and health characteristics.* National Center for Health Statistics, May 1967, Series 10, Number 34, p. 27.

Waldron, I. Sex differences in longevity. In S. G. Haynes & M. Feinleib (Eds.), *Epidemiology of aging.* Washington, D.C.: U.S. Govt. Printing Office (NIH Publication No. 80-969), 1980, pp. 163–186.

4
Psychological and Social Factors in Longevity and Survival

This chapter continues the discussion of longevity and survival. The previous chapter dealt with biological factors and the present chapter focuses on psychological and social factors. All these factors are intimately tied together and the distinctions among them are partly arbitrary.

TERMINAL DROP

Although it may be apparent that biological factors underlie much in longevity and survival, it may not be so apparent that psychological factors are also important. For example, impending death is often preceded by a "terminal drop" in cognitive functioning. This was first observed and highlighted by Kleemeier (1961, 1962), whose studies, though perhaps lacking the precision of procedure and the elegance of statistical analysis that subsequent studies had, did point to the time of death as an anchoring date, rather than the time of birth.

Kleemeier tested 13 elderly men on four occasions during the course of 12 years. Approximately every two to three-and-a-half years during this time, an intelligence test (Wechsler-Bellevue) was give to each man, and the changes in his performances were noted. Each one of the 13 men showed decrement over the span of 12 years, but the extent of decrement varied from person to person. Shortly after the last test of the series, four men died. Kleemeier observed that these four men had declined much more rapidly in their cognitive abilities than had the surviving nine men. This decline was named "terminal drop." He also analyzed the decline in scores of 70 elderly men who had but two testings. After nearly half of them died, Kleemeier found evidence that the "drop" in scores was greater among the deceased than among the living.

These observations opened possibilities not before emphasized; they also stimulated terminal drop investigations with contradictory or negative results

55

(e.g., Berkowitz, 1965; Palmore & Cleveland, 1976). In the main, however, a new study area was begun. In fact, studies appeared in such frequency after Kleemeier's early 1960s reports that a special volume was written to decribe them (*Predictions of Life Span*, edited by Palmore and Jeffers, 1971). Subsequent studies were reviewed by Siegler (1975).

Testing Terminal Drop

There are two different ways of going about testing the concept "terminal drop." In one, when predicting death on the basis of test results, it is a person's relative standing within the group at a particular time that is important. In Figure 4.1, for example, if Person A makes a very poor score and Person B a very good one, Person A is thought more likely to die in the course of the next few years than Person B. This concept is not Kleemeier's terminal drop concept; it came about subsequent to his reports but was based on his thinking. This concept implies that the poor score of Person A reflects a decline that has already occurred, but one the test-giver could not

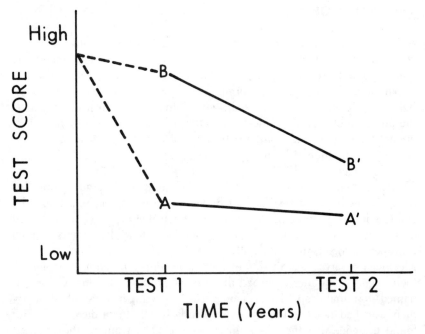

FIGURE 4.1: Two ways of testing for terminal drop: (1) Comparing test scores B and A suggests that the two groups were comparable at an earlier time—a time before it was possible for the experimenter to observe the drop. (2) Comparing curve B-B' with A-A' is a direct comparison of the extent of declines over two test periods.

observe. The other concept is Kleemeier's—it is the observed relative decline in test scores over a number of years. If, as shown in Figure 4.1, Person A scores poorly at Test 1 but scores much the same years later at Test 2, and Person B scores well at Test 1 but poorly at Test 2, Person B has the poorer potential for survival.

Retrospective Accounts

Many or most of the studies testing terminal drop were not planned for this purpose. Instead, they took the following form: First, investigators collected data on elderly people for a variety of different reasons without plans to carry out follow-up investigations regarding longevity. Then, years later, they realized that a splendid research opportunity was available: they could compare those who died with those who survived with respect to the test scores made some years before. In this way, they had a retrospective study investigating possible antecedent factors of survival and death. That is, referring to Figure 4.1, they were able to compare B and A at Test 1 (the first terminal drop concept described). When the research was longitudinal, that is, when two or more measurements were available prior to death, changes in scores over time were available for postmortem analysis (i.e., the second concept). In Figure 4.1, they were able to compare curve B-B' with curve A-A'.

Poor Performance and Prediction of Death. There were studies prior to Kleemeier's that showed that elderly people poor in cognitive abilities tend to die sooner than their more able brethren. At the time of these early studies, the concept of terminal drop was not well known. As a result, the fact that those elderly with lower abilities tended to die sooner was seen as a confounding artifact negating a main argument rather than an important fact in its own right. It is described in detail in Chapter 21 how this presents special problems in longitudinal research. For example, Jarvik and Falek (1963) examined senescent twins with the Wechsler-Bellevue intelligence test and found that fewer of the initially poor performers were alive for later retest; this clouded the results of the longitudinal study. Similarly, Riegel, Riegel, and Meyer (1967), with several tests, including a verbal achievement test, found attrition rates higher among the less able; and Baltes, Schaie, and Nardi (1971) reported similar results with a test of intelligence and of rigidity. These results complement the concept of terminal drop.

Such findings have been reported often now, and recently again by McCarty, Siegler, and Logue (1982). It is clear that selective dropout of the less able is hardly avoidable if the test-takers are elderly to start and the longitudinal study lasts long.

Types and Time of Loss. What potential there is for the use of performance scores to predict ensuing death may depend on the nature of the performance under examination. Birren (1964) compared survivors and nonsurvivors with respect to intelligence test scores made five years previously when most had been in their early 60s. Survivors and nonsurvivors were differentiated by their original performances on tests of verbal information skills, not on tests of perceptual-motor skills involving speed. The nonsurvivors had performed more poorly on the verbal tests. Eleven years later, when more of the test-takers had died, Granick and Patterson (1971) compared their scores again. This time poor performances on both verbal and psychomotor tests were seen among the nonsurvivors. Palmore (1982, p. 514) carried out an analysis of a different kind but with conclusions compatible to those of Granick and Patterson. Rather than comparing survivors and nonsurvivors, he correlated test performance scores made 25 years previously with a "longevity difference index." This index was "the difference between the number of years the panelists lived after initial testing and the actuarily expected number of years remaining based on age, sex and race. . . ." Palmore also found both verbal and nonverbal intelligence predictive of life and death years later. In this study, the nonverbal may have been a bit better as a predictor.

It should be recognized that in all of the studies, the relationship between earlier performance and later survival or nonsurvival is small, but suggestive nevertheless. To the extent that these three reports are reliable, that is, potentially repeatable, it is seen that the type of ability or loss of ability together with the time frame of prediction is important. Birren's report indicates that verbal intelligence is a better predictor within five years while the other reports show both verbal and nonverbal intelligence predict equally well over the long run.

Distance from Death. Palmore's data were based on the Duke longitudinal study. The data of this study were examined in a different way by Siegler, McCarty, and Logue (1982). They compared three groups that differed in the "distance from death" following testing. In other words, the Time 1 scores were compared in relation to the length of time the person lived following testing. It may be recognized that this is simply a refinement of the first concept in testing for terminal drop.

One group (average age 76) died within one year of testing. Another group (average age 78) died 8 to 13 years after testing. A third group was younger (average age 69); people in this group either died 14 or more years afterwards or were still alive at the time the data of the study were analyzed. Although the three groups were different in age, this fact did not seem to be important in the findings.

The data of Siegler et al. (1982) were based on an intelligence test and a memory test, and from these, four scores were developed.* Figure 4.2 shows the results of this study. It may be seen in this figure that higher scores were associated with more distance from death, that is, longer survival. Figure 4.2 suggests that terminal drop was involved with both the verbal and non-verbal scores.[†]

Critical Loss. Jarvik and Falek (1963) singled out three measures as particularly important in terminal decline; two were verbal measures (Vocabulary and Similarities tests) and one was nonverbal (Digit Symbol test). The study began with 39 twin pairs (78 people), aged 60 years or older, first tested between 1946 and 1949. Then, the 78 twins were again tested on two occasions subsequent to 1958. An "annual rate of decline" measure was computed for each person with each of the tests. It was found that an annual decrement of at least two percent on the Digit Symbol test, 10 percent on the Similarities test, or any decline on the Vocabulary test was a poor omen for survival five years following the last testing. People with two or three of these decrements showed high mortality rates: of eight people, seven died within the next five years.

Later, Jarvik and Blum (1971, p. 204) examined these "critical loss" scores in a subsample of 26 twin pairs. Fifteen twin pairs were without "critical loss" and 11 pairs were discordant in that only one twin partner showed the "loss." It is striking that in 10 of the 11 discordant pairs, "the partner with the 'critical loss'. . . succumbed earlier to death." The eleventh pair were both alive after five years, but the member with the "loss" was the more deteriorated of the pair. Of the 15 twin pairs without "critical loss," 12 pairs survived the five-year period and, of the other three pairs, one member of the pair survived.

To repeat, these results were based on the first testing carried out between 1946 and 1949 and the subsequent testings to 1958. A similar analysis was possible when tests were given during 1967–69 and then again during 1973–74. At this last test period, 8 men and 14 women still survived, having reached the ages 83 to 99. Five years later, by 1978, 5 men and 7 women had died and the critical loss index of annual rate of decline was reexamined. This time the critical loss indices did not relate to earlier death.

---

* The Wechsler Adult Intelligence Scale (WAIS) was scored in terms of the Verbal scale and the Performance scale. The Wechsler Memory Scale (WMS) was scored in terms of a verbal score and nonverbal score. The verbal was the sum of Logical Memory (immediate + delayed) and Paired Associate (hard + easy). The nonverbal score was of the Visual Reproduction subtest.

[†]The group that died first was poorer than each of the other two groups in the two WMS scores and in the WAIS Performance score. The WAIS Verbal score did differentiate the group to die first from the group to die last, but neither of these groups was significantly different from the middle group in Verbal intelligence. Thus, to this extent, the data of Siegler et al. (1982) are compatible with those of Granick and Patterson (1971), just as Palmore's data (1982) were.

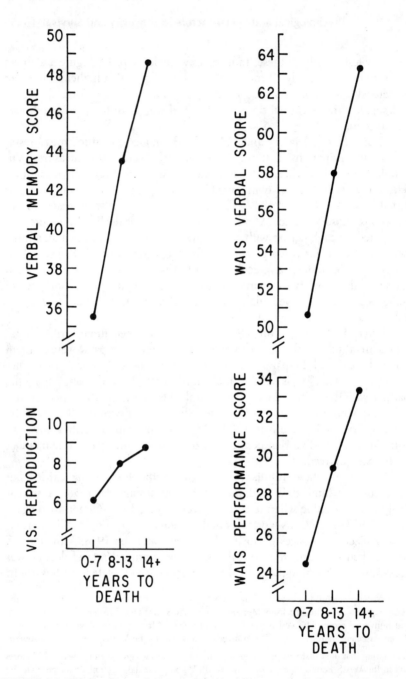

FIGURE 4.2: Verbal and nonverbal test scores made at the time prior to death (years) indicated on the abscissa. The graphs on the left are based on the Wechsler Memory Scale while those on the right are based on the WAIS. (From Siegler et al., 1982, Figure 2. Reprinted by permission of the *Journal of Gerontology*, Vol. 37, pp. 176–181, 1982.)

The reason, perhaps, was the "far-advanced ages" of the people examined. As will be seen in the next section, this is "in line with Riegel's . . . observation that the relationship between longevity and decline in test scores was greater for persons below age 65 . . ." (Steuer, LaRue, Blum, & Jarvik, 1981, p. 212).

Cooperation.　Riegel, Riegel, and Meyer (1967) tested people on three occasions. In 1956, verbal achievement and other tests were given to 380 men and women residing in northern Germany. Five years later a retest was made, and five years after this a third testing was made.

Of the 550 people originally tested, 62 died by the time of the second test period and 116 refused to be tested; at the third testing, another 100 had died. Riegel made this interesting observation: Of the 116 people surviving to the time of the second testing who refused to cooperate by allowing a retest, 43 percent did not survive the next five years to the third test period. By contrast, only 25 percent of those who were tested at Time 2 did not survive to Time 3. "Thus," said Riegel (1971, p. 141), "cooperation in retest studies is a powerful predictor of survival."

People who were tested a second time were compared to people who did not survive to the second testing with respect to the Test 1 scores. These scores were higher among the retested group. Surprisingly perhaps, this terminal drop result was larger among those aged less than 65 years than for those over 65. Drawing upon these and other results, Riegel concluded that, during the decade prior to age 65 years, death occurs more often with less able people. At older age levels, however, "death strikes randomly." Prediction of survival is, therefore, more reliable at the younger age levels.

Comparisons of both the Test 1 scores and the Test 2 scores were made between those who survived to Time 3 with those who did not. A superiority of test scores among the surviving group was seen again. The Time 2 scores separated living and dead groups at Time 3 even more than did the Time 1 scores. This again pointed to a relationship between poor initial performance and the greater likelihood of death. Riegel (1971, p. 146) attributed the very poor scores of those retested at Time 2 and failing to survive to Time 3 to "terminal drop"—"sudden deterioration, occurring during periods extending less than five years prior to death."

Personality: Coping Ability.　Personality factors as well as cognitive ability seem to undergo a "terminal drop." For a period of two-and-a-half years, four psychological tests were administered every three to four weeks to a group of residents of a home for the aged (Lieberman, 1965). The tests were the Bender-Gestalt, the Draw-a-Person, time reproduction, and a projective test of 12 line drawings. When the study was completed, the data of only 25 people were available for analysis, but, despite this, the data were clear in indicating that personality changes may occur many months prior to death. Lieberman reported his results in terms of a comparison between two groups of people. One group was composed of those who died less than three months after completing the first five testings, and another group was composed of people who were still living at least a year after completing 10 or more testings.

Unlike Riegel who emphasized relative standing in performance within a group, Lieberman emphasized that, in terms of survival, absolute levels did not distinguish among people; it was the level changing over time that was important, that is, the second terminal drop concept (A-A' vs. B-B', in Figure 4.1). Lieberman emphasized that in his study the drop did not appear to be the result of physical illness; rather it was more of psychological determination. Those residents who became seriously physically ill and recovered did not show the test performance changes shown by those who died shortly afterward.

Lieberman's data suggested to him that people close to death have lessened ability to cope with environmental demands; they have a lowered ability to organize and to integrate environmental inputs. "Individuals approaching death pull away from those around them . . . because they are preoccupied in an attempt to hold themselves together—to reduce the experience of chaos" (p. 189).

A Retrospective-Prospective Study

All these data on terminal drop point to important opportunities for prediction and, therefore, possible control of impending tragedy. It must be recognized, however, that in all these studies the data were obtained retrospectively. That is, predictions were not made and tested; instead, Test 1 scores were examined after the fact of death. It is crucial to test the validity of the terminal drop concept by prospective analyses. The prospective studies may yield the same results as the retrospective studies, but they may not. First, not all retrospective studies reported positive results (e.g., Berkowitz, 1965; Palmore & Cleveland, 1976). Second, results do not always turn out as expected, as seen in the study by Steuer et al. (1981). Retrospective analyses are but first steps to prediction of survival.

A first step in prospective analysis was made in one study (Botwinick, West, & Storandt, 1978). This study, unlike many of the previous ones, was initiated specifically for the purpose of comparing survivors and nonsurvivors with respect to test scores made earlier. This study also was retrospective, but it was conceived as the first of a two-part study, the second of which would be truly prospective. The first study was based on tests sensitive to aging processes and provided cut-off or "danger" scores based on the comparisons between survivors and nonsurvivors. These cut-off scores would then be applied and tested prospectively in the second study.

The first study assessed a wide array of functions as they relate to survival. These included cognitive abilities, perceptual and psychomotor abilities, and personality and morale characteristics. The study included information regarding health and social activities; it examined the role of age, sex, and socioeconomic status in survival. In this study, 380 men and women between the ages of 60 and 89 were tested. During the five years following the tests, 83 had died.

Approximately two-thirds of those who died and those who survived could be "predicted" by the test scores made five years previously. Simple psychomotor speed performances differentiated the survivors from the non-survivors, as did learning and memory performances. Self-ratings of health were important in the differentiation and so were two personality character-istics—depression and feeling of being in control of things. Those people with good cognitive skills and those who were relatively quick in their test performances were good bets to survive, as were those who felt healthy, in control, and not depressed.

Cut-off "danger" scores were developed and a new sample of people was tested in the second study of the two-part sequence. The second study is in the five-year waiting period to determine whether the cut-off "danger" scores hold up as meaningful predictors. After all, predictions can only be made prospectively, not retrospectively.

SOCIAL AND ATTITUDINAL FACTORS RELATED TO HEALTH

Terminal drop may mean little more than that those who are ill, or even subclinically ill, perform less well on tests than those who are well. And those who are ill are less likely to survive than those who are well. The most obvious and most persistent finding in longevity research is the importance of good health and physical functioning. In study after study, sometimes by itself, sometimes in conjunction with the other factors, it is the major one affecting longevity (e.g., Palmore, 1982). Next to health, three health habits loom large in maintaining long life. These were discussed in the previous chapter—weight control and proper diet, no cigarette smoking, and exercise and activity. Each of these three habits relates to health status and survival.

Attitudes and Adaptation to Illness

Other factors bearing on health and illness also relate to longevity. For example, attitudes toward illness and the manner in which adjustments are made seem to be very important in survival. This was seen with special

vividness in a study by Garrity and Klein (1971). They investigated the
attitudes of heart-attack patients during their hospitalization as well as how
their attitudes related to survival six months later.

Observations were made during the acute phase of the heart attack.
During each of the first five days of hospitalization the patients were rated
with respect to 21 dimensions of adaptation—dimensions such as anxiety
and cheerfulness. The patients were then categorized into two groups: one
group was characterized either by slight behavior disturbance, or by improvement in this disturbance over the five-day period; the other group was
characterized either by great disturbance or by deteriorating behavior. Six
months after hospital discharge, 12 of the original 48 patients had died: 10
of these 12 were in the behavior-disturbance group.

Garrity and Klein examined their data further and learned that the
patients with negative behavior adjustments tended to be those who had
experienced previous heart trouble. In other words, their negative attitudes
and adjustments were based on what probably were more serious heart
conditions. Thus, although it is apparent that attitudes and behavioral
adaptations toward illness may be predictive of outcome, when more is
learned, these may only turn out to be secondary concomitants of more
direct predictors.

Work and Work Satisfaction

Palmore (1969) carried out a study showing that satisfaction with work is an
important indication of long life. The total sample of men and women in
Palmore's study ranged in age from 60 to 94, but when only men aged 60 to
69 were examined, work satisfaction was found the best predictor of longevity, "even better than life expectancy." Satisfaction with work was again
found important in Palmore's 1982 analyses of survival covering a 25-year
period. Among men, work satisfaction related to longevity almost to the
same extent as physical health. The relationship between work satisfaction
and longevity was also seen in an earlier study by Rose (1964). He examined
the data of a very old population that ranged in age from 72 to 92, with
more than half being 80 to 84 years. It is extraordinary that only 21 percent
of those old people were not working at least part time. Rose (1964, p. 35)
believed that "this evidence of a refusal to 'disengage' became even more
remarkable when no relationship was found between current income and
age of complete cessation from work." The implication, but not the observed fact, is that aged people who are satisfied with their work and who
maintain useful roles live longer than those who do not.

Thus, Palmore's studies and Rose's study suggest that work satisfaction
makes for long life. This may not be as surprising as it first seems to be when

it is realized that healthy people can work and enjoy it. Sick people cannot work and cannot enjoy it. It may be poor health, rather than dissatisfaction with the work, that makes for earlier death.

Education and Economic Status

It probably is no surprise to learn that high socioeconomic status (SES) predisposes one to longer life. Several investigators, for example, Rose (1964) and Pfeiffer (1970), demonstrated that high education levels, high-status occupations, and high intelligence, all go together and make for favorable longevities. Lower status roles are associated with poor housing, poor nutrition, poor sanitation, and a host of other factors important to health and thus long life. Palmore's (1982) study pointed to financial status as the most important SES ingredient in survival—more important than education or occupational status. Interestingly, however, this was true only for men. Among women, none of the three SES factors was important.

Family Relations

Age at Childbirth. "To a doctor, a woman pregnant for the first time after 35 is an 'elderly primigravida'." So states the lead sentence in an article in *Time* magazine (Feb. 22, 1982, p. 58). Women in their 30s having babies for the first time had been seen as risky, but this has partly been changed. "Older women" in terms of pregnancy are in better shape now than they used to be and many are in better health than many younger women. The medical world no longer regards the older first-time mother as a real risk, whereas in the past, Caesarean sections were frequently routine.

Still, there are some risks in postponing childbearing. Postponing childbirth makes more likely complications due to diabetes, respiratory conditions, high blood pressure, and other ailments. There are higher risks of birth defects.

"Older mothers also face a mortality rate that edges higher with each birthday" (*Time*, p. 59). In the United States there are fewer mother deaths than one in 10,000. However, there is five times the risk for women aged 35 to 39 than for those in their early 20s.

The Not-Married. Most data point to bachelorhood or spinsterhood as a negative factor in survival later in life. Not all data point to this, but many do. Rose (1964) concluded that the maintenance of a "with spouse" status provides physical and emotional support that may be crucial in survival. Pfeiffer's (1970) data indicated that only for women is the "never married" status associated negatively with longevity. These latter data, however, are based on too few people to make reliable generalizations about men. Further, new lifestyles of women make "never married" a different status than heretofore.

Another dimension of family that may relate to longevity is the number of children—fewer children make for longer life for the parents (Rose, 1964). If this is true, the mechanism, as suggested by Rose, is that fewer children limit the economic and emotional stress placed upon the parent. The smaller number of children may also be related to higher socioeconomic status, which in turn, is related to longevity.

Death of a Loved One. There are data suggesting that loss of a close loved one can make for stress sufficient to cause the death of some older people. The notion of stress is central to the thesis of psychosomatic medicine; the thinking is that stress, such as that resulting from bereavement due to the loss of a spouse, has organic consequences that are particularly damaging to those elderly of diminished physiological reserves.

Rowland (1977) reviewed the literature bearing on death among the elderly that may be linked to the death of spouse or some other close person. In all there were less than a dozen such studies, and several of them were unclear as to whether bereavement made the difference or the poor health of the surviving member. For example, it has been speculated that the survivor who is sick and who had been cared for by the deceased spouse is particularly vulnerable when left alone without this care. This speculation suggests that it is the loss of nursing-care type of attention, not stress due to bereavement, that is associated with the death of the survivor.

The data are ambiguous, but Rowland (1977, p. 356) suggested: ". . . for some people, especially males, the loss of a significant other may be detrimental. The risk of death is highest during the first year of bereavement."

SUICIDE

Some of the life-shortening and life-lengthening factors discussed in this and in the previous chapter are at least partly under personal control. Suicide is a factor in old age but, unlike the other factors, it would seem that it is under direct, total control. This may not be so, however, if misery is strong enough.

Suicide among White People

The age–suicide pattern is different among whites, blacks, and others. There is no doubt that much of the suicide among white people in the United States is a phenomenon of the elderly. U.S. Census data show that people 65 and older made up 10.69 percent of the population in 1976 but committed 16.95 percent of the suicides. The picture is not different worldwide, with figures of 11.9 percent and 17.62 percent, respectively (McIntosh & Santos, 1981). The suicide rate among white men is particularly striking. Figure 4.3 shows with stark clarity how painful life must be for many aged white males.

Suicide rates increase among both white men and white women from childhood on. The increase in rates of men to age 20 to 24 is almost as great as the increase from middle age on. Women, however, reach a peak suicide rate in the middle years, that then declines. The greatest difference between the sexes, however, is the overall suicide rate. At no point after the pre- or very early-teens do women come anywhere near men in self-destruction.

Why do people choose to take their own lives? This question was raised

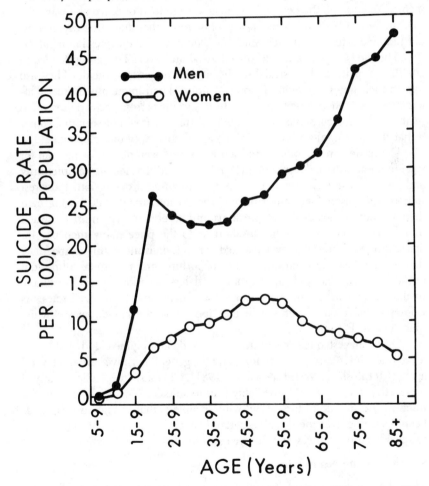

FIGURE 4.3: U.S. suicide rate by age and sex among white people in 1976, based on U.S. Census data. (Adapted from McIntosh et al., 1981. Reprinted by permission of the Haworth Press, Inc.)

by Darbonne (1969, p. 46) with an attempt to answer it by analyzing 259 suicide notes. Although the analysis did not take into account sex or ethnic group differences, the finding may nevertheless be applicable to many subgroups.

Suicide notes of younger adults (aged 20 to 39) were related to feelings of rejection, particularly concerning problems of love for a member of the opposite sex. There seemed to be an internalization of blame and guilt and self-depreciation.

Those aged 40 to 49 "left a communciation of the vanquished. They seemed unequal to the demands of life and were tired or bored and wanted a way out" (p. 49). The 50- to 59-year-olds, more than the other age-groups, did not give a reason for their suicides. There was little expression of affect.

The oldest group was categorized as 60 and over. This group tended to cite illness, pain, and physical disability as their reasons for suicide. They also told in their notes of loneliness and isolation. "Their frequently expressed affect of sorrow and seeking forgiveness from specific persons seemed most often related to having caused troubles to others" (p. 50). It will be seen in Chapter 9 that this is congruous with a major stage theory of ego development.

Depression in the more usual sense has also been offered as a reason for suicide among the elderly. Zung (1967) suggested that feelings of inferiority and loss of self-esteem are among the major causes of depression. If depression is the reason for many suicides, the greater suicide rate among men than women indicates that depressions among elderly men must be much more severe. This raises the question as to the price many men pay for opportunities achieved, never realized, or lost. It is interesting to speculate that women, having been deprived of opportunities for personal fulfillment outside of marriage and family, have had less occasion to feel personally unable or unworthy without career achievements and high social roles. As women achieve equal rights, will they too follow the suicide rates of white men seen in Figure 4.3?

Other suggested reasons underlying suicide among the elderly are loss of loved ones, interpersonal restriction, and the general negative attitudes toward aging (McIntosh, Hubbard, & Santos, 1981). Obviously, depression or any of these other factors do not invariably lead to suicide. One bright note in the trend in the suicide history of old white people is that as high as it is, it has been declining over the decades, certainly over the last 20 years. This seems to speak well of changes over the years in the lives of older adults.

Suicide among Nonwhites

Most data relating to suicides categorize people by sex and by race in terms of "white" and "nonwhite." But there are differences among the nonwhite ethnic groups. Chinese- and Japanese-Americans, like whites, have suicide rates that peak in old age. In fact, their rates exceed those of whites. The age–suicide pattern is different among blacks. Suicide rates among blacks reach a peak in young adulthood and then decline thereafter. In contrast to aged whites and Orientals, the suicide rates among old blacks are very low. Unlike with white populations, where suicide rates among the elderly have declined over the years, rates among the black elderly have increased. Is this due to declining opportunities? Or, conversely, is it due to higher aspiration levels that come with opportunity, resulting in disappointments? Are the blacks slowly being assimilated to white values and lifestyles, including suicide patterns?

Perhaps the group that is under greatest duress is the American Indian. Like blacks, American Indian suicide rates are highest among the young. Their rates are startlingly high; about 40 per 100,000 population commit suicide compared to about 12 per 100,000 among blacks. There is so much self-destruction among Indian youths (ages 15 to 34) that one explanation for the low suicide rate of the elderly Indian is that they achieved "survivor" status and are thus "a selective group"; "they are the hardiest and also as survivors may lack suicidal tendencies" (McIntosh & Santos, 1981, p. 161).

Altogether, it would seem that among all the factors leading to long or short life, suicide would be the most amenable to correction. Given the devastating motives underlying suicide, however, it may be no easier to correct this than the other factors. Improving the quality of life for those in misery, those who feel depressed, deprived, or unwanted, is a social goal hard to achieve but worthy of trying.

SUMMARY

Behavioral and social factors related to health and long life have come under study. The data indicate that cognitive abilities among the aged are predictive of the years left to live, and to a lesser extent, so are changes in personality. These "terminal drop" studies emphasize that both the level of present functioning and decline from prior levels bear on longevity. The ability to predict decline and death holds promise for the possible control of impending tragedy. All the studies bearing on this, however, have thus far been retrospective and so, before much faith can be put in them, prospective studies must be carried out. To date, only one has been started and this one is not yet complete.

Poor cognitive and personality test scores predicting early death may reflect hardly more than that those who are ill and close to death perform poorly on these tests. Poor health, including organic brain disease, are major reasons for earlier death. Social factors also relate to health and thus survival. For example, high socioeconomic levels make for health and long life, with financial well-being playing a more important role than education or occupational status. Work satisfaction seems very important to long life. Intact family status, particularly marriage, makes for long life.

Some of these factors are under personal control, at least partially. Suicide is another important consideration in the study of aging and survival because so many old men take their own lives. Theoretically, suicide is under total personal control, but in actuality this is debatable. Many older men are so physically ill, feel so depressed or rejected, are so alone or feel so guilty about the past, that death for them is preferable to life. Older women do not seem to bear such burdensome weights. Suicide among elderly men is seen mainly in white and Oriental populations, not black or American Indian. In the latter, there are extraordinarily high suicide rates among the young (people in their 20s), but not among the old.

Research prying into the psychological and social bases of short and long life holds promise. But it has just begun. There is a long journey before this research can aid in identifying the vulnerable to whom help can be given. In the meantime, improved educational opportunities, greater financial help to the needy, better medical services, counseling for those who are alone, and more organized opportunities for friendships and remarriage can go a long way in enriching lives and perhaps in prolonging them.

REFERENCES

Baltes, P. B., Schaie, K. W., & Nardi, A. H. Age and experimental mortality in a seven-year longitudinal study of cognitive behavior. *Developmental Psychology*, 1971, *5*, 18–26.

Berkowitz, B. Changes in intellect with age: IV. Changes in achievement and survival in older people. *Journal of Genetic Psychology*, 1965, *107*, 3–14.

Birren, J. E. Neural basis of personal adjustment. In P. F. Hanson (Ed.), *Age with a future*. Copenhagen: Munksgaard, 1964, pp. 48–59.

Botwinick, J., West, R., & Storandt, M. Predicting death from behavioral test performance. *Journal of Gerontology*, 1978, *33*, 755–762.

Darbonne, A. R. Suicide and age. *Journal of Consulting and Clinical Psychology*, 1969, *33*, 46–50.

Garrity, T., & Klein, R. F. A behavioral predictor of survival among heart attack patients. In E. Palmore & F. C. Jeffers (Eds.), *Prediction of life span*. Lexington, Mass.: D. C. Heath, 1971, pp. 215–222.

Granick, S., & Patterson, R. D. *Human aging II*. Washington, D.C.: U.S. Govt. Printing Office (Publication No. 71-9037), 1971.

Jarvik, L. F., & Blum, J. E. Cognitive declines as predictors of mortality in twin pairs: A twenty-year longitudinal study of aging. In E. Palmore & F. C. Jeffers (Eds.), *Prediction of life span*. Lexington, Mass.: D. C. Heath, 1971, pp. 199–211.

Jarvik, L. F., & Falek, A. Intellectual stability and survival in the aged. *Journal of Gerontology*, 1963, *18*, 173–176.

Kleemeier, R. W. *Intellectual change in the senium, or death and the I.Q.* Presidential Address, American Psychological Association, 1961 (Mimeograph).

Kleemeier, R. W. Intellectual change in the senium. *Proceedings of the Social Statistics Section of the American Statistical Association,* 1962, pp. 290–295.

Lieberman, M. A. Psychological correlates of impending death: some preliminary observations. *Journal of Gerontology,* 1965, *20,* 181–190.

McCarty, S. M., Siegler, I. C., & Logue, P. E. Cross-sectional and longitudinal patterns of three Wechsler Memory Scale subtests. *Journal of Gerontology,* 1982, 37, 169–175.

McIntosh, J. L., Hubbard, R. W., & Santos, J. Suicide among the elderly: a review of issues with case studies. *Journal of Gerontological Social Work,* 1981, 4, 63–74.

McIntosh, J. L., & Santos, J. F. Suicide among minority elderly: a preliminary investigation. *Suicide and Life-Threatening Behavior,* 1981, *11,* 151–166.

Palmore, E. Physical, mental and social factors in predicting longevity. *The Gerontologist,* 1969, 9, 103–108.

Palmore, E. B. Predictors of the longevity difference: A 25-year follow-up. *The Gerontologist,* 1982, 22, 513–518.

Palmore, E., & Cleveland, W. Aging, terminal decline, and terminal drop. *Journal of Gerontology,* 1976, *31,* 76–81.

Palmore, E., & Jeffers, F. C. (Eds.). *Predictions of life span.* Lexington, Mass.: D. C. Heath, 1971.

Pfeiffer, E. Survival in old age: physical, psychological and social correlates of longevity. *Journal of the American Geriatrics Society,* 1970, *18,* 273–285.

Riegel, K. F. The prediction of death and longevity in longitudinal research. In E. Palmore & F. C. Jeffers (Eds.), *Prediction of life span.* Lexington, Mass.: D. C. Heath, 1971, pp. 139–152.

Riegel, K. F., Riegel, R. M., & Meyer, G. A study of the dropout rates in longitudinal research on aging and the prediction of death. *Journal of Personality and Social Psychology,* 1967, 5, 342–348.

Rose, C. L. Social factors in longevity. *The Gerontologist,* 1964, 4, 27–37.

Rowland, K. F. Environmental events predicting death for the elderly. *Psychological Bulletin,* 1977, 84, 349–372.

Siegler, I. C. The terminal drop hypothesis: fact or artifact? *Experimental Aging Research,* 1975, *1,* 169–185.

Siegler, I. C., McCarty, S. M., & Logue, P. E. Wechsler Memory Scale scores, selective attribution, and distance from death. *Journal of Gerontology,* 1982, 37, 176–181.

Steuer, J., LaRue, A., Blum, J. E., & Jarvik, L. F. "Critical loss" in the eighth and ninth decades. *Journal of Gerontology,* 1981, 36, 211–213.

Zung, W. W. K. Depression in the normal aged. *Psychosomatics,* 1967, 8, 287–292.

5
Well-being

CONTENTMENT

It was concluded in Chapter 2 that many people at age 60 are vibrant, people at 70 can look forward to exciting things, and at 80, much in life can be pleasant. In brief, age should not be a deterrent to life satisfaction. Many studies of life satisfaction in later life have been carried out under various titles such as morale, successful aging, and happiness. Underlying these studies, even if implicitly, was the goal of determining what adjustments and changes could be made before old age, or during it, that can improve life. Despite these studies, specific prescriptions must remain a goal since the prescription can only be in individual terms.

Three Ingredients

There are some basic facts that apply to almost everyone's life satisfaction, however. These facts are obvious: First, there must be sufficient income. Without money to take care of needs and personal pleasures, life is hard for nearly everyone. Of course, the amount of financial resources necessary for life satisfaction is an individual matter. Second, there must be reasonably good health—life can hardly be pleasant if health is poor, especially if there is pain. Here again, however, people vary greatly in the extent of illness and pain they can endure and still be content.

The third ingredient to contentment in later life may be less obvious. Contentment in old age for most people is difficult, if not impossible, without a confidant. People of every age need someone with whom to talk, to confide, to be close. This will be elaborated later but for now it is well to simply recognize that for most older adults, the husband or wife is usually this close confidant. When either dies, the confidant is lost. It is difficult to develop a new confidant, especially in old age. Widowed people are often left alone.

Having these three ingredients—money, health, and someone to confide in—does not guarantee contentment. They are necessary, but other things are also needed, some more for one person than another.

Are Older Adults Content?

This is a rhetorical question because, first, what is meant by contentment or life satisfaction? Second, there is the issue of individual differences. It is hardly possile to lump together all older people and ask whether they are content.

Life satisfaction is assessed in two ways. The most usual is by way of a questionnaire involving statements that are endorsed or not (agree, disagree) or are endorsed to some extent (e.g., agree somewhat . . . agree very much). An example statement is, "I am just as happy as when I was younger." As reviewed by Kausler (1982, pp. 620–621), the two most popular life satisfaction questionnaires are one by Neugarten, Havighurst, and Tobin (1961) and another by Lawton (1975). The other way life satisfaction is assessed is by way of a general rating—for example, some variant of "from 1 to 7, rate your life in terms of life satisfaction."

The Old See Old Age Differently. The study by Borges and Dutton (1976), referred to briefly at the end of Chapter 2, used this latter way to assess life satisfaction. The respondents were asked to rate their past lives, their lives in the present, and what they anticipated in the future. They were also asked to rate the "average person's life" at various age intervals.

When ratings of "own life" were compared to those of "average person's life" of the same age, the older people said their own lives were better. This was in contrast to younger prople projecting themselves into the future as older. As indicated in Chapter 2, they consistently rated their future lives as less satisfying when old than did the older people already at that age. Thus, it would seem, young people saw old age for themselves in the future in more negative terms than the older people saw it for themselves in the present. The younger people thought getting old was worse than older people did.

Different Life Satisfactions for Young and Old. There is at least as much evidence that contentment is to be found in old age as the other way around. Kausler (1982, p. 622) referenced several studies, with about as many showing "increments in the magnitude of life satisfaction with increasing age" as those showing "slight decrements," or showing no differences at all. "The overall pattern suggests that there is little age change [in contentment] in the total population of adults."

Although overall life satisfaction or contentment does not seem to change with age, life satisfaction is not a single, unitary concept. Some aspects of life satisfaction decrease with age but other aspects increase (Cutler, 1979; Lieberman, 1970). There is a different profile of contentment for the old and the young.

Cutler (1979) analyzed survey data that focused on 12 different domains of life satisfaction, such as home, family, wealth, and friendships. Each respondent was asked this same question regarding each of the 12 domains: "How much satisfaction do you get from (home, family, etc.)?" Answers were ratings based on a seven-point scale.

Marriage, family, and friends provided much satisfaction for people of all ages. "As might be expected . . . satisfaction with personal health declines with age. Satisfaction with home, government, religion, and organization involvement . . . increases slightly with age" (Cutler, 1979, p. 576). Overall, the results of this study demonstrated "that persons of varying ages are likely to have widely different views as to what constitutes 'the good life' " (p. 577). When the 12 dimensions were grouped by a statistical technique called factor analysis, "the first dimension of life satisfaction for persons aged 35 to 44" included home, wealth, and area of residence. For "persons aged 65 to 74 the first dimension is defined by satisfaction with marriage and family" (pp. 577–578). Thus, there are similarities and there are differences in what brings on contentment for the old and the young.

Contentment and Personal Adjustment. There seems to be a consensus that satisfaction with life is really a matter of personality or personal adjustment. Adjustments are necessary throughout life. There are special problems in old age, there are difficulties to be met, but this is true during all phases of life. Atchley (1980, p. 240) concluded that two of the special problems of the elderly revolve around the person's independence and the stability of the person's social world. "Being able to admit one's aging and the physical and social limits it imposes, being able to redefine one's place in the social world . . . being able to take up new values . . ." are part of what is required for satisfaction in later life (p. 243).

A long-term longitudinal study suggested that men and women differ in the personal and social factors that make for life satisfaction in old age. In this study, people aged about 70 were interviewed and given the Neugarten et al. Life Satisfaction Rating Scale. The study was a longitudinal one because 40 years or 50 years prior to this the men and women had been interviewed when they were young parents. In this way, a series of correlations were available of ratings made when they were aged 30 and when aged 70. Marital adjustments and satisfaction with the husband's work were important in later life satisfaction of both men and women. The "strongest predictors for men [of life satisfaction], however, were their own emotional and physical well-being and their wives' emotional characteristics, particularly the latter" (Mussen, Honzik, & Eichorn, 1982, p. 321). Women's satisfaction, on the other hand, was related more to life circumstances such as income and leisure time. Unlike men, the personality traits of their spouses were not very important to the later life satisfaction of these women. Mussen et al. concluded that although the predictors of later life satisfaction were different for men and women, "emotional well-being during early years of marriage is predictive of relatively high LSF [Life Satisfaction Ratings] for both sexes . . ." (p. 322).

Fears of Aging

People of all ages fear becoming old, perhaps not all people, but many. It is obvious that fear spoils life satisfaction, and the pity of it is that not all fears are realistic, and not all are based on what is really important in life.

Loss of appearance and loss of sexual ability are two fears mainly young and middle-aged people have about aging. It will be seen in the next chapter that sexuality is rarely lost in later life. In fact, Comfort (1980) and many others have maintained that the old are interested in sex, practice it and always have, but they "have kept their own counsel." As to fear of losing appearance, it is true that skin wrinkles, postures stoop, and stomachs tend to bulge. Life is not lost, however, with these superficial changes. Contentment is based on values more important than these.

The old also have fears about age, but their fears seem to be different; they are mostly fears of physical breakdown. The magazine of the Johns Hopkins University reported an interesting study in which 600 elderly alumni were asked about their reactions to aging (Anonymous, 1968). It should be noted that these alumni were mainly successful people who were relatively unique in being college graduates when most people of their ages were not.

These alumni were generally positive about their lives but they reported some physical changes. They were apprehensive that these would get worse. One person said that there was much pleasure in growing old, "if the body holds up; however, the body lets one down badly." People expressed fear that they would become a burden to friends and family. They were afraid of living with great physical deterioration.

Although sexual decline may be a fear of the young, it did not seem to be a fear of the old. Loss of independence because of physical disability was an expressed fear. Surprisingly, perhaps, fear of death was not prominent. Family, friends, and lack of pressures were among the pleasures that were often expressed. One woman said that even physical problems would not be so bad if people stopped mentioning her aged physical status.

These alumni may or may not be representative of old people generally in regard to contentment in life. They did express much contentment but, as indicated, they also expressed fear that this contentment would stop because of physical change.

DISENGAGEMENT

Kalish (1975, p. 60) listed "possible definitions of successful aging" but only to indicate that these "definitions" are nothing other than false beliefs held by many people. His first "definition" bore on a presumed socially desirable way of life for the aged. Kalish indicated that social pressure directs the elderly into submissive, uncomplaining roles. Obviously, successful aging, that is, contentment in later life, does not depend on any such role—just the opposite, if this role is not for the particular individual.

Another "definition" is that successful aging involves the maintenance of middle-age activities. The admonishment is to be busy, as when young, or else life satisfaction is beyond grasp. This prescription has a long history and it is wrong for many people. An opposite prescription has also been offered and it is equally wrong for many people. This opposite view has been called *disengagement theory*. Although it really is not a theory in the formal meaning of the term, it is unique in the study of aging in that, as an idea or hypothesis, it is among the few that gave rise to many investigations.

Original Formulation of Disengagement Theory: Withdrawal for Successful Aging

The heart of the theory of disengagement rests on the observation that, in later life, people tend to become withdrawn or dissociated from others and from activity. There is very little controversy regarding this observation—it has been corroborated many times. What was controversial, and what went against the grain of many social and behavioral theorists, was the original emphasis on the role played by the individual in this withdrawal rather than the role played by the broader society in which the individual lives and works.

Cumming and Henry (1961) interviewed and tested people aged 48 to 68 living in Kansas City on five occasions over a period of three years. In addition, they examined people in their 70s and 80s on three occasions. It was, thus, an extensive study. Cumming and Henry believed the withdrawal was intrinsic with almost a biological basis. They believed the older person becomes more involved with self and less with others and with events in the outside world. This increased self-involvement, they said, was because of changed inner, psychological needs, not only because society pushes in this direction.

Even more controversial, however, was the theory's statement that, as a natural or normal process, the disengaged person is the happy person. The disengaged person is following inner-directed interests. If the disengaged behavior is compatible with the values and edicts of society, feelings of satisfaction will be high. Conversely, if the individual is not permitted to disengage, but is pushed into activity instead, morale and life satisfaction will suffer.

Reformulation: Different Types of Successful Aging

Many studies tested the theory of disengagement, and, as will be seen, the theory was found in need of reformulation. Indeed, the essential prescription—withdrawal for happiness—was attacked and found wanting.

Deprivation. One study in partial support of the original formulation was by Lowenthal and Boler (1965), who examined a great number of people and categorized them on the basis of voluntary disengagement versus involuntary disengagement. The voluntary group was defined as having little social interaction, the involuntary group as being socially deprived (i.e., by retirement, recent widowhood, or physical disability). The involuntary disengagement group had low morale but, supporting the original Cumming and Henry thesis, the voluntarily disengaged people had higher morale. Lowenthal and Boler (1965, p. 371) concluded, "It is the deprivations themselves rather than the consequent changes in social interaction that are decisive."

Activity and Well-being. As indicated, the original formulation that life satisfaction goes hand-in-hand with disengagement has not, in the main, been confirmed. In fact, just the opposite is true, but with important, often overlooked exceptions. For the most part, well-being goes with activity, not disengagement. This suggests that disengagement is neither universally natural nor normal, and it may also suggest that very often withdrawal is imposed, not voluntary. This emphasis on activity for well-being has been termed "activity theory," or as Kausler (1982, p. 620) more appropriately termed it, "engagement theory."

An important study was carried out by Maddox and Eisdorfer (1962), who measured both activity and morale of people aged 60 to 94 years. The activity included physical movement, social contacts with family and friends, participation in organizations, work patterns, and leisure-time pursuits. Morale included feelings about the self and about friends, and notions of personal usefulness and unhappiness. The people tested were divided into two equal groups based on their activity scores—there was thus a "high activity" group and a "low activity" group. Similarly, they were divided into groups of "high morale" and "low morale." This produced four typologies: high in both activity and morale, low in both, and high in one of these and low in the other. Effort was then directed to determining the characteristics of people within the four typologies.

Since the oldest people tended to be those who were lowest in activity, the poorest health, not working, and in least control of their living situation, an unambiguous analysis of the relationship between activity and morale was precluded. Within this limitation, however, the results were informative in testing the disengagement theory. Seventy-three percent of the people were either high in both activity and morale, or low in both. The original formation of the disengagement theory would suggest that only a small percentage, if any, would occupy these categories. From the disengagement theory one would predict that low activity, as an index of disengagement, would be associated with high morale, and high activity with low morale. If there were no relationship between activity and morale one way or the other, 25 percent of the people would be expected to fall into each of the four typologies. The actual results thus pointed to a positive relationship between activity and morale, providing evidence for activity or engagement theory. There was also evidence, however, that as age increased (from 60 upward), activity may decrease without affecting life satisfaction (Maddox, 1965).

Those people typed as both "low activity" and "high morale," or vice versa, fell within the expectations of the original disengagement theory. Data were not available to permit a clear-cut differentiation between these people and the remaining 73 percent, but Maddox and Eisdorfer (1962) suggested that their actual or perceived inability to maintain expected levels of activity may be what differentiated them from the 73 percent majority. In other words, if activity is beyond capability, the resulting disengagement may well lead to poor morale.

Health and Social Factors. Maddox and Eisdorfer (1962) found that high morale, whether associated with activity or inactivity, was associated with good health. Conversely, low morale was associated with poorer health regardless of the level of activity. "Satisfaction was more likely to be high when both physical and mental health states were good than when either was poor" (Maddox, 1965, p. 122).

Social factors were important in the disengagement relationships also. Those people who were highest in socioeconomic status and those who experienced a minimum of work-role change were the most likely to report both high activity and high satisfaction. Neither of these social factors, however, pointed to satisfaction when activity was low.

Interpersonal and Noninterpersonal Activity. Maddox made a distinction between activity that is primarily interpersonal and that which is primarily not. This distinction is crucial because inner, psychic changes must, almost by definition, affect interpersonal investments, but not necessarily activities that are routine.

Maddox's data suggested that it is in the interpersonal realm, more than in the noninterpersonal, where the greater decline in activity with age occurred. More important, perhaps, was the finding that "the mean satisfaction score was higher among subjects who reported high non-interpersonal and low interpersonal activity than among those for whom the relationship between subscores (type of activity) was reversed" (Maddox, 1965, p. 123). Thus, the disengagement notion received confirmation when the data were analyzed in this way. Maddox also reported, however, that the total of both types of activity (interpersonal and noninterpersonal) was a somewhat better predictor of satisfaction than either type alone, and much better when one was high and the other low.

Personality Types. Havighurst, Neugarten, and Tobin (1968, pp. 171–172) were in accord with Maddox in finding that life satisfaction was more related to activity than nonactivity, but there were many exceptions. These exceptions, they thought, were associated with "personality type, particularly by the extent to which the individual remains able to integrate emotional and rational elements of the personality."

Those people who are satisfied in disengagement are of several types. According to Neugarten, Havighurst, and Tobin (1968), among the most successful are those who are self-directed and interested in the world, but not in personal interactions with people. (In Maddox's terms, life satisfaction may be seen more frequently with disengagement from interpersonal activities than from noninterpersonal.) Such people satisfied in disengagement from interpersonal activities tend to have high self-regard, and be content and calm, even though they are withdrawn. Those who are striving, ambitious, and achievement-oriented, those to whom aging is a threat, fare less well, but they may also be content in withdrawal. Although they are preoccupied with losses and deficits and shrinking social involvements, they fight against this by closing themselves off. Those who also do relatively well with low activity are people who are passive and dependent. A medium level of activity and satisfaction is possible as long as there are one or two people on whom to lean. Another type of dependent person, one who is especially apathetic and passive, can be moderately satisfied with low activity, but this type was probably always this way.

Thus, it is seen that some do well in disengagement but most do not. For most people, activity and life satisfaction go hand in hand.

The Importance of a Confidant. The theory of disengagement is subject to still another modification—one that is crucial and one brought to light by Lowenthal and Haven (1968). Although not examined in the context of disengagement theory, it matters a great deal, it seems, whether there is a confidant on the scene, someone in whom to confide, to talk about oneself and one's problems.

> . . . it is clear that if you have a confidant, you can decrease your social interaction and run no greater risk of becoming depressed than if you had increased it. Further, if you have no confidant, you may increase your social activities and yet be far more likely to be depressed than the individual who has a confidant but has lowered his interaction level. Finally, if you have no confidant and retrench in your social life, the odds for depression become overwhelming. The findings are similar, though not so dramatic, in regard to change in social role: if you have a confidant, roles can be decreased with no effect on morale; if you do not have a confidant, you are likely to be depressed whether your roles are increased or decreased (though slightly more so if they

are decreased). In other words, the presence of an intimate relationship apparently does serve as a buffer against such decrements as loss of role or reduction of social interaction (Lowenthal and Haven, 1968, pp. 26–27).

Thus, it is seen that the disengagement theory provided much impetus for investigation and much has been found out. Even those studies not carried out with disengagement theory foremost in mind, studies such as Lowenthal and Haven's, were seen in broader perspective with the theory. In summary, the disengagement–happiness relationship is dependent upon the age of the person, the health status (both physical and mental), the personality, the social role, the type of activity in which the person engages (interpersonal or noninterpersonal), and whether or not there is a confidant.

DEATH OF A SPOUSE

A major deterrent to contentment in later life for many people is death of a spouse. For most people, death removes one of the three necessary ingredients of life satisfaction, that of confidant. It removes a major avenue of engagement. Death of a spouse after a long, satisfactory marriage leaves the survivor vulnerable and depressed. Ward (1979, p. 282) phrased it aptly: "The new widow [or widower] can no longer play the role of confidant, lover, housekeeper, or 'member of a couple.' "

Prevalence

This fate is more likely for women than men because most women marry men older than themselves, and most women die at a later age than most men. The median age of widows is 68 and the median age of widowers is 71, reflecting this fact. One in every seven or eight American women is a widow. Naturally, the percentages are much increased among older women—25 percent of those aged 60 to 64, and over 75 percent of those aged 85 and over (Lopata, 1979, pp. 35–36). A comparison between widowhood and widowerhood rates in relation to age may be seen in Figure 5.1.

Widows, Widowers, and New Roles

Difficult adjustments must be made and these are different for men and women. The new widower must now do things that he never did before. He may even feel that he should not do these things, such as taking care of and cleaning the home, doing the shopping, laundry, and cooking. Older widowed men seem to have more serious difficulties than women with personal care. The new widow, on the other hand, must now take care of business matters and go out without a man (Berardo, 1970). This is very difficult for

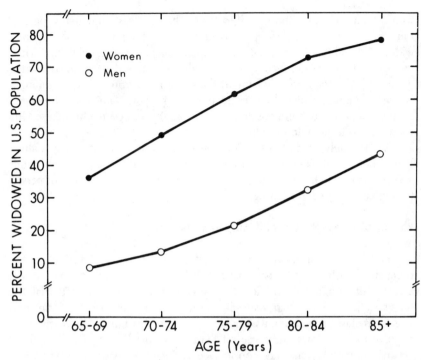

FIGURE 5.1: Percent widowhood in 1970. (From the U.S. Bureau of Census, 1973.)

many older women, some of whom never even learned to write a check. Some had rarely visited friends or gone to the cinema without their husbands. For most older women, that is, for traditional older women, the role of wife is a cornerstone in life. Widowhood brings financial problems to many women, even more so than to men (Atchley, 1980, p. 214), and this makes it difficult for them to leave the house and do things. This only exacerbates their isolation and loneliness.

Parental and Other Support

Some people get used to isolation (Lopata, 1973b), but in the end, most do suffer. Lieberman and Borman (1981, p. 3) reported that *all* the widows in their study showed lower "psychological well-being, more anxiety and depression, and lower life satisfaction." Widows and widowers seek help and solace from family and friends and many find such support, but one recent study showed that it is the widowed person's aged parents who provide this best.

Bankoff (1983, p. 229) examined questionnaires filled out by women in grief who had been widowed 18 or fewer months. The average age of these women was 52 and about half of them had at least one living parent. Bankoff found that "elderly parents play a crucial supportive role for their widowed daughters." Apparently the supportive role is so crucial, that when the aged parent cannot or does not provide it, there is depression, but when the aged parent can provide support there is a relief from this depression. It is important that when there is no parental support, "no other associate's support appears to compensate . . ." (p. 229). Not even children of the widow seem to be able to help.

Interestingly, this seems to hold only as long as the aged parent is alive. When both aged parents are no longer alive, support from widowed friends and others can help. The old parent, it seems, remains an important person throughout his or her lifetime.

Phases of Bereavement and Adjustments

Lieberman and Borman (1981), as well as others, make a distinction between the "early crisis bereavement stage" and the "transition stage" where adjustments are made and identities are formed. They reported that the "crisis stage" can last two years; it may last much longer. The "transition stage" can last an additional year or more. It seems that in the early crisis stage younger widows are worse off than older ones (Carey, 1977), perhaps because older women may consider, even practice, widowhood in more realistic terms beforehand. In the later stages of widowhood, however, the younger women have better opportunities to restructure their lives through remarriage.

Widowerhood has been researched less thoroughly than widowhood, probably because the prevalence of widowhood is so much greater. Atchley (1980, pp. 209–210) believes that "Because the male traditionally emphasizes other roles in addition to the role of husband, widowers are probably not as apt as widows to encounter an identity crisis. . . ." As will be seen in the next section, work role and self-identity can become synonymous. Since more older men than older women have work histories, more of the men have identities outside of spouse. This may be less true of the retired widowers than the working ones, but even for the working widower with little "identity crisis" there is the loss of confidant. This means a loss of an important element in life satisfaction.

Men have a better opportunity than women to reorganize their lives in remarriage. The ratio of many older women to fewer older men in the population makes men more eligible (see Figure 1.2). Men marry women younger than themselves, leaving many older widows without opportunity for remarriage. One study found that those widows who did remarry "were younger, better educated, married before to better trained men earning better incomes than women who remained widows" (Lopata, 1979, p. 161).

Not Everyone Suffers

Not every new widow suffers greatly: not every widow experiences great feelings of isolation and feelings of being different. Those who do not experience this are women who have been "socially isolated and less dependent in their social life on the presence of their husband" (Lopata, 1973a, p. 414). Death of spouse does not seem to make for great dislocation when the marriage had been less than successful, or when death followed a long illness. For such women, after a period of mourning, widowhood can be a release of drudgery of household duties and a beginning of a new independence.

Future generations of widowed elderly should not have to make so many of the painful adjustments that the current elderly widows and widowers make. Young women today do not find business matters very alien to their experience. Writing checks and driving cars, for example, are routine. Young women today are less dependent on their spouses than were young women of yesteryear. Young men today frequently carry out home care chores, finding the kitchen and laundry room part of their experience. They, too, are less dependent on their spouses. This relative independence, however, important as it is, does not bear on emotional dependency. Future widows and widowers will be more able to manage in a physical sense but the sense of isolation and feelings of being different because of being alone will doubtless remain.

There is a growing number of young men and women who are single heads of households. They may escape the pain of being alone when old but this only means that their attachments were never so great in the first place. Loss of spouse is most devastating when commitment and emotional sharing characterized the relationship. Still, not very many people would forgo such sharing, for without it, life would be barren.

WORK, RETIREMENT, AND LEISURE

Work

Since so much of life is spent at work or home care, satisfaction with these efforts becomes almost inseparable from life satisfaction. Work means so much more than the process itself; it provides an identity. People, particularly men, are often described not so much as who they are, or what kind of people they are, but by what they do for a living. Who are you? I am a scientist. What kind of person is he? He is an insurance salesman. It is not very different for women. Who are you? I am a housewife. What kind of person is she? She is a teacher. Socioeconomic status and roles played are implicit in these inquiries and answers, as may be feelings of self-worth and usefulness. The more the job or work-role provides an interest, a responsibility, an opportunity for autonomy, the less inclined the worker is to leave work and retire. More blue-collar workers than white-collar workers would prefer to retire if money were not at issue (Sheppard, 1976, p. 303).

More and more women have been entering the work force and they are staying in it longer than men. Work seems to have a different meaning for women. More men are willing to retire than women (Streib & Schneider, 1971); among blue-collar workers, at least, income is not as big a consideration for women as men in deciding whether they want to continue working (Jacobson, 1974). Many women choose to remain at work because it gives them a greater feeling of accomplishment than work at home. Palmore (1965) reported that the retirement rate is increasing among men but not among women. A working woman gets a salary and this is more than just income. It is a reward for effort. At work a woman meets friends and socializes. Thus, women become individuals apart from their husbands and children. They develop their own identities. Not all women want this, but it seems more and more do. For these women, life satisfaction depends on work.

Retirement

If so much of who and what a person is becomes defined by what he or she does in the workaday world, it is only to be expected that many of the attitudes and values regarding older people derive from their retirement status. Who are you? I am retired; I am no longer working. For a nonemployed housewife, retirement takes a different form, perhaps a less severe one, but here too her role of mother-without-children makes her a different person. The woman can still rule over her domain, her home; her husband has no domain to rule. This makes her role change easier than his except, perhaps, for the fact that with his retirement, her daily function now centers around him as never before. What strains in their relationship might have existed before this retirement will be exacerbated after it.

Successful Retirement. A desire to retire is one thing. Adjustment to retirement is another. As may be anticipated, successful retirement relates to three important factors: whether there is (1) sufficient income; (2) health; and (3) substituted satisfactions. If income is low, health is poor, and nothing satisfying replaces work, retirement holds little promise for a happy life. A retired person who is in good health and financially secure is more likely to be happy than one still working but without these attributes (Streib, 1956). It seems clear now that the old belief that retirement brings on poor health is wrong. It is true that people who retire for reasons of poor health may get worse and even die (Kingson, 1981). This health change, however, seems to be incidental to retirement. Actually, a large number of people claim improvements in health after retirement, but this is not always substantiated. In one study, more than one third of a sample of men who had retired within the previous six years claimed better health, and half the sample said retirement had no effect on health. Ekerdt, Bosse, and LoCastro (1983), however, found that these claims were not compatible with self-rated health reports made by these men both before retirement and afterwards. Despite the perception of improvement in health, the two sets of self-ratings of health disclosed no change. The perceived improvement was attributed to the reduction of prior job strains. This is not to say that actual improvement in health is a rare occurrence. Eisdorfer (1972) reported that those who retire for reasons other than health not only tend to remain well but often improve.

Retirement involves change—it is a disruption of the pattern of life. To the extent that there are large differences between the work life and the retirement life, flexibility is needed. The rigid person is not a good candidate for successful retirement (Atchley, 1980, p. 181). Neither is the "workaholic" who requires an institutional setting for the work. Preparation and planning are essential for successful retirement. Without them, life satisfaction in retirement is unlikely.

Some people shun retirement, some seek it. Many find it a positive part of life. Those who never liked their jobs, those who found their work taxing, and those who enjoy leisure are able to relish their retirement. To some it means that they finished their work, their debts to society are paid; now, they can pay attention to themselves. But people who like their jobs or who get other satisfactions from them tend not to want to leave (e.g., Epstein & Murray, 1968). In the main, the closer the worker is to retirement, the more the disinclination to retire (Riley & Foner, 1968, p. 445).

Phases of Retirement. Butler and Lewis (1977, pp. 104–105) differentiated several phases of retirement. First, there is anticipation. This could be positive or not, depending on whether retirement is voluntary or not. But even if it is voluntary, changes are taking place on the job that are often negative. For instance, other employees start pulling away socially in preparation for the parting. They begin to plan for a successor. The soon-to-be-retired person's job may also be a source of infighting among co-workers and friends. The atmosphere at work is no longer quite the same.

The second phase of retirement is the actual day of separation. This day has either been dreaded or looked forward to with pleasure. This can be an emotional event but it is short-lived. The next phase is the most difficult one, the period where adjustments have to be made in the new life of retirement. Things are different and, like it or not, changes have to be made. These changes can vary from a new career to hobbies and interests long-neglected because of lack of time. The changes can include idleness and boredom. Idleness may be fine for some, but not for many.

The fourth and last phase is the acceptance of a new life. For better or worse, there is finally recognition that another life passage has been completed. Leaving the work force is a rite of passage, similar in some ways to birth, marriage, and death. The ceremony, however, if any, is very individual and rarely, if ever, of a religious character as on the other occasions. Nevertheless, it is a crucial passage, where contentment can be either increased or decreased. Acceptance of this rite of passage is the fourth and last stage of successful retirement.

Voluntary and Mandatory Retirement. At present in the United States, retirement is mandatory at age 70 for all but relatively few people in special occupations, or for the self-employed; it used to be at age 65. It is likely that the mandatory age retirement in the future will be discontinued. All retirement, or almost all, will be voluntary, except for reasons such as health. Will this bring greater life satisfaction to those who would otherwise be obliged to leave the labor force?

To many, mandatory age retirement is wrong. This belief is based on humanistic concerns. It is obvious that to cut someone off from the work force when the worker is still competent and wants to work—and may be miserable not working—is unjust.

The other side of the argument is based on economic concerns. During the depression of the 1930s, the goal was to make jobs available for younger people by retiring older people. During World War II, when there were many jobs and workers were needed, older people were encouraged to stay at work or to do volunteer work for "the war effort." Opening up jobs for younger people is still one of the reasons given in favor of mandatory retirement.

The current emphasis on doing away with mandatory age retirement seems to be based on a combination of humanistic values and economic predictions based on demographic trends. It is expected that the number of older workers who can claim Social Security benefits and who will need financial assistance will rise and be a burden on taxpayers. Keeping the older worker at work reduces the tax drain.

Many unions and large businesses fear that older workers will not choose to retire, and younger workers therefore will not get a chance for promotion. Furthermore, they fear that minorities and women may not get an opportunity for jobs they were unable to get before because of discrimination. They also fear that "dead wood," that is, those who never contributed much to their jobs, cannot be easily pushed out without compulsory retirement.

This fear may not be realistic. With pensions and other financial opportunities, there is an increasing trend toward retiring at a younger age, rather than an older one. Next to reasons of health (Kingson, 1981) workers tend to retire as soon as there is enough money to do so (Bixby, 1976). Most early retirements, however, that is, before the age of 62, are for reasons of poor health.

Leisure Time

With retirement there is much time for leisure activity. Leisure time can be satisfying, but it can also be boring. Leisure time activity is not synonymous with having nothing to do. The retired old person with nothing to do becomes irritable, moody, complaining; there is no life satisfaction in such status. Leisure time should be filled with activity that is enjoyable, meaning-ful, and healthy. Activities done just for the sake of doing something are not satisfying.

Work and leisure are not always easy to tell apart. Leisure time and work time activities are generally distinguished by what is considered enjoyable and voluntary and what is seen as necessary and mandatory. Even this distinction, however, is not always clear because, as Ward (1979, pp. 237–238) pointed out, leisure time activity "can be as intense and meaningful as any activity (including work)." Further, what is meaningful or fun for one person is not for another. Kalish (1975, p. 113) made this clear in a colorful statement: he simply dislikes gardening. For him it's work. For others, gardening is fun. The key difference is what is personally rewarding and meaningful.

It is difficult to tell how satisfactory an activity is by just appearance. The old man sitting on a park bench talking with friends may be bored, but he may be doing exactly what he wants, even though he has an opportunity to do something else. The older woman who is doing volunteer work may seem to be doing exactly what she wants and enjoying it, but, on the other hand, she may hate it and not know what else to do.

Leisure, like the economic aspects of retirement, must involve plan-ning. Some people in their retirement are blessed with a wide variety of interests, but others are cursed with too much time. For the retired worker, time is an available commodity. This commodity can make for life satisfac-tion or the opposite.

SUMMARY

Well-being among the aged has been investigated under various titles such as life satisfaction, contentment, morale, successful aging, and others. What makes for well-being is a personal matter, but there are features in common for almost all people. Good health, adequate finances, and someone to be with and confide in are basic to life satisfaction. People vary greatly in how much money they require for happiness, but everyone needs some mini-mum amount. The same is true for health. People vary in the extent of illness and pain they can endure and still have good morale, but the very infirm can hardly be expected to enjoy life. Almost everyone needs a confi-dant to tell things to and to be told things by—someone who listens and shares. Again, people vary in how much this is needed and how often, but few are so self-involved as to be content alone without anyone else.

Loss of spouse removes the confidant for most people, leaving the widow or widower in grief and isolation. Much more study has been made of the widow than the widower, probably because of the much greater prevalence of widows. Most women marry men older than themselves, and women have a longer life expectancy than men. Widowhood has a crisis stage of much dislocation, often lasting two years, perhaps longer. There is a transition stage when life improves, and this can last another year or more. There are wide individual differences in this. Some who are widowed take years to recover and some never do. Finding a new way of life and a new identity without the deceased spouse is not an easy task for those who have had a long and satisfactory marriage.

The man left alone has problems in common with the woman alone, but he also has different problems. For the older man there may be problems in personal care. Men find it easier to remarry, however, and to reestablish a home life. The younger widow may have a more difficult time than the older widow at first, but the younger woman has better opportunity for remarriage.

Until late old age, most men and women are with their spouses and contentment is more possible for them. Are old people content? Mostly yes, as much as are young people, as judged by studies carried out to answer this question. Their pleasures may derive from different sources than young people's, but they are as content overall. One study, at least, showed that the young think that their lives when old will not be especially satisfying, but this expectation is not warranted on the basis of what older people indicate of their lives.

Young people often fear that life will be less pleasant for them when old for various reasons, including loss of appearance. Skin does wrinkle, stomachs do bulge, and postures do stoop, but these are superficial changes. Old people do not seem to worry about such trivialities. They do worry about physical breakdown, incapacity, and loss of independence. Although this is not the fate of very many old people, such fear can interfere with contentment.

A theory that stimulated much research and that bears on the prescription for well-being is called disengagement theory. The heart of this theory rests on the observation that, in later life, people tend to become withdrawn or dissociated from others and from activity. There never was much controversy regarding this observation, but there was controversy regarding whether the withdrawal is willing or whether society pushes the older person aside. Even more controversial was the belief that withdrawal is natural and normal and, as such, the disengaged, withdrawn person is the happy person.

Many studies were carried out to test this theory, and the essential prescription—withdrawal for happiness—was attacked and found wanting. For the most part, just the opposite was seen as true; well-being goes with activity or engagement, not disengagement. Various factors, however, modify the relationship between activity and well-being. Good health is so important that contentment is hardly possible without it whether activity is high or not. Socioeconomic status (SES) and work-role change are important too. Those highest in SES and those who experience a minimum of work-role changes are the most likely to report both high activity and high satisfaction. Another factor is whether the person has a confidant. If there is one, then good morale is possible even with little activity. Although most people may not be happy in disengagement, some are. Among these, the most successful, it appears, are those who are self-directed, have high self-regard, and are interested in the world but not in personal interactions with people.

Life satisfaction is also related to issues of work, retirement, and leisure. So much of life is tied to job and home care that if these are not satisfying, neither can the quality of life be. Some people want to continue working, some want to retire. Most people, it appears, would retire if they could afford it. Most early retirements, however, are for reasons of poor health. Adjustment to retirement requires planning. For retirement to be successful, again, money and health are crucial.

Retirement brings leisure time. For a satisfying life this time must be filled with activity, but not any activity. Just keeping busy will not do. Leisure time activity that is enjoyable, personally meaningful, and healthful is the road to life satisfaction in old age.

REFERENCES

Anonymous. What's it like? *The Johns Hopkins Magazine*, Spring, 1968, 27–28.

Atchley, R. C. *The social forces in later life*. Belmont, Calif.: Wadsworth, 1980.

Bankoff, E. A. Aged parents and their widowed daughters: a support relationship. *Journal of Gerontology*, 1983, 38, 226–230.

Berardo, F. M. Survivorship and social isolation: the case of the aged widower. *Family Coordinator*, 1970, 19, 11–25.

Bixby, L. E. Retirement patterns in the United States: Research policy interaction. *Social Security Bulletin*, 1976, 39(8), 3–19.

Borges, M. A., & Dutton, L. J. Attitudes toward aging. *The Gerontologist*, 1976, 16, 220–224.

Butler, R. N., & Lewis, M. I. *Aging and mental health*. St. Louis: C. V. Mosby, 1977.

Carey, R. G. The widowed: A year later. *Journal of Counseling Psychology*, 1977, 24, 125–131.

Comfort, A. Sexuality in later life. In J. E. Birren & R. B. Sloane (Eds.), *Handbook of mental health and aging*. Englewood Cliffs, N.J.: 1980, pp. 885–892.

Cumming, E., & Henry, W. *Growing old: The process of disengagement*. New York: Basic Books, 1961.

Cutler, N. E. Age variations in the dimensionality of life satisfaction. *Journal of Gerontology*, 1979, 34, 573–578.

Eisdorfer, C. Adaptation to loss of work. In F. M. Carp (Ed.), *Retirement*. New York: Academic Press, 1972.

Ekerdt, D. J., Bosse, R., & LoCastro, J. S. Claims that retirement improves health. *Journal of Gerontology*, 1983, 38, 231–236.

Epstein, L. E., & Murray, J. H. Employment and retirement. In B. L. Neugarten (Ed.), *Middle age and aging*. Chicago: University of Chicago Press, 1968.

Havighurst, R. J., Neugarten, B. L., & Tobin, S. S. Disengagement and patterns of aging. In B. L. Neugarten (Ed.), *Middle age and aging*. Chicago: University of Chicago Press, 1968, pp. 161–172.

Jacobson, D. Rejection of the retiree role: A study of female industrial workers in their late 50s. *Home Relations*, 1974, 27, 477–492.

Kalish, R. A. *Late adulthood: Perspectives on human development*. Monterey, Calif.: Brooks/ Cole, 1975.

Kausler, D. H. *Experimental psychology and human aging*. New York: Wiley, 1982.

Kingson, E. R. *The early retirement myth: Why men retire before age 62*. Washington, D.C.: U.S. Govt. Printing Office, 1981. (A report by the Select Committee on Aging, U.S. House of Representatives; Comm. Pub. No. 97-298.)

Lawton, M. P. The Philadelphia Geriatric Center Morale Scale: a revision. *Journal of Gerontology*, 1975, 30, 85–89.

Lieberman, L. R. Life satisfaction in the young and old. *Psychological Reports*, 1970, 27, 75–79.

Lieberman, M.A., & Borman, L. D. Who helps widows: the role of kith and kin. National Reporter (of the National Research and Information Center, Evanston, Ill.), 1981, 4(8), 2–4.

Lopata, H. Z. Self-identity in marriage and widowhood. *Sociological Quarterly*, 1973, 14, 407–418. (a)

Lopata, H. Z. *Widowhood in an American city*. Cambridge, Mass.: Schenkman, 1973. (b)

Lopata, H. Z. *Women as widows*. New York: Elsevier North Holland, 1979.

Lowenthal, M. F., & Boler, D. Voluntary vs. involuntary social withdrawal. *Journal of Gerontology*, 1965, 20, 363–371.

Lowenthal, M. F., & Haven, C. Interaction and adaptation: Intimacy as a critical variable. *American Sociological Review*, 1968, 33(1), 20–30.

Maddox, G. L. Fact and artifact: Evidence bearing on disengagement theory from the Duke Geriatrics Project. *Human Development*, 1965, 8, 117–130.

Maddox, G., & Eisdorfer, C. Some correlates of activity and morale among the elderly. *Social Forces*, 1962, 40, 254–260.

Mussen, P., Honzik, M. P., & Eichorn, H. Early adult antecedents of life satisfaction at age 70. *Journal of Gerontology*, 1982, 37, 316–322.

Neugarten, B. L., Havighurst, R. J., & Tobin, S. S. The measurement of life satisfaction. *Journal of Gerontology*, 1961, 16, 134–143.

Neugarten, B. L., Havighurst, R. J., & Tobin, S. S. Personality and patterns of aging. In B. L. Neugarten (Ed.), *Middle age and aging*. Chicago: University of Chicago Press, 1968, pp. 173–177.

Palmore, E. B. Differences in the retirement patterns of men and women. *The Gerontologist*, 1965, 1, 4–8.

Riley, M. W. & Foner, A. *Aging and society* (Vol. 1). New York: Russell Sage Foundation, 1968.

Sheppard, H. L. Work and retirement. In R. H. Binstock & E. Shanas (Eds.), *Handbook of aging and the social sciences*. New York: Van Nostrand Reinhold, 1976.

Streib, G. F. Morale of the retired. *Social Problems*, 1956, 3, 270–276.

Streib, G. F., & Schneider, C. J. *Retirement in American society*. Ithaca, N.Y.: Cornell University Press, 1971.

U.S. Bureau of the Census. *Census of the population: Characteristics of the population*. Part 1, Section 1, 1973.

Ward, R. A. *The aging experience*. New York: Lippincott, 1979.

6
Sexuality and
Sexual Relations

It was noted in the previous chapter that many young people fear losing sexual ability later in life. This fear may be more common to men than women. Butler and Lewis (1976, p. 19) wrote, "Most men begin to worry secretly about sexual aging some time in their thirties. . . . These worries tend to accelerate in the forties and fifties and reach a peak in the sixties. . . ." Such fears are not warranted. Although there is sexual aging, all experts agree that neither sexual needs nor sexual function ceases. People of almost all ages can and do have sexual lives.

SEXUAL REVOLUTION

There was a time when public discussion and the written record of research on sexual relations between men and women had to be indirectly and delicately expressed. It is difficult to envision now the stir that was made in 1948 when Kinsey and his collaborators reported their findings on sexual behavior of men (Kinsey, Pomeroy, & Martin, 1948), and in 1953 when findings about women were reported (Kinsey, Pomeroy, Martin, & Gebhard, 1953). Later work was more revealing but it caused less of a stir. For example, the work of Masters and Johnson (1966) was much more detailed with respect to sexual anatomy and physiological functioning. It was based much more on laboratory participation than the earlier Kinsey reports. The book by Rubin (1965), *Sexual Life After Sixty*, provided a much wider scope of information regarding very intimate details of sexual acts and problems. This too did not have nearly the social shock value of the earlier Kinsey works.

The revolution in sex research and reports did not stop here; it grew more daring and seems to have corresponded with the sexual revolution generally. Comfort's (1972) *Joy of Sex* is a frank "how-to book," replete with colored pictures with related information: For example, "In men, the only important changes over the first seven decades are that spontaneous erection occurs less often . . . ejaculation takes longer to happen . . . but given certain conditions . . . active sex lasts as long as life." (p. 224).

This was followed by *More Joy*, in which advice to people over 60 such as this was given: "Don't cut your rate of intercourse below what you've been used to, because with age sexual response, like muscular strength, is very susceptible to disuse . . ." (Comfort, 1974, p. 149). In similar fashion, Butler and Lewis (1976), in their book, *Love and Sex After Sixty*, provide a great deal of information and advice. For example, one chapter is titled, "Learning New Patterns of Love-Making" (p. 37). In another chapter they tell women how they can aid their men who have problems with impotence (p. 92). This book has not attained the popularity of Comfort's books, but it is the main "help book" directed to those in later life.

Coinciding with these "facts and advice" books are research projects asking personal sex questions. From the perspective of years ago, these are shocking, and the answers are even more so. In one study, Starr and Weiner (1981) questioned men and women aged 60 to 91 years regarding all matter of sexual experience. Their questionnaire included issues of "sexual experimentation and the ideal lover"; they asked their respondents, "How do you feel about older people who are not married having sexual relations and living together?" Starr and Weiner (p. 127) reported that, "A whopping 91 percent approved. Men (95 percent) and women (89 percent) gave similar responses, as did those who were sexually active . . . and those who were inactive. . . ." To questions regarding older men–younger women combinations, or vice versa, the endorsement of approval was about 85 percent (p. 173).

Their data suggest that the sexual revolution is not only a revolution of the young, but of many elderly people as well. This is in contrast to Hite's (1976, p. 349) conclusion that, "The sexual revolution did not include older women." Hite's questionnaire study of women, however, included very few older people even though her respondents were aged from 14 to 78 years. Hite asserted women's sexual independence—she declared women's need to take responsibility for their gratifications.

It is interesting to contrast all this with the thinking of years ago. Each of the more recent authors emphasized gratification in sexual behavior, for both men and women, for both young and old. How different it had been: Kinsey's books of the 1940s and 1950s were descriptive and gave no advice; the books of the 1960s were more daring but not nearly as assertive in emphasizing gratification. And long before, in the nineteenth century, a marriage manual counseled, "As a general rule, a modest woman seldom desires gratification herself. She submits to her husband, but only to please him; and but for the desire of maternity, would far rather be relieved from his attentions" (from Butler & Lewis, 1976, p. 55).

FREEDOM OF INQUIRY?

We have thus entered a period of greater freedom regarding sexual behavior and greater freedom to do research on sexuality and sexual relations. This freedom of research, however, may be more apparent than real; it may provide opportunities of inquiry, but it may also provide misleading results.

Generalizability

Investigators are free to inquire but people are free to not answer. The Hite report, so clear in declaring women's sexuality, was based on a mere 3 percent of the 100,000 people solicited. What can be said of those 97 percent of women who chose not to respond? Starr and Weiner were more successful because they went around giving talks to older adults on "Love, Intimacy and Sex in the Later Years." Question-and-answer periods followed these talks, and then questionnaires were distributed. Even here, only 14 percent responded. What can be said of the other 86 percent, and of the men and women who did not attend the sex talks in the first place? Is it possible that these and similar investigations are based mainly on the more "sexually liberated" people, and therefore provide an unrepresentative picture of sexuality?

There is special difficulty in obtaining generalizable sex information on older adults. In fact, with the exception of Starr and Weiner, who had respones of 800 older people, few other studies had large samples, or even ones that could be regarded as adequate. For example, in the study by Hite, age data were available on only about one-third of the respondents. Of these, only 13 were in their 60s and six in their 70s.

In the major study of Masters and Johnson, 157 women of the age range 51 to 78 years were interviewed, but only 34 were selected for study, that is, 22 percent. In comparison, 75 percent of women aged 21 to 50 years who were interviewed were selected for study, with their total number being 10 times greater than those aged 51 to 78 years. Of the 34 older women selected, only eight were aged 61 to 70 years and three 71 to 78 years. This sampling problem was not essentially different for men. The data of Kinsey et al., as will be seen shortly, are also deficient with regard to older samples.

Many investigators are either uninterested in the sexuality of older people or are uncomfortable with the idea that old people are sexual. More often than not, the elderly have been excluded from their focus of investigation. Additionally, many older people themselves, or their relatives, seem to be uncomfortable with sex research. It had been seen in one study that even when elderly people volunteered to participate in sex research studies, their relatives often became upset and insisted they withdraw (Pfeiffer, 1969, p.

152). Older people, having been reared in earlier eras when open and frank discussion of sexual life was taboo, often require special circumstances to be open and candid. Apparently this is less true of today's elderly than the elderly of yesteryear, but even now, as seen in the Starr–Weiner study, the percentage of older adults responding to sex questions is not overwhelming. It is not surprising, therefore, that most of the studies on sexuality in later life are based on relatively small sample sizes and on low subject selection rates. Nor is it surprising, in view of this difficulty, that so much of the literature on sex among the elderly is of a clinical nature.

Validity

Objective and valid information regarding sexual experience is difficult to obtain for other reasons too. Most sex research, but not all, is based on interviews or questionnaires. The honesty or correctness of the answers is unknown. Some elderly male respondents have been known to deny their disinterest or inability in sexual intercourse and have reported feats of virility instead. Others may be reluctant to disclose their thoughts and behaviors. Although this is not sufficient to negate interview methods, it is important to warrant cross-validation by interviews with spouses, when possible. In other words, a serious problem of much of the research is its unknown or uncertain validity, as well as its uncertain generalizability.

THE AGED ARE SEXUAL TOO

"All of us," Rubin (1965, p. 3) said, "have been accustomed to associate sex and love exclusively with youth. Sexual activity of any kind on the part of older persons is rarely referred to except in derogatory terms. According to our folklore, what is 'virility' at twenty-five becomes 'lechery' at sixty-five." The fact is, sexuality is a characteristic of old people as it is of young people. Although many young people may be uncomfortable with the idea of sexual relations among elderly couples (older grandparents, for example), sexual relations among the elderly are not unusual and should not be thought of as immoral. What is immoral are the restraints sometimes placed upon the aged because of false beliefs that old people are sexless people. Restraints are also placed on them because of discomfort younger people have with the sexuality of the old. Such false beliefs and restraints are dangerous, Rubin (1965) maintained, because they can make for "a self-fulfilling prophecy." In other words, sex functioning is so much a matter of attitude and belief that false expectations may make sexlessness come true. Comfort (1972, p. 224) seems less concerned about the false notion of the sexless aged. "Ours isn't the first generation to know otherwise" he said, "but probably the first one which hasn't been brainwashed into being ashamed to admit it."

Intolerance and discomfort with the idea that the aged have sexual interests and needs includes professional people who should know better. This takes a particularly inhumane form when such attitudes are held by people who have responsibilities for planning and supervision. "Many state hospitals, nursing homes, and homes for the aged practice segregation of the sexes or else permit men and women, even husbands and wives, to spend time with each other only in public dayrooms or under 'supervision' " (Pfeiffer, 1969, p. 161). These practices do more than simply ignore the sexual needs of the elderly; they negate the dignity of old people and their very existence as human beings.

SEX DIFFERENCES

Male Sexuality

Frequency of Sexual Experience. Sexuality is retained through much of life, but there is no question that the human male's sexual responsiveness wanes as he ages. In fact, "In the sexual history of the male, there is no other single factor which affects frequency of outlet as much as age. . . . Age is so important that its effects are usually evident, whatever the mental status, the educational level, the religious background, or the other factors which enter the picture" (Kinsey et al., 1948, pp. 218–219). There is only little controversy regarding this. Comfort (1972, p. 149) adds, "Men normally attain fewer orgasms but no fewer erections as they get older." Butler and Lewis (1976, p. 20) agree but advise that "comparisons of a man's present sexual status must be made in terms of his past and present history and not against a generalized 'standard.' " The reason for this is the large individual differences in sexual "potency." Starr and Weiner (1981) do not agree that potency wanes, but their data are exceptions. More will be said about this shortly.

A significant characteristic of male sexual waning is its gradualness. The age of maximum sexuality, according to Kinsey et al., is in the teens, and sexuality then drops almost linearly until age 60, at least. Until age 60, therefore, the drop from one age to another is of about the same magnitude as the drop between any other comparable age spans. This may be seen clearly in Figure 6.1. Kinsey et al. analyzed the sexual behavior of the human male in terms of six sources of orgasm, sources such as sexual intercourse, masturbation, and nocturnal emission. The total of these six sources was called "total sexual outlet." Figure 6.1 presents the Kinsey data in terms of the median number of orgasms per week from all sources, and from marital intercourse. In general, the aging pattern seen in Figure 6.1 was seen also for each of the six sources of outlet.

Kinsey et al. also had data on men over the age of 60, but the number of cases was judged too few for statistical analyses. The most important generalization from the data of the older men is that the pattern of gradually diminishing activity that started with 16-year-olds seems to continue. But even in the oldest age-groups, many men continue to have sexual lives. At 60 years of age, 95 percent of Kinsey's male respondents were still active sexually, and at age 70, nearly 70 percent were active. The number of men older than 70 was too few to judge confidently, but the indication was of a continued drop.

Table 6.1 shows that at about age 40, marital intercourse was at about 1.5 times per week. Starr and Weiner (1981, p. 48) reported that men aged 60 to 69 in their study had sexual relations at about the same time frequency: 1.5 times per week. Thus, Starr and Weiner did not observe very

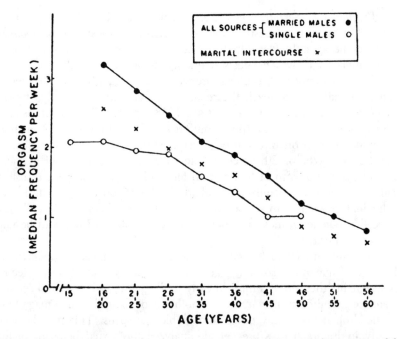

FIGURE 6.1: Sexuality, as measured by the frequency of orgasms, in relation to age of the human male. Figure from Botwinick, J. in J.E. Birren (Ed.), *Handbook of aging and the individual*. Copyright 1959 by the University of Chicago. Original data may be seen in Kinsey et al., 1948, pp. 226 and 252, Tables 45 and 46.

much waning in later life. They concluded, "Our data provides some strik-ing evidence for the conclusion that older people who remain sexually active do not differ significantly in frequency of sexual relations compared with when they were younger" (p. 48).

Further, almost 83 percent of Starr and Weiner's total sample (aged 60 to 91) was sexually active (see their Table 21, p. 268); 17 percent was inactive. This is a greater percentage than that reported by Kinsey et al.; by age 70, they said, one-quarter of the men were impotent. Comfort's (1972, p. 224) analysis was more in line with Kinsey et al. "From a quarter to a half of all couples of this age [up to 75 and beyond] have regular sex . . ."; that is, one-half to three-quarters do not. Comfort, however, believed that this need not be. He wrote, "since continued activity keeps hormone levels up, for couples who make love often it's probably to 75 percent and the other quarter will have stopped because of arthritis or other ills of age, not impotence or frigidity" (p. 224).

Starr and Weiner made an important point. When cross-sectional data such as those in Figure 6.1 are viewed, it is common to assume that "the older group will reflect the younger group many years later." This assumption may be wrong. The younger group represented in Figure 6.1 may not be like the old group in the figure. They may not change with age at all. If so, as older adults, they would be different from older people of the past. Starr and Weiner emphasized that the older people they examined were born at about the same time as the younger people Kinsey et al. examined. Kinsey et al. began interviewing people in the late 1930s and Starr and Weiner began their study in the late 1970s. This suggests that the different results of the two studies could be attributed to the different eras, 1930s and 1970s, in which the studies were conducted. Perhaps attitudes and beliefs, and therefore practices, changed over the 40 years. (This is called the cohort effect, described in detail in Chapter 20.) Given the issues of generalizability and validity discussed before, perhaps the most conservative and meaningful conclusion regarding male sexuality is that it does wane but maybe not as much as it had been thought (or as it did in the past). Further, there may be even less waning with proper attitudes and if sexual practices are maintained.

Phases of the Sexual Cycle. There are changes in the specific phases of the male sexual response. According to Masters and Johnson (1966, p. 248), with age, particularly after age 60, there is a slowing of erection, of mount-ing, and of ejaculation. There is an increase in the time after orgasm in which the male is once again ready for ejaculation. "The psychosexual pleasure of the ejaculatory process may be impaired." In the ejaculatory process "the young male . . . is aware not only of the force of the explosive contractions but also of the localized sensation of fluid emission . . . the aging male, particularly if his erection has been long maintained, may have

TABLE 6.1
Indices of Sexuality of Married and "Post-Married" Women

	50		55		60		65		70	
	Incidence %	Median Frequency Per Year	Incidence %	Median Frequency Per Year	Incidence %	Median Frequency Per Year	Incidence %	Median Frequency Per Year	Incidence %	Median Frequency Per Year
Marital Activities										
Coitus	87.5	69.4	89.2	57.9	69.7	40.7	50.0	—*	—	—
Masturbation	31.2	13.3	29.7	3.7	27.3	—	25.0	—	—	—
Sex dreams	27.0	3.1	26.0	3.0	18.2	—	18.8	—	—	—
N	160		74		33		16		3	
Post-marital Activities										
Coitus	37.0	44.8	29.3	27.2	12.5	—	0.0	—	0.0	—
Masturbation	58.8	15.0	46.6	11.3	43.8	8.0	33.3	—	25.0	—
Sex dreams	34.6	8.6	27.6	4.0	18.8	—	11.1	—	16.7	—
N	81		58		32		18		12	

AGE (YEARS)

* Number of cases is less than ten.
From C.V. Christenson and J.H. Gagnon, 1965. Reprinted by permission of the *Journal of Gerontology*, Vol. 20, p. 352, 1965.

the experience of seepage rather than of seminal fluid expulsion" (Masters & Johnson, 1966, p. 259).

All this need not be negative. Comfort (1972, p. 224) suggested that as the "ability and need to ejaculate frequently gets less, it's a good idea not to try for it every time, which will give you more mileage and no less mutual pleasure." Butler and Lewis (1976, pp. 21–22) reported in similar fashion: "The forcefulness of orgasm also lessens naturally when a couple voluntarily prolong their love-making before orgasm. Older men have a choice of an extended period of sexual pleasure with a milder orgasm or a briefer session with a more intense orgasm." Referring to the diminished frequency of orgasm, as well as to the quality of ejaculation, they continued: "Remember that love-making need not be limited to ejaculatory ability" (p. 22).

Female Sexuality

The study of female sexuality is more complex than that of the male, not only because of the heretofore greater inhibition of sexuality of the female, but also because of the greater difficulty in assessing it. The assessment of female sexuality is more difficult because, although the male rarely fails to reach orgasm in his sexual activities, much of the sexual activity of women does not result in orgasm.

Frequency of Orgasm. Different reports vary in their estimates of the frequency of female orgasm during lovemaking. Starr and Weiner (1981, p. 80) reported that 88 percent of Hite's respondents said they had orgasms during intercourse, two different magazines reported 90 and 93 percent, and their own data of much older women showed that 98.5 percent of them experienced orgasm in coitus. Eighty-six percent of their women respondents said that they achieve orgasm at the same or greater rates as when younger (p. 81).

Again, given the issues of generalizability and validity discussed before, such results remain uncertain. In fact, there are data suggesting sexual waning in women as well as in men, but the waning appears later in life. When waning does begin, it is of lesser extent than men's.

The frequency of marital coitus declines with age, but this is due mostly to the sexual waning of husbands. Accordingly, Kinsey et al. suggested that for women the frequency of masturbation may be a more appropriate index of sexuality than frequency of intercourse. Masters and Johnson (1966, p. 24) reported that masturbation decreases after age 60. Pfeiffer (1969) reported that among women aged 60 to 94 years, only about one-third acknowledged continued sexual interests. The clearest data on female sexuality during later periods of life may be those of Christenson and Gagnon (1965), who culled information from the case history files of the Kinsey laboratory.

Christenson and Gagnon directed their attention to the data of women aged 50 to 70, who either were married at the time of the interview or had been married. As may be seen in Table 6.1, they categorized the results of five age groups: 50, 55, 60, 65, and 70 years, keeping separate the data of married and "post-married" women. This table supports the contention that masturbation is a better index of female sexuality than is sexual intercourse. The "post-married" women, more deprived of a sex partner, masturbated at nearly twice the rate of the married women.

The frequency of masturbation declined with age in the "post-married" group. In the married group, the incidence of both coitus and masturbation was progressively less with each age-group. This suggests a sexual waning in women as well as men.

Difficult to Measure. It was said that diminished frequency of sexual intercourse with age by women may be more a matter of the unavailability of a male, or of the male's sexual waning, than of anything else. Kinsey et al. suggested that masturbation is a better index of sexuality, but it is a less than desirable index. Many people, it seems, are reluctant to admit masturbation even when they may feel free to declare their roles in sexual intercourse. Starr and Weiner (1981) did not doubt the reports by their respondents regarding active sexual lives, yet they were dubious about their reports of masturbation. More women (85 percent) than men (76 percent) endorsed the practice "to relieve sexual tensions," but only 47 percent of the women and 44 percent of the men said they masturbated. The suggestion is that there may be more masturbatory activity than is admitted. This suggestion was supported by the observation that half "of those who endorsed masturbation left blank the questions of participation or frequency. Others used suspiciously guarded qualifiers that were not used in other responses" (Starr & Weiner, 1981, p. 64). Thus, their data on masturbation, as well as the data of Kinsey et al., may underestimate incidence.

In the Starr–Weiner study, masturbation was "reported by 47 percent of the 60–69 year-old women, 49 percent of the 70–79 year-olds, and 34 percent of the 80-and-over group" (their Table 15B, p. 263). These percentages are vastly higher than those of Christenson and Gagnon (1965). Their report, shown in Table 6.1, indicates that from ages 60 to 70, far fewer admitted to masturbation (25.0–43.8 percent). Underestimates or otherwise, both sets of data suggest sexual waning with age.

Relative Sexual Patterns of the Two Sexes

The pattern of decline for men is gradual, starting early in life. The pattern for women is different. There is little, if any, decline in sexuality until age 60, but from that point on, there are indications of decline in women also.

In both sexes, however, the diminished sexuality is more in terms of frequency and vigor than it is of kind. For a large number of elderly men and women, sexual relations end only with death.

Men More Active than Women. Although the decline with age in sexuality is more apparent in men than in women, the sexual activities of men, for various reasons, are more frequent than those of women throughout most of their lives. Given the double standard that has been present, at least till now, it is not surprising that men are more active sexually than women; this might be expected even with an assumption that the two sexes are equal in psychobiological sexuality. This seems clear among younger people but it is less clear that this is so among older people. There are few studies comparing men and women at advanced ages. The data of Kinsey et al. (1953, p. 716), that include groups only to age 60, show that the relatively rapid decline of the male brings him to a level of activity only slightly higher than that of the female. If we extrapolate the Kinsey curves, a very dubious practice, a point would be reached, at about at 70, when both sexes would seem very similar in the frequency of attaining orgasms. The data of Starr and Weiner (1981), however, show that even in later life there is greater sexual activity on the part of men. (See their Table 21A, p. 269.) Availability of partners, not sexuality, may be the basis of this.

Conclusions of higher sexual rates by men than women were suggested in two other studies, but these also leave uncertainty. Psychiatrists interviewed people aged 60 years and older, and reinterviewed as many as they could over the next decade (Verwoerdt, Pfeiffer, & Wang, 1969). They concluded that sexuality, as indicated by declared interest in heterosexual coitus, decreased with age past 60 but with men showing more interest than women. A similar conclusion was drawn by Cameron and Biber (1973), who interrupted people in a variety of situations to ask them what they had been thinking about during the previous five minutes. Here, any sexual thought was tabulated, not only those associated directly with orgasm or coitus. It was noted that the incidence of sex thoughts decreased with age, this being so with both sexes. In all age-groups, however, including the oldest one of 65 to 99 years, men reported a higher frequency of sex thoughts "crossing their minds" than did women.

Age in Marriage. The two studies above were of interests and thoughts, not behavior. Sexual performance is another matter. This is seen in a study where it was found that the frequency of sexual intercourse between man and wife is limited mainly by the man's interest and ability. Christenson and Gagnon (1965) divided wives aged 50, 55, and 60 into three groups—one group where the wife was older than her husband, one where she was younger, and one where she was the same age as her husband. The wives with younger husbands tended to have the most active sex lives, and those with the older husbands the least active. This was true both for the incidence and frequency of sexual relations. Wives aged 50 and 55, however, who had husbands the same age as themselves experienced more orgasms than those with husbands either older or younger than they. "Thus, in the present data, at least, it seems that physical sexual fulfillment for the wife at these ages is either directly or indirectly related to the age of the husband" (Christenson & Gagnon, 1965, pp. 355–356).

LIMITING FACTORS IN SEXUAL FULFILLMENT

Women without Active Partners

It is paradoxical that men seem more sexually active than women, and yet, as seen in the previous study, it is they who are the limiting factor in women's sexual gratification in marriage. Decline in sexuality starts later in life among women than among men, and is of a lesser magnitude. All this makes for a diminution of woman's sexual fulfillment later in life. One study indicated that when sexual intercourse was stopped, it was at an age nearly a decade earlier for women than for men. The frequent reason for stopping, in addition to widowhood, was a lack of interest on the part of the men (Pfeiffer, Verwoerdt, & Wang, 1968). Comfort (1974, p. 151) recommends that, "If there's a big difference in age, the wife needs to be clued about the normal changes in male response." Rubin (1965, p. 223) recognized that many widows do not have partners, and many married women are not fulfilled. He recommended masturbation as an appropriate outlet for those without "opportunity for sexual release."

Butler and Lewis (1976, p. 15) go further. They see masturbation as contributing positively in a physiological way, as well as in a psychological way. It "can be effective in preserving lubricating ability and the muscle tone which maintains the size and shape of the vagina. In addition, it can release tensions, stimulate sexual appetite and contribute to general well-being." Butler and Lewis realize that in years past, masturbation "was strictly forbidden." They pointed out that "The Victorians invented a grotesque array of mechanical devices to make sure that children, particularly boys, would not be able to stimulate themselves. Children were warned that masturbation would cause feeble-mindedness; it could 'use up the life juices,' weaken the body and shorten life span . . ." (p. 64). Likewise, Starr and Weiner (1981, p. 55) reported that in "1914 one major publication warned parents that if their children were allowed to masturbate their impulses could get out of control and the youngsters would be 'wrecked for life.' " "Even in the 1950s," they said, "when our respondents were young parents of today's 40- and 50-year-olds the attitudes toward autoeroticism were repressive."

It would not be surprising, therefore, if masturbation made for guilt and shame. For those who are alone, and there are more women than men, masturbation is frequently recommended as an important sexual outlet that has no harmful effects and, in fact, beneficial ones. There is no place for guilt and shame.

Keeping the Male Active

Consistency of Function.   Masters and Johnson (1966, p. 262) reported that an important factor in the sexuality of older men is the "sociosexual environment within which a male lives during his sexually formative years." When the male is stimulated to a high level of sexual expression during his early years, his middle-age and older years are usually characterized by maintained sexuality. This view that high rates of sexual activity early in life are correlated with high rates in later life was also noted by Newman and Nichols (1960) when they had elderly people rate themselves on the relative strength of their sexual drives during youth and during old age. The data of the Kinsey studies (1948) also support this view. From none of these studies, however, is it possible to ascertain whether the high levels of sexual expression in youth, and thus in old age, are due primarily to social learning factors, as the above quote from Masters and Johnson would suggest, or whether the same vigorous biological system serves one in both youth and old age. What can be ascertained, and what is most relevant here, is that a high rate of sexual responding in earlier life does not result in a sexual depletion, in a sexual wearing out later in life. Perhaps just the opposite is the case. Masters and Johnson (1966, p. 262) indicated that "the most important factor in the maintenance of sexuality for the aging is consistency of active sexual expression."

Lifestyle.   Masters and Johnson indicated that most men in middle adulthood find themselves at the height of their economic needs and responsibilities. Many of these men are also in the prime of their careers, with many demands on their time and energy. These economic and career pressures, particularly when adverse, tend to decrease sexual interest. According to Masters and Johnson, it is mental fatigue, more commonly than physical fatigue, that affects sexual behavior. Although excessive physical fatigue from work and recreation does inhibit sexuality, it is the mental strain of work that is more accountable for reduced sexuality in marriage.

Overindulgence in food—and, more importantly, in alcohol—also represses sexuality. Secondary impotence is a common result of the use of alcohol, and when an older man is traumatized by this experience, he often fails to associate the impotence with the drink. This enhances self-doubt and makes for a fear of failure.

Excessive drinking only exacerbates the fear of failure; the fear is often present without alcohol.

> There is no way to overemphasize the importance that the factor "fear of failure" plays in the aging male's withdrawal from sexual performance . . . many males withdraw voluntarily from any coital activity rather than face the ego-shattering experience of repeated episodes of sexual inadequacy (Masters & Johnson, 1966, pp. 269–270).

Boredom and New Excitement. Although some aging males withdraw in the face of their fears, others seek out new sex partners to "prove" themselves. Still others, of course, seek out new sex partners for reasons other than fear of failure. A most common reason is the excitement that often comes with novelty, an excitement that may stimulate the lagging sex drive. Kinsey et al. (1948, pp. 227–229) were clear in indicating that decline in male sexuality results partly from "a loss of interest in repetition of the same sort of experience, an exhaustion of the possibilities for exploring new techniques. . . ." Masters and Johnson (1966, pp. 264–265), in a similar view, reported that "the female partner may lose her stimulative effect as her every wish, interest and expression become too well known."

The diminution of the stimulating effects of the marriage partner is attributable to factors other than the male's boredom or monotony with the repetition of the sexual act. Rubin (1965, p. 146) suggested that as wives age, their physical appearances may have a negative effect on the potency of their husbands, or they may sexually repel their husbands by slovenly habits which may develop as they grow older. "Where the wife is the basic cause of the impotence, she must be involved in measures to correct it. Sometimes the husband can be induced to accept a change that has occurred as inevitable and make the best of it." A more sanguine position is taken by Comfort (1974, p. 150): "A regular partner who ages," he said, "only gets ugly and undesirable to a loving man if she really lets herself go. Familiarity and experience more than make up for magazine looks."

Often it is neither the wife's appearance nor her habits that affect the potency of her husband, but simply that she has "lost herself in the demands of the children, in social activities, in an individual career. . . . By their own admission many of the women interviewed no longer showed concern for their husbands" (Masters & Johnson, 1966, p. 265).

For the sexually bored, unstimulated, elderly male, philanderous behavior may restore the excitement experienced in more youthful days. This excitement, however, is short-lived at best. Kinsey et al. (1948), among others, discussed the only temporary rejuvenation effect of a new partner on the male. Needless to say, the excitement of temporary rejuvenation that may come with a new partner can put such strains on his marriage as to make his excitement of dubious worth.

Women at Menopause

Despite a relative maintenance of sexual vigor, women do experience a very clear signal indicating the end of childbearing potential. This "change of life," the menopause, when menstrual periods cease, means different things to different women but, for many, it is a depressing, disturbing event. Significantly, women who have already experienced the climaeterium tend to have more positive views about the recovery period that follows. These women recognize that there is no great discontinuity to life with the menopause (Neugarten, Wood, Kraines, & Loomis, 1963). "However, there is no doubt that the end of menstruation has important implications for the emotional life of the women. For many of them, menstruation has been their badge of femininity" (Rubin, 1965, p. 126).

It is very clear that sexual desire and ability are not lost with menopause. In fact, greater sexual interest and activity are often displayed. Masters and Johnson (1966, p. 243) concluded that many postmenopausal women develop renewed interest in their husbands and in the physical maintenance of their own persons. Comfort (1974, p. 149) agrees: "Women's sexual feelings only decline after menopause if they are upset about it or think they should decline." Butler and Lewis (1976, p. 14) add that "Women in good health who were able to have orgasms in their younger years can continue having orgasms until very late in life, well into the eighties. (Indeed, some women begin to have orgasms for the first time as they grow older.)"

Health Factors

Poor health as a limiting factor in sexual fulfillment is increasingly important after age 40, and after age 60 it becomes especially important. "Any physical disability, acute or chronic, may and usually does lower the sexual responsiveness of the involved male" (Masters & Johnson, 1966, p. 268). Any physical disability lowers sexual responsiveness, at least in the male, but cardiac problems provide a major concern.

The tie between cardiovascular problems and sexual activity applies to women as well as men. Rubin (1965, pp. 199–221) pointed out that although the male is seen as the more physically active member during sexual intercourse, both the male and the female have strong pulse rate and blood pressure increases during sexual excitement. It is not just the muscular movement, it is the emotional involvement that is taxing to the cardiovascular system. The husband may not recognize the cardiac strain a recovering wife experiences because her muscular response may appear minimal to him. But it is her feelings and sexual excitement that determine the cardiovascular response, not the body movements.

Rubin also indicated that many people believe that once a heart attack occurs, sexual intercourse is no longer possible. This belief is not true. After a period of recovery, usually lasting several months, most of the coronary patients resume their sexual relations. The attack is limiting, however, and caution is recommended. Not only is the severity of the attack a factor in the resumption of sexual behavior, but so are the circumstances and emotional character of the patient. A man and wife who are compatible, whose sexual patterns are very familiar, can achieve sexual intercourse with minimum expenditure of energy and a minimum strain on the heart. For men whose sexual outlets involve the excitement of pursuit and clandestine encounters, however, the strain on the heart can be severe.

Comfort (1974, p. 148) goes further: "If you have a heart attack, you need to get gentle sex started again as soon as you can start gentle exercise. Heart attacks don't affect potency. . . . Relaxed sex, even if it's violent, only rarely provokes a heart attack—very anxious sex scenes more often do." Butler and Lewis (1976, p. 27) are more conservative. They indicate,

> Most physicians do recommend that sexual intercourse be discontinued for a period of weeks or months (roughly eight to fourteen weeks—check with your doctor) immediately following an attack, to give the healing processes plenty of time. But after that, many experts feel, sex can and should be resumed, depending on the patient's interest, general fitness and conditioning. . . . If you can walk briskly for three blocks without distress in the chest, pain, palpitations or shortness of breath, you are usually well enough for sex. . . . Masturbation can begin long before.

Rubin was of the opinion that for people with very severely damaged hearts, any coital behavior, however unexerting, may be contraindicated. For the heart patient, moderation, and relaxed or "sedate" coitus are the watchwords; delayed or extended periods of climax are to be avoided. The healthy spouse should cooperate in regard to posture and frequency, and should avoid as much as possible an atmosphere of emotional tension.

SEXUAL AGING IN PERSPECTIVE

Sexual waning is but an aspect of a general psychobiological decline that occurs naturally in later life. Sexual decline is unique only in its relation to concepts of self-worth that have been built up through the decades by exaggerated emphases and taboos. A large number of domains are much more important in daily life than sexuality. Sensory-perceptual systems, or psychomotor skills, for example, decline in later life, but do not cause the doubts and self-analyses that sexual decline often does. The value and pleasure of maintained function, be it vision or sex, ought to be appreciated and used to the limit of individual prudence.

It is worth repeating: The ability to have and enjoy sexual relations is not limited to youth. In later life, the ability is simply diminished in intensity and in frequency. It is not until very advanced age that many people seem to lose their interest in and capacity for sex. Older people should not attempt heroic feats of sexuality as they should not attempt such feats on the tennis court. But sex in the older years is normal; neither the older person nor anyone else should make restrictions, be they psychological or physical.

An ending statement of Masters and Johnson (1966, p. 270) is appropriate here:

> There is every reason to believe that maintained regularity of sexual expression coupled with adequate physical wellbeing and healthy mental orientation to the aging process will combine to provide a sexually stimulative climate within a marriage. . . . This climate will, in turn, improve sexual tension and provide a capacity for sexual performance that frequently may extend to and beyond the 80-year age level.

SUMMARY

Sex research is different from what it was in years past. The emphasis in the past was descriptive, that is, the studies charted changes in relation to age. The emphasis in the more recent literature is sexual gratification. The literature past and present, however, is similar in indicating that sexuality is not characteristic of the young alone. It is characteristic of the elderly as well, persisting for many people until the end of life.

The sexual revolution with its diminution in inhibitions made sexual research easier, but difficulties remain, nevertheless. This is especially so as the research involves older adults. Most of the research, but not all, has been based on interviews and questionnaires. The response rates to the questionnaires have been less than good and, thus, the generalizability of the findings is in question. It is very possible that it is mainly the more "liberated" and sexually active people who choose to respond, conveying limited, even false information regarding the vast majority of people. Additionally, there is rarely opportunity to check on the correctness or honesty of the information and there is reason to believe that much of it can benefit from checking. These problems of research are greater when they involve older adults because, with the exception of only one study, the number of cases investigated has been very small.

The main body of research indicates that the pattern of sexual waning is different for men and women. In men, sexuality is maximum in the teens and drops very gradually from then on. For women, sexual waning does not seem to come about until the 60s and, when it does, its extent is probably less than in men. This, plus the fact that women outlive men, makes sexual fulfillment in later life very difficult for many women. It is for these reasons that several investigators and clinicians recommend masturbation as a relief of sexual tensions. One report indicated that masturbation is not only a release of tension but "can contribute to general well-being."

The sexual ability of men is limited by a variety of factors, including one of concern with career and economic responsibilities. Most men in middle adulthood find themselves with peak demands on their time and energy. These pressures, especially when adverse, tend to decrease sexual interest. The strain of mental involvement in work is more responsible for reduced sexuality than is physical fatigue.

Self-doubt or fear of failure in sexual intercourse is another limiting factor for men. It makes some men withdraw from sexual experience, but it encourages some to attempt to "prove" themselves with women other than their wives. When proof is found, however, it usually is temporary. The fear of failure often derives from secondary impotence resulting from the inhibiting effects of alcohol, from boredom with the repetitiousness of the marital coitus, and from negative changes in the physical appearance and habits of the wife. Often, the wife loses interest in the husband, immersing herself in her children, social activities, or a new career. This can have the effect of sexually inhibiting her husband.

Women may experience emotional trauma regarding their sexuality with the onset of menopause. Menopause is a disturbing event for many but, soon, most women recognize that this causes no great discontinuity to their lives. With this realization, they tend to have less negative attitudes.

Poor health, especially cardiovascular problems, limits sexual fulfillment among both men and women. Men may be the more active member in sexual intercourse, but both men and women have strong pulse rate and high blood pressure during the excitement. Heart attacks, of course, are a special problem, but this does not mean that sexual relations cease. After a period of recovery coronary patients are encouraged to resume sexual activities. The resumption should be with moderation, however, and with a more "sedate" style.

The key words in the maintenance of sexual ability seem to be good physical and mental health, and regularity in sexual activity. The ability to perform sexually may extend to age 80 and beyond.

REFERENCES

Botwinick, J. Drives, expectancies, and emotions. In J.E. Birren (Ed.), *Handbook of aging and the individual*. Chicago: University of Chicago Press, 1959, pp. 739–768.

Butler, R. N., & Lewis, M. I. *Love and sex after sixty*. New York: Harper & Row, 1976.

Cameron, P., & Biber, H. Sexual thought throughout the life-span. *The Gerontologist*, 1973, 13, 144–147.

Christenson, C.V., & Gagnon, J.H. Sexual behavior in a group of older women. *Journal of Gerontology*, 1965, 20, 351–356.

Comfort, A. *The joy of sex*. New York: Simon and Schuster, 1972.

Comfort, A. *More Joy*. New York: Crown, 1974.

Hite, S. *The Hite report*. New York: Macmillan, 1976.

Kinsey, A.C., Pomeroy, W.B., & Martin, C.E. *Sexual behavior in the human male*. Philadelphia: W.B. Saunders, 1948.

Kinsey, A.C., Pomeroy, W.B., Martin, C.E., & Gebhard, P.H. *Sexual behavior in the human female*. Philadelphia: W.B. Saunders, 1953.

Masters, W.H., & Johnson, V.E. *Human sexual response*. Boston: Little, Brown, 1966.

Neugarten, B.L., Wood, V., Kraines, R.J., & Loomis, B. Women's attitudes toward the menopause. *Vita Humana*, 1963, 6, 140–151.

Newman, G., & Nichols, C.R. Sexual activities and attitudes in older persons. *Journal of the American Medical Association*, 1960, 173, 33–35.

Pfeiffer, E. Sexual behavior in old age. In E. Pfeiffer & E. W. Busse (Eds.), *Behavior and adaptation in late life*. Boston: Little, Brown, 1969.

Pfeiffer, E., Verwoerdt, A., & Wang, H. Sexual behavior in aged men and women. *Archives of General Psychiatry*, 1968, 19, 753–758.

Rubin, I. *Sexual life after sixty*. New York: Basic Books, 1965.

Starr, B. D., & Weiner, M. B. *Sex and sexuality in the mature years*. New York: Stein & Day, 1981.

Verwoerdt, A., Pfeiffer, E., & Wang, H.S. Sexual behavior in senescence. II. Patterns of change in sexual activity and interest. *Geriatrics*, 1969, 24, 137–154.

7
Friends, Family, and Institutionalization

The vast majority of older people live in the community and function socially much like anyone else. This means that they have friends and family and that they need them. A minority of elderly people, however, cannot continue life in the community for one reason or another, and institutions provide them with the help and support they need.

FRIENDS

People of all ages need someone to be with and with whom to share experiences. Obviously, without friends or family there is loneliness for most people; there is general dissatisfaction and feelings of not being cared for or wanted (Graney, 1975; Riley & Foner, 1968). Many of the friends old people have are of long standing, but many are new friends. New or old, however, most of the friends tend to be of the same age as the person making the friend. This is not surprising because people of the same age share common experiences. Most of the time, too, friends are also chosen to be of the same sex and marital and socioeconomic status. This makes for commonality (Hess, 1972; Riley & Foner, 1968). Kalish (1975, p. 87) expressed it so well: "Perhaps they feel more at home with people who have shared their . . . memories—of the same ball players, movie actors, automobiles, politicians, dances . . . slang . . . clothing styles."

Old people see their friends often. A report from the National Council on Aging (see Harris, 1975) indicated that two-thirds of their respondents aged 65 and over had been with a friend during the last few days and nearly all the rest had been with a friend within the last couple of weeks. Most of the friends come from the same neighborhood, so the longer the neighborhood relationships the stronger they are (Riley & Foner, 1968). Nearness of friend, however, is often more important than the intensity of the relationship. "Among older persons, themselves, distinctions are often blurred between the availability of . . . friends and the maintenance of close relationships . . ." (Lowenthal & Robinson, 1976, p. 439). Although, as will be seen, it is family more than friends that come to help in the moment of real need, Adams (1967) reported that interactions with friends are more highly valued than family because, unlike family, friendships are based on voluntary choice.

How do older people meet friends? Much like anyone else. Meeting friends is easier in houses or apartments next door than further away. Many professionals frown on age-segregated living arrangements, favoring, instead, living places where people of all ages are found. One study, at least, however, suggests that age-segregated housing may be desirable.

Rosow (1967) examined a large number of apartment buildings in Cleveland and found that most friendships among older people developed in buildings that had a high percentage of older people. Thus, he also found that most of the friendships were made between people of similar age. Similar results were reported in six retirement communities in California, that is, more friendship relationships were established in age-segregated than age-integrated settings (Sherman, 1975a,b).

Not everyone needs or wants friends, although most do. Rosow reported that those aged people who did not want friends seem to suffer poor morale when living in complexes where many older people live. The opportunities for friendship and the friendships that evolve around them make these "isolates" feel bad.

FAMILY

A Change in the Family Structure

The nuclear family has typically meant mother, father, and young children living in the household. Grandparents and other relatives, the extended family, more often than not, live nearby. This has been the American family scene for decades. When the last child grows up and leaves to set up his or her own household, the home of the middle-aged parents is called the empty nest. Many of these parents feel almost alone and saddened with the empty nest, but others feel free and relieved of responsibility. One group of investigators found so much positive feeling when the last child left home that instead of empty nest, they suggested it be called the "child-free home" (Palmore, Cleveland, Nowlin, Ramm, & Siegler, 1979, pp. 847–848). They wrote, ". . . we found *no negative* effects [of children leaving] and instead, found two significant positive effects"; both were measures of life satisfaction.

All this may be changing, however. Just as the multigenerational households of many years ago were more a matter of economic necessity than preference (Aiken, 1982, p. 157), the changing economy may make it difficult for today's young people to set up their own households. Many young adults today cannot afford to live in the same neighborhoods as their parents. A generally rising economy from the time of World War II to the 1970s has brought relative affluence to many. Since, then, however, a declining economy with expensive housing and high energy prices, with inflation that makes automobiles and other items costly, places young adults in a more dependent status. Young people need to rely more on their parents than was necessary a generation ago. Perhaps they will need to move back home for economic reasons. Should this come to pass, the empty nest will be a less common pattern.

Another change is foreseen, one that is already coming upon us, one more important than the end of the empty nest. This change is so revolutionary as to threaten American family life as it had been known. Major adjustments will be necessary, not only for the elderly, but for people of all ages.

Masnick and Bane (1980), in a study entitled "The Nation's Families: 1960–1990," predicted that the nuclear family of a husband, wife, and young children is on the way out for the majority of people. In 1960, 55 percent of American households consisted of the nuclear family with children under 15. By the end of the 1980s, this will be true for less than one-third of the households.

The reasons for this are, first, there is a declining marriage rate. By 1990 between one-third and one-half of women aged 20 to 29 will never have married. Second, the number of children born to a couple is declining. Third, more couples are divorcing. Of the 20 million new households expected to be established between 1975 and 1990, it is predicted that only three to four million will be married couples. The remaining households will be headed by adults who never married or who are divorced or widowed.

The vast majority of households in 1990 will see both parents in the labor force, if there are two parents. All this is already occurring. If there is one parent, he or she will be working. Adjustments of many kinds have to be made. Who cares for the children at home? Who provides the necessary emotional and physical support of elderly members in the extended family?

Closeness and Help

These developing changes of the family structure are still problems mainly of the future. The problems of the present are the traditional ones where the nuclear family, or the empty nest family, have aging parents nearby. Some of these aging parents are well and sources of mutual support, but some are not well and need much aid and comfort.

Concern for the elderly family member is the rule, not the exception. Family is important to the old person, and the old person is important to the rest of the family. Although the emphasis in the United States is on the nuclear family, the extended family is very much part of family life. The idea that the elderly are left destitute, that there is no emotional closeness between middle-aged children and their parents, has been labeled a "social myth" by Shanas (1979a), who interviewed a large number of families in varied living arrangements. "Older people and their children both place a value on separate households." (p. 6); accordingly, "Old people living under a single roof together with their children and grandchildren are unusual. . . ." The fact that middle-aged children live apart from old parents does not mean, however, that the old parents are neglected; just the opposite. "Joint living is not the most important factor governing the relationship . . . it is the emotional bond between parents and children" (Shanas, 1979b, p. 169).

Although old parents and their children live apart, they live close by. Shanas (1979a) indicated that about 80 percent of noninstitutionalized adults over 65 in the United States have living children. Of these, over 50 percent either live with one of their children or live within 10 minutes distance, that is, next door, down the street, or a few blocks away. Parents and middle-aged children see each other often. In fact, at the time of the interviews, over 50 percent had seen one of their children the day before and over 80 percent had seen at least one of them within the week. Shanas was not the only investigator reporting such frequent contact. There were others, for example, Cantor (1975), who investigated family relationships in "New York's Inner City." "Familial bonds are strong," she said, "and there is evidence of mutual affection and assistance between the generations. . . ." Further, "Contact between parents and children is not limited to mere visiting or 'checking up.'. . ." There are strong feelings about "the desirability of mutual interdependency . . ." (Cantor, 1975, p. 25). Over 75 percent of the elderly reported helping the middle-aged children, usually with gifts, and 87 percent of the children reported helping the parents in similar ways. The family bonds are strong at all stages of life. Even young married adults, particularly after their children are born, want to live near their parents (Troll & Bengston, 1979, p. 150). The strength of the family bond is so strong, as seen in the interviews reported by Brown (1974, p. 258), that although the elderly people broke off social contacts that were not satisfying and maintained those that were, it was otherwise with members of their immediate families. They maintained contacts "regardless of satisfaction."

Older people see and need other relatives too. Brothers and sisters become particularly important (Shanas, 1979a). At the time of interview, for example, about one-third saw a brother or sister within the week. It is clear, however, that "it is primarily children to whom the old people turn when in need of general assistance, and particularly, in times of crisis" (Robinson & Thurnher, 1979, p. 586). This has been documented by many investigators. In times of crisis, when emergency assistance is necessary, the older adult turns first to families, then to friends and neighbors (Cantor, 1975; Shanas, 1979b). Then, if all fails or is not otherwise possible, the old person turns to "bureaucratic replacements . . . social workers, ministers, community agencies" (Shanas, 1979b, p. 174).

Thus, family members need each other, help each other and, if necessary, endure each other: the notion that old people are alienated from family and friends, is a "social myth." Still, not everyone takes this position; Peterson (1979, p. 132), for example, does not. He examined elderly adults who moved into a middle-class retirement community. Peterson did not find what Shanas and others did; Peterson reported that close to 50 percent of the people did not have close living relatives. "A great mythology surrounds the wish of the older person to associate with children and grandchildren," he said. "One sentimental view is that intergeneration contacts are essential to the life satisfaction of older persons. . . ." Peterson rejected this "sentimental view," indicating that the older person values independence and prefers it to intrusion by family.

Peterson studied people moving into a retirement community and perhaps this colored his perceptions. His observations are at variance with the general picture of closeness between an old parent and a middle-aged son or daughter that other investigators have found.

Complexity of Relationships

Independence and Role Reversals. Although most investigators do not agree with Peterson regarding the closeness of family, they do agree with him that the greatest number of older adults value their independence. As much as anyone else, they want to be able to make their own decisions, to manage their own finances and arrange their own household affairs. When intrusion is resented, as Peterson suggested it is, surely it is with interference or challenge to such independence by children and grandchildren. Older people want this independence but, at the same time, they want to have close and frequent contacts with their adult children and their grandchildren.

Independence, however, often becomes progressively more difficult for the older person to retain. Aging frequently means a progressive loss of independence because of a diminishing ability to function alone. Self-reliance and self-direction are possible only when health and wealth permit it. As the older parent becomes less able to manage alone, the middle-aged child helps more and more, and in this process the older parent assumes a less dominant position. With this comes a pattern of role reversal that intensifies the longer people live. The middle-aged child or the grandchild takes on responsibilities regarding the old parent that are different from those of the past. There is a switch in the independent–dependent relationship, with the parent becoming the more dependent.

Schwartz (1979, pp. 121–125) prefers to think of this change in role relations as a switch to mutual dependence on the part of both parent and child rather than as a complete role reversal from independence to dependence. He reasons that the child is dependent on the parent from birth and, regardless of the change, some psychological dependence remains at least until the time of the parent's death. The younger person now ministering to the older parent creates a balance of mutual dependence that is a two-way street.

Schwartz maintains that the more realistic the old parent is about shifting to mutual dependence, the better he or she will respond as an adult and not as an immature person. The more realistic the son or daughter is about shifting to mutual dependence, the easier it will be to perceive the increasing physical dependency of the aging parent as mutual dependency and not as a regression into second childhood. This kind of relationship will lead to a peer-like friend relationship, Schwartz says. Mutual dependency should become the goal.

Too Much and Too Little Help. Mutual dependence maximizes the opportunity for the adult children to help the old parent and, at the same time, minimizes the chance of intrusion into the privacy and independence of the parent. Well-meaning sons and daughters who are emotionally close to their parents have problems of knowing when to stop helping. Too much help is perceived as being overly solicitous and dominating. In *You and Your Aging Parent* (1976), Silverstone and Hyman discussed this, indicating that middle-aged children can hover over their parents and overpower them. They can spend too much time with them and encourage complete dependence before it is necessary. Middle-aged children may do this, they said, because of guilt feelings, or because they may still be emotionally dependent on the parents and fear their loss. Focusing their attention on the aged parents gives the children a feeling of protecting them so that they, the children, will not be left without the parents.

Silverstone and Hyman noted also that the opposite can happen. The middle-aged children may feel that care should be given but for one reason or another do not provide it. Guilt feelings can result. Rather than blame themselves, however, they may blame someone else—the nursing home or other family members. This is often unconscious, meant to divert blame from themselves, but it does not work well. The other family members usually get angry and they place the blame where it belongs. This starts family fights.

Silverstone and Hyman emphasized that it is important for the middle-aged son or daughter to recognize that both too much and too little concern can have a negative effect. The right amount of help is often difficult to offer but can be more nearly achieved when both parent and child have a realistic understanding of what needs to be done and what feelings underlie the mutual relationships.

Miscommunication. There is yet another problem in family relationships. It is a problem of communication where people speak to each other and yet do not understand each other. They may convey mixed signals. They interact on different levels, sometimes saying one thing on one level but conveying something else on another. There are contradictory messages that require some sort of answer that often is equally contradictory, putting the person in a "double bind."

Herr and Weakland (1979, p. 147) provided a subtle example of a double bind involving an 80-year-old woman who became widowed after 55 years of marriage. She was frightened, uncertain, and confused. She became more involved with her children, but they gave her contradictory messages—the double bind. They told her that they would help her to remain independent, but if she refused their help, this would only show that she was not capable of independence. In other words, the 80-year-old mother either takes orders from her children and thus loses her independence, or she does not take them, thus seemingly admitting that she cannot take care of herself anymore. Soon, whatever she does is no good and this shows that she cannot take care of herself. After a while she begins to believe it.

To avoid the double bind it is necessary to recognize it. The second step is harder. It is necessary to understand feelings and motives; then it is more possible to speak on one level without contradiction.

Grandparents

Contrary to the stereotype of the old grandparent, most people become grandparents when they are middle-aged, in the 40s. Great-grandparenthood is becoming ever more common. Currently, about 40 percent of older people in the United States are great-grandparents (Atchley, 1980, p. 353). It is not so rare to find a very old parent living with an old child in the same household, or living nearby.

Middle-aged parents often think that their own children are a source of pleasure to their aging parents. This is usually the case, but not all grandparents feel this way. There are times when the grandparents resent being baby-sitters or being asked to perform other household responsibilities. Grandparents have lives of their own.

How Do Grandparents Respond to Grandchildren? Neugarten and Weinstein (1964, p. 200) interviewed each member of a grandparent couple and reported that "the majority of grandparents expressed only comfort, satisfaction, and pleasure" in the grandparent role. As many as one-third of the grandparents interviewed, however, expressed difficulty in the role and expressed some disappointment. Neugarten and Weinstein categorized the grandparents into five categories of "styles of grandparenting." One group liked to "provide special treats and indulgences . . . and although they may occasionally take on a minor service such as baby-sitting, they maintain clearly demarcated lines between parenting and grandparenting" (p. 202). Such grandparents tended to be over 65 more often than younger. Younger grandparents, those under 65, were of two types. One type was "character-ized by informality and playfulness." They join in specific activities just for fun. The other type of younger grandparent is opposite. This grandparent is "essentially distant and remote from the child's life." They emerge on "spe-cial ritual occasions such as Christmas" (p. 203).

The other two categories appear to be represented across the age range. They took over the parents' job, but only when invited to or when neces-sary, as when the mother worked. This was more characteristic of women than men. A last group liked to be the source of wisdom or skills, and this was true mainly of men.

Thus, perhaps only three of these categories fit the usual concept of grandparent. Neugarten and Weinstein believed that those who were infor-mal and playful as well as those who were distant did not fit the concept.

How Do Grandchildren Respond to Grandparents? A study by Kahana and Kahana (1970) showed that children aged four or five responded to grandparents according to what they got—food, presents, and love. There was little interpersonal give and take in an emotional sense other than the enjoyment of being with the family and getting presents. Older children, about eight or nine, interacted more. They went to ball games with the grandparents, played cards with them, and did other things together. These children looked up to their grandparents.

As the children moved closer to the teenage stage, say at age 11 or 12, they started to withdraw from the grandparents. By the teens, not much of a grandparent–grandchild relationship was left. A questionnaire study by Rob-ertson (1976), however, showed that as teenagers grew into young adulthood (18–26 years), there was still much feeling left, viewing the grandparents as a source of influence. They felt responsibility toward their grandparents and, like adult middle-age sons and daughters, they provided the older parent with emotional support and tangible help whenever possible.

INSTITUTIONALIZATION

The Family Cares

It is interesting to view this emotional and tangible help from a different perspective. In a feature article in *Newsweek* magazine, family relations in China were discussed, focusing on a 29-year-old telegraph operator, named Yang Liche, who was about to be married. Yang showed his tiny three-room apartment in Shanghai to the reporter and said, "that room will belong to us. Of course, my mother will move in with us for the rest of her days." The writer (Gwirtzman, 1979) indicated that although Shanghai is one of the five largest cities in the world, he found only one home for the aged there. Golden Age clubs and other social meeting institutions are not needed, nor are retirement communities. The writer was impressed with what he found: "Old people in China," he said, "seem secure, almost serene," compared with old people in the United States. He indicated that old people in China have close family lives and they have the respect of the community.

It would seem that life is better for the aged in China in many ways, yet this comparison with the aged in the Western world, certainly the United States, is unfair. On the whole, in the United States, great effort is also made to keep the aged parent at home. Butler and Lewis (1977, p. 123) reported that "most people who have families move in with relatives when they can no longer live independently." Further, the greater majority of younger adults "strive to delay the parents' institutionalization at considerable cost to themselves. In the majority of instances . . . the relocation [to the institution] occurred . . . after a lengthy period of the parent's steady mental and physical deterioration, which imposed severe psychic stress" (Robinson & Thurnher, 1979, p. 592).

Thus, in the United States, older family members are also taken care of despite the emphasis on the nuclear family. As many as 96 percent of those over 65 reside in the community, not institutions; as many as 83 percent over 85 reside in the community (Kastenbaum & Candy, 1973). Older adults are institutionalized mainly when there is little support for them in the community. People who have never married, have no children, or have few or no children nearby are the most likely to end up in institutions.

Before the debilitated old person comes to the children for help, the spouse is the primary caretaker. Since elderly men are more likely to be married than elderly women, it is the woman who is more likely to be the caretaker. Shanas (1979b, p. 171) reported that two-thirds of the "men who had been ill say their wife took care of them. Women, who are more likely to be widowed, are taken care of by their children. A child . . . is mentioned by one-third of the women as a source of help."

The elderly spouse as caretaker often has a very difficult time of it. "Men take over traditionally female tasks as necessary, women find the strength to turn and lift bedfast husbands. Husbands or wives of the elderly bedfast persons, themselves elderly, are rarely able to manage the care of the spouse without outside help" (Shanas, 1979b, p. 171).

Institutionalization Is the Last Option

After all efforts to help the aging parent have been exhausted and after the spouse or middle-aged son or daughter has done all that it is possible to do, a point may be reached where life for everyone is too painful to proceed without institutionalization. This point often is reached when the debilitated person becomes incontinent. Typically, it is the spouse who has to make the painful decision regarding institutionalization, but the decision is often made with the help of the middle-aged children. When there is no surviving spouse, the decision is up to the middle-aged son or daughter.

The decision is not easily made. Butler and Lewis (1977, p. 249) emphasized strongly that families often need help in dealing with their feelings about institutionalizing a parent. There may be guilt and suffering with the decisions to institutionalize the spouse or parent. There may be feelings of having abandoned the old person.

People often think of institutionalization as a complete severance from their loved ones, but this is not so. An important series of interviews was carried out with both institutionalized parents and their middle-aged children in which "the majority of people of both generations expressed an improvement of, or continuation of, close family ties following institutionalization" (Smith & Bengston, 1979, p. 438). It is clear, then, that institutional care often reduces stress and conflict and enhances good family relations. The decision to institutionalize should be made before the stress of caretaking becomes overpowering, but not before every effort has been made to see if the disabled parent can be maintained at home.

Butler and Lewis believe that in institutionalizing a loved one, there should be an expectation of return and not of final commitment. Visits to the old person should not stop, although they sometimes do because guilt and grief make the whole experience too painful. Not only can families visit, they can take the institutionalized adult on outings.

The older person should be prepared for institutionalization as much as possible. Butler and Lewis advise that effort be made to acquaint the elderly person with the institution beforehand. Family members might try to become part of the intake procedure. They can also get to know the institution's staff; this could work to the institutionalized member's advantage. Most important, perhaps, families can have the same responsive attitude they had before.

RELOCATION

Entrance to the institution from the household is a major relocation in life, perhaps the most major of all. Once in the institution, it may be necessary to relocate to another one. There have been fires that necessitated a second move; newer, better facilities have been built and older ones closed down; older people have been relocated from one hospital ward to another, or from one room in a nursing home to another.

Moving into an institution or moving within one was not cause for alarm until the latter 1960s when reports started to appear such as one by Blenkner (1967, p. 101), who wrote, "Older people admitted to institutions die at excessively high rates during the first year, and particularly during the first three months after admission." Blenkner asked another question: Would it be better to provide service in the person's own home even if the program of care is less good than could be provided in an institution? She raised this question as a result of her disquieting observation that aged people randomly assigned to three service programs showed mortality rates proportional to the extent of the care that had been rendered. This relationship was statistically nonsignificant, but it was alarming in its implication, nevertheless. The program of greatest care was directed toward providing better or more protected living environments, and this was associated with the highest mortality rates. The disquieting observation was not assuaged by a subsequent one, also statistically not significant. A six-month follow-up compared two groups, one with extensive service and more institutionalization, and the other with less service and less institutionalization. Again, the better service program was associated with a higher death rate.

Blenkner's concern was based not only on her own observations but on earlier ones, going back to 1961. In one study, older hospital patients were moved from one ward to another (Aleksandrowicz, 1961). In another study, nursing home applicants were studied during a period prior to institutionalization to one year following admittance (Lieberman, 1961). In both these studies higher death rates were reported with the relocations.

Lieberman (1974, p. 414) became concerned and concluded: ". . . no matter what the condition of the individual, the nature of the environment, or the degree of sophisticated preparation, relocation entails a higher than acceptable risk." By risk, Lieberman meant negative changes in overall functioning as well as ensuing death. Not all investigators reached this conclusion, however. Examining death rates, but not overall functioning, Gutman and Herbert wrote: ". . . with careful planning of the move, involuntary relocation . . . need not result in increased mortality" (1976, p. 357).

Institutional Moves: Transfer Trauma

A flurry of research investigations followed, but the evidence was mixed. What was a clear-cut social issue requiring drastic attention became a muddled area of research results. Early death in relocation came to be known by several shorthand phrases, one of which is "transfer trauma." The issue became so intense that a legal suit involving transfer trauma reached the Supreme Court of the United States, with Justice Blackmun ruling. The justice was unimpressed with the "inconclusive body of research and opinion" (Coffman, 1981, p. 48; Cohen, 1981).

What is the evidence for early death in relocation? A symposium was held to address this question and Coffman (1981), one of the symposium participants, summarized studies based on 26 groups that were relocated. His summary is in keeping with Justice Blackmun's opinion, but it does not close the door to the idea that transfer trauma may be a genuine effect, even though more limited than previously thought.

Disintegrative versus Integrative Processes. Coffman's analyses (1981) revealed that only 14 of the 26 groups showed different mortality rates with relocation, but eight of these were in the opposite direction. That is, in eight studies people survived longer with relocation. In only six studies did people die sooner with relocation. Coffman tried to determine what differentiated those moves that were related to the higher mortality rates from those moves that related to lower rates. He concluded that when the relocation involved a whole group or when the individual moved from one stable population to another, death did not come more quickly. On the other hand, when the move involved a deterioration in the support system, there was transfer trauma. That is, early death was associated with poor institutional staff, poor care, loss of contact with family, or a perceived deterioration of these supports. Coffman believed that a disintegrative process followed the loss of support systems. The process "involved long periods of high anxiety, tension, uncertainty, and confusion" (pp. 492–493). With stable moves, however, integrative processes followed, and these enabled survival. This is compatible with the conclusions of others who put the issue in other terms. For example, as already indicated, Butler and Lewis (1977), Gutman and Herbert (1976), and others concluded that preparing the resident for the move is crucial. Visits to the new site can make the difference. "The more that residents can participate in planning a relocation and influencing their new environment the better" (Kowalski, 1981, p. 518). Schulz and Brenner (1977) maintained that stress in relocation is reduced if the new environment is predictable.

Coffman (1981) believes that all moves involve both disintegrative and integrative processes but "what really matters," he said, is which predominates. It is the extent or lack of institutional support that makes the difference. If the support is there or if it is replaced quickly when absent, the move can be beneficial. It is not one factor that makes the difference, Coffman maintained; it is the totality of them. If one factor is of main importance, it is staff morale because they are the "central and powerful figures in the total support systems" (p. 493).

Make-or-Break in Relocation. Lawton (1977, p. 291) reviewed an unpublished study by Marlowe, who found increased mortality with relocation of mental hospital patients. Marlowe reported that those movers who were initially in poorest mental status either died or remained in essentially the same condition. The movers who were in the "most-adequate" condition to start, however, either improved or deteriorated most. This was in contrast to a group of nonmovers who were comparably "most-adequate"; they either improved or remained the same. Thus, Marlowe concluded that transfer trauma applied mainly to those of "most adequate" mental status. For them, it was a "make-or-break" affair; they either improved or deteriorated.

To the extent that this study can be replicated, it would suggest that relocation can be dangerous for the relatively intact if, as Coffman suggested, the process is disintegrative. Relocation can be beneficial to the relatively intact if the process is integrative. The danger is mainly in relative terms, however, because in absolute terms, death is most likely in relocation among the least intact.

Depression. The conclusions of Coffman and the others placed the basis of transfer trauma on the environment, that is, on support systems. Others have placed emphasis mainly on the individual. Although the various research reports make it clear that the sick and the weak are the most vulnerable, there seem to be personality factors that also play a role.

One such factor is depression. Miller and Lieberman (1965) examined a group of aged women who were being transferred from one Illinois state home for the aged to another. The women were free from incapacitating mental or physical illnesses and thus were not representative of a total population of a state home. A battery of tests was given to these women 2 weeks prior to their move and then again 6 and 18 weeks after the move. The test scores were examined for their possible relation to either death or negative psychological and physical health changes.

After 18 weeks in the new home, 23 of the 45 residents either died or were judged to show negative reactions. Of the psychological measures made prior to relocation, only depressive affect was significantly related to negative outcome after the move. The depressive affect was such as to involve extremely negative evaluation of the past life, a sense that the future does not exist, and the feeling that life satisfaction was impossible.

Adjustment and Hostility. Aldrich and Mendkoff (1963) investigated the relocation of 182 residents in a home for the chronically disabled, a move made necessary when the home in which they had been residing was closed for administrative reasons. Since this reason and none other was responsible for the move, a natural situation experiment was available, one in which the effects of relocation could be assessed without confounding factors such as different health and dependency statuses among the different comparison groups.

Residents with satisfactory adjustments in their initial institution survived best in the move. Residents characterized as hostile and demanding, although not surviving as well as those with satisfactory adjustments, died at a rate half of that of the neurotic residents, or those who denied their physical disabilities. Psychotics and near psychotics fared worst of all. In a subsequent study, Aldrich (1964) compared 26 elderly residents who died within three months following relocation with a like number of residents who survived the first 12 months in the new residence. Again, satisfactory adjustment in the old residence was a positive predictor of survival in the new residence. And, again, those classified as "angry and demanding" survived. This finding was exceedingly limited, however, by its small sample size: there were four angry and demanding people who survived and one person, not angry, who died during the first year.

It may seem strange at first that "angry and demanding" institutionalized people tend to survive more than some of the others, or that depressed people die sooner. There may be a reasonable explanation for this, however. When services are needed and attention is required but not spontaneously given, those who are demanding are most likely to receive the necessary help. Those who are depressed, uncomplaining, or otherwise placid in demanding the needed services do not get them and so, do not fare well.

Evidence for the survival value of angry adjustments also received support from a study by Turner, Tobin, and Lieberman (1972). Elderly persons awaiting institutionalization were tested prior to their admittance and again approximately one year after being admitted. The residents were categorized as to whether they were functioning not very differently than they had been during pre-admission, or whether they functioned appreciably less well, or died. Turner et al. (1972, p. 67) concluded that, "The particular trait factor found to be associated with successful institutional adaptation . . . loaded highly on activity, aggression, and narcissistic body image. This cluster of traits suggests that a vigorous, if not combative, style is facilitory for adaptation."

Noninstitutional Moves: No Transfer Trauma

There is a big difference between the effects of relocation on those elderly people moving to institutions because they are too sick to continue living in the community and those elderly who are healthy and move voluntarily to other quarters—perhaps smaller apartments that are easier to maintain and where medical and social service supervision is more readily available. If there is some question regarding the effects of relocation on the institutionalized elderly, there is less question regarding moves to noninstitutional residences. Older healthy community residents relocating voluntarily to desirable residences do "not incur greater risk of dying—if anything . . . the relocation may decrease the risk" (Wittels & Botwinick, 1974, p. 442). Moreover, such moves do not appear to affect overall functioning negatively. This was seen in a study where healthy movers were compared to healthy nonmovers in a variety of test performances (Storandt & Wittels, 1975). Even though the movers were in good health and there were no ill effects of the move, an effort was made to determine whether those who were inclined to depressive affect or who were low in hostility before the move were more likely afterwards to fare less well in terms of zest and vitality. This was not the case (Storandt, Wittels, & Botwinick, 1975). It is clear that voluntary moves by healthy old people are a very different matter than involuntary moves by debilitated old people.

This conclusion is compatible with that of Carp (1966, 1975) in her studies dealing with normal healthy older adults. If anything, the conclusion is understated. Carp's 1966 report was particularly glowing in the effect of voluntary relocation to a public housing project. Those who moved, compared to those who wanted to move but were turned down, were more satisfied, had higher morale, and had higher activity levels. In another similar study, satisfaction also increased following the move, as did social activity and self-rated health (Sherwood, Greer, Morris, & Sherwood, 1972). Lawton and Cohen (1974) also observed favorable effects of voluntary relocation, but their report was less glowing. Lawton and Yaffe (1970) reported that health declines in moving among some elderly people but improves among others.

SUMMARY

People of all ages need friends or family; without them there is loneliness, feelings of not being wanted, and general dissatisfaction. Many of the friends old people have are of long standing, but many are new friends. Both the old and new friends tend to be of the same age as the person making the friend; this is no surprise because people of the same age share common experiences. Availability of friendships is important: new friends who are close by are more important than old friends who are far away and hard to see. Since older people make new friends more easily when they are nearby, living in areas or houses where there are many old people seems best in terms of making friends.

As important as friends are, family is even more important to the majority of older people, especially in a time of need. The idea that the elderly are left destitute, that there is no emotional closeness between middle-aged sons and daughters and their parents, has been labeled a "social myth." Both the old parents and their offspring prefer to live under separate roofs, but this does not mean that the old parents are neglected. There are strong emotional bonds and much commitment among family members.

The relationships among family members, particularly between middle-aged children and older parents, are complex. As much as anyone else, older adults value their independence; they want to be able to make their own decisions and resent challenges to their independence. Aging frequently means a progressive loss of independence, however, because of diminishing ability to function alone. Thus, as the middle-aged son or daughter helps more and more, the older parent assumes a less dominant position. There is a role-reversal in the independent–dependent relationship, with the parent becoming the more dependent.

A problem for well-meaning sons and daughters who are emotionally close to their parents is when to stop helping. Middle-aged children can hover over their parents and overpower them; they can spend too much time with them and encourage complete dependence before it is necessary. Middle-aged children may do this because of guilt feelings, or because they may still be emotionally dependent on the parents and fear their loss. The opposite can happen too. The middle-aged children may feel that care should be given but do not give this care. Too much and too little concern can have a negative effect.

There is yet another problem in family relationships. It is a problem of communication where people speak to each other and yet do not understand each other. They may convey mixed signals, that is, say two opposite things at the same time. This puts the person in what is called a "double bind." To avoid this, it is necessary to understand feelings and motives so that it becomes possible to speak on one level without contradiction.

Middle-aged children are not the only family members in the lives of older people. There are grandchildren. Most grandparents enjoy being with their grandchildren, but not all do. There are different "styles" of grandparenting. Young grandchildren like to be with grandparents, but when they reach their teens not much relationship is left. This changes again, however, so that by young adulthood commitments to grandparents are often as intense as those of the middle-aged children.

When an aged person becomes incapacitated, the spouse is almost always the major caretaker and has a difficult time. The family help as they can, and this help is often appreciable, but the caretaker's role remains difficult. A point is reached where institutionalization is unavoidable.

People often think of institutionalization as a complete severence from their loved ones, but this is not so. In fact, one study showed that, with institutionalization, there were improvements of, or continuation of, close family ties. Institutional care often reduces stress and conflict and enhances family relations. Nevertheless, the decision to institutionalize a spouse or parent is among the most unpleasant of decisions that has to be made. The decision should be made before the stress of caretaking becomes overpowering, but not before every effort has been made to see whether the disabled person can be kept at home. Families often need help in dealing with intense feelings of guilt regarding institutionalization.

There is literature suggesting that the very process of moving into an institution, or moving from one institution to another, shortens life. This literature is referred to as studies of "relocation" or "transfer trauma." There is little question that many elderly who are very frail and debilitated respond negatively to relocation, but they would likely respond negatively without it. At first, the suggestion that death comes with relocation was so upsetting that many professional recommendations emphasized this threat. Over the years, however, the research pointed to as much benefit as harm in relocation. When negative effects were seen, it was mainly when support groups were lacking and when institutional staff morale and service were poor. Although there may be negative effects when sick people move involuntarily, this is not so when healthy people voluntarily move to better housing. Just the opposite: relocation of healthy older people is often beneficial.

REFERENCES

Adams, B. N. Interaction theory and the social network. *Sociometry*, 1967, *30*, 64–78.

Aiken, L. R. *Later life*. New York: Holt, Rinehart & Winston, 1982.

Aldrich, C. K. Personality factors and mortality in the relocation of the aged. *The Gerontologist*, 1964, *4*, 92–93.

Aldrich, C. K., & Mendkoff, E. Relocation of the aged and disabled, a mortality study. *Journal of American Geriatrics Society*, 1963, *11*, 185–194.

Aleksandrowicz, D. R. Fire and its aftermath on a geriatric ward. *Bulletin of the Menninger Clinic*, 1961, *25*, 23–32.

Atchley, R. C. *The social forces in later life*. Belmont, Calif.: Wadsworth, 1980.

Blenkner, M. Environmental change and the aging individual. *The Gerontologist*, 1967, *7*, Part I, 101–105.

Brown, A. S. Satisfying relationships for the elderly and their patterns of disengagement. *The Gerontologist*, 1974, *14*, 258–262.

Butler, R. N., & Lewis, M. I. *Aging and mental health*. St. Louis: C. V. Mosby, 1977.

Cantor, M. H. Life space and social support system of the inner city elderly of New York. *The Gerontologist*, 1975, *15*, 23–27.

Carp, F. M. *A future for the aged*. Austin: University of Texas Press, 1966.

Carp, F. M. Life style and location within the city. *The Gerontologist*, 1975, *15*, 27–34.

Coffman, T. L. Relocation and survival of institutionalized aged: a reexamination of the evidence. *The Gerontologist*, 1981, *21*, 483–500.

Cohen, E. S. Legal issues in "transfer trauma" and their impact. *The Gerontologist*, 1981, *21*, 520–522.

Graney, M. Happiness and social participation in aging. *Journal of Gerontology*, 1975, *30*, 701–706.

Gutman, G. M., & Herbert, C. P. Mortality rates among relocated extended-care patients. *Journal of Gerontology*, 1976, *31*, 352–357.

Gwirtzman, M. Restored treasure. *Newsweek*, Sept. 10, 1979, p. 15.

Harris, L., & Associates. *The myth and reality of aging in America*. Washington, D.C.: National Council on Aging, 1975.

Herr, J. J., & Weakland, J. H. Communications within family systems: Growing older within and with the double bind. In P. K. Ragan (Ed.), *Aging parents*. Los Angeles: University of Southern California Press, 1979.

Hess, B. Friendship. In M. Riley, M. Johnson, & A. Foner (Eds.), *Aging and society* (Vol. 3). New York: Russell Sage, 1972.

Kahana, B., & Kahana, E. Grandparenthood from the perspective of the developing grandchild. *Developmental Psychology*, 1970, *3*, 98–105.

Kalish, R. A. *Late adulthood: Perspectives on human development*. Monterey, Calif.: Brooks/Cole, 1975.

Kastenbaum, R. J., & Candy, S. E. The 4% fallacy: a methodological and empirical critique of extended care facility population statistics. *International Journal of Aging and Human Development*, 1973, *4*, 15–21.

Kowalski, N. C. Institutional relocation: Current programs and applied approaches. *The Gerontologist*, 1981, *21*, 512–519.

Lawton, M. P. The impact of the environment on aging and behavior. In J. E. Birren & K. W. Schaie (Eds.), *Handbook of the psychology of aging*. New York: Van Nostrand Reinhold, 1977, pp. 276–301.

Lawton, M. P., & Cohen, J. The generality of housing impact on the well-being of older people. *Journal of Gerontology*, 1974, *29*, 194–204.

Lawton, M. P., & Yaffe, S. Mortality, morbidity, and voluntary change of residence by older people. *Journal of American Geriatrics Society*, 1970, *18*, 823–831.

Lieberman, M. A. Relationship of mortality rates to entrance to a home of the aged. *Geriatrics*, 1961, *16*, 515–519.

Lieberman, M. A. Symposium—Long-term care: research, policy, and practice. *The Gerontologist*, 1974, *14*, 494–501.

Lowenthal, M. F., & Robinson, B. Social networks and isolation. In R. H. Binstock & E. Shanas (Eds.), *Handbook of aging and social sciences*. New York: Van Nostrand Reinhold, 1976.

Masnick, G., & Bane, M. J. *The nation's families: 1960–1990*. Cambridge, Mass.: Joint Center for Urban Studies of M.I.T. and Harvard Universities, 1980.

Miller, D., & Lieberman, M. A. The relationship of affect state and adaptive capacity to reactions to stress. *Journal of Gerontology*, 1965, *20*, 492–497.

Neugarten, B. L., & Weinstein, K. K. The changing American grandparent. *Journal of Marriage and the Family*, 1964, *26*, 199–204.

Palmore, E., Cleveland, W. P., Nowlin, J. B., Ramm, D., & Siegler, I. Stress and adaptation in later life. *Journal of Gerontology*, 1979, *34*, 841–851.

Peterson, J. A. The relationships of middle-aged children and their parents. In P. K. Ragan (Ed.), *Aging parents*. Los Angeles: University of Southern California Press, 1979.

Riley, M. W., & Foner, A. *Aging and society* (Vol. 1). New York: Russell Sage Foundation, 1968.

Robertson, J. F. Significance of grandparents: Perceptions of young adult grandchildren. *The Gerontologist*, 1976, *16*, 137–140.

Robinson, B., & Thurnher, M. Taking care of aged parents: a family cycle transition. *The Gerontologist*, 1979, *19*, 568–593.

Rosow, I. *Social integration of the aged*. New York: Free Press, 1967.

Schulz, R., & Brenner, G. Relocation of the aged: a review and theoretical analysis. *Journal of Gerontology*, 1977, *32*, 323–333.

Schwartz, A. N. Psychological dependency: an emphasis on the later years. In P. K. Ragan (Ed.), *Aging parents*. Los Angeles: University of Southern California Press, 1979.

Shanas, E. Social myth as hypothesis: The case of the family relations of old people. *The Gerontologist*, 1979, *19*, 3–9. (a)

Shanas, E. The family as a social support system in old age. *The Gerontologist*, 1979, *19*, 169–174. (b)

Sherman, S. Patterns of contacts for residents of age-segregated and age-integrated housing. *Journal of Gerontology*, 1975, *30*, 103–107. (a)

Sherman, S. Mutual assistance and support in retirement housing. *Journal of Gerontology*, 1975, *30*, 479–483. (b)

Sherwood, S., Greer, D. S., Morris, J. N., & Sherwood, C. C. *The Highland Heights experiment*. Washington, D.C.: U.S. Department of Housing and Urban Development, 1972.

Silverstone, B., & Hyman, H. K. *You and your aging parent*. New York: Random House (Pantheon Books), 1976.

Smith, K. F., & Bengston, V. L. Positive consequences of institutionalization: Solidarity between elderly parents and their middle-aged children. *The Gerontologist*, 1979, *19*, 438–447.

Storandt, M., & Wittels, I. Maintenance of function in relocation of community-dwelling older adults. *Journal of Gerontology*, 1975, *30*, 608–612.

Storandt, M., Wittels, I., & Botwinick, J. Predictors of a dimension of well-being in the relocated healthy aged. *Journal of Gerontology*, 1975, *30*, 97–102.

Troll, L. E., & Bengston, V. Generations in the family. In W. Burr, R. Hill, & I. Reiss (Eds.), *Contemporary theories about the family*. New York: Free Press, 1979.

Turner, B. F., Tobin, S. S., & Lieberman, M. A. Personality traits as predictors of institutional adaptation among the aged. *Journal of Gerontology*, 1972, *27*, 61–68.

Wittels, I., & Botwinick, J. Survival in relocation. *Journal of Gerontology*, 1974, *29*, 440–443.

8
Pathological Aging

This book is about normal aging, but this chapter is an exception in that is about abnormal or pathological aging. In one sense this chapter is a continuation of the previous one, where institutionalization was discussed. Many people in nursing homes or hospitals have pathological conditions; "It is estimated that about one-third to one-half of elderly patients were admitted to hospitals as younger patients and the remainder were admitted at age 65 or older" (Butler & Lewis, 1977, p. 52). It is mainly the "rising occurrence of depression and organic brain disorders" in old age that make for problems of institutionalization (pp. 55–56). This chapter on pathology is limited to one form of depression and two types of organic brain disorders.

DEPRESSION

The *Diagnostic and Statistical Manual of Mental Disorders* of the American Psychiatric Association is the major psychiatric classification guide for medical practitioners. The most recent version was published in 1980 and is referred to as DSM-III. The manual is revised periodically to reflect changes in opinions when more is learned.

The DSM-III lists several diagnostic categories of depression. The important one for present purposes is "Major Depressive Episode." This is characterized (p. 210) by an unhappy mood, "loss of interest or pleasure in almost all usual activities or pastimes." This condition is "relatively persistent" and associated with "appetite disturbance, change in weight, sleep disturbance, psychomotor agitation or retardation, decreased energy, feelings of worthlessness or guilt, difficulty concentrating or thinking, and thoughts of death or suicide, or suicide attempts." If the depression "does not involve the central nervous system" and "meets the full criteria . . . it is to be classified as a mental disorder." Depression is not only a painful state, it makes for incapacitation.

Although depression is a frequent disorder in later life, it must be noted at all times that pathology in old age is not the rule, it is the exception. Most old people do not suffer from Major Depressive Episode or from any other mental or physical disorder in the psychiatric sense. Old people suffer losses of loved ones and they mourn; they encounter hardships and feel bad, but most bounce back and continue their lives in normal, nonpathological fashion. Major Depressive Episode refers to the sick who need professional help.

Depression is Different in Old Age

The age of onset of depression "may begin at any age . . . and . . . is fairly evenly distributed throughout adult life" (DSM-III, p. 215). Since so many illnesses are more representative of the young than the old, however, (schizophrenic disorders, for example), depression looms more prominent among the old, at least in a relative sense. Depression can be brought on by infectious diseases or drugs, even those "such as reserpine," prescribed by physicians. Such depression is regarded in a different way, however. "Only by excluding organic etiology can one make the diagnosis of a major depressive episode" (p. 212).

"Although the essential features of a major depressive episode are similar in infants, children, adolescents, and adults, there are differences in the associated features" (p. 211). "Depressive Episodes of the elderly are often brief; guilt is uncommon but irritability and somatic complaints are frequent." (Blazer, 1982, p. 140). "Loss of interest in the social environment is characteristic of depressive disorders in late life. Irritability, worry, and impulses to cry are symptoms frequently exhibited by depressed older adults. However, negative feelings toward the self . . . are not nearly so common" among the depressed elderly as among depressed younger people (p. 22).

There is a difference between earlier and later life depression that is of greater importance—it is most characteristic. As indicated in DSM-III (p. 212), "In elderly adults there may be symptoms suggesting Dementia, such as disorientation, memory loss, and distractability . . . difficulty in concentration." It is for this reason that differential diagnosis between such depression and true dementia is difficult. It is so difficult, in fact, that the diagnosis "pseudodementia" has evolved. Pseudodementia indicates that dementia was thought the basic problem when actually it was depression. The distinguishing features between depression and dementia are that the major depressive episode has a more rapid onset, symptoms are usually of shorter duration, unhappy mood does not fluctuate, and disabilities are highlighted rather than denied (Blazer, 1982, p. 144). Characteristics of true dementia are opposite. Perhaps the most important distinguishing feature is that cognitive impairment is relatively continuous in dementia (more so in some dementia disorders than others) while it fluctuates widely in depressive episode. "Depression is difficult to classify" because it "may be more of a symptom than a disease entity." (Goldstein, 1979, p. 38). A major problem with the elderly "is an inability to handle multiple losses. Feelings of helplessness and reduced self-esteem are significant" (p. 38).

Treatment

Treatment for depression in late life is not very different from treatment in young adult age, except perhaps that "Nutritional deficits are a common complication . . ." (Blazer, 1982, p. 262). Treatment procedures include psychotherapy: "Common themes" among older people are wishes "to undo some of the patterns of their life" (Butler & Lewis, 1977, p. 265). (The next chapter will relate to this in Erikson's theory of development.) Older depressed "people speak of the monotony or dryness of their experiences" (p. 273). Family therapy can also help. Often young family members bring in the depressed person for help, but in the family therapy situation, there should "always be clarification as to who constitutes the 'patient.' Sometimes the older person is 'brought in' by a son or daughter, and it is quickly apparent that it is the child adult who needs help" (p. 273).

Antidepressant drugs can help (Butler & Lewis, 1977, pp. 281–292), but some of these may increase the incidence of strokes and coronary heart attacks. Tranquilizers may help, but they "often serve the provider of service rather than the served" (p. 281). That is, "there are increased numbers of people in the community whose fundamental problems in living have not been solved but who are simply pacified" with the "tranquilizer revolution" (p. 54). A major problem of drug therapy with all people, but perhaps most particularly with old people, is that, unknown to the physician, the patient is taking other drugs prescribed by another physician. Drug effects can interact and make for serious complications. Shock therapy may also help the depressed older person. With this therapy, however, the "Effects on memory must be continually assessed" and "respiratory and cardiovascular complications may occur" (p. 291).

Although depression does not appear as serious a state as organic brain disorders, the misery and debilitation it brings about makes it a major catastrophe. For those older people who suffer depressive disorder, life must be made better or else it feels hardly worth continuing.

MULTI-INFARCT DEMENTIA

All the organic mental disorders involve dementia, that is, impairment in higher mental functioning such as "memory, judgment, abstract thought . . ." (DSM-III, p. 107). The diagnosis of dementia, however, is not made if the impairments are thought to arise primarily from secondary factors such as "clouding of consciousness" or delerium, rather than organic brain changes.

"The diagnosis of Dementia is warranted only if intellectual deterioration is of sufficient severity to interfere with social or occupational functioning" (DSM-III, p. 110). This suggests that medical diagnosis is frequently a matter of personal and socioeconomic status. For example, the housewife and homemaker who has organic brain problems but who has much house help might be able to carry out her responsibilities. The homemaker without much help or who is employed, however, may not be able to carry on. A man with a supportive wife may avoid the need for medical attention and thus the diagnostic label, but the man living alone may not be able to manage. Those with sufficient income to take taxis rather than buses involving transfers might be able to appear as simply forgetful or eccentric. Those without such funds might be seen as impaired, requiring help, even institutionalization.

There are many different types of organic brain disorders; some are temporary or reversible, such as those due to nutritional and toxic problems, and some are permanent and not reversible. Among the latter, the two most frequent in later life are Multi-infarct Dementia and Alzheimer's Disease. These two are often not easy to tell apart and each may be easily confused with depression. As indicated, if depression is severe, cognitive abilities are poor, and in later life depression may be confused with dementia due to organic brain damage.

It is estimated that about 12–17 percent of older people suffering from organic brain disease suffer from Multi-infarct Dementia. Perhaps another 18 percent suffer from this condition together with Alzheimer's Disease (Tomlinson, Blessed, & Roth, 1970). Multi-infarct Dementia used to be called Psychosis with Cerebral Arteriosclerosis because this brain disorder involves the vascular system. The name change is because it used to be thought that the severity of the disease was due to the extent of damage done to the vessels in the cerebral cortex of the brain. The damage is due to either a hardening of the blood vessels (arteriosclerosis) or a narrowing of them (atherosclerosis). With this condition, there is interference with the blood flow and, as a result, insufficient oxygen and nutrients reach the brain. Now it is believed that the disorder is related not so much to the extent of vessel damage as to the repeated infarcts of the brain. That is, Multi-infarct Dementia is caused by repeated damage to different brain areas due to repeated blood vessel blockages. There are more and more areas of dead brain tissue in the brain.

Clinical Symptoms

Problems come on relatively suddenly. "Early symptoms" [of Multi-infarct Dementia] are dizziness, headaches, decreased physical and mental vigor, and vague physical complaints" (Butler & Lewis, 1977, p. 86). The course is uneven. "A person may be unable to remember one minute and regain total capacity the next" (p. 86). Although this disorder is different from Alzheimer's Disease and other similar dementia disorders, "it is almost impossible to distinguish [among them] at a single point in time on the basis of behavioral observations" (Eisdorfer & Cohen, 1978, p. 15). It is only on the basis of history and the course of the disease that differentiation is possible.

Multi-infarct Dementia is associated with a history of hypertension (high blood pressure). There is often a history of blackouts and of strokes. Unlike Alzheimer's and related diseases, this vascular disease is characterized by "stepwise deterioration in intellectual functioning that early in the course leaves some functions relatively intact" (DSM-III, p. 127). The deterioration depends on the areas of the brain destroyed. Although there is stepwise deterioration there are also fluctuating rapid changes of improvement and impairment. This "uneven and erratic downward progression" of the disorder (Butler & Lewis, p. 86) makes life hard for the family. "Families may have their hopes for a cure reinforced only to see them compromised in a series of crises" (Eisdorfer & Cohen, 1978, p. 15). Along with disturbances of memory, abstract thinking and judgment, there are also disturbances of impulse control and personality.

Possibly for some of the reasons that women live longer than men (discussed in Chapter 3), men suffer Multi-infarct Dementia more often than women (DSM-III, p. 127). "The disorder is found in middle and later life because it is a progressive disease which may remain asymptomatic until that point. Age of onset is between 50 and 70 years, with an average age of 66 years" (Butler & Lewis, 1977, p. 86).

Treatment

A sudden cerebrovascular stroke will cause confusion; it can make for a long-lasting, even permanent, condition. If it is massive enough, it can cause death. Such cerebral accidents are often associated with heart attacks. Treatment of Multi-infarct Dementia involves the basic cardiovascular problem. Therapies other than the cardiovascular ones may help; "the person can often benefit from psychotherapy, physical therapy, recreation and all the usual therapeutic supports and services" (Butler & Lewis, 1977, p. 88). But the basic problem involves the heart and cerebrovascular system.

ALZHEIMER'S DISEASE

Among the organic brain diseases, it is Alzheimer's Disease that is the major problem of the elderly. It had been thought that Multi-infarct Dementia constituted most of the dementia cases, but now it is understood that approximately half the cases are Alzheimer's (Tomlinson, Blessed, & Roth, 1970). As indicated, about 18 percent of dementia patients suffer both Alzheimer's Disease and Multi-infarct Dementia, but the former is thought more debilitating (Wisniewski & Terry, 1976, p. 267). It is not dead brain tissue stemming from blood vessel stricture that is the major problem in Alzheimer's Disease, it is brain degeneration apart from the vasculature that makes for the major problem.

It is estimated that in the United States between 0.88 and 1.2 million people suffer from Alzheimer's Disease; many more may experience the disease before death (Katzman, 1976, p. 218). Alzheimer's is the fourth or fifth leading disease killer in America, although it is not often reported as such on the death certificate (Katzman & Karasu, 1975).

Lest these facts make for inordinate fear, it is well to note that statistically, the vast majority of people will never suffer the disease. Only 2–4 percent of people develop the disorder (DSM-III, p. 125), but those who have or had close family members with the disease are at greater risk—7 or 8 percent (Henig, 1981, p. 119). "The prevalence increases with increasing age, particularly after 75" (DSM-III, p. 125). Death claims many Alzheimer patients in the very old age brackets. Katzman (1976) reported that severely demented old people compared to normal people of the same age survive only one-third to one-half the remaining years. (Thus, a crude estimate of the life expectancy of the Alzheimer patient may be made from Figure 1.1, where general population statistics are provided.)

Symptoms and Time Course

It is hard to distinguish one form of dementia from another on the basis of behavioral observations alone. Memory difficulties are a major sign in all dementias, as are difficulties in thinking and in judgment. With Alzheimer patients, particularly, there are problems of language—using the right word for the particular object, for example. Or words that are appropriate in one context are used in others (Fuld, Katzman, Davies, & Terry, 1982). Simple motor skills, such as tying bows of shoelaces, also become impaired.

Unlike Multi-infarct Dementia where the onset is more sudden and where there are ups and downs in functional status, Alzheimer's Disease comes on very gradually and the course of deterioration is progressively downhill. This is not to say that there are not better and worse days, but it is to say that what seems like a good day is only little better than before and will not remain better for long.

Effort has been made to describe the insidious beginning of the disorder and the progressive decline in terms of phases (see Schneck, Reisberg, & Ferris, 1982, for example). In phase I, there is forgetfulness—the person or the spouse notices a more frequent forgetting of where items are placed, what appointments were made, what the names of people are. There often is anxiety about this but, in the main, daily life continues without much problem. It is what Kral (1978) called "benign senescent forgetfulness." This condition may not be very different from that experienced by many older people and, in itself, is not a serious problem with dire consequences (Kral, 1978; Reisberg & Ferris, 1982). If deterioration does not continue beyond this point, Alzheimer's Disease is not indicated.

If, however, there is further deterioration, phase II of Alzheimer's Disease is said to be in progress. Here, there is confusion and clear intellectual impairment: memory for recent events is poor, as are orientation and concentration. Given lots of family and other "support systems," the phase II person may be able to manage at home, but cannot manage at work. The patient can hide his or her problem in phase I and often tries to do this, but in phase II, hiding it is not possible, certainly not for very long.

In phase III, the dementia is so evident that social relations are affected. There is disorientation such as to "confuse a spouse with a parent . . . the person cannot carry a thought long enough to remember what to do next" (Schneck et al., 1982, p. 167). At this point delusions, agitation, and other symptoms may show up.

The phase III Alzheimer patient reaches a point where complete custodial care is required. There is a loss of basic abilities, such as sitting in a chair for any length of time without being strapped in. There may be incontinence.

At present, there is no known cure for Alzheimer's Disease; however, much can be done to help the patient's family. Alzheimer's Disease is a very painful experience for family members. Often there is unjustified guilt and confusion. There is fear. Professional information and counseling of family members is more than desirable; it is crucial.

History

Until comparatively recently, Alzheimer's Disease was described as a "presenile" disorder. The medical classification actually specified that its occurrence was only at ages less than 65. When people over 65 presented with Alzheimer symptoms, the disorder was classified as "Senile Dementia." Recent clinical reports and recent autopsy analyses, however, determined that the presenile and senile conditions were indistinguishable (e.g., Katzman, 1976). Accordingly, many clinicians and investigators specializing in the disorder now refer to it as Alzheimer's Disease regardless of the age of the patient, and more are beginning to do so. Even now, however, DSM-III makes a distinction between "senile onset" of the disorder (after 65) and "presenile onset" (p. 125). The DSM-III distinction of senile and presenile onset is made, apparently, "for the purpose of historical continuity" and to maintain compatibility with other classifications (p. 124).

The name change, from Senile Dementia to Alzheimer's Disease, has continued to yet a third designation in DSM-III—Primary Degenerative Dementia. This latter change was designed to include other disease entities that are distinguishable from Alzheimer's Disease only at autopsy. Since the confirmation of the diagnosis of Alzheimer's Disease can only be made at autopsy, many professionals refer to this condition as Senile Dementia of the Alzheimer's Type (SDAT). Whether the label Primary Degenerative Dementia replaces the label Alzheimer's Disease or the label SDAT in daily usage remains to be seen.

How did the distinction at age 65 come about? How did the disorder get this name of Alzheimer's Disease? Very simply, shortly after the turn of the century, a pathologist by the name of Alois Alzheimer described the disorder when he microscopically examined the brains of several people who had died following varying episodes of dementia. All were less than 65 when they died and all had the same type of neurological evidence of this disease. All the brains were filled with neuritic plaques (sometimes called senile plaques) and with neurofibrillary tangles. These are called plaques and tangles for short. Plaques had been seen before but not tangles. In large part, many plaques and tangles define Alzheimer's Disease.

Plaques, Tangles, and Other Evidence of Disease

Plaques are found outside the nerve cells, mainly in the cerebral cortex. They appear to be degenerating bits of nerve cells including their fibers (axons and dendrites), surrounding a material called amyloid, a protein. Plaques are found in the brains of normal aged too, with perhaps as many normal old people showing them as demented people, but the number of plaques in the demented brains is much greater than in the normal brains. It has been suggested by Tomlinson et al. (1970, pp. 215–216) and frequently accepted by others, that 14 or more plaques per microscopic field characterizes the demented patient, not the normal one. The degree of intellectual deterioration is roughly correlated with the number of plaques per brain area (Blessed, Tomlinson, & Roth, 1968; Tomlinson et al., 1970).

Tangles are found in the brain cell itself. Two strands of nerve filaments in the cell wrap around each other in a spiral and get tangled. The reason this happens is unknown. As with plaques, tangles are found in the brains of the normal aged, but many more are seen in the brains of demented people. Tangles are found over most of the cortex but are seen in very high density in the hippocampus area of the brain of demented patients. Tangles are also related to intellectual ability, as suggested in an abstract of research findings by Farmer, Peck, and Terry (1976).

There are brain changes other than of plaques and tangles. Marked swelling of neurons with large, bubblelike spaces (vacuoles) are found in dementia. This is called granulovacular degeneration. Again, these changes may be found in normal aging but much more so in Alzheimer's Disease. Ball and Lo (1977) found brains of Alzheimer patients to have many times greater incidence of granulovacular degeneration than the brains of age-matched controls. Again, the hippocampus is where much of this was seen, particularly in the anterior half.

There are other brain changes as well. The ventricles of the brain are enlarged (as they are in other irreversible as well as reversible organic brain disorders.) Ventricular size and cognitive impairment in early to moderate cases have been found to be correlated (de Leon, Ferris, George, Reisberg, Kircheff, & Gershon, 1980). There is some evidence of fewer total brain neurons in dementia, but this is debated. There is shrinkage of the dendritric branchings of the neurons. There are also some biochemical changes that will be discussed briefly.

Possible Causes (Etiology)

The causes of Alzheimer's Disease are unknown at this time but there are several hypotheses. One is that Alzheimer's Disease arises from a virus that takes an extremely long time to show its effects. The evidence for this is that in some ways, the disease is similar to that which the chimpanzee and the scarpie mouse are known to get by way of slow acting viruses. A second hypothesis explaining Alzheimer's Disease relates to a defect in immunity. (It may be recalled that immunological theory was discussed in the first chapter.) It is thought that Alzheimer's Disease may be related to defects in immune processes because the plaque surrounds an amyloid body and amyloid production is linked with immune processes. These processes involve circulating proteins (called immunoglobulins) that form amyloid bodies. Since it is believed that general immunity diminishes with age, it may be that the older person is less able to defend against Alzheimer processes.

Another hypothesis is that Alzheimer's Disease is caused by *toxic agents*, most particularly aluminum. High levels of aluminum had been found in the brains of Alzheimer patients by Crapper, Kirshnan, and Dalton (1973). This hypothesis, however, is not without controversy, since not all investigators have found high levels of aluminum in Alzhemer brains. This remains an open issue (see Schneck et al., 1982).

Still another hypothesis is that Alzheimer's Disease is inherited but the evidence supporting this hypothesis is weak. Alzheimer's Disease is found in greater percentages among families than among the population at large (approximately 7–8 percent among families, about 3 percent in the population). Despite this, Katzman made clear (as indicated by Henig, 1981, p. 129) that it cannot be a simple case of genetic transmission. In identical twins, when one of the pair is inflicted, the other one runs a 60 percent chance of also being inflicted. This is high, but if it were simply a matter of genes, there would be 100 percent chance. Perhaps there is a problem of family transmission in Alzheimer's Disease, but if there is, it may be some combination of genetic predisposition and virus or other factor in the environment. The listing of all these hypotheses and the lack of certain connection of each of them to Alzheimer's Disease tells us that little is known about the disease. If little is known, little can be done about it. There is another hypothesis, however, one that leaves room for more optimism.

Treatment

The other hypothesis is linkable to treatment. In fact, treatment has been tried with some hope but many failures. It seems that the brains of Alzheimer patients lack an enzyme called choline acetyltransferase (C.A.T., for short; see Richter, Perry, & Tomlinson, 1980, for example). C.A.T. is important because it is involved in the synthesis of neurotransmitters, substances that are important in learning and memory. Learning and memory involve information that is encoded or transformed into electrical qualities to get from one brain cell to another. To get from one brain cell to another, to cross the synapse, neurotransmitters (for example, acetylcholine) must be released to diffuse across the synapse to excite the postsynaptic brain cell. If C.A.T. is missing, so will be the neurotransmitter, and learning and memory will suffer.

Alzheimer patients seem to lack C.A.T. and their learning and memory are deficient. Older normal people have less C.A.T. than young people (McGeer & McGeer, 1976) but have more than age-matched Alzheimer patients. Accordingly, it would seem that pharmaceuticals associated with neurotransmitters should help Alzheimer patients. This has been tried with some success. For example, Davis and Mohs (1982) gave the drug physostigmine to 10 Alzheimer patients. Recognition memory was improved in each of the 10 cases in the first part of the study, and 8 out of 10 in the second part. This is not to say that long-term effects have been indicated, but research is continuing and there is hope for the future. Other types of therapies have also been tried. For example, a drug that increases blood flow to the brain has been tried with some success (Funkenstein, Hicks, Dysken, & Davis, 1981). Nevertheless, it is well not to be too optimistic because the history of medical investigation in this area is full of disappointment.

PATHOLOGY IN PERSPECTIVE

Pathology or Accelerated Aging?

Is it the fate of all people, if they live long enough, to end up with organic brain problems? It seems that most of medical opinion clearly places Multi-infarct Dementia and Alzheimer's Disease in the realm of pathology, not normal aging. These dementia disorders, and others not discussed in this chapter, may have similarities to normal aging but they are qualitatively different. Thus, the answer to the question raised above is no.

Still, an argument can be raised on the other side. For example, although fewer in number than in Alzheimer brains, many normal old brains have plaques and tangles and other changes not seen in young brains, or not seen nearly as often (e.g., Tomlinson, Blessed, & Roth, 1968). Further, many of the cognitive impairments seen in demented patients are also found in mild forms in normal aging. A goodly number of aged people show a "benign senescent forgetfulness." In fact, 10 to 15 percent of community-residing older adults experience cognitive impairment not unlike that of early Alzheimer patients (e.g., Kay & Bergmann, 1980). It may make sense to think of dementia and normal aging as having something in common.

Despite this, whatever the quantitative relationship, normal aging and pathological dementia are so very different functionally that they seem to constitute different qualitative domains. Perhaps Terry was correct (as told by Henig, 1981, p. 126) when he said that when the quantitative differences become large enough, they make for qualitative differences in terms of functional disease. This thinking suggests a threshold beyond which there is pathology. To the point of threshold, however, there is no pathology. As indicated, population statistics show that the threshold is not reached in the vast majority of cases. The vast majority of people live to old ages and never reach the threshold to develop pathological status.

Reversible and Irreversible Dementia

The discussion in this chapter was limited to depression and two organic disorders, Multi-infarct Dementia and Alzheimer's Disease. Many more pathological states of the senium could have been described. Among these are reversible organic problems. It is very easy to see a dementia patient and make the mistake that it is one of the irreversible organic conditions discussed here. There are many conditions that are not nearly as serious and not nearly as long-lasting, although they seem the same.

It was said that severe depression in old age makes people appear demented. When the depression lifts, so does the apparent dementia. Infections and toxic affects of drugs and other substances make for reversible dementia (see, for example, Sloane, 1980). When these conditions are corrected, unless extensive permanent damage resulted, the dementia lifts. Nutritional deficiencies also make for dementia. Older people sometimes suffer nutritional deficiencies because they do not eat well. They do not take the trouble to prepare appetizing, wholesome meals, especially when they live alone. There may be metabolic problems. Such conditions can also make for cognitive deficiencies. When proper diet and bodily processes are restored, so are the cognitive skills.

Irreversible dementia is another matter, but as already mentioned, even here there are vast individual differences in the ability to live relatively normal lives. Butler and Lewis (1977, p. 54) indicated that even "an older person who is diagnosed as having severe brain damage . . . may function quite well in supportive milieu. Another person may have minimal brain damage but have no economic, personal and social supports and thus have more trouble functioning."

SUMMARY

By far the greatest number of old people in need of institutionalization suffer from debilitating depression or organic brain problems, or a combination of both of these. Depression is characterized by a loss of interest in most things. There is appetite disturbance, sleeping difficulties, agitation. There is a feeling of worthlessness; sometimes there is guilt. Often, life is so unbearable that there are thoughts of death and suicide attempts.

Although depression is found at all ages, it takes a different form in old age. Behaviorally, depression in old age resembles dementia; there is loss of memory, disorientation, difficulty in concentrating and thinking. Poor judgment is seen. One factor that differentiates depression from dementia is that cognitive disabilities are denied in dementia but highlighted in depression. Depression can be treated by individual and family psychotherapy, antidepressant drugs, and electroshock. When the depression lifts, so do the cognitive impairments.

The major organic brain disorders in old age are Multi-infarct Dementia and Alzheimer's Disease. All organic brain disorders involve impairments in higher mental functioning such as memory, abstract thinking, and judgment. There are two important attitudes to maintain when observing such dementia. First, some dementias are reversible. Nutritional deficiencies can make for dementia; so can toxins, including drugs prescribed by physicians. When these conditions are ameliorated, so is the dementia in most instances.

The second attitude is that not all people with dementia need to be institutionalized. It depends on severity and it depends on the "support systems," such as a caring spouse. It also depends on the demands made on the patient. The demented person may be able to manage at home and even manage social relations. It is not likely, however, that the demented person can manage at work.

Mulit-infarct Dementia, one of the two major irreversible dementias, claims about 15 percent of older people who suffer from organic brain diseases. Additionally, another 18 percent are so afflicted in combination with Alzheimer's Disease. Multi-infarct Dementia is a disease of the brain due to problems of the vascular system. Repeated attacks to the brain by the hardening or narrowing of the cerebral blood vessels make for spotted areas of dead brain tissue. Early symptoms of this disorder are dizziness, headaches, decreased physical and mental vigor, and vague physical complaints.

Behaviorally, Multi-infarct Dementia and Alzheimer's Disease are hardly distinguishable at a single observation period. They are told apart clinically mainly on the basis of past history and by observation over time. Multi-infarct Dementia comes on relatively suddenly—Alzheimer's Disease comes on insidiously. Patients with Multi-infarct Dementia almost always have high blood pressure. There are erratic swings in their symptoms. Although the general course is downward, there are ups and downs so that the patient may appear to be getting better one day, only to swing down the next. With Alzheimer's Disease the course is mainly downward. Treatment for Multi-infarct Dementia is basically cardiovascular treatment. Psychotherapy, physical therapy, and support services can all help.

Alzheimer's Disease is different in that the vasculature need not be a problem at all. It is estimated that about one-half of all dementia cases in old age suffer from Alzheimer's Disease. As indicated, an additional 18 percent suffer this disease in conjunction with Multi-infarct Dementia. The disease ends with death; it is the fourth or fifth leading disease killer.

The two most prominent brain changes in Alzheimer's Disease are neuritic plaques and neurofibrillary tangles. Plaques, found outside the brain cell, are degenerating bits of cells surrounding a fibrous protein called amyloid. Tangles, inside the brain cell, are made up of fibers twisted around each other. The number of plaques and tangles are each correlated with scores of intellectual ability.

The etiology of Alzheimer's Disease is largely unknown but there are hypotheses. Perhaps the most hopeful one is biochemical deficiency because it leaves the opportunity to cure the disorder by pharmaceuticals. Research data have suggested that brain neurotransmitters, so important in learning and memory, are deficient in Alzheimer patients. Several drugs, based on this knowledge, are currently being investigated.

REFERENCES

Ball, M. J., & Lo, P. Granulovascular degeneration in the aging brain and in dementia. *Journal of Neuropathological Experimental Neurology*, 1977, 36, 474–487.

Blazer, D. G. *Depression in late life*. St. Louis: C. V. Mosby, 1982.

Blessed, G., Tomlinson, B. E., & Roth, M. The association between quantitative measures of dementia and senile change in the cerebral grey matter of elderly subjects. *British Journal of Psychiatry*, 1968, 114, 797–811.

Butler, R. N., & Lewis, M. I. *Aging and mental health* (2nd ed.). St. Louis: C. V. Mosby, 1977.

Crapper, D., Kirshnan, S. S., & Dalton, A. J. Brain aluminum distribution in Alzheimer's disease and experimental neurofibrillary degeneration. *Science*, 1973, 180, 511–513.

Davis, K. L., & Mohs, R. C. Enhancement of memory processes in Alzheimer's Disease with multiple-dose intravenous physostigmine. *American Journal of Psychiatry*, 1982, 139, 1421–1423.

de Leon, M. J., Ferris, S. H., George, A. E., Reisberg, B., Kircheff, L. L., & Gershon, S. Computed tomography evaluation of brain-behavior relationships in senile dementia of the Alzheimer type. *Neurobiology of Aging*, 1980, *1*, 69–79.

Diagnostic and statistical manual of mental disorders (3rd ed., DSM-III). Washington, D.C.: American Psychiatric Association, 1980.

Eisdorfer, C., & Cohen, D. The cognitively impaired elderly: differential diagnoses. In M. Storandt, I. Siegler, & M. F. Elias (Eds.), *The clinical psychology of aging*. New York: Plenum Press, 1978, pp. 7–42.

Farmer, P. M., Peck, A., & Terry, R. D. Correlations among numbers of neuritic plaques, neurofibrillary tangles and severity of dementia. *Journal of Neuropathology and Experimental Neurology*, 1976, *35*, 367. (Abstract).

Fuld, P. A., Katzman, R., Davies, P., & Terry, R. D. Intrusions as a sign of Alzheimer Dementia: Chemical and pathological verification. *Annals of Neurology*, 1982, *11*, 155–159.

Funkenstein, H. H., Hicks, R., Dysken, M. W., & Davis, J. M. Drug treatment of cognitive impairment in Alzheimer's disease and the late life dementias. In N. E. Miller & G. D. Cohen (Eds.), *Clinical aspects of Alzheimer's Disease and Senile Dementia*. New York: Raven Press, 1981.

Goldstein, S. E. Depression in the elderly. *Journal of the American Geriatrics Society*, 1979, *27*, 38–42.

Henig, R. M. *The myth of senility*. Garden City, N.Y.: Anchor Press/Doubleday, 1981.

Katzman, R. The prevalence and malignancy of Alzheimer Disease. *Archives of Neurology*, 1976, *33*, 217–218. (Editorial)

Katzman, R., & Karasu, T. B. Differential diagnosis of dementia. In W. Fields (Ed.), *Neurological and sensory disorders in the elderly*. New York: Stratton International Medical Book Corp., 1975, pp. 103–134.

Kay, D. W. K., & Bergmann, K. Epidemiology of mental disorders among the aged in the community. In J. E. Birren & R. B. Sloane (Eds.), *Handbook of mental health and aging*. Englewood Cliffs, N.J.: Prentice-Hall, 1980.

Kral, V. A. Benign senescent forgetfulness. In R. Katzman, R. D. Terry, & K. L. Beck (Eds.), *Aging* (Vol. 7): *Alzheimer's Disease: Senile Dementia and related disorders*. New York: Raven Press, 1978, pp. 47–51.

McGeer, E., & McGeer, P. L. Neurotransmitter metabolism in the aging brain. In R. D. Terry & S. Gershon (Eds.), *Aging* (Vol. 3): *Neurobiology of aging*. New York: Raven Press, 1976, pp. 389–403.

Reisberg, B., & Ferris, S. H. Diagnosis and assessment of the older patient. *Hospital and Community Psychiatry*, 1982, *33*, 104–110.

Richter, J. A., Perry, E. K., & Tomlinson, B. E. Acetylcholine and choline levels in postmortem brain tissue: preliminary observations in Alzheimer's Disease. *Life Science*, 1980, *26*, 1683–1689.

Schneck, M. K., Reisberg, B., & Ferris, S. H. An overview of current concepts of Alzheimer's Disease. *American Journal of Psychiatry*, 1982, *139*, 165–173.

Sloane, R. B. Organic brain syndrome. In J. E. Birren & R. B. Sloane (Eds.), *Handbook of mental health and aging*. Englewood Cliffs, N.J.: Prentice-Hall, 1980.

Tomlinson, B. E., Blessed, G., & Roth, M. Observations on the brains of non-demented old people. *Journal of Neurological Sciences*, 1968, *7*, 331–356.

Tomlinson, B. E., Blessed, G., & Roth, M. Observations on the brains of demented old people. *Journal of Neurological Sciences*, 1970, *11*, 205–242.

Wisniewski, H. M., & Terry, R. D. Neuropathology of the aging brain. In R. D. Terry & S. Gershon (Eds.), *Aging* (Vol. 3): *Neurobiology of aging*. New York: Raven Press, 1976, pp. 265–280.

9
Personality Development: Stability and Change

The previous chapter told of abnormal development in later life with the focus on disease. This chapter tells of normal development with the focus on personality. It will be seen that the research literature is inconsistent in what it tells and that there is controversy about whether change or stability characterizes adult development.

Studies of personality in later life take many forms. Some studies are simply based on personality test and questionnaire results, others describe people in their adjustments in different phases of life situations. Only a few of the studies relate to theory or to broad concepts of development.

PERSONALITY: THREE VIEWS

Personality Does Not Change

There is a viewpoint that personality is something more than behavior. Conversely, behavior is a result of many influences in addition to personality—influences such as health status, cognitive abilities, and learned cues. Since behavior is determined by all of these, changes in behavior with age do not necessarily imply changes in personality. A statement by Costa and McCrae (1980, p. 80) is compatible with such a viewpoint: "Admittedly, many things do change with age. . . . Social roles alter drastically, and events like retirement and widowhood produce major changes in the behavior of individuals. . . . And it can be admitted that there are unmistakable age changes in the specific behaviors that express enduring traits: [for example] 'Activity' in older persons is likely to be gardening rather than football. But all these changes do not amount to change in personality."

This viewpoint obliges the personality investigator to specify beforehand those changes in behavior that are determined by, or reflective of, personality change; otherwise, any change in behavior can be seen as unrelated to personality change. By the same logic, stability of behavior can be seen as reflective of personality change.

By their choice of tests, Costa and McCrae did specify beforehand, even if implicitly, those behavior changes they accepted as reflective of personality change. As will be seen later, they found only few behavioral changes with age and concluded that personality is stable, not changing during adulthood.

Personality Changes Due to Generational Impact, Not Age

There is an alternate view, one expressed strongly by Schaie and Parham (1976). It will be seen later that they found much stability in personality in their longitudinal age comparisons but much difference among age-groups in their cross-sectional comparisons. They concluded that it is not a matter of "lack of change in personality after adolescence, as most traditional theorists might believe. . . . The change, however, is a function of specific early socialization experiences, commonly shared generation-specific environmental impact, and particular sociocultural transitions that may affect individuals of all ages" (p. 157).

The implication of this is that there is personality change but it is not a result of intrinsic maturational or biological forces. It is a result of different forces in the environments of the old and young, and these shape the personalities of the old and young differently. This suggests that if the environmental forces of tomorrow are different from the forces of today, the old of tomorrow will have different personalities than the old of today. In brief, there are personality differences across the life span but they are due to sociocultural influences.

Personality Change Because of Age

There is a third view, but one that is not held by many. Personality changes with age and the change has a maturational or biological basis. This view, contrasted with the Schaie–Parham view, reflects the old nature–nurture controversy. Schaie and Parham are clearly on the side of nurture. It will be seen that a few studies do show personality traits that change, possibly for maturational reasons.

The interactionist might insist that personality development in adulthood is a joint function of a changing biology and of forces in both the present and past environments. There are not many theorists in the study of aging that explicitly maintain this position, but stage theorists are among those that do. Typically, stage theorists do not discuss biological antecedents of personality but the demands they put on their theories imply this, even if in a most general way.

STAGE THEORIES

Stage theories have in common the idea that life's development involves stages or steps that must be climbed one by one. There is no skipping of steps, and once a step has been reached there is no return to the previous one, and there is no need for return. Each new step or stage represents an accomplishment, a problem solved in the previous stage. Further, each stage is qualitatively different from the others.

There is a force propelling passage from one stage of life to the next. This force applies to everyone in every society, in every era. This certainly suggests a biological system. Although this seems too much to ask of any theory, a true stage theory does not allow for exception. "A single case of longitudinal inversion of sequence disproves the stage theory" (Kohlberg, 1973, p. 182). "While cultural factors may speed up, slow down, or stop development, they do not change the sequence" (p. 181).

Stage theories, therefore, are specific and demanding. There are only few such theories that cover the life span; most start out with issues of development in infancy, then proceed to young childhood, late childhood, and adolescence and stop there. Some newer theories have proceeded to middle age and have stopped there; others made effort to continue to old age. These theories, in the main, have not been put to adequate test; thus, even if they have merit, it may be best to think of them as describing general developmental patterns rather than invariant sequences of life. As such, they lose their stage theory character and simply become descriptive statements of broad segments of society. They also become compatible, however, with the Schaie and Parham contention of cultural determination of personality, or with the Costa and McCrae contention of stable personality despite different behavioral patterns.

Ego Development

One theory, often cited, extends to old age. Erikson (1963) described eight stages of development, each focusing on a need or a crisis. If decisions are made well during one stage, then successful adaptation can be made in the subsequent stage. The first five stages cover life through adolescence. The sixth stage, early adulthood, focuses on the need to give of oneself and to take from someone else, as in marriage. This stage is labeled *intimacy*. Involvements with children, work, and play are part of the intensive interactions typical of this stage. The seventh stage, middle adulthood, focuses on teaching or guiding the next generation. This stage is called *generativity*. There is a dependence upon the younger generation in that, without the opportunity or ability to give in this fashion, there is over self-indulgence, and over self-concern, a babying of oneself. This makes for an immature adult. The final stage of development, old age, focuses upon self-acceptance; it is called *ego-integrity*. Failure in development through this stage leads to despair, a condition that many people do not escape. Erikson contended that good adjustment in this stage follows only when important matters have been arranged, and when the successes and failures of life have been seen as inevitable. Good adjustment in late life implies a type of fatalism, an acceptance of order in life, where even death is viewed without agony.

Life Review. How are important matters arranged to facilitate successful adjustment during this stage? One of the ways is by a *life review* (Butler & Lewis, 1973, pp. 43–44; Butler, 1975, pp. 412–414). People reminisce, they dwell in the past. For Butler, this is not an idle process; it is purposive, it occurs naturally with everyone so that unresolved conflicts are brought into the focus of attention where they can be resolved. Impending death brings out and highlights the life review—it makes the review mandatory, for little time is left to arrange one's matters. Butler indicates that, in mild form, the life review is a reminiscence that makes for nostalgia and mild regret. In severe form, anxiety and depression result. This is particularly true for those people who, when young, tended to avoid the present and emphasize the future. Depression and anxiety are also seen in the life review among those who had hurt others. A failure of the life review to resolve these conflicts, to arrange these types of important matters, makes self-acceptance difficult. It makes for failure in adjustment often seen during Erikson's eighth and final stage of ego-integrity.

Related Studies. Not many aging studies have been carried out with Erikson's final stage in mind, but several studies can be related to it. A study by Reichard, Livson, and Peterson (1962), for example, supports at least one aspect of the theory. Reichard et al. interviewed people who were still working (aged 55–66) and people who were retired (aged 67–72) and rated them for a great number of personality traits. Of these, a sample was selected as being high in acceptance of aging and another sample was selected as being low in acceptance of aging. The high group was seen as made up largely of three subgroups, and the low group was composed mostly of two subgroups. The larger of the latter subgroups was termed aggressive; they blamed others for their miseries. The smaller of the two was very much smaller and was made up of "self-haters." They were full of despair. These seemed to correspond to what Erikson indicated would result without proper resolution of the crises in the final stage of life. Those who accepted aging, however, did not seem to have the fatalistic quality Erikson expected. These people fell in three subgroups as follows: (1) they seemed to enjoy what they were doing at the moment; (2) they tended to enjoy relaxation and not having to work; or (3) they obliged themselves to keep active as a defense against getting old.

A subsequent study, in some ways similar in purpose and in procedure, was carried out by Neugarten, Crotty, and Tobin (1964). Men and women aged 50 to 90 were interviewed and tested, and rated on many dimensions. Principal-component analyses disclosed six personality types of each sex. Five tended to be similar to those reported by Reichard et al., with the sixth not seeming important, including only a few men. Neugarten et al. correlated these personality types with a rating scale of Life Satisfaction and, not unexpectedly, the better-adjusted people were rated higher in life satisfaction.

There have been other formulations of developmental sequences similar to that of Erikson, some assigning more stages to the later periods of life. In the main, however, neither these formulations nor the better-known one of Erikson provided much impetus for research and thus new information and further theory building.

Developmental Tasks

Two theories have been formulated that relate more to practical tasks that must be carried out than to personality adjustments that must be made. Schaie (1977) evolved a theory from his research on intelligence which is related as much to cognitive development as to personality. It is Piaget (e.g., 1970), of course, who is best known for theory in cognitive development, but his theory does not go beyond young adulthood. (See Chapter 15, section on "Problem Solving in Perspective," in this book.)

Schaie sees four stages of development. Common to just about all stage theories, his first stage involves the task of the developing young person to establish independence. The next stage of young adulthood involves goal-oriented behavior that must be efficient and effective. Task-specific behaviors give way to broader competency.

During middle age, there is an assumption of responsibility for others, particularly a spouse and children. This stage seems to have elements in common with Erikson's sixth stage, intimacy, and seventh stage, generativity. Schaie calls this the *responsible* stage and suggests that it extends from the late 30s to the early 60s. Here the basic skill is the integration of long-range goals. If this stage is successfully completed, many of life's problems are solved. Some people in this stage develop executive abilities, growing beyond the family to responsibility for society.

The final stage of cognitive development is the *reintegrative* stage. This stage is reached when life has become so complicated that it needs to be simplified. Retirement, disengagement (discussed in Chapter 5), and selective attention are all part of the simplification process. Responsibilities are taken on only if they have meaning and purpose.

Schaie specified the types of cognitive tasks used in the laboratory that measure or relate to each of the first three stages. Cognitive skills required in the last stage are not necessarily correlated with the skills of earlier stages, he said. This suggests that the successful person, the person who has accomplished the tasks and solved the problems through middle age, is not necessarily successful during the last stage. This is compatible with the idea that the stages in stage theories are qualitatively different. Schaie maintained that at present there are no adequate measuring devices for assessment of fourth-stage competence.

Another investigator proposed in very concrete terms the tasks of life that must be faced. Havighurst (1972) divided the adult life span into three major groupings: 18 to 30 years, similar to Schaie; 30 to 60 years; and 60 to the end of life. The tasks of the first stage include selecting a mate, rearing children, getting started in an occupation. The middle stage involves helping teenage children to become happy, responsible adults. This is similar to both Erikson's sixth stage and Schaie's third stage. This long middle stage also involves developing leisure-time activities, adjusting to physiological changes of middle age, and adjusting to aging parents.

The task of later life is of adjustments to losses. Adjustments must be made to decreasing strength and health, to retirement and reduced income, to death of spouse. There must be flexibility in developing new social roles, new relationships with age peers, and new living arrangements.

Midlife Crisis

Three Theories. "Midlife crisis" has become a popular concept, accepted by some as inevitable. Much of this thinking has derived from stage theories that have major focus on middle age but little to say beyond this period of life. "Midlife crisis" seems to be a frequent occurrence, but unless it is universal, it really is not a stage at all. The related data suggest that it is the adjustment pattern of many people in U.S. society, and perhaps elsewhere, but is not a true stage as rigorously defined.

Among the better-known midlife crisis theories is one by Levinson, Darrow, Klein, Levinson & McKee (1978) based on the study of 40 men. Their stage theory centers around the concept of life structure, that is, the basic pattern of a person's life at a given period of time. It is the relationship between the self and the world. Like other researchers, Levinson et al. see the job of the young person, aged from the late teens to the young 20s, as separation from family in order to form a basis for living in the world. During the 20s a person gains entrance into the adult world, where it is important to test what has been accomplished.

There is a settling down in the mid-30s; life becomes more stable and satisfying. From the late 30s to the mid-40s, however, stability gives way to a review and reappraisal. It is now felt that crucial choices must be made and there is little time left to do this. Levinson's studies have suggested to him that at this point in life, as many as 80 percent of men undergo a "tumultuous struggle" within themselves—the "midlife crisis."

Gould (1978) is a psychiatist who developed a similar theory. His theory was based on work with group psychotherapy patients, but he contended that patients and nonpatients share common problems and concerns about self-development. For him, as for others, the job of early adulthood is separation from parents and the development of independence. Next, there is growth of confidence and competence with a sense of being an adult. With independence achieved, during the late 20s to early 30s, there is realization that "dreams do not come true" by wishful thinking, or even by effort. Instead, effort can bring about only "what can reasonably be expected." There is family closeness in the 30s but all this gives way in the 40s. Soon, there is a pressure of time: "whatever we must do, must be done now" (p. 185). There is a search for new resolution; life becomes unstable and uncomfortable— thus, the midlife crisis. Gould (1975, p. 78) emphasized that although the sequence holds for the majority of people, "the precise ages at which changes occur are a product of an individual's total personality, life style and subculture."

Vaillant (1977), another psychiatrist, studied 95 men from an original sample of 268 college students of the 1940s. He followed them longitudinally for 30 years. He was impressed with how the patterns and rhythms of the life cycle are geared to career planning. Vaillant was concerned with adaptive or coping mechanisms that he classed as either mature or immature. He concluded that mature coping mechanisms increased to midlife. Vaillant did not focus on the "midlife crisis," but his conclusions suggested that when present, the crisis is a reflection of poor mental health, rather than an inevitable stage for every man.

Not Enough Emphasis on Stability. Costa and McCrae (1980) would agree and go further. They questioned the whole idea of midlife crisis. "Rather than look for change," they argued, "psychologists might better search for the mechanisms to promote stability" (p. 65).

Costa and McCrae (1978) developed a questionnaire to measure crises and compared the scores among various age-groups. They were not impressed with what few differences they found and referred to their 10-year longitudinal data to argue that those people with high crises scores were simply those with long-standing neuroticism. "According to our data," they said, "most men do not go through a mid-life crisis at all."

A Broader View

Stage theorists see the process of development as one of continually completing new tasks or coping with new crises. They do not provide an overview of what is accomplished by aging, of what life is really like in old age. Butler (1975, pp. 409–416), however, does provide such an overview, making the following points:

First, old age is the only period in life in which the future is less important than it had been; the present is what matters. Thus, there is a change in the sense of time. The quality of present time is more important than how much of it one has left. Older people can fully experience the now.

Second, old age is the only time when a person can experience a sense of the entire life cycle. There is an accumulation of factual knowledge and there is a sense of experience. These broad, wisdom-giving experiences can come only with age. They make resolutions of personal problems more possible. For these reasons, old people can often be good sources of advice to others; they can be good counselors. Unfortunately, however, they are not always seen as such.

Third, older people are also workaday historians. They are good reference sources, keeping a continuity with the past. Butler indicated that old people are attached to familiar objects of their past and they value them. Their homes and their possessions provide a sense of comfort and continuity with the past. Pets, scrapbooks, and keepsakes are treasured. Not only do older people maintain continuity with the past, but they want to leave a legacy for the future. Unless they are extraordinarily fixated on themselves, Butler said, they want to pass on power. The old feel fulfilled if they can do all of these things while at the same time continuing a satisfactory existence.

CHANGING ROLES AND STATUSES

There is a type of study that in some ways is similar to the stage theory study but is not identical to it. While stage theories assume an inevitable, universal, unidirectional unfolding of life, there is a type of study that investigates adjustment to transitional life events as they occur in particular societies. For example, there is an adjustment to marriage, to the empty-nest period, to retirement, widowhood, and so on. Such studies are sometimes referred to as stage theory studies, but this is incorrect because these transitions are not universal nor unidirectional. Not all people, nor all societies, go through the transitions of empty nest or retirement, for example. The results of such studies are more properly called adjustment or transition studies.

Regularity: Age Norms and Age Constraints

Adjustments to the transitions in life are not always made easily. They are governed, in part, by what is called age stratification. This means that within a particular culture, the life course is graded by what people of different ages are supposed to be like (Riley, Johnson, & Foner, 1972). Roles and statuses are attributed to people, not as individuals, but on the basis of their ages alone. Through socialization processes, people learn what is expected of them.

Age stratification lays out what is expected, what is appropriate, and what can or cannot be done. It makes for regularities in behavior by producing age norms. For example, a study was reported by Neugarten, Moore, and Lowe (1965) in which a questionnaire was given to respondents who indicated ages best to marry, get settled on a career, become a grandparent, and others. There was a remarkable congruence of opinion—best age for a man to marry was 20 to 25, for a woman 19 to 24. Most men should be settled on a career between 24 and 26. People should become grandparents between 45 and 50.

An interesting dimension to this study was a comparison between personal norms and those ascribed to society. The questionnaire was answered in two ways; one, "give your personal opinions" and, two, "tell how 'most people' would respond." Interestingly, personal opinions were less governed by perceived age norms and age constraints than those opinions attributed to most people. This was clearly so for young people in their 20s and less so for those middle-aged; however, people aged 65 and older held age norm attitudes not very different from those ascribed to people in general.

Adherence to age norms makes for age constraints. It makes for a homogenation of people. If elderly people adhere more to the age norms than young people do, they are more constrained than young people. If they are more constrained, they are governed more by what Neugarten et al. called a "prescriptive timetable" ordering their behavior. Prescriptive timetables may make for orderliness but they remove freedom of choice and can make for unfair social practices.

Irregularity in Life

Not all investigators see life as regularly patterned. Some see life full of irregularity, not at all systematic and predictable as stage or transition theories suggest. It would seem that both irregularity and regularity characterize life's patterns, but over the generations, irregularity has become more apparent. For example, Neugarten and Hagestad (1976, p. 52) see the rhythms of life changing—"ours seems to be a society that has become accustomed to

70-year-old students, 30-year-old college presidents, 22-year-old mayors, 35-year-old grandmothers, 50-year-old retirees, 65-year-old fathers of preschoolers, 60-year-olds and 30-year-olds wearing the same clothing styles, and 85-year-old parents caring for their 65-year-old offspring."

Neugarten and Hagestad argued that general behavior patterns are becoming less and less related to age norms. Age is less and less a regulator of behavior. This suggests that if Neugarten, Moore, and Lowe were to repeat their 1965 study today, in which people were asked the best ages to marry, to become a grandparent, and other such age-norm opinions, they might get different answers. A stage theorist might agree with this, but would indicate that what Neugarten and Hagestad observed as either irregularity or regularity does not alter the idea of stage development. The tasks of each stage remain the same, a stage theorist would say; it is only that people cope with these tasks in different ways and at different times of life. Stage theorists would insist that successful entry to the next stage—whether as a father or grandfather—can come about only after the problems of the previous stage have been successfully handled. What Neugarten and Hagestad were referring to, stage theorists might insist, is adjustments or transitions that involve role and status. There are both regularities and irregularities in these.

Life's Anchoring Points: Making for Order

Many people do not want to be boxed in by age constraints, but most want order or regularity in their lives. People refer to events they experienced to mark off periods. This gives structure to what occurred and what is going on. Young children may mark off birthdates or outings or gifts they received. Adolescents may refer to the start of grade school and to their first date. Adults with longer histories mark off events spaced farther apart.

Women and men mark time differently. Neugarten (1968a, pp. 95–96) reported that women marked time by such events as getting married, having babies, and children's graduation from school. Men, on the other hand, marked time by events that occurred outside the home, often by occasions that relate to the job, as, for example, promotions and changes in positions. These events are the ones that have special meaning in life and function as organizing or anchoring points.

Beginning sometime in middle age there is an ordering of time that is different. Sometime in middle age there is a beginning awareness that time is finite. Everyone knows that life does not go on forever, but a point is reached when this is felt. At this point, life takes on a different reality; perhaps this is the basis for midlife crisis when it occurs.

When this realization of finite existence is felt, "Life is restructured in terms of time-left-to-live, rather than time-since-birth" (Neugarten, 1968a,

p. 97). For example, a young person might say, "I am 20 years old." An old person might say, "I have 10 good years left, I want to retire soon." This is an important turning point. With this restructuring of time there is the formulation of new perceptions of self, time and death" (Neugarten, 1968b, p. 140).

Sex Role Development

Neugarten and Gutmann (1958) presented a picture to men and women of two age-groups, a middle-aged one (40–54 years) and an older one (55–70 years). This picture, seen as Figure 9.1, is of four people: an elderly man and a woman and a younger man and woman.

This picture was shown with the instruction to tell a story about the figures in it; to assign ages to each figure and feelings that each might have for the others. By this procedure, feelings and ideas were thought to be projected, thus reflecting inner, psychic dimensions of their personalities.

This thematic apperception test (TAT) showed interesting sex role attributions. Neugarten and Gutmann (1958, p. 53) reviewed the responses to Figure 9.1 and wrote:

> Most striking was the fact that with increasing age of respondents, the Older Man and Older Woman [of Figure 9.1] reversed roles in regard to authority in the family. For younger men and women [aged 40–54] the Older Man was seen as the authority figure. For older men and women [aged 55–70] the Older Woman was in the dominant role, and the Older Man, no matter what other qualities were ascribed to him, was seen as submissive. [Moreover] women, as they age, seem to become more tolerant of their own aggressive, egocentric impulses, while men, as they age, of their own nurturant and affiliative impulses.

Thus, a reversal in sex role seemed to have taken place later in life. Why should such a reversal take place? Gutmann (1975) speculated that the different sex roles of men and women come about because of social or practical need, not because of biological differences. Sex role specialization, he conjectured, takes place in early parenthood as a result of pressures in taking care of children. The new mother must inhibit aggressive and competitive impulses that might detract from her nurturant care of the offspring. The father, on the other hand, must not express dependency needs or affiliative instincts; instead, he must show aggressiveness, authority, and an ability to achieve what is necessary. When the child grows up, however, both parents can revert to tendencies more true to their basic character. Older men can be more submissive and nurturant and older women can be more aggressive and competitive. In other words, men and women have

FIGURE 9.1: A family scene. (Figure copyright © by the Committee on Human Development, University of Chicago. Reprinted by permission of B. L. Neugarten and the Committee on Human Development.)

basically the same disposition, but parenthood and other demands of society make for sex-role differentiation.

This hypothesis may seem unlikely, yet an interesting study was carried out that gave it partial support. Feldman, Biringen, and Nash (1981) classified people according to their places in eight periods of the family life cycle—periods such as adolescence, parenting, empty nest, and grandparents. Each person was given a questionnaire of adjectives or short phrases that were either masculine or feminine in nature. Each person had to rate, from 1 to 7, how each of the items related to him or herself. The ratings were factor-analyzed (a mathematical technique designed to simplify the data by grouping the responses into several clusters) and nine factors or clusters were seen. These were investigated in relation to the eight periods of the life cycle.

This complex study was not in total support of Gutmann's speculation but supported it in part. For example, men, more than women, saw themselves as leaders. This self-description began in early adulthood and continued through life. At about the time of the empty nest, however, the two sexes were not as different as previously. Similarly, women saw themselves as more compassionate and tender than did the men and this was so through most of the periods of life. The two sexes, however, saw themselves equally tender during the married-childless stage and the grandparent stage. Grandfathers saw themselves as more compassionate and tender than the other men. Thus, as Gutmann suggested, the greatest sex difference occurred during active parenting. When the children grew up and left home, the two sexes saw themselves more similarly.

Not all the findings supported Gutmann's thinking; many sex differences were seen early in life that remained throughout. Sex role differentiation across the life span is an interesting area of research but little more than this is known about it as it includes older adults. It should be noted that even if more evidence becomes available indicating that men and women are most different through child-caring ages and least different during old age, a biological basis of this change cannot be ruled out.

WHAT PERSONALITY TESTS SHOW: NEW AND OLD STUDIES

Personality tests and questionnaires have been given to people of different ages in order to describe how they differ. The results of such studies have been contradictory and confusing for reasons in part having to do with experimental method. First, as will be described in great detail in Chapter 20, the simple comparison of two or more age-groups (i.e., cross-sectional studies) leaves the researcher unsure about whether differences between groups are due to maturational changes or to the different cultural influences of old and young. Schaie and Geiwitz (1982, p. 128) went so far as to say that with cross-sectional studies "we may . . . be wasting our time looking for age changes in personality." This is an overstatement if the goal of the research is limited to describing age differences in personality for whatever reason. It is not an overstatement if the goal bears on the issue of maturation versus culture, that is, the question of what young people today will be like when old. Probably no line of research can answer this question with real confidence.

Personality research has suffered from another more immediate problem. Results found in one study are not always found in another. This is partly because different experimental designs have been used and different age-groups have been tested, making for different questions being asked. The older personality studies were mainly cross-sectional. Some of the newer studies have been more sophisticated in utilizing a design called "cross-sequential" that is a combination cross-sectional and longitudinal study (see Chapter 20 for detailed description). To date there have been at least four such studies and, for the most part, these have shown that personality behaviors are remarkably stable across the adult life span. This is different from what many of the older, simpler cross-sectional studies have shown.

Cross-sequential Designs

The 16 PF. Three cross-sequential studies utilized part or all of a test called the 16 PF (short for 16 personality factors). This test is made up of a series of statements, each followed by three alternative choices. For example, one statement might be, "Money cannot bring happiness." The alternative choices might be yes (or true), no (or false), or sometimes (or occasionally). From the test answers, 16 personality traits are measured.

One cross-sequential study was by Schaie and Parham (1976), another by Costa and McCrae (1978), and a third by Siegler, George, and Okun (1979). A fourth study utilized a different test and this will be described shortly, but all of these four studies have this in common: People of wide age range were given the test once and then were given it again some 7 to 10 years afterwards. In each of the studies, the crucial test of age change or age stability rested largely, although not solely, on the difference between the scores at the first testing and those of the second, 7 to 10 years later. Each of the three PF studies ended with conclusions impressed more with the stability than the change in personality behaviors with age. Given that periods of the comparison were only 7 to 10 years, however, and that the people tested were of wide age range, this may not be very surprising.

Schaie and Parham divided adults aged 22 to 77 years into six-year groupings (e.g., 22–28, . . . , 71–77) and gave them parts of the 16 PF once and then again seven years later. Over the seven-year interval the whole group showed little change. Increased age was associated only with decreased excitability and decreased jealousness and suspiciousness. There was a greater "practical, down-to-earth mindedness."

This was the longitudinal part of the study. The cross-sectional part showed many differences between the age groupings, but these were not regarded as due to maturational differences. These differences were attributed to cultural differences. In accord with the longitudinal part, cross-sectionally, the older age-groups were less excitable than the younger ones and more practical. Opposite to the longitudinal data, however, the older people were more jealous and suspicious. Additional findings were that the older people were more outgoing, more internally restrained, conservative, and conscientious (ego-strength). They were more dependent on the group.

Costa and McCrae (1978) also utilized the 16 PF, but the ages of the people they tested were very different, as were the age groupings. Groups aged 25 to 40, 41 to 46, and 47+ were compared across two test periods, 10 years apart. Longitudinally, only one personality trait showed change: over the 10 years they became less dependent on the group. Schaie and Parham (1976) did not observe this longitudinally but found just the opposite cross-sectionally. Costa and McCrae did not find as many cross-sectional age differences in personality behaviors as did Schaie and Parham. In agreement with them, Costa and McCrae found increased conscientiousness with age, but in disagreement found increased liberal thinking (not conservatism as Schaie and Parham reported). Unlike Schaie and Parham, they found increased tendermindedness with age.

The observations of Siegler et al. (1979) were different still, but the age range of the people they tested was also very different. Siegler et al. had no one in their study younger than 46. Their age groupings were in two-year intervals, the youngest cohort was 46 to 47 and the oldest was 68 to 69. There were four test periods covering a span of approximately eight years.

Unlike Schaie and Parham, and Costa and McCrae, not a single difference among age-groups was observed, not cross-sectionally, not longitudinally. The test was the same even if there were some minor differences, but the age range of people tested was different, as were the age groupings. Can these have made for the differences in results? This unanswered question tells much regarding the confusion and conflicting results seen in these personality studies.

All these results taken together are confusing, perhaps reflecting the fact that if longitudinal data are required to answer questions of personality behavior change in later life, age comparisons greater than 7 to 10 years are required. Greater agreement in what constitutes appropriate age groupings would be helpful.

The older and simpler cross-sectional studies comparing very disparate age-groups were simpler to understand but were not without their own confusion. Sealy and Cattell (1965), and before them Cattell (1950), compared people of different ages on the 16 PF and found older adults were more sober, serious, and cautious in manner. Fozard (1972) found this too, but Botwinick and Storandt (1974, pp. 50–51) did not. Neither was this age pattern found in the cross-sequential studies.

The GZTS.   Douglas and Arenberg (1978) tested intellectually superior men ranging in age from the 20s to the 70s with the Guilford-Zimmerman Temperament Survey (GZTS). The men were divided in age decades, thus the 20s, 30s, . . . ,70s. Approximately seven years later they were tested again. The GZTS has 10 scales, each representing a different personality trait. In the longitudinal phase of the study, scores on 5 of the 10 scales showed change between the first testing and the second one but performances on only two of the scales were attributed to age (maturation); the others were attributed to cultural effects.

Douglas and Arenberg reported that on one trait scale, after age 50, there is a decrease in the pace of activity. There is a decrease in liking for action that "may sometimes be impulsive." The second trait scale involves interests people have that can be described as "masculine," and this showed decline. It would be of interest to discover whether masculinity in men truly decreases with age, or whether it is the need that young men may have to think of themselves in "macho" terms that changes with age.

The other three scales that showed longitudinal changes over the seven-year period were Friendliness (agreeableness), Thoughtfulness (introspective, evaluative thinking about the past), and Personal Relations (tolerance and cooperativeness). These declined over time. Douglas and Arenberg reported that the decline in Personal Relations reflects lessened trust and lessened inclination to think well of others and institutions. Schaie and Parham (1976), by contrast, found otherwise. They found that jealousy and suspicion decreased in their longitudinal analysis.

The decrease that Douglas and Arenberg found in the Thoughtfulness score with age seems to be at variance with Butler's notions of the "life review." It will be recalled that Butler believed that old people engage in this meditative process that helps resolve conflicts. The decrease Douglas and Arenberg reported reflects a lessened tendency to indulge in analytic and evaluative thinking.

Stability More Than Change.   In the main, the cross-sequential investigators were more impressed with the many traits that did not change with age than they were with the relatively few that did. In fact, Schaie and

Parham (1976, p. 157) concluded, "stability of personality traits [with age] is the rule rather than the exception." This conclusion is not unlike the one of Neugarten et al. (1964, p. 187) based on their cross-sectional research, that is, "personality type was independent of age."

Stability was seen in other ways. McCrae, Costa, and Arenberg (1980) had a third testing with the GZTS. The timing of the three test periods and the people who were available for each of them resulted in these three age-groups at the time of the first test: 17 to 44, 45 to 59, and 60 to 97 years (mean ages: 34, 52, and 70). The second testing was five to eight years after the first, and the third testing was on the average six to seven years afterwards. The purpose of this study was to determine the "constancy of personality structure." A separate factor analysis was carried out with the test scores of each of the three test sessions. Three factors were disclosed that were similar across the test sessions. This "invariance in personality structure across age groups" (p. 882) was taken as further evidence that personality does not change with age.

In another study based on these data, Costa et al. (1980) correlated each of the 10 GZTS scores across three periods of testing. The coefficients of correlation ranged from .59 to .87, indicating stability of personality of another sort. These coefficients suggest that a person relatively high in one trait when young will remain relatively high in that trait when older. This does not mean that there will not be decline or increase, it simply means relative standing in the group will remain stable.

Less impressive, perhaps, but still indicative of this type of stability was evidence seen by Siegler et al. (1979) in their 16 PF study. Correlation coefficients across the eight-year period of retests were about .50. Although this is not great, it is about the same order of magnitude as the reliability of the test itself (as determined by a one-week test–retest reliability test).

Taken together, these cross-sequential studies show change with age but they also show stability—stability of the sort that reflects maintenance of trait and also stability that reflects relative standing in the cohort across time.

Older, Cross-sectional Studies

Conformist and Passive Patterns. When Neugarten and Gutmann (1958) showed Figure 9.1 to their middle- and older-aged participants, they found that the latter—those mainly in their 60s—saw the young male in the figure as conformist and passive. The younger group—those mainly in their 40s—saw the young male figure as energetic, aggressive, and achieving.

There have been other TAT studies and, as reviewed by Chown (1968), the results were compatible with those of Neugarten and Gutmann. These studies showed that with increasing adult age there was a decreasing intensity and frequency of emotions. This seems similar to the decrease in excitability that Schaie and Parham reported. The studies also showed decreasing achievement needs, and decreasing feelings of mastery of the environment. Conformity and self-control were seen to be emphasized with increasing age, while self-indulgence was seen to be deplored. In some ways, this was also seen with the Edwards Personal Preference Schedule, an "objective" questionnaire (Gavron, 1965; Schaie & Strother, 1968; Spangler & Thomas, 1962).

Introversion. Chown (1968) reviewed studies dealing with tests of introversion-extraversion. Among these was a study by Gutman (1966), who gave the Maudsley Personality Inventory to people aged 17 to 94 years. He found that introversion increased with age. This was also found with a test devised by Heron given to a great number of people aged 20 to 80 years (Heron & Chown, 1967). An examination of the specific correlation coefficients between age and introversion, however, showed them to be extremely small, even though they were statistically significant. This indicates that, although there is a tendency for greater introversion as people become older, age alone does not account for it. Cross-sectional evidence for greater introversion of the old relative to the young was also found with the 16 PF (Sealy & Cattell, 1965), as well as with the Minnesota Multiphasic Personality Inventory (MMPI) (Calden & Hokanson, 1959; Slater & Scarr, 1964). Given the small correlations between age and introversion, and the results based on cross-sequential studies, these cross-sectional conclusions must be viewed as merely suggestive, certainly not definitive.

Depression. "Depression is the most frequent psychological difficulty encountered in the aged . . . at least one basic concomitant of successful aging is the ability to tolerate depression" (Zinberg & Kaufman, 1963, p. 66). Depression as measured by the MMPI depression scale often shows increases in later life (e.g., Botwinick & Thompson, 1967; Britton & Savage, 1966; Swenson, 1961). Again, however, not all studies show this (Botwinick & Storandt, 1974, p. 52).

Physical loss as well as the loss of a loved one can make for depression, but the depression seems to be less severe than found in clinical cases (Gallagher, Breckenridge, & Thompson, 1982). Busse (1961) indicated that although depression among the old is often due to loss, depression among the young is based more often on shame or guilt and on self-hate. The treatment programs for these two sources of depression are different. Busse and Pfeiffer (1969, p. 210) suggest that treatment programs for the aged who are mildly depressed be geared toward restoration of a feeling of self-worth. Their recommendation is that social engagement be encouraged.

Hypochondriasis. The three MMPI scales most likely to show increases with age form a logical unity: depression, introversion, and hypochondriasis. The latter trait can be described as an "anxious preoccupation with one's own body or a portion of one's own body which the patient believes to be either diseased or functioning improperly" (Busse & Pfeiffer, 1969, p. 202). Zinberg and Kaufman (1963, p. 52) maintain that depression and physical problems are so often related that "what comes first is very hard to determine." MMPI hypochondriasis has been reported by Calden and Hokanson (1959), Swenson (1961), and others. Hypochondriasis as seen in patient groups, at least, is more prevalent among women than men.

Busse and Pfeiffer see hypochondriasis as an escape from feelings of personal failure. The sick role may be easier to tolerate than the role of failure. The older person, for example, in losing a job through retirement when work was the sole interest, in losing social and financial security, and in finding no good replacements for them may find solace in the role of the sick person, even when there is no special incapacitation. It is unclear how prevalent hypochondriasis is in the general population of older adults, but it is clear that most old people are not impaired by bodily complaints that are basically mental in origin.

COPING WITH STRESS

McCrae (1982) carried out an interesting study testing two divergent sets of hypotheses. One set referred to Pfeiffer's 1977 contention that in coping with stress, older people tend to resort to "more primitive" defense mechanisms—"unmodified anxiety, depression-withdrawal, . . . denial . . ." (p. 651). On the other hand, Vaillant (1977) contended that in the course of development to at least middle age, more mature mechanisms are employed such as altruism, humor, and sublimation.

McCrae mailed out questionnaires and received replies from 150 men and women aged 21 to 90. Each person was asked to list three events in the past six months that were stressful. Each person was then given a list of 50 coping mechanisms with instructions to check the ones that had been used in dealing with the three stressful events.

McCrae concluded from the results of this study that, "In most respects older people . . . cope in much the same way as younger people; where they employ different mechanisms it appears largely to be a function of the different types of stress they face." When differences were found, it was that "older individuals were less inclined than younger men and women to rely on the theoretically immature mechanisms of hostile reactions and escapist fantasy" (1982, p. 459). Thus, it is seen that neither personality nor types of coping patterns change very much in old age.

SUMMARY

Some investigators are more impressed with the stability of personality through adulthood to old age than they are with the changes. Others might agree but point to some personality changes, indicating that they are due to socialization processes, not maturational or biological processes. Still others, however, are impressed with the similarity of changes among people with various life stages. To them, maturation plays a role in development, and this includes personality.

Stage theories imply a maturational basis for change because a true stage theory does not allow for an individual exception in any society, at any time. There is a progression from one stage to another that is universal and unidirectional. Cultural factors may speed up, slow down, or stop the progression, but do not change it. Stage theories as they include the older person have not been put to proper test. They may have merit, nevertheless, if they are thought of as adjustment theories, describing a mainstream pattern for many people in U.S. society, but not all people.

Most of these stage theories start with young people and their need to become independent of parents and to establish individual identities. Most theories point to a long midlife period, the first part of which is stable and oriented to family. There is a sense of responsibility to others and a sense of giving. Some theories focus on a subsequent period of personal reevaluation that involves turmoil and tumultuous struggle; this is the male midlife crisis. The data suggest, however, that this crisis is not an inevitable transition point for every man, and more, not all investigators even believe that most men experience the crisis. The end part of life, when successful, is seen as a period of reflection, an acceptance of reality and a continuance of adjustments necessary for contentment.

Most personality studies, particularly the older ones, are cross-sectional studies. One showed a change with age in time perspective. The young focus on time since birth, the old focus on time left to live. Women mark time by events in the family—marriage date, childbirth, children's graduation from school. Men more often mark time by occasions relating to career, for example, promotions, change of jobs.

In the course of development, people learn what is expected from them. They learn what behaviors are "proper" at one age but not another. Age norms are developed this way, but soon, these become age constraints. People are boxed in by what is expected and it becomes difficult to do what may be desired. Some investigators believe that this is changing so that more and more, age will not be a factor in what people do or what social roles they carry out.

Social roles are not only age-related, they are sex-related. Women are seen as nurturant and affiliative, men are seen as more competitive and aggressive. Cross-sectional studies show that these differences in the sex roles diminish in later life, and in one study, at least, men and women were seen reversing these roles when older. It has been suggested that men and women are not basically different in these ways but the demands and pressures of parenthood and career make such sex-role differentiation necessary. As children leave the home and the demands of parenting are no longer present, men and women revert to what is basic to their characters and thus become more similar. Avaialable research data are in partial support of this contention.

Cross-sectional studies have also shown that older people are more conformist and passive than younger people. The young are more energetic, aggressive, and adversarial. Cross-sectional studies have also shown that older people are more introverted, more depressed and, to an extent, more hypochondriacal than younger people. Despite these differences, coping mechanisms in stressful situations appear similar in old and young.

More recent studies have stemmed from dissatisfaction with cross-sectional methods for personality study. The more recent studies have been based on complex, cross-sequential designs, but they have been limited by the difficulty in accruing longitudinal data over many years. Each of the studies has been limited to age comparisons of only 7 to 10 years. These have shown more stability than change, but among the changes that have been noted are less excitability with age, a decrease in the pace of activity, and a decrease in taking impulsive actions. With age, more practical attitudes were seen.

REFERENCES

Botwinick, J., & Storandt, M. *Memory, related functions and age.* Springfield, Ill.: Charles C. Thomas, 1974.

Botwinick, J., & Thompson, L. W. Depressive affect, speed of response, and age. *Journal of Consulting Psychology,* 1967, *31,* 106.

Britton, P. G., & Savage, R. D. The MMPI and the aged: Some normative data from a community sample. *British Journal of Psychiatry,* 1966, *112,* 941–943.

Busse, E. W. Psychoneurotic reactions and defense mechanisms in the aged. In P. H. Hock & J. Zubin (Eds.), *Psychopathology of aging.* New York: Grune & Stratton, 1961.

Busse, E. W., & Pfeiffer, E. Functional psychiatric disorders in old age. In E. W. Busse & E. Pfeiffer (Eds.), *Behavior adaptation in late life.* Boston: Little, Brown, 1969.

Butler, R. N. *Why survive? Being old in America.* New York: Harper & Row, 1975.

Butler, R. N., & Lewis, M. I. *Aging and mental health.* St. Louis: C. V. Mosby, 1973.

Calden, G., & Hokanson, J. E. The influence of age on MMPI responses. *Journal of Clinical Psychology,* 1959, *15,* 194–195.

Cattell, R. B. *Personality: A systematic, theoretical, and factual study.* New York: McGraw Hill, 1950.

Chown, S. M. Personality and aging. In K. W. Schaie (Ed.), *Theory and method of research on aging.* Morgantown, West Va.: West Virginia University, 1968, pp. 134–157.

Costa, P. T., & McCrae, R. R. Objective personality assessment. In M. Storandt, I. C. Siegler, & M. F. Elias (Eds.), *The clinical psychology of aging.* New York: Plenum Press, 1978, pp. 119–143.

Costa, P. T., & McCrae, R. R. Still stable after all these years: Personality as a key to some issues in adulthood and old age. In P. B. Baltes & O. G. Brim (Eds.), *Life-span development and behavior.* New York: Academic Press, 1980, pp. 65–102.

Costa, P. T., McCrae, R. R., & Arenberg, D. Enduring dispositions in adult males. *Journal of Personality and Social Psychology,* 1980, 38, 793–800.

Douglas, K., & Arenberg, D. Age changes, cohort differences, and cultural change on the Guilford-Zimmerman Temperament Survey. *Journal of Gerontology,* 1978, 33, 737–747.

Erikson, E. H. *Childhood and society* (2nd ed.). New York: W. W. Norton, 1963.

Feldman, S. S., Biringen, Z. C., & Nash, S. C. Fluctuations of sex-related self-attributions as a function of stage of family life cycle. *Developmental Psychology,* 1981, 17, 24–35.

Fozard, J. L. Predicting age in the adult years from psychological assessments of abilities and personality. *Aging and Human Development,* 1972, 3, 175–182.

Gallagher, D., Breckenridge, J. N., & Thompson, L. W. Similarities and differences between normal grief and depression in older adults. *Essence,* 1982, 5, 127–140.

Gavron, E. F. Changes in Edwards Personal Preference Schedule needs with age and psychiatric status. *Journal of Clinical Psychology,* 1965, 21, 194–196.

Gould, R. Adult life stages: Growth toward self-tolerance. *Psychology Today,* 1975, 8, 74–78.

Gould, R. *Transformations: Growth and change in adult life.* New York: Simon & Schuster, 1978.

Gutman, G. M. A note on the MMPI: Age and sex differences in extroversion and neuroticism in a Canadian sample. *British Journal of Social and Clinical Psychology,* 1966, 5, 128–129.

Gutmann, D. Parenthood: A key to the comparative study of the life cycle. In N. Datan & L. H. Ginsberg (Eds.), *Life-span developmental psychology.* New York: Academic Press, 1975, pp. 167–184.

Havighurst, R. J. *Developmental tasks and education* (3rd ed.). New York: David McKay, 1972.

Heron, A., & Chown, S. M. *Age and function.* London: Churchill, 1967.

Kohlberg, L. Continuities in childhood and adult moral development revisited. In P. B. Baltes & K. W. Schaie (Eds.), *Life-span developmental psychology.* New York: Academic Press, 1973, pp. 179–204.

Levinson, D. J., Darrow, C. N., Klein, E. B., Levinson, M. H. & McKee, B. *Midlife Crisis.* New York: Ballantine Books, 1978.

McCrae, R. R. Age differences in the use of coping mechanisms. *Journal of Gerontology,* 1982, 37, 454–460.

McCrae, R. R., Costa, P. T., & Arenberg, D. Constancy of adult personality structures in males: Longitudinal, cross-sectional and time of measurement analyses. *Journal of Gerontology,* 1980, 35, 877–883.

Neugarten, B. L. The awareness of middle age. In B. L. Neugarten (Ed.), *Middle age and aging.* Chicago: University of Chicago Press, 1968, pp. 93–98. (a)

Neugarten, B. L. Adult personality: Toward a psychology of the life cycle. In B. L. Neugarten (Ed.), *Middle age and aging.* Chicago: University of Chicago Press, 1968, 137–147. (b)

Neugarten, B. L. Crotty, W. F., & Tobin, S. S. Personality in middle and late life. New York: Atherton Press, 1964.

Neugarten, B. L., & Gutmann, D. L. Age-sex roles and personality in middle age: A thematic apperception study. *Psychological Monographs: General and Applied*, 1958, 17, Whole No. 470.

Neugarten, B. L., & Hagestad, G. O. Age and the life course. In R. H. Binstock & E. Shanas (Eds.), *Handbook of aging and the social sciences*. New York: Van Nostrand Reinhold, 1976, pp. 35–55.

Neugarten, B. L., Moore, J. W., & Lowe, J. C. Age norms, age constraints and adult socialization. *American Journal of Sociology*, 1965, 70, 710–717.

Pfeiffer, E. Psychopathology and social pathology. In J. E. Birren & K. W. Schaie (Eds.), *Handbook of the psychology of aging*. New York: Van Nostrand Reinhold, 1977, pp. 650–671.

Piaget, J. Piaget's theory. IN P. H. Mussen (Ed.), *Carmichael's manual of child psychology* (3rd ed.). New York: Wiley, 1970.

Reichard, S., Livson, P., & Peterson, P. G. *Aging and personality*. New York: Wiley, 1962.

Riley, M. W., Johnson, M., & Foner, A. *Aging and society: a sociology of age stratification*. New York: Russell Sage, 1972.

Schaie, K. W. Toward a stage theory of adult cognitive development. *Journal of Aging and Human Development*, 1977, 8, 129–138.

Schaie, K. W., & Geiwitz, J. *Adult development and aging*. Boston: Little, Brown, 1982.

Schaie, K. W., & Parham, I. A. Stability of adult personality traits: Fact or fable? *Journal of Personality and Social Psychology*, 1976, 34, 146–158.

Schaie, K. W., & Strother, C. R. Cognitive and personality variables in college graduates of advanced age. In G. A. Talland (Ed.), *Human behavior and aging: Recent advances in research and theory*. New York: Academic Press, 1968.

Sealy, A. P., & Cattell, R. B. Standard trends in personality development in men and women of 16 to 70 years, determined by 16 PF measurements. Paper read at British Psychological Society Conference, April 1965.

Siegler, I. C., George, L, K., & Okun, M. A. Cross-sequential analysis of adult personality. *Developmental Psychology*, 1979, 15, 350–351.

Slater, P. E., & Scarr, H. A. Personality in old age. *Genetic Psychological Monographs*, 1964, 70, 229–269.

Spangler, D. P., & Thomas, C. W. The effects of age, sex and physical disability upon manifest needs. *Journal of Counseling Psychology*, 1962, 9, 313–319.

Swenson, W. M. Structured personality testing in the aged: An MMPI study of the gerontic population. *Journal of Clinical Psychology*, 1961, 17, 302–304.

Vaillant, G. E. *Adaptation to life*. Boston: Little, Brown, 1977.

Zinberg, N. E., & Kaufman, I. Cultural and personality factors associated with aging: An introduction. In N. Zinberg & I. Kaufman (Eds.), *Normal psychology of the aging process*. New York: International Universities Press, 1963.

10
Cautious Behavior

There is a persistent belief that increasing age makes for increasing cautiousness or conservatism. There are research data in support of this belief, but there are also data indicating otherwise. Even when the aged are seen as more cautious, there are those who believe that "the differences between means of age groups are frequently so slight and individual differences so great that these age trends may have little practical significance" (Pressey & Kuhlen, 1957, p. 405). There are many types of cautiousness and many contexts. Some of these reflect a relationship between age and cautiousness and some do not. Those that do may indicate the areas where older people seem to feel vulnerable.

CAREFULNESS

Some of the studies resorted to the concept of cautiousness in *post hoc* explanation of data collected for other purposes. Other studies, however, investigated cautiousness directly. One hypothesis derived from these studies is that for a variety of reasons, older adults as a group experience a loss of self-confidence. There is the expectation or fear of failure and possibly rejection. These threatening consequences inhibit venturesome behavior and result in cautiousness. This confidence hypothesis, as will be seen, requires further test.

Valuing Accuracy

The old are thought to be cautious in the avoidance of mistakes, valuing accuracy over speed. This was seen in a psychomotor study by Welford (1951) where "the subjects in their thirties appeared to maintain the speed of those in their twenties, but at the expense of accuracy. From the forties onwards accuracy was restored at the expense of speed."

Although these results are interpretable in the framework of cautiousness, Welford did not prefer to do so. In fact, he brought up the concept of cautiousness in order to refute it; he believed the determining characteristics of the slowing in performance of the elderly were not volitional. Welford suggested that the slowing in behavior, even if related to increased accuracy, was due, not to a preference, but to limitations in perceptual mechanisms and in translation mechanisms that control movement (Welford, 1958). More recent studies bearing on this issue are described in Chapter 13.

The unsettled controversy, therefore, is whether aged people are purposefully slower than need be in order to achieve more accuracy, or whether accuracy is simply a by-product of slowing biopsychological mechanisms. This controversy has been cast in terms of a *motivation hypothesis* in the case of purposeful slowing, versus a *consequence hypothesis* in the case of the slowing mechanism position (Botwinick, 1959, p. 763). It is to be noted that, whichever hypothesis is more correct or explains more of the data, the accuracy of the elderly is often greater than that of the young only in a relative sense. Often, as in Welford's (1951) study, the younger people are both more speedy and more accurate despite the speed–accuracy trade-off. Sometimes, however, the older people are more accurate in an absolute sense.

Avoidance of Mistakes: The Omission Error

In a wide variety of contexts—in learning studies, perception studies, tests of intelligence—the older person often makes a characteristic error: The older person fails to respond. The older person gets marked wrong for not answering the question, sometimes more often than answering it incorrectly. Perhaps the older person chooses to not respond when unsure of the answer even if it can be offered. This is called the omission error. Even with instructions to guess, even when encouraged to respond quickly and not worry about being wrong, the inclination of the older person to make the omission error is strong.

An early empirical demonstration of this phenomenon was seen in the classic 1928 publication, *Adult Learning*, by Thorndike, Bregman, Tilton, and Woodyard (pp. 171–172):

> We have also compared old with young . . . in respect of the proportion which omitted elements are of omitted plus wrong. If age is accompanied by an increase in caution or a decrease in impulsiveness in intellectual operations the old would be expected to write no answer rather than a wrong answer oftener than the young. . . . There are many irregularities, but the general influence of age is clearly toward a substantial increase in the percent which the number of omissions is of the number of wrongs.

Thorndike et al. demonstrated the propensity of the aged to the omission error in the course of intelligence testing. The omission error by the aged has been seen in other situations as well. In learning studies, for example, Korchin and Basowitz (1957) demonstrated it with paired-associate procedures, and Eisdorfer, Axelrod, and Wilkie (1963) with serial learning procedures. The omission error has been seen many times over the years. It has been seen in perceptual studies but as reported by Basowitz and Korchin (1957), not in all contexts. This suggests that the generalization regarding the omission error and age must be referred to specific procedures or operations.

Basowitz and Korchin (1957) presented two tasks to old and young people. In one, the Gestalt Completion Test, the main ability tested was perceptual integration of fragmented parts of pictures. The task was to put together in one's mind the parts of the pictures that have been presented in a mixed pattern. In this task, the omission error by the elderly was prominent. In the second task, Concealed Figures, the error was not prominent. The ability tested here was to identify a simple figure embedded in a complex background that masks it. It is possible that in this study the instructions to the test-takers and the requirements of the task were such as to minimize the omission error. The test-taker simply had to specify whether he or she could identify the figure. It was not necessary to trace it out or to make perceptual decisions. As will be seen later, instructions that are structured to minimize ambiguity, minimize cautious omission errors among the elderly.

Confidence in Responding

If older people are characterized by the omission error, one hypothesis to account for this is that they require more certainty from a situation before venturing a response, possibly because they lack confidence in themselves. Without certainty there is a greater chance of failure. The omission error may stem from just such a desire for more certainty—better not respond than be wrong. It staves off failure and maximizes self-esteem.

Need for Certainty. Basowitz and Korchin (1957, p. 96) in their perception study concluded that with increased age there is "the need for a high degree of certainty before committing oneself." In their learning study, Korchin and Basowitz (1957, p. 68) concluded: "Despite the injunction to guess, it may be that older persons require greater certainty before they are willing to report. . . . This tendency to inhibit response in the uncertain situation may reflect a more profound personality defense of the aged through which the recognition of inadequacy is avoided." The need for greater confidence can stem from a lack of self-confidence.

The need for certainty was also suggested in a very different type of study. Adults of two diverse ages were compared in their judgments as to which of two vertical bars was the shorter (Botwinick, Brinley, & Robbin,

1958). The two bars were presented simultaneously; sometimes the difference in their length was great and easy to distinguish, sometimes it was small and difficult to distinguish. For all practical purposes, there was no time limit to view the two bars. The older people were generally slower than the young in making the judgments, and this was more so with the difficult discriminations than with the easy ones.

Following this, both the old and young adults were obliged to make their judgments more quickly by the simple expedient of reducing the time allowed for viewing the two bars: they were shown the bars for only a fraction of a second. People of both age-groups made their judgments more quickly than before, but the improvement in speed of response was greatest among the older people with the difficult discriminations. The old people were slowest when they had a long time to make the difficult judgments; their speed improved greatly in judging these very same bars when they were pushed to be quicker by the experimental procedure. These findings suggested that: "It is as if the older person takes a longer time with the difficult discrimination when he has this time to take, but relative to his ability to discriminate correctly, the older person may not require this added time" (Botwinick et al., 1958, p. 6). This extra time can be thought to reflect the need on the part of the older people for greater certainty—perhaps a need for greater confidence in being correct before responding. This conclusion is similar to those involving the omission error. Older people seem to want more certainty or want more confidence in being correct before venturing a response.

In a follow-up of these discrimination studies, Silverman (1963) put the confidence hypothesis to a more direct test. He matched two adult age-groups in their ability to recognize words shown for very brief exposures. His matching of age-groups was based on their performances under instructions that forced a response, that is, each person had to guess the word, if necessary. Silverman then compared the two age-groups in their responses when they were under instructions to be "sure they had recognized it . . . to say nothing at all and wait for the next word if they were not sure" (p. 372).

In the matching procedure, Silverman obliged response regardless of whether the person felt sure and wanted to respond. Choosing young and old adults who performed equally well, and then giving them the opportunity to respond only when sure, the confidence hypothesis was considered confirmed if the older group gave fewer responses than the younger group. The older group did give fewer responses.*

---

*Silverman considered the hypothesis only partially confirmed because the level of statistically significant age differences was not great ($p < .10$). The t-value was 1.99 with 22 subjects in each age-group. A one-tailed test of significance would be appropriate in this case; had Silverman carried out such a test, his results would show statistically significant age differences at less than the .05 level.

Self-ratings. A lack of self-confidence is but one hypothesis that might account for a desire on the part of older people for more certainty before responding. There are other hypotheses, of course, but none have really been put to proper test. A few studies, however, bore on the confidence hypothesis with negative or equivocal results.

Elderly and young adults were asked to rate themselves with respect to their self-confidence in responding to two types of questionnaires (Botwinick, 1970). In one situation no knowledge or information was required; in the other, information was involved but it was not ordinarily available to the responder, nor was it essential for response. Confidence might be a more important factor when information is involved than when it is not.

The no-information questionnaire was a true-false version of the 60-item Depression scale (D-scale) of the Personality test, MMPI (Hathaway & McKinley, 1956). Each item was answered true or false and, in addition, checked on a four-point scale going from "extremely confident" to "not at all confident" in the response. In similar fashion, 24 items of the information questionnaire* were checked on a four-point scale, going from "nearly certain" to "very uncertain."

The results of this study were not at all in accord with the expectation that the old adults would show themselves as less self-confident than the young adults. In the questionnaire involving information, old and young adults were similar in their declared levels of self-confidence. In the questionnaire not involving such information, the two age-groups were different, but it was the younger group, not the older, that declared itself to have less confidence.

These data, then, do not lend support to the idea that older adults lack confidence, and so they do not lend support to the hypothesis that this is the basis of their cautious behavior. There are two considerations, however, that need to be examined before rejecting the hypothesis. First, it is conceivable that questions and answers regarding self-confidence do not reflect the true facts. Conceivably, conscious responses may reflect the opposite. They may reflect an effort to minimize or even deny a loss or lack of confidence in oneself. Second, in not all contexts do older people demonstrate cautious

---

*The questionnaire was a slightly modified version of the "Band-Width" procedure used by Wallach and Kogan (1965, pp. 112–115), which was based upon "The Category Width Scale" of Pettigrew (1958).

Each item of this questionnaire started with a declarative statement, as, for example, "Most men in the world are around five feet, seven inches tall." One part asked a question regarding the maximum dimension (fastest, longest, most) and the second part asked a question regarding a minimum dimension. In the example given, the first part asked, "How tall is the tallest man in the world?" The second part asked, "How short is the shortest man in the world?"

behavior. Perhaps it is not to be expected, therefore, that in all contexts will they demonstrate a lack of confidence.

Estimating Success. A very different study also failed to support the confidence idea. Young adults and two different age-groups of older ones were given lists of words to learn. Before starting, they were shown examples of the words and asked to predict the number of them they would be able to learn (Bruce, Coyne, & Botwinick, 1982). If the older people had been less confident than the younger ones, or more cautious for whatever the reason, it would have been reasonable for them to predict learning fewer words. They did predict learning fewer words than the younger people, but not so much fewer that the age-groups were significantly different in this. For all practical purposes, therefore, the old and young predicted learning a similar number of words but the fact is that the old actually learned fewer words. Thus, the old might have been well advised to be less confident, but they were not. No less confidence was also suggested when both old and young were given as much time to study the words as they wanted. The old did not take any more time to study the words than did the young despite their poorer learning performances.

This study, then, again questioned the adequacy of the confidence hypothesis. Together with the study described previously involving self-ratings, this one suggests that the confidence hypothesis is either not correct or incomplete. It is possible that older people do tend to require more confidence in being correct before venturing a specific response to a specific test item (as suggested in the several studies described before), but they may not lack confidence once a response is made (as seen in the self-rating study) or when undertaking a task (as seen in the learning study). A questionnaire study on risk, described later, also indicates that older adults seem to exercise caution in venturing a response to a specific situation when they have the opportunity to do so.

Minimizing the Omission Error

If the older person knows the answer to a question or can make a good guess of the answer but is unwilling to provide it because of a desire for more certainty, then the older person will score less well on tests than a younger person who requires less certainty. Several studies were designed with this thinking, with efforts made to induce the older person to take a chance on being wrong, if necessary.

Birkhill and Schaie (1975) noted what Thorndike et al. (1928) did, *viz.*, older adults taking intelligence tests often leave out answers. Birkhill and Schaie gave an intelligence test called the Primary Mental Abilities. Their study was complicated, but it can be simplified for present purposes in focusing on two of their four groups of older people. Money reward was given for correct answers but money was lost by the test-takers for incorrect responses and for omission errors. They made the rewards and losses for one group such that the omission error became very costly. For another group, the omission error cost little and, therefore, could be made comfortably. Birkhill and Schaie reported that the scores of the old people taking the tests were higher when they were induced to forgo the omission error because it was unrewarding to do so. The implication is that when omission errors are noted, it does not necessarily mean the person does not know the correct answer or has no idea of it.

A study with a similar idea was based on the learning of paired associates. With one group of older people Leech and Witte (1971) used the standard procedure of rewarding only the correct response. Another group was rewarded for all responses, right or wrong. The reward was money; more was given for the correct response than the wrong one, but no money at all was given for the omission error. Again, the inducement to forgo the omission error resulted in better performance.

A version of this study was attempted by Erber, Feely, and Botwinick (1980) with mixed results. The basic finding of Leech and Witte was observed with older people of lower socioeconomic status (SES) but not higher SES. The higher SES group approached the experimental learning task with less of a tendency to make the omission error and thus, perhaps, the monetary reward was not effective with this group for this reason. The learning task was made more difficult in a subsequent study and a larger money reward was given. This study again failed to show better performances with the inducement to minimize the omission error (Erber and Botwinick, 1983).

Structure and Direction

Clear directions and highly structured tasks minimize differences among age-groups in their performances. Korchin and Basowitz (1956) presented young and elderly adults with a series of 13 pictures, the first of which was a cat that, with successive changes in the picture series, gradually became a dog. The greatest ambiguity of percept, that is, dog or cat, was found in the middle pictures in the series. A sample of this picture may be seen in Figure 10.1.

When Korchin and Basowitz presented this cat–dog series, they found that older adults tended to shift from cat to dog later in the series than did the young adults. Moreover, they tended to vacillate more from dog to cat

FIGURE 10.1: A series of 13 pictures was shown to each person, one picture at a time. Each picture was a combination of a cat and a dog, with the first picture in the series being most clearly a cat and the last picture in the series being most clearly a dog. The middle pictures in the series were the most ambiguous, being about as much cat as dog. Pictures 1, 7, and 13 in the series are presented here. (From "The Judgment of Ambiguous Stimuli as an Index of Cognitive Functioning in Aging," by Sheldon J. Korchin and Harold Basowitz, in *Journal of Personality* 25, 81–95, copyright 1956 by Duke University Press. Figure 1 on p. 84.)

in the successive pictures. The older people could be said to be cautious in modifying their percept to dog.

A subsequent similar study was carried out, but with a variation of the procedure (Botwinick, 1962). The variation in procedure led to a variation of results, once again emphasizing the importance of specifying the conditions of measurement. The same cat–dog series was presented to young and old adults, and, in addition, a 22-picture series of a triangle merging into a circle was given. In this study, the shift was made *earlier* in the series by the older people than by the younger.

The task in the latter study was more structured than that in the Korchin–Basowitz study and the directions were less ambiguous. In the Botwinick study, uncertainty was minimal. When Korchin and Basowitz showed the pictures they asked, "Is it more like a cat or more like a dog?" The older people vacillated back and forth and then made the final shift late in the series. When Botwinick showed the pictures, the need to shift was clearly emphasized; the beginning and end points of the series were shown at the start of the experiment. Opportunity to vacillate back to initial percepts was not given since the experiment was terminated with the first shift.

This suggested that, given appropriate structure and direction rather than an opportunity to determine structure and direction by oneself, the older person will perform with minimum difficulty. This was seen also in a cognitive task rather than a perceptual one. Brinley (1965) tested old and young people in a series of cognitive tasks, some of which required shifting from one operation to another. The tasks were given with three different instructions: the person (1) had to discover what was required (least structured); (2) needed to keep in mind a sequence of instructions; and (3) was told explicitly what the test required (most stuctured). Again, the older people performed most adequately in the structured situation and less well in the unstructured one.

DECIDING ALTERNATIVES

Wallach and Kogan (1961) gave an interesting questionnaire to young and elderly adults. This questionnaire consisted of 12 "life situations," each one involving a central character who faced a decision. The decision was whether to embark on a course of action that, if successful, would bring much gain, but if not successful, would result in serious loss. Each person responding to the questionnaire reviewed the 12 "life situations" and advised the central character in the decisions. The advice revealed gambling propensities since the decision was made on the basis of the probability of success deemed necessary to take the action.

The first item of the 12 is presented as an example of the questionnaire.

(1) Mr. A, an electrical engineer who is married and has one child, has been working for a large electronics corporation since graduating from college five years ago. He is assured of a lifetime job with a modest, though adequate, salary, and liberal pension benefits upon retirement. On the other hand, it is

very unlikely that his salary will increase much before he retires. While attending a convention, Mr. A is offered a job with a small, newly founded company with a highly uncertain future. The new job would pay more to start and would offer the possibility of a share in the ownership if the company survived the competition of the larger firms.

Imagine that you are advising Mr. A. Listed below are several probabilities or odds of the new company's proving financially sound. *Please check the lowest probability that you would consider acceptable to make it worthwhile for Mr. A to take the new job.*

—— The chances are 1 in 10 that the company will prove financially sound.

—— The chances are 3 in 10 that the company will prove financially sound.

—— The chances are 5 in 10 that the company will prove financially sound.

—— The chances are 7 in 10 that the company will prove financially sound.

—— The chances are 9 in 10 that the company will prove financially sound.

—— Place a check here if you think Mr. A should *not* take the new job no matter what the probabilities.

Eleven other situations were presented, each in the same manner as the first one. Each was scored on the basis of the probability of success deemed necessary to take the indicated action: A score of 9 (chances in 10) represents a conservative decision—a requirement of high likelihood that the action would lead to success. A most incautious person would be scored as 1 (chance in 10 of succeeding). Refusal to advise the risky alternative regardless of its probability of success was scored as 10 (chances in 10). The higher the score, the less risk is indicated in the choice and the more cautious the responder is taken to be.

Older People Are More Cautious Than Younger People

Wallach and Kogan (1961) compared young men with older men, and young women with older women in regard to cautiousness. In both comparisons, the older group was seen as the more cautious. The analysis focused on the content of the "life situations." Both older men and women seemed to be especially cautious in decisions involving financial matters. Not surprisingly, perhaps, for them the lure of substantial financial gain was not worth the possible loss of money-in-hand. Some of the 12 "life situations" reflected cautiousness in later life in one of the sexes, rather than in both. Wallach and Kogan reported that the older men seemed more cautious than the younger men in items dealing with professional failure and with death. Older women were more cautious than younger women in items concerning defeat in a game and in unsuccessful marriage. With the possible exception of the risk-of-death item differentiating only males, and the peculiarity of the game situation differentiating the females, Wallach and Kogan suggested the results were in accord with cultural expectation.

Different Problems for Young and Old

A perusal of the 12 "life situations" indicated that they mostly involve problems and activities of young adults. The central characters go into new business ventures, play football, apply to graduate schools, marry. Although some of these are activities elderly people engage in too, for the most part they typify concerns of young adults. To offset this, an investigation was carried out with "life situations" about aged central characters facing problems representative of their own age-group. Would aging patterns in cautiousness be exacerbated when problems and consequences were tied more intimately to their circumstances?

In addition to the 12 "life situations" of Wallach and Kogan (1961), 12 others were written about aged people (Botwinick, 1966). A total of 24 situations were thus available, making a 24-item questionnaire. As before, each of the items called for a decision based upon a desired probability of outcome before venturing a risk: the higher the desired probability, the more cautious the responder was considered to be.

Needs, Problems, and Cultural Determination. Cautiousness was investigated in relation to the age and sex of the respondents, and also their level of education as a crude index of socioeconomic status. The different "life situations" of the young and aged central characters were taken as reflecting needs and problems of their respective generations (Botwinick, 1966).

The basic result of Wallach and Kogan (1961) was again seen in this study. The older adults responded in a more cautious manner than the younger adults; they seemed to want more assurance that the outcome would be favorable before recommending an action. Men and women were not very different in their levels and patterns of cautiousness. Neither were the education groups different in levels of cautiousness, but their patterns were different with respect to the 24 "life situations." This suggested that socioeconomic factors may determine the specific approaches to various problems, but not the overall extent of cautiousness.

A cultural role may be indicated in regard to aging. When elderly people in Botwinick's study were compared with those in Wallach and Kogan's, cautiousness was demonstrated by way of different "life situations." Since Wallach and Kogan investigated people mostly from eastern Massachusetts and Botwinick examined people mostly from central North Carolina, it was suggested that the cautiousness in later life may be manifest in culturally different contexts.

Disinclination to Risk. It will be recalled that each respondent decided whether to embark upon a course of action in each of 24 "life situations," and was characterized by the average of these 24 decisions (1, 3, 5, 7, 9, or 10 chances in 10). A different method of analysis was also made. Rather than comparing groups on the basis of these average probability levels, comparisons were made on the basis of the number of times each probability level was chosen. For example, one person might have chosen 1 one time; 3 two times, 5, 7, and 9 five times each; and 10 six times. The combined total of these for each respondent was 24, the number of "life situations."

Figure 10.2 shows the number of times each probability level was chosen by age, sex, and education groups. Perhaps the most prominent feature in Figure 10.2 is the tendency of elderly adults to choose the number 10 alternative—the alternative that does not advise risk regardless of the likelihood of the success in the outcome. This tendency is clearly apparent in each of the three education groups of men and in the middle education grouping of women. *

Why do elderly people, possibly men more than women, shy away from risky courses of action regardless of their likelihood of success? It was suggested that older people either "were disinclined toward making decisions and taking actions, or they were more willing than the young Ss [people] to continue with involvements which were far from ideal (or both of these)" (Botwinick, 1966, p. 352).

RELUCTANCE TO ACT VERSUS CAUTIOUSNESS

A distinction may be made between two types of cautiousness: one takes the form of a reluctance to make decisions and to act, and the other takes the form of behaviors that minimize risk even if it means minimizing potential gain. Is the number 10 alternative a very cautious response that minimizes risk to nearly zero, or is it something else—a reluctance to decide or to act, to be involved? In other words, is the number 10 alternative on a quantitative continuum with the other choices involving risk, or is choice of the number 10 alternative a qualitatively different phenomenon?

*Older women with college degrees tended less to the number 10 alternative than did the less well educated older women. This was seen with highly educated men also, but they did resort to the number 10 alternative more than did the younger men ($p < .05$). The age comparison for women of the lowest education group was based on a very small number of elderly women. Perhaps this comparison would best not be given serious attention.

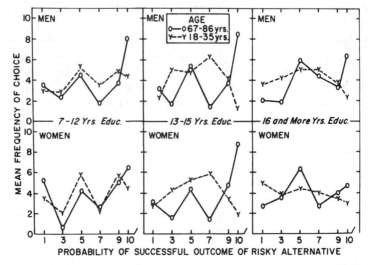

FIGURE 10.2: Mean frequency of choice among six alternatives in the decisions of young and elderly adults. Abscissa values are ordered fom lesser to greater cautiousness. Alternative "1" represents a decision to follow a course of action which has a low likelihood of success. There are rewards if it does succeed, but there are negative consequences if it does not. Alternative 9 is to follow this course only if there is a high likelihood of its success. Alternatives 3, 5, and 7 are middle-value alternatives. Alternative 10 is not to follow the course of action regardless of the likelihood of success. (From Botwinick, 1966, Figure 1. Reprinted by permission of the *Journal of Gerontology*, Vol. 21, pp. 347–353, 1966.)

When Risk Cannot Be Avoided

An attempt to answer this question was made by repeating the previous, 1966 study, except that the number 10 alternative was left out altogether (Botwinick, 1969). The thinking was that, if the choice of the number 10 alternative was a very cautious response and quantitatively on the same continuum as the others, then when not available, the respondent would simply go to the next most cautious option, that is, the choice recommending action only if there are 9 chances out of 10 that success would be the outcome. On the other hand, if the number 10 alternative was qualitatively different from the others, then the respondent would be faced with a different problem and might choose any of the options.

The same 24-situation questionnaire was given to two age and sex groups, and this time only to the more highly educated groups (i.e., 13–15 and 16-and-more years of education, not the 7–12 year group). The results were very different in this study than they were in the studies by Wallach and Kogan (1961) and Botwinick (1966). Age differences in cautiousness were not seen at all! The implication is quite clear: In the earlier studies, the cautiousness on the part of the elderly probably was due more to their avoidance of risk situations than to their gambling propensities when risk could not be avoided.

Avoidance of Risk

Two Studies Compared.   Some of the older people tested in this latter study were the same ones tested in the earlier study, some 23 to 40 months previously. Figure 10.3 provides the two sets of results: the dashed line in the figure shows the percentage (of 24 opportunities) each alternative was chosen when risk was unavoidable (Botwinick, 1969). The solid line shows the percentage when risk was avoidable by resorting to the number 10 alternative (Botwinick, 1966).

The same people, responding in both situations, chose the option to not venture risk regardless of the probabilities in nearly 30 percent of the

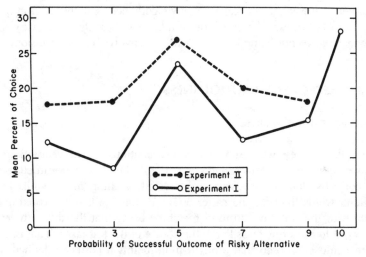

FIGURE 10.3: The same questionnaire of 24 "life situations," with one difference, was presented to elderly persons on two occasions, designated here as Experiment I and Experiment II. The one difference was that in Experiment I, six alternative choices for each situation were available, with the choice labeled 10 on the abscissa being one to avoid risk regardless of the probabilities of successful outcome. In Experiment II, this alternative was not available, leaving only five possibilities to choose among, with alternative 9 being the most cautious response and alternative 1 being the most risky. When alternative 10 was available, near 30 percent of the choices were for this option. When it was not available, alternative 5 was the most common choice, not 9. This suggested that gambling propensities of the elderly are similar to those of young. (Figure 1 from Botwinick, 1969. Permission to reprint this figure was given by the *Journal of Genetic Psychology*.)

occasions, but, when not permitted this option, rather than go to the next most cautious one (alternative 9), they tended to choose the middle levels of cautiousness. These middle levels were similar to those young people selected, both when the number 10 alternative was available and when it was not.

Disengagement. Why did the elderly seem to avoid making decisions when it was possible for them to do so? It is interesting to speculate. The studies on perception and learning described before were interpreted in terms of older people requiring a higher "confidence level . . . before responding" (Botwinick, et al., 1958), "a defensive reluctance to venture response for fear of recognizing their inadequacy" (Basowitz & Korchin, 1957, p. 96), and an "increase in overall anxiety . . . [which] may result in withdrawal from the situation" (Eisdorfer, 1965, p. 22). In each of these studies the older people either responded with latencies much longer than seemed necessary or did not respond at all. The choice of the number 10 alternative (no decision of risk) may be analogous to these in that it may represent some form of omission pattern.

The omission pattern seems related to disengagement, as discussed in Chapter 5. For whatever reason, many elderly people withdraw from people and from activities. Choice of the number 10 alternative is an easy way of disengaging, of not being bothered with the involvement of decision.

MANY ASPECTS OF CAUTIOUSNESS

Wisdom in Cautiousness

A vocabulary test was used to measure cautiousness in decision making among the elderly (Okun & Di Vesta, 1976). The test-taker earned "points" by correctly defining the words of the test, earning more points for the difficult words than for the easier ones. All the words were graded in difficulty with the unique feature of the study being that the difficulty level of the word to be defined was left to the choice of the test-taker. That is, a hard word could be chosen that brought more points if correctly defined, or an easy one could be chosen that brought fewer points. Obviously there was more risk of failure in the choice of the hard word with the big point payoff.

In this study, there was no rational basis for choosing either a hard word or an easy one since the experimenter manipulated the points so that one strategy was as likely to be successful as another. In this uncertain situation the elderly again were more cautious. They tended to choose easier words while younger adults tended to choose more difficult ones.

A second study was different in that there was a rational basis for choosing hard or easy words (Okun & Elias, 1977). The experimental arrangements were such that sometimes it was smarter to go for a hard word (better chance of making more points) and sometimes it was a better strategy to choose an easier word. In this latter study, where there was a basis for strategy, the elderly were not more cautious than the young. The old and young were the same—even their shifts in the choice of word difficulty level based on experimental payoffs were the same.

Putting the two studies together, it would seem that the elderly may be more cautious when there is no reason to be otherwise. When, however, there is reason to take risks, they seem to be no more cautious than anyone else. It seems wise to be risky only when there is reason to be so.

More Than One Kind of Cautiousness

The foregoing indicates that people will be cautious in one context but not necessarily in another. In addition, different types of cautiousness were described in this chapter, and it is very possible some people display one type of cautiousness but not another. This suggests that the generalization that old people are cautious may be misleadingly broad.

Okun, Siegler, and George (1978) were interested in determining empirically whether there are different types of cautiousness. They gave both the risk-taking vocabulary test of the Okun and DiVesta study and the risk questionnaire of the Wallach and Kogan study to the same people. If a person was generally cautious some correlation would be expected, but performances on these two procedures were uncorrelated. When the scores on each of these procedures were correlated with omission error scores in a laboratory learning task, correlations were seen but they were small. This suggests that cautiousness is a multivariate construct. A subsequent study confirmed this thinking in that when the two risk-taking procedures were given along with a third one, correlations among these three sets of performances were small (Okun, Stock & Ceurvorst, 1980).

The study of cautiousness and age therefore might best be conceived in multivariate terms. Factor analytic studies can be planned; contexts in which cautious behavior is seen can be varied. A determination of the types of cautiousness elderly people display and the specific contexts in which they are displayed would be useful.

SUMMARY

Cautious behavior takes many forms and is seen in varied contexts. The research literature indicates that older adults appear more cautious than younger adults in some of the forms and some of the contexts, but not all.

Investigators researching cautiousness in later life have either measured cautious behavior directly or have inferred cautiousness from performance in studies of learning, perception, psychomotor skills, and intelligence. Two features stand out in these studies; one, the old perform in a way to suggest that they value accuracy over speed. They seem to want to be sure of being correct before they venture response and, perhaps as a result, their performances are slow. This is not to say all old people are like this or that no young person is, but in the main, valuing accuracy seems to be generally characteristic of older people.

The second feature that stands out in the literature is that in these learning, perception, and other studies, the older person often does not respond to a question or test item. Rather than guess or provide an answer that may be wrong, older people persist in not responding even when encouraged to guess and told that being wrong is all right. Again, accuracy seems to be valued. Not responding is called the omission error.

Several studies have been devoted to eliminating the omission error on the part of the elderly by rewarding them to respond even if wrong, or by making the omission error costly to them. A few but not all of these studies have shown that such efforts resulted in better performance scores. This suggests that many older people may know more than they normally show on tests. Making the omission error when a correct answer might be given is a type of cautiousness that is not beneficial.

It has been hypothesized that a lack of self-confidence underlies this disinclination to venture response unless fairly certain of being correct. It was suggested that if a person lacks confidence, then being wrong is ego-threatening and one way to stave off failure is simply not to respond. This hypothesis was not supported in two studies when neither showed older people lacking confidence. The hypothesis was not totally rejected, however; instead, a refinement of the hypothesis was suggested based on several of the studies examined together. The old may be less confident than the young and less willing to respond when unsure of the answer to a particular test question, but they do not necessarily lack confidence in starting a task or once a response has been made.

Cautious behavior was measured more directly in a series of studies in which elderly and young adults responded to a questionnaire of "life situations." In each situation, a central character was depicted who faced a conflict. The responder had to advise the central character as to whether to embark upon a course of action that, if successful, would bring much gain. If the action were not successful, however, there was no gain and even loss. The respondent had an opportunity to be cautious or not by indicating the likelihood of success demanded from a course of action before advising it.

One study showed that elderly people required a greater likelihood of success than younger people before advising the risk. Thus, the elderly were seen as more cautious. A second study, however, revealed that the greater cautiousness of the elderly was largely attributable to an option they often exercised—an option not preferred by the younger adults. The older respondents often chose not to recommend the course of action that could lead to gain regardless of its probability of success. This suggested that the old, again, were cautious in the sense of not committing response. When this option to avoid risk was no longer made available to them, however, they were no different than the young in their risk taking. These questionnaire studies taken together showed that the elderly may appear cautious in avoiding decision but once obliged to venture some risk, their betting propensities are much the same as those of the young.

REFERENCES

Basowitz, H., & Korchin, S. J. Age differences in the perception of closure. *Journal of Abnormal and Social Psychology*, 1957, 54, 93–97.

Birkhill, W. R., & Schaie, K. W. The effect of differential reinforcement of cautiousness in intellectual performance among the elderly. *Journal of Gerontology*, 1975, 30, 578–583.

Botwinick, J. Drives, expectancies, and emotions. In J. E. Birren (Ed.), *Handbook of aging and the individual: Psychological and social aspects*. Chicago: University of Chicago Press, 1959, pp. 739–768.

Botwinick, J. A research note on the problem of perceptual modification in relation to age. *Journal of Gerontology*, 1962, 17, 190–192.

Botwinick, J. Cautiousness in advanced age. *Journal of Gerontology*, 1966, 21, 347–353.

Botwinick, J. Disinclination to venture response versus cautiousness in responding: Age differences. *Journal of Genetic Psychology*, 1969, 115, 55–62.

Botwinick, J. Age differences in self-ratings of confidence. *Psychological Reports*, 1970, 27, 865–866.

Botwinick, J., Brinley, J. F., & Robbin, J. S. The interaction effects of perceptual difficulty and stimulus exposure time on age differences in speed and accuracy of response. *Gerontologia*, 1958, 2, 1–10.

Brinley, J. F. Cognitive sets and accuracy in the elderly. In A. T. Welford & J. E. Birren (Eds.), *Behavior, aging and the nervous system*. Springfield, Ill.: Charles C. Thomas, 1965, pp. 114–149.

Bruce, P. R., Coyne, A. C., & Botwinick, J. Adult age differences in metamemory. *Journal of Gerontology*, 1982, 37, 354–357.

Eisdorfer, C. Verbal learning and response time in the aged. *Journal of Genetic Psychology*, 1965, 107, 15–22.

Eisdorfer, C., Axelrod, S., & Wilkie, F. L. Stimulus exposure time as a factor in serial learning in an aged sample. *Journal of Abnormal and Social Psychology*, 1963, 67, 594–600.

Erber, J., & Botwinick, J. Reward in the learning of older adults. *Experimental Aging Research*, 1983, 9, 43–44.

Erber, J., Feely, C., & Botwinick, J. Reward conditions and socioeconomic status in the learning of older adults. *Journal of Gerontology*, 1980, 35, 565–570.

Hathaway, S. R., & McKinley, J. C. Scale 2 (Depression). In G. S. Welsh & W. G. Dahlstrom (Eds.), *Basic readings on the MMPI in psychology and medicine*. Minneapolis: University of Minnesota Press, 1956, pp. 73–80.

Korchin, S. J., & Basowitz, H. The judgment of ambiguous stimuli as an index of cognitive functioning in aging. *Journal of Personality*, 1956, 25, 81–95.

Korchin, S. J., & Basowitz, H. Age differences in verbal learning. *Journal of Abnormal and Social Psychology*, 1957, 54, 64–69.

Leech, S., & Witte, K. L. Paired-associate learning in elderly adults as related to pacing and incentive conditions. *Developmental Psychology*, 1971, 5, 180.

Okun, M. A., & Di Vesta, F. J. Cautiousness in adulthood as a function of age and instructions. *Journal of Gerontology*, 1976, 31, 571–576.

Okun, M. A., & Elias, C. S. Cautiousness in adulthood as a function of age and payoff structure. *Journal of Gerontology*, 1977, 32, 451–455.

Okun, M. A., Siegler, I. C., & George, L. K. Cautiousness and verbal learning in adulthood. *Journal of Gerontology*, 1978, 33, 94–97.

Okun, M. A., Stock, W. A., & Ceurvorst, R. W. Risk taking through the adult life span. *Experimental Aging Research*, 1980, 6, 463–473.

Pettigrew, T. P. The measurement of correlates of category width as a cognitive variable. *Journal of Personality*, 1958, 26, 532–544.

Pressey, S. L., & Kuhlen, R. G. *Psychological development through the life span*. New York: Harper, 1957.

Silverman, I. Age and the tendency to withhold responses. *Journal of Gerontology*, 1963, 18, 372–375.

Thorndike, E. L., Bregman, E. O., Tilton, J. W., & Woodyard, E. *Adult learning*. New York: Macmillan, 1928.

Wallach, M. A., & Kogan, N. Aspects of judgment and decision making: interrelationships and changes with age. *Behavioral Sciences*, 1961, 6, 23–36.

Wallach, M. A., & Kogan, N. *Modes of thinking in young children*. New York: Holt, Rinehart & Winston, 1965.

Welford, A. T. *Skill and age: An experimental approach*. London: Oxford University Press, 1951.

Welford, A. T. Psychology and social gerontology in Europe. *Journal of Gerontology*, 1958, 13, 51–67, Supplement no. 1.

11
Contact with the Environment: The Senses

In the previous chapter on cautiousness, it was said that often, older people appear reluctant to commit themselves to a response unless sure that they are correct. This is also sometimes seen in the measurement of sensory thresholds. For example, in tests of hearing, very low-level sounds are presented—so low that it is difficult to tell whether it was heard or imagined. A decision regarding this must be made and the old, more often than the young, in not being sure that they are correct, decide that there was no sound heard. All this must be taken into consideration in giving tests of sensory ability. Newer tests and research studies based on the method and theory of signal detection do take this into consideration, but the older ones based on the older psychological methods do not.

This chapter deals with the basic information of seeing, hearing, and other senses. Much of what is described in this chapter is based on the older methods of investigation because most of the literature is of long standing. Nevertheless, the literature of seeing and hearing, at least, is very reliable. In fact, the studies are among the most reliable in behavioral research. Nothing major to date found with the newer methods controverts what was discovered with the older ones. This is more so for seeing and hearing than the other senses, but to an extent it is so for the others too. The older observations are so reliable that Helson (1968, p. 53) concluded, "Probably in no other area of psychological investigation are the findings so clear-cut and consistent: old people simply don't see, hear, or otherwise perceive as acutely . . . as do younger people."

The literature of sensory and perceptual differences among age-groups is both extensive and technical. Corso (1971), in reviewing the literature, listed more than 100 references. The list grew very much longer in 1977 with Birren and Schaie's edited volume that included four chapters on this topic alone. A more recent volume devoted three chapters just to the newer method of signal detection and age (Danziger, 1980; Hertzog, 1980; Williams, 1980).

The next chapter also deals with sensory and perceptual issues; thus, some of the information of the next chapter could have been placed here and vice versa. A major determinant in placing the information here was that it more nearly applied to common experience and common needs of daily living.

SEEING

When people talk about seeing they usually mean how clear things look—how much detail can be spotted. For scientists studying visual sensation and perception, however, various aspects of seeing ability are examined.

Visual Acuity

Acuity is what most people mean when they talk about seeing ability, yet this index is among the least well documented. In fact, Corso (1971, p. 91) wrote, "Experimental data on age and visual acuity are meager." Visual acuity is measured with the aid of charts such as the Snellen chart. Letters or numbers are varied in size with the knowledge of what can be seen by the "normal eye" over a specified distance. If, for example, the "normal eye" can see a letter of a certain size at a distance of 40 feet but the person tested can see the object when 20 feet away, but no further, this is reported as 20/40. There are variations of this index, but all of them are designed to measure the smallest visual angle at which the object could be correctly seen. (The farther away the person is from the object, the smaller the visual angle at the eye. This is measured by lines drawn from the eye to the top and the bottom of the object.)

Up to ages 40 to 50, little change in acuity has been noted, but after this time there is marked decline. By age 70, without correction, poor vision is the rule rather than the exception (e.g., Chapanis, 1950; Hirsch, 1960).

Accommodation

In addition to the decline in visual acuity at far distances, there is loss in ability to focus on near objects (Duane, 1931; Friedenwald, 1952; Hofstetter, 1954). This becomes apparent to almost everyone sooner or later. People become farsighted, that is, they do not see well those things up close; they find it hard to read. This is called presbyopia. This happens because the lens gets less elastic, becoming more dense or compact from continued cell growth. Thus, the lens does not change shape as easily as before and does not accommodate to viewing objects at close range. Bifocal eyeglasses take care of this problem by minimizing the need for the lenses of the eyes to change shape.

Although almost everyone recognizes this decline by later life, many do not realize that the loss of accommodation is gradual, beginning very early in childhood. The greatest decline in close distance vision, however, comes about for most people between the ages 40 and 55, as determined by longitudinal study (Brückner, 1967). It declines thereafter at a lesser rate.

Cataracts and Glare

A problem for many old people is cataracts; perhaps 20–25 percent of those in their 70s have this problem. The lens of the eye becomes opaque or clouded so that rays of light are scattered in making their way through the visual system. When the clouding is severe, sight is much impaired. Additionally, the scattering of light makes for problems of glare. In such cases, the lens has to be removed surgically. This has become a very commonplace procedure that greatly increases the person's ability to see. Glasses or contact lenses must then be used as a replacement for the natural lens that has been removed. More and more, lenses are surgically implanted.

Cataracts and the scattering of light rays that makes for glare are uncomfortable. Maybe this is the reason so many of the elderly seem to prefer dark, even dingy sitting rooms rather than bright, sunny ones. When the opaque lens, the cataract, is removed, not only is sight improved, but glare problems diminish, if not disappear altogether (Fozard, Wolf, Bell, McFarland, & Padolsky, 1977).

Illumination

If too little light reaches the retina, it is hard to see but people adjust to this automatically by simply raising the level of ambient light. Older people need greater levels of illumination than do younger people. When the level of ambient light is increased, elderly people are helped relatively more than are younger people, although their vision never reaches the same level of acuity (Weston, 1949). Among the reasons older people need more light is that they have smaller eye pupils than younger people (Birren, Casperson, & Botwinick, 1950); it is through the pupil that light reaches the retina. There is an approximate linear decrease in the amount of light reaching the retina from age 20 to age 60 years (Weale, 1965).

The need for greater illumination is seen in many circumstances. For example, it is seen when driving at night, or when there are many shadows; these are not the safest situations for the elderly. Not seeing a street curb because it is in shadow may lead to falls. Depth perception is impaired in later life (Bell, Wolf, & Bernholz, 1972) and this is exacerbated when there is low illumination.

There is conflict here. Older people need lots of illumination, yet high illumination can make for glare, especially among those who have cataracts or who are developing them. A practical solution in the conflicting needs between glare reduction and more illumination is to leave the control of lighting as much as possible to the individual. It has been suggested that environments should be lit for the "older eye," or at least the "average-age eye," rather than for the "young eye" as is now the practice (Fozard et al., 1977, p. 582).

Adapting to the Dark

There are two dimensions to dark adaptation: (1) how long it takes to develop maximum seeing ability, and (2) how good a level is eventually reached. There is little doubt that the level reached by the old is not nearly as good as that reached by the young. Birren and Shock (1950) showed this, as did McFarland and Fisher (1955), and Domey, McFarland, and Chadwick (1960) among others. This relationship between age and the final level of dark adaptation is so clear that rarely in psychological work are correlations so consistently high. McFarland, in several of his studies, reported correlations of approximately 0.90.

The other dimension of dark adaptation is more controversial: Does it take longer for the old to reach their own level of adaptation in the dark than it does the young? Birren and Shock's (1950) data suggested not—only the level was displaced with age. The old saw less well in the dark, but, given this as a base line, they got to this level at the same rate as did the young. On the other hand, Domey et al. (1960) concluded from their study and from the literature overall that the rate of dark adaptation as well as the final threshold level decrease with age. They concluded that the old not only see less well when finally dark-adapted, but it takes them longer than the young to get to their optimum level.

Dark adaptation has important practical significance. Birren (1964, p. 92) referred to automobile driving at night, and McFarland (1968, p. 18) to piloting airplanes in overcast skies as tasks that could be both difficult and dangerous for older people.

Color Vision

Colors are different for old and young; some seem to be almost as clear and vivid and as easily told apart by old people as they are by younger ones, but some colors are not so clear. The lenses of the eyes also yellow with age and this makes for a filtering of the shorter wavelengths of light. The shorter wavelengths of light are the blues and violets, while the longer lengths are the yellows and reds. This yellowing of the lenses may not be the whole reason for the aging effect on color vision, but it seems to be the main one.

Several studies have shown that with increasing age there is special difficulty in discriminating among the blues, blue-greens, and violets, with much greater success in discriminating among the reds, oranges, and yellows. Gilbert (1957) showed this in a rather straightforward way. She tested people of wide age range in a task of matching chips of various colors. People aged 10 to 19, perhaps surprisingly, were not as good in this matching as were people in their 20s. People in the 20s were best in this task; after this age, there was a gradual decline in color matching ability. Although the decline was seen in all colors, including the red part of the spectrum, the decline was greatest for the blue part.

A difficulty in distinguishing between blues and greens, or such similar colors, can make for special problems if not recognized. For example, if a physician prescribes medication in the form of pills—two green ones in the morning and three blue ones in the evening—there must be some basis for distinguishing the two kinds of pills. Color coding of home appliances, of power tools, and the like, ought to be arranged with color vision abilities of the elderly in mind.

Brightness Discrimination and Personal Status

Like colors, brightnesses are not as discernible in later life as they are in earlier adulthood. Weiss (1959) pointed out that, although only a few studies are available to document this fact, there is evidence showing that discriminating different brightnesses (i.e., contrast sensitivity) declines with age. This can also have practical consequence. Referring to an old study by Zinner (1930), Weiss reported that astronomers over age 50 could not differentiate as many brightnesses among stars as could their younger colleagues. (Contrast sensitivity is discussed in the next chapter in a different way.)

Brightness is not only a dimension of white, it is a dimension of all colors. It would not be unexpected, therefore, that elderly people would have difficulty in discriminating brightnesses of various colors, as well as white. Increasing the level of illumination can be helpful in making finer discriminations among different brightnesses.

Although brightness and color discrimination may be impaired in later life, these and other types of visual discriminations may be dependent on personal status. For example, Danziger (1979) compared young, middle-aged, and older adults in their ability to detect differences in the size of openings at the top of two circles (Landoldt rings). The openings in the two circles were sometimes the same, and sometimes one was larger than the other. The difference in the size of the two openings was varied, thus the difficulty in stimulus discrimination was varied.

Danziger found that the three age-groups were similar in their ability to make the discriminations. This did not correspond with other changes in visual abilities so Danziger sought reasons for his findings. He concluded that he may have tested an unusual group of older adults. The older people he tested were superior in intelligence, in health, and in other ways to most of the older people tested in the other studies. Danziger concluded that this fact may have been the reason other investigators reported loss with age in the ability to make visual discriminations and he did not. The implication is that other investigators reporting differences with age in brightness discrimination and other visual abilities, might have observed smaller, fewer, or no differences at all had their test groups been selected differently.

Retinal Damage

Visual abilities do decline with age, but it is well to keep in mind that most old people can and do correct their visual problems with eyeglasses and get along very well. Schaie and Geiwitz (1982, p. 348) indicated that "most people do not experience serious problems with vision until age eighty or later." Further, when they do, it is usually because of damage to the retina. Schaie and Geiwitz (1982, p. 348) reported that damage to the retina comes about mainly from faulty blood circulation. Although retinal damage may be more of a disease than a normal process, some damage is seen "in most people by the age of fifty-five to sixty-five." Unless such damage is at an advanced state, however, it is not debilitating. It is mainly the very old who show much advanced stage damage.

HEARING

The decline in hearing ability with age has been documented many times both in the laboratory and in the clinic. Schaie and Geiwitz (1982, p. 349) reported that hearing impairments begin in middle age and rise sharply after age 60. By the 70s as many as 75 percent have some problem. About 15 percent of people over 65 are legally deaf.

Butler and Lewis (1977, pp. 37–38) indicated that hearing loss makes for greater isolation than does visual loss. Hearing loss is associated with depression. "Onlookers," they said, "may mistake the hard-of-hearing as mentally abnormal or 'senile.' " "Hearing defects create irritation in others because they interfere so markedly with communication. The loud, badly articulated speech of the deaf person and the need to shout and speak slowly make simple conversations frustrating" (p. 111). Later, information will be provided on how to talk with the hearing-impaired older person.

Even given all this, however, hearing loss with age may be overestimated. This is seen in studies that were concerned with nonsensory personality factors that contribute to measured hearing loss (Craik, 1969; Rees &

Botwinick, 1971; Potash & Jones, 1977). Although finding clear evidence of hearing loss in old age, these investigators also found that the old were less inclined to report hearing faint test stimuli. As indicated earlier, the old were more cautious in that when not very sure that they heard the auditory stimuli, they more often than the young said they did not hear the faint sounds. This pattern may present the old as being more hard of hearing than they really are.

Pitch Threshold

Presbycusis. Hearing loss in old age is not equal across all frequencies of sound. High-pitched tones, such as those a soprano can reach, are progressively less audible for the elderly while those of lower pitch are better heard. So many studies have documented this by now that several reports have taken to combining the various studies. For example, Kryter (1960) compared the results of five studies and Spoor (1967) compared the results of eight. The problem of high tone disability (presbycusis) is depicted in Figure 11.1, extracted from the report by Spoor.

The "normal" human ear can hear sounds ranging in pitch from 20 vibrations per second to 20,000 per second. The very bass sounds or the very soprano sounds, however, have to be much louder than the middle frequency sounds if they are to be hard. In the measurement of hearing ability,

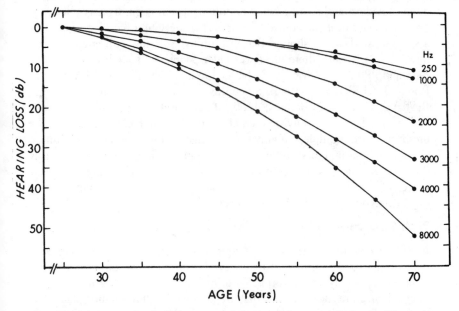

FIGURE 11.1: Hearing loss for different tone pitches in relation to age of men. Age 25 years is taken as the base line, i.e., no hearing loss. (Selected data from Table 3 of Spoor, 1967.)

a wide range of sound frequencies is presented and the loudness level (measured in decibles, dB) necessary to hear each frequency is recorded. When it is said that the old suffer presbycusis, it means that the sounds have to be made progressively louder as the frequencies are increased.

Figure 11.1 shows that the decline with age is relatively slight with tones of frequencies less than 1,000 vibrations per second (Hz). A 1,000 Hz tone is similar to that heard on the piano when a note two octaves above middle C is played. Although the decline with age in hearing tones lower than 1,000 Hz is slight—it is only about 5 dB from age 25 to 50 years—it is progressive; that is, the decline is somewhat greater, for example, between ages 75 and 85 than it is between 25 and 35.

Presbycusis becomes really apparent after age 50 with pitches above 1,000 Hz. As the frequencies are increased, loudness levels must be raised progressively for the older person to hear the tones at all. For men at age 50, with tones approximately 4,000 Hz (the highest note on the piano), the hearing loss is 17 dB or more; at age 75, the loss is more than 47 dB. The higher the frequency and the older the person, the louder will the tone need to be to be heard. For practical, everyday purposes, however, high-tone deafness for frequencies above 3,000, perhaps 4,000, Hz is not too important.

Environmental Factors. For some reason, this aging pattern is more pronounced with men than with women. It has been suggested that men are subject to greater "noise pollution" than are women because their jobs more often provide such hazards. Noise pollution, it is thought, damages hearing, even if slowly, over the course of years. This suggestion received support in a series of studies that showed that in primitive societies with environments low in such hazards there are fewer older people with presbycusis (Rosen, Bergman, Plester, El-Mofty, & Sath, 1962; Rosen, Plester, El-Mofty, & Rosen, 1964; Bergman, 1966). Since this was not found in all studies (e.g., Reynaud, Camara, & Basteris, 1969), it may be that only part of the problem of presbycusis is environmental, but this is not certain. Causes for presbycusis are multiple, ranging from changes in the inner ear to presumed changes in the auditory cortex. Deterioration in the auditory sense organ (the cochlea) has been demonstrated, but these changes have not been sufficient to account for the loss in hearing sensitivity. It is thought that higher nervous system centers are also involved.

Pitch Discrimination

If older people hear tones of varying pitch less well than younger people, it may not be surprising to find that they also discriminate among tones less well. More, it may not be surprising to find that the tones that are least well discriminated are the very ones that are not heard well in the first place. On the other hand, all this might not necessarily follow if each of the tones to be discriminated is made as functionally loud for them as for young people.

Konig (1957) presented people with tones 40 dB above their own individual thresholds. Although such tones do not seem very loud to the person tested, they were designed to be loud enough to be easily heard. Konig found that from ages 25 to 55, the ability to discriminate between tones decreased slightly, but after 55 the decrease was marked. The age difference in pitch discrimination was relatively small with tones 500–1,000 Hz, but with tones of frequencies above 1,000 Hz, the age difference was greater. Thus, it is seen that the age curve for pitch discrimination follows a trend similar to that of pitch threshold.

Speech Communication

If hearing is poor, speech communication suffers. Communication suffers in relation to the magnitude of problems with pitch threshold and pitch discrimination. It was seen that the old have special problems with high-frequency tones and special problems discriminating among such tones. Certain speech sounds are higher in frequency than others; consonants are higher frequency than vowels. Thus older people have more trouble hearing whether the spoken word was "*bat*" or "*cat*" than whether it was "*fun*" or "*fan*." Most women have higher frequency speech than most men. For the aged, therefore, women will be harder to understand than men. Young children and teenagers tend to have high-frequency speech; they will be harder to understand than adults.

Rapid speech calls for more rapid integration of inputs; also, sounds run into each other with rapid speech. Many older people have problems with this. Difficulties also arise when there are background noises. If there is a noisy air conditioner or traffic sounds, for example, the older listener may have trouble communicating. Not that background distractions are necessarily more confusing to the old than to the young, but starting as the elderly do with high-tone problems and pitch-discrimination problems, added background noise can be most burdensome (see Corso, 1977, pp. 545–547).

Audiologists and others have studied problems of speech communication and one of them, Hull, developed what he called "thirteen commandments for talking to the hearing-impaired older person" (see *Asha*, 1980, p. 427). These "commandments" are presented as Table 11.1. Abiding by these "commandments" can be very helpful when communicating with older people who have hearing problems.

TASTE

Vision and audition are more easily investigated than the other senses and thus there are many more reliable reports of them. In fact, the data on human sensation other than vision and audition are sparse and often of limited generality.

TABLE 11.1
Talking to the Hearing-Impaired Older Person*

1. Speak at a slightly greater than normal intensity.

2. Speak at normal rate, but not too rapidly.

3. Speak to the elderly person at a distance of between three and six feet.

4. Concentrate light on the speaker's face for greater visibility of lip movements, facial expression and gestures.

5. Do not speak to the elderly person unless you are visible to him or her, e.g. not from another room while he or she is reading the newspaper or watching TV.

6. Do not force the elderly person to listen to you when there is a great deal of environmental noise. That type of environment can be difficult for a younger, normally hearing person and even more difficult for the hearing impaired elderly.

7. Never, under any circumstances, speak directly into the person's ear. The listener cannot make use of visual clues, plus the speaker may be causing an already distorted auditory system to further distort the speech signal. In other words, clarity may be depressed as loudness is increased.

8. If the elderly person does not appear to understand what is being said, rephrase the statement rather than simply repeating the misunderstood words. An otherwise frustrating situation can be avoided in that way.

9. Do not *over* articulate. Over articulation not only distorts the sounds of speech, but also the speaker's face, thus making the use of visual clues more difficult.

10. Arrange the room (living room or meeting room) where communication will take place so that no speaker or listener is more than six feet apart and all are completely visible. Using this direct approach, communication for all parties involved will be enhanced.

11. Include the elderly person in all discussions about him or her. Hearing impaired elderly persons sometimes feel quite vulnerable. This approach will aid to alleviate some of those feelings.

12. In meetings or any group activity where there is a speaker presenting information (church meetings, civic organizations, etc.) make it mandatory that the speaker(s) use the public address system. One of the most frequent complaints among elderly persons is that they may enjoy attending meetings of various kinds, but all too often the speaker, for whatever reason, tries to avoid using a microphone. Many elderly persons do not desire to assert themselves by asking a speaker who has just said, "I am sure that you can all hear me if I do not use the microphone" to *please* use it. Most persons begin to avoid public and organizational meetings if they cannot hear what the speaker is saying. This point cannot be stressed enough.

13. Above all, treat elderly persons as adults. They, of anyone, deserve that respect.

*Recommendations by Raymond H. Hull, Ph.D., Department of Communication Disorders, University of Northern Colorado. Used with permission of Raymond H. Hull and *Asha*, June 1980, Vol. 22, p. 427.

The Basic Tastes

The sense of taste decreases with age but the implication of this is unclear. The basic tastes are thought to be salty, sweet, bitter, and sour. The earlier studies were mixed as to what happens to these taste abilities as a person becomes old. For example, in one study carried out with 100 people aged 15 to 89 years, changes in each of the four tastes were minor, if at all, up to the later 50s. After this time, there was decline in the ability to taste substances with these attributes (Cooper, Bilash, & Zubek, 1959). In an earlier study (Bourlière, Cendron, & Rapaport, 1958), elderly people were less able to detect sweet substances than were young adults. Old men also showed deficiency in detecting salty tasting substances but old women did not. This sex difference, however, was not observed by Cooper et al.

These studies were not carried out with the more sensitive and probably more reliable methods available today and, as a result, did not disclose the continuous nature of the loss with age. Among the more recent studies, Moore, Nielsen, and Mistretta (1982) investigated sensitivity to sweet taste, and Grzegorczyk, Jones, and Mistretta (1979) investigated sensitivity to salty taste. Both sets of investigators employed a method of forced choice (which will be discussed and described at the end of this chapter).

Moore et al. (1982) tested men and women aged from 20 to 88 with 20 different concentrations of sucrose concentrations. In contrast to the older studies, gradual loss in sweet sensitivity with age was seen, but the loss was smaller than had been reported in the earlier studies. Further, there were large individual differences, especially among the old. Moore et al. reported that large age changes in taste sensitivity are not to be expected because first, contrary to previous belief, little if any loss in taste buds is found with age, except perhaps among the very old, and second, taste buds are continually replaced in adulthood.

Grzegorczyk et al. (1979), investigators from the same laboratory, used the same method to test for salt sensitivity. Their results were similar to those of Moore et al. (1982)—among people aged 23 to 92, there was a continuous but small loss in salt sensitivity. In this study, however, loss to age 60 was not nearly as great as the loss beyond this age. These investigators believed the loss even after age 60 was "not high enough to suggest a substantial taste deficit."

Tasting Normal Foods

The investigators of these salt and sucrose studies emphasized that data of thresholds do not necessarily relate to information of "suprathreshold intensities." That is, a person can be insensitive to weak tastes but can be very sensitive in differentiating stronger tastes as found in normal food. If old people are less sensitive to weak solutions of sucrose and salt, are they also less sensitive to normal food tastes?

The answer appears to be, yes. Schiffman (1977) presented two age-groups of people (average ages 20 and 73) with a group of 24 common foods in the categories of fruits, vegetables, meat, dairy products, and others. Each person in the two age-groups was blindfolded and allowed to smell and taste each food but not to swallow it. After tasting each food, they had to identify and rate them.

The foods were correctly identified more frequently by the young than the old. More old people than young commented on the weakness or lack of taste or smell of the foods. In addition to better identification of the foods, the young discriminated among them more adequately than the old. Schiffman believed that loss of smell may have even been more important than the loss of taste in the food sensitivities.

Taste ability is governed by many factors, smell being one of them. Some studies, but not all, showed that smoking is a factor; it diminishes ability to taste. Attitudes toward food and eating are important. Whether a meal is enjoyable depends on a lot more than just taste sensitivity. Eating is a social experience as well as a gustatory one. Eating alone all the time can make a good meal into a dull one. The aged can and do enjoy their meals, but those who do not often fail for reasons other than loss in taste sensitivity.

SMELL

Taste and smell go together experientially, as indicated in Schiffman's (1977) food study. People seem to find food less tasty when their noses are clogged because of a cold or allergy.

The data on smell sensitivity are even sparser than on taste. Two studies suggested that smell sensitivity does not decline with age (see Engen, 1977, pp. 556–557). In one of these studies, however, insufficiently few people were tested, and in the other study, unusually superior people were tested. As Danziger (1979) concluded in his visual discrimination study, testing superior older adults in smell sensitivity may yield results different from those of testing more representative populations.

Other studies reported poorer smell sensitivity among the aged. The more usual laboratory procedure is to use simple, specific odors, as for example, camphor, but Schiffman and Pasternak (1979) resorted to real food items. This time just their odors were presented, not solids taken by the mouth. Old and young were compared in sensing 14 odors of commercial additives. The additives were in the categories of fruit odor, vegetable, meat, butter, and chocolate odor. The 14 items were presented two at a time so that each item was compared with each of the other 13. The two items in a pair were compared on a scale ranging from same to different. Following this, each of the 14 odors was rated on another scale, ranging from good to bad.

Schiffman and Pasternak (1979, p. 79) concluded, "the ability to discriminate food odors was considerably diminished in elderly subjects. Elderly subjects were best at discriminating fruits from the rest of the stimuli, and preferred fruits to the rest of the stimuli as well."

Schiffman and Pasternak briefly reviewed much of the literature on olfaction with age and indicated that all but one study showed a decrease in sensitivity for specific smells such as camphor. According to Schiffman and Pasternak, the one study that showed no decrease was based on faulty interpretation of the data.

A subsequent study used odors of a different kind: almond extract, bubble gum, horseradish, leather, pencil shavings, and others (Schemper, Voss, & Cain, 1981). More old people (65–88) than young (17–20) failed to recognize the odors based on a type of multiple choice task. When only those old and young people who recognized the odors equally well were chosen for further tests, the old were found less able to identify the odors when the multiple choice opportunities were not present. This observation of better performance in recognition than in identification is similar in some respect to the superiority of recognition memory to recall memory, as will be described in a later chapter.

PAIN

There is much clinical evidence that old people do not feel pain as intensely as do younger people. Several internal diseases of the aged do not seem nearly as painful to them as they would to younger adults. Minor surgery can often be performed on old people without inflicting severe pain; coronary thrombosis occurs often without the agony found in young people. Paradoxically, however, subjective sensory complaints are very common in old age.

Weiss (1959, p. 530) reviewed the literature on pain thresholds in later life and concluded that, although the aged seem to be spared many of the agonies of disease and surgery, the "statistics as to the incidence of these clinically observed changes are few." The fact is, the laboratory data are not only few, they often show no age change in pain sensation at all. Part of the inconsistency in the literature lies in the difficulty of measuring pain. The feeling of pain, and certainly the reporting of it, appears to be related to personality and to cultural influences.

One of the better older studies, one that does corroborate clinical experience, was reported by Schludermann and Zubek (1962). Radiant heat was applied with a projector to five different parts of the body while the person lay on an air mattress. The instructions emphasized that it was not a test of the ability to endure pain but of the ability to perceive the first trace of it. Each person was given a stopwatch that was to be started when the heat apparatus was turned on, and stopped when pain was first felt.

The time it took to become aware of the pain stimuli increased slightly with age up to 60 years; after this age the increase was more noticeable. A more recent study, also using a method of radiant heat, investigated sex differences as well as differences between young and middle-aged adults (Clark & Mehl, 1971). A signal detection analysis disclosed that men of these two age categories were not different in detecting heat stimuli, but women were. Middle-aged women seemed to decline in ability to feel thermal pain. Perhaps one of the reasons for this sex difference is that the middle-aged men, more than the middle-aged women, endured greater pain than the younger adults before reporting it.

Harkins and Chapman (1976) electrically stimulated the pulp of teeth to induce pain, also applying a signal detection analysis. Testing men, they found results similar to Clark and Mehl (1971) and different from Schludermann and Zubek (1962). Young and elderly men were similar in their ability to detect the pain stimulus, that is, electrical shock. When two shocks were applied, however, one more noxious than the other, the older men were not as able to discriminate between them as were the younger men. Thus, in this index of pain stimuli discriminations, pain sensitivity was seen to undergo a decline with age. A similar study on women yielded the same results as on men (Harkins & Chapman, 1977).

As in the Clark and Mehl study of men, the older people examined by Harkins and Chapman were less willing to report the sensation as pain, but this time only when the pain stimuli were relatively mild. When the electrical shocks to the tooth pulp were perceived as strong, the elderly were not reluctant to report pain. This reluctance on the part of the elderly to report pain unless strong is analogous to what has been found in the hearing tests, that is, reluctance to report hearing the low-level sound.

TOUCH

The threshold of touch, like that of pain, varies with the part of the body stimulated. In 1971, Corso (p. 101) wrote that the "data are noticeably absent in the area of tactile sensitivity with age effects." The data are only a little bit less absent today. The older studies of tactile sensitivity and age were carried out with the less sensitive psychophysical methods and perhaps it is for this reason that in 1964, Birren (p. 101) concluded, "touch sensitivity remains unchanged from early adulthood through about age fifty to fifty-five, with a rise in threshold thereafter." More recent data, based on better methods, show that touch sensitivity declines with age in a more continuous way, just as do the more recent data on taste sensitivity.

Among the best of the studies on touch sensitivity was one based on stimulation of the pad of the index finger (Thornbury & Mistretta, 1981). Common to many tactile studies, fine, bristle-like filaments, varied in thickness, were applied to the skin. Unlike other studies, the forced choice method was used. Thornbury and Mistretta tested people aged 19 to 88 and found increasing loss of sensitivity across the age range; however, although a large proportion of the older people had thresholds that were higher than the average of younger people, there were great individual differences among the old. In fact, "A large percentage of our older subjects correctly identified the least intense . . . filament. . . ." Moreover, "the age-related increased tactile threshold may not be great enough to grossly interfere with functional behaviors" (p. 38). By functional behaviors, the investigators meant "the ability to locate, manipulate, and identify objects in the environment" (p. 39). These results and conclusions are similar to those based on taste sensitivity where the same method of forced choice was used.

A study more closely related to manipulation and identification of objects in the environment was carried out by Thompson, Axelrod, and Cohen (1965). They had people of two age-groups palpate, without looking, a variety of differently shaped forms made of masonite. The task was to identify these forms with those represented on a visual display. The older group (60–77) identified the forms less well than the young group (18–34), but this was attributed as much to deficits in searching the visual display as to deficits in touch sensitivity.

In a similar study, Kleinman and Brodzinsky (1978) had people explore an irregular form with the right hand and match it to one of several others that were explored with the left hand. All this was done without the benefit of being able to see the forms. People of average age 76 were less able to do this than people of average ages 41 and 19, who were similar in their performances. Compatible with the conclusion of Thompson et al. (1965), the poor performances of the older adults were attributed at least in part to poorer exploratory touch strategies.

Related to touch sensitivity is vibration sensitivity. Verrillo (1980) found decrease with age in vibratory sensitivity in males and females aged 8 to 74. This decrease, however, was found only with high-frequency vibratory stimuli, not low-frequency. The people tested were categorized into mean age-groups 10, 20, 35, 50, and 65 years. Although there was progressive decrease over the entire age range with high-frequency stimulation, the sharpest decrease was between 50 and 65 years.

MEASURING SENSATION

It has been indicated in several places in this chapter that the methods of measuring sensory processes have undergone change. The change has come about in the last two decades or so with progressive momentum. The older, traditional psychophysical methods have given way to the theory and method of signal detection. This method provides measures of both sensitivity and the criterion people use in decisions. It is thus a better method because it takes into consideration the reluctance people might have in identifying the presence of low-intensity inputs. When criteria in decision processes are not of interest but only measures of sensitivity are, more and more the method of forced choice is being used. These different methods of measuring sensory ability are briefly described in this section.

Psychophysical Measurement:
Absolute and Difference Thresholds

The most common of the older psychophysical methods takes this form: In visual research, for example, a series of lights is presented, each light less bright (or more bright) than the preceding one. The task is to determine the least bright light that can be seen. Similarly, in auditory research, a series of sound-tones is presented, each tone less loud (or more loud) than the preceding one. The task is to determine the least loud tone that can be heard. This method of determining the *absolute threshold* for seeing or hearing is still used in many places.

Another method, similar in concept, is to compare two lights or two tones to determine how similar in intensity they can be and still be told apart. This method of *difference threshold* is not used as often in the clinic as the method of absolute threshold, but it is used even if unsystematically. For example, in a routine eye examination, a point is reached where the patient seems to be reading a line of small print equally well with two very similar correction lenses. The examiner will say, "Is it clearer with this lens or with this one?" The patient may have a difficult decision in choosing the better lens.

Signal Detection

Difficulty in decision is found also with the methods of absolute thresholds. An example of this may be seen when at home reading or watching TV and a rustle is heard in the next room. The rustle is so faint, however, that it is not clear whether it is imagined or whether something is going on. A decision has to be made whether it is imagined or something real. Difficulty in decision, and individual differences in decision processes, led to a newer way of measuring sensory ability. This newer way, the method of signal detection, is used increasingly in both laboratory and clinic.

The theory and method of signal detection are based on the recognition that decision involves choice and people are different in how they make their choices. This affects sensory threshold measurements. The theory of signal detection (Green & Swets, 1966) distinguishes between what is regarded as a more biologically determined measure of sensory ability and a more personality determined measure of the reluctance (or proclivity) in saying, "Yes, I see that light," or "I hear that tone." "The rustle in the next room is real." The more biological measure, the ability to detect low-level stimuli, is called sensitivity (d'). The personality measure is called criterion or response bias. (There are several such measures, but the most commonly used one is β.) If the old are more cautious or more conservative in saying, "Yes, I see that light" when it is very dim, they will have a higher β score.

In its simplest but not complete form, signal detection measurement is based on a procedure such as this: The stimulus or signal (e.g., light or tone) is sometimes presented and sometimes not. When the signal is faint, it is hard to tell whether or not it was presented. In any case, a choice must be made: yes, it was presented or no, it was not. After a series of trials, a four-fold table is set up: (1) Signal presented and a yes response, (2) signal, a no response, (3) no signal, a yes response, (4) no signal, a no response. When the signal is presented and the person says, yes, it is called a "hit." When a signal is not presented but the person says, yes it was, it is called a "false alarm." A person with a high β score—older people if they are more cautious than younger people in signal detection studies—will have fewer hits but also have fewer false alarms.

Higher Response Bias among the Aged. Higher criterion scores among aged people were found in several studies, but not all. Craik (1969), Rees and Botwinick (1971), and Potash and Jones (1977) found higher criterion scores among the elderly in auditory perception studies. Hutman and Sekuler (1980) found higher criterion scores in a visual perception study with one measure but not with another. Clark and Mehl (1971) found middle-aged adults more cautious in this way than younger adults in a study of pain perception. Similarly, Harkins and Chapman (1976, 1977) found elderly people less likely to report a pain stimulus as painful, although only for low-intensity stimuli. Just the opposite was true for high-intensity stimuli. Danziger and Botwinick (1980) carried out a weight-lifting sensitivity study and reported higher criterion scores for old people than for young. All these results suggest that traditional tests of sensory acuity might overestimate the magnitude of sensory deficits in later life. If the older person says no, there is no light (tone) when there was one, this might be due to a reluctance to say yes, rather than to an inability to detect the stimulus. That older person will be seen as sensorily deficient when, in fact, this may not be the case.

Response Bias of Old and Young Is Similar. Not all studies showed higher response bias or criterion scores among the elderly. Danziger (1979) did not find this in a visual perception study, nor was it found in another weight-lifting sensitivity study (Watson, Turpenoff, Kelly, & Botwinick, 1979). What differentiates these findings from those above?

Danziger (1980) pointed to the fact that in most instances where higher criterion scores were found among the elderly, so were lower d' scores. In other words, when detection ability or sensitivity is different between age-groups, criterion differences will probably be noted. It seems that d' and β tend to be correlated empirically, even if not theoretically; thus, when old and young are similar in sensitivity, they tend also to be similar in response bias. This is not always the case, but it often is. For example, Rees and Botwinick (1971) showed independence of d' and β, as did Potash and Jones (1977), but these may be exceptions, or unique to auditory perception studies.

Method of Forced Choice

The implication of all this is that response bias can have a bearing on detectability or vice versa, even though theoretically this should not be. A method has been designed that negates the role of response bias in the measurement of sensory ability but this method also precludes the possibility of measuring response bias. The method is of forced choice, where a stimulus condition is paired sequentially with a no-stimulus condition; for example, a salt in water solution (stimulus) is paired with just water (no stimulus). Sometimes the stimulus is presented first, sometimes it is presented second. The person taking the test must tell whether the stimulus was presented first or whether the stimulus was presented second in the paired sequence. Clearly, if the stimulus is sufficiently weak, it will be difficult to discriminate it from the no-stimulus. Here, choice is not a matter of criterion, or cautiousness, because a choice is forced. There is some loss of information with this procedure over a complete signal detection analysis, but it does do away with the response bias problem. The studies of Grzegorczyk et al. (1979) on salt taste sensitivity, Moore et al. (1982) on sucrose taste sensitivity, and Thornbury and Mistretta (1981) on touch sensitivity were based on the forced choice method. This method is an advance and preferable to the older psychophysical methods. It is preferable to the method of signal detection unless there is special interest in measuring criterion or response bias.

SUMMARY

Probably in no other area of psychological investigation are the findings as clear-cut as they are in sensory age changes. Old people do not see or hear as well as young people do, and decline in sensitivity is present also in taste, smell, touch, and possibly pain.

The ability to see detail at far distances declines with age, although up to the 40s and 50s this decline is very slight. The decline in ability to see things well that are up close is more apparent, becoming noticeable in the middle 40s, although the decline starts very early in life. Other visual processes also change, for example, the ability to differentiate colors and brightnesses, the ability to see in the dark, and probably the time it takes to adapt to the dark. Raising the level of illumination is especially helpful to older people. Cataracts are a problem but surgical techniques are so well developed that cataracts are no longer major life events. Problems of glare are usually corrected with cataract removal.

Hearing ability also declines with age, but the loss is not equal across all frequencies of sound. High-pitched tones are progressively less audible for the elderly while those of lower pitch are better heard. Before age 50 the decline is relatively slight; little loss with age is seen with tone frequencies less than 1,000 Hz. There is evidence that this auditory change may be due partly to environmental insult.

Old people not only have difficulty in hearing high-frequency tones, they have difficulty in discriminating among them. In normal, daily speech, consonants are high-frequency sounds and vowels are lower ones. Difficulty with consonants affects the very important business of speech comprehension and communication. There are "rules" for speaking to hard-of-hearing older adults and these were listed.

The data on human sensation other than vision and audition are more sparse and lend themselves less well to making generalizations. Studies of taste show that simple tastes such as sweet and salty decline gradually with age but the decline is small and there are large individual differences. Taste for food items declines with age, but there is a lot more to enjoying food than taste sensitivity. The sense of smell is related to the sense of taste; the pattern of decline is similar for both senses.

There is clinical evidence that old people do not feel pain as intensely as do younger people, but, paradoxically, subjective sensory complaints are very common in old age. The scientific studies on pain thresholds in later life are few and often show no age change in pain sensation at all. When differences between young and old are seen, it is more in discriminating between intensities of pain than in pain thresholds.

Despite these losses in all sense modalities seen in the laboratory, older people, by and large, do very well in their normal day-to-day activities. Most of the studies are based on threshold determinations, but the published literature tells little about suprathreshold stimulation in natural circumstances. For example, it is one thing to say that older people cannot see small print size that young people can see. It is another thing to say that the ability to see TV programs is not very different for old and young.

Different methods of sensory measurement sometimes provide different types of information. For example, the method of forced choice may show gradual decline in sensitivity with age when older psychophysical methods may show no decline to middle age. The earlier methods may show greater decline in old age than is seen by the forced choice method. The different methods of measuring sensitivity were discussed, as was the role of response bias in measuring sensitivity.

REFERENCES

Asha (a journal of the American Speech-Language-Hearing Association), 1980, 22, 423–428 (an interview with three speech-language pathologists).

Bell, B., Wolf, E., & Bernholz, C. D. Depth perception as a function of age. Aging and Human Development, 1972, 3, 77–88.

Bergman, M. Hearing in the Mabaans. Archives of Otolaryngology, 1966, 84, 411–415.

Birren, J.E. The psychology of aging. Englewood Cliffs, N.J.: Prentice-Hall, 1964.

Birren, J.E., Casperson, R.C., & Botwinick, J. Age changes in pupil size. Journal of Gerontology, 1950, 5, 216–221.

Birren, J.E., & Schaie, K.W. Handbook of the psychology of aging. New York: Van Nostrand Reinhold, 1977.

Birren, J.E., & Schock, N.W. Age changes in rate and level of visual dark adaptation. Journal of Applied Physiology, 1950, 2, 407–411.

Bourlière, F., Cendron, H., & Rapaport, A. Modification avec l'age des seuils gustatifs de perception et de reconnaissance aux saveurs salée et sucrée chez l'homme, Gerontologia, 1958, 2, 104–111.

Brückner, R. Longitudinal research on the eye. Gerontologia Clinica, 1967, 9, 87–95.

Butler, R. N., & Lewis, M. I. Aging and mental health. St. Louis: C. V. Mosby, 1977.

Chapanis, A. Relationships between age, visual acuity and color vision. Human Biology, 1950, 22, 1–33.

Clark, W.C., & Mehl, L. A sensory decision theory analysis of the effect of age and sex on d', various response criteria, and 50% pain threshold. Journal of Abnormal Psychology, 1971, 78, 202–212.

Cooper, R.M., Bilash, I., & Zubek, J.P. The effect of age on taste sensitivity. Journal of Gerontology, 1959, 14, 56–58.

Corso, J.F. Sensory processes and age effects in normal adults. Journal of Gerontology, 1971, 26, 90–105.

Corso, J.F. Auditory perception and communication. In J.E. Birren & K.W. Schaie (Eds.), Handbook of the psychology of aging. New York: Van Nostrand Reinhold, 1977, pp. 535–553.

Craik, F.I.M. Applications of signal detection theory to studies of ageing. In A.T. Welford

(Ed.), *Interdisciplinary topics in gerontology* (Vol. 4). Basel and New York: S. Karger, 1969, pp. 147–157.

Danziger, W. L. *Adult age differences in sensitivity and response bias in a visual discrimination task*. Ph.D. Dissertation, Washington University, St. Louis, 1979.

Danziger, W. L. Measurement of response bias in aging research. In L. W. Poon (Ed.), *Aging in the 1980s*. Washington, D.C.: American Psychological Association, 1980, pp. 552–557.

Danziger, W. L., & Botwinick, J. Age and sex differences in sensitivity and response bias in a weight discrimination task. *Journal of Gerontology*, 1980, 3, 338–394.

Domey, R.G., McFarland, R.A., & Chadwick, E. Dark adaptation as a function of age and time: II. A derivation. *Journal of Gerontology*, 1960, 15, 267–279.

Duane, A. Accommodation. *Archives of Ophthalmology*, 1931, 5, 1–14.

Engen, T. Taste and smell. In J.E. Birren & K.W. Schaie (Eds.), *Handbook of the psychology of aging*. New York: Van Nostrand Reinhold, 1977, pp. 554–561.

Fozard, J.L., Wolf, E., Bell, B., McFarland, R.A., & Padolsky, S. Visual perception and communication. In J.E. Birren & K.W. Schaie (Eds.), *Handbook of the psychology of aging*. New York: Van Nostrand Reinhold, 1977, pp. 497–534.

Friedenwald, J.S. The eye. In A.L. Lansing (Ed.), *Cowdry's problems of aging* (3rd ed.). Baltimore: Williams & Wilkins, 1952.

Gilbert, J.G. Age changes in color matching. *Journal of Gerontology*, 1957, 12, 210–215.

Green, D. M., & Swetz, J. A. *A signal detection theory and psychophysics*. New York: Wiley, 1966.

Grzegorczyk, P. B., Jones, S. W., & Mistretta, C. M. Age-related differences in salt taste acuity. *Journal of Gerontology*, 1979, 34, 834–840.

Harkins, S.W., & Chapman, R.C. Detection and decision factors in pain perception in young and elderly men. *Pain*, 1976, 2, 253–264.

Harkins, S. W., & Chapman, C. R. The perception of induced dental pain in young and elderly women. *Journal of Gerontology*, 1977, 32, 428–435.

Helson, H. Comments on McFarland's paper. In K.W. Schaie (Ed.), *Theory and methods of research on aging*. Morgantown, West Va.: West Virginia University, 1968, pp. 53–55.

Hertzog, C. Applications of signal detection theory to the study of psychological aging: A theoretical review. In L. W. Poon (Ed.), *Aging in the 1980s*. Washington, D.C.: American Psychological Association, 1980, pp. 568–591.

Hirsch, M.J. Data cited by Weymouth, F.W. Effect of age on visual acuity. In M.J. Hirsch & R.F. Wick (Eds.), *Vision of the aging patient*. Philadelphia: Chilton, 1960.

Hofstetter, H.W. Some interrelationships of age, refraction, and rate of refractive changes. *American Journal of Optometry and Archives of the American Academy of Optometry*, 1954, 31, 161–169.

Hutman, L. P., & Sekuler, R. Spatial vision and aging. II: Criterion effects. *Journal of Gerontology*, 1980, 35, 700–706.

Kleinman, J. M., & Brodzinsky, D. M. Hepatic exploration in young, middle-aged, and elderly adults. *Journal of Gerontology*, 1978, 33, 521–527.

Konig, J. Pitch discrimination and age. *Acta Oto-Laryngologica*, 1957, 48, 473–489.

Kryter, K.D. Damage-risk criteria for hearing. In L.L. Beranek (Ed.), *Noise reduction*. New York: McGraw-Hill, 1960.

McFarland, R.A. The sensory and perceptual processes in aging. In K.W. Schaie (Ed.), *Theory and methods of research on aging*. Morgantown, West Va.: West Virginia University, 1968, pp. 9–52.

McFarland, R.A., & Fisher, M.B. Alterations in dark adaptation as a function of age. *Journal of Gerontology*, 1955, 10, 424–428.

Moore, L. M., Nielsen, C. R., & Mistretta, C. M. Sucrose taste thresholds: age related differences. *Journal of Gerontology*, 1982, 37, 64–69.

Potash, M., & Jones, B. Aging and decision criteria for the detection of tones in noise. *Journal of Gerontology*, 1977, 32, 436–440.

Rees, J., & Botwinick, J. Detection and decision factors in auditory behavior of the elderly. *Journal of Gerontology*, 1971, 26, 133–136.

Reynaud, J., Camara, M., & Basteris, L. An investigation into presbycusis in Africans from rural and nomadic environments. *International Audiology*, 1969, 8, 299–304.

Rosen, S., Bergman, M., Plester, D., El-Mofty, E., & Sath, M. Presbycusis study of a relatively noise-free population in the Sudan. *Annals of Otology*, 1962, 71, 727–743.

Rosen, S., Plester, D., El-Mofty, E., & Rosen, H.V. High frequency audiometry in presbycusis: a comparative study of the Mabaan tribe in the Sudan with urban populations. *Archives of Otolaryngology*, 1964, 79, 18–32.

Schaie, K. W., & Geiwitz, J. *Adult development and aging*. Boston: Little, Brown, 1982.

Schemper, T., Voss, S., & Cain, W. S. Odor identification in young and elderly persons: Sensory and cognitive limitations. *Journal of Gerontology*, 1981, 36, 446–452.

Schiffman, S. Food recognition by the elderly. *Journal of Gerontology*, 1977, 32, 586–592.

Schiffman, S., & Pasternak, M. Decreased discrimination of food odors in the elderly. *Journal of Gerontology*, 1979, 34, 73–79.

Schludermann, E., & Zubek, J.P. Effect of age on pain sensitivity. *Perceptual and Motor Skills*, 1962, 14, 295–301.

Spoor, A. Presbycusis values in relation to noise induced hearing loss. *International Audiology*, 1967, 6, 48–57.

Thompson, L.W., Axelrod, S., & Cohen, L.D. Senescence and visual identification of tactual-kinesthetic forms. *Journal of Gerontology*, 1965, 20, No. 2, 244–249.

Thornbury, J., & Mistretta, C. M. Tactile sensitivity as a function of age. *Journal of Gerontology*, 1981, 36, 34–39.

Verrillo, R. T. Age related changes in sensitivity to vibration. *Journal of Gerontology*, 1980, 35, 185–193.

Watson, C. S., Turpenoff, M., Kelly, W. J., & Botwinick, J. Age differences in resolving power and decision strategies in a weight discrimination task. *Journal of Gerontology*, 1979, 34, 547–552.

Weale, R.A. On the eye. In A.T. Welford & J.E. Birren (Eds.), *Behavior, aging and the nervous system*. Springfield, Ill.: Charles C. Thomas, 1965.

Weiss, A.D. Sensory functions. In J.E. Birren (Ed.), *Handbook of aging and the individual*. Chicago: University of Chicago Press, 1959, pp. 503–542.

Weston, H.C. On age and illumination in relation to visual performance. *Transactions of the Illuminating Engineering Society* (London), 1949, 14, 281–297.

Williams, M. V. Receiver operating characteristics: The effects of distribution on between-group comparisons. In L. W. Poon (Ed.), *Aging in the 1980s*. Washington, D.C.: American Psychological Association, 1980, pp. 558–567.

Zinner, E. Die Reizempfindungskurve Ztschr. *Psychol. Sinnesphysiol*, 1930, 61, Abt. II, 247–266.

12
Processing Sense Information

Donald W. Kline, Ph.D.*

STIMULUS PERSISTENCE

If a person responds to a stimulus and then must respond to a second stimulus shortly afterward, the second response is often different from the first one, even if the two stimuli are identical. One explanation of this is that the first stimulus, in its neural representation, has not been "cleared through the nervous system" before a response must be made to the second stimulus. Since neural transmission of the first stimulus is not complete, the person is not optimally ready to process the second stimulus. The trace of the first stimulus persists, so to speak, leaving the responder either relatively refractory to subsequent stimulation or responsive but in a different way.

Older persons are typically slower than younger ones in carrying out almost all tasks. At least some of this slowness may be due to stimulus traces that persist longer in the nervous system of older persons. For example, Welford (1969, pp. 4–5) referred to a study by Jeeves in which speed of response was measured to each of two stimuli separated by brief time intervals. When the two stimuli were very close in time, the response to the second stimulus was slower than to the first one. Welford reported that among young adults aged 18 to 33 years, after about 300 milliseconds elapsed following the first stimulus–response sequence, the response to the second stimulus was as fast as to the first. But among older adults, aged 58 to 71 years, an interval of 500 milliseconds was necessary for this to be the case. The neural impulses of the first stimulus, together with those of the associated responses, persisted longer in the older group than in the younger and left the older group less prepared for the second stimulus.

Stimulus persistence is a theory or a model more than it is a fact, but many data seem to fit the model (Axelrod, 1963). For this reason, the notion of stimulus persistence is useful.

*Department of Psychology, University of Notre Dame, Notre Dame, Indiana.

TEMPORAL RESOLUTION OF DISCRETE STIMULI

Stimulus Persistence in Explanation

Critical Flicker Fusion. A traditional and frequently used measure of visual efficiency is critical flicker fusion (CFF). When a light goes on and off at a very fast rate, it will be seen as being on continuously, that is, a steady-state light. CFF is the lowest rate of a flickering light source that appears to be on continuously. CFF is taken as an index of the visual system's limited ability to track rapid changes in illumination. This limitation appears to be due to neural components in the retina since the photoreceptors can track flicker at rates much higher than the CFF. The exact rate of flashing at which a light appears fused (steady-state) depends on a variety of factors, including the adaptation state of the retina, color of the light, retinal location, size of the light, and the light time/dark time ratio.

Among the better replicated findings is that the fusing point comes at lower rates among older persons than among younger ones. In other words, the old see a fused, steady-state light at slow off–on rates where the young would see the on–off character of the light. Weale (1965) reviewed several studies and concluded that between age 20 and 60 years, the average decline is about 7 cycles per second. On the average, young adults perceive fusion at a flicker rate of about 40 cycles per second (Misiak, 1947) and old persons at slower rates.

A portion of the decline in CFF can be attributed to a reduction with age in effective level of light reaching the retina (due primarily to a decline in pupil size and increased opacity of the lens). This does not explain most of the decline, however. Coppinger (1955) showed that an increase in illumination lowers the rate more among the young than the old. On this basis, Weiss (1959) concluded that neural factors must also be involved. Similarly, when Weekers and Roussel (1946) compared CFF with and without induced pupil dilation, the difference between the young and old groups was only halved. In similar manner, Falk and Kline (1978) found that viewing the light through a small aperture (i.e., an artificial pupil) had only a small effect on the CFF. A more direct demonstration of neural involvement was seen in a study by Semenovskaia and Verkhutina (cited in Weiss, 1959). They bypassed the effects of age on the optical media of the eyes altogether by stimulating the retina directly with pulsating electrical current. They found that the resulting electrical CFF was still significantly lower for old persons. Their CFF measures were similar to the levels reported by Weekers and Rousel with dilated pupils.

Stimulus-persistence theory may explain these results. If the trace of the first light flash persists longer in the older person's nervous system than in the younger person's, it has the same effect as a longer duration flash. Each flash will tend to fuse with the trace of the preceding flash. McFarland, Warren, and Karis (1958) presented data consistent with this suggestion. As they varied the flash so that more and more of the cycle was taken up by the light on, fusion of the flashes came about more readily, that is, thresholds for CFF were lowered. When there was long light-on time, the old and young were more similar in CFF threshold. It is as if the stimulus made for a persisting trace in all people, including young ones. But when there was little light-on time it was the old group, much more than the young group, that perceived fusion.

Click Fusion. An auditory analogue of this visual fusion has been seen in studies utilizing sound clicks (Weiss & Birren, reported by Weiss, 1959, p. 523; Weiss, 1963). In these studies, two sound clicks were presented in rapid order to both ears of a person who tried to determine whether it sounded like two clicks or a single fused one. The difference between a young group and an over-65-year group was not great, but was similar to that seen in CFF: fusion of the two clicks came about more readily for the old. Again, the young perceived objective reality better than did the old.

Trains of clicks, 1 to 10 in number, were also presented and these were varied in the rate of delivery. "On the whole, older subjects reported significantly fewer clicks than younger subjects" (Weiss, 1959, p. 523). Perhaps persistence of the stimulus trace of the earlier part of the train of clicks fused with later parts to make differentiation more difficult.

Fusion of Discrete Shocks. Axelrod, Thompson, and Cohen (1968) stimulated the fingers of the hand with mild shocks. The ability to perceive the shocks as separate stimulations was measured with two groups of people aged 21 to 34 and 65 to 75 years. Each person was told that sometimes the shocks would be applied simultaneously and sometimes successively. The task was to judge whether they were presented together or separately.

Successive shocks were presented in two ways: both shocks were applied to one hand, or the first shock was applied to one hand and the second shock to the other. In line with the stimulus-persistence model, the old fused the successive presentations more readily than did the young. The temporal thresholds were higher for the bimanual stimulations than for the unimanual ones, and this was more so among the old than among the young. That is, fusion took place more readily with two stimulations to one hand than one stimulation to each of the two hands; this was particularly the case among the elderly. Axelrod et al. (1968) explained the higher temporal thresholds of the bimanual stimulation on the basis of interhemispheric interaction. That is, with two hands more synapses of both brain hemispheres are involved than in the one-hand situation. Thus, with the aged, especially when a greater number of synapses are involved, there appeared to be "greater persistence of evoked activity . . . [giving] rise to a greater increase in temporal threshold . . . " (Axelrod et al., 1968, p. 193).

Testing for Stimulus Persistence

Corresponding Stimulus Halves. The studies that have been examined so far have been applied to the stimulus-persistence model in retrospective or *post hoc* fashion. Of course, the best test of this or any other scientific model is through prospective studies that evaluate the accuracy of the model's predictions. Several such prospective studies have now been carried out to determine the utility of the theory of stimulus-persistence.

If stimuli persist longer in the nervous systems of older people, then they should be better than the younger people in identifying a stimulus when it is presented in two halves separated by a time interval. This proposition was investigated in a study where half of each letter of a word was presented as the first stimulus and the other half of each letter was presented as the second stimulus (Kline & Orme-Rogers, 1978). The results of this study showed that the older adults identified more total words than the young in "strong support for the stimulus-persistence model" (p. 76).

Dark Interval Threshold. There is an experiment called the dark interval threshold which is similar to the CFF experiment except that instead of a continously pulsating single light, two different flashes of light in quick succession are used. The dark interval threshold is the shortest duration between two flashes at which a person can discriminate the pair as two flashes rather than a single fused flash. Amberson, Atkeson, Pollack, and Malatesta (1979) tested 72 female participants of different ages and found that although the difference was statistically significant only between the youngest (20–29) and oldest (70–79) groups, the dark interval threshold rose with age from about 65 msec to approximately 95 msec. This study, then, is also in support of the stimulus-persistence hypothesis.

Continuity of Form. Rather than light flashes, as with the CFF or with the dark interval thresholds, it is possible to flash a structured stimulus such as a circle on and off to determine the apparent continuity of the form rather than the steady-state of unstructured light. Walsh and Thompson (1978) presented a circle that was alternated cyclically with a blank field (i.e., no stimulus). The goal of the study, similar to CFF, was to determine whether older adults would more readily see a continuous circle than would younger adults. The latter might more readily see the alternating or cycling character of the display. The results of this study did not support the stimulus-persistence notion—in fact, just the opposite. It was the young adults who maintained the illusion of a circle over long blank intervals. Kline and Schieber (1981a) noted that a variety of factors could have contributed to this result. These included the luminance and contrast conditions of the display and lack of adequate practice to help older people to establish a stable judgment criterion.

When Kline and Schieber repeated the study taking these factors into account, the results were otherwise—the persistence of the target circle was significantly greater among the elderly participants. The difference in outcome between the two studies, however, was with the young groups; the estimates of circle persistence were highly similar between the two older groups in both studies. The young group in the second study was able to perceive the oscillating character of the stimulus at shorter durations of the blank field.

Color Fusion. There is also evidence of greater persistence with age in the mechanisms responsible for color vision. When red and green lights of the appropriate wavelengths are presented to the eye at the same time, it results in the perception of yellow. If there is a sufficiently brief interval between the red and green lights, this will also result in the perception of yellow. Kline, Ikeda, and Schieber (1982) used this effect to compare age-groups in their abilities to integrate sequentially presented red and green flashes. In the manner of CFF, it was predicted that the colors would fuse to yellow more readily among the old than the young. The prediction was supported: the older people reported yellow over longer intervals (time separations) between the red and green flashes. Kline et al. concluded that this age difference in color fusion was due more to alterations in neural mechanisms than to changes in the optical apparatus of the eye, or in the photoreceptors. This conclusion was based on the fact that the luminance level of the color displays was not a factor in the differences with age in color fusion.

Color Afterimages. Temporal resolution by the mechanisms of color vision has also been investigated through examination of afterimages. The mechanisms responsible for color vision operate in a way such that if a person fixates on a color patch for a short while and then looks at a neutral background, the person will see an image that is the color complement of the original color patch. If, for example, a person looks at a green patch for a while and then a neutral background, a red image of the patch will be seen. Up to a point, the longer the original patch is viewed, the longer lasting will be the resulting complementary afterimage. Stimulus-persistence theory would predict that such negative afterimages would last longer in the older nervous system. There is evidence that this is the case.

Kline and Nestor (1977) had young and old observers fixate on a green patch surrounded by a red background field. Following this, they fixated on a white area until the afterimage (a red image on a green background) could no longer be seen. Directly consistent with the stimulus-persistence theory, the afterimages lasted longer among the old.

Perceptual Aftereffects

Somewhat similar to afterimages are aftereffects. If a person views one stimulus and then views a second one that replaces it, the perception of the second stimulus is affected by the experience with the first one. In other words, the first stimulus leaves an aftereffect that influences perception of the second stimulus. The stimulus-persistence hypothesis would predict that aftereffects would be longer-lasting among older than younger persons. It is not yet clear, however, whether this is the case. There are only a few studies of the relationship between age and aftereffects and they are inconsistent in their support of the stimulus-persistence hypothesis.

Figural Aftereffect. Axelrod and Eisdorfer (1962) carried out a study comparing young (18–34) and older (60–76) persons with respect to the duration of both a figural and kinesthetic aftereffect. In the figural aftereffect task, the person fixated on a dot to the left of which was a black rectangle. When this rectangle was replaced by another one that was further to the left of the dot, it looked even further away than it actually was. The magnitude of this aftereffect was determined by having a person set a movable pointer to the right of the dot the same distance from it as the rectangle on the left appeared to be. No differences were found between the young and old age-groups in either their susceptibility to or duration of the aftereffect, an apparent blow to the stimulus-persistence idea. Later, however, Eisdorfer and Axelrod (1964) discovered an artifact in the study and reanalyzed the data. The reanalysis revealed that the elderly were generally less susceptible to the aftereffect, but once the aftereffect was established, even at the lower level, it persisted longer. This may be seen in Figure 12.1. After removing the fixation stimulus (dot), the size of the aftereffect diminished rapidly among the young but more slowly among the old, although not significantly. Given the lower aftereffect level among the elderly, the direction of these figural aftereffect results was in support of the stimulus-persistence model. The kinesthetic study was deemed invalid because of the artifact.

Spiral Aftereffect. Another type of aftereffect was also investigated. If a two-dimensional spiral is rotated by a motor and a person fixates on it for a period of time, the spiral will appear to rotate in the opposite direction for some time after it is actually stopped. The stimulus-persistence model would lead to the prediction of longer spiral aftereffects among older persons. So far, however, there is not much evidence in support of this prediction. Griew and Lynn (1960) reported that with fixations of 30 seconds on the rotating spiral, the aftereffect was briefer among the old than among the young, just the opposite of prediction. This was seen again in a subsequent study by Griew, Fellows, and Howes (1963).

In this later study, however, the duration of fixation was varied. As may

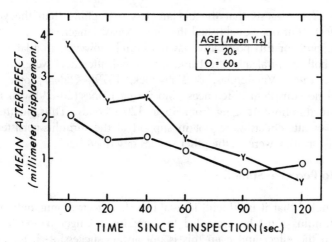

FIGURE 12.1: Magnitude of figural aftereffect as a function of the time since inspection. (Drawn from Figure 4 of Eisdorfer & Axelrod, 1964.)

be seen in Figure 12.2, after 15 seconds, 30 seconds, and 45 seconds of focusing on the rotating spiral, the aftereffect among the old (60–81 years) was shorter lasting than among the young (18–25). After 60 seconds of viewing the rotating spiral, however, the older people had longer aftereffects than the younger ones. The crossing of curves in both this figure and in

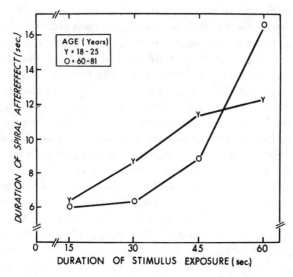

FIGURE 12.2: Duration of spiral aftereffect as a function of stimulus exposure duration. (From Table 1 of Griew et al., 1963.)

Figure 12.1 suggests that the old are less susceptible than the young to aftereffects, but once established they may persist longer.

Support for this possibility was not found, however, in a later study in which both a spiral aftereffect and a waterfall aftereffect were investigated (Coyne, Eiler, Vanderplas, & Botwinick, 1979). Older people (60–69) showed no consistent differences from younger ones (20–29) with stimulus exposure durations ranging from 45 to 120 seconds. Thus, in the main, studies of aftereffects were not in support of the stimulus-persistence hypothesis, as they were in the other studies described here.

Time to Perceive Stimuli

It was noted that it is difficult to establish aftereffects among older persons. The stimulus must be presented to them for a longer period of time to establish the effect and even this is not always successful. It is as if more time is required to transform the stimulus into effective nervous energy. There is evidence to support this idea.

Eriksen, Hamlin, and Breitmeyer (1970) carried out two experiments in which they compared three adult age-groups (30–35, 40–45, and 50–55 years). In the first experiment, they measured ability to visually identify the location of gaps in circles when the circles were exposed for varying periods of time. In this study, unlike the others, every person in each of the age-groups was matched for visual acuity. Thus, the three age-groups were similar in this kind of visual ability. Even so, Eriksen et al. (1970) found that it took progressively more time for the older persons to perceive the stimulus, despite the fact that the oldest person was only 55. This is a typical finding; older persons are almost always disadvantaged by brief exposures or quickly paced tasks regardless of the type of task. This could explain why aftereffects are difficult to induce among older people.

In another part of the study, Eriksen et al. (1970) tested the same three groups of people, adjusting the stimulus materials in size and critical detail for each individual. The adjustments were such that for each person the stimuli would yield 75 percent correct detections for a specified duration and brightness level. In this way all persons were responding to stimuli of equal difficulty in terms of individual perceptual ability.

The experimenters then varied both the exposure duration and illumination of each stimulus so as to keep the total light energy reaching the retina at a constant level. In doing this, they found that the older people took longer to detect the stimuli. That is, the older adults integrated the light energy over a longer interval and so were able to compensate for their higher light thresholds. Eriksen et al. (1970) concluded that older adults have a longer critical duration in time–intensity reciprocity relationships in the identification of form.

All these studies together suggest that older persons have more difficulty in processing inputs and that it takes them longer to do so. Once the inputs are incorporated into the perceptual system, however, they persist longer. These characteristics often hinder performance, but in some instances such as in the study of corresponding letter halves, they are helpful.

VISUAL MASKING

The formation of a percept begins with sensory information. If this information is interrupted, then the percept will not be formed. One way of studying interruption is by way of visual masking studies. These studies are similar in some ways to the fusion experiments, but instead of investigating the fusion of corresponding stimuli, one stimulus is masked (obliterated or degraded) as a result of a second stimulus that is presented just before or just after it. In this experiment the stimulus that is masked is called the test or target stimulus (TS); the stimulus that diminishes the visibility of the TS is called the masking stimulus (MS). When the MS follows the TS, it is called backward masking; when the MS precedes the TS it is called forward masking.

Studies on visual masking have found that older persons are susceptible to masking over longer intervals. That is, an MS separated from a TS by a relatively long time interval masks the TS for the old but not the young. This is consistent with the notion of stimulus persistence and also suggests that the old process information more slowly than the young.

Backward Masking

Kline and Szafran (1975) presented digits as a target stimulus and an array of short horizontal and vertical line segments (visual noise) as a masking stimulus). Both the target stimuli and the masking stimuli were presented to the same eye (monoptic stimulation). In a subsequent study, Kline and Birren (1975) presented the TS (single digits) to one eye and the visual noise MS to the other (dichoptic stimulation). Both studies showed similar results. Older people were more susceptible to masking than the younger people, that is, the TS and MS had to be separated by more time in order for the old person to see the TS (digits).

Peripheral and Central Processing. Walsh, Till, and Williams (1978) reported similar results when letters of the alphabet were masked by a pattern of line segments in a monoptic backward masking task. Walsh et al. attributed the greater susceptibility to masking on the part of the elderly to slower speed of "peripheral perceptual processing." Walsh et al. referred to Turvey's (1973) criteria in distinguishing peripheral from central processes. In this view, peripheral processes include the retina, the lateral geniculate nucleus, and the primary visual cortex. This is very different from the more traditional neurophysiological distinction between peripheral and central processes, where peripheral processes refer to sites outside the central nervous system but, perhaps, include the retina.*

Walsh (1976) also examined age differences in the effects of backward dichoptic masking when the TS was a letter and the MS a random pattern of lines. The elderly were again more susceptible to masking and this time this was attributed to "central perceptual processing" as defined by Turvey (1973). Till and Franklin (1981) compared the relative contributions of peripheral and central processing to the masking. They concluded that age differences in central processing are significantly larger than those in peripheral processing. This suggests that age differences in stimulus persistence are associated more with central than peripheral neural processes.

Perceptual processing speed apparently can be modified with training. Hertzog, Williams, and Walsh (1976) provided practice to reduce the amount of time needed to process the target stimulus. That is, they carried out the TS–MS sequences over many trials. They found that both young and old reduced their times, and to a similar extent. After practice both old and young were able to see the TS with smaller time separations between TS and MS. The ability to modify stimulus-persistence effects is all the more interesting if the effects are thought to have a neurophysiological base. It seems especially important to replicate these results, especially since Kline and Birren (1975) did not observe significant practice effects in their backward dichoptic masking study.

Signal-to-Noise Relationships. Masking studies have been interpreted in terms of stimulus persistence or in terms of a loss with age in the speed of perceptual processing. Salthouse (1980), however, has proposed an alternative interpretation: The susceptibility of older persons to backward masking might stem from an age-related reduction in the ability to perceive the signal relative to background "noise" levels (i.e., the ratio between target stimulus strength and background perceptual noise in the nervous system). He tested this hypothesis in a study in which he manipulated the signal-to-noise ratio through variations in duration and discriminability of the TS. Salthouse confirmed the signal-to-noise hypothesis in that as the TS (signal) was increased (and the noise level kept constant), the older adults were able to see the TS at short interstimulus intervals.

---

*Turvey made this distinction between peripheral and central processing based on the time–energy relationships between TS and MS. According to Turvey, in peripheral masking, TS energy is multiplicatively related to the interstimulus interval (ISI) necessary to escape masking (i.e., target energy X ISI = a constant). On the other hand, central masking is not energy dependent; the target duration and the ISI are additively related (i.e., target duration + ISI = a constant).

Forward Masking

Coyne (1981) carried out a study of forward masking (where MS precedes TS). His study yielded results consistent with those of backward masking studies. The critical interstimulus interval between the TS (letters) and MS (visual noise) necessary to escape masking was determined for three age-groups: a young group (19–31), an older group (61–69), and a still older one (71–79). Both old groups required more time to escape masking than did the young group, but there was no difference between the two old groups.

It is thought that backward masking involves both summation and interruption of stimulus traces but that forward masking primarily involves only summation of the visual traces of the MS and TS. Accordingly, Coyne in his forward masking study concluded that older adults integrate energy over longer intervals than younger persons. This result is in accord with the data of Eriksen et al. (1970), based on the time required to perceive stimuli. It is also consistent with the stimulus-persistence hypothesis.

Coyne also examined the effects of practice in forward masking. Although practice reduced the critical interstimulus interval necessary to see the TS, the practice effects were comparable among the three age-groups. These results are similar to those of Hertzog et al. (1976) in the effects of practice in backward masking. This suggests that the increase with age in susceptibility to forward masking would not be eliminated by practice.

VISUAL CHANNELS

The stimulus-persistence model is generally useful in accounting for a variety of changes that occur with age in sensory–perceptual processes. As a precise scientific model, though, its utility is limited in that it does not specify either the mechanisms that underlie the changes, or their loci (other than references to the nervous system). Accordingly, Kline and Schieber (1981b) proposed a transient–sustained shift hypothesis to account for age differences in stimulus persistence in the visual system.

The transient–sustained shift hypothesis is based on physiological and psychophysical evidence that different types of visual stimuli are detected by different neural channels in the visual system. The human visual system seems to contain at least two classes of channels, the *transient* and the *sustained*. These channel types differ in their ability to detect stimuli of different temporal characteristics and different size.

Transient and Sustained Channels

Sustained channels are slow to respond, produce a persistent response when stimulated, and can integrate stimulus energy over relatively long periods of time. They are best at detecting stable high-spatial-frequency stimuli. Transient channels, on the other hand, respond best to low-spatial-frequency stimuli and handle the detection of stimulus change such as flicker or motion. When activated, transient channels respond quickly and briefly. They also appear to inhibit the persistence in the sustained channels.

Studies based on the Contrast Sensitivity Function, as will be seen shortly, show that young and old are not very different in detecting stationary low spatial frequencies, but are different in detecting high spatial frequencies. Low spatial frequencies correspond to large objects, and high spatial frequencies to small objects. When the stimuli are transient (i.e., moving or flickering), the elderly appear to be less sensitive than the young in the detection of the low spatial frequency gratings (see below). Thus, Kline and Schieber's (1981b) transient–sustained shift hypothesis suggests that when with age there is loss in the effectiveness of the transient visual channels, the older observer comes to depend relatively more on the sustained channels. Certainly, the overall visual functioning of the older visual system seems to resemble more the characteristics of sustained channels than transient ones. If the effectiveness of the transient channel is impaired in old age and the sustained channels predominate, one would expect to see greater persistence and longer stimulus integration times. As noted, this is what the studies on temporal resolution show. The Kline and Schieber hypothesis, therefore, assumes a differential aging of the transient versus the sustained channel, with a resulting "shift" to sustained-type functioning.

Contrast Sensitivity

Stable Stimuli. It was indicated that this shift hypothesis is based in part on the Contrast Sensitivity Function (CSF). Spatial and size discrimination abilities subserved by the visual channels are assessed by reference to this function. In the CSF experiment a series of dark and light bars (gratings) are presented and the contrast between the light and dark bars is varied. The thickness and closeness of the bars (spatial frequency) can also be varied. A fine grating is one with high spatial frequency and a coarse grating is of low spatial frequency. Thus, spatial frequency refers to the number of repetitions of the bars per unit of space on the retina. As contrast and spatial frequency are varied, the observer has to indicate when the grating can no longer be seen (i.e., tell the difference between the bars and the spaces between them). Detecting the presence of a very high frequency grating is basically the same as a visual acuity task.* By determining the contrast needed to detect spatial frequencies from low to high, the CSF provides a more com-

*Figure 12.3 shows a range of spatial frequencies from 0.5 to 16 cycles per degree. The low spatial grating of 0.5 cycles per degree corresponds roughly in size to two bars (one light and one dark) within the width of a quarter of a dollar coin when viewed at a distance of 27 inches. The grating of 16 cycles per degree corresponds in size to 32 light and 32 dark bars in the space of the quarter at 27 inches.

plete assessment of the spatial discrimination capacity of the visual system than does a traditional acuity test.

The first studies of CSF and age reported mixed results. More recent, better controlled investigations, however, show clear age differences in CSF, particularly with high and intermediate spatial frequencies (e.g., Arundale, 1978; Derefeldt, Lennerstrand & Lundh, 1979; Owsley, Sekuler, & Siemsen, 1983; Kline, Schieber, Abusamra, & Coyne, 1983). The results of Owsley et al. may be seen in Figure 12.3. Although much of the relative inability with age to detect finely structured gratings is associated with changes in the eye's

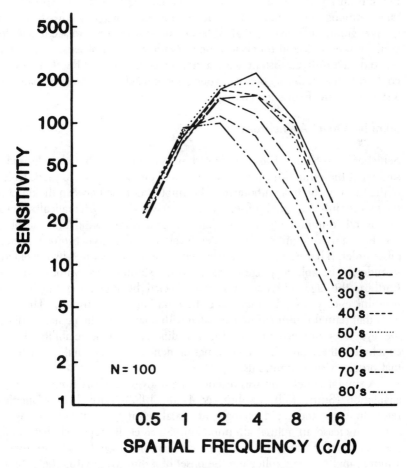

FIGURE 12.3: Age and contrast sensitivity as a function of spatial frequency of grating. (From *Vision Research*, 23: 7, Owsley, Cynthia, Sekuler, Robert, & Siemsen, Dennis. Contrast Sensitivity Throughout Adulthood. Copyright 1983, Pergamon Press, Ltd. Reprinted with permission.

optical system, it is possible that some of the inability is due to differences with age in the visual channels that process high-spatial-frequency stimuli (Owsley et al., 1983).

Moving Stimuli. The lack of age differences at low spatial frequencies observed in the CSF is not consistent with the transient–sustained shift hypothesis (that the old come to rely on sustained channels to the relative neglect of transient channels). This may be, however, because the CSF uses stationary gratings that are much less likely than moving stimuli to expose differences in transient channel functioning. There is some evidence for this. Owsley et al. (1983) compared age-groups in contrast sensitivity when the stimulus was a one cycle per degree grating moving at two different rates. Among the young, sensitivity is enhanced when a low-spatial-frequency grating is moving, that is, less contrast is required to see it. Owsley et al., however, found much less motion enhancement of sensitivity among the old, a result consistent with a transient–sustained shift. This was in contrast to the similarity between young and old subjects when compared on a stationary low-frequency grating.

Stimulus Offset Asynchrony

Schieber and Kline (1982) presented two visual stimuli (a circle and a square) at the same time and both young and old people had to judge which of the two was the first withdrawn. The amount of time between the offset of the two stimuli (i.e., their offset asynchrony) was varied systematically as was the overall duration of stimuli. Schieber and Kline found that the older people required significantly greater levels of offset asynchrony to detect offset order. That is, more time between stimuli was required by the elderly in order to be able to judge correctly which stimulus was withdrawn first. Further, this age difference was not affected by increasing the level of stimulus energy (i.e., by increasing the duration of the stimuli). This suggests that retinal illumination associated with changes in the ocular media of the eye does not account for the age difference in detectability. It was concluded, therefore, that aging brings on deficits in the neural mechanisms that process visual "transients."

A similar conclusion was reached in a study of recovery from early light adaptation (Sturr, Kelly, Kobus, & Taub, 1982). Early light adaptation refers to large and rapid changes in visual sensitivity that accompany an abrupt increase in retinal illumination. Sturr et al. reported that young people showed a more vigorous response than older people and also showed a more rapid recovery following the onset of a dim white visual field. Since the adapting field consisted primarily of low-spatial-frequency components, the slower response pattern of the older observers suggested a loss with age in transient visual channels.

The Shift Hypothesis and Reaction Time

Kline et al. (1983) tested the shift hypothesis in the context of reaction time. Age differences in reaction time were measured in relation to gratings of varied spatial frequency. The results of this study are seen in Figure 12.4. Reaction time increased with increases in spatial frequency, and this was even more so among the old than the young. This result could be accounted for only partly by age differences in contrast sensitivity (see Figure 12.3). First, the correlation between spatial frequency and reaction time was higher among the young than among the old. Thus, the visibility of the grating was a better predictor of reaction time in the young than the old. This was more apparent with the low spatial frequencies, where contrast sensitivity was completely unrelated to reaction time in the old group. Second, in this study, age-group differences in reaction time did not follow directly those in contrast sensitivity. The largest age difference in contrast sensitivity occurred at intermediate spatial frequencies but as can be seen in Figure 12.4, the greatest reaction time differences were at the highest spatial frequencies.

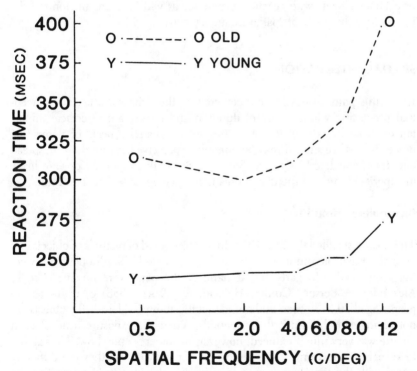

FIGURE 12.4: Reaction time of young and old adults as a function of spatial frequency of the reaction stimulus. (From Kline et al., 1983. Reprinted with permission by the *Journal of Gerontology*, Vol. 38, pp. 211–216, 1983.)

Therefore, although some of the increase in reaction time in the old group at higher spatial frequencies is undoubtedly due to contrast sensitivity losses, at least one other factor seems to be involved. This might be a decline in the speed of the visual channels and/or a change in the relationship between visual channel types, perhaps a transient–sustained shift. As can be seen in Figure 12.4, reaction time increased sharply among the young from 8 cycles per degree, which is about the range that distinguishes the transient and sustained channels (Kulikowski & Tolhurst, 1973). Among the old, reaction time increased steadily from 2 cycles per degree, perhaps due to increasing dependence on the slower sustained channels. Overall, therefore, these data suggest an age-related slowing in the transient visual channels that process low spatial frequencies, and a contrast sensitivity loss, plus some sustained visual channel slowing at the high spatial frequencies.

Although reaction time studies typically use stimulus contrast levels higher than the one used in this study, it nonetheless raises a question as to the meaning of age differences in reaction time when, as in most all studies, the spatial frequency characteristics of the stimuli are not specified. The next chapter deals with reaction time and, as will be seen, in none of the literature is this issue of spatial frequency considered.

SPATIAL INTEGRATION

Up to this point discussion has centered on the temporal aspects of perceptual processing where issues of duration and timing are of critical importance. Now the discussion will turn to the spatial aspects of perceptual processing where stimuli may be difficult to perceive because they are spread out, fragmented, or disguised. Studies indicate that older persons are likely to experience more difficulty in organizing perceptions of such stimuli.

Incomplete Stimuli

There is a test called the Street Test that is composed of pictures of objects and animals. Each picture looks as it would be in solid black silhouette if it were not segmented into parts and if none of the parts were missing. Crook, Alexander, Anderson, Coules, Hanson, & Jeffries (1958) gave this test to people aged 20 to 50 years and found that the ability to identify the objects did not change in this limited age period. When the exposure time of each picture was very much reduced, however, the older people showed less ability to recognize the forms. This study did not indicate whether the difficulty rested with the time required to perceive the stimulus or in integrating the stimulus parts. Other research suggests that it is, at least in part, the latter.

A test called the Hooper Visual Organization Test (Hooper, 1958) was devised to help in the diagnosis of organic brain pathology. A person is presented with drawings of simple objects that have been cut into parts so that each drawing can appear as a type of jigsaw puzzle. The task is to name the object, which can be done only by a spatial reorganization and integration of the parts. Hooper reported that the test performances among young adults are superior to those of older ones. The finding that older perceivers are likely to be disadvantaged when the stimuli are irregular and/or unfamiliar was also reported by Kline, Culler, and Sucec (1977). They asked young, middle-aged, and old adults to identify 10 words, when each letter of the words was formed by the unclosed white area between black blotches. The letters were somewhat irregular in their appearance, and so the task was similar in some ways to the Street Test based on objects. The word task was very easy for young people but almost impossible for older people; only one of the 16 older people correctly identified any of the words. This study was repeated (Kline, Hogan, & Stier, 1980), but instead of using inconspicuous words made irregular by black blotches, more traditional block-style letters were used. In this study, both young and old people performed extremely well.

Danziger and Salthouse (1978) in their study of identifying incomplete figures suggested that the difficulty old people have rests in their less efficient utilization of the available information.

Parts Embedded in Confusing Backgrounds

There is other evidence of decreased ability of older persons to integrate spatial information. Both Crook et al. (1958) and Basowitz and Korchin (1957) gave people of different ages a version of the Gottschaldt hidden figures test. In this task, two-dimensional geometric figures are embedded in a confusing complex of additional lines so that the figure melds into the background of lines. The task is to identify the figure. Many abilities are involved in this task, including spatial rearrangement of the forms. Crook et al. did not observe significant differences with age in identifying the figures but Basowitz and Korchin did. It may be recalled that the oldest person in the Crook et al. study was 50 years; the average age of the older group in the Basowitz and Korchin study was 70 years. Thus, ability to identify concealed figures is age-related but it seems, to age 50 there is little, if any, decline.

Hidden figures, both visual and tactile, were used by Axelrod and Cohen (1961). The tactile version involved examining figures by touch and finding them by touch when embedded in more complex contexts. Here too, with both the visual and the tactile versions, the old were found to have greater difficulty than the young in identifying the figures. Axelrod and Cohen also measured touch sensitivity to determine whether this could account for their results. Touch sensitivity was not related to tactile embedded figure performance and it was thus concluded that the deficit reflected a "higher order" perceptual function than tactile acuity.

COMPENSATORY ADJUSTMENTS

Although there are obvious deficits in later life in sensory perceptual processing, the magnitude of the deficits in overall functioning is often less than might be expected. This is so because it is possible to make compensatory adjustments to response deficits. Some of these compensations appear as changes in personality, such as the increase in cautiousness described in Chapter 10. Some of them involve changes in strategy so as to make use of skills or abilities that are still relatively strong. This might involve taking a more efficient approach to a problem or relying on a different sensory modality. Szafran (1968), for example, found that older airline pilots tended to select strategies that optimized signal detection in auditory and visual discrimination tasks, thus compensating for age declines in sensory mechanisms. Other adjustments are also possible but, unfortunately, they have hardly been studied. It is here, perhaps more than in other areas, where good work can be very important both for basic science and for the welfare of older adults.

In the previous chapter, recommendations were made for speaking to older people who have auditory sensory difficulties (see Table 11.1). One recommendation was to advise the hard-of-hearing to observe lip movements. Visual input can supplement or even supplant sensory-perceptual information other than auditory. For example, in walking up and down steps, older people often watch what they are doing while young people do this less often. Other adjustments are possible, as seen in driving a car. It is possible for the older person to drive more slowly, to rely on well-known routes, or to avoid high traffic times. The older driver may supplement his skills by depending on someone else to navigate. Such compensatory adjustments are often made automatically without awareness. Studies examining such adjustments and developing suggestions that can be applied consciously would be most helpful.

SUMMARY

Sensory-perceptual processes provide the means for us to interact with the external world. With age, however, there are a variety of changes in these processes that limit the interaction. For example, if a person responds to a stimulus and then must respond to a second one which follows shortly after the first, the second response is often different from the first. It is as if the neural trace of the first stimulus persists for a while leaving the responder either refractory to subsequent stimulation or responsive in a different way. It has been suggested that this stimulus persistence is greater in older persons. Although it is more a model or theory than an established fact, this notion can explain much of the data concerning age differences in sensory/perceptual functioning.

The stimulus-persistence hypothesis can explain the age-related fusion of closely occurring stimuli such as flashes of light (CFF), or pairs of clicks, or discrete electric shocks. The stimulus-persistence hypothesis, however, has been applied to these data in *post hoc* fashion, whereas the most appropriate evaluation of any scientific model is through prospective studies. More recent studies that have applied the model prospectively are generally supportive of the stimulus-persistence hypothesis, but not totally.

For example, if the stimuli are constructed appropriately, older persons appear to be superior to younger ones in identifying a word when it is presented as two corresponding halves separated by a time interval. Similarly, the dark interval threshold study shows a lengthening with age in the interval between two flashes necessary for the flashes to be seen as separate, rather than fused.

The data in regard to the perceived continuity of a form when it is presented alternately with a blank field can similarly be explained by stimulus persistence.

The stimulus-persistence notion can be applied to the processes of color vision. Older persons appear to fuse lights of different wavelength more readily than young people. This results in a new color over greater time intervals. Older people also form more enduring complementary afterimages.

Studies of visual masking are related to studies of temporal fusion in that one stimulus will mask or obliterate another one if the time interval between them is short enough. These studies show that whether the masking stimulus precedes the target stimulus (forward masking) or follows it (backward masking), the results are supportive of greater stimulus persistence in old age. That is, older people require more time between the two stimuli to escape the masking effect.

Studies of perceptual aftereffects in elderly persons have provided little support for the stimulus-persistence model. Earlier investigations suggested that although older persons are less susceptible to aftereffects, the aftereffects seem to last longer once established. A more recent study, however, failed to confirm this result. Since the duration of aftereffects constitutes a direct test of the stimulus-persistence model, these data represent a significant challenge to the stimulus persistence model in its present simple form.

Although the stimulus-persistence model is very helpful in accounting for a wide variety of age changes in sensory/perceptual processes, its usefulness as a scientific model is limited because it does not indicate the mechanisms of persistence or their loci. One model that attempts to address these shortcomings in vision is the transient–sustained shift model. This model indicates that the older visual system comes to be dominated by the slow-responding sustained channels as a result of a decline in the effectiveness of the fast-responding transient channels.

Information about the spatial discrimination abilities of the visual channels comes primarily from studies of the Contrast Sensitivity Function (CSF). In the CSF experiment, an assessment is made of the amount of contrast required to detect visual gratings of varying degress of fineness (spatial frequency). When the gratings are stationary, the major loss with age is in discriminating intermediate and high spatial frequencies. This loss appears to be due largely to changes in the optical media of the eye. This is not supportive of the transient–sustained shift idea of loss in the transient neural channels that handle low spatial frequencies. The transient channels, however, are best tapped by stimuli that flicker or move. When a low spatial frequency stimulus is in motion, there is a significant age difference in its detection, as would be predicted by the transient–sustained shift idea. Studies of early light adaptation, of detection of stimulus offset order, and of reaction time to gratings of different spatial frequency are also in accord with this model.

There are also changes with age in more global aspects of perception. Studies of spatial integration where issues of exposure duration and timing are less emphasized also show that older people have difficulty. Older adults perform less well in tasks where the integration of dissociated stimulus parts is required. They fill in missing stimulus elements less well and they do not perceive stimuli in more complex backgrounds as readily as do younger people.

A type of research that is greatly needed is in the area of compensations for sensory/perceptual deficits. These compensations take on a variety of forms including changes in task strategy, bisensory compensatory adjustments, and alterations in the allocation of attentional resources. Such research could advance basic scientific understanding as well as contribute greatly to the welfare of older persons.

REFERENCES

Amberson, J. I., Atkeson, B. M., Pollack, R. H., & Malatesta, V. J. Age differences in dark interval threshold across the life-span. *Experimental Aging Research*, 1979, 5, 423–433.

Arundale, K. An investigation in the variation of human contrast sensitivity with age and ocular pathology. *British Journal of Opthalmology*, 1978, 62, 213–215.

Axelrod, S. Cognitive tasks in several modalities. In R. H. Williams, C. Tibbitts, & W. Donahue (Eds.), *Processes of aging* (Vol. 1). New York: Atherton Press, 1963, pp. 132–145.

Axelrod, S., & Cohen, L. D. Senescence and imbedded-figure performance in vision and touch. *Perceptual and Motor Skills*, 1961, 12, 283–288.

Axelrod, S., & Eisdorfer, C. Senescence and figural aftereffects in two modalities. *Journal of Genetic Psychology*, 1962, *100*, 85–91.

Axelrod, S., Thompson, L. W., & Cohen, L. D. Effects of senescence on the temporal resolution of somesthetic stimuli presented to one hand or both. *Journal of Gerontology*, 1968, *23*, 191–195.

Basowitz, H., & Korchin, S. J. Age differences in the perception of closure. *Journal of Abnormal and Social Psychology*, 1957, *54*, 93–97.

Coppinger, N. W. The relationship between critical flicker frequency and chronological age for varying levels of stimulus brightness. *Journal of Gerontology*, 1955, *10*, 48–52.

Coyne, A. C. Age differences and practice in forward visual masking. *Journal of Gerontology*, 1981, *36*, 730–732.

Coyne, A. C., Eiler, J. M., Vanderplas, J., & Botwinick, J. Stimulus persistence and age. *Experimental Aging Research*, 1979, *5*, 263–270.

Crook, M. N., Alexander, E. A., Anderson, E. M. S., Coules, J., Hanson, A., & Jeffries, N. T., Jr. *Age and form perception*. USAF School of Aviation Medicine, Randolph AFB, Tex., 1958, Report No. 57-124.

Danziger, W. L., & Salthouse, T. A. Age and the perception of incomplete figures. *Experimental Aging Research*, 1978, *4*, 67–80.

Derefeldt, G., Lennerstrand, G., & Lundh, B. Age variations in normal human contrast sensitivity. *Acta Opthalmologia*, 1979, *57*, 679–689.

Eisdorfer, C., & Axelrod, S. Senescence and figural aftereffects in two modalities: A correction. *Journal of Genetic Psychology*, 1964, *104*, 193–197.

Eriksen, C. W., Hamlin, R. M., & Breitmeyer, R. G. Temporal factors in visual perception as related to aging. *Perception and Psychophysics*, 1970, *7*, 354–356.

Falk, J., & Kline, D. W. Stimulus persistence in CFF: Underactivation or overarousal? *Experimental Aging Research*, 1978, *4*, 109–123.

Griew, S., Fellows, B. J., & Howes, R. Duration of spiral aftereffect as a function of stimulus exposure and age. *Perceptual and Motor Skills*, 1963, *17*, 210.

Griew, S., & Lynn, R. Constructive "reaction inhibition" in the interpretation of age changes in performance. *Nature*, 1960, *186*, 182.

Hertzog, C. K., Williams, M. V., & Walsh, D. A. The effects of practice on age differences in central perceptual processing. *Journal of Gerontology*, 1976, *31*, 428–433.

Hooper, H. E. *The Hooper visual organization test—Manual*. Beverly Hills, Calif.: Western Psychological Services, 1958.

Kline, D. W., & Birren, J. E. Age differences in backward dichoptic masking. *Experimental Aging Research*, 1975, *1*, 17–25.

Kline, D. W., Culler, M. P., & Sucec, J. Differences in inconspicuous word identification as a function of age and reversible-figure training. *Experimental Aging Research*, 1977, *3*, 203–213.

Kline, D. W., Hogan, P. M., & Stier, D. L. Age and the identification of inconspicuous words. *Experimental Aging Research*, 1980, *6*, 137–147.

Kline, D. W., Ikeda, D., & Schieber, F. Age and temporal resolution in color vision: When do red and green make yellow? *Journal of Gerontology*, 1982, *37*, 705–709.

Kline, D. W., & Nestor, S. The persistence of complementary afterimages as a function of adult age and exposure duration. *Experimental Aging Research*, 1977, *3*, 191–201.

Kline, D. W., & Orme-Rogers, C. Examination of stimulus persistence as the basis for superior visual identification performance among older adults. *Journal of Gerontology*, 1978, *33*, 76–81.

Kline, D. W., & Szafran, J. Age differences in backward monoptic visual noise masking. *Journal of Gerontology*, 1975, *30*, 307–311.

Kline, D. W., & Schieber, F. What are the age differences in visual sensory memory? *Journal of Geronotology*, 1981, 36, 86–89. (a)

Kline, D. W., & Schieber, F. Visual aging: A transient/sustained shift? *Perception and Psychophysics*, 1981, 29, 181–182. (b)

Kline, D. W., Schieber, F., Abusamra, L. C., & Coyne, A. C. Age, the eye, and the visual channels: Contrast sensitivity and response speed. *Journal of Gerontology*, 1983, 38, 211–216.

Kulikowski, J. J., & Tolhurst, D. J. Psychophysical evidence for sustained and transient detectors in the visual system. *Journal of Physiology*, 1973, 232, 149–162.

McFarland, R. A., Warren, B., & Karis, C. Alterations in critical flicker frequency as function of age and light:dark ratio. *Journal of Experimental Psychology*, 1958, 56, 529–538.

Misiak, H. Age and sex differences in critical flicker frequency. *Journal of Experimental Psychology*, 1947, 37, 318–332.

Owsley, C., Sekuler, R., & Siemsen, D. Contrast sensitivity throughout adulthood. *Vision Research*, 1983, 23, 689–699.

Salthouse, T. A. Age differences in visual masking: A manifestation of decline in neural signal/noise ratio? Paper presented at the Thirty-third Annual Scientific Meeting of the Gerontological Society, 1980, San Diego, Calif.

Schieber, F., & Kline, D. W. Age and the discrimination of visual successiveness. *Experimental Aging Research*, 1982, 8, 159–161.

Sturr, J. F., Kelly, S., Kobus, D. A., & Taub, H. A. Age-dependent magnitude and time course of early light adaptation. *Perception and Psychophysics*, 1982, 31, 402–404.

Szafran, J. Psychophysiological studies of aging in pilots. In G. A. Talland (Ed.). *Human aging and behavior*. New York: Academic Press, 1968. pp. 37–74.

Till, R. E., & Franklin, L. D. On the locus of age differences in visual information processing. *Journal of Gerontology*, 1981, 36, 200–210.

Turvey, M. T. On peripheral and central processes in vision: Inferences from an information-processing analysis of masking with patterned stimuli. *Psychological Review*, 1973, 80, 1–52.

Walsh, D. A. Age differences in central perceptual processing: a dichoptic backward masking investigation. *Journal of Gerontology*, 1976, 31, 178–185.

Walsh, D. A. & Thompson, L. W. Age differences in visual sensory memory. *Journal of Gerontology*, 1978, 33, 283–297.

Walsh, D. A., Till, R. E., & Williams, M. V. Age differences in peripheral perceptual processing: A monoptic backward investigation. *Journal of Experimental Psychology: Human Perception and Performance*, 1978, 4, 232–243.

Weale, R. A. On the eye. In A. T. Welford & J. E. Birren (Eds.), *Behavior, aging and the nervous system*. Springfield, Ill.: Charles C. Thomas, 1965.

Weekers, R., & Roussel, F. Introduction a l'étude de la fréquencée de fusion en clinique. *Ophthalmologica*, 1946, 112, 305–319.

Weiss, A. D. Sensory functions. In J. E. Birren (Ed.), *Handbook of aging and the individual*. Chicago: University of Chicago Press, 1959, pp. 503–542.

Weiss, A. D. Auditory perception in aging. In J. E. Birren, R. N. Butler, S. W. Greenhouse, L. Sokoloff, & M. R. Yarrow (Eds.), *Human aging: A biological and behavioral study*. P. H. S. Publication No. 986. Washington, D.C.: U. S. Government Printing Office, 1963.

Welford, A. T. Age and skill: motor, intellectual and social. In A. T. Welford (Ed.), *Interdisciplinary topics in gerontology* (Vol. 4). Basel and New York: S. Karger, 1969, pp. 1–22.

13
Slowness of Behavior

TWO VIEWS OF
SPEEDED PERFORMANCE

The Consequence View

It was seen that sensation and perception become altered in later life and it will be seen in subsequent chapters that cognitive abilities are also affected. There is a close relationship between these functions and speed of behavior. For example, if there is difficulty detecting objects, or in making visual discriminations, or in solving problems, response times in carrying out these tasks increase. This suggests that speed of performance may be used as a measure to examine a variety of different abilities. Few behavior scientists would argue with this, except perhaps to question whether speed of performance is the best measure that can be used, especially in investigating differences among age-groups. If perceptual or cognitive abilities are under test, other measures may be preferable. Additionally, slowness can result from age changes in muscles and peripheral neural mechanisms. The question of best measure comes up often, for instance in the context of mental testing where the choice is between tests of "power" (accuracy, knowledge) or tests of "speed." Most investigators opt for power tests or for a combination of the two.

The Determinant View

There is an alternate view regarding speed and age. In the alternate view, slowness of behavior with age is not a consequence of failing sensory perceptual or cognitive functions as much as these are consequences of a general slowing down of central nervous system (CNS) functioning. In this view, slowness of behavior is thought to be a reflection of CNS slowing and, as such, a determinant of perceptual and cognition abilities. Birren (1964, pp. 111–112), for example, concluded, "the evidence indicates that all behav-

229

ior mediated by the central nervous system tends to slow in the aging organism. . . . In the view favored here, slowness of behavior is the principal manifestation of a primary process of aging in the nervous system." In a similar vein, Birren, Woods, and Williams (1980, p. 305) wrote, "loss in speed is a reflection of a general mediating process in the central nervous system. This process appears to lead to a general slowing in speed of behavior, which in turn is reflected across a number of specific behaviors." It is as if there is a central power source that when functioning optimally, not only makes for fast behavior of all sorts, but through it, makes for good performances of all sorts.

Supporting a Position

Thus, there are two divergent views: one is that slowing of behavior with age is a consequence of failing perceptual and cognitive systems, the other view is that speed of behavior, as a reflection of CNS functioning, determines functional ability in many if not all systems. The former view is the traditional one, so traditional in fact, that most investigators take it for granted and may not be aware of the other one. Accordingly, in investigating memory, for example, not many would bother to measure speed of performance, preferring instead the more traditional measures, such as the number of items correctly remembered.

Only a few protagonists explicitly defend the traditional, consequence view because there are so very few investigators who do not maintain this mainstream position. This will change, however, since the number of investigators taking the determinant view now seems to be growing. The change has already begun with the consequence view defended and the determinant view challenged. Hartley, Harker, and Walsh (1980, p. 243) declared, "For three reasons we believe that the speed-of-processing explanation (determinant view) is an unproductive research hypothesis for memory investigations." The three reasons relate to incongruities between specific findings in traditional memory studies and predictions made from the determinant view. Kausler (1982, pp. 257–258) also felt the need to criticize the determinant position. He said, "there should be no exceptions" to the universality of the speed loss with age as a result of slower CNS functioning. ". . . All behaviors should be affected by slowing down. But this is clearly not true."

If to date only little argument has been raised among the adherents of the consequence position, it has been otherwise among adherents of the determinant position. Adherents of the determinant position have raised arguments frequently. Birren was an early voice, but there are others now. For example, Salthouse and Kail (1983) maintained that rate of processing, that is, speed of performance, represents an important dimension in understanding the causes of differences among age groups in cognition. Salthouse (1980; 1982), Waugh and Barr (1980), and others maintained that it is not capacity or the strategies that people develop in learning and memory tasks that distinguishes their abilities but, instead, the general slowing of behavior.

HOW GENERAL IS THE SLOWING?

A Most Replicated Finding

How universal is the slowing with age? It is not seen in all studies, but it is seen very, very often. It has been seen so often that Salthouse (1984) introduced his chapter by quoting many investigators who had referred to the slowing with age in terms such as these: " 'most pronounced,' . . .' most strongly substantiated,' . . .' most characteristic,' . . . " and many other similar ones. Still, presented in this way, the generality of the speed loss with age may be misleading.

Poor Prediction of Performance Speed from Age

Individual differences in speed of response are greater among the old than the young (e.g., Botwinick & Thompson, 1968). In fact, some old people perform more quickly than some young people. This means that prediction of an individual's speed scores on the basis of age alone is poor. Based on reports in the literature over the years, Salthouse (1984) listed over 50 coefficents of correlation between age and many different kinds of speeded behaviors. All coefficients are positive, reflecting slowing with age, but the range is large, going from 0.15 to 0.64 with a median of 0.45. This means that over a wide band of different kinds of behaviors, age accounted for only between 2 and 41 percent of the variance of speed of performance, with a median of 20 percent. As a universal characteristic and as one to explain much of perceptual and cognitive functioning, this is not a very impressive accounting. Thus, the slowing of behavior with age may be important in accounting for failing abilities, but much room is left for other explanations.

WHAT IS THE EVIDENCE FOR CENTRAL SLOWING?

If slowness of behavior with age is important as an index of a slow functioning central nervous system, or one that is otherwise functioning suboptimally, it must be shown that central mechanisms are much more important than peripheral mechanisms in accounting for the slowing. Much of the research literature bearing on this issue is based on studies of reaction time.

Peripheral Mechanisms

Studies have been directed to determining whether the loss of speed with age can be explained on the basis of alterations in the sense organs and other peripheral neural mechanisms. If it can, speed loss would not be seen nearly as important to the processes of perception and cognition as it would if the speed loss were due mainly to alterations within the central nervous system.

Sensory Factors. Knowing that reaction time (RT) is slower when the intensity of stimulation is weaker, and that sensory ability diminishes with age, it was thought that the RTs of the old might be slower than those of the young because the stimuli calling for response are functionally weaker for the old. Accordingly, auditory stimuli were made functionally equal in intensity for old and young, but the results showed that the old remained slower (Botwinick, 1971). This ruled out a sensory basis for the slowing with age.

Motor Factors. In a similar vein, Botwinick and Thompson (1966) ruled out motor factors in accounting for RT differences with age. RT was segmented into two components, a premotor (PM) component and a motor (M) component. The premotor component was measured as the time from when the stimulus was presented to when the forearm muscle of the responding arm was activated. The motor component was measured as the time between this muscle activation and the finger lift in the RT study. It was found that both PM and M times were slower among the old than the young but, in both age-groups, motor time was not nearly as important as premotor. The motor time constituted only 16 percent of total RT, while the premotor constituted 84 percent. This study suggested, therefore, that RT slowing with age could not be explained by motor factors, just as it could not be explained by sensory factors.

This was corroborated by LaFratta and Canestrari (1966), who measured both motor and sensory nerve conduction velocities directly. They stimulated the wrists of people while recording the action potentials, both of the index finger (sensory transmission speed) and the area of the hand below the thumb (motor transmission speed). Although both sensory and motor transmission speeds declined with age, the extent of decline was small relative to that of voluntary RT. Just as motor time was slow relative to total RT, these peripheral nerve transmission speeds could not account for the slowing with age.

Length of Neuromuscular Pathways. A different kind of study but with a similar conclusion regarding the rate of peripheral factors was carried out by Birren and Botwinick (1955). They argued that since it takes time for neural impulses to make their way across the neuromuscular pathways, the longer the pathway, the longer the RT should be. If the peripheral pathway accounts for the slowing with age, old people should be slower than young people to the extent that the pathway is long.

To investigate this, RT of the foot (longest pathway), jaw (shortest), and finger of the hand (middle length) were measured in comparing age-groups. The results of this study, like the others, provided no support for the hypothesis that peripheral factors account for the slowing with age. The difference in RT between old and young was essentially the same with each of the response modes.

Central Mechanisms

Thus, peripheral mechanisms do not account for the slowing with age, but what direct evidence is there that the central mechanisms do? Central mechanisms require translation of input and association to correct responses. Is this where the age-slowing is seen? There are not many studies bearing on this question, and those that do, bear on it only indirectly.

Brain Function–Reaction Time Relations: EEG. Surwillo (1961, 1963) examined RT in relation to electroencephalogram (EEG) activity. The alpha waves of the EEG are blocked (reduced in frequency) when a person is stimulated by an environmental event. When this occurs, the person is said to be aroused, activated, or alerted. Surwillo reported that in such an alerted state, RTs are quicker. He found a correlation of 0.72 between RT and alpha period (the inverse of alpha frequency). "It appears," Surwillo (1963, p. 112) concluded, "that frequency of the EEG is the central nervous system factor behind age-associated slowing in response time."

This conclusion, although possibly correct, does not fit his finding that the correlation between age and RT was very low, the coefficient being only 0.19, accounting for only less than 4 percent of the variance. Further, with smaller samples, narrower age ranges, and some methodological changes, neither Birren (1965) nor Boddy (1971) were able to replicate Surwillo's results. Thompson and Botwinick (1968), measuring change in EEG amplitude rather than frequency or period, also failed to find a relation with RT. Woodruff (1975) did find a relation between RT and alpha period, but with only about half the magnitude of relationship that Surwillo found. Thus, it seems if EEG activity (a central factor) can account for RT slowing with age, it is of limited extent at best.

Contingent Negative Variation (CNV). In the RT task, one signal serves to inform the person that a second signal is on the way. The first signal functions as an alerting or warning signal for the second, which calls for the response. The first warning signal starts a sequence of electrical activity of the brain, which is called contingent negative variation, or CNV for short. The amplitude of the CNV is related to RT, as seen in some, but not all studies.

Loveless and Sanford (1974, p. 59) compared old (58–75) and young (20–23) people and found "a considerable relationship between CNV and

RT." Thompson and Nowlin (1973) found this also but among young (18–32) people only, not old (66–89). Despite relationships with RT in each of these studies, the CNVs in each study were unrelated to age.

All these EEG and CNV results together form an inconclusive picture regarding the central locus of RT slowing with age. There is evidence supporting the notion of a central nervous system control of the slowing—that is, the determinant position—but there is at least as much evidence questioning or even denying such support. Perhaps the greatest support of the notion of CNS control of speeded performance comes from studies showing slow RTs among patients with both diffuse and focal brain damage (see Light, 1978, pp. 4–5). This slowing of behavior with brain damage, however, is not necessarily a unique event, qualitatively different from over-all behavioral decline measured in a variety of ways.

Cardiovascular Functioning. The heart and blood vessels play basic roles in providing nourishment to the brain through blood circulation. If the heart and blood vessels function improperly, brain function may become impaired. As with the CNV, Lacey and Lacey (1970) reported that heart rate also undergoes change during the interval between warning and reaction signals in an RT task. The heart rate slows, and this is associated with quick RT. As with CNV, however, Thompson and Nowlin (1973) reported that this association is seen only among the young. They did not find a relationship between heart rate deceleration and RT among the old.

This is compatible with a finding by Birren (1965), namely, that if the stimulus occurs during the heart's contraction (R-wave), RT is slower than when the stimulus occurs during different phases of the heart cycle. Again, however, this was found so only among the young people, not old.

If RT is unrelated to cardiac rhythms among elderly people, it does seem to be related to overall cardiac status. Abrahams and Birren (1973) compared the RTs of men behaviorally predisposed to coronary heart disease with those of men not so disposed and found that the predisposed men were slower in response. In similar manner, Spieth (1965) found that in serial RT tasks (in contrast to discrete RT trials) those who had cardiovascular disorder had slower RTs. People with some cerebrovascular disorder had even slower RTs. A later study by Light (1978) also pointed to this.

Botwinick and Storandt (1974) did not examine people with medical problems; instead they compared elderly and young adults who were "normal volunteers." Simple RTs were measured after categorizing each person on the basis of answers to a questionnaire designed to assess cardiovascular well-being. Those who reported more cardiac symptoms were slower in response, but the extent of the symptom–Rt relationship was not great. Moreover, the relationship held no more so for the old than for the young.

Congruence of Central and Autonomic Functioning. Thompson and Marsh (1973) suggested a way to integrate some of the diverse EEG, CNV, and cardiovascular data. They suggested that among young people the CNS and autonomic nervous system (ANS) function congruently to produce high-level performance, but the two systems are more often incongruent among the elderly, resulting in poorer performances. Their evidence for this suggestion was that measures of heart rate change (ANS) and of amplitude of CNV (CNS) were unrelated among the elderly performing an RT task but were related among the young.

This congruence hypothesis is innovative and deserves further investigation. The evidence for CNS control of RT slowing in later life, as measured by EEG and CNV, is not very impressive. The evidence for cardiovascular control of the speed loss is likewise equivocal. It is possible, however, that evidence for central control of speed loss with age may yet be found if CNS activity is investigated concomitantly with ANS activity.

TASK DIFFICULTY AND MODELS OF SPEED LOSS

These studies of the locus of the slowing of behavior with age focused on peripheral and central mechanisms conceived in psychophysiological terms. There is another type of study that also is concerned with the locus of slowdown, but here the locus is conceived in terms that sound physiological but really are not. In these studies there is concern with "central processes" and with "CNS," but they are concepts more than they are anatomical structures or physiological functions.

The typical research strategy is to determine how quickly one task is carried out in relation to another one. Differences among task performances are then attributed to differences in the demands placed on central processes, that is, the CNS. In a typical aging study, the tasks are varied in difficulty or complexity and age differences in the times it takes to do the difficult tasks relative to the easy ones are explained in terms of the single central mechanism, the CNS. The thinking is that if there is excessive slowness among the elderly in carrying out the difficult task, it is because the older person's CNS is not up to meeting the demands of this task.

The RT experiment provides a good example of this. In the RT experiment, responding to a single, simple stimulus requires attention and response preparation. Responding to five stimuli, with each requiring a different response, calls for a decision in addition. The notion that the central nervous system is the central power source underlying all behavior would suggest that there is nothing unique in the five-choice decision task that is not present or accounted for in the simple one. Another way of saying this is that a person's speed of performance with the simplest of tasks is a basis for predicting speed of performance with the most difficult task. With regard to aging, the thinking is that if the old are slower than the young in simple, easy situations, they should be that much slower in difficult situations because more demand is placed on the CNS. It is the issue of "that much slower," however, that has called for much theorizing, model building, and research.

The Additive Model

Two names in particular, James Birren and Alan Welford, are identified with the issue of speed of response because of their long-standing shared belief that it is a key to understanding behavioral age changes of many different kinds. Despite their shared belief, they have tended to view the nature of the speed loss differently. By and large, Welford has tended to an additive model whereas Birren has tended to a multiplicative model. Although Welford (1977) recognized inconsistencies in the available literature, he proposed that within limits, the data pointed to a constant increment in speed loss with age with variations in task difficulty. That is, the difference between old and young in speed of performing an easy task is the same as the difference in performing a difficult one. (Welford's observations were limited to variations in task difficulty within a single type of task as in the example of simple to five-choice RT, but the model can possibly be extended to variations in task difficulty across different types of tasks.) The additive model can be written this way: Response Time of the Old equals Response Time of the Young plus a constant, or $RT_o = RT_y + c$. Figure 13.1 presents this model with hypothetical data such that the constant is 20 seconds. In Figure 13.1, a young age-group carried out an easy task in 20 seconds, an intermediate task in 30 seconds, and a difficult task in 50 seconds. The old carried out these tasks in 40, 50, and 70 seconds, respectively. Thus there was a constant 20-second difference between old and young regardless of the difficulty level of the task.

The Multiplicative Model

A model that appears to be in greater favor is the multiplicative model. This one is also shown in Figure 13.1. There is also a constant difference between old and young across task difficulty, but the constant is a multiplicative factor. With the same response times of the young (i.e., 20, 30, and 50), the multiplicative model in the figure shows a twofold increase among the old across each difficulty level (thus, 40, 60, and 100 seconds). The multiplicative model can thus be written as: $RT_o = RT_y(c)$. In Figure 13.1, the constant is 2.

   A Single Mechanism.   Cerella, Poon, and Williams (1980) examined 18 published studies, each very different in the types of tasks used. In each of them, however, speed of response was measured in relation to variations of task difficulty. In each of the 18 studies, elderly people were compared with the younger people in their 20s or 30s. Cerella et al. found a remark-

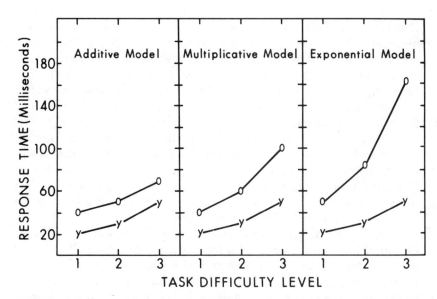

FIGURE 13.1: Hypothetical data of response time (RT) as a function of task difficulty as conceptualized with use of three models. The function described by the additive model is of the form: RT of old adults (o) = RT of the young adults (y) plus a constant, or, $RT_o = RT_y + c$ (where $c = 20$ seconds in this figure). The function described by the multiplicative model is $RT_o = RT_y(c)$ (where $c = 2$ in this figure). The function described by the exponential model is: $RT_o = RT_y^c$ (where $c = 1.3$ in this figure).

able similarity across studies with support seen for the multiplicative model (although their study did not address this model directly.)

Cerella et al. (1980, p. 337) concluded that their results suggest "a single mechanism operating equally in difficult and easy conditions, the mechanism of performance slowing [with age]." This conclusion was strengthened when they asked, "To what extent does consideration of type of task increase accuracy of prediction?" For example, does a complex mental function such as memory make for different results than those of the less complex reaction time? "The answer," they said is no, "virtually none at all" (p. 338).

This single mechanism position is really a form of the determinant view where the mechanism is the viability of the CNS. It determines how good memory will be or how good RT will be. In the multiplicative model, it is a matter of proportionate slowing in performance.

Different Conclusions. The multiplicative model is of interaction between age and task difficulty and the additive model is of a constant age difference in speed of behavior across difficulty levels.* It was seen that

---

*This is so with linear response measurements but not necessarily others, as for example logarithms. Similarly, this is so with variations in task difficulty described in linear or ordinal terms but not necessarily others.

Cerella et al. in their analysis of 18 studies found support for the multiplicative model, that is, they found interactions. Paradoxically, Welford (1977) referred to three of these 18 studies among others in support of the additive model, not the multiplicative one. Welford tended to view task difficulty differently from Cerella et al.; he analyzed it in terms of nonlinear scaling (see previous footnote). Thus, the same data can be viewed in different theoretical perspectives, making for some ambiguity.

The ambiguity is even greater than this because, unlike Cerella et al., Waugh and Vyas (1980, p. 566) found support for the additive model without resorting to Welford's type of scaling. They said their results were "consistent with a growing body of evidence that it simply takes the older subject longer (by a constant amount in a given task) to identify *any* signal or select *any* response." This is the additive model.

The additive model does not point to a single CNS mechanism of slowing, but rather, points to something less important. As Greene (1983, p. 47) indicated, the additive model suggests "that age-related slowing arises from variables orthogonal to . . . required CNS processing, as for example, in input/output components." The thinking is that difficult tasks require more from central neural processes than easier ones, but if a constant increment with age is found across all levels of task difficulty, this cannot result from CNS slowing, but from sensory and motor functions, that is, peripheral mechanisms, instead. A visual defect, for example, will add an equal increment of slowing to performances on all levels of task difficulty.

The Exponential Model (Increasing Rate of Change)

Greene (1983) developed a "dynamic model" where the prediction, as with the multiplicative model, is of increasing age differences in speed of response with task difficulty. In his model, however, the increase is not relative; the increase is of progressively greater magnitude; of an increasing rate, rather than a constant rate. Greene's model is complex, but its basic character is exponential. His model was very much simplified here to depict it in Figure 13.1. In Figure 13.1, Response Time of the Old equals Response Time of the Young to the exponent 1.3 (i.e., $R_o = RT_y^{1.3}$). Thus, in Figure 13.1, in going from the easy to the intermediate to the difficult task, the young again are responding in 20, 30, and 50 seconds, respectively, but the response times of the old in this figure are 49, 84, and 162 seconds, respectively.

The exponential model can be differentiated empirically from what Greene calls the "static" multiplicative model only when there is a minimum of three levels of task difficulty. A significant interaction between age and task difficulty level when there are only two difficulty levels can be seen as supporting either the multiplicative or the exponential model. The latter more than the former model must apply only to a limited range of task difficulty levels; otherwise the time taken to do the task would be so long as to preclude measurement.

Greene suggested that the continuously increasing differences between age-groups in speed of response as the tasks become more difficult, that is, exponential change, is compatible with the speculations of Birren et al. (1980) regarding losses in neuronal connectivity with age. Greene (1983, p. 50) said, "If it were the case that each neuronal connection was subject to a fixed probability of irreversible loss over time, then it is mathematically straightforward to show that the number of intact neuronal connections will decline exponentially with age. . . . If latency is inversely related to the number of remaining neuronal connections, it can then itself be expected to increase exponentially with age."

Models and the Determinant Position

It seems too much to expect any one model to correctly represent all the data. It would seem that some functions may more appropriately be described or predicted by one model and other functions by another model. To the extent that this is true, a single-mechanism theory, the determinant position, does not appear very reasonable—unless it is maintained in a most general, nonspecific way. Cerella, Poon, and Fozard (1981, p. 620) had an interesting view; they suggested that there is a "weak form" of the speed hypothesis and a "strong form." "In its weak form the hypothesis predicts that some slowing will be observed in all mental processes; in its strong form the hypothesis predicts that the extent of slowing will be the same in all mental processes." Almost all studies (but not all) support the weak form of the hypothesis, but there are differences of opinion regarding the strong form.

In its weak form—a general, nonspecific slowing with age—the speed hypothesis loses much of its value. There is little more to be said than that older people are slower than younger ones. The strong form of the hypothesis is important because it bears on the determinant position and the models. It was seen that there is disagreement regarding this.

It would seem that for the present, at least, the single-mechanism notion may best be seen as heuristic, applying to some data and not others. Seen as heuristic, the single mechanism is not synonymous with the CNS. It may be useful, nevertheless, because it can help integrate varied and diffuse behavioral functions that otherwise would seem to have little in common.

COGNITIVE PROCESSING TIME

The foregoing was a theoretical discussion of how inferences of central processing can be made from an analysis of speed of performance on tasks varied in difficulty. Now, examples of actual studies will be presented.

Phases of Processing Information for Memory

Activating Representations in Memory. Hines, Poon, Cerella, and Fozard (1982, p. 175) asked, "Does it take a stimulus longer to activate one of its internal codes in older people than in younger people?" Said in another way, do older adults extract the meaning of a stimulus as quickly as younger people? To answer this question, Hines et al. had people indicate whether two single digits, separated by variable time intervals, were the same or different. In another, more difficult task, they had people indicate whether two different digits were both even or both odd. The odd–even judgments were more difficult than the same–different judgments, and in this way, there was a variation in task difficulty. Hines et al. reported the older people were generally slower, but more so with the more difficult judgments. One interpretation, therefore, is that it does take older people longer to extract meaning from information.

Searching Memory. Sternberg (1969) devised a procedure based on recognition memory to estimate the rate at which people search their stores of information. Anders, Fozard, and Lillyquist (1972) used this procedure to compare people of three age-groups—young, middle-aged, and older. In this procedure people memorize only a few items of information so well that the accuracy of their responses in tests of recognition memory is no longer an issue. Only the speed of searching memory for these items is at issue. In this Sternberg procedure, one item is presented at a time to which a response is made, "yes" or "no," to reflect whether the item was in the earlier memorized list. Time to respond is measured, that is, rate of search of what is already well-established in memory.

Anders et al. (1972) presented lists of 1, 3, 5, and 7 digits in length with the idea that it takes longer to search many items of information than a few items; the longer the list, the more difficult the task. Their results are seen in Figure 13.2. The slopes of the curves of the older groups were steeper than that of the younger group, indicating that among the older people the rates of search were particularly slow as the search task became more difficult. Thus, rate of search, as well as memory, is seen as less good among the aged.

Madden's (1982) results were in support of this, but they were not as clear-cut. He also used a Sternberg type of task but with a somewhat different procedure. He presented letters and digits for search, varying them in a variety of ways to make the task easier or more difficult. Madden presented his results in two experiments, one in which the items were memorized, as in the study of Anders et al. (1972), and the other in which the items were available for viewing until response was made. Madden also reported that search times were progressively longer among the aged as the number of items to be searched was increased, but this was not so for each one of the variations of task difficulty.

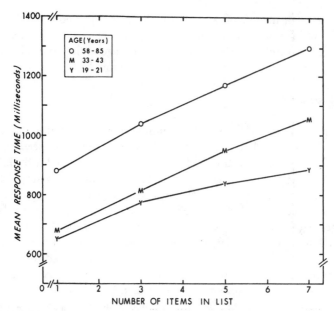

FIGURE 13.2: Mean recognition response time as a function of the number of digits in a list. (Figure was developed from Figure 1 of Anders et al., 1972).

Not all studies reported disproportionate slowing among the elderly when tasks increased in difficulty. Marsh (1975) carried out a Sternberg procedure but did not find elderly and younger people more different in their search rates when the task was difficult as compared to when it was easy. Search of five items in memory made for no greater difference in response speed between old and young than search for one item. These results challenge the others above but remain an exception.

Encoding and Response Selection. Salthouse and Somberg (1982a) compared old and young in a Sternberg type of task when the information (digits) was clearly seen and when it was not. The latter was arranged by superimposing a series of dots over the digits. The idea was that the less-easy-to-see information would be harder to encode, that is, to learn and remember. Salthouse and Somberg also varied the difficulty of the required responses in that the easy response simply required pressing one key to indicate that the digit was among those seen before and another key to indicate otherwise. The difficult response also required this but in addition, the digit seen before had to be identified. Memory load was varied in the studies in that there was either one digit or four digits.

In keeping with the task difficulty hypothesis, Salthouse and Somberg found that compared to the young, older people were relatively slower when the information was less clear, when there was more information to recognize, and when the response was more difficult. They concluded that their results were in support of the multiplicative model and, by implication, the determinant position. There was slowing with age at the point of encoding, memory, and response preparation, and execution.

Mental Rotation

Memory processes are frequently examined from the determinant perspective but there are other processes that can be examined—speed of mental rotation, for example. In this study two figures are presented with the task of determining whether they are identical figures or mirror images. This task becomes more difficult as one of the figures is rotated because the rotated figure has to be manipulated or rotated mentally to determine its relation to the other figure. The greater the rotation, the greater the difficulty.

Gaylord and Marsh (1975) carried out such a task and found that older adults were slower than younger ones in this task of mental rotation. As in the Sternberg search task, when difficulty was increased—as the rotation was greater—the aged were that much slower than the young.

Jacewicz and Hartley (1979) suggested that the figures Gaylord and Marsh used in the rotation task might have been disadvantageous to older people. They reasoned that the figures were abstract or meaningless and most older people are far removed from schoolwork where abstract considerations are customary. Accordingly, they repeated the study but used the familiar alphabet as figures instead. In addition, to eliminate the time taken to glance from the standard figure to the rotated one, only a single rotated letter-figure was presented. The task was simply to indicate whether it was a standard letter or an image of one (as for example, B or ꓭ).

In this study, both older and younger people were students in a university and so, unlike in other studies, the age groups were matched for education level and type of daily activity. In this study, old and young were not different in the speed of mentally rotating the letters. Mental rotation speed was slowed as the rotation angle increased, but not more for the old than the young.

The results of this study, then, and those of Gaylord and Marsh (1975) were at odds. Cerella et al. (1981) raised the fact that the older adults in Jacewicz and Hartley's (1979) study were not as old as those tested in most studies—they were between 53 and 62 years. Further, they were unusual in that they were university students. Accordingly, Cerella et al. repeated this study with older (66–77) adults engaged in more typical activities. They reported results comparable to those of Gaylord and Marsh, not those of Jacewicz and Hartley. It would seem, therefore, that more typical older adults, at least those over 65, are slower in mental rotation (spatial orientation) processes than younger adults, and become even slower as the task becomes more difficult.

REACTION TIME

These studies of cognitive processing time involved quick response, but none of them involved reaction time (RT) in the traditional or classical sense (as in the psychophysiological studies described before). The bulk of the research literature on cognitive processing and age is relatively recent, but the bulk of the traditional RT literature is older.

Traditional RT is only a special case of the slowing of behavior with age; in fact, RT is not always correlated with other speed measures (e.g., Birren, Botwinick, Weiss, & Morrison, 1963). Choice RT involves decision or other cognitive or perceptual processes, but simple RT only calls for attending to the onset of an event for the purpose of making a quick discrete response to it. Much has been learned about simple RT and age. To be sure, there is slowing with age but there is more to it than just this. For example, when an environmental event comes as a surprise, older people are particularly slow to respond (e.g., Botwinick & Brinley, 1962). They can improve with practice, however, learning how to anticipate the event (Botwinick & Thompson, 1967). Actually, older people improve with RT practice regardless of whether the event comes as a surprise or not; they often improve more than younger people do. Nevertheless, it is not likely that they will become as quick as young people regardless of the extent of practice (Salthouse & Somberg, 1982b).

Valuing Accuracy

Most investigators assume that the slowing of RT on the part of older people is outside of their control. There is an alternate view that older people are slower on purpose because they value accuracy and will sacrifice speed to this end (see also Chapter 10). The available evidence suggests that both views are partly correct. Salthouse (1979) carried out three studies; in the first, a choice RT task was presented such that a pattern of lights was presented on the left side of a display and another pattern of lights on the right. If the two patterns were the same, a response button on the right was to be pressed, but if the two patterns were different, a button on the left was to be pressed. Baseline RTs were measured and then each person was instructed to increase their response speeds. A reward of 2¢ was given for RTs that were faster than the individual baseline RT, but 1¢ was charged for incorrect response. Each person was then encouraged to be even faster with 4¢ given for very fast RTs and then encouraged to be faster still with 6¢ given as reward for each response.

Salthouse found that old and young were alike in that when their RTs were slower, they were more accurate. They were different, however, in both their RTs and their levels of accuracy. Increased age was associated with slower behavior but increased age was also associated with more accurate behavior. These results lent support to the idea that at least some of the slowing in later life could be attributed to a valuation of accuracy.

This experiment was repeated with some procedural changes designed to eliminate emphasis on accuracy. Salthouse (1979) compared people aged 18 to 25 years with people aged 63 to 87 and the results were different. The old were slower than the young, but in this experiment they were not more accurate than the young. In fact, the old were less accurate than the young at slow RT levels. A third experiment was in essential agreement with the second. Taking the three studies together, Salthouse (1979, pp. 819–820) wrote: "While a greater emphasis on accuracy as opposed to speed is definitely a factor contributing to the slower performance of older adults, it probably cannot account for all the age differences in speed of performance."

Feedback

Several studies have shown that feedback (i.e., knowledge of results) is motivating in that it quickens RTs, but Hines (1979) showed that it does so at the expense of accuracy. Older people (55–74) were compared to younger ones (18–26) in a choice RT task such that either a key was pressed to indicate that two letters were the same (e.g., A-A or A-a) or another was pressed to indicate that they were different (e.g., A-B).

Approximately half the people in each age-group carried out this task without feedback, while the others were given information as to both their response speeds and whether their responses were correct. Again, the old were slower than the young overall, but it was the feedback results that were of special interest; they were surprising. Feedback speeded the RTs of the young but slowed them of the old. Feedback made for more errors in both age-groups but more so among the young. Thus, overall, the old made fewer errors than the young, especially in the feedback condition.

Hines did not argue from these data that the elderly value accuracy and will forgo speed to achieve it, but his data suggest the possibility. Feedback was motivating for the young and served to speed them up only to make for more errors. On the other hand, feedback did not affect response speeds of the elderly in this way, and their accuracy was decreased only a little. It is as if the elderly tried to be accurate even if they paid the price of speed. Again, therefore, at least part of RT slowing with age might be attributed to a valuation of accuracy.

SUMMARY

The study of the slowness of behavior with age has occupied an important place in aging research. Several prominent investigators have maintained that speed of performance is a reflection of central nervous system (CNS) functioning, and as such, it bears on perception, cognition, and a variety of other kinds of abilities. This was labeled the "determinate position" in this chapter because the status of the CNS, as reflected by speed of performance, determines ability in tasks of perception, cognition, and others. If older people are slower than younger people, it is because the CNS of the older person is less up to the demands of task requirements.

This determinant view is in contrast with the more traditional "consequence position." Most investigators seem to accept the fact that if perceptual abilities decline with age, or cognitive abilities decline, then performances on such tasks will be slower as a result. The consequent position is simply that speed of performance is one of several response measurements; it may be the best one in some instances and not in others. Memory performances, for example, can be scored either in terms of items recalled, or in terms of how long it takes to recall the items.

Investigators working from the determinant (CNS) perspective develop models centered around speed of performance. Investigators working from the consequence perspective develop models specific to the domains of interest. The models within the determinant perspective have taken three forms, each in mathematical terms. One model, the additive model, indicates that as the task becomes more difficult, the response speed of the young and of the old will slow to an equal extent, thus: $RT_o = RT_y + c$, where c is a constant. This model sugests that peripheral factors play a large role in the slowness in behavior with age since sensory or motor disability should contribute equally to easy and difficult task performances.

Another model is the multiplicative model. Here, both young and old will again be slower in performance with difficult tasks, but since difficult tasks place greater demand on the CNS, the slowing among the old will be relatively greater. The relative slowing, however, will again be constant, thus $RT_o = RT_y(c)$. If $c = 2$, for example, this model indicates that the old will be twice as slow as the young at any given level of task difficulty.

A third model is similar except that instead of a relative but constant increase, the slowing with age in relation to task difficulty is increasing, thus: $RT_o = RT_y^c$. This is an exponential model, much simplified from how it has been presented in the literature.

The exponential model, even more than the multiplicative, is compatible with the idea that as neural elements within the CNS drop out with age, or otherwise function more slowly, the differences between old and young in speeded performances will be exacerbated.

The heart of the determinant position is that old people are slower than young people in just about every kind of function. What is the research evidence supporting this? It is clear that in most studies, but not all, older people are slower than young people. This finding is so pervasive as to be among the most strongly substantiated and least disputed. Nevertheless, a prediction of a person's speed of performance on the basis of age alone is very poor. A long list of studies shows coefficients of correlation between age and speed performance ranging from 0.15 to 0.64 with a median of only 0.45. The median correlation indicates that only 20 percent of variance is explained by age.

The research evidence that speed performance can be linked to specific central neural mechanisms is mixed; certainly it is not strong. The belief that speed performances are reflections of CNS functioning receives its greatest support indirectly. Efforts to relate speed performances to peripheral mechanisms such as sensory and motor factors have shown that these play a minor role supporting the CNS hypothesis. When more direct measurements of electrocortical reactivity (EEG, CNV) are made, however, the relations between these and speed performances tend to be seen mainly among young people, not old.

Cardiovascular functions are tied to brain functions in that nutriments are circulated by the blood to the brain. As with electrocortical activity, what relation there is between speed performances and cardiac function is also seen more among the young than the old. The data do show, however, that those people with cardiovascular deficiency are slower in their performance. This may bear on the idea of CNS control of speeded performance, but again, only indirectly.

Most of the older literature of speeded performance with age was of reaction time and the more recent literature is of more complex perceptual and cognitive functions. Simple reaction time is particularly slow among elderly people when there is an unexpected need to respond, with little time to prepare. Older people become quicker with practice, however, improving more than young people do. Older people seem to value accuracy and may not respond as quickly as they might in order to maximize their chances of being correct. As the tasks become more complex, involving learning and memory, mental manipulation, response selection, and other abilities, the response slowing with age is greatest at the most complex levels.

REFERENCES

Abrahams, J. P., & Birren, J. E. Reaction time as a function of age and behavioral disposition to coronary heart disease. *Journal of Gerontology*, 1973, 28, 471–478.

Anders, T. R., Fozard, J. L., & Lillyquist, T. D. Effects of age upon retrieval from short-term memory. *Developmental Psychology*, 1972, 6, 214–217.

Birren, J. E. *The psychology of aging*. Englewood Cliffs, N.J.: Prentice Hall, 1964.

Birren, J. E. Age changes in speed of behavior: Its central nature and physiological correlates. In A.T. Welford & J. E. Birren (Eds.), *Behavior, aging and the nervous system*. Springfield, Ill.: Charles C. Thomas, 1965, pp. 191–216.

Birren, J. E., & Botwinick, J. Age differences in finger, jaw, and foot reaction time to auditory stimuli. *Journal of Gerontology*, 1955, *10*, 429–432.

Birren, J. E., Botwinick, J., Weiss, A. D., & Morrison, D. F. Interrelations of mental and perceptual tests given to healthy elderly men. In J. E. Birren, R. N. Butler, S. W. Greenhouse, L. Sokoloff, & Marian R. Yarrow (Eds.), *Human aging*. HEW, PHS Publication No. 986. Washington, D.C.: U.S. Government Printing Office, 1963, Chapter 10, pp. 143–156.

Birren, J. E., Woods, A. M., & Williams, M. V. Behavioral slowing with age: Causes, organization, and consequences. In L. W. Poon (Ed.), *Aging in the 1980s*. Washington, D.C.: American Psychological Association, 1980, pp. 293–308.

Boddy, J. The relationship of reaction time to brain wave period: A reevaluation. *Electroencephalography and Clinical Neurophysiology*, 1971, *30*, 229–235.

Botwinick, J. Sensory-set factors in age difference in reaction time. *Journal of Genetic Psychology*, 1971, *119*, 241–249.

Botwinick, J., & Brinley, J. Aspects of RT set during brief intervals in relation to age and sex. *Journal of Gerontology*, 1962, *17*, 295–301.

Botwinick, J., & Storandt, M. Cardiovascular status, depressive affect, and other factors in reaction time. *Journal of Gerontology*, 1974, *29*, 543–548.

Botwinick, J., & Thompson, L. W. Components of reaction time in relation to age and sex. *Journal of Genetic Psychology*, 1966, *108*, 175–183.

Botwinick, J., & Thompson, L. W. Practice of speeded response in relation to age, sex, and set. *Journal of Gerontology*, 1967, *22*, 72–76.

Botwinick, J., & Thompson, L. W. Age differences in reaction time: An artifact? *The Gerontologist*, 1968, *8*, 25–28.

Cerella, J., Poon, L. W., & Fozard, J. L. Mental rotation and age reconsidered. *Journal of Gerontology*, 1981, *36*, 620–624.

Cerella, J., Poon, L. W., & Williams, D. H. Age and the complexity hypothesis. In L. W. Poon (Ed.), *Aging in the 1980s*. Washington, D.C.: American Psychological Association, 1980, pp. 332–340.

Gaylord, S. A., & Marsh, G. R. Age differences in the speed of a spatial cognitive process. *Journal of Gerontology*, 1975, *30*, 674–678.

Greene, V. L. Age dynamic models of information-processing task latency: A theoretical note. *Journal of Gerontology*, 1983, *38*, 46–50.

Hartley, J. T., Harker, J. O., & Walsh, D. A. Contemporary issues and new directions in adult development of learning and memory. In L. W. Poon (Ed.), *Aging in the 1980s*. Washington, D.C.: American Psychological Association, 1980, pp. 239–252.

Hines, T. Information feedback, reaction time and error rates in young and old subjects. *Experimental Aging Research*, 1979, *5*, 207–215.

Hines, T., Poon, L. W., Cerella, J., & Fozard, J. L. Age-related differences in the time course of encoding. *Experimental Aging Research*, 1982, *8*, 175–178.

Jacewicz, M. M., & Hartley, A. A. Rotation of mental images by young and old college students: The effects of familiarity. *Journal of Gerontology*, 1979, *34*, 396–403.

Kausler, D. H. *Experimental psychology and human aging*. New York: Wiley, 1982.

Lacey, J. I., & Lacey, B. Some autonomic central nervous system interrelationships. In P. Black (Ed.), *Physiological correlates of emotion*. New York: Academic Press, 1970, pp. 205–227.

LaFratta, C. W., & Canestrari, R. E. A comparison of sensory and motor nerve conduction velocities as related to age. *Archives of Physical Medicine and Rehabilitation*, 1966, *47*, 286–290.

Light, K. C. Effects of mild cardiovascular and cerebrovascular disorders on serial reaction time performance. *Experimental Aging Research*, 1978, *4*, 3–22.

Loveless, N. E., & Sanford, A. J. Effects of age on the contingent negative variation and preparatory set in a reaction-time task. *Journal of Gerontology*, 1974, 29, 52–63.

Madden, D. J. Age differences and similarities in the improvement of controlled search. *Experimental Aging Research*, 1982, 8, 91–98.

Marsh, F. R. Age differences in evoked potential correlates of a memory scanning process. *Experimental Aging Research*, 1975, 1, 3–16.

Marsh, G. R., & Thompson, L. Psychophysiology of aging. In J. E. Birren & K. W. Schaie (Eds.), *Handbook of the psychology of aging*. New York: Van Nostrand Reinhold, 1977.

Salthouse, T. A. Adult age and the speed-accuracy trade-off. *Ergonomics*, 1979, 22, 811–821.

Salthouse, T. A. Age and memory: Strategies for localizing the loss. In L. W. Poon, J. L. Fozard, L. S. Cermak, D. Arenberg, & L. W. Thompson (Eds.), *New directions in memory and aging*. Hillsdale, N.J.: Lawrence Erlbaum Associates, 1980.

Salthouse, T. A. *Adult cognition*. New York: Springer-Verlag, 1982.

Salthouse, T. A. Speed of behavior and its implications for cognition. In J. E. Birren & K. W. Schaie (Eds.), *Handbook of the psychology of aging* (2nd ed.). New York: Van Nostrand Reinhold, 1984.

Salthouse, T. A., & Kail, R. Memory development throughout the life span: The role of processing rate. In P. B. Baltes and O. G. Brim (Eds.), *Life span development and behavior* (Vol. 5). New York: Academic Press, 1983.

Salthouse, T. A., & Somberg, B. L. Isolating the age deficit in speeded performance. *Journal of Gerontology*, 1982, 37, 59–63. (a)

Salthouse, T. A., & Somberg, B. L. Skilled performance: effects of adult age and experience on elementary processes. *Journal of Experimental Psychology: General*, 1982, 111, 176–207. (b)

Spieth, W. Slowness of task performance and cardiovascular diseases. In A. T. Welford & J. E. Birren (Eds.), *Behavior, aging and the nervous system*. Springfield, Ill.: Charles C. Thomas, 1965.

Sternberg, S. Memory scanning: Mental processes revealed by reaction time experiments. *American Scientist*, 1969, 57, 421–457.

Surwillo, W. W. Frequency of the "alpha" rhythm, reaction time and age. *Nature*, 1961, 191, 823–824.

Surwillo, W. The relation of simple response time to brain-wave frequency and the effects of age. *Electroencephalography and Clinical Neurophysiology*, 1963, 15, 105–114.

Thompson, L. W., & Botwinick, J. Age differences in the relationship between EEG arousal and reaction time. *Journal of Psychology*, 1968, 68, 167–172.

Thompson, L. W., & Marsh, G. R. Psychophysiological studies of aging. In C. Eisdorfer & M. P. Lawton (Eds.), *The psychology of adult development and aging*. Washington, D.C.: American Psychological Association, 1973, pp. 122–148.

Thompson, L. W., & Nowlin, J. B. Relation of increased attention to central and autonomic nervous system states. In L. F. Jarvik, C. Eisdorfer, & J. E. Blum (Eds.), *Intellectual functioning in adults*. New York: Springer Publishing, 1973, pp. 107–123.

Waugh, N. C., & Barr, R. A. Memory and mental tempo. In L. W. Poon, J. L. Fozard, L. S. Cermak, D. Arenberg, & L. W. Thompson (Eds.), *New directions in memory and aging*. Hillsdale, N.J.: Lawrence Erlbaum Associates, 1980.

Waugh, N. C., & Vyas, S. Expectancy and choice reaction time in early and late adulthood. *Experimental Aging Research*, 1980, 6, 563–567.

Welford, A. T. Motor performance. In J. E. Birren & K. W. Schaie (Eds.), *Handbook of the psychology of aging*. New York: Van Nostrand Reinhold, 1977.

Woodruff, D. S. Relationships among EEG alpha frequency, reaction time, and age: A biofeedback study. *Psychophysiology*, 1975, 12, 673–681.

14
Intelligence

CONTROVERSY

No area of study of aging has seen as much heated controversy as that of intelligence. It is not that the available data are contested or in doubt, it is how they are interpreted that is in question. The debate is whether intelligence declines with age or is maintained to at least the 60s, perhaps later. The debate seemed to start with a strong no-decline-with-age position by Baltes and Schaie (1974), who wrote, "Aging and IQ: The myth of the Twilight Years." There were rebuttals and counterrebuttals that included "Faith Is Not Enough: A Response to the Baltes-Schaie Claim That Intelligence Does Not Wane" (Horn & Donaldson, 1977). The public debate terminated but not the private ones, which included more and more investigators. There still are differences of opinion.

Tests and Methods of Investigation

There is no controversy that when two or more age-groups are compared in intelligence test performances, that is, when cross-sectional investigations are carried out, older people perform less well than younger people. This is not so with all tests, but it is with many of them. There is controversy as to which tests are the more meaningful and best to use. There is also controversy as to whether cross-sectional studies are meaningful for analysis of age patterns in the first place. Longitudinal studies are regarded as more meaningful, that is, where the same people are tested two or more times over a period of years. More complicated experimental designs are better still, for example cross-sequential analyses (see Chapter 20). The controversy regarding intelligence and age, therefore, centers around the tests that are used and the methods of collecting data. The controversy centers around what the results based on these methods mean.

Intelligence—What Is It?

In a general way everyone knows what intelligence is, but in a specific way efforts in definitions have been exasperating. Matarazzo (1972), after a thorough, exhaustive examination of the literature, devoted one whole chapter of 27 pages to "The Definition of Intelligence: An Unending Search." He followed this by two other chapters which included more specific considerations of definition.

Biological and Genetic Characteristics. One definition of intelligence is that it is some "under-the-skin" capacity or potential. It is the "theoretical limit of any individual's performance. It is never actually measured, since functioning abilities always fall somewhat below the capacity ceiling" (Jones, 1959, p. 700). This limit is based on the biology or genetics of the person, recognizing that experience and environmental opportunities or limitations modify intellectual performance. In any case, a person cannot perform beyond what is innately possible.

Measuring Behavior. The above definition places intelligence in the realm of the inferred but never observed. Another definition of intelligence relates more to observed behavior, not capacity or theoretical limit. With this definition, the concept of biology or genes is not necessary; it is only necessary to ask what can the test-taker do now. Environmental constraints may hurt one individual and environmental opportunities may benefit another; in either case the tests simply measure functional intellectual performance.

Validity of Adult Intelligence Tests

Adult intelligence tests have come under attack in recent years, particularly for use with older adults, because what is measured is often not relevant to their daily lives. Schaie (1978), for example, maintains that the lives of adults, particularly older adults, are better evaluated in terms of "competence" rather than intelligence as measured by standard tests. By competence he means the manner in which their daily lives are carried out and the adequacy with which life problems are solved. Schaie would prefer tests which are "ecologically valid," that is, tests bearing on competence.

Others have been of a similar mind. Demming and Pressey (1957) asserted that tests used to measure intelligence of older people should deal with problems indigenous to them. Traditional intelligence tests often involve items more indigenous to children or very young adults. Accordingly, Demming and Pressey (1957, pp. 144–145) constructed a test comprising information items very practical in nature, items more related to the needs of adults. They reported results of a test based "on use of yellow pages of a telephone directory, on common legal terms, and on people to get to perform services needed in everyday life." They found a *rise* in scores through middle and later years with this test, even with the same people who declined in their test scores with the conventional tests.

In similar fashion, Gardner and Monge (1977, p. 340) developed tests after having asked people "to describe in as much detail as possible a problem they had faced recently and which required some thought on their part to solve." The test items included information about diseases and other medical issues specific to various adult ages, matters related to death and dying, modes of transportation used in the past 75 years, financial matters, ability to follow directions, and others. These tests were given to adults aged 20 to 79 along with a traditional test of achivement. In line with the findings of Demming and Pressey, age decline was seen with the traditional test but, in the main, not with their tests of "adult-relevant" items.

All this suggests that our present array of tests is lacking in "ecological validity" for older people. Tests need to be constructed with reference to the purpose for which the test is administered in the first place. The present traditional tests have been useful when administered in the clinic to determine how a patient compares to his or her cohort, or in neuropsychological examination. The tests have also been useful in research. For these purposes but not for the prediction of daily life competence, adult tests of cognitive ability are useful. Very low test scores and perhaps very high ones relate to competence, but not those in between.

IQ AND INTELLIGENCE

The notion of IQ has become so popular that it is often used to mean intelligence. They are not the same thing. First, not all tests of adult intelligence have IQ scores. They simply have test scores that relate to the concepts of intelligence described before. Second, IQs are calculated differently in different tests and thus mean different things. The notion of IQ has become popular because tests for children have it and the most frequently used adult test has it—the Wechsler Adult Intelligence Scale (WAIS).

The Age Factor in WAIS IQ

The WAIS IQ is based on the idea that older people perform less well than younger people and that this is "normal" or expected. This expectation is the basis of the IQ. Observe Figure 14.1, developed from the standardization norms of the most recent revision of the test, WAIS-R (Wechsler, 1981). This figure shows that if a 25-year-old man and a 70-year-old man each makes the same IQ score of 100 (the average IQ), the actual performance of the older man is poorer than the younger one. The IQ has an age correction as part of the definition.

Figure 14.1 shows that to achieve an IQ of 100, a person aged 25 to 34 must make a score of 114.5, while a person aged 70 to 74 must make a score of only 81. Therefore, for the young person the "age debit" is 14.5; for the old person, the "age credit" is 19. The intelligence test scores are 114.5 and 81, the IQs in both instances are 100. If in one man's lifetime there is neither decline nor improvement in his intelligence test score, his IQ will go up as he gets older.

IQ—A Necessary Index?

The IQ has become so much a part of common parlance and so much a part of the psychologist's thinking that it seems likely that IQ will be here for a long time. Still, an argument can be made that there really is little need

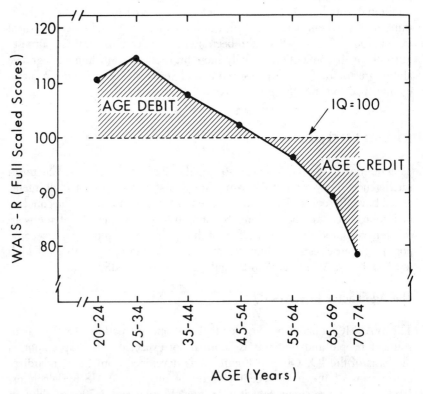

FIGURE 14.1: WAIS-R Full Scaled scores as a function of age. Data were obtained from Table 20 of the WAIS-R Manual (Wechsler, 1981, pp. 97–109) by culling sum of scaled scores of IQs of 100.

for it and since it has been so often misused, intelligence tests might be better without the IQ.

The measure, IQ, serves as a quick aid in evaluating a person's status relative to his or her cohort (taking into account experiential and environmental opportunities the person has had). But it is not a necessary measure—it is only necessary to have scores such as 114.5 and 81, as above, along with the information of what is "normal" or expected for an age-group. The physician in making blood pressure measurements does not convert them to an "age-corrected" blood pressure quotient, nor does the eye doctor "age-correct" measures of visual acuity to a visual acuity quotient. Both these functions change with age but the physician knows what is expected for an age-group and what is pathological.

Although the IQ is convenient as a gauge of a relative standing in a particular age-group, it does cloud the meaning of the actual performance and functional mental status to the extent that faulty research projects have even been carried out with it. There have been many studies where IQs of people of different ages were correlated with other performance or physiological measurements. This can fail to disclose a genuine correlation, for example, between intelligence and learning ability, because the intelligence scores of people of different ages are adjusted toward a common mean.

Meaning of Low Scores of the Aged

In a practical sense what do the low scores of older people, as seen in Figure 14.1, really mean? Does it mean that older people should be kept from important jobs, jobs of great responsibility? Does it mean that 25- to 34-year-olds, those scoring highest on the WAIS-R, ought to be the only ones to maintain executive roles? Decidedly not. First, the previous discussion of "ecological test" validity would suggest that the test scores are not adequate to predict life competencies, certainly not by themselves. Second, the data in Figure 14.1 are group data, a statistical representation of populations. A given old person may have extraordinarily high intelligence when compared to anyone. Correlations between chronological age and intelligence tend to be below .50, often much below this, explaining only about one-quarter of the variance, at most. Thus, predictions of IQ when knowing age alone, while better than chance, are hardly useful for any but the most gross purpose. A third reason why older people ought not to be excluded from important jobs is that, even if test scores and age were more highly correlated, intelligence is only one of the important ingredients necessary in carrying out responsibility. To be a successful executive, for example, wisdom, patience, courage, social adeptness, and a variety of skills, not just intelligence, are important. It would be a tragic mistake to think that people of any age can be successfully evaluated for responsibility by test scores alone.

Why bother with the description of age decline in intelligence if it is so limited in what it conveys? First, this information, though limited, is important. Intelligence is an essential ingredient of much successful behavior. Second, as indicated, tests are useful for research purposes. We want to learn which abilities change with age and which do not. We want to learn through research how help may be given to improve intellectual skills.

A CLASSIC AGING PATTERN

Figure 14.1 does not tell the whole story, and this is another reason the test score is not to be taken as the basis of prediction. As indicated earlier, not all tests show age decline and of those that do, some show it as less great than do other tests. Different tests measure different aspects of intelligence and not all aspects are equally important for predicting job performance or any other specific activity.

Verbal and Performance Tests

The WAIS tests are made up of 11 subtests: six are grouped in what is called the Verbal scales and five are grouped in the Performance scales. (These are poor designations, or labels, because all measures are based on performance. Further, not all six Verbal scales are clearly verbal, nor are the Performance tests devoid of verbal aspects. Nevertheless, these two labels are much in use and the groupings have proven useful.)

There is a pattern of Verbal and Performance scores that has been demonstrated in so many research projects that it has been called the "classic aging pattern": The tests in the Verbal grouping, in the main, tend to hold up fairly well in aging, but the tests in the Performance grouping do not. Figure 14.2, based on the WAIS-R norms, demonstrates this.

This classic aging pattern, relative maintenance of function in Verbal skills as compared to Performance skills, has been seen many times with a variety of different populations. Cross-sectional studies show this, as do longitudinal studies, although the latter are few in numbers and are often based on other tests.

Studies over the years have indicated that of the six WAIS Verbal tests the three holding up best with age are Information, Vocabulary, and Comprehension. The Performance test that shows most decline is the Digit Symbol, with Picture Arrangement and Block Design next. What do these particular tests reflect? The Verbal functions, particularly the three holding up best with age, are "determined by what [elderly people] already know rather than by what new information they can elicit from the situation" (Birren, 1952, p. 404). These Verbal abilities reflect "stored information or

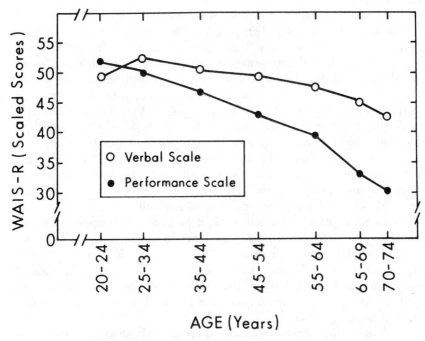

FIGURE 14.2: WAIS-R Verbal and Performance scores as a function of age. Data were obtained from Table 20 of the WAIS-R Manual (Weschsler, 1981, pp. 97–109) by culling sum of scaled scores of IQs of 100. (The Verbal scaled scores were multiplied by 5/6 to develop a common base with the Performance scaled scores.)

general intellectual achievement. . . ." The Verbal subtests are "simple and unambiguous; the subject either knows or doesn't know or recognize what is called for" (Birren, Botwinick, Weiss, & Morrison, 1963, pp. 150–151). Verbal tests seem to measure the manipulation of familiar materials in familiar ways. On the other hand, the Performance tests seem to measure the manipulation of unfamiliar materials, perhaps in unfamiliar ways (Schonfield & Robertson, 1968). These tests involve speed (especially Digit Symbol) and tend to call for manipulative skill (Block Design). They involve perceptual-integrative functions and the processing of new information.

Fluid and Crystallized Intelligence

There is another grouping of abilities that are based on other tests and that corresponds to an extent with the Verbal and Performance dichotomy. The grouping has been labeled crystallized and fluid intelligence. The crystallized grouping, like the Verbal scales of the WAIS, involves tests such as information and comprehension, and the fluid grouping involves tests such

as reasoning and figural relations. Not surprisingly, fluid intelligence declines with age and crystallized intelligence does not—some crystallized
measures even increase to at least age 60 (e.g., Horn & Cattell, 1967).

Horn and Cattell have published many studies, both individually and
together, elucidating the concepts of fluid and crystallized intelligence, but
Horn (e.g., 1970, 1978), in particular, has been concerned with issues of
development and aging. Unlike the grouping of Verbal and Performance
skills, the concept of crystallized and fluid intelligence relates directly to
biological and cultural factors in intelligence. Crystallized intelligence is
mainly the result of education and acculturation but, like all behavior, it is
based on physiological mechanisms, particularly the brain and nervous
system. Fluid intelligence, on the other hand, is more nearly a function of
the state of the brain, although it is clearly influenced by experiential
circumstances. Fluid intelligence might be expected to increase through
childhood to maturity if the brain mechanisms continue to develop
throughout this period. Conversely, if they diminish from maturity to old
age, then fluid intelligence might be expected to decline. Crystallized
intelligence, being more dependent on continued experience and learning,
may be expected to increase, or at least to be maintained. The data
support these expectations.

Although the notions of fluid and crystallized intelligence are important, for most purposes intellectual skills can be investigated and applied
without reference to biological antecedents. Only when biologically oriented
questions in research or in the clinic are asked is it necessary to think in
these terms.

Tests Involving Speed

Thus, Verbal and crystallized tests show relative maintenance of function
with age while Performance and fluid tests do not. Often, but not always,
the Performance-fluid tests involve speed of response and this, it has been
claimed, is unfair to the older person because of a natural slowing of behavior with age.

Speed Tests Unfair?   The argument that speed tests are unfair to older
test-takers is of long standing. The argument bears on what speed of response is thought to mean. The previous chapter highlighted a viewpoint
that sees the ability to perform quickly as central to almost every kind of
behavior. This viewpoint sees the ability to perform quickly as a reflection of
an optimally functioning central nervous system. It is as if there is a "central
power source" that, when low, causes the related behavior to be slow.
Obviously, those who maintain such a position would argue for the importance of tests involving speed in the assessment of intelligence.

The opposite argument is that ability to do things quickly is more a matter of muscles than of brain and is of no importance to intelligent behavior. This position may be the more popular one in aging research, going back at least to 1936 with Lorge's study. He matched people in three age-groups on the basis of scores they made on a power test (nonspeed test). He then found that the older groups performed less well on speed tests. Lorge's conclusion was not that older people perform relatively well with one grouping of tests and poorly on another group, but that "speed obscures sheer mental power in older adults" (p. 105).

These two diametrically opposed viewpoints are still prevalent today. One is that speed tests are of special importance in the assessment of intellectual ability since they reflect central nervous system functioning. The other is that speed tests are unfair to older people in that they obscure sheer intellectual ability. A third viewpoint is that speed is one type of measurement not qualitatively different from other types to assess ability. There is nothing special or unique in speed measurements in reflecting central nervous system functioning that is not also so for nonspeed measurements. (This is the consequence position described in Chapter 13.) Both this third viewpoint and the first place value on speed tests but for different reasons.

Eliminating Speed from Tests. Several studies were carried out just to see the effects of speed requirements in a test when comparing age-groups. There is an important test called the Primary Mental Abilities (PMA) that was developed by Thurstone and Thurstone (1949). The PMA has several subtests that are given with prescribed time limits. Schaie, Rosenthal, and Perlman (1953) gave these tests (except one of them—Word Fluency) to people aged 53 to 78 divided into four age-groups. They gave these tests with time limits in the prescribed way, but they allowed the people to complete the tests in their own time. This had the result of making for greater age differences in the test scores: the younger people were better able to take advantage of the extra time. These results, therefore, argued that the time limits, that is, the need to work quickly, were not disadvantageous to the older test-takers.

The WAIS utilizes time differently from the PMA. Bonus scores are given for quick response to specific items and some responses are not credited at all if they are too slow. Storandt (1977) matched old people (65–75 years) and young ones (20–30) on the basis of the nonspeeded Verbal tests; then she compared them on four of the Performance tests and one of the Verbal tests that involve speed in the scoring. The comparison was based on three scoring methods: (1) the standard method of time limits and bonuses for quick responses, (2) no time limits and no bonuses, and (3) time limits but no bonuses.

Storandt found that removal of bonus scores for quick response made the scores of old and young more similar but, except for the Picture Arrangement subtest, the scores of the old were still lower. The main thrust of these results, then, is that the elimination of speed scoring does not bring the scores of the old up to the level of those of the young. This conclusion is compatible with earlier studies by Klodin (1976) and Doppelt and Wallace (1955).

The Digit Symbol Test. Among the WAIS tests, the Digit Symbol is most clearly based on speed. It will be recalled that this test differentiates between old and young more than any of the others. If a speed test is unfair to the elderly person, then this has to be the most unfair. It is no surprise that the Digit Symbol Test has been singled out for special investigation.

The WAIS Digit Symbol test involves a display of digits from 1 to 9, reading left to right. Beneath each digit is an associated symbol. The task is to write as quickly as possible the appropriate symbol under the particular digit whenever it appears on the test. The more symbols written during the allowed time, the higher the score. Is this a matter only of speed? Is there nothing more to this test than just how quickly symbols can be copied?

Storandt (1976) had old and young adults simply copy symbols as quickly as possible without reference to digits. She did this to get a measure of motor speed independent of other factors that may be involved in the task—factors such as visual search (i.e., looking for the symbol that goes with the digit) or coding (matching the digit and symbol) or perhaps memory (remembering which two go together).

In addition to the copying of symbols, Storandt gave the test itself. She found that approximately 50 percent of the time to do the test could be attributed to the time it takes simply to write down the symbols; the other 50 percent could be attributed to factors other than motor speed. The old were slower than the young both in motor speed and in the nonmotor speed component. The Digit Symbol test, therefore, was seen as reflecting differences with age for reasons in addition to simple slowing that could be attributed to muscle groups.

Several studies have been devoted to determining the specific factors, other than motor speed, that may underly the poor performances of old people on the Digit Symbol test. None has disclosed them. Erber (1976) sought to determine whether lack of test practice was detrimental to older people. She provided practice but the old did not reach the performance levels of the young. Grant, Storandt, and Botwinick (1978) also provided practice, and in addition, thought lack of motivation might be an answer. They provided inducements for quick response, but this did not bring the old up to the levels of the young. Lair and Moon (1972) tried the social incentives of praise and reproof with no apparent positive effect. Erber, Botwinick, and Storandt (1981) had their old and young test-takers memorize the pairings of digits and symbols. Old and young memorized the pairings to an equal extent. This did not help the older people at all. Salthouse (1978), in a different type of study, similarly ruled out memory as the basis of the poor scores of older people.

Thus, all this research did not provide information of what it is that makes the scores of old people on the Digit Symbol test so low. Perhaps speed in the sense of "central power source," as described in the previous chapter, is a sufficient explanation, perhaps not. Whatever the explanation, the Digit Symbol test does seem to be a test of intellectual ability, not just motor speed. Wechsler (1955) reported correlations of .63 to .69 (depending on the age-group) between Digit Symbol performance and full-scale WAIS score.

GENERAL INTELLIGENCE AND THE IMPORTANCE OF EDUCATION

Organization of Abilities

When many tests are given to many people, it becomes exceedingly difficult to organize the great mass of data and to impart meaning to it. There are mathematical methods that organize data into relatively few structural groupings, based upon the pattern of correlations among the different test scores. These methods—factor analysis and principal component analysis—therefore help determine constellations of mental abilities.

Many studies have shown that the single most important element in the organization of intelligence is general ability. It is overall ability, rather than any one specific ability, that most distinguishes one person from another. This is about as true for old people as it is for young people. (For reviews of factor analytic studies see Botwinick, 1967, pp. 13–20; Matarazzo, 1972, pp. 261–276.)

One of the studies on the organization of intelligence in relation to age was particularly important because it focused upon the role of education in intelligence. Birren and Morrison (1961) reanalyzed the WAIS standardization data of the 11 WAIS subtests placing both age (ranging from 25 to 64) and education in the same matrix of correlations. That is, the age and education of each person were correlated with the WAIS subtest scores just as if age and education were scores themselves. Birren and Morrison extracted a large component of general intelligence which accounted for approximately half of the variance. Interestingly, the age of the person was not at all important to this general intelligence component. The education level of the person, however, was very important. It contributed to general intelligence as much as any one of the 11 WAIS subtests.

Although age was not important to the component of general intelligence, age was very important in their second component that accounted for approximately 11 percent of the total variance. Birren and Morrison referred to the second component as an Aging component; it contained subtests "positively related to age, e.g., vocabulary, and a group negatively related to age, e.g., digit symbol." They wrote that, "This aging component may have within it at least two concurrent, independent processes operating in opposite directions" (Birren & Morrison, 1961, p. 368). This was the classic aging pattern in different form.

Since their results suggested that the educational level of a person is more important than his or her age in general mental ability, Birren and Morrison (1961) emphasized the need to focus on education in the analysis of age patterns in intelligence. In fact, they said that the failure to control or remove the effects of education by statistical or experimental methods exaggerates the decremental effects of aging because older people tend to have fewer years of schooling.

Removing the Effects of Education

The control or removal of the effects of education can be accomplished either by statistical techniques such as covariance analysis or by selection procedures such as testing only people who meet a specific criterion of education level. In other words, selection is not based on representative or random sampling but on choosing people with similar amounts of schooling.*

Green (1969) carried out a study doing this. He gave the WAIS to people of four age-groups—25–29, 35–39, 45–49, and 55–64—and found the classic aging pattern: relative maintenance of Verbal scores and decrement in both Performance and Full Scale scores. Then he matched the age-groups in education levels. Figure 14.3 shows the effects of this matching. Instead of maintenance of Verbal skills, there was a statistically significant rise with age. Performance scores did not decline, except for the Digit Symbol task performances. WAIS Full Scale intelligence did not show decline.

Which of the curves in Figure 14.3 are more meaningful, the open-circle curves of more representative sampling or closed-circle curves of matched education groups? It depends on the questions asked. As people are normally found in the community, representative sampling is the way to investigate. For questions regarding the influence of education, matched sampling may be appropriate. (More appropriate, however, are statistical techniques to determine the magnitude of the influence of education level; see Chapter 21.) Questions based on matched samples relate more to definitions of intelligence in terms of theoretical capacity. Questions based on representative sampling relate more to definitions of intelligence in terms of ability at the time of testing.

---

*Such a procedure, it must be noted, makes for highly artificial age comparisons because most older adults have less schooling than most younger ones. If the level selected is high, it selects older people who do not represent their cohort in that they are more highly educated. If the level is low, it selects younger people who do not represent their cohort in that they are less highly educated. Since it is not clear whether high education makes for high intelligence, or whether it is that high intelligence makes for high levels of education, matching old and young on the basis of education may be throwing out the baby with the bath water. It may be comparing superior old with average or inferior young, or vice versa.

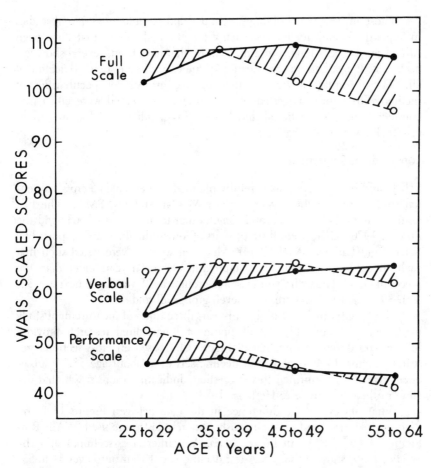

FIGURE 14.3: WAIS scaled scores as a function of age. Open circles represent a random stratified age sampling of a Puerto Rican population and the closed circles represent these age-groups matched on the basis of education. (Drawn from Figure 1 and Table 3 of Green, 1969.)

LONGITUDINAL STUDIES

There are many investigators who examine data such as presented in Figures 14.1 and 14.2 and conclude that they have little bearing on what really happens to intelligence in the course of aging. These investigators maintain that the different age-groups have lived through such different cultural influences and have had such different experiences, that it is the effects of these, rather than of age, that are reflected in the figures. These investigators might refer to Figure 14.3 and point out how radically the cultural influence of education changed the picture.

Those investigators holding such a position point to longitudinal studies in support. There are not very many longitudinal studies that have been carried out for very long, but among those that have been, several show less decline with age than do cross-sectional studies and some show no decline at all. These results, however, often involve artifacts or peculiarities of method. One study suggested that if artifacts of method were taken into consideration, cross-sectional and longitudinal studies would show similar results (Botwinick & Siegler, 1980).

Longitudinal Sequences

Schaie and his collaborators carefully planned and executed a cross-sequential study based on the test of Primary Mental Abilities (PMA). The first testing was in 1956, the second longitudinal testing was in 1963, and the third in 1970. There were thus 14 years of longitudinal research reported by Schaie and Labouvie-Vief (1974). Men and women were tested such that each succeeding age-group was approximately seven years older than the preceding one. Thus, the youngest age-group was 25 years, the next was 32, then 39, etc., to 67. There were seven groups all told.

The longitudinal part of this 14-year, three times of measurement study may seen in Figure 14.4. This figure of longitudinal research provides information different from that of Figure 14.1 based on cross-sectional research. Figure 14.4 suggests that decline sets in at about age 53. A subsequent reanalysis confirmed this suggestion, indicating more substantial decline in the 60s (Schaie & Hertzog, 1983).

What makes for the difference in the data between Figure 14.1 and Figure 14.4? First, and most obviously, different tests were used (WAIS-R in Figure 14.1 and PMA in Figure 14.4). An earlier cross-sectional study by Schaie (1959) showed that PMA test decline is not seen until ages 51 to 55. Thus, the longitudinal sequences and the cross-sectional data are not very different.

Second, both the WAIS and the PMA are comprised of subtests. Figure 14.2 shows that groupings of WAIS Verbal tests reflect a different age pattern than groupings of the Performance tests. The PMA subtests can be categorized in a similar fashion. The Reasoning, Space, and Verbal Meaning tests show age patterns not very different from what is seen in Figure 14.4. The Word Fluency and Number tests, however, showed longitudinal decline beginning in young adulthood.

Third, there is a special problem in longitudinal research. As a study is carried out over the years, people drop out of the study. It is not a random dropout, it is a selective one where mainly the superior-scoring older people remain in the study and the poorer scorers do not. (This was discussed in the context of "terminal drop" in Chapter 4.) Thus, if it is mainly superior

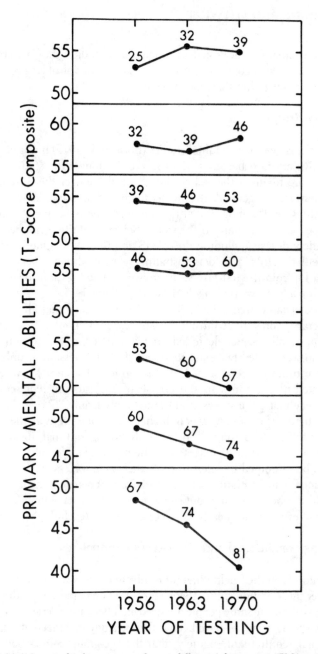

FIGURE 14.4: Longitudinal age curves of seven different cohort groups: PMA test scores as a function of age. (Drawn from data provided by Schaie; reported in different form in Schaie and Labouvie-Vief, 1974.) Numbers refer to mean age of groups.

people who remain to be tested in longitudinal studies, the data are not of representative older people but of intellectually superior older people. This limits the generalization that may be made.

Selective Attrition

Based on a review of longitudinal studies (Botwinick, 1977) it was concluded that selective attrition becomes more severe the longer the study is continued, the more frequent the test sessions, and the longer the time intervals between sessions. In general, the greater the constraints and demands placed on the test-takers, the more the attrition and the more likely that mainly the superior people will remain in the study. Selective attrition has been found with a variety of tests including the WAIS and the PMA. One WAIS study was particularly striking in demonstrating selective dropout because it demanded a lot from the test-takers. There were 11 test sessions over a period of approximately 20 years. This is shown in Figure 14.5.

To understand Figure 14.5, it must be recognized that all data points reflect average scores made during the first test session only. At longitudinal test session 1, all the people tested are represented; at test session 2, only people who were tested twice are represented. At test session 3, only people tested three times are represented, and so on to test session 11, where only people tested all 11 times in the course of 20 years are represented. To repeat, in each case the scores are of test session 1 only.

This figure shows how much higher the scores were at the first test session for those who remained in the study throughout than for those who dropped out early in the 20-year study. The results of all longitudinal studies must thus be examined to determine whether there was severe dropout. The cross-sectional data of Figures 14.1 and 14.2 are of people in general (that is, include those who might drop out subsequently); the data of long-term longitudinal studies are more nearly of selected samples (exclude the drop outs).

Comparing Longitudinal and Cross-sectional Analyses

Do longitudinal studies yield different results than cross-sectional studies? To best answer this question simultaneous cross-sectional and longitudinal comparisons based on the same people are needed. There are several such studies, but thus far there seems to have been only one study that meets an important experimental requirement, namely, that the age-group comparisons in the cross-sectional and longitudinal studies be as identical as possible. For example, if there is a 12-year age range in the longitudinal comparisons, there should be a 12-year age range in cross-sectional comparisons. Comparing groups very different in age in one kind of study while comparing groups more similar in age in another kind is not at all meaningful in determining whether

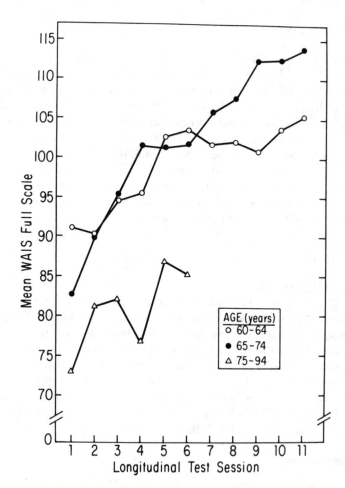

FIGURE 14.5: Mean WAIS Full Scale score *at the time of first testing* as a function of the number of longitudinal test sessions. Only subjects who were tested on all test sessions up to and including the abscissa test number are represented here. For example, subjects represented at test session 11 comprise only those who had been tested on 10 previous occasions. (From Siegler & Botwinick, 1979, Figure 1. Reprinted by permission of the *Journal of Gerontology*, Vol. 34, pp. 242–245, 1979.)

cross-sectional and longitudinal studies yield similar or different results. (See Botwinick & Arenberg, 1976).

Botwinick and Siegler (1980) were able to arrange simultaneous 12-year age comparisons in both cross-sectional and longitudinal studies with the age comparisons limited to approximately ages 62 to 74. Compatible with other analyses—for example, comparing the longitudinal sequences of Figure 14.5 with the earlier cross-sectional PMA study—Botwinick and Siegler found very similar age patterns in the two types of analyses.

PHYSICAL STATUS

Many of the investigators who believe that intelligence does not decline with age until late in life point to various studies showing that older people in poor health perform less well than those in good health. They point to data bearing on terminal drop, perhaps to figures such as 15.5 of selective dropout, then to longitudinal comparisons that show little or no age decline. They then conclude that it is mainly the unhealthy who show decline with age and who drop out, not the normal, healthy aged. This may be. The other side of the argument is that age is associated with medical problems, and so to select for study only those who are healthy is analogous to selecting for study only old people with high levels of education. The selection makes for an artificial, unrepresentative sample.

General Health

Although several studies have shown that unhealthy people perform less well than healthy ones, one study was unusual in that it compared two groups of basically healthy people, but one more healthy than the other. One group was very select in that it comprised old men without any evidence of medical problem, as determined by intensive medical examination. These men were compared to others who had very minor medical problems, so minor as to fit the usual medical concept of "normal." This latter group performed less well than the extraordinarily healthy group, not on all tests but on several of them. The Performance tests more than the Verbal tests differentiated the two groups (Botwinick & Birren, 1963).

Vascular Problems

Other studies focused on cardiovascular problems specifically. Wilkie and Eisdorfer (1971) carried out an unusual study where intellectual loss over a 10-year period was linked to high blood pressure. At the time of initial testing, people aged 60 to 69 and 70 to 79 were divided into three groups: normal blood pressures, borderline pressures, and high blood pressures. They retested these people 10 years later and focused on the change in scores over this time.

The high blood pressure group among those aged 60 to 69 at the start of the study declined most. The decline was seen with the Full WAIS score and the Performance score, but not the Verbal. The normal blood pressure group showed similar decline, but not as much. Surprisingly, the borderline group showed improvement over the course of years. In possible explanation, Wilkie and Eisdorfer (1971, p. 962) referred to a contention by Obrist

(1964): "mild elevations of BP [blood pressure] may be necessary among the aged to maintain adequate cerebral circulation."

The intelligence test data based upon those aged 70 to 79 years at the start of the study were marred by the significant fact that none of the high blood pressure group completed the 10-year study. Both the normal and borderline groups declined in their test performances over this period of time, with perhaps a greater decline for the borderline group.

A different type of vascular study was conducted by Hertzog, Schaie, and Gribbin (1978). They analyzed part of the PMA data depicted in Figure 14.4 in terms of various categories of vascular problems. They also found that test scores were poorer among those with cardiovascular problems; those people having atherosclerosis and cerebrovascular disease were particularly poor in the test of Psychomotor Speed. Those with these diagnoses were most likely to drop out of the study. People without cardiovascular problems and those who had high blood pressure were most likely to stay in.

Taken together, these studies suggest that older people in good health, those with relatively undamaged cardiovascular systems, with, perhaps, enough mild elevation of blood pressure to nourish the brain in face of some naturally occurring arteriosclerosis, tend to maintain their intellectual abilities better than their less healthy counterparts. This augers well for the future, when more medical control over the states of our vasculatures will be available.

Hearing Loss

Even simple hearing loss apparently affects intelligence test performances. Granick, Kleben, and Weiss (1976) correlated measured hearing ability with intellectual performance in two samples of people: one comprised the atypically healthy men discussed under "General Health" above; the other comprised aged women, each with some significant medical problem but free of emotional pathology. Both the atypically healthy men and not-so-healthy women showed the typical age decline in auditory function of high tone loss. In both groups, however, these declines were in the normal range for their ages (mean about 76 years).

Hearing losses were correlated with cognitive test performances, including those on the WAIS. The results showed associations between hearing losses and test scores for both samples such that the greater the hearing loss, the poorer the performance. Unlike the data of general health, the Verbal tests reflected this more than the non-Verbal tests. The tests more resistant to normal aging were among those most related to hearing loss. It was concluded that "aged subjects may be more intellectually capable than their test performances suggest . . ." (Granick et al., 1976, p. 434).

MODIFICATION STUDIES

A different type of study has been developed, having as its premise that tests measure what people can do at the present time but not what they are capable of doing with help and experience. This type of study explores individual plasticity, that is, the person's possible range of tested behavior. It is an effort, in a sense, to more clearly measure the theoretical limits of intelligence rather than the under-the-limit performances that are almost always measured. There is also another purpose to these studies. By exploring the limits of intelligent behavior, there is an exploration of those factors that may provide help for better function. Such research is sometimes called modification or intervention research.

One type of modification study involves the concept of transfer; a study by Plemons, Willis, and Baltes (1978) is typical. The basic research strategy is first to give one or more tests, at least one of which is of fluid intelligence, the type of test on which old people do poorly. Then, intensive training on a similar test is given, pointing out its characteristics and teaching approaches and responses that are successful. Following this training, other tests are given and these vary from ones similar to the training test to others very different. The very different tests are of crystallized intelligence. The purpose is to measure transfer effects. This pattern is referred to as pretest, training, and posttest. The posttests are given at varying time intervals, up to about six months in some studies. The older persons who have been trained are contrasted in their test scores with comparable older persons who have not received the training, that is, a control group.

The results of these studies have been positive in that benefit of the training was apparent, but the results have also been limited. For example, Plemons et al. found continuous improvement through 23 weeks after training but only when the test was very similar to the training test. With another fluid intelligence task, one somewhat different from the training task, the control and training groups performed equally well after 23 weeks. Similar studies with similar results were reported by Blieszner, Willis, and Baltes (1981) and Willis, Blieszner, and Baltes (1981).

Other modification studies take the form of training in spatial perspective-taking, for example, the ability to see geometric forms from the perspective of a different location. This perspective-taking calls for the ability to rotate patterns in mind, thus having characteristics in common with the Space test of the PMA. Schultz and Hoyer (1976) provided such training to people aged 61 to 88 and, in addition, provided feedback, that is, indicated when a response was correct and when it was not. In this study, the effects of training were only partially beneficial. As in the transfer studies, training helped performance only in regard to the test similar to the training test, but not others.

Zaks and Labouvie-Vief (1980) used a different method of training to facilitate spatial perspective-taking. They provided older adults "the opportunity to take the role of another in 'real-life' social situations . . ." (p. 218). This was done by way of social interactions and group discussions in the presence of a group leader. The older adults receiving such training performed better than those without such training. Perhaps older adults in their normal, daily interactions do not have many opportunities to so involve themselves with others and, accordingly, tend not to perform as well on spatial perspective tasks as younger people.

Other modification studies simply take the form of practicing the same task. The results of these studies have been generally positive but not completely. Schultz and Hoyer did not find that practice helped on perspective-taking but Hofland, Willis, and Baltes (1981) reported improvement with practice on two fluid intelligence tests. Taub (1973) practiced old and young people on the Digit Span task, and as seen earlier, Erber (1976) and Grant et al. (1978) practiced old and young on the Digit Symbol task. Hoyer, Hoyer, Treat, and Baltes (1978–1979) practiced them on a letter cancellation task. In each of these studies, both old and young improved, but with the old not reaching the levels of the young. In fact, in some of these studies, the young improved more than the old.

Comparing old and young in intervention or practice studies is a better procedure than that of trying to modify the performances of the old without a comparison group. Having a comparison group provides the opportunity of possibly learning the mechanisms or reasons for the poor performances of the elderly.

SUMMARY

There is no controversy regarding the data of cross-sectional studies of intelligence. The data show that older people perform less well than younger people, the extent depending on the type of test functions measured. For example, one cross-sectional study with the test of Primary Mental Abilities (PMA) showed that it was not until about age 50 that scores became successively lower with increasing age. The Wechsler Adult Intelligence Scale (WAIS-R), on the other hand, showed that beginning by about age 30 scores became increasingly lower. There is controversy, however, in what this means.

Both the PMA and WAIS-R are made up of different subtests, each showing different age patterns. Those tests and subtests that measure mainly verbal skills, skills that have long ago been learned and often practiced, tend to be well maintained in later life. Some of the verbal tests are sometimes referred to as crystallized tests, indicating that the functions they measure are largely dependent upon environmental opportunities.

Those subtests that measure reasoning and perceptual-integrative abilities sometimes requiring speed do not hold up well with age. Such tests are sometimes called fluid intelligence tests, implying a largely biological basis for the measured abilities.

Not all investigators attribute this cross-sectional pattern to age. Many believe that cross-sectional studies do little more than compare groups born in different eras and as such, the patterns reflect their respective cultural opportunities and values, rather than age. In other words, many believe that cross-sectional group comparisons are not of age in the maturational sense, but of different cultural influences instead.

A better way to measure aging effects, it is maintained by those who hold this view, is to do longitudinal studies. A major problem with longitudinal research, however, is that people drop out of the study. Moreover, they do not drop out randomly; it is usually those who perform poorly that drop out. Thus, many people of superior intelligence remain, limiting the generality of the study. There is reason to believe that many of the poor-scoring dropouts are people in poor health. This suggests that age, as such, does not make for decline, but poor health does. The counterargument is that, at the present time at least, age and poor health are related. It would make for artificial, unrepresentative sampling to exclude the elderly with medical problems from studies.

Contrary to popular opinion, longitudinal studies provide information that is not very different from that of cross-sectional studies when issues of dropout are evaluated. Some longitudinal studies show less decline than cross-sectional studies, and some show decline starting later in life. In the main, however, like the cross-sectional studies, they show decline in fluid functions and relative maintenance of crystallized functions. Unfortunately, such information is easily misapplied. Within normal limits, performances on tests of intelligence, whether cross-sectional or longitudinal, have little relevance to the needs and activities of adults in their everyday lives. Test performances have value in the clinic, however, and they certainly have value in the research laboratory, but if older people are classified in terms of job potential or other role competence on the basis of the intelligence test score, the test is incorrectly used.

The performances on tests of intelligence must be evaluated in terms of a person's experiential and environmental opportunities. For example, it has been demonstrated many times that the more schooling a person has had, the higher the intelligence test score is likely to be. Today's young adults have had more schooling than today's old adults. This has a bearing on their respective test performances. This suggests that some of the age patterns of today may be different tomorrow. If crystallized intelligence is based more on acculturation than is fluid intelligence, it is in the former where most of tomorrow's gain among the elderly would be seen.

A newer type of study has appeared in recent years. This study focuses more on what can be done to improve the intellectual abilities of the elderly than on regarding these abilities as static. Training and practice sessions are provided in these studies and measurements are made of the derived benefits. These studies have shown that the old, like the young, have more potential than is typically measured by the tests.

REFERENCES

Baltes, P.B., & Schaie, K.W. Aging and IQ: The myth of the twilight years. *Psychology Today*, 1974, 7, 35–40.

Birren, J. E. A factorial analysis of the Wechsler-Bellevue Scale given to an elderly population. *Journal of Consulting Psychology*, 1952, 16, 399–405.

Birren, J.E., Botwinick, J., Weiss, A., & Morrison, D.F. Interrelations of mental and perceptual tests given to healthy elderly men. In J.E. Birren, R.N. Butler, S.W. Greenhouse, L. Sokoloff, & M.R. Yarrow (Eds.), *Human aging: a biological and behavioral study*. Washington, D.C.: U.S. Government Printing Office, 1963.

Birren, J.E., & Morrison, D.F. Analysis of the WAIS subtests in relation to age and education. *Journal of Gerontology*, 1961, 16, 363–369.

Blieszner, R., Willis, S. L., & Baltes, P. B. Training research in aging on the fluid ability of inductive reasoning. *Journal of Applied Developmental Psychology*, 1981, 2, 247–265.

Botwinick, J. *Cognitive processes in maturity and old age*. New York: Springer Publishing Co., 1967.

Botwinick, J. Intellectual abilities. In J.E. Birren & K.W. Schaie (Eds.), *Handbook of the psychology of aging*. New York: Van Nostrand Reinhold, 1977, pp. 580–605.

Botwinick, J., & Arenberg, D. Disparate time spans in sequential studies of aging. *Experimental Aging Research*, 1976, 1, 55–61.

Botwinick, J., & Birren, J.E. Cognitive processes: Mental abilities and psychomotor responses in healthy aged men. In J.E. Birren et al. (Eds.), *Human aging: A biological and behavioral study*. Washington, D.C.: U.S. Government Printing Office, 1963.

Botwinick, J., & Siegler, I. C. Intellectual ability among the elderly: Simultaneous cross-sectional and longitudinal comparisons. *Developmental Psychology*, 1980, 16, 49–53.

Demming, J.A. & Pressey, S.L. Tests "indigenous" to the adult and older years. *Journal of Counseling Psychology*, 1957, 2, 144–148.

Doppelt, J.E., & Wallace, W.L. Standardization of the Wechsler Adult Intelligence Scale for older persons. *Journal of Abnormal and Social Psychology*, 1955, 51, 312–330.

Erber, J. T. Age differences in learning and memory on a digit-symbol substitution task. *Experimental Aging Research*, 1976, 2, 45–53.

Erber, J. T., Botwinick, J., & Storandt, M. The impact of memory on age differences in digit symbol performance. *Journal of Gerontology*, 1981, 36, 586–590.

Gardner, E. F., & Monge, R. H. Adult age differences in intellectual abilities and educational background. *Experimental Aging Research*, 1977, 3, 337–383.

Granick, S., Kleben, M.H., & Weiss, A.D. Relationships between hearing loss and cognition in normally hearing aged persons. *Journal of Gerontology*, 1976, 4, 434–440.

Grant, E. A., Storandt, M., & Botwinick, J. Incentive and practice in the psychomotor performance of the elderly. *Journal of Gerontology*, 1978, 33, 413–415.

Green, R. F. Age-intelligence relationship between ages sixteen and sixty-four: A rising trend. *Developmental Psychology*, 1969, 1, 618–627.

Hertzog, C. K., Schaie, K. W., & Gribbin, K. Cardiovascular disease and changes in intellectual function from middle to old age. *Journal of Gerontology*, 1978, *33*, 872–883.

Hofland, B. F., Willis, S. L., & Baltes, P. B. Fluid intelligence performance in the elderly: intraindividual variability and conditions of assessment. *Journal of Educational Psychology*, 1981, *73*, 573–586.

Horn, J. L. Organization of data on life-span development of human abilities. In L. R. Goulet & P. B. Baltes (Eds.), *Life-span developmental psychology.* New York: Academic Press, 1970.

Horn, J. L. Human ability systems. In P. B. Baltes (Ed.), *Life-span development and behavior.* New York: Academic Press, 1978.

Horn, J.L., & Cattell, R.B. Age differences in fluid and crystallized intelligence. *Acta Psychologica*, 1967, *26*, 107–129.

Horn, J.L., & Donaldson, G. Faith is not enough: A response to the Baltes-Schaie claim that intelligence does not wane. *American Psychologist*, 1977, *32*, 369–373.

Hoyer, F. W., Hoyer, W. J., Treat, N. J., & Baltes, P. B. Training response speed in young and elderly women. *International Journal of Aging and Human Development*, 1978–1979, *9*, 247–253.

Jones, H.E. Intelligence and problem-solving. In J.E. Birren (Ed.), *Handbook of aging and the individual: psychological and biological aspects.* Chicago: University of Chicago Press, 1959.

Klodin, V.M. The relationship of scoring treatment and age in perceptual-integrative performance. *Experimental Aging Research*, 1976, *2*, 303–313.

Lair, C. V., & Moon, H. W. The effects of praise and reproof on performance of middle-aged and older subjects. *Aging and Human Development*, 1972, *3*, 279–284.

Lorge, I. The influence of the test upon the nature of mental decline as a function of age. *Journal of Educational Psychology*, 1936 *27*, 100–110.

Matarazzo, J.D. *Wechsler's measurement and appraisal of adult intelligence* (5th ed.). Baltimore: Williams & Wilkins, 1972.

Obrist, W.D. Cerebral ischemia and the senescent electroencephalogram. In E. Simonson & T.H. McGavack (Eds.), *Cerebral ischemia.* Springfield, Ill.: Charles C. Thomas, 1964.

Plemons, J. K., Willis, S. L., & Baltes, P. B. Modifiability of fluid intelligence in aging: A short-term longitudinal training approach. *Journal of Gerontology*, 1978, *33*, 224–231.

Pressey, S.L., & Kuhlen, R.G. *Psychological development through the life span.* New York: Harper and Brothers, 1957.

Salthouse, T. A. The role of memory in the age decline in digit-symbol substitution performance. *Journal of Gerontology*, 1978, *33*, 232–238.

Schaie, K. W. Cross-sectional methods in the study of psychological aspects of aging. *Journal of Gerontology*, 1959, *14*, 208–215.

Schaie, K. W. External validity in the assessment of intellectual development in adulthood. *Journal of Gerontology*, 1978, *33*, 696–701.

Schaie, K.W., & Hertzog, C. Fourteen-year short-sequential analyses of adult intellectual development. *Developmental Psychology*, 1983, *19*, 531–543.

Schaie, K.W., & Labouvie-Vief, G. Generational versus ontogenetic components of change in adult cognitive behavior: A fourteen-year cross-sequential study. *Developmental Psychology*, 1974, *10*, 305–320.

Schaie, K. W., Rosenthal, F., & Perlman, R. Differential mental deterioration as factorially "pure" functions in later maturity. *Journal of Gerontology*, 1953, *8*, 191–196.

Schultz, N. R., & Hoyer, W. J. Feedback effects on spatial egocentrism in old age. *Journal of Gerontology*, 1976, *31*, 72–75.

Siegler, I. C., & Botwinick, J. A long-term longitudinal study of intellectual ability of older adults: The matter of selective subject attrition. *Journal of Gerontology*, 1979, *34*, 242–245.

Schonfield, D., & Robertson, E.A. The coding and sorting of digits and symbols by an elderly sample. *Journal of Gerontology*, 1968, 23, 318–323.

Storandt, M. Speed and coding effects in relation to age and ability level. *Developmental Psychology*, 1976, 12, 177–178.

Storandt, M. Age, ability level, and method of administering and scoring the WAIS. *Journal of Gerontology*, 1977, 32, 175–178.

Taub, H. A. Memory span, practice, and aging. *Journal of Gerontology*, 1973, 28, 335–338.

Wechsler, D. *Manual for the Wechsler Adult Intelligence Scale*, New York: Psychological Corporation, 1955.

Wechsler, D. *WAIS-R manual*. New York: Psychological Corporation, 1981.

Wilkie, F., & Eisdorfer, C. Intelligence and blood pressure in the aged. *Science*, 1971, 172, 959–962.

Willis, S.L., & Baltes, P.B. Intelligence in adulthood and aging: contemporary issues. In L.W. Poon et al. (Eds.), *Aging in the 1980s*. Washington, D.C.: American Psychological Association, 1980, pp. 260–272.

Willis, S. L., Blieszner, R., & Baltes, P. B. Intellectual training research in aging: Modification of performance on the fluid ability of figural relations. *Journal of Educational Psychology*, 1981, 73, 41–50.

Zaks, P. M., & Labouvie-Vief, G. Spatial perspective taking and referential communication skills in the elderly: A training study. *Journal of Gerontology*, 1980, 35, 217–224.

15
Problem Solving: Forming Concepts

A LARGE VARIETY OF TASKS

Laboratory studies of problem solving sometimes take the form of games people like to play. Sometimes they take the form of situations that are similar or related to practical tasks found in life outside the laboratory. Most times, however, the studies involve very abstract tasks that are artificial or contrived. Therefore, questions of ecological validity might be asked, much as they were in the previous chapter on intelligence.

There are many problem-solving tasks that have been used in the laboratory, almost as many as the published accounts reporting them. The single thread relating many of these tasks is that they require the formation or identification of concepts.

Categorizing

Perhaps the simplest type of concept-formation problem is that of undirected categorization or classification. The general pattern of these tasks is to present a person with an array of objects with the instruction to group the objects in any way that seems reasonable. No specific grouping plan is suggested.

Several studies were based on this task with similar results: the young more often than the old categorize by superior concepts (e.g., Cicirelli, 1976; Denney, 1974; Denney & Denney, 1982; Kogan, 1974; and others). For example, Denney (1974) presented many people ranging in age from 35 to 95 years with an array of cutouts varied in shape (triangle, square), color (red, orange, and blue), and size (large and small). Denney found that there were two kinds of categorization; either a design was made with the stimuli, or there was a grouping based on the concept shape, color, or size. It was mainly those over 60 who resorted to the design category—the category devoid of concept. Even among those over 60, however, the majority categorized by concept.

In similar fashion, Kogan (1974) presented old adults (62–85) and college students with line drawings of common objects. Cicirelli (1976) presented these same drawings to children, young adults aged 19–21, and old people in their 60s, 70s, and 80s. Three levels of concept were seen. One involved grouping by a superordinate concept. This is regarded as a superior concept because it involves a broad idea in grouping (for example, the idea of fruit grouping an orange and a banana). Another concept seen as less superior involved grouping by physical attributes (e.g., large items versus small items). A third, low-order concept was grouping by functional or thematic relationship (e.g., a knife cuts an orange). Both investigators found that sorting by the high-level superordinate concept decreased among the older groups. Sorting by physical attributes was seen to the age of 20 but not afterwards. Sorting by functional or thematic groupings increased progressively from age 20.

A compatible result was reported by Bromley (1956), who gave a modified Shaw test to people of four age-groups (17–35, 35–51, 51–66, and 66–82 years). He presented them with four wooden blocks that could be arranged in a variety of different ways, for example, according to height, weight, position of notch, and others. Fifteen relatively high-level concepts, called Grade A concepts, could be formed with these blocks, but many other, poorer concepts could also be formed. Bromley found that the quantity of Grade A concepts declined with age and this was related to performance on the Wechsler intelligence test.

These studies on categorization, then, were similar in what was observed. Older people formed lower level concepts.

The Game of Twenty Questions

Forming Hypotheses.   Denney and Denney (1982) used a version of the game "20 questions" to determine how well and how quickly a concept is formed. This game was used by one or both of these investigators in a half-dozen or more studies with similar results. This particular 20-question game involves 42 photographs of objects or animals; for example, scissors, dogs, milk, lamp, a pig. The task is to identify the one or two pictures that the investigator has in mind by asking questions such as to allow only a yes or no answer. The goal is to identify the picture with the fewest number of questions possible. An effective question such as, "Is it an animal?" eliminates many possible pictures. An ineffective question such as "Is it that picture?" eliminates only one.

Denney and Denney tested people in the five age decades—30s to 60s—and reported that increasing age was associated with decreasing frequency of superior questions. Older people often asked questions that eliminated only one object. This suggested that the older people did not have good hypotheses in forming the concept of the picture in question. Denney and Denney explored this suggestion by also presenting a categorizing task. Following the 20-question game, they said to the people who played, "Look at all the pictures and choose two that are alike or that go together in some way." They found that those who categorized thematically, for example, "the cow goes in the barn," tended to ask poor questions in the 20-question game. Conversely, those who formed high-order concepts, for example, "You can ride in both of them," tended to ask good questions. This suggests that the ability to develop good concepts underlies good performances in both the categorization task and the 20-question game.

   Salient Characteristics.   Denney (1980) wanted to see whether elderly people perform better on more practical or familiar tasks than they do on the 20-question concept task. She used the 20-question game once more and this time also used regular playing cards. The idea was to identify the card she had in mind. Those aged 30 to 50 were equally good in both the 42-object game and in the playing-card game. Those aged 60 to 90, however, were very much better with the playing cards. In fact, they were almost as good as the younger game players. Denney (1980, p. 562) attributed this to "salience of the dimensions by which the stimuli could be classified." In other words, the categories of playing cards are more apparent: for example, there are four suits, face cards or number cards, cards numbered higher than six and cards lower. "Salience of dimension" made the task more do-able and the older adults performed better.

   West, Odom, and Aschkenasy (1978) carried out a study in which the categories were also varied in their apparency, but here, the basis of apparency was "perceptual salience." West et al. determined perceptual salience by the ability of people to recognize similarities between objects. They found that the perceptually salient stimuli made for better performances in a concept task that required combining or coordinating information. Unlike what Denney's (1980) study might suggest, however, the effect of saliency was comparable for young (18–22) and older adults (60–78).

Tasks Resembling Real Life Problems

In a study by Bernadelli, reported by Welford (1958), people were presented with an electrical problem meant to simulate the servicing of radios. The apparatus consisted of a small number of boxes each with six terminals on top, connected underneath by resistors. Each person was given one such box along with a resistance (ohm) meter, and a circuit diagram. The diagram showed the connections between the terminals in the box, but it did not show which terminals in the diagram corresponded to which ones on the box. The job was to deduce the correspondence.

Welford reported that it was necessary for older adults to ask more questions than younger adults, that is, to take more meter readings. Often, the older problem solvers asked questions to get information they already had, that is, their questioning was redundant. This suggested to Welford that the older people had difficulty giving meaning to their meter readings. He also concluded that once they had the information, they had more difficulty in remembering it for later application.

A conceptually similar problem was carried out by Clay (Welford, 1958) but instead of electrical connections, the problem was cast in terms of a horse race in one case and automobiles on the road in another. These tasks called for finding a button that corresponded to a light. Clay found that with increased age, from the 20s to the 50s, performances became progressively poorer in solving these problems. Again, the older problem solvers required more apparatus readings. It was noted that many people wrote notes to help themselves recall and interpret the information, minimizing the need for an excessive inquiry. This tendency to write notes was correlated with good performance, and it decreased with increasing age.

Abstract Laboratory Tasks

Redundant Inquiry and Disorderly Search.   Most problems used in the laboratory are more abstract and less practical than those tasks simulating life situations, even though they are conceptually related in some ways. For example, Jerome (1962) used the "Logical Analysis Device" that had a series of lights and associated button switches circling a center light. The task was to learn complex relationships among the peripheral lights and to use these to turn on the center light. This was a very difficult task, and to accomplish it three concepts had to be formed. One concept was called effector: one peripheral light must be lit for one or more other peripheral lights to turn on. A second concept was called combinor: two lights must be lit for another to go on. The third concept was called preventor: one light when turned on prevents another from turning on. These three concepts had to be integrated in sequence, making Jerome's problem-solving task very difficult.

To solve the task, it was necessary to press the buttons to learn the three concepts. In accord with Welford, redundant inquiry was seen among the older problem solvers. That is, they asked questions (pressed the buttons) to obtain information they already had. In fact, Jerome (1962, p. 814) reported that redundant inquiry was the most prominent feature in the "strikingly inferior" performances of the older problem solvers (mean age 66) relative to the younger ones (mean age 23).

Jerome observed that the inquiries of the elderly—their search for information—was characterized by a lack of order. They did not have explicit knowledge of the goal until very late in the exploratory effort. There was considerable fluctuation and haphazard questioning rather than concentration on a single path to the goal. This unordered search brought information only randomly, making it difficult to distinguish the relevant from the irrelevant. Before long, the older people were overwhelmed by the multitude of irrelevant facts, and this made for frequent repetition of the redundant questions.

This was also seen years earlier by Clay (1954, p. 12). Her conclusions were similar to Jerome's: The old "were unable to build a solution in a logical way with the more complex problems. . . . The younger subjects encountered similar difficulties . . . but were methodical in dealing with them. They followed their initial plan more closely. . . ."

Memory. In agreement with Welford, Jerome thought that the disorderly search of the elderly could be related to a failing memory. Accordingly, he tried to minimize the factor of memory by teaching and encouraging them to take notes. Jerome reported that, although the younger people seemed to find the notes helpful, the older ones said that they could not make use of notes and saw no reason for writing them. Their notes tended to be indecipherable, even to themselves.

Brinley, Jovick, and McLaughlin (1974) also thought memory might be a key issue in problem solving, but their study showed this in certain situations only. They tested the idea of memory in problem solving in two ways. One way was by presenting a series of relatively easy tasks that were varied with respect to the amount of information that had to be remembered. The other way was to vary opportunities to view the information that was needed, rather than keep it in mind. Brinley et al. (1974, p. 188) found that memory as involved in these two variations was not a factor in the poorer performances of the older problem solvers. They concluded, however, that the older problem solvers "seemed to have greater difficulty in storing, retaining, and utilizing information needed to solve problems when this information was more complicated from a logical point of view." This conclusion suggested that memory was an important component in the difficulties older people have in problem solving but only in regard to how difficult they find the task in the first place.

Random Performance. Perhaps the most typical or traditional concept formation problem used in the laboratory is that of concept identification. With this task, objects of multiple characteristics are viewed with the goal of identifying the characteristic that the experimenter has in mind (or has displayed along with others). A study by Offenbach (1974) is typical. He presented either a square or a circle (shape), each of which was either red or blue (color), either large or small (size), and positioned to either the right or left. The goal was to form one of these concepts, the one Offenbach had in mind (as for example, circle, irrespective of the color, size, or position). The problem solver could learn this in the course of several presentations of the objects during which Offenbach would say "correct" whenever a circle was present and "incorrect" when it was not. To develop the concept circle, it is necessary to develop a hypothesis regarding the circle and either keep or reject it with subsequent information in later presentations.

Offenbach gave this problem to children (aged 7–11) and to both college students and older adults (aged 65–87). He found that the older adults performed more poorly than the others. The reason they performed so poorly, Offenbach indicated, was that their behavior seemed unsystematic and random. They seemed to handle each presentation (trial) as if there were no previous ones. If the older people had hypotheses, good ones were as apt to be rejected as poor ones, possibly because they could not impart meaning to the information "correct" and "incorrect." This is much like what Jerome reported in his study and what Welford indicated in regard to the meter readings with the simulated radio. The performances of the older people in Offenbach's study were so poor as to be almost random.

ABSTRACT AND CONCRETE THOUGHT

This type of concept indentification task, the one most typically used, just about always shows very poor performances on the part of the elderly. Arenberg (1968), however, demonstrated that this does not necessarily mean older people cannot think logically. He presented his abstract concept identification tasks in more familiar ways and demonstrated that although some old people were unable to think at high levels with one form of the task, they were much more able with another form of the same task. His research set a pattern for later investigators.

Meaningfulness of the Task

Arenberg (1968) presented stimuli that involved nine elements within the three categories shape, color, and number. For shape he might have used a square, a circle, and a triangle; for color, he might have used red, blue, and yellow; and the number might have been 1, 2, or 3. The task was to form the concept Arenberg had in mind (much as in the study by Offenbach, 1974). For example, a single trial might be of two red triangles, with the information "yes" or "no." If this was the first trial with the information "yes," then the concept could be triangle, red, or 2. If one red triangle was presented next with the information "no," the concept, 2 could no longer be considered.

In accord with Offenbach's observations, this task was so difficult for Arenberg's elderly problem solvers that only a few could do it. Arenberg himself was a problem solver, however, and came up with an ingenious solution that enabled many older people to carry out the task. Instead of the abstract categories of shape, color, and number, he used concrete food categories: beverage, meat, and vegetable. Instead of a series of trials, the presentation of these foods constituted a series of meals. Instead of saying yes or no, Arenberg told that one of the meal items was poisoned. Thus, he said "died," when a poisoned food was presented and "lived" when none of the food items was poisoned. An example used by Arenberg may be seen in Table 15.1. In this example, having a meal of coffee (beverage), lamb (meat), and peas (vegetable) caused death because one of the three foods was poisoned. Another meal of coffee, veal, and peas also caused death; thus, coffee and peas remained as possibly poisoned. A meal of coffee, lamb, and corn, in not causing death, left peas as the poisoned food.* (The reader may want to substitute shapes for beverages in Table 15.1, colors for meats, and numbers for vegetables, to see that the logical characteristics of the task are exactly the same.)

The important point here is simply that when the problem was framed in the familiar, concrete way (poisoned foods), the older people could solve the problem much more readily than when it was formed in the less familiar, abstract way (shape, color, number). This is not to say that the performances of the elderly (60–77) in Arenberg's study were up to those of the young (17–22). They were not, but more of the old could do these problems in the concrete, poisoned food presentation than in the abstract presentation.

Young people can also benefit when tasks are made concrete. Hayslip and Sterns (1979) also used a poisoned food task, contrasting the performances with those on comparable abstract problems. Their results suggested that both the young and old performed better on the poisoned food task and, apparently, to an equal extent. Paradoxically, middle-aged people performed better on the abstract task. This latter result requires replication before it can be accepted as reliable.

Rogers, Keyes, and Fuller (1976), also presented both abstract and concrete poisoned food tasks, but only to elderly adults. They found performances on the two tasks similar statistically (although the number of trials to solution on the poisoned food task was only about 60 percent of that on the comparable abstract task). Thus, not all studies point to the clear advantage

---

*In this example, coffee is a negative instance in that, although death does not occur with it, important information is learned, nevertheless. The example could have included as a last meal tea, veal, and peas with death resulting. Here peas is an example of a positive instance; it is the only food item that caused death when appearing with others that did not. Negative and positive instance tasks are discussed later.

TABLE 15.1
An Example of a Poisoned Food Problem

Step	Meals (Instances)	Lived or Died	Possibly Poisoned Foods
1.	Coffee, lamb, peas	Died	Coffee, lamb, peas
2.	Coffee, veal, peas	Died	Coffee, peas
3.	Coffee, lamb, corn	Lived	Peas

Note: If after Step 2, the problem proceeded with the meal of coffee, beef, peas with the information, "Died," or with the meal of milk, beef, and rice with the information, "Lived," no solution would yet be possible because these meals provide redundant information.
From Table 1 of Arenberg, 1968. Reprinted by permission of the *Journal of Gerontology*, Vol. 23, pp. 279–282, 1968.

of concrete tasks. Nevertheless, arranging for tasks that are familiar, concrete, and personally meaningful can only help older adults—there do not appear to be data suggesting that doing so will make for poorer performances by older adults.

Solution Preferences

Some older people not only prefer tasks that are concrete to those that are abstract, they also tend to perform in concrete fashion. Bromley (1957) gave tests of logical inference and generalization to people aged 17 to 82 years. The tests were made up of proverbs that required interpretation. There were two types of proverb tests. In the first, there were 14 proverbs that were scored on the basis of whether a principle was abstracted or generalized, a principle was not abstracted but a relevant explanation was given, or the interpretation was hardly more than the literal statement of proverb itself, i.e., a concrete response. The second test was one of multiple choice. It consisted of 10 proverbs, each with three explanations: again the generalized, functional, and concrete. Each person was asked to record the "best," "next best," and "worst" explanation.

When people were divided into three age-groups of approximate mean ages 27, 47, and 67 years, it was found that increased age was associated with a decrease in the tendency both to form the higher order generalization (first test) and to choose it when given an opportunity to do so (second test). The rejection of the higher order concept when not required to generate it by one's own thought seems particularly important. Either such a concept is not recognized for what it can do, or if it is, it is not as preferred as sticking close to the specific detail. This adherence to the concrete can be very limiting. It is possible, however, that it is not age so much as education level that is reflected in the preference for concrete concepts and the relative inability to form abstract ones. Higher education is associated with abstract thinking. By and large, older people tend to have less formal education than young people. This factor may underlie much of Bromley's data and those of the other investigators.

RIGIDITY

People who rigidly adhere to problem solutions that do not work, perform poorly, but it is unclear whether rigidity makes for poor cognitive performances or vice versa. Perhaps it is poor cognitive skill that makes the old person appear rigid and not the other way around. If a new solution is not at hand, perhaps only the old one can be offered. In any case, rigidity was seen in Hartley's (1981, p. 706) poisoned food study. He found poorer performances among older (56–87) people than youger (36–51) ones, such as to indicate that those who could not solve the problems "are less flexible in their thinking: They arrive at a hunch about part of the solution before the available evidence warrants it and they stay with that hunch despite the available information. . . . Age differences, in this interpretation, would result as progressively more individuals slip from flexible to inflexible thinking." Some studies support this contention but some do not.

Reversal Shifts

Wetherick (1965) presented cards with four letters on them, for example, *CFJP*. The task was to form a concept, for example, the letter *C*. With this concept, cards would be sorted in one group if they had the letter *C* on them, and in another group if they did not. A different problem might involve another letter, or two letters, for example, *C* and *J*. Cards with both these letters would be sorted in one group and those cards without both letters could be in another.

    As soon as the concept was attained, Wetherick introduced the next task with the instruction that a differnt letter or pair of letters were important to the solution. Four tasks were employed with each person learning one concept and having to shift to another until all four were learned. People aged 21 to 30 years, 42 to 47 years, and 60 to 70 years were matched on the basis of the Progressive Matrices test scores and compared on these tasks. "Despite the equation on the basis of non-verbal intelligence, all four tasks showed evidence of a disinclination in old subjects to change an established concept even where it was demonstrably wrong" (Wetherick, 1965, p. 94).

Thus, a type of rigidity or inflexible thinking on the part of the elderly was seen, even when their cognitive skills, that is, intelligence, were comparable to those of the young.

Reversal and Nonreversal Shifts

When the same relevant items are used in switching from one task to another but with their values changed, this is called a reversal shift. In Wetherick's tasks, the letter C may be the concept in one task, but it is a letter other than C in a subsequent task.

A nonreversal shift task involves a change to completely different stimulus dimensions. If, for example, some of Wetherick's letters had been red and some blue, the nonreversal shift would be from a task where the letter C is correct to a task where the color blue is correct. Letters are irrelevant in the second task and colors are irrelevant in the first.

Rogers et al. (1976) used both reversal and nonreversal shift tasks in testing adults aged 57 to 85 years. A young control group was not tested in this study since the main purpose was to determine which type of shift was the more difficult for older people. Typically, studies with older children and young adults show that the reversal shift is more difficult. In this study, however, there was little difference in the two. Although the performances on the shift tasks were not as good as those on the initial tasks, Rogers et al. ruled out rigidity as the reason—"very few individuals perseverated with the previous solutions response" (p. 673). Other studies with procedures similar to reversal and nonreversal problems also questioned the idea that rigidity was the basis of problem solving difficulty (e.g., Nehrke & Coppinger, 1971; Nehrke & Sutterer, 1978). These studies, unlike the one by Wetherick, suggested that forming concepts is the primary problem and not rigidity, at least as seen in shifting solutions within a dimension.

SPECIAL DIMENSIONS OF THE TASK

Irrelevant Information

The problem solvers in Hartley's (1981) poisoned food study often failed to identify the poisoned food (failed to attain the concept) because they overlooked the relevance of the dimension (food item). They also failed, however, because irrelevant dimensions were not properly evaluated. Moreover, those who failed the task were more confident than those who succeeded in that the irrelevant dimension was implicated in the solution. The misdirection caused by irrelevant information has been noted in several studies. For example, Hoyer, Rebok, and Sved (1979) presented a concept identification task where the number of irrelevant concepts was varied. Cards were matched to a standard such that on each card were objects with four possible dimensions (color, form, number, and positioning of the objects on the card). One dimension was relevant to the concept formation match and the others were irrelevant. There were either zero, one, two, or three of these irrelevant dimensions. Hoyer et al. observed that elderly people (62–85 years) relative to young (18–21) and middle-aged (42–56) people were disproportionately slow and made more errors in concept identification as the number of irrelevant items increased.

Redundant Information

Redundant information can also make the task more difficult. It was seen before that Welford (1958), Jerome (1962), and others concluded that older problem solvers obtain more redundant information than younger ones because they ask the same questions over and over again. Redundant information can do more than waste time or get in the way; like irrelevant information, it is often the source of misdirected behavior.

Arenberg (1968) found that redundant information was a special difficulty for the older problem solver. For example, it is seen in Table 15.1 that with the second meal, either coffee or peas is poisoned but lamb is not. A new meal of coffee, beef, and peas with the information "died" is redundant (because by the rules of the procedure, additional poisoned foods are not introduced). Another meal of three other foods such as milk, beef, and rice, with the information "lived" (none of these items is poisoned), is similarly redundant. Arenberg found that such redundancy made for errors on the part of the older problem solvers when it hardly ever made for errors on the part of the young.

Negative Instance

Another feature of the task that may make it difficult for the older problem solver is negative information. The absence of an event (negative instance) can have the same information value as the presence of an event (positive instance), but the former seems to be more difficult to use. Wetherick (1965) believed that the elderly find it particularly difficult to make proper use of negative instances.

For older people, the difficulty may be less with negative instance problems than with problems where both negative and positive instances (mixed instances) are present. Wetherick (1966), in describing three experiments, found that when older adults were confronted with problems that involved both positive and negative instances, they had difficulty in applying operations appropriate to the positive instances. In a later report, Wetherick (1969) hypothesized that even in the world outside the laboratory this is true, often making old people appear rigid or unwilling to change their ways when, in fact, it may be nothing other than their inability to profit from negative instance information in the context of mixed instance situations. The mixed instance situation is characteristic of most life contexts.

Not all data support this view. Arenberg (1968, p. 281) examined the negative instance problem as one of shift or change from a positive instance. Based upon Wetherick's (1965) results, Arenberg hypothesized that "the old would be more likely than the young to continue a previous mode of operation." Arenberg found that, although concept attainment was not as good among his 60- to 77-year-olds as among his 17- to 22-year-olds, the negative instance problem was not differentially difficult for them when it followed a positive instance problem. The results, therefore, did not confirm the hypothesis of special difficulty in later life in drawing conclusions from negative instances in a mixed context. Accordingly, the results did not suggest inflexibility in changing or shifting concepts. Arenberg attributed the differences between his results and those of Wetherick (1965) to a considerably greater burden on memory in the solution of Wetherick's problems. "It is not unreasonable," Arenberg (1968, p. 281) concluded, "that negative instances, which are seldom rich in information, are likely to be forgotten or inadequately processed when memory is taxed."

Brinley et al. (1974) were more in agreement with Arenberg than with Wetherick. They presented three tasks, each different in the sequencing of information so that performances on mixed-instance tasks could be compared to those on a single-instance task. There were three trials to each task. With one task each of three trials was of positive instance; with another task one trial was positive, followed by two negative-instance trials; and with a third task one trial was of negative instance between two positive-instance trials. Although these three tasks and their different sequences made for different degrees of difficulty in solving the problems, the effect of sequencing was not greater for the old than for the young. Thus, the mixed instance problems were not differentially harder for the older problem solvers.

These studies together do not argue strongly for the idea that the negative instance task or the mixed instance task is a special problem for the aged. These studies add to the literature in suggesting that laboratory problem solving in general is difficult for the elderly with the negative and mixed instance solutions just being part of the general difficulty.

MODIFICATION STUDIES

The previous chapter, on intelligence, included an ending section with this same heading of modification studies. Both with intelligence tests and with problem-solving tasks, investigators have attempted to help older people improve their performances by various kinds of training. Since intelligence tests and problem-solving tasks are sometimes similar, and since the training techniques are similar, some of the modification studies described in the previous chapter might have been included here and vice versa.

The results of the modification studies have been mixed, but with enough success to allow room for optimism. In these studies, older people often show more potential than they demonstrate in the course of the more traditional problem-solving studies. A sampling of modification studies is presented to indicate their diversity and varied successes.

Training in Orderly Search

Young (1966) was so impressed with the lack of order on the part of older people in solving Jerome's (1962) difficult logical analysis problems that she made an effort to train them to reduce redundant inquiry and maximize orderly progress toward a clear goal. First, Young explained what needed to be learned and how to make notes to reduce the memory load. Then she helped each person solve a practice problem, indicating again the important details necessary for successful solution.

After this, a test problem was given. If successful solution was achieved, the next problem was given. If success was not achieved, the correct solution was illustrated, using a procedure "designed to impose order on the search of information" (Young, 1966, p. 506). This procedure involved item-by-item correction as necessary. The whole training procedure included nine one-hour practice sessions.

This training study was among the unsuccessful ones. Those tested were of two groups, one aged 29 to 45 years and the other 45 to 76 years. At every difficulty level, fewer older than younger people achieved solution. At every level, the older adults made at least twice as many inquiries as did the younger ones. Even after training, Young's conclusions were similar to those of Jerome and Welford, viz., the older people had difficulty in giving meaning to the information that was elicited.

Long-term Successful Effects

A training program by Sanders, Sterns, Smith, and Sanders (1975) was more successful, probably because their problem tasks were easier. They started with a very simple problem and built to more difficult ones. The main features for solution were pointed out, and as the more difficult tasks were introduced, additional principles for successful solution were explained. Practice opportunities were provided and, as necessary, so were the answers. All this was done gradually and with much patience. Success was seen when some of their test-takers, aged 64 to 84, began to solve problems that in other studies many people of similar age could not solve. A subsequent study based on similar training procedures showed even more success since more difficult problem-solving tasks were performed well (Sanders, Sanders, Mayes, and Sielski, 1976).

These were short-term successes but Sanders and Sanders (1978) reported success after one year. A few of their successfully trained people were retested one year later. The tests were not the same ones used originally, but the principles for solution were the same. After one year those with prior training were superior in their performance to those with no taining or those who simply practiced the problems.

Practice

A less dramatic effect, but one still of consequence, was demonstrated by Labouvie-Vief and Gonda (1976). The tasks were different from those of Sanders et al. (1975; 1976), but shared with them the need of finding the rule or concept necessary for correct solution. Women aged 63 to 95 years were divided into four groups, each provided with different experiences. One group was taught how to plan and guide themselves in solving the problems; another group was taught this also but, in addition, they were taught how to overcome anxiety and cope with failure. There were two control groups; one had no training at all, the other was given an opportunity to work or practice with the problems but nothing else.

The results were partly expected, partly not. The special training, both with and without the anxiety reduction, made for better test performances than did no training. This was so, however, only when tests were given soon afterwards. When retests were made about two weeks afterward the results were mixed. Sometimes one training procedure proved somewhat better, sometimes the other. The biggest surprise was that practice alone, although not particularly helpful in immediate testing, was the only procedure that had clear positive effects two weeks later.

Modeling

It was seen how in a version of the 20-questions game, older adults tended to ask inefficient questions that eliminated only a few wrong alternatives. Denney and Denney (1974) used a modeling technique to aid them in learning how to ask better questions, that is, form better concepts. They simply had older people observe a model asking efficient questions. This simple procedure proved very effective. Very soon after the modeling, the older adults also asked efficient questions. This was demonstrated again in a later, similar study by Denney, Jones, and Krigel (1979).

Evaluating Training

These modification studies, in the main, show that given sufficient training in developing skills and in gaining experience with unfamiliar tasks, the elderly will improve their performances. The studies show that the elderly are plastic; they can learn and have potential ability to solve problems. Some of these modification studies fall short, however, in that they do not test for long-term effects. They fall short additionally because they do not point out areas of deficiency in problem solving.

Giambra and Arenberg (1980, pp. 257–258) suggested a way that future studies should go. They suggested adopting a thinking aloud procedure where problem solvers "made their thoughts public." They suggested that the problem solvers should "verbalize all thoughts they were aware of and that are pertinent to solving the problem." Giambra and Arenberg pointed out that thinking aloud is not introspection "since it does not require the problem solver to evaluate and analyze the thoughts, mental events or ideas." Thinking aloud, they maintained, provides the experimenter with information of those mechanisms or those underlying qualities that make performances good or poor. It is on these qualities that training studies might best focus.

PROBLEM SOLVING IN PERSPECTIVE

In no chapter in this book are the data as consistently unfavorable to the elderly as they are here. The types of tasks used in the problem-solving laboratory just are not suited to what many older people can do. This raises the issue of ecological validity, the issue brought up at the beginning of this chapter. It is far from clear that the studies of problem solving bear on the competence older adults show in their normal, daily lives. Many older adults agree with this.

Everyday Problems

Denney and Palmer (1981, p. 323) referred to data based on interviews with people aged over 65 to determine whether they thought their "abilities to reason, think and solve problems had changed over the course of their adult lives. Of these individuals 76% reported that they thought that these abilities increased with age, 20% reported no change, and only 4% reported that these abilities declined with age." When these respondents were confronted with facts from the laboratory, a majority (52%) said they were referring to a different type of problem. Of these, 40% said they meant "everyday problems" and 28% said they meant "financial problems—which are also presumably everyday problems." In other words, those older people who were interviewed tended to see themselves as good, everyday problem solvers. In fact, most thought they were better than they had been when young.

Piaget's Stages and Problem Tasks

There is a growing literature on adult development based on the stage theory of Piaget which bears on everyday competency. This literature has not been discussed here although the modification studies on spatial perspective described in the previous chapter stem from or relate to Piaget's stage theory.

Stage theories were discussed in Chapter 9, where it was said that a true stage theory does not allow for regression. That is, once a stage is reached, there is no return to the previous stage. Piaget's stage theory of cognitive development ends with a fourth stage called "formal operations." It is thought that by age 14 or 15, no later than age 20, this stage of logical reasoning is reached. This presents a problem for Piagetian stage theorists because laboratory performances of the elderly are poor in tasks seemingly related to the stage of formal operations. Since there cannot be regression to earlier stages, there is a question regarding the applicability of Piagetian theory to adult development.

This problem was addressed by Piaget (1972), whose contention is compatible with what was indicated above in regard to everyday problems. He indicated that the ability to perform well on tasks associated with the final stage of formal operations, that is, tasks of abstract and logical thought, is found in the areas of personal aptitudes and occupational specialization. A lawyer, for example, may reason well in the context of verbal argument involving juridical concepts but may not reason well in the context of tasks such as those often used in the laboratory. A carpenter may apply logical thought to a problem of building a house but may fare poorly on concept identification tasks in the laboratory. It may be inferred from Piaget's contention regarding aptitudes that lack of knowledge and experience with laboratory tasks may make the older problem solver appear inadequate as a person when, in fact, this is simply not so. This is another aspect of ecological validity.

Individual Differences

Even in the laboratory outside of everyday problems, not everything is bleak. It is always important to remember that individual differences are large among the aged as well as among the young. Even with Jerome's (1962) very difficult tasks—those involving center lights that had to be turned on—even when the older problem solvers were "strikingly inferior" to the younger ones, there were individual differences. Not every old person performed in this "strikingly inferior" way. This was seen in a study by Arenberg (1974), who used a procedure similar but not identical to that of Jerome.

Arenberg tested people between the ages of 24 and 87 in a combination cross-sectional and longitudinal study. Cross sectionally, those over 60 years performed less well than those under 60 years, but longitudinally the results were more favorable to the elderly. After seven years of longitudinal follow-up, decline was seen only in those aged over 70. Before age 70, there was no decline. It is true that the longitudinal analysis was limited to select, superior-performing problem solvers, but the point is that there are superior-performing problem solvers among the elderly. It is important to realize that when discussing "the elderly" and "the old," not all people fit the general or group trend.

The Role of Education

Kesler, Denney, and Whitely (1976) gave a large variety of problem-solving tasks to people aged 30 to 50 and 65 to 81. They carried out a correlational analysis where age, intelligence, education, and occupation were examined in relation to problem-solving performances. Both education and intelligence were related to problem-solving ability but, most important, age was not. Most older people have less formal education than most younger people. This may well account, at least in part, for both their lower intelligence-test and problem-solving scores.

The importance of education was also seen in a study by Heyn, Barry, and Pollack (1978). They presented a series of questions of logical inference regarding arithmetic calculations. Three age-groups were compared: 20 to 30, 40 to 50, and 60 to 70. Unlike other studies that showed progressively poorer performances with increased age, Heyn et al. found the middle-aged group the best, and the youngest and oldest groups equal. Notably, the middle-aged group had significantly more education than the younger and older groups, which were equal in education. Here again, education was important, more than age. In similar fashion, Tesch, Whitbourne, and Nehrke (1978) compared four age groups of people who were similar in their educational attainment and who resided in a common environment (Veterans Administration domiciliary). Tesch et al. found that the four age-groups were also similar in their performances in a spatial perspective taking task (egocentrism), one associated with Piaget's final stage of cognitive development.

Young people today have much formal education. It may well be that as they age and become old, their backgrounds will enable them to continue being good problem solvers.

SUMMARY

There are so many different types of tasks used in the laboratory to investigate problem solving that they are difficult to classify. A common theme running through many of them, however, is that of forming concepts through logical reasoning. Many studies based on these tasks have reported very poor performances by older adults. The concept identification task appears particularly devastating for older people, with one study reporting such poor performances as to be below those of children aged 7 to 11.

Many problem-solving tasks involve the acquisition of information by asking questions in one form or another. These questions, based on hypotheses, receive answers that many older problem solvers do not seem to understand. They seem not to impart appropriate meaning to the answers. Often, they ask the same questions over and over again, only to obtain the information they have already received. Many older people seem to have difficulty in remembering the information when the logic underlying it is complicated. Many ask questions in disorderly ways, not seeming to have knowledge of the goal until very late in their exploratory efforts. Their search for information is often random. They seem thrown by redundant and irrelevant information.

Older adults seem to prefer tasks that are concrete rather than abstract. They sometimes perform better with concrete tasks even when their logical characteristics are identical to abstract ones. They not only prefer concrete tasks, they tend to perform in concrete ways. One study showed that they prefer concrete answers to higher level abstract answers even when the latter were provided.

The studies reporting very poor performances by the elderly must be evaluated in perspective; otherwise misleading inferences may be drawn. First, the tasks used in the laboratory are highly artificial, bearing little or no resemblance to what goes on in the real world. Old people seem to handle their affairs well enough in the real world, these problem-solving studies notwithstanding. Interviews with older adults indicated that a majority of them believed they were better at solving daily-life problems than they had been when young. There is reason to believe that if studies were carried out with tasks based on personal aptitudes and occupational specialization, the results would be otherwise. An engineer, for example, may reason well in the course of designing a bridge but fare poorly on abstract tasks typically used in the laboratory.

Second, even with laboratory tests, there are vast individual differences. Even with very difficult tasks, many older people have been observed to perform well. For example, in one longitudinal study using very difficult tasks, no decline to age 70 was observed. It is important to realize that in describing "the elderly" and the "old," not all people fit the general or group trend.

Third, educational level is related to problem-solving success. One study showed that educational level and intelligence level are related to problem-solving ability but that age is not. Old people, as a group, have less formal schooling than young people and may be expected to perform less well than young people on this basis alone. Another study showed that with age-groups matched for education and type of living context, no differences were found in performing a task which older people typically carry out poorly.

Finally, a series of studies have been carried out to evaluate teaching techniques designed to help the older problem solver to perform at better levels. These studies, as a group, have had mixed success but with enough room for optimism to suggest that the simple administration of tests or problems to solve does not take into consideration the potential abilities that old people have.

REFERENCES

Arenberg, D. Concept problem solving in young and old adults. *Journal of Gerontology*, 1968, 23, 279–282.

Arenberg, D. A longitudinal study of problem solving in adults. *Journal of Gerontology*, 1974, 29, 650–658.

Brinley, J. F., Jovick, T. J., & McLaughlin, L. M. Age, reasoning, and memory in adults. *Journal of Gerontology*, 1974, 29, 182–189.

Bromley, D. B. Some experimental tests of the effect of age on creative intellectual output. *Journal of Gerontology*, 1956, 11, 74–82.

Bromley, D. B. Some effects of age on the quality of intellectual output. *Journal of Gerontology*, 1957, 12, 318–323.

Cicirelli, V. G. Categorization behavior in aging subjects. *Journal of Gerontology*, 1976, 31, 676–680.

Clay, H. M. Changes of performance with age on similar tasks of varying complexity. *British Journal of Psychology*, 1954, 45, 7–13.

Denney, N. W. Classification abilities in the elderly. *Journal of Gerontology*, 1974, 29, 309–314.

Denney, N. W. Task demands and problem-solving strategies in middle-aged and older adults. *Journal of Gerontology*, 1980, 35, 559–564.

Denney, N. W., & Denney, D. R. Modeling effects on the questioning strategies of the elderly. *Developmental Psychology*, 1974, 10, 458.

Denney, N. W., & Denney, D. R. The relationship between classification and questioning strategies among adults. *Journal of Gerontology*, 1982, 37, 190–196.

Denney, N. W., Jones, F. W., & Krigel, S. W. Modifying the questioning strategies of young children and elderly adults. *Human Development*, 1979, 22, 23–36.

Denney, N. W., & Palmer, A. M. Adult age differences on traditional and practical problem-solving measures. *Journal of Gerontology*, 1981, 36, 323–328.

Giambra, L. M., & Arenberg, D. Problem solving, concept learning and aging. In L. W. Poon et al. (Eds.), *Aging in the 1980s*. Washington, D.C.: American Psychological Association, 1980, pp. 253–259.

Hartley, A. A. Adult age differences in deductive reasoning processes. *Journal of Gerontology*, 1981, 36, 700–706.

Hayslip, B., & Sterns, H. L. Age differences in relationships between crystallized and fluid intelligences and problem solving. *Journal of Gerontology*, 1979, 34, 404–414.

Heyn, J. E., Barry, J. R., & Pollack, R. H. Problem solving as a function of age, sex and role appropriateness of the problem content. *Experimental Aging Research*, 1978, 5, 505–519.

Hoyer, W. J., Rebok, G. W., & Sved, S. M. Effects of varying irrelevant informatiion on adult age differences in problem solving. *Journal of Gerontology*, 1979, 34, 553–560.

Jerome, E. A. Decay of heuristic processes in the aged. In C. Tibbitts & Wilma Donahue (Eds.), *Social and psychological aspects of aging*. New York: Columbia University Press, 1962, pp. 802–823.

Kesler, M. S., Denney, N. W., & Whitely, S. E. Factors influencing problem solving in middle-aged and elderly adults. *Human Development*, 1976, 19, 310–320.

Kogan, N. Categorization and conceptualizing styles in younger and older adults. *Human Development*, 1974, 17, 218–230.

Labouvie-Vief, G., & Gonda, J.N. Cognitive strategy training and intellectual performance in the elderly. *Journal of Gerontology*, 1976, 31, 327–332.

Nehrke, M. F., & Coppinger, N. W. The effect of task dimensionality on discrimination learning and transfer of training in the aged. *Journal of Gerontology*, 1971, 26, 151–156.

Nehrke, M. F., & Sutterer, J. R. The effects of overtraining on mediational processes in elderly males. *Experimental Aging Research*, 1978, 4, 207–221.

Offenbach, S. I. A developmental study of hypothesis testing and cue selection strategies. *Developmental Psychology*, 1974, 10, 484–490.

Piaget, J. Intellectual evolution from adolescence to adulthood. *Human Development*, 1972, 15, 1–12.

Rogers, C. J., Keyes, B. J., & Fuller, B. J. Solution shift performance in the elderly. *Journal of Gerontology*, 1976, 31, 670–675.

Sanders, R. E., & Sanders, J. A. Long-term durability and transfer of enhanced conceptual performance in the elderly. *Journal of Gerontology*, 1978, 33, 408–412.

Sanders, J. A. C., Sterns, H. L., Smith, M., & Sanders, R. E. Modification of concept identification performance in older adults. *Developmental Psychology*, 1975, 11, 824–829.

Sanders, R. E., Sanders, J. A. C., Mayes, G. J., & Sielski, K. A. Enhancement of conjunctive concept attainment in older adults. *Developmental Psychology*, 1976, 12, 485–486.

Tesch, S., Whitborne, S. K., & Nehrke, M. F. Cognitive egocentrism in institutionalized adult males. *Journal of Gerontology*, 1978, 33, 546–552.

Welford, A. T. *Aging and human skill*. London: Oxford Univ. Press, 1958.

West, R. L., Odom, R. D. & Aschkenasy, J. R. Perceptual sensitivity and conceptual coordination in children and younger and older adults. *Human Development*, 1978, 21, 334–345.

Wetherick, N. E. A comparison of the problem-solving ability of young, middle-aged and old subjects. *Gerontologia*, 1964, 9, 164–178.

Wetherick, N. E. Changing an established concept: a comparison of the ability of young, middle-aged and old subjects. *Gerontologia*, 1965, 11, 82–95.

Wetherick, N. E. The inferential basis of concept attainment. *British Journal of Psychology*, 1966, 57, 61–69.

Wetherick, N. E. The psychology of aging. *Occupational Therapy*, 1969, 32, 15–17.

Young M.L. Problem-solving performance in two age groups. *Journal of Gerontology*, 1966, 21, 505–509.

16
Learning and Memory: The Encoding of Information

THE SIMILARITY OF LEARNING AND MEMORY

Learning and memory are two sides of the same coin—at least the two are highly correlated. This can be recognized by considering the obvious fact that if a person does not learn well, there is little to recall. Conversely, if memory is poor, there is no sign of having learned very much. Learning has to do with how information "gets in," and memory has to do with how this information gets into "storage" and later is retrieved or brought up for use. This distinction between learning and memory, however, is more easily made conceptually than operationally.

One study in particular demonstrates this. Hulicka and Weiss (1965) gave a paired-associate learning task* to elderly people (60–72 years) and to younger ones (30–44 years) after having divided them into subgroups. To one subgroup of each age, the paired-associate lists were presented an equal number of times (15 trials) to everyone. To another subgroup of elderly and young people the lists were presented until a criterion of learning was achieved. Everyone reaching the same criterion was presumed to have reached the same level of extent of learning. A group of elderly people was then given training beyond the criterion (overlearning).

Five minutes and 20 minutes after this learning, all were tested for their recall of the paired associates. Some in the learning-to-criterion condition and in the overlearning condition were tested again one week later. In the condition of equal experience but not the same extent of learning, that is, 15 trials to all, the younger adults performed better than the older ones both in the learning and in the memory tests. In learning-to-criterion groups,

*The paired-associate task involves a list of paired stimuli, very often words or letters. For example, one study paired the letters TL with the word INSANE, as one of the several paired associates in a list to be learned. After exposure to the paired associates, a person having learned them will respond with the word, INSANE, when presented with the stimulus TL. Procedurally, the paired associates are first presented for study (learning), then the first members of the pairs are presented without the associates for response (recall).

although the older people required more trials to be brought to the common level of learning provided by the criterion, they were seen as very similar to the young in their recall scores measured 5 minutes, 20 minutes, and one week later. The coefficients of correlation between learning and memory were about 0.92.

This study by Hulicka and Weiss (1965) argued clearly that what is remembered is dependent upon what is learned. Although not all studies have shown such a clear tie between learning and memory (e.g., Gordon & Clark, 1974; Harwood & Naylor, 1969; Wimer, 1960), in the main, most studies reflect that learning and memory performances, if not perfectly correlated, are at least correlated to an important extent.

WHAT IS LEARNED AND REMEMBERED?

Tulving (1972) suggested two categories of what is learned and remembered, calling them episodic and semantic, or as Kausler (1982) prefers, episodic and generic. Episodic memory, as the name suggests, is memory for specific episodes, events, or items. Questions such as these relate to episodic memory: "What words did you learn yesterday?" "What is his birthdate?" Memories based on such learning do not last unless this information is worked on and made part of the broader store of semantic or generic memory. For example, if one of the words learned yesterday was "table" (episodic information), it probably will not be long remembered even though the meaning of the word *table* is clear to everyone. There are personal involvements and experiences with "table" and if the word *table* learned yesterday is integrated with these experiences (or the birthdate becomes an important part of a relationship), then these episodic facts can become part of semantic memory and be longer remembered. Episodic memory is more nearly rote learning. Semantic memory involves meaningful organization of information and relating it to what is already known. Although most investigators think of the two as a dichotomy, Craik and Simon (1980, p. 108) suggested that "episodic and semantic memories describe end points on a *continuum*, with moderately specific generic memories lying between extremes." The earlier aging studies dealt more with episodic learning and memory while the more recent studies deal more with semantic or generic memory.

LEARNING-MEMORY AND PERFORMANCE

Even in the earlier episodic literature it was recognized that a distinction must be made between learning-memory as an internal process and performance as an external act that is based on the process. We see only the act and not the process. If the performance is poor, we infer that learning-memory is poor, but the inference may be wrong. The performance, the expression of what had been learned and remembered, may be poor simply because the conditions and opportunities for expression are poor. Some of the literature that seemed to suggest that older people are deficient in the acquisition and retention of information was later seen as reflecting suboptimum opportunities to express what they knew.

It was also recognized that a most frequent suboptimum opportunity revolved around tasks requiring speed of response. Time constraints come into play at two places—one is at the point of learning, or as it is now commonly called, the point of encoding (i.e., when external information is translated to neural representations or traces). The other place time constraints come into play is at the point of expression of what is known (i.e., at the point of performance). Ability to encode quickly, that is, the ability to process information during short time intervals, is taken as a reflection of learning ability. Ability to respond quickly during short time intervals, however, is not. Recognizing this, much of what had been seen as a learning deficit on the part of older people is now seen as simply a response limitation.

Canestrari (1963) was among the first to recognize this. He presented old (60–69) and young (17–35) people with a list of paired associates to learn and varied the stimulus-pacing conditions. Two were rapidly paced, under the control of the experimenter; the third condition was one in which the learner controlled the apparatus and paced the procedure as desired. Thus, the paired associates could be studied for as long as needed, and the time to respond could be as long as needed.

Canestrari reported that self-pacing made for the best performances among the older learners and the fastest pacing made for the poorest learning. Although the young performed better than the old in each of the conditions, the differences between them decreased from fastest to self-pacing conditions. Canestrari reported that both old and young controlled the apparatus, not so much to gain additional time to study the paired associates, as to allow more time for response. His study suggested that allowing more time for expressing newly learned information was particularly important to older people. Other studies followed with similar results (e.g., Arenberg, 1965; Eisdorfer, 1965; Kinsbourne & Berryhill, 1972; Monge & Hultsch, 1971; Smith, 1976).

The importance of time constraints in responding was seen even more clearly in a totally different kind of study. Perone and Baron (1982) presented young (18–27) and elderly (67–75) men with a task that required learning a sequence of button presses that lit a sequence of lights. There were two conditions, one in which the sequence changed periodically, requiring new learning, and one where the sequence remained constant, permitting performances to become stable based on what was well-learned.

In the latter condition, learning was no longer an issue, only the time allowed for response was an issue. Perone and Baron reported that the young performed their well-learned sequence well whether the pacing was fast or self-paced. The old, however, were disrupted with the fast pacing and their performances were poor.

Each of these studies showed that older people benefit from both longer time periods for studying information and, perhaps even more so, longer time periods for responding. These studies demonstrated, therefore, that performance differences among age-groups are not synonymous with cognitive differences.

ENCODING

Learning-memory involves three functions: getting information in, keeping it in, and getting it out when needed. Getting information in is learning or encoding; keeping it in is called storage; and getting at this information when needed is called retrieval. The previous discussion of study time versus performance time is really a discussion of time to encode versus time to retrieve plus time to convey what had been learned and stored.

Where in the sequence do older people have their greatest difficulties—in encoding? storage? retrieval? A particularly good analysis regarding this question was provided by Smith (1980, p. 41). He indicated the sequence of encoding, storage, retrieval is not differentiated by all investigators. "Storage to some," he said, "means encoding and to others means maintenance of information during the retention interval," that is, during the period of time from when the information is learned to when it is retrieved. This difference in how investigators conceive of the learning-memory process makes for a difference in conclusions regarding the question of where in the sequence older people have their greatest difficulties. Smith was clear in how he answered this question: "The weight of evidence does suggest that processing differences [encoding differences with age] exist, storage deficits do not exist, and retrieval deficits may exist but are difficult to measure because of encoding differences between age groups" (p. 42). The latter refers to the fact stressed before, *viz.* that young adults typically learn more in a laboratory task than old adults, and so they have more to remember or retrieve.

Encoding is the main topic of the present chapter, with storage and retrieval in the next chapter. This is an arbitrary arrangement, made for convenience only. The processes are hardly separable and, in fact, retrieval comes into play in the present chapter also. How do people learn? How do they get information in for memory storage and retrieval? They work on it in different ways, as will be seen shortly, but it is easier to work on some types of information than others, and it is easier to work in some contexts than others.

Contexts for Learning-Memory

Supportive and Challenging Instructions. Older adults seem to learn better in supportive contexts than challenging ones, at least as seen in a study by Ross (1968). She presented a paired-associate learning task with three types of instructions. One was a "neutral" instruction as in the typical study, a second instruction was "supportive" ("I need your help"), and a third was "challenging" (this is a "test of your intelligence"). The three instructions were given to people in two age-groups (18–26 and 65–75 years).

One-half hour following measurements of what was learned with each of these learning procedures, the task was given again, but it was the results of the initial learning of a list of difficult associations that were the most impressive. The results, shown in Figure 16.1, demonstrated the importance of the emotional context that the experimenter establishes: with the challenging instructions, the older people required approximately one-third more trials to learn the paired associates than with the other instructions. The performances of the older people were clearly best in the supportive situation. On the other hand, the performances of the young were good throughout; they were not at all influenced by whether the context was supportive or challenging.

This study was also carried out with lists that were easier to learn. The different contexts were important only with the difficult list, however, perhaps because the easy lists were too easy to show the effects. Also, the effects of instructions were not apparent in the later relearning of the lists. Thus it seems with difficult materials, at least, supportive contexts can aid and challenging contexts can harm the performances of the elderly in the short term, if not the long term.

Two other studies, both of psychomotor learning, showed compatible results. The results of the study by Lair and Moon (1972) were similar to those of Ross in that elderly adults showed decrement in learning performance with reproof instructions and they showed gains with praise, but this also was not sustained. Bellucci and Hoyer (1975) did not have reproof or challenging conditions, but they compared a condition of praise ("non-contingent positive feedback") with a neutral (control) condition. Both old and young benefited from the praise, but the old did so more than the young.

These studies together suggest that the elderly in particular learn poorly with reproof or challenges to their self-worth. They seem to benefit from praise, but this improvement may not be long-lasting.

Rewarding the Omission Error. In a wide variety of studies—learning, perception, almost any kind—many older people tend to a type of error that fewer younger people make. It is called the omission error; rather than respond when unsure, or respond by guessing, many older people simply say "I don't know" or simply fail to respond. The experimenter marks this incorrect,

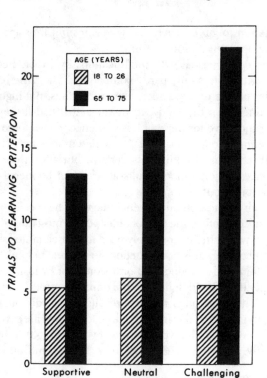

FIGURE 16.1: Mean number of trials taken to learn a paired-associate task in relation to three types of instructions. (Data from Table 1 of Ross, 1968.)

and so the scores of older people may be lower than they would otherwise be with guessing or taking a chance when unsure. (See Chapter 10.)

Leech and Witte (1971) capitalized on this tendency to the omission error by developing a potentially important study. The typical teaching pattern is to reward correct responses and not reward wrong ones. Animal trainers, parents, teachers, and others know this and try to do this. Leech and Witte, however, reasoned that if the elderly do not respond—if they make the omission error, perhaps for fear of being wrong—then it would be hard for them to learn because learning tends to be poor if responses are not given. Accordingly, all responses made by the older people were rewarded, right or wrong, but the correct responses were given greater reward than the wrong ones. In the face of all learning theories, the results showed that the old people getting rewards for both correct and incorrect responses learned more quickly and better than those who were rewarded in the traditional way only for correct responses. These data showed that what may seem like a learning inability on the part of the elderly may not be that at all. It may be a disinclination to guess or respond when unsure, thus appearing unable or minimizing opportunities for learning.

This study was repeated with modifications by Erber, Feely, and Botwinick (1980) with results only partly compatible. The basic result was seen only with older people of lower socioeconomic status, not higher. Since the reward was monetary in this study, it was suggested that it may have constituted a greater incentive for those of less affluence to overcome the tendency toward the cautious omission error. Subsequent research (Erber & Botwinick, 1983) left this possibility less certain, but altogether, it does seem that performances of some older adults at least can be increased by reward conditions that bring out response.

Studies such as these should be encouraged. The specific reward conditions that are most effective, the type of older people most helped by them, and the situations in which these most apply need to be ascertained since in not all situations are special rewards or instructions to respond helpful. For example, Taub (1967) attempted to reduce the omission error by instructing people to respond to every item, but despite this, the omission errors continued at about the same rate. These and other negative results may be discouraging, but it is worth bearing in mind that rewards for failing to respond are easy to provide, as are supportive contexts of the type provided by Ross (1968). Further, they are not at all costly. These can help the older learner and are worth trying.

Personal Relevance and Familiarity of Information

Older people, it seems, are often benefited greatly, even disproportionately, in learning studies when the material is personally familiar and relevant. Conversely, they are seen as more unable when the task is unfamiliar. Hulicka (1967) presented a traditional paired-associate task to elderly testtakers (65–80 years) and reported that they just dropped out of the study—the attrition rate reached 80%. "Many refused . . . to exert themselves to learn 'such nonsense,' and others complained they could not read the small print . . ." (p. 181).

Accordingly, Hulicka changed the task and made it more meaningful. Instead of letters such as TL associated with words such as INSANE, she presented the stimulus components in terms of occupations, such as BANKER. Surnames of four or five letters were the response associates, as for example SLOAN; thus one paired associate could have been, BANKER-SLOAN. When the task was so changed, the older people carried it out much more readily even though their performances were below those of the younger adults performing this task. [This result is not unlike that of Arenberg (1968) in his poisoned food problem-solving study described in the previous chapter.]

One study even showed that not only can familiarity help, but it can bring up the performance of the elderly to a higher level than that of the young (Barrett & Wright, 1981). In this study, two lists of 28 words each for learning and memory were developed. One list had words more familiar to old people than young—words such as "blotter" and "fedora." The other list had words more familiar to young people—words such as "tweeter" and "ripoff." Older people (63–75 years) and younger people (18–24) were compared in learning both lists with the finding that the "older adults actually showed higher recall . . . , than younger adults . . . on the old [words] list. On the young [words] list, older adults recalled fewer words . . . than younger adults . . . " (Barrett & Wright, 1981, p. 197). Not all studies show disproportionate benefit to the elderly with familiar materials, even though most do. One study showed that, if the task is very difficult, familiarity of information may not help at all (Wittels, 1972).

Mnemonics (Aids to Learning-Memory)

Arenberg (1980) urged that a priority be given to research designed to benefit the older learner. He recognized the fact of brain cell loss and central nervous system dysfunction that limits what some older people might be able to accomplish. Changes in these "structural processes," he said, can only be accepted. There are "control processes," however, and it is with these that most help can be provided. These processes should be our concern. "It may be," he said, "that some older people are impaired primarily by poor control processes, whereas others are impaired structurally" (p. 68). Help can be given to the former older adults; less help can be given to the latter.

The Method of Loci. To this end, an old and interesting mnemonic, the method of loci, was tried out (Robertson-Tchabo, Hausman, & Arenberg, 1976). This techinque goes back to the time of the ancient Greeks. Entertainers on the stage have used this technique in demonstrating great feats of memory; they have been seen to call for a long list of items and later repeat these items perfectly in the order they were brought up.

First, Robertson-Tchabo et al. gave people mostly in their 60s and 70s a list of 16 nouns to learn and remember in any order they chose. Their performances were recorded. Next, they were asked to picture in their minds the interiors or their homes and to take imaginary walks through them, stopping at 16 places—places such as the entrance foyer, the different rooms, furniture or anything else in the rooms. The only rule was that these locations must be sites that would be reached in succession on their imaginary walks.

When this progression of loci was well-rehearsed and fixed in mind, the learners associated each of 16 noun-words with each of the 16 loci. They were then asked to picture what the noun represented and the stopping places together, "for example, an 'alligator' in the 'entrance hall.' " The word could be pictured in any way, even silly ways, just so long as it was pictured with the site. Rehearsal of sites and associated noun-words was carried out on each of three days, with a test of the noun-words following. It was found that the elderly recalled more of the 16 words after their "walks" through their homes than they had at first without the aid of the method of loci. Further, they recalled more than a control group that had not been taught the method of loci.

On the following day, when tests were made again, it was found that these older adults did not resort to the mnemonic unless instructed to do so. Thus it seems the method of loci can be helpful to the aged, but it is not a device that is used by them spontaneously even after learning it. As will be seen, this finding seems to prevail almost regardless of the type of mnemonic device that is used. Many old people do not spontaneously resort to specific techniques for encoding, but when instructed to do so, they are benefited, sometimes greatly.

Verbal Mediation and Visual Imagery. Keeping pictures in mind as when taking imaginary walks is a type of mediation that has been used in paired-associate learning studies. Mental pictures can be formed or verbal associations can be applied to the paired associates, and excellent, really extraordinary performances have been seen on the part of the elderly when they resorted to such imagery or to verbal associations.

Hulicka and Grossman (1967) were among the first to recognize that older people, unlike younger ones, tend not to make use of such mediational techniques unless instructed to do so. When they are instructed on these techniques, however, they improve considerably. In fact, when Hulicka and Grossman compared elderly people (mean age 74 years) with young ones (mean age 16 years) in paired-associate learning, they found that with mediation, the elderly improved more than the young, although not reaching the same level of performance. In one condition, the instructions were hardly more than "form an image of the pair"; in another condition it was "form an image of the scene suggested by the phrase" provided by the experimenter to link the associate pairs (Hulicka & Grossman, 1967, p. 47). Not all studies reported such success (e.g., Nebes & Andrews-Kulis, 1976), but others did (e.g., Rowe & Schnore, 1971).

There was a suggestion in the data of Hulicka and Grossman (1967) that when older people do use mediators, they tend to use verbal rather than visual-imagery mediators. This was also seen by Whitbourne and Slevin (1978). Canestrari (1968) examined this suggestion by providing both kinds of mediators to people of two age-groups (16–27 and 50–73 years) in learning paired-associate words. The two age-groups were each divided into three subgroups: one subgroup of each age was given the paired-associate task in a standard way; a second subgroup was provided visual mediators (sketch draw-ings that illustrated the word pairs); a third subgroup was provided with a verbal mediator for each word pair. The latter was a short phrase that contained both words of the pair, for example, "a short box"—the last two words being the paired associates.

The results of this study may be seen in Figure 16.2: the old benefited greatly from the mediators, and the young were benefited hardly at all, mak-ing very few errors in the course of learning irrespective of the experimental variation. Perhaps the list was too easy for them; perhaps they supplied their own mediators. Canestrari found that the two types of mediators, verbal and visual, were very similar in their effectiveness for the older learners.

The older learners in this study were aged 50 to 73 years. A later study suggested that it may be the younger people in this age bracket who benefit most from mediation but a still later one suggested otherwise. Mason and Smith (1977) tested people within three age-groups for free recall of words in a list, but only the middle-aged (40–59 years) benefited from instructions to use visual imagery; the younger (20–39) and older (60–80) learners did not. This study suggested that mediation instructions are most useful for the middle-aged. Rabinowitz, Ackerman, Craik, and Hinchley (1982), however,

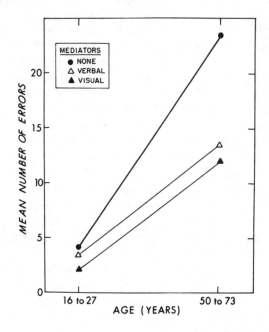

FIGURE 16.2: Mean number of errors made in learning paired associates as a function of age. The task was learned in a standard way, with verbal mediators, and with visual mediators. (Data from Figure 1 of Canestrari, 1968.)

unlike the researchers above, found both young (17–24) and elderly (61–75) people benefiting by imagery instructions. In their study, the paired associates were varied in how related they were. Imagery helped most in learning when the word pairs were most related, but as indicated, both young and old learners benefited equally from imagery.

Self-generated and Experimenter-generated Mediators. A study by Treat and Reese (1976) indicated that simple instructions to use mediators may be more helpful to the elderly than providing the mediators for them. They tested two groups of people, one aged about 30 and the other about 70 years. There were three subgroups of each age: one had to learn paired associates with no instructions regarding mediators; another group was told to generate their own image mediators; and a third group was given the mediators for learning. The older learners benefited from their own image mediators but not those provided by the experimenter. In this study, stimulus-pacing schedules were varied. The self-generated imagery was useful in learning by the elderly when there was a sufficiently long period of time allowed for response, not when the pacing schedule was very rapid. In this study, like the one by Rabinowitz et al. (1982), both the young and the old benefited from instruction.

Treat, Poon, and Fozard (1981) carried part of this study one step further. Young (18–22) and older (60–79) men and women were again given paired associates to learn within the three instruction conditions (the standard way of no imagery; generate own imagery; and experimenter-provided imagery). This time, however, they were tested on three occasions at two-week intervals. Again, the imagery instructions were beneficial to the older learners, this time bringing them to the levels of the young. Further, the older learners tended not to use imagery spontaneously after the first two-week period. This is not unlike the results seen with Ross' (1968) supportive contexts study described before, and with use of the method of loci examined by Robertson-Tchabo et al. (1976). Benefits of such mnemonic devices appear to be short term; they are not taken up and used spontaneously by older people even after learning how to use them.

Most of these studies together led Burke and Light (1981) and Kausler (1982) to conclude that older people are limited in their ability to develop mediators or organizational strategies (mediational or processing deficiency) but not so completely that they cannot. Even when they can develop mediators, however, they tend not to (production deficiency). The reason may be a lack of practice in using mediators. One study showed that after practice, older adults may spontaneously resort to imaginal mediators (Treat, Poon, Fozard, & Popkin, 1978).

Auditory Augmentation of Visual Information. Arenberg (1968) sought to determine whether auditory augmentation of visual information would help in learning. He had older men (60–86 years) and younger men

(17–22 years) learn four digits, with each of three methods. One method simply involved viewing the visual information that was to be learned (visual only). A second method also involved viewing but, in addition, the experimenter read each digit aloud as it appeared (visual with passive auditory augmentation). The third method was similar, but instead of experimenter augmentation, the learners themselves said each digit aloud as it appeared (visual with active auditory augmentation).

Arenberg found that auditory augmentation helped the older learner: the difference between age-groups in learning and recalling the four digits was decreased substantially with either of the two conditions of auditory augmentation. Although the young learners were aided by the auditory augmentation too, the older were aided more. The active auditory role was superior to the passive auditory role in learning the visual information, but not more for one age-group than the other.

Arenberg (1976) followed up this study with another one, disclosing a new dimension. He presented 16 words for learning to men of two age-groups (17–19 and 60–70 years), using the same three conditions as in his earlier study: visual alone, visual plus auditory augmentation by experimenter, visual plus auditory augmentation by self. It is well known that the words presented both at the beginning and at the end of the list are remembered better than those presented in the middle. As will be seen in the next chapter, many investigators believe that there are at least two different kinds of memory stores. The words presented at the end of the list are thought to be recalled from one of these stores—primary memory—and the words from the beginning of the list, from the other store—secondary memory. Arenberg found, as he did before, that the old, as well as the young, benefited in recall from the auditory augmentations, but this was true only with the words at the end of the list (primary memory). With words at the beginning of the list, both active and passive auditory augmentation made for poorer learning among the elderly. Thus, it would seem that with information that requires organization for longer-term storage, auditory implementation may detract, particularly among older adults.

Comparing Sensory Inputs. It is clear that Arenberg was able to improve performances by passive and active auditory augmentation of some visual information at least, but it is not clear whether it was the auditory input, irrespective of the visual one, that improved performances. A study by McGhie, Chapman, and Lawson (1965) suggested that auditory stimulation alone would make for better performances by the elderly than visual information alone. A possible reason for this is that information is thought to be stored first in verbal code. Since it is believed that the acoustic input is more rapidly translated to this verbal code than the visual input, it might be expected that the auditory information would make for better performances (Waugh & Barr, 1980, p. 255).

Taub (1975) carried out a study where the effects of visual and auditory inputs were compared without augmentation. The results were in partial agreement with those of Arenberg. Taub presented two types of information; one was digits, as was Arenberg's, and the other was passages of meaningful prose. The latter requires meaningful organization for secondary memory storage while the digits, particularly a very short string of numbers, are stored mainly in primary memory (see next chapter).

Half the women of each of three age-groups (19–31, 41–60, 61–78) both read the prose passages silently to themselves and viewed the digits. The other half listened to the experimenter, who both read the passages aloud to them and called out the digits. Thus, there was a visual and an auditory presentation both of meaningful prose and of unrelated digits. Unlike in Arenberg's studies, there was no augmentation of sensory input; there was just a comparison between sensory mode presentations.

Taub found that silent reading (visual) of the prose passages made for better recall than did the experimenter reading (auditory). Thus, it was seen that visual input was better for this type of information. This was seen also by King (1968), Dixon, Simon, Nowak, and Hultsch (1982), and McDowd and Botwinick (1984). One reason for the superiority of the visual over the auditory presentation is that reading permits review of the material while hearing it does not. Although visual prose information was better learned than auditory prose, just the reverse was true for digits in Taub's study—the auditory input was better. This latter result is in agreement with Arenberg, except that Taub found this so for all age-groups, not more for one than for the other.

Taub (1976) followed up this study with another one, inquiring whether reading silently was better for learning and recall than reading aloud (i.e., visual versus visual plus active auditory, similar to Arenberg). Women aged 21 to 36 were compared to women aged 60 to 80 in both these types of reading. Both types of reading were equally good for both age-groups, with recall scores higher for the young than for the old. These results may be seen as in disagreement with those of Arenberg (1976) since he found secondary memory impaired by auditory augmentation; recall of prose information is secondary memory.

A general conclusion of all these studies might be that to the extent the information, such as prose, is meaningful and lends itself to thoughtful analysis, visual presentation may be more desirable than auditory. On the other hand, to the extent that the information is simple and the items are unrelated, auditory input, or auditory augmentation of visual stimuli, may be more desirable. This is true to the extent that the items are limited in number, no more than just a few. Resorting to the appropriate sensory mode for the appropriate information may be thought of as another aid to encoding for the elderly.

Spontaneous Organization of Information

Meaningful and Meaningless Information. It was said before that older adults handle information that is familiar, personally relevant, and meaningful better than meaningless information. This was seen in the studies by Hulicka (1967) and Barrett and Wright (1981), among others. In a relative sense, therefore, personally meaningful information for learning is more important to the old than the young. Personally meaningful information, however, is not synonymous with meaningfulness in all its forms. Meaningfulness of information takes many forms, and one of them is the extent to which it can be organized.

Among the first studies on organization and age was one carried out by Heron and Craik (1964). They tested English people in digit span (i.e., the largest number of digits they could recall in order). The digits, however, were presented in the Finnish language. In this way, the English people were tested for the recall of auditory information that to them was meaningless. Young adults (20–35 years) and adults in their 60s were matched such that, on the average, both age groups repeated correctly 3.6 Finnish digits. These matched adults were then given an English digit span test (meaningful information), and the two age-groups were compared. The younger group repeated correctly 8.3 digits on the average, the older group repeated only 6.8 digits.

These results were attributed to a reduced efficiency with age in the ability to organize information. Meaningful material can more easily be organized than meaningless material and, thus, any deficiency in the organizing process would be more apparent with meaningful than with meaningless information.

Corroboration of this analysis was seen in a later study by Craik and Masani (1967) where verbal materials were varied from a series of random words, or words of a sentence in scrambled order, to meaningful sentences. It was assumed that the meaningful sentences were more amenable to organization than the less meaningful verbal materials that had to be learned in relatively unorganized form. Craik and Masani found that differences in learning between age-groups were greater with the meaningful sentences.

Taken together, these studies give credence to the notion that, to the extent material is meaningful and can be organized for learning and retention, the older person (although performing better than with meaningless material) will show up less well than younger persons. These conclusions may seem at variance with those based on studies of familiarity and personal relevance of the information. The difference seems to be that the studies on familiarity involved study materials that left little opportunity for organization. Meaningfulness in the sense of familiarity refers more to personal relevance than to opportunities to organize.

An important point in the study by Craik and Masani has been corroborated in later studies by others. The differences between age-groups were seen mainly with older people of inferior verbal facility, that is, inferior verbal intelligence. Verbal facility plays an important role in organization for learning.

Measures of Organization. Hultsch (1974) also found that older adults do not take advantage of opportunities to organize information as well as younger people do. He gave people of wide age range lists of words to learn and analyzed their performances with two measures of spontaneous organization. One measure was of order—how faithfully the learners followed in their recall performances the order in which the words were presented. The second measure was also of order, but of a different kind. The measure was of similarity in the order in which words of one list were recalled during a particular trial, to the order in which words of a second list were recalled during the same trial. Hultsch found that with both measures, spontaneous "organization showed an overall age effect. As chronological age increases, less [spontaneous] organization of material is exhibited" (Hultsch, 1974, p. 306).

Clustering. Denney (1974) reached a similar conclusion. She presented two lists of words for learning: one list had words in it that were similar (e.g., ocean and sea) and the other list had complementary words (e.g., music and piano). Denney sought to measure organization in terms of the amount of "clustering" of words from the same category, that is, similar or complementary. Like Hultsch, Denney found that the younger people had more spontaneous organization in the recall in that they clustered more than did the older people. "In fact, not one of the elderly subjects clustered significantly . . ." (Denney, 1974, p. 474). In this study, as in the others, learning ability was highly correlated with such organization.

Data suggesting that older people do not spontaneously categorize or cluster information to enhance learning was seen in subsequent studies, somewhat different in kind. For example, Sanders, Murphy, Schmitt, and Walsh (1980) had some learners rehearse the learning materials out loud, others rehearsed it to themselves. Both manners of learning were with word-lists containing 16 words divided into four different categories. Again the older learners (63–85) did not spontaneously take advantage of the categorizing opportunities while the younger learners (29–47) did. Sanders et al. concluded that the "old adults' rehearsal is best characterized as inactive and essentially nonstrategic. Indeed, their rehearsal primarily consisted of a single mention of each item seen . . ." (p. 556). On the other hand, "Young adults' rehearsal was active, serially organized early in the list, and then categorically organized for the rest of the list" (p. 550). Other studies, very different in format, resulted in similar conclusions (see, for example, Howard, McAndrews, and Lasagna, 1981).

Instructed Organization for Learning

The Alphabet As an Aid.   In the preceding studies, either organizational processes were inferred from the opportunities presented in the information, or organizational patterns were measured. In either case, the organizing processes were spontaneous and undirected. As indicated, all these studies showed that elderly adults do not tend to spontaneously organize or categorize information that they are trying to learn, at least they do not do it as readily as younger adults do. Accordingly, their performances suffer. Instructions to organize, however, provide different results. This was seen in a series of studies by Hultsch (1969, 1971, 1975).

Hultsch demonstrated that older people can be instructed to organize information, and when so instructed, they improve their learning-memory performances appreciably. In the first of these studies, long lists of words were learned (1) without instructions to organize, (2) with instructions to organize but without any indication as to how, and (3) with instructions to "organize your recalled words alphabetically . . . note their first letters, and make an attempt to associate the word with the letter" (Hultsch, 1969, pp. 674–675). Hultsch found that the instructions most explicit in how to best organize the material helped the oldest people (45–54 years) most of all. This suggested that those older people who perform poorly do so partly because of poor approaches or efforts in organizing information. When helped in these efforts, they show good ability to learn.

An important finding in this study, like that in the study by Craik and Masani, was that the results applied only among those middle and older age persons of low verbal facility. In Hultsch's study, the older people of high verbal facility were not benefited differentially by instructions that provided aid in organization. This distinction between types of older people is an advance in the aging literature because individual differences, though large, are often overlooked.*

Categorizing.   A subsequent study by Hulsch (1975) was even clearer in demonstrating that older people can be helped in organizing information. He presented 40 words for learning, four from each of 10 different categories. For example, 10 words may have been in the category "fruit." Hultsch

---

*This was highlighted in a study by Bowles and Poon (1982). They compared old and young adults on a memory test and found that the groups performed similarly. They observed, however, that the memory scores of the older group were distributed bimodally, that is, the older group seemed to be made up of two subgroups, one performing better than the other. The better-performing subgroup comprised adults with relatively high verbal facility and the poor-performing subgroup comprised adults of lower verbal facility. The high subgroup was comparable in verbal facility to the young adults, and they were also comparable in memory performance. On the other hand, the other subgroup was lower in verbal facility than the young group and was poorer in memory performance.

asked half the learners to recall the words after providing them with the category names and he asked the other half to recall the words without the category names. The oldest group (65–83) benefited most from the category names; the names served to organize the information and as cues or hints in recall.

Thus, this study was comparable to the others in showing that older adults tend not to process information spontaneously in ways that aid learning but they can be instructed to do it. When so instructed, their performance levels improve, often more than those of younger adults with such instruction, although not achieving the high levels of the young. This summary conclusion, however, is not without its doubters. Waugh and Barr (1980, p. 255) provided data to show that "older subjects in fact gave slightly more evidence of grouping spontaneously than did younger . . . ," that is, they spontaneously organized information for learning more than younger people did. Waugh and Barr's data seem to be exceptions; most data fit the conclusion indicated.

VERBAL AND NONVERBAL INFORMATION

Most of the studies discussed in this chapter were based on the encoding of verbal information. It was implicitly assumed that all the conclusions based on these studies applied equally well to nonverbal information. Only very recently has this assumption been put to test. The aging literature of nonverbal learning is just beginning and is still sparse. Nevertheless, a few research patterns have emerged. Some studies have simply been concerned with learning and remembering pictures of objects or faces. Other studies have contrasted such learning with that of verbal materials. Still others have been concerned with spatial information; these latter studies are described in Chapter 18.

Encoding Picture Information

In one study, black-and-white slides of individual male and female faces were shown to three groups of people—one aged 17 to 39, another aged 60 to 88, and a third of moderately impaired dementia patients of similar age as the older group (Ferris, Crook, Clark, McCarthy, & Rae, 1980). A recognition memory test followed; as will be seen in the next chapter, recognition tests are thought to mimimize retrieval processes and are thus thought to be tests mainly of encoding. Ferris et al. found old and young normal groups different in their ability to encode the faces. As with verbal information, the old were not as good. Differences between the two older groups, however, were not observed.

Pictures Better Than Words

In similar manner, Winograd, Smith, and Simon (1982) presented black-and-white line drawings of objects. In this study, the names of the objects were also presented so that it was possible to compare age-groups (college students and adults aged 50 to over 80) with respect to learning and memory of both the nonverbal items and their verbal designations. Again, the older people performed less well with both types of information. Both age-groups tended to learn and recall somewhat more of the picture information than the word information, with the extent of the picture superiority approximately the same for both groups.

Levels of Learning

Smith and Winograd (1978) had three different instructions for learning pictures of faces. The intent was to have some people in each of the two age-groups (50–80 and 18–25) learn the information well, some learn it poorly, and some be in between. This type of study, called an "orienting task" study, is more often carried out with verbal information as described in detail in Chapter 18. The general finding in these studies is that the instruction making for the best learning helps young people most.

Smith and Winograd (1978) measured recognition memory of pictures of faces following the instructions and found that memory performances improved from the first instruction level to the third. Unlike that found in the verbal-learning studies, however, where the improvement is greater for the young, they found the best instruction equally effective for old (50–80) and young (18–25) people. Smith and Winograd concluded that the reason for the difference in results was that faces are less readily organized and thus less well encoded than words, and so the young could not take advantage of their greater ability.

In light of the later Winograd et al. (1982) study where the recall for pictures was better than for words, the conclusion regarding organization of picture information does not seem correct. It remains to be seen in future research whether, for some reason, older adults demonstrate deficiency in encoding verbal information and less deficiency in encoding nonverbal information.

SUMMARY

There are by far more studies of learning and memory than any other type of study in the field of experimental psychology of aging. For this reason, the studies are described in three chapters, this one and the next two. Early in the study of learning and age, it was recognized that older adults do not learn things as quickly as younger adults do, but they can and do learn. It was also recognized that, in the laboratory at least, much of what appeared to be a learning deficit in old age was really nothing more than a response limitation. That is, many laboratory tasks required quick responses—too quick for many older people to demonstrate what they had learned. Several studies showed that when ample time was allowed them, the elderly were much more adequate in their learning abilities than had been thought.

There are situations that bring out relatively good performances on the part of the elderly and there are situations that do otherwise. Supportive contexts have been seen to bring out good performances, while challenging or critical contexts have been seen to result in poor performances. Another type of situation relates to the condition of reward. Many older people are reluctant to respond unless sure of their answer; many refuse to guess. Accordingly, they do not supply answers to questions on learning and other types of tests when, with the same knowledge, younger people might. Thus, older people make the "omission error" and are marked wrong, only to achieve poor learning-memory scores. A few studies were designed to encourage older people to respond, regardless of whether they were confident of the answer or even knew it at all. This was done by the expedient of giving monetary rewards for any response, but more money for the correct ones. Some of these studies, but not all, showed better learning on the part of the older people with such reward contingencies. It is clear from these studies, then, that encouraging older people to respond by rewards and providing them with supportive contexts can help. This is so easy to arrange and so inexpensive to provide that there seems little reason not to follow such prescriptions in relating to older people.

Additional aid to the elderly in learning can be provided by the form in which information is presented. Vastly superior performances will be seen with information that is familiar and relevant than unfamiliar. The manner in which the information is presented is also important. For example, presenting prose for silent reading makes for better recall than reading it aloud to them. Auditory presentation of a sequence of unrelated digits, however, makes for better recall than visual presentation. These aids help the older adult even if their performance levels are not brought up to those of younger adults.

Older adults are also helped to learn if taught to use mnemonic devices. There are several aids to learning that have been investigated, one of which is called the method of loci. Learners take imaginary "walks" through their homes, stopping at places and things they know well, as for example, the foyer, living room, chairs, lamps. Each item to be memorized is then associated with a room or a furniture piece. This technique has helped the older learner. Another aid in learning is mediation, that is, generating a visual image or a verbal association to pairs of items. The older learner has been helped by this too. The older learner is also aided when taught how to organize or categorize information. Each of these—the method of loci, imagery and verbal mediation, organization or categorizing techniques— often help the older person more than the younger because the younger person tends to do well enough without them. It is mainly older people of relatively low verbal facility who perform more poorly than the young, and it is they who benefit most from the aids. Despite the utility of these mnemonic devices in the benefit they provide, older people do not tend to use them spontaneously, even after being taught how. Additionally, older people do not tend to take as much advantage as younger people of the organization of information that is intrinsic in different types of materials. As a result, they do not learn as much of it as younger people.

The studies providing these findings were based mainly on learning verbal information. A new literature is developing that is based on nonverbal information. This includes learning of faces and objects, as well as learning and memory of the spatial location of items. Older people perform less well with such information too. One study showed that picture information is better retained than verbal information. Studies on nonverbal information together with verbal, in the context of aids of learning, can indicate how to present information to the elderly so that they can best learn and remember.

REFERENCES

Arenberg, D. Anticipation interval and age differences in verbal learning. *Journal of Abnormal Psychology*, 1965, 70, 419–425.

Arenberg, D. Input modality in short-term retention. *Journal of Gerontology*, 1968, 23, 462–465.

Arenberg, D. The effects of input condition on free recall in young and old adults. *Journal of Gerontology*, 1976, 31, 551–555.

Arenberg, D. Comments on the processes that account for memory declines with age. In L. Poon, J. L. Fozard, L. S. Cermak, D. Arenberg, & L. W. Thompson (Eds.), *New directions in memory and aging*. Hillsdale, N.J.: Lawrence Erlbaum Associates, 1980, Chapter 3, pp. 67–71.

Barrett, T. R., & Wright, M. Age-related facilitation in recall following semantic processing. *Journal of Gerontology*, 1981, 2, 194–199.

Bellucci, G., & Hoyer, W. Feedback effects on the performance and self-reinforcing behavior of elderly and young adult women. *Journal of Gerontology*, 1975, 30, 456–460.

Bowles, N. L., & Poon, L. W. An analysis of the effect of aging on recognition memory. *Journal of Gerontology*, 1982, 37, 212–219.

Burke, D. M., & Light, L. L. Memory and aging: The role of retrieval processes. *Psychological Bulletin*, 1981, 90, 513–546.

Canestrari, R. E., Jr. Paced and self-paced learning in young and elderly adults. *Journal of Gerontology*, 1963, 18, 165–168.

Canestrari, R. E., Jr. Age changes in acquisition. In G. A. Talland (Ed.), *Human aging and behavior*. New York: Academic Press, 1968, pp. 169–188.

Craik, F. I. M., & Masani, P. A. Age differences in the temporal integration of language. *British Journal of Psychology*, 1967, 58, 291–299.

Craik, F. I. M., & Simon, E. Age differences in memory: The roles of attention and depth of processing. In L. W. Poon, J. L. Fozard, L. S. Cermak, D. Arenberg, & L. W. Thompson (Eds.), *New directions in memory and aging*. Hillsdale, N.J.: Lawrence Erlbaum Associates, 1980.

Denney, N. W. Clustering in middle and old age. *Developmental Psychology*, 1974, *10*, 471–475.

Dixon, R. A., Simon, E. W., Nowak, C. A., & Hultsch, D. F. Text recall in adulthood as a function of level of information, input modality, and delay interval. *Journal of Gerontology*, 1982, 37, 358–364.

Eisdorfer, C. Verbal learning and response time in the aged. *Journal of Genetic Psychology*, 1965, *107*, 15–22.

Erber, J. T., & Botwinick, J. Reward in the learning of older adults. *Experimental Aging Research*, 1983, 9, 43–44.

Erber, J., Feely, C., & Botwinick, J. Reward conditions and socioeconomic status in the learning of older adults. *Journal of Gerontology*, 1980, 35, 565–570.

Ferris, S. H., Crook, T., Clark, E., McCarthy, M., & Rae, D. Facial recognition memory deficits in normal aging and senile dementia. *Journal of Gerontology*, 1980, 35, 707–714.

Gordon, S. K., & Clark, W. C. Application of signal detection theory to prose recall and recognition in elderly and young adults. *Journal of Gerontology*, 1974, 29, 64–72.

Harwood, E., & Naylor, G. F. K. Recall and recognition in elderly and young subjects. *Australian Journal of Psychology*, 1969, 21, 251–257.

Heron, A., & Craik, F. I. M. Age differences in cumulative learning of meaningful and meaningless material. *Scandinavian Journal of Psychology*, 1964, 5, 209–217.

Howard, D. V., McAndrews, M. P., & Lasagna, M. I. Semantic priming of lexical decisions in young and old adults. *Journal of Gerontology*, 1981, 36, 707–714.

Hulicka, I. M. Age differences in retention as a function of interference. *Journal of Gerontology*, 1967, 22, 180–184.

Hulicka, I. M., & Grossman, J. L. Age group comparisons for the use of mediators in paired-associate learning. *Journal of Gerontology*, 1967, 22, 46–51.

Hulicka, I. M., & Weiss, R. L. Age differences in retention as a function of learning. *Journal of Consulting Psychology*, 1965, 29, 125–129.

Hultsch, D. Adult age differences in the organizaton of free recall. *Developmental Psychology*, 1969, *1*, 673–678.

Hultsch, D. Adult age differences in free classification and free recall. *Developmental Psychology*, 1971, *4*, 338–342.

Hultsch, D. Learning to learn in adulthood. *Journal of Gerontology*, 1974, 29, 302–308.

Hultsch, D. Adult age differences in retrieval: Trace development and cue dependent forgetting. *Developmental Psychology*, 1975, *11*, 197–201.

Kausler, D. H. *Experimental psychology and human aging*. New York: Wiley, 1982.

King, D. J. Retention of connected meaningful material as a function of mode of presentation and recall. *Journal of Experimental Psychology*, 1968, 77, 676–683.

Kinsbourne, M., & Berryhill, J. L. The nature of interaction between pacing and the age decrement in learning. *Journal of Gerontology*, 1972, 27, 471–477.

Lair, C. V., & Moon, W. H. The effects of praise and reproof on performance of middle aged and older subjects. *Aging and Human Development*, 1972, 3, 279–284.

Leech, S., & Witte, K. L. Paired-associate learning in elderly adults as related to pacing and incentive conditions. *Developmental Psychology*, 1971, 5, 180.

Mason, S. E., & Smith, A. D. Imagery in the aged. *Experimental Aging Research*, 1977, 3, 17–32.

McDowd, J., & Botwinick, J. Rote and gist memory in relation to type of information, sensory mode, and age. *Journal of Genetic Psychology*, 1984.

McGhie, A., Chapman, J., & Lawson, J. S. Changes in immediate memory with age. *British Journal of Psychology*, 1965, *56*, 69–75.

Monge, R. H., & Hultsch, D. Paired-associate learning as a function of adult age and the length of the anticipation and inspection intervals. *Journal of Gerontology*, 1971, *26*, 157–162.

Nebes, R. D., & Andrews-Kulis, M. E. The effect of age on the speed of sentence formation and incidental learning. *Experimental Aging Research*, 1976, *4*, 315–331.

Perone, M., & Baron, A. Age-related effects of pacing on acquisition and performance of response sequences: An operant analysis. *Journal of Gerontology*, 1982, *37*, 443–449.

Rabinowitz, J. C., Ackerman, B. P., Craik, F. I. M., & Hinchley, J. L. Aging and metamemory: The roles of relatedness and imagery. *Journal of Gerontology*, 1982, *37*, 688–695.

Robertson-Tchabo, E. A., Hausman, C. P., & Arenberg, D. A classical mnemonic for old learners: A trip that works. *Educational Gerontology*, 1976, *1*, 215–226.

Ross, E. Effects of challenging and supportive instructions in verbal learning in older persons. *Journal of Educational Psychology*, 1968, *59*, 261–266.

Rowe, E. J., & Schnore, M. M. Item concreteness and reported strategies in paired-associate learning as a function of age. *Journal of Gerontology*, 1971, *26*, 470–475.

Sanders, R. E., Murphy, M. D., Schmitt, F. A., & Walsh, K. K. Age differences in free recall rehearsal strategies. *Journal of Gerontology*, 1980, *35*, 550–558.

Smith, A. D. Aging and the total presentation time hypothesis. *Developmental Psychology*, 1976, *12*, 87–88.

Smith, A. D. Age differences in encoding, storage, and retrieval. In L. W. Poon, J. L. Fozard, L. S. Cermak, D. Arenberg, & L. W. Thompson (Eds.), *New directions in memory and aging*. Hillsdale, N.J.: Lawrence Erlbaum Associates, 1980.

Smith, A. D., & Winograd, E. Adult age differences in remembering faces. *Developmental Psychology*, 1978, *14*, 443–444.

Taub, H. A. Paired associates learning as a function of age, rate, and instructions. *Journal of Genetic Psychology*, 1967, *111*, 41–46.

Taub, H. A. Mode of presentation, age, and short-term memory. *Journal of Gerontology*, 1975, *30*, 56–59.

Taub, H. A. Method of presentation of meaningful prose to young and old adults. *Experimental Aging Research*, 1976, *2*, 469–474.

Treat, N. J., Poon, L. W., & Fozard, J. L. Age, imagery, and practice in paired-associate learning. *Experimental Aging Research*, 1981, *7*, 337–342.

Treat, N. J., Poon, J. L., Fozard, J. L., & Popkin, S. J. Toward applying cognitive skill training to memory problems. *Experimental Aging Research*, 1978, *4*, 305–319.

Treat, N. J., & Reese, H. W. Age, pacing, and imagery in paired-associate learning. *Developmental Psychology*, 1976, *12*, 119–124.

Tulving, E. Episodic and semantic memory. In E. Tulving & W. Donaldson (Eds.), *Organization of memory*. New York: Academic Press, 1972.

Waugh, N. C., & Barr, R. A. Memory and mental tempo. In L. W. Poon, J. L. Fozard, L. S. Cermak, D. Arenberg, & L. W. Thompson (Eds.), *New directions in memory and aging*. Hillsdale, N.J.: Lawrence Erlbaum Associates, 1980.

Whitbourne, S. K., & Slevin, A. E. Imagery and sentence retention in elderly and young adults. *Journal of Genetic Psychology*, 1978, *133*, 287–298.

Wimer, R. E. A supplementary report on age differences in retention over a twenty-four hour period. *Journal of Gerontology*, 1960, *15*, 417–418.

Winograd, E., Smith, A. D., & Simon, E. W. Aging and the picture superiority effect in recall. *Journal of Gerontology*, 1982, *37*, 70–75.

Wittels, I. Age and stimulus meaningfulness in paired-associate learning. *Journal of Gerontology*, 1972, *27*, 372–375.

17
Memory Stores: Storage and Retrieval

Why do we forget things we once knew? Efforts in answering this important question have not been successful and perhaps because of this, newer theoretical perspectives have bypassed the question, placing more emphasis on encoding or learning. The newer thinking is that faulty memory is largely a consequence of inadequate or incomplete encoding. This answer is not completely satisfying; still, the newer perspectives have much to offer, as will be seen in the next chapter. The newer perspectives add to the older ones to make for better understanding.

The older perspectives conceptualize learning-memory as a three-component process—encoding, storage, and retrieval. Encoding was discussed in the previous chapter and both storage processes (retaining information) and retrieval processes (accessing this information for use) are discussed here. Some investigators place storage with encoding, as for example, Drachman and Leavitt (1972), but here, storage will be seen as retention of information during a specific time interval—from when it was encoded to when it is retrieved. In this chapter, different memory stores are also discussed.

STORAGE

Delayed Memory Tests

Several studies suggest that information can be lost in storage; if so, once lost, it can never be retrieved. Storage loss is suggested by studies that show that the amount of information originally acquired is greater than the amount of information available after a lapse of time. For example, the study by Hulicka and Weiss (1965), described in the previous chapter, demonstrated that when old and young learned paired associates, there was memory loss when later tested for retention. This was found also with meaningful prose information (Gordon & Clark, 1974) and with drawings of common objects (Harwood & Naylor, 1969). These studies showed equal or greater memory loss among the elderly, suggesting the possibility of storage process difficulties in later life.

Theories of Forgetting

Disuse: Trace Decay.   The foregoing suggests that information once in storage does not necessarily remain there. Why is this? Psychological theories of forgetting are few and inadequate. In the older literature, two main theories were popular. One is the theory of disuse. This theory has it that forgetting comes about because of a lack of practice or a lack of use of the retained material—"use it or lose it" is the catch phrase. Information simply fades or decays with time unless exercised. This theory is a poor one because it is circular. Why does information get lost? Because it fades away.

Interference.   The second theory of forgetting is interference. In fact, for many years, this was really the only viable theory that psychologists had. The study of interference has taken two main forms in laboratory studies: (1) There is the proactive inhibition study (or simply proaction) where learning one task is made more difficult because of having learned one just previously (negative transfer). (2) There is the retroactive interference task (or simply retroaction) where learning a second task interferes with the recall of what was learned in a first task. For many years, interference theory was the most popular one to explain memory loss in old age. The elderly, it was maintained, are more susceptible to the effects of interference than the young. After reviewing much of the literature on interference and age, Craik (1977, p. 397) concluded, "However plausible that view may be it has not been supported by empirical studies carried out since 1958 and the view must be rejected."

This may be a premature conclusion because there are types of interference other than proaction or retroaction. Interference is seen during encoding with distraction while learning or with divided attention while carrying out two or more tasks simultaneously. Interference is seen with information in storage when an experience interferes with or modifies it. Interference is also seen at the point of retrieval in recalling information or in executing a response.

Talland (1965) reported that older people suffer disproportionately when two operations are involved simultaneously. Similarly, Taub (1968) concluded that "rehearsing" of one event while recalling another one in "storage" was differentially deleterious to the elderly. Arenberg (1980, p. 70) put it succinctly and colorfully: "An older person may encounter no more difficulty remembering an unfamiliar telephone number than a young adult, but I would be surprised if the frequency of survival of a number following an interruption between locating it and dialing it would be as high for the older caller."

RETRIEVAL AND RECOGNITION MEMORY

Once information is encoded and stored it must be retrieved if it is to be used. Thus, retrieval is basic to recall. A failure of retrieval is seen with the experience, "I have it at the tip of my tongue, I know his name but I can't come up with it now." Later in conversation the name is recalled.

Recall memory is said to involve the search and retrieval of information from storage. It is as if there is a large bank of information, and to recall any part of it, a search is necessary; when the information is found, it is retrieved. Recognition memory, on the other hand, is thought to bypass retrieval. All that is required is a matching of the information in storage with the information in the environment. [There are other views of recognition memory, as for example that by Tulving and Thomson (1973), but in the main, this is the prevailing one.] Here is an example of a typical question bearing on recall memory: Who was the third President of the United States? The correct answer requires a "search of the data bank" and the "retrieval" of the information, Thomas Jefferson. Here is a question bearing on recognition memory: Among these five names, which is of the third President of the United States? A "match" is required; retrieval is not thought of as part of the process.

Superiority of Recognition over Recall

Many investigators now take it for granted that recognition memory is superior to recall, and that differences among age-groups are greater in recall memory than in recognition. These beliefs underlie the contention that retrieval deficits constitute a major problem in memory loss with age. Some recent literature contests these beliefs, although they are not totally refuted.

What controversy related to the issue of recognition memory and age began with a study reported by Schonfield and Robertson (1966). They presented one list of words for learning and recall and another list for learning and recognition memory. They found that the recognition scores were higher than recall scores for each of the age-groups tested (20s, 30s, 40s, 50s, 60–75). Moreover, although recall dropped continuously with age, recognition was equally good among all the age-groups.

Since the time of this study, superiority of recognition memory over recall has been demonstrated many times but most of the studies subsequent to Schonfield and Robertson's reported fall-off of recognition memory among the aged, although not to the same extent as recall memory (e.g., Erber, 1974). Repeated findings such as Erber's led Burke and Light (1981, p.52) to conclude, "Reliable age differences in recognition have been obtained with a variety of materials [such as] words . . . nonsense syllables . . . sentences . . . prose passages . . . pictures of objects . . . and photographs of faces. . . ." The studies reviewed by Burke and Light, although showing that recognition memory fails with age, are compatible with Schonfield's results in showing greater fall off in recall memory. This points to a retrieval deficit in later life.

Are the Aged Relatively Better in Recognition Memory?

Guessing on Multiple Choice Tests. White and Cunningham (1982) contested the conclusion that recognition memory holds up better with age than recall memory. They argued that recognition (multiple choice) tests allow for guessing, which may be the basis of many of the results reported in the various studies. To support this argument, first they repeated the basic Schonfield and Robertson study with similar results, and then they rescored the recognition data with corrections for guessing. (Since there were five alternatives in the multiple choice test, the recognition score was calculated as number correct minus one-fourth the number wrong). When they did this their results were otherwise. Recognition memory remained superior to recall, but the difference between recall and recognition was no greater among those aged 60 to 70 than those aged 20 to 30. A comparable result, at least conceptually, was reported by Harkins, Chapman, and Eisdorfer (1979) based on a signal detection analysis.

Older adults guessing in recognition memory tasks and benefiting from this is totally at variance with much of what was said in Chapter 10 on cautiousness in later life. It is also at variance with what was said in the prevous chapter regarding rewarding all responses in learning experiments. It was maintained that the elderly are reluctant to venture response unless they feel sure that they are correct and so do not guess. There is a discrepancy here: In partial resolution of this discrepancy, it is to be noted that the better learned information is, the less the need for guessing. If the elderly learned fewer of the words than the young, they had greater need to guess and more occasion to do it, benefiting accordingly.

It must not be overlooked that in the study by White and Cunningham (1982), the recognition scores of both age-groups, even corrected for guessing, were better than the recall scores. Irrespective of age comparisons, therefore, the elderly are seen to benefit from a reduction in the retrieval load in the recognition task.

Number of Alternatives and Guessing. The notion of guessing is compatible with the observation that the greater the number of alternatives in the multiple choice recognition task, the more likely differences between age-groups will be observed. The thinking is that the greater the number of alternatives, the less the likelihood that the guess would be correct. Several studies together suggest this. Perlmutter (1978) had a one-choice situation (was the word seen before or not, a 50% guessing chance). She found superiority of the old over the young on this recognition test. Her older test-takers were highly educated, and this could have made a difference. Kapnick (1971) presented up to 40 words for learning and also had a 50% chance test (the target or learned word was opposed with one distractor word). No age differences were observed. Erber (1974) had five alternatives (one target and four distractors) after learning 24 or 60 words and found age differences. Botwinick and Storandt (1974) presented only 8 words for learning and found age-groups different when all 8 had to be identified within a list of 32 words. Kausler and Kleim (1978) confronted the issue squarely: they found age-groups similar in recognition memory when the learned word was opposed by one other, as did Kapnick, but found age-groups different when the learned word was opposed by three others.

Controlled-lag Recognition

There is a type of recognition memory study that is called, "continuous recognition" or "controlled-lag recognition." A very long list of words is presented one at a time, some words repeating several times, and some not. The task is to identify the words seen before and those not. The task is a long one and there is good opportunity to chart changes in recognition memory over time. Some investigators believe that this is a more realistic way to test for recognition memory since in everyday life people are not typically confronted with a number of alternatives for recognition but, instead, information continuously appears and there is the need to identify it.

At least four controlled-lag studies were reported in which adult age-groups were compared. There were variations in procedure but, overall, comparable results were reported. Wickelgren (1975) compared 18- to 24-year-olds with 60- to 82-year-olds and found that forgetting took place over time, as indicated by poorer recognition performances toward the end of the study than the beginning. The older adults performed less well than the younger. This was seen also by Erber (1978), Rankin and Kausler (1979), and Poon and Fozard (1980). Wickelgren concluded that it was not that the old were deficient in recognition memory but that they were deficient in encoding. That is, the older people recognized fewer words at the beginning of testing than the younger ones, but their rates of forgetting were no different.

Thus, this controlled-lag memory study, the studies based on corrections for guessing, and the studies bearing on the number of alternatives in the multiple choice test, place much doubt on the suggestions of prior studies, viz., retrieval deficit accounts for memory problems in later life. If it does, it certainly does not appear to be the sole basis of memory loss in old age. Encoding is also a basis, perhaps the main one.

RETRIEVAL AND CUED RECALL

Cuing Minimizes the Retrieval Load

Providing hints during retrieval, that is, cued recall, helps in the retrieval process by reducing the required cognitive work. The retrieval load in cued recall tasks can be conceptualized as falling in between that in free recall and typical recognition memory tasks. In cued recall, a hint is given; in recognition tasks, the complete item is provided. Free recall tasks have no cues and the retrieval load is greatest.

Perlmutter (1979) carried out a study that showed very clearly how the effects of cuing fall in between recognition memory and free recall. People aged 18 to 22 were compared to people aged 59 to 69 with respect to free recall and recognition of words, and also with respect to cued recall. The latter was done by providing common associates of the learned words.

Figure 17.1 shows the results of this study. In keeping with the idea that cued recall falls in between free recall and recognition, the memory scores of both age-groups did increase from free recall to cued recall to recognition memory. This figure, however, shows a result contrary to expectation. Although differences between age-groups did decrease from free recall to recognition memory, and from cued recall to recognition memory, the age differences were larger with cued recall than with free recall. The large differences between age-groups in cued recall led Perlmutter (1979) to the

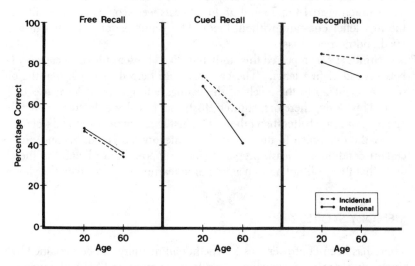

FIGURE 17.1: Intentional and incidental memory measured in three ways as a function of age. From Perlmutter, 1979, Figure 1. Reprinted by permission of the *Journal of Gerontology*, Vol. 34, pp. 533–539, 1979.

conclusion that in her study, the older adults were ineffective in the use of retrieval cues.

Cuing Helps Older People. Perlmutter's (1979) conclusion that the elderly were ineffective in the use of retrieval cues was correct in a relative sense only. Figure 17.1 shows improvement among the elderly with cued recall over that of non-cued recall, even if the improvement was greater among the young. Thus, cuing, like the presentation of correct items among the alternatives in recognition tasks, helps the elderly irrespective of comparisons with the young. As indicated, the reason is that tasks of cued recall and recognition both provide retrieval support.

A study by Hultsch (1975), briefly described in the previous chapter, showed a result somewhat different from that of Perlmutter. He also compared cued and non-cued recall, this time among young adults (18–34) and two groups of older adults (50–64 and 65–83 years). He grouped the words to be learned in categories and for cued recall, he provided the category names. For non-cued recall, he simply asked for the recall of the words with the category names withheld. The results of Hultsch's study were different from those of Perlmutter's in that cuing helped the oldest age-group more than the others. It is seen, therefore, that cuing helps the older person, perhaps more than the younger and perhaps not, but in either case, the old benefit from the retrieval support provided by cues.

The Type of Cue Is Important. Drachman and Leavitt (1972) had a different kind of cue for retrieval support. They also presented lists of words but the cues at recall in this study were the first letters of each word. Men and women aged 18 to 26 and 58 to 89 years were compared in recall with the first letter cues and without them. The young performed better in both cued and non-cued tasks.

Smith (1977) repeated this study but, like Hultsch, provided category labels instead of first letters. The category cues helped so much that the old were brought up to the levels of the young; both groups performed equally well. This study, therefore, showed, first, that it makes a difference what the cue is—some are better than others. The first letters of the words did not make nearly the difference to the elderly that category labels did. Second, under certain conditions at least, proper retrieval supports are so helpful to the elderly that they will not be seen as poorer in learning-memory than the young.

MEMORY STORES

There has been controversy as to whether all memory can be explained by a single mechanism or whether short-term memory (STM) and long-term memory (LTM) are to be explained by different mechanisms. The controversy was framed in terms of one or two mechanisms of memory (with the two-mechanism position now called dual process or dual store). Actually, a third store was disclosed (Sperling, 1960), and this was called sensory memory. This resulted in the conception of a multistore model of memory. Further, the concepts of STM and LTM have been elaborated so that these two stores are often thought of as a very brief primary memory (PM) lasting only about a second, and a longer term secondary memory (SM) that can be differentiated from still a longer term memory, called tertiary memory (TM). We thus begin our discussion with sensory memory, proceed to PM, then SM, and last, TM.

Sensory Storage in a Multistore Model

Two different types of experiments indicate that there is a type of sensory memory so brief that in the visual mode, at least, it lasts no longer than a few tenths of a second. Neisser (1967) called this visual memory "iconic memory." Sensory memory in the auditory mode is called "echoic memory," but this is more difficult to measure. Little work has been carried out in echoic memory and apparently no aging research has been done with it.

Visual Masking. Iconic memory is hardly more than a very brief image—almost an afterglow in the visual system. The image remains briefly after the stimulus is no longer present, but but those experiencing this do not know it. Neisser (1967) and Atkinson and Shiffrin (1968) conceived of this brief iconic image as the beginning of the visual memory process. Longer-term memory, they suggested, builds from this in that the iconic information can be "read out" and processed for longer term storage.

One way iconic memory is measured is by the visual masking experiment discussed in Chapter 12. There is controversy whether the icon, that is, the sensory memory, is longer lasting among the elderly than among the young or whether it is less long lasting. The position taken in Chapter 12 is that it may be longer lasting in old age. If so, it would seem that the elderly have a head start in the memory process because there is more time to attend to the icon and process it for longer term storage. As Walsh and Prasse (1980) suggested, however, it takes the elderly more time to "read" the icon and process it, thus what advantage may be there to start is soon diminished.

Partial Report. There is a second way of measuring visual sensory memory, the method of partial report developed by Sperling (1960). He noted that sensory memory is so very brief that it is gone before people can report it. To cope with this, Sperling had people report only part of the memory, and from this partial report he estimated the total.

Sperling (1960) presented letters and digits in three rows (by tachistoscope) for only 50 msec. Following this very brief display, a tone was sounded to indicate which of the three rows to report. Since the person viewing the display did not know which row would have to be reported, the whole image had to be attended in order to "read out" the indicated row from the total. Sperling found that the ability to report correctly all the digits and letters in the row far excelled the ability to report the whole display. That is, the percentage correct of the row information was much higher than the percentage correct of the whole display. The reason is that the image of the whole display is gone during the time the report is made. A similar experiment was designed by Averbach and Coriell (1961), but instead of three rows of digits and letters they used two rows of eight letters each. More important, instead of tones indicating the row to report, they used visual markers. These markers, like the tones in Sperling's study, were presented at varying intervals following the termination of the display.

Immediately after the 50 msec. exposure of the display was terminated, the report was remarkably accurate, 76 per cent, depending upon the specific procedure. As the auditory or visual signal indicating what to report was delayed, the accuracy of the visual image (partial report) declined. After one second, as much as half the information could be lost.

Only few aging studies of sensory memory have been reported and so only tentative generalization is possible. It is clear that it is very difficult to measure sensory memory among the aged. Abel (1972) made an effort to do so and could not without resorting to stimulus exposure durations of 500 msec, rather than 50. It is thus more likely that she measured some longer term memory by partial report rather than sensory memory. Walsh and Thompson (reported by Walsh, 1975), also indicated difficulty in measuring sensory memory. They tested 10 older adults (60–68 years) and only two gave evidence of sensory memory. On the other hand, 9 younger adults (18–24) were tested and all demonstrated sensory memory. Their data suggested that the two older people who could give partial reports showed more rapid decay of the icon than found among the young. (Although this is compatible with their conclusions based on visual masking studies as seen in Chapter 12, it is not compatible with the main conclusion drawn in that chapter, *viz*; the icon persists longer in the aged.)

Salthouse (1976) also tested sensory memory in the elderly and was more successful in that more of the older people could do it. He had to resort to a longer stimulus duration of 100 msec, however, raising a question of whether he measured sensory memory in the Sperling sense. In any case, in keeping with the findings of Walsh and Thompson, he also found that older people (60–75) were poorer in partial report (sensory memory) than younger people (18–30). These results suggest that older people are disadvantaged at the first stage of information processing for longer term storage.

Primary Memory (PM)

Sensory memory is preperceptual or precognitive in the sense that it is as yet nothing but an unprocessed image. The next memory store, primary memory, is cognitive but barely so. It still is not what most people think of when they think of memory. Waugh and Norman (1965) referred to PM as a temporary memory of what had just occurred. PM is of the "psychological present," not of the past—it is almost a "read out" of what was just experienced. It is more "a temporary holding and organizing *process* than a structured memory *store*" (Craik, 1977, p. 387). A person hears a short string of numbers, such as a phone number, and repeats it perfectly. Minutes, even seconds later, it is not available for recall—it is no longer in storage. As brief a memory as PM is, however, it is longer term than sensory memory. It is a different memory system: PM is a cognitive system, sensory memory is not.

Although PM depends on cognitive processing, it is the physical dimensions of the input that are processed, not the more meaningful aspects of it. If the input is auditory, for example, phonemic or sound qualities reverberating in the auditory nervous system play a role; if it is visual, the size or shape of things may be processed. The significance of the input or how it relates to things is not part of PM. Significance and relationships are part of SM. PM is a memory store of very limited capacity. A short string of numbers, for example, can be held in PM, but a long string must be handled differently; it must be processed to become part of SM. A short string of numbers can be part of PM and SM at the same time, but a long string is only of SM.

Memory Span. The longest number of items that an be recalled in order is called memory span. Craik (1977) maintained that memory spans involving even as few as five items exceed the limited capacity of PM; thus, even the recall of five items "involves the retrieval of one or more items from secondary memory" (p. 393). This reasoning suggests that what differences are found in memory span with age might be attributable to secondary memory. When the span is so long that it can only be learned with practice, it is called supra-span, which clearly involves SM.

Thus, PM is measured by memory span tasks. Digits, letters, even words are presented with the instructions to repeat or recall these immediately afterwards. Does aging affect PM measured in this way? If PM is defined as a store not exceeding three or four items of information, then more often than not age-groups will be seen as similar in PM. If it is defined as a larger store than this, say memory-span length, that is, the longest string of letters that can be repeated correctly, often but not always, older adults will be seen performing less well. (See review by Burke and Light, 1981).

Item Order. Another way of measuring PM is to present a list of words with the idea that recall of the last few in the list represents retrieval from PM. The first few words in the list are considered SM words. Typically, recall is better for SM and PM words than for the middle words in the list. Arenberg (1976) carried out such a procedure and found 17- to 19-year-olds performing better than 60- to 70-year-olds in both PM and SM. The extent of difference between age-groups was the same for PM and SM.

More recently, Parkinson, Lindholm, and Inman (1982) carried out a similar study but utilized several different measures of PM that had been recommended in the literature (for example, the last four items in the list, seven or fewer items between presentation and recall, and others based on more complicated formulas). Age differences (18–24 versus 58–89) were found in all PM measures, with the older performers doing less well.

Wright's (1982) study was very similar to that of Parkinson et al. (1982), but different results were reported. One of the measures used by Wright was identical to that used by Parkinson et al., yet Wright reported no significant age differences between young people of average age 23 and older people of average age 71. Such mixed results, as indicated, also are found in traditional memory-span studies.

All these PM studies taken together suggest some diminution with age in PM, although not so clearly that it is observed in every study. If PM is defined in terms of three or four items of information, rather than more, age differences are less likely to be observed.

Secondary Memory (SM)

Information is thus thought to flow from a sensory store to the holding process of PM. The next store in the chain is secondary memory, and it is here, for the first time, that memory is very close to what most people mean when they say "memory."

Although the primary memory store is limited in the number of items that can be retained, SM is limitless. Although PM is short-lived, SM is longer term. Depending on how it is conceived, SM can last a lifetime. In this chapter, a distinction is made between SM and tertiary or very long-term memory, but very many investigators believe this distinction is wrong. "SM should not be thought of as 'intermediate memory,' " Craik (1977, p. 400) said. "Characteristics of SM performance after 30 seconds . . . are identical to those observed after months or years." SM will last long if much quality cognitive work is carried out during the learning-memory process.

SM is the heart of what most of the scientific literature on memory is about; much of this literature was described in the previous chapter in a different context. The previous chapter indicated that older adults, relative to younger ones, do not spontaneously carry out much quality cognitive work. They do not take advantage of intrinsic organizational characteristics within information to enhance their learning-memory processes; they do not spontaneously utilize mediational or organizational strategies. They can be taught to do these things and so benefit, but in time, they fall back to old patterns and once again show relatively poor SM.

Tertiary (Very Long-term) Memory

It may never be determined unequivocally whether "characteristics of SM performance after 30 seconds . . . are identical to those observed after months or years," as the earlier quote of Craik (1977, p. 400) indicates, or whether very old memory is something different from shorter term memory in terms of process and factors governing the process. The reason for this is that it is extremely difficult, if at all possible, to rigorously research memories of years and decades ago, while, at the same time, controlling, or even knowing about the amount of information originally encoded and stored. Further, it is impossible to control the amount and kind of processing of memories in storage over years. Recognizing that tertiary memory (TM)—memory of events long ago—can be researched only with assumptions that may be untenable, and by methods that are relatively crude, various researchers have made efforts to learn about TM and age.

Memory of Personal Experiences. A literature is beginning to develop that focuses on memory for either events, personages, or objects that are known to have been part of the experiences of those tested, or are presumed to have been. Such memory is sometimes referred to as "everyday memory." Among the first of such studies was one by Schonfield (1969), who simply asked people to recall the names of their former teachers. He found that recall of their names dropped continuously from those aged in their 20s to those age 70 and over.

This study shares a methodological problem in common with other studies of this type in that the age of the memory is confounded with the age of the person remembering. The first grade teacher's name is a 14- or 15-year-old memory for a 20-year-old, but a 64- or 65-year-old memory for a 70-year-old. A similar study was carried out by Bahrick, Bahrick, and Wittlinger (1975), who tested for memory of both the names and faces of classmates recorded in high school yearbooks. Like Schonfield, they found a drop in recall scores from those recently graduated (aged about 18–22) to those who graduated many years ago (aged in their 60s). Bahrick et al. (1975, p. 65) also tested for recognition memory, and the results were otherwise. Although recognition of names showed loss with age, recognition of faces "is retained virtually unimpaired for at least 35 years."

In a subsequent study Bahrick (1979) asked for recall of street names in the area that people had lived as college students. In this study, effort was made to adjust the memory scores for the number of visits made to the college over the years. The recall pattern was similar to those seen in the other studies: much decline was noted in the first year after graduation with further, but less, decline afterwards.

Presumption of Memory. Clinical experience and common everyday folklore suggest that memories of long ago are retained in old age better than are memories of more recently acquired information. When tests are made of this presumption, however, the results are mixed.

Warrington and Silberstein (1970), and soon after, Warrington and Sanders (1971), carried out studies that were typical of others to follow. In the first study, questionnaires of past news events were developed and given to adults of three ages: less than 40 years, 40 to 54, and 55 and over. The news events were of the year 1966 in one questionnaire and 1967 in the other. Thus, all those tested were adults at the time the news event occurred. This fact differentiates the two Warrington studies from some of the others and seems to account, at least in part, for the mixed results. Warrington and Silberstein (1970, p. 509) reported "a trend for performance on the recall task to decline with age but not on the recognition task."

A more thorough investigation was seen in the Warrington and Sanders (1971) study. A questionnaire of past events was given again, but this time pictures of well-known people were also given. Events from the years 1930 to 1968 were sampled, but people in their 40s, 50s, 60s, and 70s were tested on only those sets of questions they experienced as adults. Warrington and Sanders found that both recall and recognition performances dropped with age, with recall dropping more. Squire (1974) found similar results with past news information in comparing medical inpatients in their 50s, 60s, 70s, and 80s. Thus, the results of each of these TM studies are in keeping with the pattern seen in many studies of shorter term memory performances. Warrington and Silberstein (1970) found, contrary to folklore, that memory for the more recent events was better retained than for the more distant, and this was true for all age-groups.

Memory and/or Information. In both the Warrington and Sanders (1971) study and the Squire (1974) study, the older adults were also compared with younger adults or with high school students who were not old enough to have experienced the news events as adults. In these comparisons, the younger people performed less well than the older ones. This was seen also in a study where questions about TV shows were asked rather than news items (Squire, Chance, & Slater, 1975), in a study with questions of well-known racehorses (Squire & Slater, 1975), and in a study comparing middle-aged and older adults with regard to knowledge of melodies of the 1920s though the 1970s (Bartlett & Snelus, 1980). The middle-aged hardly knew any of the melodies from the 1920s and '30s (when they were very young) while the older people knew these melodies. Each of these studies showed, therefore, that information test items that are dated relative to the age of the test-taker may be inappropriate for tests of TM. The middle-aged people may never have known the melodies to remember and the young people in the other studies may never have known the TV shows or the racehorses to remember.

One view of memory tests, therefore, is that items should be of information recent enough to have occurred during the lifetime of the person taking the test. An alternative view is that if the same test is to be given to old and young, the old will be penalized in not being able to show what they know if there are no dated information items. Perhaps these TM tests and questionnaires are better thought of as tests of information than of memory.

Old People Know Old Things. A study by Botwinick and Storandt (1974) indicates this. They gave adults ranging in age from 20 to 79 a series of information questions having to do with news events, not unlike those of Warrington and Sanders (1971). The events covered four time periods, each 20 years: the most recent events were of the 1950s and 1960s, the most distant were events of 1890–1909. In between were events of 1930–1949 and 1910–1929. In this study, aging was not deleterious to performance as it was in the Warrington studies or in the Squire (1974) studies. Age-groups were similar in their funds of information. This was seen again in a study by Storandt, Grant, and Gordon (1978) and again in a study by Botwinick and Storandt (1980).

Other studies based on similar procedures reported superior performances among the elderly in news information. Perlmutter (1978) used the same news item test as did Botwinick and Storandt and found 60- to 75-year-olds superior to 20- to 25-year-olds. The people she tested were of generally superior education and this may have been a basis for the difference in results. Similarly, Poon, Fozard, Paulshock, and Thomas (1979) gave a questionnaire of different news events to people aged from 29 to 69 and found increased age associated with superior recognition memory.

The key to understanding why all these studies reported similar or superior performances among the elderly while Warrington and the others did not rests with the datedness of the information. This is brought out clearly in Figure 17.2, based on the Storandt et al. (1978) study where a questionnaire of items related to the world of entertainment was given along with the items of past news information. As seen in Figure 17.2, older people knew more of the older information and younger people knew more of the more recent. The middle-aged were best in information of intermediate date.

Estimates of Total Knowledge. Lachman and Lachman (1980, p. 287) wanted to learn about "total knowledge" and developed an interesting and innovative way to do it. They were concerned with "information that is relatively permanent . . . acquired during a lifetime of formal education and day-to-day experience." They gave people of average ages 20, 52, and 71 a test comprising 95 items of information covering current events, movies, sports, history, and the Bible. First, a recall test was given with instructions to indicate those items that were "don't know" or "can't remember." Following this, a recognition (multiple choice) test was given of those items not correctly answered in the recall test. The multiple choice items were answered with the notation, "wild guess," when appropriate.

Total knowledge was calculated by combining the correct recall scores

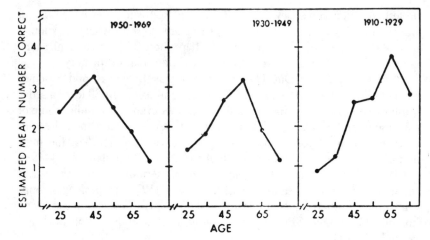

FIGURE 17.2: Long-term memory for events and personages in the world of entertainment that were well-known during different time periods. Note that younger people know the more recent information, older people know the more dated information, and middle-aged people know information of intermediate date. (Adapted from Storandt, Grant, & Gordon, "Remote memory as a function of age and sex. *Experimental Aging Research*, 1978, 4 (5), 365–375. Taken by permission of the editors of *Experimental Aging Research*, copyright Beech Hill Enterprises, Inc., 1978.)

with the recognition scores but subtracting from this sum the correctly answered items noted in recall as "don't know," and in recognition as "wild guess." This total knowledge score was seen to increase from age 20 to 52 and remain constant to age 71.

Lachman and Lachman (1980) reasoned that older people, having experienced more things, have a greater store of information. Recalling an item of information from a greater "data base" is harder than from a smaller one. Efficiency of recall, they maintained, has to be estimated in relation to the data base. Accordingly, they developed an efficiency index: number of items recalled relative to the number of items in storage, that is, number recalled/total knowledge. This ratio was constant from age 20 to 52 to 71. It may be concluded, therefore, that tertiary memory as measured this way is maintained with age. In this study, there was evidence of improvement in total knowledge from young to middle age and no decline thereafter. "Efficiency in recall" remained constant with aging.

Laboratory Learning. All these studies on tertiary memory were based on tests of information acquired long ago or presumed to have been acquired long ago. If the experimenter attempts to teach new information for long-term recall, rather than rely on unknown past histories, the obvious disadvantage is that the experimenter might have to wait years, if not a lifetime, to measure the old memories. Clearly, the experimenter in this type of study is limited as to how old the memories can be at the time of measurement. Fozard, Waugh, and Thomas (1975) were limited to about two and a half years.

These investigators presented people with 100 picture postcards, representing many different kinds of scenes and environments—oceans, airports, persons, and other. The postcards were presented one at a time by slide projection. Immediately after viewing the 100 slides, a test of recognition memory was given. The test was based on 20 of the 100 pictures with each one paired with one not in the original series. The task was to identify the one seen before.

Three groups—median ages 35, 50, and 67 years—were compared in this immediate test of recognition memory. They were also compared in a later test given either 4, 8, 16, 32, 65, or 130 weeks afterward. Fozard et al. (1975) found that most of the decline in recognition memory occurred over the first 4 weeks but it was only at that time that the three age-groups differed. A small number of the oldest people performed poorly, but otherwise, age was not seen as very important in forgetting.

SUMMARY

Once information is encoded (learned), it is stored and later retrieved as needed. The previous chapter dealt with encoding, and it was seen that this process was carried out less well among the elderly than the young. Storage, that is, the maintenance of memory, may also be less good among the elderly, but this is less clear. Storage loss is suggested by studies that show the amount of information originally acquired is greater than the amount available after a lapse of time.

Information in storage is thought to be lost because of trace decay and because of interference. Trace decay is an old explanation and now rarely used because it is hardly more than a restatement of the idea that a memory has been forgotten. Interference is a broad concept, but in general it means that one memory process interferes with another, limiting the expression of one of them or, perhaps, obliterating it. Not everyone agrees that storage loss is a viable concept, or if it is, that the aged suffer such loss more than the young. When storage loss is seen as a problem, however, the explanations of trace decay and interference are offered. The reason for the disagreement of whether storage maintenance is a viable concept is that distinction among the processes of encoding, storage, and retrieval is more of a heuristic than a clear fact of nature. For example, if memory is less good after a lapse of time, it may not be storage loss at all, it may be that the information was not learned well in the first place. Or it may be a retrieval difficulty. For example, it is common to forget a person's name, only to remember it later.

From tests made at first, storage loss may be incorrectly inferred, but from tests made later, retrieval difficulties are disclosed.

Recall memory involves retrieval, but it is less clear whether retrieval is part of recognition memory (as in multiple choice tests). In either case, the retrieval load is lightened in recognition situations because the correct alternative is available as a reminder or cue. Recognition memory, therefore, is typically superior to recall memory.

Many studies have shown that the difference between old and young in recall is greater than the age difference in recognition memory. Since the retrieval load is greater in recall, many investigators have concluded that memory loss in old age is largely a deficit in retrieval. More recent studies, however, questioned the generality of the basic finding of greater differences with age in recall than recognition memory, and accordingly, questioned the conclusion of retrieval deficit. Two studies indicated that guessing goes on in the multiple choice recognition tests and if scores are corrected for guessing, the age difference in recognition memory is no less than in recall. Strengthening this observation are studies in which the number of alternative choices in the recognition memory test are varied. The fewer the choices, the more likely a guess is correct and the more similar the age-groups in recognition memory. These studies suggest that retrieval difficulty with age is not so easily inferred as had once been thought.

Although age-groups might be no less different in recognition memory than recall, all age-groups are typically better in recognition memory than recall because of the cue value of the correct alternative, that is, the hint or reminder it provides. There is a type of recall test, called cured recall, that falls in between free recall and recognition memory. In tests of free recall, the information originally learned must be retrieved without aid. In tests of cued recall, a reminder is given that helps memory, but the reminder is not as complete as that in recognition memory. Thus, memory is best in the recognition test, next in cued recall, and poorest in free recall. Cuing helps older people, but not necessarily more than it helps younger people; it depends on the type of cue.

An older model of memory differentiated between short-term and long-term memory. More recently a distinction has been made between primary memory (PM) and secondary memory (SM). The former is a very short-term store lasting but a second or so and limited to but five or fewer items of information. It is memory of what is going on right now—it is more of a holding process than a true memory storage system. SM is what most people think of when they say "memory." This system includes memory of all durations and is limitless with regard to how much can be stored. There is no doubt that SM declines with age, but the data are less clear with regard to PM. To the extent that a strict definition of PM is maintained—that is, to the extent that only few items of information are involved—PM is less likely to be seen declining with age.

In this chapter, a distinction was made between very old, long-term memory and memory more recently acquired. The former was called tertiary memory (TM) and the latter SM. Most investigators, it seems, do not make this distinction even though there is utility in it. Some studies have reported that the aged are less good in TM, but others have reported otherwise. The reason for this disagreement relates to the nature of the test items. Old people tend to know or remember very old information while younger people tend to know more recent information. The different results in the TM studies reside in how dated the information items are. Studies showing poorer performances among the aged are limited to test items of events that occurred in the adult experiences of the test-takers.

In addition to PM, SM, and TM, there is another store, sensory memory. This store is preperceptual or precognitive. Sensory memory is very short-lasting, about one-third of a second. It is hardly more than an image of a stimulus in the visual system, and an echo in the auditory system. One model of information processing has it that information in this very brief sensory memory store can be processed or worked on to make it longer lasting. As such, it can become part of PM, which in turn can be processed for SM and TM. Older people require more time to process sensory memory information for longer term memory, leaving them disadvantaged at the first stage of the information-processing sequence.

The age pattern in this information-processing model of memory stores, therefore, is: (1) sensory memory, if not impaired, at least is not processed as efficiently in old age; (2) PM may hold up better, but (3) SM is clearly impaired; (4) TM may or may not hold with age, but even if not, the old have a large store of information, as large as that of younger people. This store is largely of occurrences of long ago.

REFERENCES

Abel, M. *The visual trace in relation to aging.* Unpublished doctoral dissertation, Washington University, St. Louis, Mo., 1972.

Arenberg, D. The effects of input condition on free recall in young and old adults. *Journal of Gerontology,* 1976, *31,* 551–555.

Arenberg, D. Comments on the processes that account for memory declines with age. In L. Poon, J. L. Fozard, L. S. Cermak, D. Arenberg, & L. W. Thompson (Eds.), *New directions in memory and aging.* Hillsdale, N.J.: Lawrence Erlbaum Associates, 1980, Chapter 3, pp. 67–71.

Atkinson, R. C., & Shiffrin, R. M. Human memory: A proposed system and its control processes. In K. W. Spence & J. T. Spence (Eds.), *The psychology of learning and motivation* (Vol. 2). New York: Academic Press. 1968.

Averbach, E., & Coriell, A. S. Short-term memory in vision. *Bell Systems Technical Journal*, 1961, *40*, 309–328.

Bahrick, H. P. Maintenance of knowledge: Questions about memory we forgot to ask. *Journal of Experimental Psychology: General*, 1979, *108*, 296–308.

Bahrick, H. P., Bahrick, P. O., & Wittlinger, R. P. Fifty years of memory for names and faces: A cross-sectional approach. *Journal of Experimental Psychology*, 1975, *104*, 54–75.

Bartlett, J. C., & Snelus, P. Lifespan memory for popular songs. *American Journal of Psychology*, 1980, *93*, 551–560.

Botwinick, J., & Storandt, M. *Memory, related functions and age*. Springfield, Ill.: Charles C. Thomas, 1974.

Botwinick, J., & Storandt, M. Recall and recognition of old information in relation to age and sex. *Journal of Gerontology*, 1980, *35*, 70–76.

Burke, D. M., & Light, L. L. Memory and aging: The role of retrieval processes. *Psychological Bulletin*, 1981, *90*, 513–546.

Craik, F. I. M. Age differences in human memory. In J. E. Birren & K. W. Schaie (Eds.), *Handbook of the psychology of aging*. New York: Van Nostrand Reinhold, 1977.

Drachman, D., & Leavitt, J. Memory impairment in the aged: Storage versus retrieval deficit. *Journal of Experimental Psychology*, 1972, *93*, 302–308.

Erber, J. T. Age differences in recognition memory. *Journal of Gerontology*, 1974, *29*, 177–181.

Erber, J. T. Age differences in a controlled-lag recognition memory task. *Experimental Aging Research*, 1978, *4*, 195–205.

Fozard, J. L., Waugh, N. C., & Thomas, J. C. Effects of age on long term retention of pictures. *Proceedings of the Tenth International Congress of Gerontology*, Jerusalem, Israel, 1975, *2*, 137. As reported by Fozard, J. L., & Poon, L. W. in Research and training activities of the mental performance and aging laboratories (1973–1976). Technical Report 76-02, GRECC, Veterans Administration, Boston, 1976.

Gordon, S. K., & Clark, W. C. Application of signal detection theory to prose recall and recognition in elderly and young adults. *Journal of Gerontology*, 1974, *29*, 64–72.

Harkins, S. W., Chapman, C. R., & Eisdorfer, C. Memory loss and response bias in senescence. *Journal of Gerontology*, 1979, *34*, 66–72.

Harwood, E., & Naylor, G. F. K. Recall and recognition in elderly and young subjects. *Australian Journal of Psychology*, 1969, *21*, 251–257.

Hulicka, I. M., & Weiss, R. L. Age differences in retention as a function of learning. *Journal of Consulting Psychology*, 1965, *19*, 125–129.

Hultsch, D. Adult age differences in retrieval: Trace development and cue dependent forgetting. *Developmental Psychology*, 1975, *11*, 197–201.

Kapnick, P. L. *Recognition memory of verbal material of varying lengths as a funcition of age*. Unpublished doctoral dissertation, Washington University, St. Louis, Mo., 1971.

Kausler, D. H. *Experimental psychology and human aging*. New York: Wiley, 1982.

Kausler, D. H., & Kleim, D. M. Age differences in processing relevant versus irrelevant stimuli in multiple item recognition learning. *Journal of Gerontology*, 1978, *33*, 87–93.

Lachman, J. L., & Lachman, R. Age and the actualization of world knowledge. In L. Poon, J. L. Fozard, L. S. Cermak, D. Arenberg, & L. W. Thompson (Eds.), *New directions in memory and aging*. Hillsdale, N.J.: Lawrence Erlbaum Associates, 1980, Chapter 18, pp. 285–311.

Neisser, U. *Cognitive psychology*. New York: Appleton-Century-Crofts, 1967.

Parkinson, S. R., Lindholm, J. M., & Inman, V. W. An analysis of age differences in immediate recall. *Journal of Gerontology*, 1982, *37*, 425–431.

Perlmutter, M. What is memory aging the aging of? *Developmental Psychology*, 1978, *14*, 330–345.

Perlmutter, M. Age difference in adults' free recall, cued recall, and recognition. *Journal of Gerontology*, 1979, *34*, 533–539.

Poon, L. W., & Fozard, J. L. Age and word frequency effects in continuous recognition memory. *Journal of Gerontology*, 1980, *35*, 77–86.

Poon, L. W., Fozard, J. L., Paulshock, D. R., & Thomas, J. C. A questionnaire assessment of age differences in retention of recent and remote events. *Experimental Aging Research*, 1979, *5*, 401–411.

Rankin, J. L., & Kausler, D. H. Adult age differences in false recognitions. *Journal of Gerontology*, 1979, *34*, 58–65.

Salthouse, T. A. Age and tachistoscopic perception. *Experimental Aging Research*, 1976, *2*, 91–103.

Schonfield, D. Age and remembering. Duke University Council on Aging and Human Development, *Proceedings of Seminars*. Duke University, Durham, N.C., 1969.

Schonfield, D., & Robertson, E. A. Memory storage and aging. *Canadian Journal of Psychology*, 1966, *20*, 228–236.

Smith, A. D. Adult age differences in cued recall. *Developmental Psychology*, 1977, *13*, 326–331.

Sperling, G. The information available in brief visual presentations. *Psychological Monographs: General and Applied*, 1960, *74*, 1–28.

Squire, L. R. Remote memory as affected by aging. *Neuropsychologia*, 1974, *12*, 429–435.

Squire, L. R., Chance, P. M., & Slater, P. C. Assessment of memory for remote events. *Psychological Reports*, 1975, *37*, 223–234.

Squire, L. R., & Slater, P. C. Forgetting in very long-term memory as assessed by an improved questionnaire technique. *Journal of Experimental Psychology: Human Learning and Memory*, 1975, *104*, 50–54.

Storandt, M., Grant, E. A., & Gordon, B. C. Remote memory as a function of age and sex. *Experimental Aging Research*, 1978, *4*, 365–375.

Talland, G. A. Three estimates of the word span and their stability over the adult years. *Quarterly Journal of Experimental Psychology*, 1965, *17*, 301–307.

Taub, H. A. Age differences in memory as a function of rate of presentation, order of report, and stimulus organization. *Journal of Gerontology*, 1968, *23*, 159–164.

Tulving, E., & Thomson, D. M. Encoding specificity and retrieval processes in episodic memory. *Psychological Review*, 1973, *80*, 352–373.

Walsh, D. Age differences in learning and memory. In D. S. Woodruff & J. E. Birren (Eds.), *Aging*. New York: D. Van Nostrand, 1975.

Walsh, D. A., & Prasse, M. J. Iconic memory and attentional processes in the aged. In L. W. Poon, J. L. Fozard, L. S. Cermak, D. Arenberg, & L. W. Thompson, (Eds.), *New directions in memory and aging*. Hillsdale, N.J.: Lawrence Erlbaum Associates, 1980.

Warrington, E. K., & Sanders, H. I. The fate of old memories. *Quarterly Journal of Experimental Psychology*, 1971, *23*, 432–442.

Warrington, E. K., & Silberstein, M. A questionnaire technique for investigating very long term memory. *Quarterly Journal of Experimental Psychology*, 1970, *22*, 508–512.

Waugh, N. C., & Norman, D. A. Primary memory. *Psychological Review*, 1965, *72*, 89–104.

White, N., & Cunningham, W. R. What is the evidence for retrieval problems in the elderly? *Experimental Aging Research*, 1982, *8*, 169–171.

Wickelgren, W. A. Age and storage dynamics in continuous recognition memory. *Developmental Psychology*, 1975, *11*, 165–169.

Wright, R. E. Adult age similarities in free recall, output order, and strategies. *Journal of Gerontology*, 1982, *37*, 76–79.

18
Newer Perspectives in Learning-Memory

DEPTH OF PROCESSING

In the two previous chapters on learning and memory, a distinction was made among the processes of encoding, storage, and retrieval. There is now a deemphasis on this distinction and also a deemphasis on multistore models of memory, just described. A newer theory—depth of processing—places almost all of the emphasis on encoding. The idea is that the duration of memory depends mainly, if not totally, on the quality and extent of information processing. If information is very well learned (deeply processed), it will be long remembered. Conversely, if it is poorly learned (shallowly processed), it will soon be forgotten.

There is much to recommend this theory, as data bearing on it demonstrate, but there is an associated shortcoming. The theory is often applied in circular manner such that if information is deeply processed, it is thought that it will be long remembered. If it is not long remembered, however, it is explained after the fact that the information was not deeply processed in the first place. Despite this circularity, the theory is viable since predictions can be made of the types of processing that make for good memory and these predictions can be tested in the laboratory.

Four Concepts

Shallow and Deep Processing. The depth of processing view is attributed to Craik and Lockhart (1972) and has been modified and expanded in several places, including a report by Craik and Simon (1980, pp. 97–98). There are four aspects to this view of learning-memory. First, to place information in storage, more correctly in the theory of depth of processsing, "for the purposes of perception and comprehension," information is processed simultaneously in two qualitatively different ways. One way is of " 'shallow' levels of analysis [that] are concerned with sensory and physical aspects of stimuli . . . [the other way is of] deeper levels of analysis [that] are progressively concerned with abstract, semantic, associative processes." Some information is more amenable to shallow processing than others, and some information can hardly be retained without deeper processing. In either case, however, shallow and deep processing go on together, each to some extent. The "memory trace is the record of those operations [of shallow and deep processing, with the] . . . deeper processing . . . associated with more durable traces."

This has a bearing on the concept of memory stores, described in the previous chapter. Craik (1977) allowed that there were two stores, primary memory and secondary memory, with the former associated with shallow processing and the latter with deep. More recently, Craik and Simon (1980) appear to have minimized the distinction between these two types of memory stores by emphasizing that shallow and deep processing go on together. It is possible to conceptualize primary and secondary memory on a continuum of a single system, the determining characteristic being the degree of shallow processing relative to deep. Primary memory is associated with more shallow processing and secondary memory with deeper. No distinction need be made between secondary and tertiary memory, as indicated at the end of the previous chapter; the extent and quality of deep processing determines how long-lasting secondary memory will be.

Elaboration. The second concept in the depth of processing theory is that of "elaboration." Depth refers to the difference between shallow and deep processing but elaboration "refers to the extensiveness or richness of processing carried out at any level of depth." Elaboration, then, is synonymous with quality of processing. Craik and Simon (1980, p. 97) gave these examples of extensiveness or richness: proofreading or color matching "require extensive processing at shallow levels" in that physical aspects of stimuli are attended. Reading for meaning, on the other hand, requires "minimal sensory analysis, but extensive deep processing."

Distinctiveness of Information. The third concept is that the more distinctive information is, the more easily identified it is from other information and, as such, the easier it is to process and thus retain. Conversely, the more deeply and elaborately information is encoded, the more distinctive it becomes. Another way of saying this is that something that stands out can better be perceived and processed for memory than something in the background. And learning something well makes it stand out.

Encoding and Retrieval. The fourth concept is the only one that focuses on retrieval, as contrasted to encoding. Craik and Simon (1980) maintain that retrieval processes and encoding processes are each to be described in terms of depth and elaborateness. Just as encoding involves some combination of shallow and deep processing, each with some level of elaboration, so does retrieval in recall. Further, memory is best when the types of processing in retrieval operations are compatible with those in encoding operations. This is not unlike the thinking of Hovland (1951, pp. 676–677) in his theory of "changed cues and expectations." Hovland's is an old theory that simply maintains that recall is best when the conditions during recall are most similar to those that were present during learning. For example, having learned directions to a particular address while going there, it may be difficult to remember these directions when not in the neighborhood of that address. This is not identical to Craik's notion, but it points in the same direction. For Hovland, expectations are important in recall. If information is asked in unexpected, strange ways, there is greater likelihood of poor recall than when expectations are met by questions framed in accustomed ways and in contexts similar to those in which the information was learned.

The Orienting Experiment

Most of the research related to aging that bears on this thinking has been concerned with the first concept, that is, shallow and deep processing. The literature indicates that older people do not process information as deeply as younger people and the elaborative character of their processing is not as extensive or as rich. Older adults "fail to process deeply both at encoding and retrieval unless their processing is guided appropriately" (Craik & Simon, 1980, p. 100).

This conclusion evolved in the course of many different types of studies, but none more than those based on the orienting experiment. In the orienting experiment, different instructions are given to different people, focusing them on different aspects of information. In this way, some people will process mainly in a shallow way, others in mainly a deep way, and others in between. In learning a list of words, for example, shallow processing instructions might be to attend to a specific letter of the words (sensory, physical dimensions) while deep processing instructions might be to form images of the words or to judge whether the words were pleasant (semantic, associative dimensions). Prediction based on the theory is that deep processing instructions would make for better learning and memory than shallow. Most studies based on this orienting experiment support this prediction. Deep processing, even without intention to learn, makes for good performances; in fact, some studies, but not all, have shown that deep processing without intention to learn made for better performances than intentional efforts that, presumably, were not based on such deep quality processing.

Studies based on the orienting task typically contrast unintentional (incidental) learning with intentional. It is in incidental learning that differing instructions are given. Although some instructions orient some people to shallow processing and others to deep, typically no mention is made in either case that tests of memory will follow. In intentional learning, on the other hand, instruction on how to process the information is not given but the learner is told that there will be a test of memory.

Elderly People Do Not Process Deeply. A good number of aging studies based on the orienting task have now been reported and most of these have shown that although older people are better in their incidental learning performances with instructions for deep processing than for shallow, the difference between the two is not as great as among younger people. In one study, for example, Eysenck (1974) gave five different instructions: the instruction for the most shallow processing was to count the letters of each of the words to be learned. (Attending to physical aspects of stimuli, it was said, makes for shallow processing.) The instruction for the deepest processing was to form images of the words. Eysenck found that as processing proceeded from shallow to deep, learning-memory improved but more so for younger people (18–30) than for older ones (55–65). Unlike what some other studies have disclosed, however, none of this processing made for learning-memory performances that were as good as those with intentional learning.*

Figure 18.1 shows the results of another study in which there were five different instructions, two of incidental learning and three of intentional learning (Erber, Herman, & Botwinick, 1980). One incidental instruction given to young (18–31) and old (65–77) adults was to examine each word in the learning list to see whether they contained the letters *E* and *G* (shallow processing). The other incidental instruction was to examine each word and determine whether it was pleasant or unpleasant (deep processing). There was a simple instruction to learn the words (intentional learning), an instruction to learn the words while examining them for *E*s and *G*s (intentional plus shallow), and an instruction to learn the words while examining them for pleasantness–unpleasantness (intentional plus deep processing).

---

*In the main, these results were compatible with other studies based on processing words, i.e., Walsh (1975); White (described by Craik, 1977); Perlmutter (1978); Zelinski, Walsh, and Thompson (1978); Mason (1979); and Erber, Herman, and Botwinick (1980). There were variations in procedure among these studies and some variations in what was found, but the basic notion that the elderly do not process as deeply as the young was concluded by all.

White and Erber et al. did not find results compatible with this conclusion when recognition memory was tested, only when recall was. Perlmutter, on the other hand, found compatible results only with recognition memory, not recall. In contrast, Mason's results of both recall and recognition memory showed the deep processing deficit among the elderly. Zelinski et al. measured recall two minutes after the words were presented and again 48 hours later. Their results were compatible with the main conclusion only with the delayed recall, not the earlier recall as measured in the other studies.

Simon, Dixon, Nowak, and Hultsch (1982) provided orienting instructions in regard to

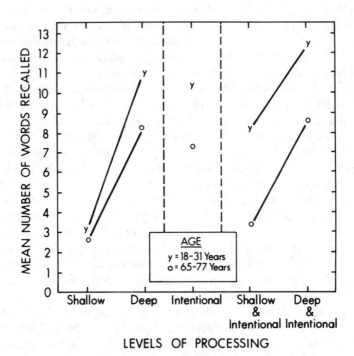

FIGURE 18.1: Mean number of words recalled as a function of depth of processing. Shallow processing resulted from instructions to examine each word in the test for letters *E* and *G*. Deep processing resulted from instructions to examine each word with regard to whether it was pleasant or unpleasant. Instructions to learn the words were labeled "intentional." (Data from Table 1 of Erber et al., 1980)

Figure 18.1 shows that the old and young adults were hardly different with shallow processing while their learning-memory performances with deep processing were different. As indicated in the footnote, this was taken as evidence that the elderly do not or cannot process information as deeply as the young. Figure 18.1 also shows that deep processing without intention to learn made for performances as good as those of intentional learning, if not better.

---

meaningful prose. In this study, orienting instructions had no effect at all on the older people, but it did on the young. Till and Walsh (1980) varied orienting instructions preceding both free and cued recall. The deepest processing instruction made for better free recall among the young than the elderly, but equal cued recall. (This study will be described later.)

Smith and Winograd (1978) measured recognition memory of pictures of faces. Unlike in most of the verbal learning studies above, old and young benefitted equally from deep processing instructions. Winograd, Smith and Simon (1982) provided orienting instructions regarding the learning of pictures and also, the names of the pictures. Here, contrary to all the other studies, orienting instructions had no effect at all.

It is to be noted that these results and the similar ones reported in most of the orienting studies are in contrast to the studies by Hultsch and others, described in Chapter 16. Those studies demonstrated that specific instructions to learn, together with specific processing strategies on how to do it, helped the old more than they helped the young. The orienting studies showed that with no instruction to learn and with relatively oblique processing strategies, the old are helped less than the young. Perhaps in the studies described in Chapter 16, more than in those based on the orienting task described here, the older people were "guided appropriately," as Craik and Simon (1980) indicated was necessary.

Divided Attention. In the Erber et al., (1980) study, represented in Figure 18.1, intentional learning together with processing the information as instructed made for interesting results. Among the old, there was little improvement in memory performance in going from shallow processing to the combination of shallow plus intentional learning. On the other hand, there was sizable improvement among the young. Similarly, there was no improvement among the old in going from deep processing alone to the combination of deep plus intentional processing, but there was improvement among the young. This led to the conclusion that "the old have more difficulty than the young in dealing with two instructional components simultaneously . . ." (Erber et al., 1980, p. 341).* This conclusion was suggested by the thinking of Craik (1977) and Craik and Simon (1980), where it was maintained that divided attention between simultaneous tasks is more of a problem for the old than the young. Wright (1981, p. 612) was in agreement in her studies of divided attention but added, "it is not divided attention among stimuli, per se, which is responsible for the [age] decrement but rather division of attention or capacity among competing mental operations." Overcoming the effects of interference from competing operations during encoding or recall, therefore, was seen as more of a problem for the elderly than the young.

AUTOMATIC AND EFFORTFUL PROCESSING

Deep and elaborative processing "is especially effortful, [it] takes more 'cognitive energy,' and so such processing drops first as the person ages. . . . [However], deep processing that is highly practiced can be carried out with relatively little expenditure of effort" (Craik & Simon, 1980, p. 107). According to theory, such highly practiced processing should not drop out with

---

*This conclusion is also supported by the comparisons in Figure 18.1 between the intentional and the combination instructions. The decline was greater among the old in going from intentional to the combination shallow plus intentional instruction, and the improvement in performance was smaller in going from intentional to the combination deep plus intentional instruction.

age. There is a growing literature on the contrast between effortful processing and processing that requires little effort; the latter is called "automatic
processing."

This literature and theory had its formal beginnings with a publication
by Hasher and Zacks (1979). They conceived of automatic and effortful
processing on the opposite ends of a continuum; effortful processing, they
said, diminishes ability to successfully engage in other effortful activities.
For example, with deep, effortful processing for secondary memory (such as
in the use of mnemonic devices, discussed in Chapter 16, or in processing
with orienting instructions, described just before), little room is left for other
involvements. With practice and expertise, however less effort is required;
the task becomes more and more automatic, making it possible to attend to
other things. Divided attention situations are more easily dealt with if one or
more of the situations call for automatic processing. An experienced bicy-
clist, for example, can carry a package or two while riding, or read a brief
note; a new learner cannot do this.

According to Hasher and Zachs (1979), automatic processes, unlike
effortful ones, are not improved by practice. Additionally, unlike effortful
processes, automatic ones do not require awareness or attention. Although
automaticity can result from having practiced functions that once were
effortful, some processes are inherently automatic. The inherent ones, they
said, involve spatial, temporal, and frequency-of-occurrence information.
Such information should come as easily to the old as the young because
these "are ones for which humans are genetically 'prepared'" (Hasher &
Zacks, 1979, p. 356).

Frequency of Occurrence Information

Hasher and Zacks (1979, Experiment 2) presented several lists of words to
old (56–80) and young (18–24) people, each different in regard to the
frequency with which words in the list were repeated. The task was to judge
the relative frequency of occurrence of the words—an automatic process
task, predicted to be no harder for the old than the young. The results of this
study, however, were not in total accord with prediction: the two groups
were different in that the young were progressively closer to the mark as the
words repeated more frequently. Other support was found for their theory,
however, in that, first, both age-groups increased their estimates of the
frequency of occurrence of words as the word frequencies actually increased
in the lists. Second, instructions that frequency estimates would be required
were no more useful to either age-group than instructions that did not
disclose this. As indicated, the theory has it that intention to process automatic functions does not improve performance over that which comes nat-

urally, since people are genetically prepared. Awareness and attention are not important to automatic processing.

Attig and Hasher (1980) thought that conservative tendencies on the part of the old might have been the reason they made lower estimates of frequency when the actual word-frequencies were relatively high. That is, Attig and Hasher thought that when words were repeated as many as four times in the list, the older people might have felt it too risky or assertive to declare such high estimates (see Chapter 10). Accordingly, Attig and Hasher repeated the original study but this time, to avoid the issue of conservative tendency (response bias), instead of simple estimates of word frequency, young (18–34), middle-aged (35–51), and older (60–77) people had to compare two words at a time and indicate the word that they heard more frequently.

In this study, the aging results were compatible with theory—the three age-groups were comparable in their frequency judgments. The Hasher–Zacks theory was supported, then, indicating that aging does not affect automatic processing. Attig and Hasher (1980, p. 69) reported, "College students, prepared for this test of frequency information, were no more sensitive than were elderly persons who were not so prepared." Kausler and Puckett (1980) carried out a very similar study with word information presented visually, rather than auditorily as in the Attig and Hasher study. Their results were very similar, lending support to the theory.

Temporal Information

Hasher and Zacks (1979) suggested that frequency-of-occurrence, temporal, and spatial information are automatically processed and that age-groups should not be different in these. The data appear to support their contention with regard to frequency-of-occurrence information, but the data are not yet in with regard to temporal information since there appears to have been but one study. This study supported the theory.

McCormack (1981) gave elderly (60–75) and younger (17–29) adults a list of words auditorily, with instructions to half of the people of each age-group to study them so that they could indicate later where the words belonged in the temporal order given. The other half of each age-group were instructed to simply concentrate on each word with no mention made of temporal order. The focus of interest in this study was not memory for the words themselves but memory for their locations in the list (the automatic process).

In the first part of the study, "the younger subjects exhibited superior location memory but this was attributed to a pronounced tendency on the part of the elderly to be conservative with assigning words to early and late locations" (McCormack, 1981, p. 509). This is conceptually similar to what Hasher and Zacks (1979) found with the word frequency estimations when the words appeared relatively often. When this conservative tendency in McCormack's study was corrected by a special scoring method, the two age-groups were similar in their recall of temporal order. This study, then, is conceptually similar to the one by Attig and Hasher (1980), as are the results. Although the theory received support in the temporal domain, more than one study is needed to confirm a theoretical position.

Spatial Information

Recall of Location.   Studies on processing spatial information do not provide evidence in support of Hasher and Zacks' (1979) formulations of automatic processing, not at least as it is inferred from the comparison of age-groups. One way of measuring spatial memory involves the presentation of objects in well-defined places, then removing them and asking for their replacement after a lapse of time. Spatial memory is said to be good to the extent that the objects are replaced correctly in their locations. This is intentional learning and memory, but from the Hasher and Zacks' perspective, intentional and incidental processing should lead to comparable results in automatic processing.

Several studies of spatial information were carried out, not necessarily in test of the notion of automatic processing, but bearing on the issue nevertheless. Perlmutter, Metzger, Nezworski, and Miller, (1981) placed miniature buildings on a map, and later people of two age-groups (18–24 and 60–69) had to indicate where the buildings had been when the map without them was shown. Performance was better among the younger people, suggesting that this task involved effortful processing.

A similar study, one comparing middle-aged (31–59) and older (65–85) adults included two conditions: one, a three-dimensional panorama of organized relationships—a street, houses, a parking lot, and so on; the other, a series of cubicles or cubbyholes that varied in size with no organized relationships (Waddel & Rogoff, 1981). In each of these arrangements—organized and not—items such as cars, animals, people, and others were placed for later recall.

The two age-groups were similar in their spatial recall performances with the organized display, but the middle-aged were superior with the nonorganized display. The Hasher and Zack's theory holds that spatial processing is automatic and, thus, age-groups should be similar in their performances. Again the data were not in support of the theory.

Spatial and Picture Information.   Utilizing a different kind of spatial memory procedure, Park, Puglisi, and Lutz (1982) presented line drawings of everyday objects either on the left side of a display or on the right side. Older people of average age 70 and college-age people were tested for memory following instructions to half in each group to simply try to learn and remember the drawings. Instructions to the other half were to remember the drawings and also whether they were on the right or left side. Automatic processing theory would suggest that both half-groups would remember the spatial information equally well.

In keeping with the prediction of automatic processing, spatial recall (right or left) was similar for old and young when the instructions were simply to study the drawings. When told to study both the drawings and their locations however, the old performed less well than the young. In this study, spatial recall was measured for only those items correctly recognized, thus it was not a test of total spatial memory. Based on such a measure, it was concluded that "Instructions to study item location apparently had a facilitative effect on spatial recall for college students but a detrimental effect on spatial recall for elderly persons" (Park et al., 1982, p. 334). Notions of automatic processing would predict that instructions would not have a bearing on the performances of either age-group, and that age-groups would not differ. As indicated, this prediction was not confirmed.

Spatial and Verbal Information. In a study that was similar in some ways, Schear and Nebes (1980) presented a grid of 25 squares in a 5 by 5 arrangement. Each of 7 letters were placed on one of the squares to form a spatial arrangement. Both the letters and their spatial arrangements were varied, with people of average age 19 and average age 70 compared with respect to the recall of both the letters and the spatial arrangements. The older group performed less well in both types of recall, again indicating that spatial information is processed effortfully.

One spatial information study did confirm Hasher and Zacks' (1979) thinking. McCormack (1982) had 16 cards, each with four words arranged vertically. After briefly viewing these cards (of 64 words), women aged 61 to 74 and 17 to 31 were given 128 cards, each with but one word on it. Half these cards had words seen before and half had new words. The task was to discard the new words and to sort the old ones into the original four-slot spatial (vertical) order. Half the women of each age were told of the task requirement in advance, and the other half were not—instead they were told to remember the words. In accordance with the predictions of Hasher and Zacks, McCormack found that neither the awareness of the task requirement, nor the age of the women taking the test, related to spatial location memory. The two age-groups performed equally on this task. The two age-groups were different, however, with regard to recognition memory of the words themselves.

McCormack repeated this study with only an "unaware" group (i.e., not told of the spatial location test to follow). He presented only one word on a card instead of four, but varied the spatial location of the one word. Tests of free recall followed tests of spatial memory. Again, age was unrelated to spatial memory, but memory of the words themselves was better among the young.

All these studies taken together, with the exception of the one by McCormack (1982), suggest that Hasher and Zacks' (1979) formulations may need to be modified. It seems that processing spatial information may be effortful, not automatic, but frequency-of-occurrence and temporal information do seem to be processed automatically. Perhaps there are varieties of spatial information with some requiring effortful processing and some not.

MEANINGFUL INFORMATION

Studies of effortful processing of new information, not studies of automatic processing, constitute most of the literature of learning and memory. Most of these effortful processing studies have dealt with words that are learned in the laboratory, and a few of them have dealt with nonverbal information such as pictures or objects. Thus, most laboratory studies reviewed in Chapters 16, 17, and the present one have dealt with highly artificial information and contexts. These studies, in lacking "ecological validity," have come under criticism, and for this reason the more recent studies have dealt with more meaningful information.

In the main, meaningful sentences or prose paragraphs have constituted most of the more ecologically valid information used in learning and memory studies. Tests based on such information are different from tests of rote memory of words because meaningful information can be understood and remembered in different ways. A list of words, for example, can only be remembered verbatim; each word must be recalled exactly. In meaningful prose recall, however, the gist of the information can be recalled, where the ideas are there but the word order and even the words can be different.

Gist and Verbatim Recall

Specific and General Information. Cohen (1979, Experiment 3) investigated the recall of very short stories of only about 300 words in length. People aged 65 to 95 and 18 to 29 listened to these stories and tried to remember as much about them as they could. Cohen analyzed the stories into 48 facts or propositions, and so he could measure recall in relation to these facts. Six of the 48 facts were general or summary in character, representing "the gist of the story," and the others were more specific. Although exact verbatim reproduction was not required for correct recall, the six items more nearly represented a test of gist recall while the remainder more nearly represented a test of verbatim recall.

Cohen found that the younger people recalled more of both types of information, but the difference between age-groups was greater when the information was of a more general or summary kind, lending itself to gist recall. Cohen's results, therefore, suggest that the aged are at least as disadvantaged in gist recall as they are in other types of recall. As will be seen, some studies corroborate this conclusion but others do not.

Newspaper Information. Dixon, Simon, Nowak, and Hultsch (1982, p. 358) used newspaper articles to test for gist recall and reported results compatible with those of Cohen (1979). They measured recalls immediately after the articles were presented to people aged 18 to 32, 34 to 56, and 60 to 81, and also one week later. They found that "younger adults remembered the text materials better than middle-aged and older adults under both immediate and delayed recall conditions." Dixon et al. concluded that, "These data suggest that age-related performance differences may occur even with the gist recall of presumably ecologically valid materials" (p. 363).

Taub and Kline (1978) also found that age-groups were different (21–36 versus 60–80) with materials amenable to gist recall, but their results indicated that this may not be seen in the early stages of learning and memory. Paragraph information was presented four times (trials) to chart improvement in gist recall. In this study, the two age-groups performed similarly through the first two trials, but after this, the young recalled more.

Information More Amenable to Verbatim Recall. A study based on similar ideas was conducted by McDowd and Botwinick (1984). They used paragraphs from Wechsler's (1945) memory test that were made up of a lot of specific facts. For this reason, unlike the short paragraphs that Taub and Kline (1978) used, or the newspaper articles that Dixon et al. (1982) used, verbatim recall is more likely than gist with the Wechsler information. For this reason, too, perhaps, the results of McDowd and Botwinick were different from the others.

McDowd and Botwinick (1984) found that gist recall was no better among younger adults aged 20 to 29 than among older adults aged 60 to 69 and 70 to 79, but the verbatim recalls, constituting most of what was remembered, were poorer among the older adults.

The evidence indicates, therefore, that when information is amenable to gist recall, there is at least as large an age difference in memory as seen in verbatim recall studies. When the informaton is more artificial and thus more likely to be recalled in a verbatim way, the elderly are clearly disadvantaged.

Comprehension

Several investigators questioned whether it is not so much the learning and remembering of meaningful information that differentiates age-groups, as much as the ability to comprehend the information in the first place. Comprehension seems to involve two simultaneous processes that can be separated to an extent. One is obvious and needs little explanation. Very direct information can be understood at face value, as for example, "This is a car." The meaning is simple and easily comprehended without further thought. The other process occurs much more often. There is more implied in most information than at first is apparent and inferences are required. For example, to understand the information, "Here are keys, bring me the car," it is assumed that one of the keys will work to start the engine and that the car is parked in some known place. Simple meaning and inference together, therefore, make for comprehension. Some meanings and some inferences are easy, as those in the examples of the car, but others are difficult.

Simple Meaning. Feier and Gerstman (1980) tested for simple meaning by presenting sentences of animals doing things, such as, "The giraffe kicked the hippo that bumped into the cow." This sentence and all the others they used, involved two actions—in the example sentence, there is the giraffe's kick and the hippo's bump. (Actually, an inference is involved here too, that of the giraffe's kick causing the hippo to bump the cow.) People in five age-groups (18–25, 52–58, 63–69, and 74–80) responded to these sentences by manipulating animal-objects to demonstrate the two actions, thereby demonstrating comprehension of the sentences.

Not many errors were made in this very simple task, and some people did not make errors at all; still, overall, the older people made more errors than the younger ones. Up to age 63 to 69, no age pattern was reliable, but after this age, comprehension declined.

A comparable result was seen in an earlier study by Taub (1979). He presented three short passages of prose and asked questions about them while the passages were still available for viewing. Taub found, as did Feier and Gerstman, that young people (19–36) comprehended the text meanings better than the older people (55–83), as judged by their answers to the questions. Taub also asked questions about the passages later when the passages were removed from sight, to test for memory, as contrasted to comprehension. He found that the old performed less well in this too, although comprehension was better than recall in both age-groups.

An important aspect to this study was that the extent of difference between age-groups in comprehension was the same as the extent of the age differences in memory. Thus, Taub (1979) concluded that "acquisition" (comprehension) underlay the memory difference between age-groups.

Memory. Belmore (1981) concluded just the opposite. She presented a series of short paragraphs, each one composed of only three simple sentences. Following each of these short paragraphs, two sentences were provided; one was a direct paraphrase of one of the three sentences, and the other was a plausible inference based on information in the paragraph. Half the paragraphs and half the inferences were correct in reflecting the information, and the other half were incorrect. After people aged 58 to 74 and 17 to 21 read these three-sentence paragraphs, they indicated whether the paraphrases and inferences were correct.

This was done immediately after the paragraphs were read and then it was done again about 20 minutes afterwards. Belmore reported that the two age-groups were similar immediately after, both with the paraphrase information and with inference-comprehension; however, the results were otherwise in regard to delayed memory. The older people were less accurate than the younger ones in responding to both the paraphrase and the inference items. These results led her to conclude that the main problem in later life is not simple comprehension nor inference-comprehension, but memory.

Inferences.   Belmore's (1981) study was of both simple meaning and inference comprehension. Cohen (1979) specifically compared the two. He presented a series of short, tape-recorded passages to young (18–29) and old (65–95) people, who had to answer two types of questions: one simply required the reproduction of the facts in the passages, again, not necessarily in the original wording, and the other required inferences because the information in the passages was implicit, not being stated openly. Cohen found old and young similar in comprehending the fact information. The old performed more poorly, however, in drawing inferences.

Thus, Feier and Gerstman (1980) reported some difference with age in simple meaning comprehension and so did Taub (1979). Belmore (1981) found no difference at first with either simple meaning or inference comprehension but did find it after a period of delay. Like Belmore, Cohen (1979) reported no age difference in simple meaning comprehension, but unlike her, he found the old performed less well with inference information.

Walsh and Baldwin (1977) were more in support of Belmore with regard to inference. They carried out a different kind of study where they had a series of four-sentence paragraphs. The four sentences together formed an idea, but they were presented either one at a time, or two at a time, or three or four at a time. Since each sentence conveyed only a part of the idea, Walsh and Baldwin could determine in tests of memory what had been retained directly from the sentences and what was inferred from each sentence in forming the idea. The sentences in this study were of concrete ideas; later Walsh, Baldwin, and Finkle (1980) repeated this study with sentences based on abstract ideas and reported similar results.

They found that the old (60–79) were no worse than the young (18–20) in their inference performances. The age-groups performed similarly both in recognizing the prose content and in integrating the information to form the idea that could only be accomplished by the inference process.

Comprehension with Orienting Instructions. Just as the distinction between learning or encoding and memory is fuzzy (see Chapter 16), so is the
distinction between encoding and comprehension. In fact, Till and Walsh
(1980) made an effort to manipulate or vary comprehension levels by manipulating levels of encoding through the use of orienting instructions. They
presented sentences such that an inference was implicit in each one. One
sentence, for example, was "the audience stood up and continued to clap
loudly." The implication is that a speaker or a performer pleased the audience; perhaps an encore was desired. Till and Walsh tested for recall of
these sentences in two ways, one by free recall and one by cued recall. The
cues, in this case, were inference cues—in the example given the cue was
"encore."

Till and Walsh (1980) carried out three studies in which they manipulated comprehension levels by three orienting instructions. One was a shallow processing instruction—estimate the number of words in each sentence.
A second instruction (intermediate level) was to think about the meaning of
the sentence and judge whether the sentence was pleasant or unpleasant.
The third, deepest level of processing was to write a word that reflected the
meaning of each sentence. This made for the best level of comprehending
the implicational sentences. The basic research question was: if old and
young can be brought up to high, comparable levels of comprehension,
would they still differ in recall?

The basic results may be seen in Figure 18.2, where free and cued
recall scores are shown. This figure shows that with the deepest instruction,
comprehension levels were highest. In this situation the elderly were much
poorer than the young in free recall. At the same time, they were no
worse—perhaps even superior—in implication cued-recall. This was not so
with lower levels of comprehension resulting from less deep processing.
These results suggested that memory ability of the old is not as good as that
of the young because they do not comprehend information (in the implicational sense) as well. When brought to high levels of comprehension, however, and provided with proper implicational cues, the old can be brought
up to the memory performance levels of the young. This conclusion is
compatible with that of Taub (1979).

METAMEMORY

"Most people know what they do and do not know," Lachman, Lachman,
and Thronesbery (1979, p. 543) declared. To this, it may be added, most
people have an idea of what they will and will not be able to remember.

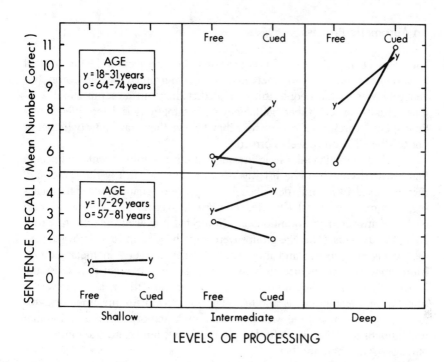

FIGURE 18.2: Free and cued recall as a function of levels of processing in two age-groups. (Data from Tables 1 and 3 of Till and Walsh, 1980. Upper functions from their Experiment 3 and lower functions from their Experiment 1.)

Lachman et al. indicated that knowing about knowing is called *metacognition* and knowing about remembering is called *metamemory*. There are a few research reports in aging that deal with metamemory.

Metamemory is important because in knowing what can be remembered, plans and strategies in daily living can be made to suit individual purposes. People do this routinely, not giving much thought to the process. For example, if a series of phone calls need to be made the next morning, many people simply write them down in a list, not leaving the task to memory. If the shopping list is long, the individual items will be written in note form. On the other hand, if only one or two phone calls need to be made, or only one or two items need to be bought, these may be left to memory. Metamemory is thus important in everyday affairs; several investigators believe that faulty or overestimated metamemory might possibly account for some of the memory problems in later life. If a person incorrectly believes that a long list of items will be remembered easily, too little or inadequate effort may be made to memorize it.

An Automatic Process

Lachman et al. (1979; p. 544) measured the accuracy and efficiency of metamemory: accuracy of metamemory is determined by the correspondence between what people think or predict they can remember and what they actually do remember. Efficiency of metamemory is determined by the time spent "searching for an answer they believe they may know (whether or not this belief is objectively correct)."

Lachman et al. had a long list of questions regarding events and people that are well-known. (The list was the same one, or nearly the same one, that was used in a study described in the previous chapter under the heading, "Estimates of Total Knowledge.") People aged 19 to 22, 44 to 53, and 65 to 74 answered the questions and indicated how well they thought they knew the answers. The age-groups were equally good in their knowledge of the events and people and they were also equally good in metamemory. More questions were correctly answered when they thought they knew the answers than when they thought they did not know them, and this was as true for one age-group as another. The same held for metamemory efficiency, that is, more time was spent searching memory for information that was thought to be known than thought unknown, but again, not more so for one age-group than another.

This study, then, showed that both accuracy and efficiency of metamemory is maintained into old age. Lachman and Lachman (1980, p. 302) indicated that "metamemorial processes which figure in everyday information-processing are rapid, non-attention-demanding, and unconscious." This defines everyday metamemory as an automatic process; as such, it might not be expected to vary in different age-groups.

Old and New Information

Perlmutter (1978) also concluded that metamemory holds with age. She presented questions of old information that were similar in some ways to those asked by Lachman et al. (1979), and she also presented tests of new word-list learning. Young (20–25) and older (60–65) adults had to recall the old information and predict whether, later, they would be able to remember the "I don't know" items when presented in a recognition test. The new word learning test was handled differently: old and young were instructed to study the words and predict how many they would be able to recall and recognize.

Perlmutter found that with both old and new information, the elderly were no different from the young in accuracy of metamemory, that is, the difference between prediction and memory performances was the same for the old as the young. This despite the fact that the elderly remembered more old fact information than the young, but remembered less new word information.

Metamemory of new information (paired associates) was investigated with similar results by Rabinowitz, Ackerman, Craik, and Hinchley (1982). This study was different from the others, however, in that predictions were made after a brief study period, rather than from "don't know" items in recall tests.

In accord with the studies above, older adults (61–75) made predictions that were as good as those of younger adults (17–24) even though they remembered fewer words. "The metamemory results were remarkable in their complete absence of any age-related differences" (Rabinowitz et al., 1982, p. 694).

Over- and Underestimation

The results of each of these studies clearly pointed to the similarity between old and young in metamemory. The next two studies, however, pointed to differences with age, but only one of these indicated poorer metamemory on the part of the aged.

In the first of the two studies, old and young estimated their memory spans (i.e., the longest number of items that could be recalled in order) and then they were given memory span tests. Murphy, Sanders, Gabriesheski and Schmitt (1981, p. 187) reported, "The overall accuracy of span estimation [i.e., metamemory] was found to be the same for young [17–29] and old [60–80] subjects, but the direction of error was different for the two groups. In general, the young adults underestimated their spans . . . while the elderly overestimated. . . ." The old had smaller memory spans than the young but their predictions of what they would do were lower, even if they did overestimate.

Bruce, Coyne, and Botwinick (1982) also found overestimations on the part of the elderly, but not underestimations on the part of the young. Thus, the results of this study were different from the others in that age-groups were different in metamemory. Bruce et al. presented several lists of words for learning to people in three age-groups. They were shown examples of the words they would be asked to learn, and then they were compared with respect to the predictions they made. The results were compatible with the other studies in that the young (18–31) remembered more words than either of the two older groups (60–69 and 70–79) but, as indicated, were incompatible with the other studies in that the elderly showed poorer metamemory accuracy.

Recall Readiness (Memory Monitoring)

There is an aspect of metamemory that is different from straight prediction, although it would seem to be related to it. If a person is presented with material to learn, and if as much time as is needed to learn it is allowed, then it would seem that time spent learning is a good index of metamemory. In other words, it is expected that given good metamemory, a fast learner would take less time to study the material and a slow learner would take more time. Additionally, it is expected that more time would be spent studying difficult material and less time on easy material.

Murphy et al. (1981) recorded the time old and young spent studying the span information in relation to the difficulty of it, that is, the number of span items to be learned. Although the older people recalled fewer items than the younger people, they took less time for study. Additionally, younger adults increased their study times over three levels of difficulty, but the older adults increased their study times only from the second to the third level. Such results are characteristically interpreted in terms of poorer "recall readiness" on the part of the elderly, that is, they do not know in the course of studying when they are adequately prepared. This indicates a poorer metamemory among the aged; they show a "metamemory deficiency." Another possibility, however, is that it is not recall readiness so much that differentiates the old from the young but, instead, a disinclination on the part of the old to pressure themselves in effortful processing.

Murphy et al. made an effort to test the metamemory deficiency notion in a second experiment by emphasizing the need for accuracy and, more important, by indicating that they would determine when to stop studying, not the person taking the test. When this was done, old and young performed more nearly alike. In fact, the performances of the elderly resulting from this "forced time" of studying were no worse than the performances of the younger people when they themselves determined study times. Murphy et al. (1981, p. 190) concluded that the aged can be helped in learning and memory "by simply insuring that . . . [they] take enough time in studying the items."

This is an important result and conclusion, having practical consequences and warranting further investigation. This is particularly so since such age differences in recall readiness (or memory-monitoring, as it is sometimes called), were not observed by Bruce et al. (1982). They allowed as much time as wanted but they did not force studying time. In their study, young adults, mainly in their 20s, took no more time to study words than the older adults in their 60s and 70s. This interesting discrepancy in results might be related to the different types of information and types of subject populations in the two studies.

SUMMARY

The two previous chapters covered theoretical perspectives and related investigations of learning-memory in relation to age. These focused on encoding, storage, and retrieval processes and on a multistore model of memory. A newer theory, discussed in this chapter, conceives of learning-memory in more unitary terms, deemphasizing both storage and retrieval processes, and multistore models. The newer theory sees learning-memory mainly in terms of encoding. The idea is that the duration of memory depends mainly on the type and quality of information processing.

The main feature of this theory, depth of processing, is that there are two qualitatively different types of information processing that go on simultaneously. There is shallow processing that is carried out primarily in relation to physical and sensory aspects of stimuli, and there is deep processing that is carried out in relation to abstract, semantic, and associative aspects of stimuli. The greater the amount of deep processing relative to shallow, the longer-lasting the memory. Several studies have suggested that older people tend not to process as deeply as younger people, and for this reason, the theory has it, older people have poorer memory. This conclusion has evolved in the course of many different types of studies, but mainly one based on the orienting task. In this type of study, different instructions are given, one that makes for shallow processing, one that makes for deep, and others in between. Although deep level instructions make for better learning-memory than shallow levels among both old and young, the old tend to perform most differently from the young (least well relatively) with deep processing.

Most of these studies have been based on processing highly artificial information such as lists of words, but recent trends have been to studies based on more significant or "ecologically valid" information. Meaningful sentences, prose paragraphs, or newspaper articles have been used; this kind of information can be learned and remembered in a variety of gist ways rather than in a verbatim way that is required with the more artificial information. Most studies show that gist memory of the more meaningful information follows the same age pattern as the verbatim, that is, the old perform less well.

Several investigators questioned whether the reason for this is that older people do not comprehend the information as well in the first place. Obviously, if information is not understood, it is difficult to learn and retain. Comprehension is of two kinds: one is of understanding the direct meaning of information, the other is based on drawing inferences from it. Most information, even simple kinds, requires some inference. Data bearing on this question are mixed, but there is evidence that comprehension of both kinds is poorer among the elderly.

A major study in this area suggests that faulty or inadequate comprehension might underlie some memory problems in old age, but certainly not all. In this study, both old and young were brought up to high levels of comprehension and still their memory performances in terms of free recall were different. When comprehension cues were provided, however, old and young were much alike in recall. This study indicated, therefore, that with high levels of comprehension, memory performances of the aged can be brought to the high levels of the young by proper cues. With lower comprehension levels, however, memory performances will not be as high even with cues.

High levels of comprehension and deep levels of encoding come about through effort. Perhaps it is for this reason that older people process less deeply. Effortful processing is contrasted with automatic. Effortful processing of one set of information makes it difficult to attend to another set. Older people, it seems, have a special difficulty with tasks of divided attention. Divided attention should be less of a problem, or no problem at all, with automatic processing. Automaticity comes about from extensive practice of effortful functions. Experts do not expend the energy on tasks that novices do. Automaticity also comes about from capacities thought to be present from the start, that is, genetic. As such, unlike effortful processes, automatic ones are not improved by attention or practice. According to theory, automatic processes include the ability to detect the frequency of occurrence of information and the temporal character of information and to recall the spatial location of things. According to the theory, old and young should be different in effortful processing, as indeed they are, but they should be the same in automatic processing.

There are several studies regarding frequency-of-occurrence information, and they support the theory in that this presumed genetically based function is no different for old and young. Only one study of temporal processing was reviewed, and this study also supported the theory—old and young were no different. Studies on the recall of spatial information, however, did not support the theory. With one exception, the studies showed the old performing less well than the young.

Recent research interest has focused on metamemory, that is, what people think they do or can remember. In the course of everyday living, typically, metamemorial activity is carried out without conscious intent, attention, or effort and is thus an automatic process. For example, if a sizable number of phone calls need to be made, most people make up a list of them, rather than leave it to memory. This is done automatically, without thoughtful effort. As an automatic process, metamemory is not expected to decline with age. Most studies support this expectation, but not all. When differences with age are seen, it is that the elderly overestimate what they will be able to learn and remember and underestimate the time and perhaps the effort that will be required. When obliged to expend the effort and time in learning, their performances improve.

REFERENCES

Attig, M., & Hasher, L. The processing of frequency of occurrence information by adults. *Journal of Gerontology*, 1980, 35, 66–69.

Belmore, S. M. Age-related changes in processing explicit and implicit language. *Journal of Gerontology*, 1981, 36, 316–322.

Bruce, P. R., Coyne, A. C., & Botwinick, J. Adult age differences in metamemory. *Journal of Gerontology*, 1982, 37, 354–357.

Cohen, G. Language comprehension in old age. *Cognitive Psychology*, 1979, 11, 412–429.

Craik, F. I. M. Age differences in human memory. In J. E. Birren & K. W. Schaie (Eds.), *Handbook of the psychology of aging*. New York: Van Nostrand Reinhold, 1977.

Craik, F. I. M., & Lockhart, R. S. Levels of processing: A framework for memory research. *Journal of Verbal Learning and Verbal Behavior*, 1972, 11, 671–684.

Craik, F. I. M., & Simon, E. Age differences in memory: The roles of attention and depth of processing. In. L. W. Poon, J. L. Fozard, L. S. Cermack, D. Arenberg, & L. W. Thompson (Eds.), *New directions in memory and aging*. Hillsdale, N.J.: Lawrence Erlbaum Associates, 1980.

Dixon, R. A., Simon, E. W., Nowak, C. A., & Hultsch, D. F. Text recall in adulthood as a function of level of information, input modality, and delay interval. *Journal of Gerontology*, 1982, 37, 358–364.

Erber, J., Herman, T. G., & Botwinick, J. Age differences in memory as a function of depth of processing. *Experimental Aging Research*, 1980, 6, 341–348.

Eysenck, M. W. Age differences in incidental learning. *Developmental Psychology*, 1974, 10, 936–941.

Feier, C. C., & Gerstman, L. J. Sentence comprehension abilities throughout the adult life span. *Journal of Gerontology*, 1980, 35, 722–728.

Hasher, L., & Zacks, R. T. Automatic and effortful processes in memory. *Journal of Experimental Psychology: General*, 1979, 108, 356–388.

Hovland, C. I. Human learning and retention. In S. S. Stevens (Ed.), *Handbook of experimental psychology*. New York: Wiley, 1951, Chapter 17, pp. 613–689.

Kausler, D. H., & Puckett, J. M. Frequency judgments and correlated cognitive abilities in young and elderly adults. *Journal of Gerontology*, 1980, 35, 376–382.

Lachman, J. L., & Lachman, R. Age and the actualization of world knowledge. In L. Poon, J. L. Fozard, L. S. Cermak, D. Arenberg, & L. W. Thompson (Eds.), *New directions in memory and aging*. Hillsdale, N.J.: Lawrence Erlbaum Associates, 1980, Chapter 18, pp. 285–311.

Lachman, R., Lachman, J. L., & Thronesbery, C. Metamemory through the adult life span. *Developmental Psychology*, 1979, 15, 543–551.

Mason, S. E. Effects of orienting tasks on the recall and recognition performance of subjects differing in age. *Developmental Psychology*, 1979, 15, 467–469.

McCormack, P. D. Temporal coding by young and elderly adults. *Developmental Psychology*, 1981, 17, 509–515.

McCormack, P. D. Coding of spatial information by young and elderly adults. *Journal of Gerontology*, 1982, 37, 80–86.

McDowd, J., & Botwinick, J. Rote and gist memory in relation to type of information, sensory mode, and age. *Journal of Genetic Psychology*, 1984.

Murphy, M. D., Sanders, R. E., Gabriesheski, A. S., & Schmitt, F. A. Metamemory in the aged. *Journal of Gerontology*, 1981, 36, 185–193.

Park, D. C., Puglisi, J. T., & Lutz, R. Spatial memory in older adults: Effects of intentionality. *Journal of Gerontology*, 1982, 37, 330–335.

Perlmutter, M. What is memory aging the aging of? *Developmental Psychology*, 1978, 14, 330–345.

Perlmutter, M., Metzger, R., Nezworski, T., & Miller, K. Spatial and temporal memory in 20 and 60 year olds. *Journal of Gerontology*, 1981, 36, 59–65.

Rabinowitz, J. C., Ackerman, B. P., Craik, F. I. M., & Hinchley, J. L. Aging and metamemory: The roles of relatedness and imagery. *Journal of Gerontology*, 1982, 37, 688–695.

Schear, J. M., & Nebes, R. D. Memory for verbal and spatial information as a function of age. *Experimental Aging Research*, 1980, 6, 271–281.

Simon, E. W., Dixon, R. A., Nowak, C. A., & Hultsch, D. F. Orienting task effects on text recall in adulthood. *Journal of Gerontology*, 1982, 37, 575–580.

Smith, A. D., & Winograd, E. Adult age differences in remembering faces. *Developmental Psychology*, 1978, 14, 443–444.

Taub, H. A. Comprehension and memory of prose materials by young and old adults. *Experimental Aging Research*, 1979, 5, 3–13.

Taub, H. A., & Kline, G. E. Recall of prose as a function of age and input modality. *Journal of Gerontology*, 1978, 33, 725–730.

Till, R. E., & Walsh, D. A. Encoding and retrieval factors in adult memory for implicational sentences. *Journal of Verbal Learning and Verbal Behavior*, 1980, 19, 1–16.

Waddell, K. J., & Rogoff, B. Effect of contextual organization and spatial memory of middle-aged and older women. *Developmental Psychology*, 1981, 17, 878–885.

Walsh, D. Age differences in learning and memory. In D. S. Woodruff & J. E. Birren (Eds.), *Aging*. New York: D. Van Nostrand, 1975.

Walsh, D. A., & Baldwin, M. Age differences in integrated semantic memory. *Developmental Psychology*, 1977, 13, 509–514.

Walsh, D. A., Baldwin, M., & Finkle, T. J. Age differences in integrated semantic memory for abstract sentences. *Experimental Aging Research*, 1980, 6, 431–443.

Wechsler, D. A standardized memory scale for clinical use. *Journal of Psychology*, 1945, 19, 87–95.

Winograd, E., Smith, A. D., & Simon, E. W. Aging and the picture superiority effect in recall. *Journal of Gerontology*, 1982, 37, 70–75.

Wright, R. E. Aging, divided attention, and processing capacity. *Journal of Gerontology*, 1981, 36, 605–614.

Zelinski, E. M., Walsh, D. A., & Thompson, L. W. Orienting task effects on EDR and free recall in three age groups. *Journal of Gerontology*, 1978, 33, 239–245.

19
Creativity and Contribution

It has been seen that intelligence declines with age, problem solving in the laboratory declines, as do learning and memory abilities. To be sure, not all aspects of these important functions decline, but many do. From this it may be expected that creativity also declines with age. On the other hand, much of cognitive skill remains relatively intact in later life and accordingly it may be expected that creativity does not decline. All this suggests that, as with so many issues, there is disagreement and controversy. The answer depends, in part, on how creativity is viewed—where the emphasis is in the definition.

WHAT IS CREATIVITY?

There are two main ways of defining creativity and each can provide a different answer to the question, Does creativity decline with age? One definition emphasizes the process or the act of doing, even of just being. The other relates to a special kind of product or the accomplishment of the creative process.

McLeish (1981) reviewed a variety of thoughts and opinions regarding creativity, mainly as set forth by psychoanalysts and other personality theorists. One view is that creativity is the process of being aware of life around, of sensing and responding. A collateral view is that creativity is a change in personality that maximizes opportunities for a happy life. A somewhat different view, one proposed by a chemist, is that creativity is a combination of parts already available that form a new thought or new product. From perspectives such as these, everyone can be creative, although not everyone is. Being aware and experiencing, changing oneself so as to improve life, developing new ideas or products—these are possible for everyone—old and young, bright and not so bright.

For others, creativity is defined by an extraordinary product or accomplishment based on creative processes. The accomplishment or product must be novel, original, and unique. Further, it must be relevant to a social need, that is, the product must either be appropriate to common concerns (for example, scholarly contributions or inventions) or as meeting esthetic needs (for example, art works and great theatrical performances). In all instances, however, the product must be extraordinary. It is with this definition that there is controversy regarding the answer to the question, Does creativity decline with age?

The Role of Intelligence and Thought

If creativity is defined by unique, original, and novel contributions, it might be expected that high-level intelligence and high-level thought are basic to creativity. It is not clear, however, that this is so. Extraordinarily creative people have been found to score highly in intelligence tests, but this has not accounted completely for their unusual contributions. The reason for this, it is believed, is that intelligence tests measure only one type of thought process.

A distinction is made between convergent and divergent thinking. Convergent thinking is needed to solve problems of logical reasoning of the type discussed in Chapter 15. Divergent thinking is needed to be creative. Convergent thinking is measured by standard intelligence tests, divergent thinking typically is not. Getzels and Jackson (1962, p. 14) wrote:

> The conventional IQ test requires that the subject know the common association to a stimulus and the accepted solution to a problem. . . . He is not asked to innovate, to speculate, to invent . . . if the answer is "novel" it is likely to be scored wrong. In short, the conventional IQ test tends toward the evaluation of those cognitive processes that have been called convergent, retentive, and conservative, more than those processes . . . that have been called divergent, innovative, and constructive.

On the basis of tests of both creativity and intelligence, Getzels and Jackson identified two groups of children: a high-intelligence, low creativity group, and a low-intelligence, high-creativity group. In a similar fashion Wallach and Kogan (1965) identified four groups of children: two bearing the same designations as the groups of Getzels and Jackson, and two being identified as either high or low in both intelligence and creativity. The foregoing suggests that creativity is possible in the face of a relatively low conventional test intelligence.

McLeish (1981, pp. 97–98) presented viewpoints of various scholars on the relationship between intelligence and creativity, one of which was particularly interesting. The "fascinating question . . . [was raised] whether some forms of intelligence are not actual blocks to creative achievement." Some people may be "highly programmed into exactly logical thinking [and] are frequently inhibited from creative solutions that they might reach." It is through a more innovative or divergent thinking that creativity is achieved.

Thus, according to some, intelligence as typically measured is not only imperfectly correlated with creativity, it may be negatively correlated. This does not seem to be the general view, however. It would seem that most accept the view that traditional intelligence is a factor in creativity but certainly not the sole factor.

Methods of Identifying Creativity

There are no universal standards for identifying creativity; in fact, there is strong disagreement about how creativity is to be identified. There are three most common ways of identifying creative people or their products: one has been to make use of judgments by qualified experts, another refers to uniqueness of psychological test scores, and a third way is to refer to the frequency with which creative people have been cited in the literature. For example, the qualified expert method was used by Barron (1963) to identify creative writers, by Simonton (1977) to identify composers, by MacKinnon (1962) to identify architects, and by Roe (1953) to identify scientists. In similar fashion experts have been called upon to rate products rather than people. For example, experts of various disciplines rated science projects of senior high school students which were submitted for a national competition. The applicants were then classified on the basis of their rated projects and given many tests for comparative purposes (Parloff & Datta, 1965).

The use of qualified experts for evaluation presupposes their ability to make judgments by applying criteria of creativity rather than other criteria. This supposition may be wrong, however. The experts may unwittingly use criteria related to prominence rather than creativity. Prominence can result from frequent and popular solutions that are not necessarily creative; from holding rank in university, government, and commercial organizations; and from activities in professional societies.

The second method of identifying creative people is by the uniqueness of psychological test scores. The criteria with this method may be more precise than those with ratings of experts, but in the final analysis, uniqueness and creativity are not identical. Accordingly, data that are based on this method of identification are often designated with labels other than creativity. For example, Barron (1955) studied originality by giving 100 people several tests and selecting the 15 of them who were most different in their test scores, and 15 who were most similar. These two groups were then compared.

The third method used to identify creative people is that of referring to the frequency with which they have been cited in the literature. Like the other two, this method has flaws, but it can be useful. Lehman's (1953) research, the masterwork of creativity in relation to age, is based on this method in combination with expert appraisal.

CREATIVE PEOPLE

Lehman's 20 years of research on the quantity and quality of creative output were summarized in his book *Age and Achievement* (1953). In the Foreword to the book Terman wrote that Lehman "established with reasonable finality, and for many fields of endeavor, the age levels at which man's most creative work has been done" (Lehman, 1953, p. v). Since the appearance of this book, Lehman has published many additional studies elaborating important aspects of the creativity–age relationship, but his work was not without its critics.

It is a tribute to Lehman's work that it has stirred so much controversy, but none so vehement perhaps as that of McLeish (1981, p. 105). He wrote that Lehman's "Numerous erroneous conclusions are still being reproduced . . . as though coming on tablets of stone. In fact, in spite of all the statistical busywork put into Lehman's thesis, his conclusions on the peaking [at an early age] of creative powers in the arts are simply grotesque." McLeish left the door open for the possibility that creativity peaks early in life among scientists, but he soon closed this door as well.

McLeish and others notwithstanding, Lehman's (1953) study is not to be dismissed so readily; certainly it is not to be dismissed on the basis of emotion in the absence of serious rebuttal based on research findings. It will be seen that there has been such serious rebuttal, but the issue remains unsettled nevertheless.

The Masterwork:
Charting Creativity across Age

Lehman provided information regarding the sciences, medicine, philosophy, the arts, practical invention, and other areas. His book dealt mainly with deceased persons of earlier centuries, but some of his later work focused upon the still living (e.g., Lehman, 1963). His general method was to tabulate by age-groups the frequency with which quality productions were listed in expert historical accounts. For example, in examining the creative years of chemists, Lehman referred to a written history of chemistry in which the names of several hundred chemists were listed along with the dates on which they made their contributions. Often, he submitted such listings to university teachers for further evaluation. In investigating the relation between age and creativity in philosophy, Lehman canvassed 50 standard books dealing with the history of philosophy. His assumption was that philosophers whose writings are cited in numerous books are likely to be more important than those mentioned in a few.

Lehman's basic results and conclusions are found in numerous publications with each one including much data; for this reason, only a general picture can be provided here. The important finding for which most criticism is levied is that within most fields of endeavor, the maximum production rate for quality work occurred during the age decade 30 to 39 years. That is, a higher percentage of all quality work is produced during this age period than any other. Figure 19.1 shows this in combining the works of several disciplines. Lehman also found that this is earlier in life than the age of the maximum production rate for less distinguished work by the same individuals.

It is possible to view Figure 19.1 in either pessimistic or optimistic terms. Optimistically, Lehman reported that although the rate of creative production peaks at ages 30 to 39, decline afterwards is gradual. Further, it is even more gradual for quality products of lesser level. Figure 19.1 shows that creative contributions of even the topmost quality are found well beyond age 30 to 39, remaining at substantial rates through the 50s.

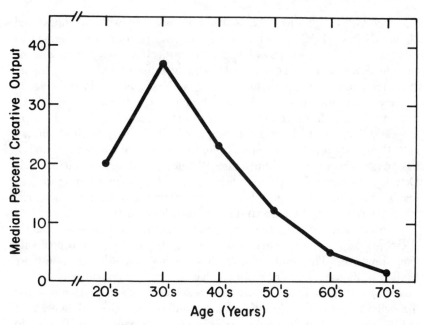

FIGURE 19.1: Percentage of creative output as a function of age. This is a generalized curve representing a combination of various fields of endeavor and various estimates of quality. (Data from Lehman, 1953, p. 242, Table 34.)

Figure 19.1 does not reflect what else Lehman found. He reported that the specific relations between creativity and age are dependent not only upon the types of measures used (i.e., quantity vs. quality), but also upon the field of endeavor investigated. For example, although creative contributions by chemists peaked in the early 30s, those of astronomers peaked in the mid-40s, and psychologists peaked in the late 30s. Later studies of psychologists by Lyons (1968) and Zusne (1976) showed very similar results. Figure 19.1 is based on the average of the various fields and so characterizes Lehman's results only in a general way.

There is hardly an article by Lehman in which he does not stress the fact that man's usefulness is not limited by his age, despite his findings of peak creativity early in life. Individual variations at all ages are so great that prediction for any one individual is not feasible. Even in group trends, however, we can look forward to a high rate of worthy even if less outstanding contributions in later years. For example, in the study of philosophers who had long lives, the peak age of quantity production was not in the 30s but from 60 to 64 (Lehman, 1953, p. 323).

Criticism and Rebuttal

Different Longevities. Lehman's work was not without critics, and Dennis (1956a, 1958), more than anyone else, performed this important function in a scientific way. Dennis was critical of Lehman because he combined information pertaining to men of different longevities. Figure 19.1, for example, might include data of producers, all reaching the age of 30, fewer reaching the age of 40, and still fewer age 60. Dennis argued that since all the significant contributions of short-lived people can occur only in the early decades, and since the long-lived people can contribute during both their early and late decades of life, the practice of combining longevities exaggerates, or even manufactures, the decrements seen in Figure 19.1. Dennis recognized that Lehman was aware of this, even referring to Lehman's tables that pointed to this issue. He was critical of Lehman, however, for not highlighting the problem of combined longevities.

To demonstrate the artifact of combining different longevities, Dennis (1956b, 1966), in two studies, analyzed only the creations of people who lived long lives. The results of both these studies were different from those typified in Figure 19.1. The pertinent data of the 1966 study may be seen in Figure 19.2. This figure shows that peak performance years are found throughout most of the adult life span. Even in the arts, the poorest example of this, 20 percent of the productions were found at ages above 60 years. In the humanities, 41 percent of the productions were done after 60 years of age, and 61 percent after 50 years.

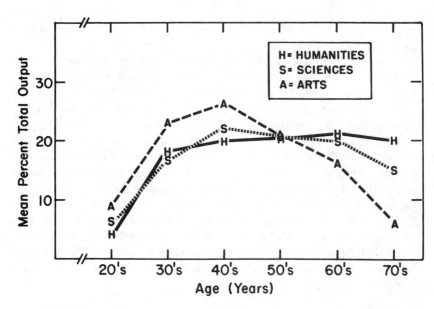

FIGURE 19.2: Percentage of total output as a function of age. The humanities, sciences, and arts are represented by the means of several specific disciplines. (Data from Dennis, 1966, p. 2, Table 1).

Quality versus Quantity: Difficulty in Evaluating Quality.   Lehman (1956, 1958) rejected Dennis' argument, believing that because older people put out relatively few high-quality products, the effect of combining information pertaining to men of different longevities was small. Lehman believed that Dennis' data, seen in Figure 19.2, are due to the fact that he emphasized quantity of output, while in his own work Lehman emphasized superior quality. Dennis (1966) recognized this but contended that it is difficult to arrive at an unbiased evaluation of quality.

Dennis contended that analysis of quality through biographies and citations contains systematic errors favoring a person's early work, artificially making for the curves seen in Figure 19.1. First, he said, an historian of science may be more likely to mention a young person's pioneering work than subsequent investigations that develop and validate the earlier ones. Second, critics and historians find it harder to evaluate the more recent work (i.e., the work of later life) and tend not to designate it as masterwork. Third, because of the increased number of creative workers from one generation to the next, competition increases, making it difficult for a person's later work to be evaluated as superior. A related fourth point was made later by Zuckerman, (1977, p. 165). Since the population of scientific contributors has been expanding exponentially, "the young make up a hefty percentage at any given time, and so they will produce a large aggregate of contributions."

Dennis' (1958) argument, in brief, is that the reason the ratio of significant work to total work appeared to decline over time is because of systematic historian error. He provided data to substantiate this belief. Lehman (1960) rejected this argument and reinterpreted Dennis's ratio data as simply showing that over the years, great contributions have been increasing at a slower rate than have lesser ones. The reason for this, he thought, was that problems have become more difficult to solve and, also, there has developed a greater emphasis on publication. These factors together have combined to reduce the ratio of quality to quantity of contributions, with the old producing little of the existing quality contributions.

As in so many arenas of controversy, the arguments on both sides are compelling and agreement is not to be had. Perhaps the most cogent argument Dennis levied was the one of the different longevities of the contributors. Over the years, this argument has been emphasized by others, with at least one research effort based on it.

Great Composers

Simonton (1977) used a clever experimental design to contend with the methodological problem of the different longevities of the various creative contributors. He also contended with the issues of quality versus quantity. Simonton analyzed the lives and works of 10 eminent classical composers, dividing their compositions into major and minor contributions.

The 10 composers were chosen from a listing of eminent composers based on a survey of members of the American Musicology Society. The members were asked to rank composers born before 1870 in terms of their eminence. The top 10 were selected for study. Simonton's study was thus based on the lives and works of Bach, Beethoven, Mozart, Haydn, Brahms, and others of similar quality.

Dennis (1966) contended with the problem of short- and long-lived composers by restricting his sample to only long-lived contributors. Simonton (1977) contended with the problem by the use of a time-series design based on five-year age periods. The first five-year age period was different for each composer and included the years when the composer began production. The last five-year period was also different for each composer since it included the year of the composer's death. Thus, there were a different number of five-year age periods for each composer, with each composer contributing to the analysis only over his own productive life span. Productivity scores were analyzed in terms of deviations from each composer's mean.

There were two measures: one was the total number of works. For each composer, each work was assigned to one of the five-year periods. Each work, however, was given a weighting based on its importance; for example, an art song was weighted as much less important than an entire opera. A second measure used to assess production was total themes, that is, the number of themes composed in each five-year period. If more than one theme was credited to a given work, all themes listed for that work were counted. Thus, this measure also weights the contributions since larger works tend to have more themes.

Simonton (1977) wanted to test the validity of Lehman's conclusions versus those of Dennis. Simonton analyzed total works and total themes, but he also analyzed the proportion of major works to total works and the proportion of major themes to total themes. He found that the ratio of major works to total works was unrelated to age. These results did not support Lehman's position. Further, although the percentage of major themes to total themes was age-related, the extent of decline was very small, and based mainly on one composer.

Simonton also analyzed total productivity (rather than the ratio of major works to total works) and this analysis was more in support of Lehman's results. Total works peaked at age 45 to 49 and then declined to approximately the level of early years. Total themes, however, peaked at age 30 to 34 and then declined but not nearly to the level of early years. In fact, the thematic production rate later in life was so high relative to the pre-30 to 34 age period, that over the life span an upward pattern was seen.

Simonton's results, therefore, once again can be seen to argue on both sides of the Lehman-Dennis controversy. Simonton's ratio measures—major works to total works—were constant across age. Total works, however, were age-related. These two indices examined together indicate that major or creative contribution must have also been age-related, in fact related in a nearly identical way. This lends support to Lehman's position. On the other hand, Dennis' contention regarding quality and quantity also receives support. Dennis maintained not only that it is difficult to differentiate between quality contribution and quantity contribution without great error but that quality contribution occurs in those periods of life when there is also quantity of contribution. In other words, quantity and quality are correlated. Simonton's data showed this.

From biographical accounts, Simonton was able to assess several personal and social factors that might relate to creativity. Dennis suggested that increased competition might affect evaluations of creativity to the disadvantage of the older contributors. Simonton found this so with regard to total themes but not total works. He also found that health status affected both total themes and total works but that health did not account for the age patterns.

Nobel Prize Winners

Identifying creative talent is also possible by reference to those who have been recognized with the award of high honors. For scientists, the Nobel Prize is among the highest honors, if not the highest. This prize was awarded the first time in 1901 and has continued almost every year since then. The decisions on awards are made by independent committees of leading scientists.

Manniche and Falk (1957) covered the period of 1901 to 1950 in investigating the ages during which the Nobel Prize winners in chemistry, physics, and physiology or medicine did their award-winning work. The result of this investigation were compatible with Lehman's findings. Over the years, in physics, the average ages ranged from 33 to 38; in chemistry the range was 34 to 42. Winners in physiology and medicine were a bit older, ranging from 39 to 44. Zuckerman (1977) extended this analysis to cover the years through 1972. The results remained approximately the same, with little or no change in the age trend over the 71 years the analyses covered.

It might be noted that Dennis' argument regarding short- and long-lived people can apply here, although it hardly seems likely. It is possible to argue that short-lived people cannot receive the Nobel Prize for work done in old age whereas long-lived people can. Given the narrow range of ages in which the award-winning work was done, at least from 1901 to 1950, this argument does not seem strong.

Manniche and Falk (1957) also investigated the ages at which the award was made, rather than when the work was done. They found that the scientists were 11 to 15 years older, on the average, when they received the awards. The range was large, however, with the shortest interval between the work and the award being one year, and the longest interval 37 years. Zuckerman (1977) made a similar analysis covering the years 1901 to 1972, with similar results. The average period between when the research was done and when the award was made was 12 years.

In similar fashion, Shin and Putnam (1982) also investigated the age during which the Nobel Prize winners received the award, extending the period to 1975. They included winners in literature, a category that was added later in the history of the award. The average age of the winners was about 52, similar to that reported by Zuckerman. In literature the average age of the award was 62. Over the course of 74 years of the awards, there was a slight age trend upward in when they were made. These data by Shin and Putnam, Manniche and Falk, and Zuckerman, bearing on the time of receipt of the award, highlight the difference between when creative work is done and when it is recognized. National and international prominence is a poor key of present-day creativity, if it is one at all.

Top Chess Players

It is unclear that top-level chess play calls for the same level of creativity demonstrated by great composers or by Nobel Prize winners, but it is clear that top-level chess play calls for high-level thought with clever planning of strategies and responses. "Chess is an ancient game that has undergone no significant rule changes in the past century, meaning that there will be few if any generational confoundings [cohort differences] related to the time when the game was learned" (Charness, 1981, p. 24). All this may make top-level chess a good candidate for study of creative accomplishment. Chess players compete in tournaments, and the best of these are called "international masters" or "grandmasters." Only players of such class are permitted to compete in international tournaments. Their successes and failures in tournaments are recorded in journals. Such chess players may be thought to exhibit creative thinking, certainly high-level thinking, in their competitions.

Elo (1965) developed a chess-rating scale and applied this to the play of grandmasters during the period 1885 to 1963. This was a longitudinal study in that Elo tracked individual careers and noted accomplishments in relation to age. Compatible with the data of Lehman, peak tournament performance was seen at the approximate age of 36. Unlike the data of Lehman, however, the performances at age 63 were no different from those at age 21.

Charness investigated more ordinary players than the grandmasters, but still people who devoted much time to tournament play and who were good enough to have been nationally rated. Charness did not examine their tournament skill in relation to age; instead he purposely selected people aged 16 to 64 to be approximately equal in skill. Charness asked the players to choose a best chess move, then after several plays, he gave them an unexpected memory test of the preceding moves. He also had players evaluate rapidly an end-game position.

With these players, where the selection procedure made age and skill uncorrelated, it was found, not surprisingly, that both the accuracy in choosing a move and end-game evaluation were unrelated to age. Age, however, was related to memory of the preceding moves—the older players having poorer recall. The older players did not group the information for memory as well as did the young. Charness found that the better players, regardless of age, had better recall than poorer players. It is conceivable, if not probable, that the older players had had better memory in the past and, accordingly, it is possible to conjecture that in the past their chess skill had been better. As young players, therefore, they might have been superior to the young players in the study.

Decline in Creativity

Evaluation—Summary. All evidence together does seem to show that in terms of creativity, young people contribute substantially and old people contribute less so. In criticism of this contention by Lehman, the more recent literature emphasizes Dennis' argument regarding the different longevities of the contributors. It will be recalled that this cogent argument was met by Lehman with the response that older people put out so relatively few high-quality products that the effect of combining people of different longevities is small. Simonton's analysis of great composers, based on a time-series design to cope with Dennis' argument, was at least in partial support of Lehman. He also showed decline in creativity; total production rates were maximum among those in their early 30s with quality effort, as contrasted to total effort, seemingly showing a similar age pattern.

Dennis also argued that because of the increased number of creative workers from one generation to the next, competition increases, making it difficult for later work to be evaluated as superior. Data bearing on this argument are mixed. Simonton's analyses of composers supported this argument for total themes but not for total productivity. The data of Nobel laureates might suggest that the argument is not valid for scientists. The ages when the award-winning works were done were remarkably similar over the years since 1901. Increased competition might be expected to have shifted the ages over the years. Admittedly, these data do not negate Dennis' argument; it may still be maintained, but perhaps with less conviction. Zuckerman's (1977) argument is related. She maintained that increases in the number of young scientific workers over time (the change in population demography) make it probable that a young person will win the Noble Prize. This argument is also weakened by the relatively constant age pattern of when Nobel laureates did their work. Thus, it can be concluded that Lehman's data, as unacceptable as many investigators seemed to have found it, has withstood reasonably well the tests of argument and of data.

Why Decline? Not all older people stop quality work but, as indicated, very many do. Quantity of work is better maintained; however, even though some older people produce more at the end of their lives than ever before, there is fall off in quantity too. Thus, there is decline and the question is, Why? The reasons offered in explanation are really conjectures because the related research data are not available.

First, as suggested at the start of this chapter, aspects of cognitive abilities decline with age, and this may have a bearing on creativity and productivity. Work factors have a bearing, as seen in still another criticism of Lehman's work. Bjorksten (1946) suggested that as a person advances in a field and attains recognition, administrative, social, financial, and other noncreative responsibilities grow. Thus, Lehman's data may reflect output only in the context of available time. Bjorksten suggested that perhaps a more meaningful index of creativity is output in the time available to produce. To support this argument, Bjorksten interviewed a "small number of successful chemists within the writer's acquaintance" and obtained information regarding the percentage of creative working time available to them. This time was found to decrease with age at about the same rate as did the creative productions.

Lehman did not refer to Bjorksten's article, but readily admitted that circumstances may be unfavorable for older people. He did not accept these circumstances, however, as the basis for the decrement. He pointed to the fact that production rate for quantity holds up better with age than does quality. "Should one consider," he wrote, "that older men foolishly devote their time and energy to the publication of mere quantity to the neglect of the quality of their output?" (Lehman, 1953, p. 309).

Johnson (1972, p. 275) went one step further, representing an argument just counter to that of Bjorksten—"young men usually created their masterpieces when they were burdened with occupational and domestic problems. Eminent thinkers of fifty have arrived, they are generally established—with facilities, assistance and the prestige smooths away many difficulties." Johnson continued, "These same thinkers at thirty had to find and hold jobs, perhaps to move several times, and to compete with their peers for support and a place to work." Despite this, their "abundant energy . . . and enthusiasm for new ideas" allowed them to be creative.

Lehman (1953) offered 16 possible causes for the decrement with age. Among these were diminution in physical vigor, physiological capacity, and health; unfortunate family experiences; poorer education; complacency, inflexibility, and lowered motivation. Simonton's data support Lehman's conjecture with regard to the relationship between health and accomplishment, but age decrements were seen even when health conditions were taken into account.

Creative at All Ages

Creative Old People. Lehman was as aware as anyone else that individual differences are large. He was so aware, in fact, that he devoted a whole chapter, "Older Thinkers and Great Achievements," in his book, *Age and Achievement,* to this topic. This chapter comprised brief biographies of 94 older persons who did notable creative work late in life, sometimes their most important work. Of the 94, there were 29 who did their work of note at 80 and over, the others at 70 and over. Some of this work could not have been created at an earlier age because it took nearly a lifetime to accumulate the necessary information.

Lehman pointed out that in addition to creative accomplishments, older people have maintained roles of leadership with distinction. Although Lehman believes that leadership positions are awarded on the basis of previous achievement, many people served late in life with much distinction. For example, several Supreme Court justices have served well past 80, with Holmes not retiring until 90. Gladstone was Prime Minister at 84. Churchill served as Prime Minister the second time from age 77 to 81. The peak age for leadership varies with the type of role, but often falls between the ages of 50 and 70.

Pressey and Pressey (1967) referred to this chapter by Lehman and also to an older listing by Hubbell (1935), who provided an even broader list of people who "performed distinctive service" after the age of 74. The Presseys wanted to evaluate the contributions of those aged over 80 who had done important work. They eliminated the ancients on the ground of insufficient evidence and selected for study only those who were important enough to be given three or more pages in the *Encyclopedia Brittanica*.

Michelango was the chief architect of St. Peter's from age 72 until his death at 89. Thomas Hobbes continued his brilliant writing career until his death at 91, and Voltaire still published at 83. Benjamin Franklin was influential until his death at 84, as was Thomas Jefferson at 83. Jefferson's last years were devoted to planning the University of Virginia. Goethe completed *Faust* at 82, and Victor Hugo was still writing after 80, as was Tennyson. As already noted, Gladstone and Churchill continued their brilliant political careers into their 80s.

Types of Accomplishments. Nevertheless, Lehman believed that, with exceptions, the work of old age differs from work done earlier in life. The creative work of old age, he said, is more likely to involve the preparation for publication of material used earlier in college lectures. The creative work is more likely to involve writing of personal memoirs, or recording and interpreting what has been obscured during most of a lifetime. Older people are more likely to write important textbooks. In older age, creative effort is more likely to include the assembling of knowledge from a wide variety of fields. It is likely to involve the completion or revision of work planned or begun earlier. Lehman added that creative productions in old age are more likely to involve discussions of the problems of old age and to include writing of general and specialized histories.

Why such accomplishments and not the kind more typical of young people? One possible reason is that, "Compared with older adults, young adults are enthusiastic and blessed with fresh perspective" (Schaie & Geiwitz, 1982, pp. 163–164). Another possibility is simply that, "Older scientists tend to lose touch with the developing heart of their discipline, their knowledge becomes obsolete. . . . This process has nothing to do with intellectual creativity itself but is a result of the patterns of education and specialization in science" (Shin & Putnam, 1982, p. 222). Another reason, indicated before, is that some works can be done only by the elderly since it takes a lifetime to accumulate the information and it takes the breadth of experience to integrate it.

Wisdom and Humanitarian Achievements. Pressey and Pressey (1967), in reviewing their list of creative old people, would have none of this. They were convinced that the men they studied were not merely following through on achievements of earlier, prime years. Instead, they believed that some of these men did their greatest work beginning in their 60s. The old people they studied, although extremely varied in their work, had a lot in common. The Presseys indicated that all these great men, in their later years, had important perspectives on their work and their times. They had wide contacts and experience; they had tasted failure as well as success; they had loves and losses, hopes and disappointments. Most important, all had attained wisdom.

These great men had goals and purposes and they had the discipline needed to achieve them. Interestingly, Pressey and Pressey concluded that these goals and purposes in old age became increasingly benevolent. In their words, these men were characterized by their "wisdom and their persistent and powerful drive toward increasingly humanitarian achievements" (1967, p. 184).

Characteristics of the Creative Person

Background. Johnson (1972, p. 274) reviewed several analyses of creative people and concluded that, "The creative geniuses that we know about from records of the past came predominantly from middle class families and had the benefits of a good education, although in some cases a rather irregular education." This is compatible with Zuckerman's (1977, pp. 61–64) observations of Nobel Prize winners: they "come in disproportionate numbers from middle and upper middle occupational strata. . . ." She also wrote that they have a high representation in the "Ivy League or other elite college" (p. 82).

Personality. Roe (1953), MacKinnon (1962), Barron (1963), and others were interested in the creative person, and each has contributed to a general picture. Creative people have been described as original, flexible, strong in dedication, and independent in thought and values. They have been described as open to new experiences, as disciplined, as paying attention to their own thoughts and feelings. Many are highly intelligent, tending to focus upon the broad implications of problems rather than on small details. Reports are that creative people tolerate ambiguity and prefer complexity. They can live with conceptual disorder and need not impose organization immediately. Although there are a few indications that creative people may be more troubled psychologically than their less creative counterparts, it has been reported that they have better resources to deal with their troubles.

In Chapter 9, personality was discussed and reference was made to Cattell's test of 16 personality factors. As told by Johnson (1972, p. 276), Cattell "read many biographies and autobiographies of scientists and inventors to work out a generalized description of them [based on these 16 factors]. . . . On the average, these scientists were . . . withdrawn, skeptical, internally occupied, precise, and critical." They were frequently dominant; they were "introspective, restrained, brooding, and solemn, but this is not incompatible with a high level of resourcefulness and adaptability." There was also some evidence that scientists and inventors possess "greater ego strength and emotional stability than the average," but artistic and literary geniuses may show "more signs of psychopathology . . . than . . . scientists."

Resistance to Social Influence. "Biographical data of the creative genius give evidence of strong motivation toward intellectual goals in spite of frustration, indeed, often in spite of strong opposition from family, friends and social norms" (Johnson, 1972, p. 274). This resistance to social pressures was also seen by Simonton (1977, p. 802), studying the great composers. The composers were

> remarkably immune from a wide range of external forces. Such impersonal social factors as warfare and civil turmoil have no noticeable impact, nor do such personal influences as social honors and tribulations of private life. On the contrary, we gain a picture of the creative genius as one whose productivity perseveres, no matter what the environment may bring in the way of rewards, anxieties or distraction.

This resistance to social influences, although apparently characteristic of the person of extraordinary contribution, does not appear true of people of lesser status, even when they too are of note. In fact, just the opposite seems indicated. Shortly, contributions of highly trained university faculty members will be discussed. Although among these may be people of true genius, as a group they are not as esteemed as Nobel laureates or great composers. Resistance to social influences does not seem to characterize them. Cole (1979, p. 969) was of the opinion that their productivity was "influenced by the scientific reward system," that is, they sought "recognition by publishing." Cole hypothesized that those whose publication rates declined with age were the very people who had not been rewarded in the past for their publications. Similarly, Bayer and Dutton (1977, p. 279) suggested that "the influence of changing market conditions over time" was a factor in publication rates.

Thus, it would seem that the truly creative march to the sounds of their own drumming. The others, are responsive to the social rewards in the world around them.

CONTRIBUTION

Lehman insisted that in studying the accomplishments of the great people in history, a distinction can be made between their products that are truly creative and those that are simply noteworthy. Dennis disagreed, at least to the extent that he believed that it is hardly possible to distinguish between the two without much error. Both Lehman and Dennis were in agreement, however, that there is much contribution that is worthwhile whether or not it is acclaimed as creative. Cole (1979) examined such contributions, focusing on scientists in academia. Cole chose to examine contributions of scientists of varying ages during a single period of history rather than mixing different periods of history, as Lehman did. He also carried out a longitudinal investigation, indicating that he believed both these methods were preferable to that used by Lehman.

Scientific Publications during a Single Period

Cole examined published papers of a random sample of scientists working in prestigious departments of Ph.D.-granting institutions. The publications were limited to the years 1965 to 1969. Quality of publication was gauged by the number of times the publication was cited. Cole found that both quantity and quality were age-related but not in the way Lehman indicated. Although the peak age of production across disciplines was 40 to 44, "In most of the fields studied the scientists over the age of 60 were not much less productive than those under 35" (Cole, 1979, p. 963).

This observation was based on frequency counts of publications. It is true that the difference between old and young was not large in numbers, but it was large in percentage terms. At ages under 35, there were 6.1 publications during the years 1965 to 1969. At ages 60 and over, there were 4.6 publications. This difference, although only 1.5 publications, is about one-quarter of the publications of the younger group and one-third of the older. Thus, although Cole's data do not conform to the function seen in Figure 19.1, they do not suggest a vastly different picture: they suggest a later peak and a slower decline than Lehman's data show for quantity production of superior scientists.

As to quality, Cole used the index of number of citations. The results were similar to those based on quantity. For these highly trained scientists, quality production again peaked in the 40s with little difference among age-groups in terms of frequency but greater difference in terms of percentage. Thus, it can be said that productive scientists remain productive most of their lifetimes with some diminution in their outputs at later ages.

A Longitudinal Study

Cole (1979) also carried out a longitudinal study of mathematicians. Mathematicians who earned Ph.D. degrees between 1947 and 1950 were examined with regard to their publications over the subsequent 25 years. Cole found that productivity was fairly constant over this time, varying very little from the 5-year period soon after the degree was awarded to the period 1970 to 1974, about 25 years later. In addition, the number of citations in the literature of their publications did not vary over the 25 years (except for the first 5-year period, when the citations were fewer).

This might suggest that Lehman was incorrect in saying creativity is found mainly among the young. Two facts mitigate such a conclusion, however. First, once again, the mathematicians might have been well-trained and esteemed, but this does not necessarily mean they were creative. Second, the mathematicians selected for longitudinal study could not be considered especially productive in research publications. Their average number of publications ranged from 2.3 to only 2.8 per 5-year period. The average number of citations ranged from .84 to 1.4. This again suggests that among less extraordinary people at least, reduction of contribution with age is not a foregone conclusion.

Producers and Nonproducers

A study by Bayer and Dutton (1977) is in the same tradition. They investigated Ph.D.s teaching in universities and colleges, including junior or community colleges, with regard to publications and other research-professional contributions. Instead of analyzing these in relation to age, however, they analyzed the contributions in relation to "career age." Career age was defined as years since attaining the Ph.D., but this was very highly correlated with chronological age and both yielded the same results.

Bayer and Dutton (1977, p. 272) reported that there was "a peaking at about five to 10 years of career age" which, it would seem, corresponds to a chronological age of the 30s, similar to that seen in Figure 19.1 based on Lehman's data. Bayer and Dutton made the interesting observation that over the next 25 years, there was "only a slight decline in the proportion of highly productive faculty members, but a substantial proportionate increase in nonproducers" (p. 272). Despite this, the proportion of producers to nonproducers among the older faculty (those more than 25 years past Ph.D.) was similar to that among the youngest faculty (0 to 4 years past Ph.D.).

These data suggest that among well-trained, bright scientific contributors, age is not a necessary factor in how much contribution is to be expected: "career age [and therefore, chronological age] . . . is a poor predictor of research-professional activity" (Bayer & Dutton, 1977, p. 279). Once again, therefore, the life of contribution can be very long-lasting.

Daily Lives of Old People

Pressey (1958) was interested in the great contributors throughout history, but he was also interested in the accomplishments of people of more ordinary abilities and opportunities. Pressey recognized that important contributions are made by many people, not just by the great, or even by highly trained academicians. Pressy was interested in very old people and the contributions they make in their daily lives. He wanted to know whether many of them continue to be useful past 80.

Pressey searched for material in case records, reports by university students, and clippings about older people. These three sources yielded a total of 290 persons aged 80 to 89 and 23 aged over 90. These people, although more ordinary than the famous men written up in encyclopedias, were by no means ordinary. Their very long lives made them different, as did the fact that they were important enough to have been noted in case records, reports, and clippings.

Pressey found that most of these people aged 80 and above were working part time or occasionally, but a few were still working full time. Two men past 90 were active presidents of small-town banks, another was a bank teller, a 90-year-old woman continued her insurance business. Pressey concluded that the accumulation of experience, knowledge, and wisdom that makes "the greats" valuable as leaders also makes the people of lesser ability extremely valuable. Opportunity to continue making contributions is a keynote, he said. Professional and self-employed people have had the greatest chance to continue their interests, and this is the reason they were so strongly represented in Pressey's sample.

All these studies show that creativity or a lesser form of achievement is not necessarily limited to the young. If not greatness, or even recognized notable achievement, then at least continued usefulness and feelings of self-worth are possible at any age. Perhaps creativity and achievement in old age should not be judged in terms of what has been done in the past but what is being done in the present. Given the opportunities for continued usefulness and self-respect, very many people are capable of contribution in old age.

SUMMARY

Creativity is recognized through extraordinary products and accomplishments that are relevant, novel, original, and unique. Such products and accomplishments are believed to come from divergent, innovative, and constructive thinking, more than from logical and analytical thinking. Creative people and their works have been identified for study by experts and by the frequency with which creative works have been cited in the literature. Creative people and their works, identified in this way, have been studied to determine the peak ages of creative production. Lehman's study is the main one; he found that in many fields of endeavor, much of the truly creative work is done early in life—between 30 and 39 years—with gradual decline after this period. The peak years of lesser work, but work that is still noteworthy, come later than 30 to 39 and the decline is more gradual.

These conclusions have been contested through the years with two main criticisms: One is that Lehman combined the data of creative historical figures who died early in life with those who lived long. The short-lived could only have produced early in life and long-lived could have produced both when young and when old. Combining the two makes for a picture of early life production, when this may not be so. In fact, one investigator, Dennis, charted the productions of only long-lived people and found that peak performance years were seen throughout the life span.

Lehman argued that these results did not negate his basic findings because Dennis charted all the productions of creative people, not just the truly creative ones, as he did. Further, Lehman said, the older contributors produced so little that was creative that combining the longevities made little difference. Dennis then levied the second criticism: He said that distinguishing between more creative and less creative works from citations in the literature only makes for systematic errors in favor of younger workers. Lehman denied this.

This controversy has continued over the years; in the main, however, much subsequent data were generated to support Lehman, even if with some question. First, a study of great composers, based on an experimental design to cope with the argument of combined longevities, also found peaking of creative effort early in life—by one measurement in the 30s, by another measurement in the 40s. Studies of Nobel Prize winners showed that many of them did their award-winning work when in their 30s. Top-level chess players, although perhaps not in the same league of creativity as Nobel laureates and great historical figures, also achieved their major successes when in the 30s.

Despite these studies, controversy about creativity and age still reigns, and the issues of combined longevities and the ability to differentiate the creative product from the simply noteworthy remain. There is no controversy, however, that a person's usefulness is not limited by age alone. All protagonists agree that there have been very many people who at very late age produced important work and even the most important works of their lives.

Creative people seem to come mainly from middle-class families and to have the benefit of a good or superior education. Creative people are seen as original, flexible, and disciplined. They have also been seen as withdrawn, introspective, and skeptical. Creative people are often dominant. Perhaps more than any other trait, they seem to be resistant to social pressures and social rewards. They create independently of social forces. This does not seem to apply to people of lesser creative stature, even when such people are noteworthy in their own right. Such people, average university faculty members, for example, seem to be responsive to social rewards and pressures, and their production rates seem dependent on them.

Very old people in everyday walks of life have also been studied with respect to their contributions. Even at very old age—past 80 and in the 90s—many have continued in the labor force making daily contributions through work. Such contributions have been made largely among those who have had the opportunity to continue their occupational interests. Not all old adults have this opportunity.

REFERENCES

Barron, F. The disposition towards originality. *Journal of Abnormal and Social Psychology*, 1955, *51*, 478–485.

Barron, F. *Creativity and psychological health.* New York: Van Nostrand, 1963.

Bayer, A., & Dutton, J. Career age and research-professional activities of academic scientists: Tests of alternative nonlinear models and some implications for higher education faculty policies. *Journal of Higher Education*, 1977, *48*, 259–282.

Bjorksten, J. The limitation of creative years. *Scientific Monthly*, 1946, *62*, 94.

Charness, N. Aging and skilled problem solving. *Journal of Experimental Psychology: General*, 1981, *110*, 21–38.

Cole, S. Age and scientific performance. *American Journal of Sociology*, 1979, *84*, 958–977.

Dennis, W. Age and achievement: A critique. *Journal of Gerontology*, 1956, *11*, 331–333. (a)

Dennis, W. Age and productivity among scientists. *Science*, 1956, *123*, 724–725. (b)

Dennis, W. The age decrement in outstanding scientific contributions: Fact or artifact? *American Psychologist*, 1958, *13*, 457–460.

Dennis, W. Creative productivity between ages of 20 and 80 years. *Journal of Gerontology,* 1966, *21,* 1–8.

Elo, A. E. Age changes in master chess performance. *Journal of Gerontology,* 1965, *20,* 289–299.

Getzels, J. W., & Jackson, P. W. *Creativity and intelligence.* New York: Wiley, 1962.

Hubbell, R. A. Men and women who have performed distinctive service after the age of 74. *Wilson Bulletin for Librarians,* 1935, *9,* 297–304.

Johnson, D. M. *Systematic introduction to the psychology of thinking.* New York: Harper & Row, 1972.

Lehman, H. C. *Age and achievement.* Princeton, N.J.: Princeton University Press, 1953.

Lehman, H. C. Reply to Dennis' critique of *Age and Achievement. Journal of Gerontology,* 1956, *11,* 333–337.

Lehman, H. C. The influence of longevity upon curves showing man's creative production rate at successive age levels. *Journal of Gerontology,* 1958, *13,* 187–191.

Lehman, H. C. The age decrement in outstanding scientific creativity. *American Psychologist,* 1960, *15,* 128–134.

Lehman, H. C. Chronological age versus present-day contribution to medical progress. *Gerontologist,* 1963, *3,* 71–75.

Lyons, J. Chronological age, professional age, and eminence in psychology. *American Psychologist,* 1968, *23,* 371–374.

MacKinnon, D. W. The nature and nurture of creative talent. *American Psychologist,* 1962, *17,* 484–495.

Manniche, E., & Falk, G. Age and Nobel Prize. *Behavioral Science,* 1957, *2,* 301–307.

McLeish, J. A. B. The continuum of creativity. In P. W. Johnson (Ed.), *Perspectives on aging.* Cambrige, Mass.: Ballinger, 1981, pp. 95–115.

Parloff, M. B., & Datta, L. Personality characteristics of the potentially creative scientist. In J. H. Masserman (Ed.), *Science and psychoanalysis* (Vol. 8). New York: Grune & Stratton, 1965, pp. 91–106.

Pressey, S. L. Jobs at 80. *Geriatrics,* 1958, *13,* 678–681.

Pressey, S. L., & Pressey, A. D. Genius at 80; and other oldsters. *Gerontologist,* 1967, *7,* 183–187.

Roe, A. *The making of a scientist.* New York: Dodd, Mead, 1953.

Schaie, K. W. & Geitwitz, J. *Adult development and aging.* Boston: Little, Brown, 1982.

Shin, K. E., & Putnam, R. H. Age and academic-professional honors. *Journal of Gerontology,* 1982, *37,* 220–229.

Simonton, D. K. Creative productivity, age, and stress: a biographical time-series analysis of 10 classical composers. *Journal of Personality and Social Psychology,* 1977, *35,* 791–804.

Wallach, M. A., & Kogan, N. *Modes of thinking in young children.* New York: Holt, Rinehart & Winston, 1965.

Zuckerman, H. *Scientific elite: Studies of Nobel laureates in the United States.* New York: Free Press, 1977.

Zusne, L. Age and achievement in psychology. *American Psychologist,* 1976, *31,* 805–807.

20
Research Methods

THREE RESEARCH METHODS

What research information we have is only as meaningful as the research method we use and the interpretations we make. Most of what we know about aging and old age is based on comparisons of people in different age-groups. This method, the cross-sectional method, while useful, can lead to faulty conclusions. Observe the following.

The Cross-Sectional Method

In a talk, Robert Kastenbaum told of an interesting cross-sectional observation he made. He said:

> Occasionally I have the opportunity to chat with elderly people who live in the communities near Cushing Hospital. I cannot help but observe that many of these people speak with an Italian accent. I also chat with young adults who live in these same communities. They do *not* speak with an Italian accent. As a student of human behavior and development, I am interested in this discrepancy. I indulge in some deep thinking and come up with the following conclusion: as people grow older they develop Italian accents. This must surely be one of the prime manifestations of aging on the psychological level.

This, of course, was said with tongue-in-cheek, but the message is serious and important. Descriptive statements of differences among age-groups do not necessarily reflect aging processes; the differences may reflect cultural backgrounds.

All this is very obvious in Kastenbaum's observation at Cushing Hospital. See how different all this is when his observation is paraphrased:

> Occasionally I have the opportunity to chat with elderly people who live in the communities nearby Cushing Hospital. I cannot help but observe that many of

these people are slow in their behaviors—their reaction times are slow. I also chat with young adults who live in these same communities. They are *not* slow—they have fast reaction times. As a student of human behavior and development, I am interested in this discrepancy. I indulge in some deep thinking and come up with the following conclusion: as people grow older they become slow. This must surely be one of the prime manifestations of aging on the psychological level.

In the original Kastenbaum observation, it is easy and reasonable to infer that the elderly people with Italian accents were immigrants, or at least grew up in a *culture* where English was not the primary or sole language spoken. The elderly people were of a different *generation*, born in a different era than the young people, and it is these cultural-generational influences, not maturational-age influences, that made for Italian accents. Background cultural and generational differences have come to be called *cohort* differences.

In the paraphrased reaction time observation, it is not so easy and probably not so reasonable to infer that the elderly people were slow because of cohort differences. The effects of *age* or *maturation* seem to be a better inference, but in fact, it may be a wrong inference. It may be that cohort is responsible for the slowing or it may be some combination of age and cohort. The fact is that *in cross-sectional research, age and cohort are intrinsically confounded*, that is, they are mixed together.

Research investigators have spent much time trying to tease apart this intrinsic confound of age and cohort. There are several plans or rules of how to do this, and some of them will be discussed later, but it should be kept in mind at all times that, in the end, age and cohort are inseparable in most observations. Only in the most obvious instances, one such as Kastenbaum's, can separation be made with confidence. Age and cohort are confounded because in most studies both age and cohort are defined by year of birth.

The Longitudinal Method

Many investigators have become so concerned about the cohort effect in cross-sectional studies that they have looked to longitudinal studies for clear age effects. Just as the inference of age could be wrong in a cross-sectional study, however, it could also be wrong in a longitudinal study. The reason is that there is a confound in both types of studies, although the confounds are different.

Repeated Measures. In longitudinal studies, the same people are examined during two or more periods of time, with, typically, a number of years between examinations. It is expected that changes with age will occur and these changes will be observed across these examination periods. People change for reasons other than age, however, and such changes can affect the observations. Changes of this kind, the result of mainly environmental influences occurring between or during examination sessions, are called time-of-measurement effects, or simply time effects. (Sociologists call them period effects, for time period effects.)

Here is an example of time effects: As reported in 1954, Nelson tested college students with regard to their liberalism, described on a continuum from conservative to liberal. He then tested these same people 14 years later. Nelson found that liberal attitudes increased over this 14-year period. He could have concluded that liberalism increases with age during this part of life.

Nelson, however, did something unique for that time. He also tested a sample of new college students at the same time that he made the 14-year retest of the initial sample. He found that the scores of the new sample and the retest sample were the same. The new college students and the alumni were equally liberal. Nelson also found that the two samples of college students were different; the new sample tested 14 years later was more liberal. It was easy to conclude from this that environmental influences, that is, time effects, were the important influences over the 14 years, not aging. This inference becomes more meaningful when it is noted that the 14-year period preceding the 1954 Nelson publication was a period of growing social liberalism. It is possible that had this study been conducted during the latter 1970s to 1980s, an opposite time effect would have been noted, an increased conservatism.

The point is that as the same group of people is tested over time, that is, as repeated measurements are made, the observed changes may be true age or maturational effects, but they may also be time effects. Not only attitudes and values are influenced by time, characteristics seemingly more resistant to enviromental change are affected. For example, Tilton (1949) found time effects associated with gains in intelligence test scores between the period of World War I and II. Thus, it can be said, just as cross-sectional comparisons confound age and cohort effects, *the longitudinal method confounds age and time effects.*

Independent Measures. There is a method of research that is analogous but not identical to the repeated-measures method of longitudinal research. It is called independent-measures or independent-samples research. This method may be thought of as falling in between the cross-sectional method and the repeated-measures method, although like the repeated-measures method, the confound is age and time.

Planning independent-samples research takes this form: A large, relatively homogeneous sample is selected for study. Then it is divided into as many similar or identical subsamples as there are plans for times of measurement. Thus, for example, three subsamples may be identified, with one tested at Time 1, a second subsample at Time 2, and the third subsample at Time 3. The three subsamples are regarded as comparable to start so that only age differentiates them during the different times of measurement. The first subsample at the first time of testing is younger than the second subsample at the second time; that in turn is younger than the third subsample at Time 3.

It is as if a cross-sectional comparison is made of the three age-group subsamples tested at different times. Since all three of the subsamples are from the same cohort, however, the comparison does not involve cohort; it involves age and time.

There are advantages to the independent-measures method over the repeated-measures method, such as not having to be concerned with practice effects from Time 1 to Time 2. Also, there is the advantage of minimizing selective subject attrition (which will be described in the next chapter). On the negative side, it is not possible to chart individual change with independent-samples research. The thing to remember is that in independent-samples research—as in longitudinal, repeated-measures research—the confound is age and time of measurement.

The Time-Lag Method

Thus far two major research methods in developmental research have been discussed: (1) cross-sectional comparisons where age and cohort are confounded and (2) longitudinal comparisons where age and time of measurement are confounded. There is a third research method and it is growing in importance in aging research. This method is called time lag.

The time-lag comparison was seen in the study by Nelson (1954). In that study, it will be recalled, college students were tested, then they were retested 14 years later. At the time of retest, new college students were tested; they were the same age as those originally tested 14 years prior. Thus, there were two college groups of the same age, but tested 14 years apart. This is the time-lag comparison; age is not involved in this comparison.

The two college-age groups were of different cohorts. They were tested at different items. Thus, *the time-lag comparison confounds cohort and time of measurement*. It is to be noted that when any two of the comparisons are arranged—cross-sectional, longitudinal, or time lag—the third is available automatically, that is, without planning for it.

DEFINING AGE, COHORT, AND TIME

The discussion has been of the confounded variables age, cohort, and time. What do they really mean and how have they been defined operationally?

Age

In almost all studies, age is operationally defined by year of birth or years since birth, but this does not tell very much. In a general way everyone knows what age means, yet when it comes to formal definition, it really is not that easy. Birren and Renner (1977, p. 4) provided an interesting definition: aging, they said, involves changes of people or animals "living under representative environmental conditions." These environmental conditions are those in which the "organisms evolved or are commonly found." In applying this definition, we see that human organisms reared in the early 1900s had one environment and those reared in the 1960s had another. Thus, even with careful definition, age and cohort are confounded. Glenn (1981, p. 362) took this one step further. Age effects, he said, is "a shorthand way of saying 'effects of biological, psychological, and social changes which tend to accompany chronological aging.' "

Ordinarily, age effects are regarded as maturational-biological effects, but the Birren-Renner definition together with the Glenn definition make age a psychological and sociological concept as well as a biological one. The logic of this is more apparent in some observations than others. For example, growth in height and weight is clearly a biological effect, but the magnitude of growth is related to nutritional background. Nutrition—or, more properly, extent of malnutrition—varies from culture to culture and from one socioeconomic status within a culture to another. Another example is health or biomedical status. Diminished biomedical status is associated with age. Still, as an age effect, the importance of personal health habits and sociological opportunities to exercise habits cannot be denied. They are part of biomedical status. Age is a complex variable defined by the calendar, but it is incorrect to think of age solely in biological terms.

Cohort

Cohort, like age, is most often operationally defined by year of birth. Unlike age, however, cohort is defined by cultural, environmental, or generational backgrounds. The idea is that people born in the period 1910 to 1920, for example, have more in common with each other in a cultural sense than they have with people of a different cohort, 1950 to 1960, for example.

Rosow (1978) refers to this as a demographic notion of cohort. A cohort is a group of people born or entering a system at the same time who age together. Although this is the way cohort is usually defined, Rosow points out that other definitions of cohort are more meaningful. The more meaningful definitions of cohort, however, are more difficult to investigate in aging studies.

The concept of cohort is more meaningful when it includes groupings of people, not by year of birth, but by exposure to specific sociohistorical events, for example, war and depression. The concept of cohort is also more meaningful when it is defined by groupings of people exposed to specific personal events, for example, marriage and retirement. A cohort, seen in this light, consists of people who shared common experiences. It is related to year of birth, but is not identical to it.

There is a problem with the concept of cohort as commonly investigated in aging studies. It is commonly assumed that cohort trends are monotonic, that is, in one direction only. For example, it is frequently assumed that each succeeding cohort is superior to the previous one in regard to health, performance, or other characteristics. The culture, it is assumed, is continuously improving. This may not be. Cohort differences resulting from war or economic depression are not necessarily continuous, monotonic functions.

Another problem is that cohort, like age, indexes a variety of factors, some of them very individual. For example, one cohort may have had a war impact, another cohort may have had a depression impact, but people experience war and depression differently. One person during war may have killed others on the battlefield and experienced terror. Another person may have built up a thriving business and started a family. Similarly, two people may have been adults during the same economic depression, but with basically different experiences. One person may have been poor to start but another became poor afterwards. It would be an advance in aging studies to incorporate the concept of cohort in this way. It is obvious, however, that it is very difficult to do so.

Time

Time effects can be defined by two classes of variables. One class is of environmental variables and the other is of person variables.

Environmental Effects. Environmental influences are probably the most important factors in time effects. In fact, Schaie (1967, p. 129) emphasized the environmental effects almost to the exclusion of others; he wrote that time effects "denotes that state of the environment within which a given set of data were obtained . . . changes in the state of the environment may contribute to the effects noted in an aging study."

Environmental influences are often difficult or even impossible to distinguish from the cultural influences defined by cohort effects. The distinguishing feature is that environmental influences are presumed to have impact only between and during the times of measurement. Cultural influences defined by cohort effects, on the other hand, are thought to be lifelong, most often beginning at birth.

It would seem that more often than not, cohort-cultural effects would be larger than time-of-measurement–environmental effects. This is so because, typically, cohort effects are encompassed by many more years than are time-of-measurement effects. Extensive and important change can occur in just a few years, however; with the tempo or rate of environmental change increasing, time-of-measurement effects may be expected to grow in importance in future longitudinal investigations.

Examples of environmental–time effects include societal changes in values and attitudes (as in the Nelson study), changes in the state of the general economy, changes in opportunities for social or cognitive stimulation (such as enrichment programs at school), and the advent of new technology such as television during the 1940s and 1950s and computers more recently. Environmental influences may also be seen in a more specific, less global way in the laboratory. If the longitudinal or independent-samples study continues very long, the laboratory equipment may deteriorate or the calibration may inadvertently change. New equipment may replace old, with all this making for unknown increases or decreases in the measurements during the various times of testing. The experimenter may mistakenly infer that people changed with age when it was really time effects such as these.

Subject Effects. People tested in the course of longitudinal investigation change for reasons other than age. They experience decreases or increases in personal income, they marry, they become widowed, they become sick. Their motivation and interests change. In the repeated-measures study, people may improve through practice. All this can have a bearing on the measurements.

COMPLEX EXPERIMENTAL DESIGNS

In recent years, investigators have taken to the use of research designs that are very complex. This practice appears to be increasing because, it is believed, through such designs aging processes can best be understood. These designs are complex mainly because of the mechanics of carrying them out; in concept, however, they are quite simple. They are developed from the basic methods of cross-sectional, longitudinal, and time-lag comparisons.

Cross-Sequential Design

A design developed from a series of simultaneous cross-sectional and longitudinal studies is called the cross-sequential design. This design is seen in Table 20.1 (cells A through I, exclude cells K and J). In the cells of this table, the lower-case letters represent the test scores or the measurements made during the observation sessions.

In the cross-sectional part of the analysis, cohorts 1910, 1920, and 1930 are compared; their ages are seen in the upper left corners of the cells. Thus, the cross-sectional comparison is measurements $a + b + c$ versus $d + e + f$ versus $g + h + i$. The longitudinal part of the analysis is of measurements made during 1960, 1970, and 1980. Note that this longitudinal comparison can be made whether the measurements are repeated or independent. Thus, the comparison is of $a + d + g$ versus $b + e + h$ versus $c + f + i$, or, more briefly, I versus II versus III.

From such a design, it is possible to infer the relative contribution of age/cohort and age/time to the observed changes or measurements that were made. Later, the type of inferences that have been made or can be made will be described. For now, it is only necessary to recognize that the *cross-sequential design involves two confounds: the cross-sectional age/cohort and the longitudinal age/time.*

It is to be noted that this design is nothing other than a series of simultaneous cross-sectional and longitudinal analyses. For example, cells A, D, G constitute one cross-sectional comparison, and cells B, E, H another. Similarly, cells A, B, C are one longitudinal comparison and D, E, F another. Just as in the simple case where if one cross-sectional comparison and one longitudinal comparison are available, the time lag comparison is automatic, the same applies to the complex designs except some cells have to be dropped and others added. This is seen in the next design—the time-sequential design. The interdependence of the three variables has been referred to as the two-component or bifactor model (Baltes, 1968).

Time-sequential Design

When different time-lag groups are compared in conjunction with the cross-sectional comparisons, the design of the study is called time-sequential. For this design, cell A of Table 20.1 has to be replaced by cell J, and cell I has to be replaced by cell K. The time-lag comparison then is of measurements $d + g + j$ versus measurements $b + e + h$ versus $k + c + f$ (or I versus II versus III). Note that each group is comprised of 40-, 50-, and 60-year-olds. Thus, across the times of measurement, the ages are the same but the cohorts are different. Once again, with the time-lag comparison, the confound is cohort and time.

TABLE 20.1
Three Sequential Designs

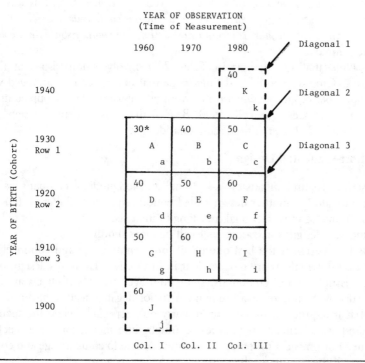

YEAR OF OBSERVATION
(Time of Measurement)

Design	Cells	Confound	Comparisons
Cross-Sequential	A through I	Age/Cohort	Row 1 vs 2 vs 3
		Age/Time	Col. I vs II vs III
Time-Sequential	All, but not A and I	Age/Cohort	Diagonal 1 vs 2 vs 3
		Cohort/Time	Col. I vs II vs III
Cohort-Sequential	B, C, D, E	Age/Time	d + b vs e + c
		Cohort/Time	b + c vs d + e
	E, F, G, H	Age/Time	g + e vs h + f
		Cohort/Time	e + f vs g + h

*Numbers refer to mean ages of cohorts; upper case letters refer to cell designations, lower case letters refer to observation measurements.

389

The time-sequential design also permits age comparisons, with each age-group involving more than one cohort. In this comparison, the scores $d + b + k$ are compared to $g + e + c$ versus $j + h + f$. In this way, *the time-sequential design involves two simultaneous confounds: a cross-sectional study with an age/cohort confound and a time-lag comparison with a cohort/ time confound.*

Note that the designs in Table 20.1 involve comparisons of three groups. Cross-sequential and time-sequential designs can be arranged with any number of group comparisons, from two upwards. Two-group comparisons may be seen with cells A, D, B, E as the cross-sectional design, and cells D, G, B, E as the time-sequential design.

Cohort-sequential Design

A series of simultaneous cross-sectional and longitudinal comparisons will also provide for another design called cohort-sequential. Baltes (1968) prefers the name cross-sectional and longitudinal sequences to that of cohort-sequential design, for reasons that will be clear shortly.

This design is the best one of all for separating age and cohort effects because these effects are independent in this design. Even this design, however, is not without confounds, since both age and cohort effects are confounded with time of measurement. A major negative feature of this design is that it requires so much time to carry out, especially when the focus of interest is age effects. It requires so much time that it has little practical value. For practical purposes it is hardly possible to compare age and cohort groups if they are more than just a very few years apart.

In Table 20.1 the comparison $b + c$ versus $d + e$ is a cohort comparison, 1930 versus 1920. Note that in this design, both cohort groups are of the same age (40 and 50 years). The comparison $d + b$ versus $e + c$ is an age comparison, 40-year-olds versus 50-year-olds. Note that each group is of the same cohort (1920–1930). Thus, age and cohort are independent in this design.

Another, similar set of cohort and age-group comparisons can be made: (1) $e + f$ versus $g + h$ (1920 versus 1910), and (2) $g + e$ versus $h + f$ (50- versus 60-year-olds). Observe that to compare but two age and two cohort groups, it takes three times of measurement. This is the simplest, that is, least extensive cohort-sequential design possible; only two-group comparisons are involved. Three-group comparisons, or more than three, require extended times of testing. It is seen in Table 20.1 that it takes 20 years (1960 to 1980) to make the 10-year age-group and 10-year cohort-group comparisons. As indicated, there are two sequences of such comparisons that are possible.

The cohort-sequential design of Table 20.1 is easier to comprehend when it is presented in a different form, as in Table 20.2. Part A of the table is of comparisons of cohort 1930 versus 1920, and ages 40 versus 50. Part B is of cohort 1920 versus 1910, and ages 50 versus 60.

Note that each cohort is measured at a different time (in Part A, 1970 and 1980 versus 1960 and 1970) and each age-group is measured at a different time (1970 and 1960 versus 1980 and 1970). Thus the *cohort-sequential design involves two confounds: age/time and cohort/time.*

DISENTANGLING THE CONFOUNDS

Effort has been made to use these complex designs, as well as the simpler methods that make them up, to separate the three confounded effects—age, cohort, and time. Can the separation be made?

Much effort has gone into trying, but after many years of such effort, the answer seems to be "no," not unless some restrictive assumptions are made and not unless we are satisfied with conclusions that are more in the nature of good, logical possibilities than hard, firm facts.

Decision Rules

More than anyone else, it was Schaie (1965) who first focused on the three confounded variables with suggestions of how to deconfound them. He formulated six "decision rules" to do this and his own work was based on

TABLE 20.2
The Cohort-sequential Design*

	Birth Cohort (Year)	AGE (YEARS) 40	50
Comparisons A	1930	1970	1980
	1920	1960	1970
		AGE (YEARS) 50	60
Comparisons B	1920	1970	1980
	1910	1960	1970

*This table presents in different form the experimental design seen in Table 20.1 by cells B, C, D, E (comparisons A) and by cells E, F, G, H (comparisons B). The dates 1960, 1970, and 1980 represent times of measurement.

some of these rules. The rules involve comparisons of the complex designs just discussed, particularly the cross-sequential and time-sequential analyses. Adam (1978) and others demonstrated that Schaie's rules do not hold up, at least not with the statistical technique of analysis of variance to which Schaie applied these rules. The reason the rules do not stand up is that the three comparisons—cross-sectional, longitudinal, and time lag—are not independent. Further, and perhaps more important, within each comparison, the confound remains unless often untenable assumptions are made. Later, George, Siegler, and Okun (1981) showed that the three comparisons can be separated despite their dependence, at least in the cross-sequential design, by complex multiple regression analyses, but the basic problem of confound within each of these comparisons remains.

Nevertheless, logical estimates of the roles played by the three variables—age, cohort, time—can be made with some of Schaie's decision rules, but only if the rules are properly applied and only if common sense prevails over the often untenable assumptions.

It is not necessary here to go over all of Schaie's six rules; only the first will be described to indicate how a logical estimate can be made. The first rule is based on a comparison between results of the cross-sequential and time-sequential designs. Specifically, the comparison is between the longitudinal effect in the cross-sequential design (age/time) and the time-lag effect in the time-sequential design (cohort/time). If age/time effect is significant, and the cohort/time is not (or if both significant, the former is larger), then it is concluded that age is the important factor in the longitudinal comparisons of the cross-sequential design. Conversely, if cohort/time is significant and not age/time, then it is concluded that time of measurement is the important effect in the longitudinal comparison of the cross-sequential design.

The reasoning is this: It is assumed that cohort/time confound is only a time effect, not cohort. If this is small or zero that is, if time is small or zero, then the important age/time confound is only age. Conversely, if the cohort/time effect is large, that is, if the time effect is large or larger than the age/time effect, then time is the important factor in the age/time confound.

Two assumptions are made here, assumptions basic to all six of Schaie's rules and, in fact, basic to most other schemes of separating the confounds. First, it is assumed that only one effect of the confound is causal, not both. Second, each of the effects—age, cohort, time—is linear and additive in the same direction as the others. Obviously, the assumptions may be wrong—perhaps are most often wrong—but as a first estimate or approximation, they do enable a determination of the prominent effect.

Schaie's decision rules and assumptions fall most short when they are abbreviated in application, as they frequently are. Also, the necessary assumptions are inappropriate if left untested. In fact, the assumptions are no better than opposite ones would be. For example, first, in the time-sequential design, it is assumed that the time-lag effect (cohort/time) is only a time effect. There is no more basis for assuming this than that cohort is the only effect. Second, in the cross-sequential design, the longitudinal comparison is assumed to be a time effect, not age. It could just as well be age, not time.

There are other decision rules where other assumptions are made. For example, in the comparison of cross-sectional groups in the time-sequential design (age/cohort), it is assumed that age is the only effect. Cohort could as reasonably be the only effect. Conversely, in the cross-sequential design, the cross-sectional comparison (age/cohort) is only a cohort effect. Age could be the only effect. If these and other assumptions are made without test, if there is no further analysis, then the separation of effects is incorrectly made; separation is made by assumptions that may be wrong. Unfortunately, this has been the practice in several studies, and in effect, by this practice the confounds have been separated by fiat.

Weight of Evidence

Age, cohort, and time can be separated in less complicated and probably better ways, again, if the separation is seen merely as a logical inference, perhaps a hypothesis. Earlier, Nelson's (1954) study on liberalism was described. The results of this study are diagrammed in Figure 20.1. As seen in this figure, the age/time of measurement effect was statistically significant in the longitudinal comparison, and so was the cohort/time of measurement confound in the time-lag comparison. The age/cohort comparison, however, was not significant in the cross-sectional comparison. It is assumed in Figure 20.1 that if neither age nor cohort was significant in one comparison, they could not have been significant in other comparisons. Thus, since age (or cohort) was not significant in the cross-sectional comparison, age is not significant in the longitudinal comparison. Therefore, it must be time. Similarly, since cohort (or age) was not significant in the cross-sectional comparison, cohort was not significant in the time-lag comparison. Only time of measurement could have accounted for the significant results in both the longitudinal and time-lag comparisons. (This exercise only formalizes what was concluded logically before in describing Nelson's study.)

Here is another example: In 1969, Woodruff and Birren (1972) gave the California Test of Personality to college alumni. These alumni had taken this same test 24 years earlier when they had been college students. In 1969, Woodruff and Birren also gave this test to young college students who were the same age as the alumni had been 25 years earlier. Thus, like Nelson,

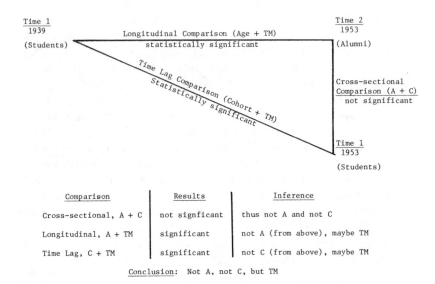

Comparison	Results	Inference
Cross-sectional, A + C	not signficant	thus not A and not C
Longitudinal, A + TM	significant	not A (from above), maybe TM
Time Lag, C + TM	significant	not C (from above), maybe TM

Conclusion: Not A, not C, but TM

FIGURE 20.1: Data from the study by Nelson (1954). A scale of liberalism was given; it is concluded that the time period from the first to second testing fostered liberal attitudes.

they had longitudinal, cross-sectional, and time-lag comparisons. As seen in Figure 20.2, the longitudinal (age/time) change was not significant. The time-lag difference (cohort/time) was significant, and so was the cross-sectional difference (age/cohort). Thus, longitudinally, age and time of measurement were not factors. Given the assumption that if these are not factors in one comparison, they are not factors in another, then it is concluded that neither age nor time of measurement was important in the time-lag or cross-sectional analyses. This leaves only cohort. It was concluded that cohort change made for better adjustment patterns during the 1969 testing than in the earlier one, a generation before.

Here is another example: Whitbourne and Waterman (1979) had a similar study in which in 1976 they gave a test called the Inventory of Psychosocial Development to alumni who 10 years earlier had been given the same test. At the time the alumni were tested, a new college age-group was tested, making for a time-lag comparison.

As seen in Figure 20.3 both the longitudinal (age/time) and cross-sectional (age/cohort) differences were significant, but the time lag (cohort/time) was not. Thus, cohort and time of measurement were seen as unrelated to the dependent measure, leaving age as the explanatory variable. It was concluded that with age, psychosocial development improved.

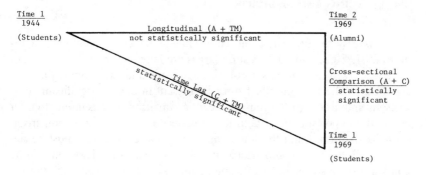

Comparison	Results	Inference
Longitudinal, A + TM	not significant	thus not A and not TM
Time Lag, C + TM	significant	not TM (from above), maybe C
Cross-sectional, A + C	significant	not A (from above), maybe C

Conclusion: Not A, not TM, but C

FIGURE 20.2: Data from the study by Woodruff and Birren (1972). The California Test of Personality was given with the conclusion that something in the backgrounds of people born in the 1920s made for better social adjustment when of college age than people born in the late 1940s, i.e., a cohort effect.

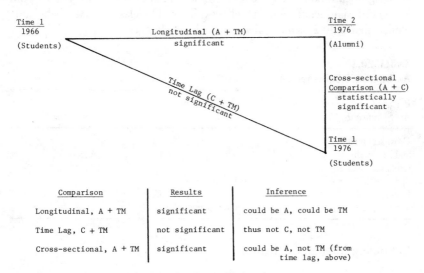

Comparison	Results	Inference
Longitudinal, A + TM	significant	could be A, could be TM
Time Lag, C + TM	not significant	thus not C, not TM
Cross-sectional, A + TM	significant	could be A, not TM (from time lag, above)

Conclusion: Not C, not TM, but A

FIGURE 20.3: Data from the study by Whitbourne and Waterman (1979). The Inventory of Psychosocial Adjustment was given with the conclusion that increasing age made for better psychosocial adjustment.

395

It is easy to summarize the basic analysis pattern diagrammed in Figures 20.1, 20.2, and 20.3. A summary is presented in Table 20.3. To infer an effect, two comparisons must be significant and one comparison not significant. The inferred effect must be present in the two significant comparisons and absent in the nonsignificant comparison. For example, to infer age as the important effect, both the cross-sectional, age/cohort comparison must be significant and the longitudinal age/time comparison must be significant. Both these comparisons involve age. The time-lag, cohort/time comparison must not be significant because this comparison does not involve age.

Each of the three studies diagrammed in Figures 20.1, 20.2, and 20.3 was based on a comparison of only two groups in each of the cross-sectional, longitudinal, and time-lag comparisons. The same scheme for separating the confounds could be applied when there are more than two groups to compare, that is, cross-sequential and time-sequential designs. In fact, Douglas and Arenberg (1978) compared six or seven groups, depending on the particular analysis, and made decisions similar to those seen in the figures.

Douglas and Arenberg (1978) gave a personality test comprising 10 scales. Of these 10, 5 scales reflected cross-sectional differences and 5 reflected longitudinal changes but only 3 of the 5 coincided (that is, only 3 were significant both cross-sectionally and longitudinally). Further, 1 of the 3 showed significant time-lag effects. Thus Douglas and Arenberg concluded that only 2 of the scales reflected age changes.

TABLE 20.3
An Inference Scheme

If These Comparisons Are Significant	And This One Is Not	Then Infer
Cross-sectional and longitudinal	Time lag	Age
Cross-sectional and time lag	Longitudinal	Cohort
Longitudinal and time lag	Cross-sectional	Time

Evaluating Inference Schemes

Above all, it must be recognized that Schaie's decision rules and the simpler inference scheme summarized in Table 20.3 are only schemes, guides to logical conclusions that may be wrong. If a scheme leads to an inference that does not appear logical or to make common sense, the inference should be questioned.

As already indicated, it should also be recognized that any scheme is based on several assumptions that are often wrong. Thus, any scheme is no better than the assumptions. Further, other schemes can be developed, or the one summarized in Table 20.3 can be modified. Neither the scheme nor the inference is seen molded in concrete.

Thus, compliance with common sense, underlying assumptions, and modification of schemes are important considerations. These will be taken up in turn.

Compliance with Common Sense. A study of intelligence was carried out utilizing a cross-sequential design (Botwinick & Siegler, 1980). The longitudinal confound (age/time) was significant but the cross-sectional confound (age/cohort) was not. Time-lag comparisons were not made, but given that only one of the two comparisons was significant, it is most unlikely that the time-lag comparison would also have been significant (Palmore, 1978).

If we use our scheme with these data, it would appear this way: If there is longitudinal significance, either age or time of measurement is important. If cross-sectional comparisons are not significant, neither age nor cohort is important. This leaves time as a possibility in the longitudinal comparison. In the assumed significant time-lag comparison (cohort and time), only time can be significant because cohort was not significant in the cross-sectional comparison. Thus, if not age or cohort, then time of measurement underlies the significant longitudinal comparison.

It does not seem to make good common sense to conclude that some factor in the environment or in the test conditions during the 1960s or 1970s when these data were collected made for decline in intelligence test scores of older adults. It is possible, of course, that something in the environment, that is, time of measurement effects, was important, but it seems much sounder to conclude that age was the factor in the decline.

Actually, in this study the cross-sectional and longitudinal curves were similar, and despite the tests of significance, it was concluded that both the cross-sectional and longitudinal analyses indicated similar results.

Assumptions. Underlying the schema seen in Table 20.3 are these assumptions: As already indicated, first, one and only one of the confounded effects is important in the data. It is either age, or cohort, or time, not two or three of them. Actually, there is no reason why two or three of the variables cannot be significant. If the results are such that each of the three comparisons (cross-sectional, longitudinal, and time-lag) is significant, then to infer one, and only one, of the variables, it is necessary to assume that one of the significant comparisons is not significant (Palmore, 1978). There really is no basis for such assumptions in most instances. Second, whatever the importance of these effects, they are linear and additive—that is, the cross-sectional confound is age plus cohort; the longitudinal confound is age plus time; the time lag is cohort plus time. The fact is that the confounded variables may not be additive; it may be even more likely that they are multiplicative. Third, in cross-sequential and time-sequential analyses, it is assumed that the effects do not interact. For example, it is assumed that no one age/cohort group changes over time more or less than does another age/cohort group. It is assumed that they change the same way and to the same extent. If one age-group changes differently than the others, then the inference of age or cohort is not as meaningful as the interaction. *

It is not to be expected in most data that these assumptions are tenable. It is well to make such assumptions in order that a logical inference can be drawn, but in the end, the inference should be held as tentative and in question because of the assumptions.

This is seen in a study by Glenn (1981). He analyzed Gallup poll data on alcohol drinking behavior in a cross-sequential design. There were six age/cohort groups (cross-sectional comparison) and three age/time-of-measurement conditions (longitudinal comparison). Glenn concluded that cohort effects explained the differences in drinking habits—the younger cohorts drank more. However, Glenn was able to get additional information— "side information," information outside the main body of data under analysis. This side information was of comparable data collected at a subsequent date. This additional information suggested that both age and time seemed important, but in opposite ways. More drinking was going on in the 1970s as compared to the 1960s and 1950s, and in the course of this time, younger people had increased their drinking more than older people. Note that this conclusion, unlike the scheme of Table 20.3, attributes drinking to two effects simultaneously, each in the opposite direction—more drinking in time from 1950 to 1970, but less drinking from younger to older cohorts.

Modification of the Inference Scheme. Glenn modified his inference scheme when more data were available. Costa and McCrae (1982) recommended an inference scheme that was compatible with but not identical to that of Table 20.3.

---

*Palmore (1978, pp. 284–285) suggests that in the complex designs where there is more than one set of relationships (for example, in Figure 20.1 there are three cross-sectional, longitudinal, and time-lag relationships), one set be analyzed at a time. That is, one set of cross-sectional, longitudinal, and time-lag comparisons "be analyzed separately to determine whether the patterns are similar or different across different age ranges, cohorts, or time periods. If they are similar, then the effects are probably additive and linear; and one can combine age groups, cohorts, or time periods. . . . If the patterns are not similar, the effects may be curvilinear or fluctuating and caution should be exercised in attempting to summarize or interpret the results."

Costa and McCrae had a large variety of data to analyze. They had both cross-sectional and time-sequential data collected with both the method of independent samples and repeated measurements. The latter was represented by both two times of measurement and three times of measurement. In this manner, Costa and McCrae had eight sources of variation: three were age/time, four were age/cohort, and one was cohort/time. (Costa and McCrae labeled the two age/time effects in the repeated-measures design as age/time/practice.)

To infer the importance of an effect, Costa and McCrae (1982, p. 245) demanded from their data that the effect had to "be a factor in all statistically significant comparisons." They had so many sources of variation that, unlike what is indicated in Table 20.3, they could be more demanding on one hand and less on another.

They were less demanding in that they did not insist that any one or any number of eight sources of variation be significant; they simply insisted that the inferred factor—age, cohort, or time—be present in each of the effects that was significant. They were more demanding in that the effect had to be present in *all* the many tests that were significant. When, as was the case with one of their observations, seven sources of variation involving age were significant and one not involving age was not significant, it was logical to infer that age was the important factor. Age was the only variable present in all seven significant effects and it was the only one absent in the one not significant (cohort/time).

This inference scheme of Costa and McCrae is different from that of Table 20.3 only in that they had more effects available for analysis. Otherwise, their logic and the logic underlying Table 20.3 are similar.

A Practical Viewpoint

Is Separating the Confounds Worth the Effort?   There is a tremendous amount of labor, time, and money involved in carrying out these complex designs and these schemes for separating the confounds. It is worth all this? The answer has to be controversial; it certainly has to be related to the questions asked.

Obviously, if a cross-sectional study showed significant differences among groups, and the differences were mistakenly thought due to age when in fact they were due to cohort, then much wasted effort is involved in all subsequent research designed to specify those aspects of age important to the measurements. In this light, separating the confound may be seen as cost effective. Assuming or estimating that age underlies the cross-sectional differences is not the same as knowing it, or having the weight of evidence indicating it.

Still, when all is said and done, what does separating the confounds leave us with? Actually, we are left with disappointingly little. We are left wanting to know what the inferred effect means. For example, let us assume that we carry out a study where a logical inference of age is made. It was seen earlier in this chapter how difficult and how ambiguous the definition of age is. It will be recalled that Glenn (1981, p. 362) defined age by saying that "age effects" is "a shorthand way of saying 'effects of biological, psychological and social changes which tend to accompany chronological aging.'" The conclusion of Costa and McCrae (1982, p. 247) may be seen as even more discouraging: "When an effect is attributed to 'aging' or to 'cohort' or to 'time,' it has not yet been explained. These are all 'dummy' variables, representing some unidentified process that they index and with which they covary. It is particularly dangerous to assume that an aging effect is equivalent to a maturational effect."

Thus, after separating the confounds, "some unidentified process" must still be sought and understood. The process is no less difficult to understand when the inference is cohort or time, rather than age—it may even be more difficult. For the gerontologist, cohort and time are not the focus of concern; they are mainly of interest to sociologists. For the gerontologist, cohort and time are "nuisance" effects to be investigated mainly to better understand aging effects. Separating the confounds is not the end of the line, it is but the beginning.

To come back to the original question, Is it worth it? The answer has to remain with the individual investigator. Without separation, the investigator may go off in directions that can fail. With separation, the work has barely begun. This conundrum is typical of research. If the answers to difficult questions were known, research would not be a very interesting or worthwhile pursuit.

When Only Cross-sectional Data Are Available. It is rare to have data based on as many different kinds of measurement methods as were seen in the study by Costa and McCrae. Even the relatively simple two-group comparisons in each of the cross-sectional, longitudinal, and time-lag methods are difficult to arrange. They certainly are very difficult to arrange with an adequate, extended time interval between test periods. Most often only cross-sectional data are available. What can be said of simple cross-sectional analyses?

First, cross-sectional studies are adequate for determining differences between and among age/cohort groups. For most practical purposes, descriptive statements or knowledge regarding differences are all that are needed; issues regarding maturational effects or cultural effects make little difference. Most political poll information, health or food preference information, height and weight information, many kinds of information, does not require separation of effects. The descriptive value of the cross-sectional information is not necessarily negated by the knowledge that cross-sectional differences observed today may not be observed in the future because cohort may underlie the differences and not age.

Logical judgment can play a role in explanation in cross-sectional studies even when carried out without accompanying longitudinal and time-lag comparisons. Religious beliefs, for example, or liberalism, would more likely be a function of culture or cohort than would visual acuity or reaction time. Recognizing that it is possible that the latter may also be cohort related, a more reasonable interpretation is age, not cohort. At least on the level of a working hypothesis, age can be seen as the important effect.

Unacceptable, however, is an increasing tendency to automatically consider cross-sectional differences as due to cohort effects. In fact, several investigators have taken to viewing cross-sectional comparisons as almost synonymous with cohort comparisons. If this tendency has any merit, it is only to counteract what had been the dominant tendency in the past—to assume that age and age alone underlies cross-sectional comparisons. As said so many times already, cross-sectional comparisons confound age and co-hort effects; knowing this, common sense and good judgment can go far in estimating what the data indicate.

SUMMARY

The time-honored method of cross-sectional analysis has come under attack in recent years because when comparing people of different ages, we are also comparing people who have been influenced differently by their respective cultural backgrounds. The influence of having grown up during the early 1900s is different from the influence of growing up during the 1950s or 1960s. The different cultural influences, not age, may underlie the cross-sectional comparisons. The cultural differences have been given the short-hand name of cohort. It is not possible to tell from cross-sectional compari-sons which of the two effects—age or cohort—is the more important because age and cohort are confounded.

For many purposes, it matters little whether age or cohort is more important. In national polls where voting preferences are stated, or in health surveys, or even in laboratory studies where simple descriptions are impor-tant, the cross-sectional method remains adequate. It is only when explana-tion is an issue that the cross-sectional method is wanting.

Many investigators have pointed to longitudinal studies as the way to determine true age effects. Such studies, however, also have the problem of confound. Longitudinal comparisons confound age and time-of-measure-ment effects. Time effects are often indistinguishable from cohort effects because both involve environmental influences; cohort effects are thought to exert their influence in the course of the whole lifetime, but the effects of time are seen as functional only during and between the observation periods in the longitudinal analysis. Examples of time effects are the impacts of television in the 1950s and 1960s and the prevalence of computers more recently. Special enrichment programs that make for cognitive stimulation are another example, economic downturns are another. All these and others can contribute to time effects, making age an incorrect inference in longitudinal studies.

Environmental influences are not the only ones involved in time effects. Changes that are unrelated to age occur among those being examined. For example, a person may be highly motivated during one observation period but not motivated in another; a person may be sick or in mourning of a loved one during one observation period and not during another. Such non-age-related personal factors can interact with true age changes to influence the observations.

A third method of group comparison is becoming increasingly more important in developmental research even though age is not a factor in this comparison. When one age-group is examined during one period of time and later, at another period of time, a different group of the same age is examined, the comparison is called time lag. These groups of the same age, examined during different time periods, are of different cohorts. Thus, the time-lag comparison confounds cohort and time.

These three methods—cross-sectional, longitudinal, and time lag— have been incorporated in complex experimental designs. When a series of cross-sectional and longitudinal comparisons are made simultaneously, the design is called cross-sequential. This design simultaneously compares age/ cohort groups, age/time groups, and the interaction between them. A second design, called time-sequential, simultaneously compares cross-sectional and time-lag groups. Here, differences among age/cohort groups and among cohort/time groups are analyzed along with the interaction between them.

A third complex design, called cohort-sequential, is the best one of the three for separating age and cohort effects because age and cohort are independent in this design. Both age and cohort, however, are confounded with time effects. From a practical point of view, this design is more applicable to studies of infant or child development than adult development because it takes so many years to carry out if the focus of interest is adults of very different cohorts and ages.

Recent interest has focused on separating the confounds of age, cohort, and time. To this end, the cross-sectional, longitudinal, and time-lag designs have been carried out simultaneously, and sometimes the more complex cross-sequential and time-sequential have been carried out simultaneously. A schema has been developed to make the separations based on the weight of evidence, but the schema is to be taken only as a guide to logical inference, not as a rule to be followed blindly. For an effect to be inferred, it has to be present in two statistically significant comparisons and absent in one comparison that is not significant. For example, for age to be inferred as the important effect, the age/cohort (cross-sectional) comparison has to be significant and the age/time (longitudinal) comparison also has to be significant. The cohort/time (time-lag) comparison, on the other hand, has to be nonsignificant.

This schema has merit but, if followed blindly, it may lead to very erroneous conclusions. Several assumptions underlie the schema analysis, and they are not always tenable. Common sense and logic must accompany the analysis separating the confounded variables.

REFERENCES

Adam, J. Sequential strategies and the separation of age, cohort, and time-of-measurement contributions to developmental data. *Psychological Bulletin*, 1978, 85, 1309–1316.

Baltes, P. B. Longitudinal and cross-sectional sequences in the study of age and generation effects. *Human Development*, 1968, 11, 145–171.

Birren, J. E., & Renner, V. J. Research on the psychology of aging: Principles and experimentation. In J. E. Birren & K. W. Schaie (Eds.), *Handbook of the psychology of aging*. New York: Van Nostrand Reinhold, 1977, pp. 3–38.

Botwinick, J., and Siegler, I. C. Intellectual ability among the elderly: Simultaneous cross-sectional and longitudinal comparisons. *Developmental Psychology*, 1980, 16, 49–53.

Costa, P. T., & McCrae, R. R. An approach to the attribution of aging, period, and cohort effects. *Psychological Bulletin*, 1982, 92, 238–250.

Douglas, K., & Arenberg, D. Age changes, cohort differences, and cultural change on the Guilford-Zimmerman Temperament Survey. *Journal of Gerontology*, 1978, 33, 737–747.

George, L. K., Siegler, I. C., & Okun, M. A. Separating age, cohort and time of measurement: Analysis of variance and multiple regression. *Experimental Aging Research*, 1981, 7, 297–314.

Glenn, N. D. Age, birth cohort, and drinking: An illustration of the hazards of inferring effects from cohort data. *Journal of Gerontology*, 1981, 36, 362–369.

Nelson, E. N. P. Persistence of attitudes of college students fourteen years later. *Psychological Monographs*, 1954, 68, 1–13.

Palmore, E. When can age, period, and cohort be separated? *Social Forces*, 1978, 57, 282–295.

Rosow, I. What is cohort and why? *Human Development*, 1978, 21, 65–75.

Schaie, K. W. A general model for the study of developmental problems. *Psychological Bulletin*, 1965, 65, 92–107.

Schaie, K. W. Age changes and age differences. *Gerontologist*, 1967, 7, 128–132.

Tilton, J. W. A measure of improvement in American education over a twenty-five year period. *School Sociology*, 1949, 69, 25–26.

Whitbourne, S. K., & Waterman, A. S. Psychosocial development during the adult years: Age and cohort comparisons. *Developmental Psychology*, 1979, 15, 373–378.

Woodruff, D. S., & Birren, J. E. Age changes and cohort differences in personality. *Developmental Psychology*, 1972, 6, 252–259.

21
Operational Issues and Special Concerns in Aging Research

Experimental designs important in developmental research were discussed in the previous chapter with emphasis on separating the confounded variables of age, cohort, and time of measurement. The longitudinal method is basic to all plans for separating the confounds, and this method is growing in importance. There are specific difficulties with it, however, among which is the bias in sampling through subject attrition. This sampling problem and others are discussed in this chapter along with common research practices.

SELECTING SAMPLES OF PEOPLE FOR STUDY: THE PROBLEM OF GENERALIZATION

Research investigators are correctly concerned about whom they test. For example, Schaie and Geiwitz (1982, pp. 17–18) wrote, "Subjects are generally presumed to be a *sample* of a larger population; the sample we want is one that is *representative* of the larger group. But there are many ways a sample becomes unrepresentative, making *generalization* of the results uncertain, perhaps invalid. . . ." They indicated that, "In adult development people with more money, more education, and better jobs are usually included in samples more often than less fortunate individuals. . . . There is a rather desperate need for studies of women, minorities, and the working class."

Bias in Selection

Salthouse (1982, p. 32) suggested some reasons for the frequent bias of unrepresentative sampling. "First, because individuals cannot be forced to participate in a project . . ." investigators rely on volunteers. Volunteers may not be representative of the total population. "Second, since volunteers are needed, investigators often attempt to recruit participants from groups or institutions where there is greatest likelihood of obtaining volunteers." Members of such groups or institutions may also not be representative of the general population. Salthouse offered a third reason for bias in sampling—subject pools. It is common for laboratory investigators to establish lists of people who are available for testing. People on such lists are phoned and recruited for testing, time and time again. "The problem with this practice is that once an individual participates in a single project he or she is no longer as representative of the population as before participation." Practices such as these make for bias, limiting the possibilities of generalization.

Validity in Generalizing

External Validity. The ability to generalize from the subject sample to the population at large is called external validity. This is only one of several kinds of external validity (Campbell & Stanley, 1966); the one above and another are particularly important in aging studies. The one above relates to the applicability of a finding in the laboratory to the "real world" outside the laboratory. Clearly, if laboratory results cannot be generalized to the living world—if the laboratory situation is not "ecologically valid"—the laboratory results are of lessened general value and are said to lack external validity.

Another type of external validity relates to different cultures or environments. For example, it was seen in Chapter 11 that in Western, industrial society, there is an increased difficulty with age in hearing high-frequency sounds (presbycusis). It was also seen that in more primitive societies where there is little or no "noise pollution," such "age effects" may not be nearly as prevalent, if they exist at all. The laboratory finding of presbycusis may not be generalizable beyond noisy industrial societies.

Internal Validity. If it is true that presbycusis is seen only in noisy industrial cultures and not in "noise free" cultures, then the inference of high-tone deafness as an age effect is wrong. Such problems in hearing may be due more to environmental factors than to biological factors. Not only does the laboratory finding and inference of age effect lack external validity, it can be said that the inference lacks internal validity. Internal validity is defined by the identification of the effect responsible for the observation.

The question of internal validity comes into play in a large variety of contexts, not only ones as broad as the comparison of different cultures. When Salthouse discussed typical subject-recruiting practices that make for poor external validity, he also indicated how such practices can make for poor internal validity. In soliciting volunteers among groups or institutions that are convenient, it is common to solicit young people from different groups or institutions than those where old people are found. Salthouse (1982, p. 32) indicated: "If young adults are recruited from college class-rooms while older adults are recruited from senior citizen clubs or retire-ment organizations, the two age groups will differ in many ways other than age. If any of these other factors is related to the measure of interest the age relationship will be impossible to interpret." The question of internal valid-ity is raised because it may be impossible to identify the effect responsible for the observation.

More Than One Study. Much of the research on aging is based on the practices that Salthouse (1982) indicated, and so, much of the research must be questioned as to external and internal validity. Still, Salthouse remains optimistic because, he believes, aging research is no different or no less reliable than other areas of research. He made clear that "no area of science has an abundance of critical studies which unequivocally resolve an issue to the complete satisfaction of everyone. Nearly all research reports have certain flaws or weaknesses that limit the conclusions that can be drawn" (p. 37). Confidence in the conclusions, he suggested, comes with similar findings among several studies on the same issue. A single study should not constitute the basis for a fact.

Matching (Equating) Age-groups

It was said that selecting people for study, with the older people coming from senior citizen clubs and the younger from college classrooms, reduces internal validity because "the two age groups will differ in many ways other than age." The fact is that even if the two age-groups were selected from the same source and even if there were perfect representative sampling, the two age-groups would differ in important ways other than age. A perfect repre-sentative sampling procedure, for example, would select young people with more formal education than old people; the young people would be of generally better health than the old people. This is what was meant in the previous chapter by the confound of age and cohort effects.

How have research investigators dealt with this issue of confound? How should they deal with it? One common practice has been to match or equate age-groups with respect to the confounded factor thought very important. After such matching, the age-groups are compared with respect to the mea-sure of interest. For example, it was said that representative sampling would result in age-groups different in the amount of their representative formal educations. In years gone by, people did not go to school for as long a period as they do now. One common research practice, then, is to match or equate age-groups with respect to education level, or whatever other factors seem important. If, for example, old and young are to be compared in intelligence test scores, education level is very important because education levels and intelligence test scores are highly correlated.

Limited Generalization. Such a matching procedure makes for difficulties. Matching or equating age-groups on the basis of years of education makes for either an unrepresentative number of highly educated old people, or an unrepresentative number of poorly educated young people. If the results of a study turn out the same way by matching as by representative sampling, that is, if intelligence test scores were found lower in old age both in representative and matched sampling, then it could be concluded that intelligence is lowered in old age or among older cohorts. If only matched samples were compared, nothing could be said about the extent of age or cohort differences in the representative sample, but it could be said that the old scored lower despite matching for education.

It may be recalled that in Chapter 14 a study by Green (1969) was described where he compared age-groups with respect to intelligence in both representative and matched samples. His results were different from the hypothetical ones above. As seen in Figure 14.3, he found by representative sampling that intelligence test scores declined with age and cohort. When he equated age-groups on the basis of education level, he obtained different results. There was little or no general decline in intelligence with age, and Verbal intelligence actually increased. What can be said about Green's results—the finding of little or no age and cohort difference in measured intelligence after matching for education? It can be concluded that with such unrepresentative sampling, no group differences were observed, or in the case of Verbal intelligence, the differences were opposite to that seen in the general population. Green concluded that there are no age differences in intelligence. A better conclusion might have been that there are no age differences in intelligence except those which are associated with the matching variable, education. If the matching variable (in this case, education) and age are intrinsically related, generalization has to be limited in this way. At best, matching provides for some abstract age–intelligence relationship; at worst, misleading information is acquired. (As indicated already, the education–intelligence relationship is but one example of a great variety of possible examples. Matching for health or income, and therefore socioeconomic status, is another.)

Controlling More Than Intended. There are other problems in matching. If we match on some criterion variable, as in the example of education level, we really do not know the basis of the matching. A high-school diploma was an achievement in the 1920s; a college degree was not for the common man. Those who graduated from college in the 1920s may have come from uncommon families or may themselves have been uncommon people. The old adult with a college degree may be cut of a different cloth than the young adult of today with a college degree.

Further, education, or any other matching variable for that matter, is related to a host of other variables—variables both known and unknown. This was pointed out by Elias and Wright (1976) and by others. When we match on one of these, we are not only involving other variables, but we are involving them in unknown ways. This is so because the correlations between the matching variable and the others may differ from age-group to age-group. Again the example of education: college graduates now aged 75 may be representative of a wealthy class or a scholarly class; college graduates aged 25 are more likely to come from a variety of socioeconomic classes and from a wide variety of backgrounds with regard to scholarship. In other words, education and socioeconomic status are probably more highly correlated among the elderly than among the young. If so, matching for education may well make for an age or cohort difference in socioeconomic background. In brief, matching on one variable may make for group differences in other, related variables that, in turn, may correlate with the dependent variable, intelligence in our example.

The common practice of matching groups, then, is unsatisfactory. Representative sampling is also unsatisfactory, however, even though it avoids problems of limited generalization and of unintended involvement of related variables. It is unsatisfactory because it ignores the importance of the correlated or confounded variable. What can be done about this? A practical solution will be suggested shortly, but first, another common practice.

Covariance Analysis. The statistical technique of analysis of covariance has been incorrectly used in place of matching or equating age-groups. This technique "partials out" the effect of the confounded variable (education in the example given) from the observation of interest (intelligence). This technique is incorrectly used in place of matching because both techniques do the same thing. Covariance analysis accomplishes statistically what the matching of samples accomplishes by experimental selection procedures. The problems associated with one technique are the same as with the other.

A major assumption in the analysis of covariance is that the covariate (education) is independent of age. This assumption is violated in our example, because, paradoxically, it is the very dependence that is the basis for the analysis in the first place. Violating the assumption of independence amounts to "throwing the baby out with the bath water." If the correlation between age and education were perfect, and education is related to intelligence, there would be no way of demonstrating an age-intelligence relationship with covariance analysis, even if there was one in reality.

A *Practical Solution.* Camp and Maxwell (1981, p. 171) properly maintained that the study of aging "still lacks a methodology which will yield unbiased results" in adjusting for the confound between the covariate and independent variable (i.e., between education and age in the example). The analysis of covariance can be used correctly only when the investigator is able to control assignment to the comparison groups. This cannot be done with age because people cannot be assigned at random to different age-groups. The confound between age and education thus remains inherent. For this reason, Camp and Maxwell said: "We cannot even hope to properly adjust for confounding influences on age differences . . . we gerontological researchers must be knowledgeable about potential sources and *directions* of bias, and limit our conclusions accordingly" (p. 171).

There is a practical solution, however, one that will inform us about sources and directions of bias. First, an analysis should be carried out based on representative sampling, without reference to the confounded variable. In the example given, age differences in intelligence can be investigated without reference to education levels. This might be done by way of analysis of variance.

Then an analysis of covariance can be carried out, with education as the covariate, recognizing that the major assumption of independence between education and age is violated. This will tell us what the covariate, education, contributes to the relationship between intelligence and age.* With the example given, the goal is to know (1) the relation between age and intelligence, (2) the relation between education and intelligence, (3) the relation between age and intelligence partialling out education, and (4) the relation between education and intelligence, partialling out age. Knowing all this, we will know all that it is possible to know about the data. By this procedure a representative sampling is available, permitting generalization. The contributions of all the presumed important variables are known, and this should permit more meaningful generalization.

---

*This is not to suggest that analyses of variance and covariance are the only methods for this purpose. They are not, and in fact are not even the best. Hierarchical multiple regression analysis is mathematically comparable and preferred. Education can be placed in the regression equation first and age second; then the process can be reversed; step in age first and then education. This will make it easier to see the respective contributions to variance of both age and education.

Variance and covariance analyses are special cases of the regression analysis. They are appropriate when the independent variable is qualitative; age, however, is a quantitative variable (George & Okun, 1976). In the variance analysis, age is treated as a nominal variable, e.g., old versus young, and accuracy of measurement is lost.

LONGITUDINAL STUDIES

Selective Attrition

There is a special problem of sampling in longitudinal studies that also limits generalization. The problem is selective subject attrition. Selective attrition in longitudinal research was discussed in Chapter 14 in the context of intelligence testing. It was said that the more frequent the test sessions, the longer the time intervals between sessions and, in general, the greater the constraints and demands placed on the test-takers, the more likely they will drop out of the study. There is selectivity, however, in that it is mainly the less able test-takers who will drop out; the more able ones tend to remain.

This was also seen in Chapter 4, in the discussion of "terminal drop." One reason the less superior drop out from the longitudinal study is that their rate of death is higher than those who are superior and stay in. This is particularly true for test-takers who are old to start. Death is but one reason for dropout; there are also others. The important point here, however, is that there is selectivity in dropout for whatever the reason.

Figure 14.5 is a clear example of the selectivity seen in one study. In not all longitudinal studies is the selective attrition so apparent or so great. When, however, the dropout is great, the remaining sample is no longer representative of the general population. Generalization thus becomes limited to the extent of the dropout rate. This is one reason longitudinal studies show less decline than cross-sectional studies—those remaining in long-term longitudinal studies may be an unrepresentatively superior and hearty breed.

There is a related issue: because of selective dropout, continued long-term longitudinal testing can obfuscate findings of age decline that were seen earlier in the longitudinal investigation. Figure 21.1 from a study by Siegler and Botwinick (1979) shows this. In this figure, the obfuscation is more prominent among those aged 60 to 64 years (left half of figure) than those aged 65 to 74 years (right half of figure). Figure 21.1 is based on the same 20-year longitudinal study as that of Figure 14.5.

There were 11 test sessions: Figure 21.1 shows four sequences—the scores of those who completed the first three of the 11 test sessions (7 years of longitudinal research), the scores of those who completed the first 4 of the sessions (10 years), the scores of the first 7 sessions (15 years), and finally, the scores of all 11 test sessions (20 years). In the age-group 60 to 64 years, note the relatively flat functions covering the first 12 years of the 15-year and 20-year curves as compared to the declines seen during the briefer 7- and 10-year longitudinal curves. (That is, compare the first six data points of the

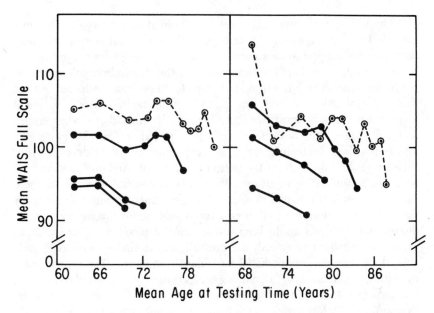

FIGURE 21.1: People aged 60 to 64 years (left half of figure) and 65 to 74 years (right half of figure) at the start of the study were tested over the course of approximately 20 years. The first 7, 10, and 15 years of longitudinal research are represented by solid circles; 20 years of longitudinal research are represented by dashed lines. (From Siegler & Botwinick, 1979, Figure 1. Reprinted by permission of the *Journal of Gerontology*, Vol. 34, pp. 242–245, 1979.)

upper two curves with all the points of the lower curves.) In the older group, 65 to 74 years, the massive drop from the first test session to the second in the 20-year sequence beclouds the stability seen from the second session on, that is, from the age early 70s to late 80s.

The point, again, is that not only can continued longitudinal testing make for progressively unrepresentative samples (Figure 14.5), but this unrepresentative sampling can make the longitudinal age trend itself appear more stable than may otherwise be indicated (Figure 21.1).

Advantages and Disadvantages

Despite all this, because longitudinal investigation is really the only way to chart age change (as contrasted to age difference), longitudinal study is the method of choice, all things being equal. If it is not possible to carry out cross-sectional and longitudinal studies simultaneously, then longitudinal investigation by itself is the more desirable. All things are not equal, however; the longitudinal method is much more difficult to carry out. There are advantages and disadvantages.

On the side of advantages, the longitudinal method is the only one possible for charting changes over time of the individual person. Not only does this method permit measurement of average changes for the individual, it also permits analysis of intra-individual (within the individual) variations. Such analysis often has value, not only for theoretical purposes but for practical applications as well. For example, if during the period of testing at Time 1 a person's performance scores *vary* by 10 units (that is, the person's scores fluctuate little) but during the testing period at Time 2 they *vary* by 100 units (they fluctuate greatly), the experimenter might develop hypotheses regarding the state of the person being tested. At Time 2, there may be a loss of interest or motivation to maintain sustained attention or there may be a transient personal problem. The experimenter might also look for signs of arteriosclerosis or other conditions making for inconsistency. Cardiovascular problems could keep the amount of blood reaching the brain variable; since the brain needs the nourishment carried by the blood, variable blood supplies may make for variable performances. The experimenter may suspect nervous system pathology, especially if cardiovascular disease is not apparent. It is only in longitudinal research that the individual may be so examined. Unfortunately, such analyses are not often carried out.

Longitudinal research has other advantages too. It is becoming almost routine in long-term longitudinal projects to examine, retrospectively, differences that had existed between survivors and those who have died. This is the "terminal drop" study described in Chapter 4. Another advantage was seen in the previous chapter. If there is any possibility of separating the confounds age, cohort, and time, longitudinal investigation is crucial.

There are disadvantages to the longitudinal method and these involve the great costs in time and money. Much patience is required by the investigator. Often, outmoded procedures have to be continued when newer and better ones are available. Often, too, it is necessary to carry through many years some of the mistakes and poor decisions made at the start of the study.

The logistics of data storage and data analysis are burdensome in longitudinal research, especially when large quantities of data are collected over many years of work. They have been so burdensome in some instances that many years of work have been negated because the mass of data became unmanageable. Fortunately, advances in computer technology have made the continuous recording and storage of data less of a problem than in the past. Moreover, many directors of long-term longitudinal research projects, especially interdisciplinary projects involving many measurements, have learned to consult with statistical experts from the very beginning. This avoids the confusion, disappointment, and waste that can result when data are collected and stored in forms that are unusable or misleading.

Weighing the advantages and disadvantages, it can only be concluded that without longitudinal research, a serious lack of information would result. The important and needed information, however, comes at a high cost. The investigator who contemplates the start of a longitudinal study should think twice before beginning. The investigator should ask again and again whether the question requires longitudinal investigation and, if so, whether the question is worth answering.

Independent Samples Research

Some of the disadvantages of the longitudinal method can be overcome by resorting to the method of independent-samples research. This method was discussed in the previous chapter with the comment that it falls somewhere in between the repeated measures of longitudinal research where the same people are tested and then retested, and the age-group comparisons of the cross-sectional method. In the independent-samples method, part of a group is tested at Time 1, another part is tested at Time 2, a third part is tested at Time 3 and so on. It is as if a cross-sectional comparison is made of people of the same cohort but tested at different times and so at different ages.

Schaie and Geiwitz (1982, pp. 24–25) recommended this method of independent samples, particularly if carried out simultaneously with the longitudinal, repeated-measures method. "What do we gain from the independent-samples procedure?" they ask. "First," they answered, "we gain a replication of sorts of the repeated-measures study, a second look at the same trends." Individuals can be followed only by the repeated-measures method, but the independent method does "allow us to estimate the effects in the repeated-measures study of such problems as losing subjects due to their inability or unwillingness to be retested . . . ," that is, selective subject dropout.

Although this is true, there is a dropout problem in the method of independent samples. There is a dropout in the cohort from which the yet-to-be-tested subjects are selected. In other words, people targeted for testing at Time 2 may die or become sick, or otherwise refuse to be tested, making for a type of subject attrition not easily identified. This is one reason, perhaps the major reason, that it was seen in at least one independent-samples study that the age declines, although not as large as in cross-sectional research, were greater than in longitudinal, repeated-measures research (Botwinick, 1977, pp. 598–599, describing studies by Schaie and associates). The attrition problem in independent-samples research may be less severe than in longitudinal, repeated-measures research, but it is there nevertheless. It is for this reason that Arenberg (1982) suggested that in planning an independent samples study, the investigator identify *beforehand* the subjects to be tested at Time 1, Time 2, Time 3, and so on. The identification should be on the basis of random selection and this should make the independent samples "unbiased and reasonably equivalent" with respect to the dropout problem.

Another advantage of the independent-samples study is that when the data are compared to those based on the repeated-measures study, the possibility of practice effects are indicated. The independent samples are inexperienced with the test procedures while the repeated-measures groups have already had "practice" with the tests. Thus, the problem of practice effects is absent in independent-samples research and the problem of subject attrition is minimized.

CROSS-SECTIONAL RESEARCH

There is no reason to believe that the sampling problem of selective subject attrition is unique to longitudinal research. The problem is present in cross-sectional research as well. It is conceivable that the problem is even more severe. It takes the form of selective subject availability. It was seen at the very beginning of this chapter that there is a typical bias in subject recruitment practices. Those who refuse or who are not contacted for investigation may be the poorer performers. There is hardly a way of determining whether this is so, or what the extent of this is. For example, in a study of visual perception and age, only subjects are selected who have adequate seeing levels to meet the requirements of the experiment. Further, subjects with poor vision who may meet the requirements of the study may not be available for study because of difficulty in coming to the laboratory. More old people than young may be expected to fail meeting the requirements, or to be otherwise unavailable for testing. Such "attrition" can make age differences appear less great than they might be in the general population.

GRADIENTS

Thus both cross-sectional and longitudinal measures are biased, but in different ways. Therefore, comparisons between cross-sectional and longitudinal measures are open to question. This is so for another reason as well: Cross-sectional measurements are made during one period of time and longitudinal measurements are made during two or more periods of time. Schaie (1970) developed a method that takes care of the latter issue, but only at the expense of highly artificial, abstract age functions. He developed a method of constructing gradients, and much of his own work relates to them. (It should be noted that age gradients and age curves are two different things.)

Longitudinal Gradients

Table 20.1 will serve as a point of reference to understanding gradients. In this table, only cells A through G need be considered. Cell A in Table 20.1 represents a group of subjects aged 30 years; let the average test score for this group be 100. Let the longitudinal follow-ups of this cohort show scores of 70 and 40 (cells B and C, respectively). Similarly, let the cohort born in 1920 have scores of 40 and 35 for ages 40 and 50, respectively (i.e., cells D and E). These data are drawn as curves in Figure 21.2(A), by the heavy solid lines, ABC and DE.

The longitudinal gradient is constructed in Figure 21.2(B). The longitudinal segment AB goes from 100 to 70, a drop of 30 points; this is connected to longitudinal segment DE, going from 40 to 35, a drop of 5 points. In this way, the longitudinal gradient in Figure 21.2(B) is based on two longitudinal sequences, one involving two observations of the 1930 cohort, and one sequence involving two observations of the 1920 cohort.

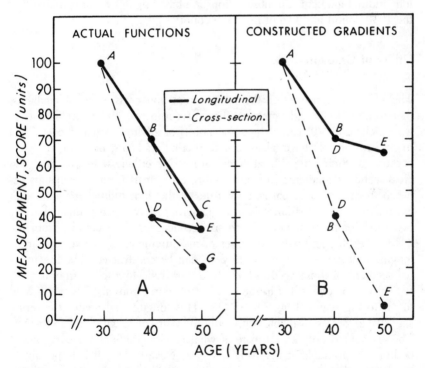

FIGURE 21.2: Hypothetical measurements or scores of people categorized into three age-groups. Part A of the figure refers to cells A, B, C, D, E, and G of Table 20.1; Part B connects disparate age comparisons (see text).

It may be seen that the level of the constructed gradient in Figure 21.2(B) is irrelevant—only the shape is meaningful. Instead of a function with the scores 100, 70, and 65 for ages 30, 40, and 50, respectively, the scores could just as easily have been shown as 70, 40, and 35 for ages 30, 40, and 50, respectively.

Cross-sectional Gradients

Table 20.1 shows that cohorts born in 1930, 1920, and 1910 were tested in 1960 (cells A, D, G). If the scores of this cross-sectional age comparison were 100, 40, and 20, respectively, the function may be described by the dashed line ADG in Figure 21.2(A). Similarly, dashed line BE is a cross-sectional comparison, with scores of 70 and 35 (see cells B and E).

The cross-sectional gradient in Figure 21.2(B), like the longitudinal gradient, is based on connecting disparate comparisons. Also, as with the longitudinal gradient, the observations are based upon two measurements of the 1930 cohort and two of the 1920 cohort.

Utility of Gradients

The effect of constructing the longitudinal and cross-sectional gradients, therefore, is to provide opportunities for comparing the two gradients in what Schaie (1970) calls "the same points of environmental impact." Not many investigators have taken to constructing gradients, however, probably because of their artificial, abstract nature. Nevertheless, longitudinal and cross-sectional gradients can have utility even apart from comparisons between them. This is particularly true of the longitudinal gradient. For example, in several studies six or so age-groups have been compared across two times of measurement. With six age decades, for example, from the 20s to the 70s, and with two times of measurement, say 10 years apart, a longitudinal gradient covering 60 years can be constructed. The longitudinal segment of those aged in the 20s to start (reflecting scores from age 20s to 30s) can be connected to the segment of scores from age 30s to 40s, and so on to the segment age 70s to 80s. This longitudinal gradient covering age 20s to 80s is available with only 10 years of longitudinal follow-up. The gradient is only an estimate of what the longitudinal age curve might be but it is available at relatively low cost. Nevertheless, it is important to emphasize that the estimate of longitudinal change by way of gradients may be wrong. Again, age gradients and age functions are not the same thing.

SPECIFIC RESEARCH CONCERNS

There are a variety of research errors, or at least poor practices, that recur. Those that are often encountered in aging research are discussed below.

Comparing Cross-sectional and Longitudinal Sequences

The cross-sequential design, discussed in the previous chapter and outlined in Table 20.1, is made up of a simultaneous series of cross-sectional and longitudinal comparisons. It is relatively easy to cross-sectionally compare two or more age/cohort groups, for example, 20-year-olds with 70-year-olds. More work is involved in comparing people in each of the decades from the 20s to the 70s, but this also is not difficult. Obviously, this is a whole lot simpler to do than to carry out longitudinal comparisons from ages 20s to the 70s.

Investigators have tended to take a shortcut by comparing people of diverse ages cross-sectionally while simultaneously following people over much briefer periods of time. Several studies have compared people cross-sectionally who differed in age as much as 40 to 50 years, while at the same time making longitudinal measurements covering only 7 to 10 years. This is understandable because it is difficult enough to carry out 7 to 10 year follow-ups. Such studies are valuable but they fall short if the data are meant to answer questions regarding comparisons between the cross-sectional and longitudinal data. Comparing a 40 to 50 year difference to a 7 to 10 year change does not make a whole lot of sense. One study went so far as to include a 20-year cross-sectional comparison (from age 55 to 75) but only a 6-month longitudinal comparison. The meaningfulness of the comparison between cross-sectional and longitudinal functions is related directly to how similar or disparate are the age-groups in the two types of functions.

A meaningful cross-sequential design, or at least the best one, is where the cross-sectional and longitudinal age groupings are identical. This is rarely found in the literature, but it was seen in studies depicted in Figures 20.1, 20.2, and 20.3. In these studies, however, there were only two age-groups that were compared in each of the cross-sectional and longitudinal measurements. One study compared four age-groups of identical age ranges (Botwinick & Siegler, 1980). If cross-sectional and longitudinal age-groups are very disparate in age ranges, the conclusions that are drawn may be wrong (Botwinick & Arenberg, 1976).

Control Groups

Most students and certainly almost all investigators now seem aware of the need for a control group in assessing the effects of drugs, therapy, and other modification or intervention techniques. Not everyone, however, seems aware of the need for a control group when inferences are made as to the mechanisms or basis of difficulty requiring modification. This was mentioned in Chapters 14 and 15, under the heading "Modification Studies," and only brief reference to the issue will be made here.

In several studies efforts were made to train older people to perform well in tasks that are typically hard for them. The purpose of these studies was to demonstrate a plasticity with age—an ability to change and to improve. Other studies had been carried out for the purpose of inferring the reasons why the tasks were hard for old people in the first place. The thinking was that if appreciable improvement was seen with behavioral intervention procedures—teaching and guidance, for example—it would be unlikely that the original problem was of biological origin; rather, it was likely to be of experiential or psychological origin.

This thinking is incomplete at best. If improvement of elderly people's performances is observed after modification training, no inference can be made regarding the basis of original difficulty, that is, biological or experiential. Similar training might help young groups as much or more even though they had little of the original difficulty that the older people had. In fact, this was seen in at least one study where old and young were provided both practice opportunities and incentive to improve (Grant, Storandt, & Botwinick, 1978). Improvement by both young and old was seen but not more for one age-group than another. The purpose of a young control group is not for testing the effectiveness of the intervention, but for ascertaining a possible basis of difficulty. In the study by Grant et al., had improvement on the part of the elderly been found greater than that of the young, a biological basis of original difficulty could not be ruled out, but an experiential basis as an explanation might have a better foundation. Without a young control group, no inference can be made as to the basis of a problem.

Change Scores

Another recurring issue is change scores. There are very many studies in a wide variety of contexts where the focus of concern is change. Does this teaching procedure make for better learning or change than that procedure? Does this drug make for greater improvement in health than that one? Does this teaching procedure or that drug have greater effects on the old than the young? The list of questions can be continued. Much of aging research is based on questions such as these—there is measurement at Time 1, then at Time 2, perhaps at subsequent times, to determine change resulting from some experimenter-manipulated event.

This is a very typical study, and often psychologists subtract Time 2 scores from Time 1 scores and compare age-groups on these difference scores. Arenberg (1982) pointed out that physiologists and chemists tend to measure change in terms of proportions, rather than differences. Thus, in the example he gave—a change from 100 to 50 is equivalent to a change from 400 to 200—both are changes of one-half the original measurement. Psychologists in comparing difference scores would compare 100–50 versus 400–200, or 50 versus 200.

Which is better, a difference score or a proportion, to note change? Actually, neither is very good, unless special conditions are met, ones that are not often found. Difference scores do not take initial level into consideration. For example, it is much easier to shave strokes off a golf score with training and practice when the overall play is in the 100s than when it is in the 70s. An improvement of 5 strokes at 100 means something very different than an improvement of 5 strokes at 70. Proportions do not take actual differences into account. Further, both difference scores and proportions are unreliable measures.

Two statistically identical methods are recommended to analyze change. One is the use of residual scores. Time 1 measures are regressed or correlated with Time 2 scores; then the individual Time 2 scores are subtracted from the slope or regression line to get the residual scores. Or, perhaps more simply, a covariance analysis is carried out with Time 1 scores as the covariate. Age-groups are then compared with respect to the residualized or adjusted scores.*

Individual change in an absolute sense is not known by residual score analyses, but in most instances this is not the important issue. In most instances, questions such as posed earlier are the points of interest, that is, does this teaching procedure or this drug make for more change than that one? Does this age-group change more than that one?

Transforming Data

Arenberg (1982) also considered the problem of transforming data when distributions are skewed. It is common and advisable to transform data to normal distributions before applying statistical analyses that are based on the assumption of normality. Arenberg cautioned against this, however, when the major hypothesis is an interaction. Here is an example of a question

---

*The residual change score analysis involves one dependent measure and one independent (age) measure. George (1982) indicated that more than one independent variable can be examined in relation to the residualized change score. Further, there may be more than one dependent measure. In other words, the interest may be of the relationship between patterns of independent variables and patterns of dependent variables. In such cases, she recommends a canonical correlational analysis.

where interaction is of interest: "Do the old improve more than the young when we provide extra training?" Or, in the example Arenberg provided, "Are the old relatively slower in choice reaction time than in simple reaction time?" Arenberg's contention applies to all issues of interaction.

Arenberg developed hypothetical reaction time data to demonstrate what transforming scores can do to interactions. His data were such that reaction times of a young group increased from 200 to 400 msec. going from simple to choice reaction time. On the other hand, reaction times of an old group increased from 300 to 600 msec. The increase was 200 msec. for the young and 300 for the old, a statistically significant difference. If the data were transformed by log transformation, however, to attain normality of distribution, the increase would be from 2.30 to 2.60 for the young, and from 2.48 to 2.78 for the old: a difference of .30 for the young and a difference of .30 for the old—an identical increase and thus having no significant interaction.

Arenberg indicated that the t-test and analysis of variance are not affected much by the violation of the assumptions of normality of distribution. The implication therefore is that if it is interaction that is important, transformations of the data are often contra-indicated.

A better solution, however, would be residual score analysis or the covariance analysis, using simple reaction time as the covariate. Going from simple to choice reaction time is really nothing other than a change score.

Factorial Invariance

Does a test or procedure used with one age-group measure what it does in another age-group? How can one tell? Cunningham (1982) suggested that the test measures the same thing in both age-groups if the variable in question correlates with other variables in the same way and to the same extent in both age-groups. If it does not, then the measurement means something different in one age-group than another.

Here is an example of this: Normally, vocabulary test scores correlate very highly with general tests of intelligence. In fact, it is common to use vocabulary tests as quick estimates of intelligence. If it were found that vocabulary test scores correlate highly with intelligence test scores in one age-group but not another, it would have to be questioned whether the vocabulary test measures the same thing in both age-groups. The conclusion that the vocabulary test measures different things in different age-groups would be on even stronger foundation if it were found that the vocabulary test scores correlate with a large number of variables very differently in one age-group than another. Another way of saying this is that the construct validity of the test is different or poor in one or the other of the age-groups.

This hypothetical result with vocabulary tests is not one that tends to be found in the literature, but it does demonstrate the concept of the meaning of a measurement.

Cunningham took this thinking further. If many variables are measured and correlated with one another, a factor analysis can be carried out. If a procedure or several procedures measure something different in one age-group than another, then the factor structures would be different among the different age-groups. For example, one factor may account for general ability in one age-group but it may take several factors to account for abilities in another age-group. In the latter case of several ability factors, abilities are said to be differentiated. When there is a single factor, abilities are not differentiated and each of the tests measure an aspect of the same ability, even if not to the same extent. With several factors accounting for abilities, tests associated with one of the factors measure something different from tests associated with another of the factors.

When different age-groups are similar in factor structure, that is, when abilities are either not differentiated within each of the age-groups or are differentiated in the same way in each, it is said that there is factorial invariance. With factorial invariance we can be confident that whatever we measure in one age-group, we also measure in another.

Individual Differences

Investigators often ignore the fact that although age-groups may differ, individual differences in all age-groups tend to be large. One study pointed to this. It was inadvertently discovered in a study comparing old and young in reaction time that diverse habits of exercise among the young may have been an important factor in the findings (Botwinick & Thompson, 1968). Many of the young people were school athletes but others hardly exercised at all. This made for large individual differences in reaction time. Accordingly, an age analysis was made of reaction time on the basis of whether the old and young did much exercise. There were 17 young people in the study who did little exercise, and 13 elderly people who similarly did little exercise. With a criterion of a reaction time of 18 msec., 5 of these young people made poorer scores than 9 of these elderly ones. That is, 70 percent of these nonexercising elderly people were superior in their responses to 30 percent of the corresponding younger people. It was concluded that if all age comparisons were made "on the basis of some such combination of percentages and . . . [criterion score] . . . much of the age difference which may seem impressive at first would lose its interest" (Botwinick & Thompson, 1968, p. 27). The overlaps between old and young are often neglected in aging studies.

AGE AS AN INDEPENDENT VARIABLE

A final issue is less a research concern than a conceptual consideration. What kind of variable is "age," the variable around which this whole book revolves? Is it an independent variable? An independent variable in research is one that the investigator manipulates to determine whether its variations are associated with variations of the dependent variable (behavior in psychological studies). Studies in aging take the form of determining the association between age and the dependent variable, but, obviously, the investigator cannot manipulate age. Age-groups can be compared cross-sectionally or longitudinally, but age itself is not under the investigator's control. Thus, age is not a true independent variable, but most often, it is treated as if it is.

Over the years, dissatisfaction has been expressed with the use of age as an independent variable. Dissatisfaction took extreme form in the comments of Bijou and Baer (1963) and Baer (1970). They argued that age *per se* is not germane to the purpose of studying developmental patterns.

Causality

It is not difficult to argue for this extreme position. Age, as a concept, is difficult to define. It was seen in the previous chapter that biological change alone does not define age; psychological and sociological change are also part of the definition. It is clear that however age is defined, it is intimately associated with time. In one sense, age and time are synonymous. Independent variables are thought to "cause" things to happen, but time does not "cause" anything. Time does not have physical dimensionality to impinge upon the sensorium, and it does not have meaning independent of the psychological, social, and biological significance that is imparted to it. (It is this which underlies much of the philosophers' age-old concern with the meaning of time, and, it seems, the scientists' more recent concern with the definition of aging.)

It is possible to argue that time is a crude index of many events and experiences, and it is these indexed events and experiences that are "causal." If we study these events and experiences, the argument goes, we need not be concerned with the crude index of time, that is, age. In other words, we need not be concerned with age to understand what had been "caused" by the time-indexed variables. In this way, age *per se* is not germane to the purpose of studying developmental patterns. Further, these time-indexed variables, unlike age itself, can be manipulated experimentally while holding related factors constant. Unlike age, therefore, these variables are true independent variables; they can be regarded as explanatory as well as descriptive.

Although all of the foregoing is correct, it is also correct that much of what we regard today as explanatory, or causal, may not be so regarded tomorrow when more immediately "causal" factors are known. Explanation and causality in science are matters of improving approximations, of determining better empirical associations. Age may be used as an explanation or predictor until better ones become available. For example, knowing the age of a person, we can predict blood pressure levels within very broad, crude limits. Knowing about the state of arteriosclerosis, our prediction would be more accurate. Neither age nor arteriosclerosis would be as useful as information regarding the efficiency of the cardiac muscle. Knowing all these together, our predictions are best. Predictability, that is, explanation based upon the degree of association, constitutes one definition of causality in science.

There is an important social reason, even if not a scientific one, for maintaining that age *per se* is germane to the purpose of studying developmental patterns. If age is regarded as irrelevant in studying developmental patterns, then focus will be only on function, not on the person. If focus is not upon the person as well as the function, then we end up with a cadre of cardiovascular specialists, for example, but few geriatricians. The problems of old age are too extensive and too important to negate a geriatric specialty. Our present knowledge of aging processes is too meager, and our social needs too great, to insist on study of only what appears to be the more immediate, causative variables. A good working hypothesis is that a specific focus upon age *per se* will not only be relevant to our social goals, but will lead to a more precise delineation of the variables that are more immediately "causal."

Two Research Stages

Just as the extreme position of classifying age as irrelevant is not satisfactory, so is the insistence that the more precise, more immediate "causal" conditions be left uninvestigated. Both need to be examined, perhaps in a two-stage process: first by studying age functions, and then by subsequent research for the purpose of elucidating and modifying the age functions (Baltes & Goulet, 1971). Although not all problems may lend themselves to these two research stages, many do.

Three studies provide an example to elucidate this research strategy; each of the three studies is what Baltes and Goulet (1971) would call part of the second stage. The first stage involves an extensive literature demonstrating that in a wide variety of situations, elderly people are slower in responding to stimuli than are younger people—reaction time (RT) increases as adult age increases.

One study of the second stage posed the question as to whether sensory loss in later life is responsible for the slowdown. For example, elderly people have hearing losses—does this account for their slowness in an auditory RT? In one study, the loudness of the stimulus was adjusted on an individual basis for the purpose of determining a more immediate, precise "cause" of the RT slowing with increasing age (Botwinick, 1971).

A second study investigated a state-of-the organism variable as a "cause" of the slowdown. Several stage-one studies suggested that older people tend to be more depressed than younger people. Since depression is often defined in terms of psychomotor slowing, it was thought that this state may be a "cause" of RT slowing. A depression scale was administered, and the scores were correlated with RT measures (Botwinick & Thompson, 1967).

A third study also examined a state-of-the-organism variable, but here the investigators manipulated the states. The question underlying this study involved the assertion that EEG activation makes for quick RTs. Since EEG activation may be different in young and old, the response slowing with age might be explained by age changes in levels of EEG activation. Thompson and Botwinick (1968) varied EEG activation by manipulating the foreperiod or preparatory interval in an RT experiment.

The results of each of these three stage-two studies was negative in the sense that the more refined explanations regarding the RT slowdown with age were not demonstrated. The point here is that, although stage-two studies must follow the stage-one study for a fuller understanding, stage-one studies provide a type of understanding in their own right. Some stage-one studies constitute the only information we have at the present time.

SUMMARY

Representative samples are sought for study in aging research so that generalizations based on the data may refer to the population at large. Typically, however, study samples of older adults are far short of being representative because volunteers from special groups or institutions are selected. Further, once so selected, they are often placed on subject pool lists that are maintained by laboratory investigators. Once a person from such a list is tested, he or she is no longer as representative in subsequent testing. All this limits opportunities for generalization, or as it is sometimes said, the data lack external validity.

Other matters also limit generalization. For example, the laboratory situation may have little bearing on "life in the real world." Also, what seems to hold in one culture may not in another. This makes inferences difficult and can challenge the very meaning of the observation. The meaning of an observation, that is, the identification of the effect responsible for it, is called internal validity.

Even perfect representative sampling in aging research can make for problems. Representative sampling will provide the investigator with various age-groups of people that are very different in many ways other than age, as for example, levels of education. The reason for this is that older adults when young tended not to go to school for as long a time as younger people go today. Thus, if the study is of education-related performances, for example, intelligence test scores, the investigator is left uncertain. The reason for uncertainty is that the older adults would be expected to score less well on intelligence tests than younger adults on the basis of education differences alone.

One strategy that has been found frequently to cope with such situations is to match or equate age-groups on the basis of education (or on the basis of some other variable considered important). After such matching, age-groups are compared with respect to intelligence (or some other measure). This common matching procedure is not a good one. First, it makes for unrepresentative groups. In the example of education, it makes for either unrepresentatively highly educated old people or unrepresentatively poorly educated young people. This limits generalization to the population at large. Second, when a match is made with one variable, many unknown variables may also be associated. For example, associated with education level are socioeconomic status, health status, and, perhaps, personal characteristics. All these limit generalizability.

Various statistical techniques have been employed to cope with this sampling problem, but in one way or another all are wanting. The best that seems possible is to sample representatively and then to determine relationships among the variables at issue. Correlations and partial correlations will offer as much information as is possible to accrue.

Sampling problems are present in both cross-sectional and longitudinal studies. In longitudinal research there is the problem of selective attrition among those people who are tested. As a longitudinal study progresses over time, the more able people tend to stay in the study and the less able tend to drop out. This is particularly so among older adults. This also limits the generalization of results. Independent-samples research and cross-sectional research also involve subject selectivity that limits generalization, but it takes the form of initial subject availability.

In addition to problems of sampling and generalization, this chapter was concerned with specific research practices. An increasingly popular method of data collection is that of simultaneous cross-sectional and longitudinal comparisons. Many investigators have taken to making cross-sectional comparisons of groups widely different in their ages, while simultaneously making longitudinal comparisons of groups not nearly as different in their ages. This is all right just so long as the cross-sectional and longitudinal analyses are not compared. If this comparison is required, then the age-groups and age ranges of the cross-sectional and longitudinal sequences must be the same. Cross-sectional and longitudinal gradients (as contrasted to actual cross-sectional and longitudinal age functions) can be useful in making appropriate comparisons. The method of constructing such gradients was shown.

Change score analysis is sometimes carried out in ways that are wanting. Many studies involve two or more age-groups that are compared with respect to changes in their behaviors resulting from some intervention or treatment (as for example, training or drugs). Often, scores made at Time 1 are subtracted from scores of Time 2, but this is not a good practice. The reason is that initial levels are not taken into consideration. Also, difference scores are unreliable. Residualized scores or covariance analysis is preferable and should be carried out in place of difference scores.

Another research practice is the transformation of data to effect normal distributions. It was indicated that this practice may not be appropriate to test hypotheses regarding interaction. Transformations may indicate no interaction when linear measures indicate otherwise. Still another issue relates to the question of whether a particular test measures the same thing in an older population that it does in a younger. Factorial invariance or simpler correlational analyses can help to answer this question.

The chapter was concluded with a discussion of age as an independent variable. Age indexes a variety of factors that may be seen as "causal." Age itself can be seen as "causal," however, and sometimes it is the only explanation we have.

REFERENCES

Arenberg, D. Learning from our mistakes in aging research. *Experimental Aging Research*, 1982, 8, 73–75.

Baer, D. M. An age-irrelevant concept of development. *Merrill-Palmer Quarterly*, 1970, 16, 238–245.

Baltes, P. B., & Goulet, L. R. Exploration of developmental parameters by manipulation and simulation of age differences in behavior. *Human Development*, 1971, 14, 149–170.

Bijou, S. W., & Baer, D. M. Some methodological contributions from a functional analysis of child development. In L. P. Lipsitt & C. C. Spiker (Eds.), *Advances in child development and behavior* (Vol. 1). New York: Academic Press, 1963, pp. 197–231.

Botwinick, J. Sensory-set factors in age differences in reaction time. *Journal of Genetic Psychology*, 1971, 119, 241–249.

Botwinick, J. Intellectual abilities. In J. E. Birren & K. W. Schaie (Eds.), *Handbook of the psychology of aging*. New York: Van Nostrand Reinhold, 1977.

Botwinick, J., & Arenberg, D. Disparate time spans in sequential studies of aging. *Experimental Aging Research*, 1976, *1*, 55–61.

Botwinick, J., & Siegler, I. C. Intellectual ability among the elderly: Simultaneous cross-sectional and longitudinal comparisons. *Developmental Psychology*, 1980, *16*, 49–53.

Botwinick, J., & Thompson, L. W. Depressive affect, speed of response, and age. *Journal of Consulting Psychology*, 1967, *31*, 106.

Botwinick, J., & Thompson, L. W. Age difference in reaction time: An artifact? *The Gerontologist*, 1968, *8*, 25–28.

Camp, C. J., & Maxwell, S. E. Nonrandom assignment and the analysis of covariance in aging research. *Experimental Aging Research*, 1981, *7*, 169–173.

Campbell, D. T., & Stanley, J. C. Experimental and quasi-experimental designs for research. Chicago: Rand McNally, 1966.

Cunningham, W. R. Factorial invariance: A methodological issue in the study of psychological development. *Experimental Aging Research*, 1982, *8*, 61–65.

Elias, J. W., & Wright, L. L. Matching, the null hypothesis and the aging variable: Would the real age effect please stand up. *Experimental Aging Research*, 1976, *2*, 261–267.

George, L. K. A canonical correlation technique for analyzing patterns of change. *Experimental Aging Research*, 1982, *8*, 67–72.

George, L. K., & Okun, M. A. Misuse of analysis of covariance in aging research revisited. *Experimental Aging Research*, 1976, *2*, 449–459.

Grant, E. A., Storandt, M., & Botwinick, J. Incentive and practice in the psychomotor performance of the elderly. *Journal of Gerontology*, 1978, *33*, 413–415.

Green, R. F. Age-intelligence relationship between ages sixteen and sixty-four: A rising trend. *Developmental Psychology*, 1969, *1*, 618–627.

Salthouse, T. A. *Adult cognition*. New York: Springer-Verlag, 1982.

Schaie, K. W. A reinterpretation of age related changes in cognitive structure and functioning. In L. R. Goulet & P. B. Baltes (Eds.), *Life span developmental psychology: Research and theory*. New York: Academic Press, 1970, pp. 485–507.

Schaie, K. W., & Geiwitz, J. *Adult development and aging*. Boston: Little, Brown, 1982.

Siegler, I. C. & Botwinick, J. A long-term longitudinal study of intellectual ability of older adults: The matter of selective subject attrition. *Journal of Gerontology*, 1979, *34*, 242–245.

Thompson, L. S., & Botwinick, J. Age differences in the relationship between EEG arousal and reaction time. *Journal of Psychology*, 1968, *68*, 167–172.

Index